THE INDEPENDENT SUDAN

The Independent Sudan

by

MEKKI SHIBEIKA

B.A. (Beirut), Ph.D. (London)

Formerly Professor of Sudan History

University of Khartoum

ROBERT SPELLER & SONS, PUBLISHERS, INC.

New York 36

TABLE OF CONTENTS

PREFACE

This book has its own history. Its nucleus was a successful Ph.D. Thesis presented to the University of London. It dealt with the events of the Mahdiya from its start in 1881 until the death of al-Mahdi in 1885. It was based mainly on documentary evidence in Khartoum, Cairo and London archives. When finishing my thesis and still in London the Public Record Office was opened to scholars to 1902. I took this opportunity and collected material relevant to events of the Sudan conquest in 1898 and the Condominium Agreement of 1899. Six more chapters and the original thesis were published by Oxford University Press subsidized by the Sudan Government under the title 'British Policy in the Sudan 1882-1902.'

When the book was out of print I was approached by Robert Speller and Sons for a book on the History of the Sudan as a contribution to a series of Official Histories. I wrote three additional chapters, two on the Turco-Egyptian period (1820-1882) and one on the administration of Khalifah 'Abdullahi, who succeeded al-Mahdi (1885-1898). These chapters were based on documentary evidence also in Khartoum and Cairo. Mr. Speller advised me to write an introductory chapter tracing developments from ancient times to 1820 and several chapters carrying the story from 1900 to Independence Day in January 1956. I complied with his wishes and the final result is the book which I present to readers.

I must make it clear, however that there should be a sharp distinction between these final additions and the main body of the book. The genuine historical part which is the result of my own efforts and for which I exhausted all the available sources which are open to scholars is that part of the book which starts from 1820 and ends in 1900. For the introductory chapter I have to acknowledge fully the efforts of Mr. A. J. Arkell in his book 'A History of the Sudan to A.D. 1821, the Athlone Press (London 1955). For the chapters after 1900 I have acknowledged the authorities consulted and on certain occasions I have to offer my own interpretation of events. This last part, i.e. after 1900, is not yet history from the point of view of historical scholarship, as the archives are not yet all open and many of the personalities are still alive. Yet a narrative of facts and motives could give a tentative picture.

M. SHIBEIKA

University of Khartoum

INTRODUCTORY CHAPTER

The Sudan Before 1820

Ancient Egyptian Civilization seemed to have stopped at the first cataract south of Aswan. The land between Aswan and Wady Halfa now called Nubia, and inhabited by a brown Mediterranean people had, however, its contacts with Egypt from the first Egyptian dynasty. In spite of its barren rocky nature this land of Nubia attracted the attention of the pharaohs at such an early date, mainly because of the quarries which were suitable for statues. This Egyptian military penetration in Nubia culminated in what amounted to a conquest by Seneferu of the 4th dynasty. His inscriptions spoke of the destruction of 'Ta Nehesi and the capture of 7000 prisoners and 200,000 cattle and sheep. The exaggeration in the figures is obvious, but it indicated the south-ward move of the Egyptian higher civilization in the land of a less civilized people. Subsequent Egyptian activities were centered around quarrying stones; boats were built, attempts were made to open channels through the first cataract and chiefs were compelled to submit to Egyptian authority. There is evidence to show that these Nubians were recruited in the Egyptian army in their fights against the Asiatic Bedouins.

These quarrying activities were followed by trading caravans which penetrated a considerable distance southwards. One of these caravan leaders, Harkhuf by name, had undertaken four journeys and brought to Egypt in one of these 300 donkeys laden with merchandise. The time it took him in one of these journeys indicated that he might have departed away from the river into Kurdufan or even Darfur.

The lack of a strong Government in Egypt towards the end of the sixth dynasty seemed to have its effect on the Egyptian control over Nubia. People south of the 2nd cataract and on the desert east and west came into Nubia with a considerable number of cattle. This is one of the evidences showing that that area could support a larger number of animals than it can now due to desiccation since that time. It is highly probable that these desert people gravitated towards the Nile because of desication in their original land.

The re-establishment of a strong central government in the 11th dynasty with a capital in Upper Egypt (Thebes; modern Luxor) inevitably renewed the interest of Egypt in Nubia, which was perma-

nently occupied. A feature of this phase was the erection of a series
of forts on the Nile bank between Shellal and Wady Halfa and a
little to the south; the purpose of these forts was to control the trade
traffic on the Nile and protect these Egyptian posts from any possible attack from the Nomads on the desert. Kerma, south of Wady
Halfa, was identified as a capital of a line of Egyptian Governors-
general. The main feature of this period was gold-mining activities
in which Nubians took part. At the beginning resistance was made
to this reoccupation, but gradually as Nubians themselves were
recruited in the Egyptian army, and had taken to the Egyptian way
of life and comradeship in arms resistance was appreciably reduced.
This served as a prelude to the next phase, which was almost complete Egyptianization of Nubia.

Under the Egyptian New Kingdom frontiers were pushed still
southwards to the 4th cataract. Ahmes, the first king of the 18th
dynasty, started the reoccupation of Nubia after he had defeated the
Asiatics. Thutmose I (1540-1501, 1496-1493 B.C.) rounded off this
reconquest (1530-1520 B.C.) up to the 4th cataract, beyond which
expansion along the Nile would not be easy. There is archeological
evidence to show that the ancient Egyptians had a post at Kurqus
50 miles south of Abu Hamad. It is possible that they might have
occasional influence along the Nile south of Kurqus up to the 6th
cataract.

Although the military strength of Egypt under Ahmes and Thutmose I proved to be so formidable that there was no resistance at
the beginning, yet with the death of the latter there started rebellions
in Nubia, thinking that it was only the personality of the King that
constituted the strength of Egypt. A strong military expedition which
crushed the resistance put an end to any rebellious activities for the
time being. There followed a period of peace interrupted occasionally
by expeditions to restore peace. Archeological missions brought to
light the buildings, objects, etc., which prove the Egyptianization of
the Northern Sudan. The administration was vested in a viceroy,
usually chosen from the royal entourage with a commander of bow-
men under him. Officials were mostly Egyptians or Egyptianized
Nubians. With all this influence all lands south of Aswan were considered to be a foreign territory and only officials, soldiers, priests,
etc., came to Nubia. There was no what could be called "systematic"
colonization. The Nubian troops under their commander and the

viceroy played an influential part in the struggle for power which was the characteristic of the closing years of the New Kingdom in Egypt. The centre of gravity seemed to have moved from Thebes in Upper Egypt to Napata (present Marawi area) in Cush. By this time Cush (Nubia) expanded southwards through the desert and established a second capital at old Meroe (near Kabushiya in Shandi District).

This Kingdom of Cush was not content with asserting its independence but planned and executed a project of invading Egypt possibly under the inspiration of the Priests of Amen Re'. Kashta (751 B.C.) was the first Cushite King to have control of Upper Egypt; but was not recognized by the full title of Pharaoh. It was his son Piankhi who systematically completed the conquest of Egypt. The Stela commemorating these conquests was found near the great temple of Amen Re' in 1862 and is now in the Cairo Museum. Although he was in full control of all Egypt, he did not establish a central administration for both countries. He was satisfied with receiving tribute from the princes of the Delta as king of Cush and Upper Egypt. Shabaka, the brother of Piankhi, transferred his capital from Napata to Thebes, as the king of Cush and Misr (Egypt).

Just at this time the Assyrians were asserting their authority in western Asia. It seems that the Cushites in Egypt encouraged the little Kingdom of Judah to resist the Assyrians. A Cushite army under Taharqa was sent to relieve the siege of Jerusalem, but before any fighting took place the Assyrians were compelled to raise the siege and evacuate Palestine because of plague.

After the death of Shabaka, Shabatka succeeded to the throne and on his death Taharqa was proclaimed King. It was he who was first defeated by Esarhaddon and then Ashur-banipal, the Assyrian kings. Both Upper and Lower Egypt passed to the Assyrians, who appointed Egyptian princes as vassals. Tanwetamani who succeeded Taharqa made an attempt to restore his Egyptian dominion. He succeeded in Upper Egypt, because the princes there accepted his authority, but in Lower Egypt some remained loyal to the Assyrians and fought against him. Before he could defeat such rebellious princes the Assyrians appeared in the scene and dealt the final blow to him in Egypt after which the Cushites retreated to their home in the Sudan. For a period of about 75 years the Cushite Kings not only united Egypt and the Sudan but Cush was a world power. After this retreat from Egypt Cush survived for about a thousand years first with its capital at Napata and later at Meroe.

CUSH AFTER THE RETREAT FROM EGYPT

This Cushite Civilization was ancient Egyptian in all its elements, although some Greek and Roman influences found their way to it through Egypt. The gradual loss of contact with Egypt and the final removal of the capital to Meroe were associated with gradual decline and deterioration in culture and civilization. Meroe proved to be more suitable as a capital than Napata because of its potentialities as grazing land and the growth of iron industries. There is evidence to show that Meroe was a supplier of iron implements to neighboring territories.

Around 225 B.C. the Cushite King, Ergamenes, seemed to have resumed friendly contacts with Egypt and perhaps with other territories. As a result of this move there was greater prosperity in Meroe under him and his immediate successors. It was in this period that women appeared as queens with full sovereign power. One of these queens took the opportunity of the absence of the Roman garrison in Egypt in an Arabian campaign and raided Aswan and Philae and pulled down the statues of Augustus. The Romans reacted by occupying the Halfa-Shallal reach and erasing Napata, the traditional and most venerated capital of Cush. Indian influence during this period, probably through the Kingdom of Axum in Ethiopia, revealed itself in the presence of Indian cloth and the idea of artificial reservoirs for storing rain-water. The story of the Roman mission in Nero's time to the Sudan and their report of the unworthiness of the country to be a part of the Roman Empire was clear evidence of the deterioration and poverty of the Kingdom of Meroe.

The final destruction to Meroe came from its neighboring state of Axum under Ezana who put on record the following:—

". . . . I, 'Ezana, the son of 'Ella 'Amida, a native of Halen, king of Axum and of Himyar and Raydan and of Saba, and of Salhen, and of Seyamo and of Beja and of Kāsu (Cush—Meroë), king of kings . . . made war upon Nōbā, for the peoples had rebelled and had boasted of it . . . . , "They (the Axumites) will not cross the river Takkāzē (the River Atbara)," said the peoples of Nōbā. And they were in the habit of attacking the peoples of Mangurto and Khasā and Bāryā and the blacks and of making war upon the red peoples.

Twice and thrice they had broken their solemn oaths, and had killed their neighbors without mercy, and they had stripped our deputies and messengers whom I sent to enquire into their raids, and had stolen their weapons and belongings. And as I had warned them, and they would not listen but refused to cease from their evil deeds and betook themselves to flight, I made war on them . . . and fought with them on the Takkāzē, at the ford of Kemalkē. They fled without making a stand, and I pursued them for 23 days, killing some and capturing others . . . I burnt their towns, both those built of bricks and those built of reeds, and my army carried off their food and copper and iron . . . and destroyed the statues in their temples, their granaries, and cotton trees and cast them into the river Sēdā (Nile). And I came to Kāsu (Cush) and fought a battle and captured prisoners at the junction of the rivers Sēdā and Takkāzē. And the next day I despatched the army Mahazā, and the army Harā, and Damawa and Falha and Serā up the Sēdā to raid the country and the cities built of bricks and of reeds. The cities built of bricks were 'Alwā (Sōba) and Daro . . . and after that I sent the army of Halen and the army of Laken down the Sēbā against the four towns of the Nōbā which are made of reeds. . . . The towns built of bricks which the Nōbā had taken were Tabitō and Fertōti. And my peoples reached the frontier of the Red Nōbā and they returned in safety, having defeated the Nōbā and spoiled them by the might of the Lord of Heaven. And I planted a throne in that country at the place where the rivers Sēbā and Takkāzē join. . . ."

The present state of our knowledge does not enable us to ascertain the extent of the Meroetic state westwards. But bits of evidence show that there was Meroetic influence in Kurdufan and Darfur and possibly still further westwards. Excavations need to be carried out before this theory can be confirmed in whole or in part. It is guessed that members of the royal family fled to the west. Periods of hostile and friendly contacts were recorded between the Bija in the Eastern Sudan and the Nubians in Lower Nubia on one hand and the Romans in Egypt on the other, but nothing is heard of about the center of Meroetic civilization after the destruction of their towns by Ezanā.

The Bija and the Nubians who were in contact with Egypt seemed to have been given permission under a treaty to pay visits to the temple of Isis and were being paid subsidies to keep peace in the frontiers. The Romans, after the official recognition of Christianity by the State, could not tolerate pagan worship in their dominion. So the temple of Isis at Philoe (near Aswan), which was frequented by the Bija and the Nubians was destroyed and its priests were imprisoned. This move was followed by the conversion of the Nubians to Christinity, a common bond more secure than treaties. As the Christian Church in the Byzantine Empire was divided at the time the race for domination was reflected in Nubia. The Manophysites won the race when Julian in 543 A.D. succeeded in converting the King of the Nubians to a Christianity that was at least nominal.

The Christian religion spread in the Sudan afterwards until three Christian Kingdoms were established; Nobatia with its capital at Bellana and later moved to Faras, 'Alwa with its capital at Soba (near Khartum) and Mukurra with its capital at old Dongola. In A.D. 569 Mukurra was converted to Orthodox Christianity. At the same time Longinus, a disciple of the exiled Patriarch Theodosius left Constantinople and confirmed the work of Julian in Nobatia. After a difficult journey he trekked southwards until he reached 'Alwa and converted Christians there to the Monophosites faith.

ISLAM AND ARABS (A.D. 600-1500)

The Muslims expanded in the direction of Persia first and then into Syria and Palestine before 'Amr Ibn al-'As conquered Egypt in 640 A.D. The Roman influence at the time was at its lowest ebb and resistance came only from the Roman Garrisons. The two Nubian Kingdoms of Nobatia and Mukurra seemed to have united to resist the Muslim invasion from Egypt under 'Abdalla Ibn Sarh who succeeded 'Amr as Viceroy of Egypt. There was no decisive victory for the Muslims but the Nubians began to pay tribute of slaves, although frequent raids on southern Egypt were maintained. 'Abdalla had to outfit another expedition which was also resisted by the Nubians and this time included the most southern Nubian Kingdom of 'Alwa. The capital of Mukurra (old Dongola) was bombarded and a treaty with the King, which remained for over 600 years, was concluded. By it the Nubians had to supply as tribute about 360 slaves to the Muslims near Aswan. The Muslims had, in return, to give to the Nubians gifts of wheat, barley, lentils, cloth and horses.

The upheaval which took place in the Near East as a result of the victory of the Abbasids over the Omayyads in 750 A.D. had its repercussions in the Sudan. Some Ommayyads fleeing from massacre and through Abyssinia. In 831 we have on record that the chief of the Bija Kanun, Ibn 'Abdel Aziz, concluded a treaty with the Muslims in Egypt, by which he agreed to pay as a tribute to the Khalifa a hundred camels or three hundred dinars every year. In return the Bija were allowed to visit Egypt but unarmed and agreeing not to damage mosques erected in their country. This is a clear evidence that some Muslims, mainly nomads, found their way to the Bija country and erected mosques for worship.

As it would be expected, the Nubians were not punctual in paying their tribute and the Muslim government in Egypt retaliated by cutting off their supplies of food and incited the Bija to raid Nubia. When relations reached such a stage Zakaria, King of Nubia, sent his son George to Baghdad to appeal to the Khalifa. George's mission was a success. He returned with a large order on the treasury of Egypt provided that the tribute should be paid. It seemed that George represented to Baghdad the difficulty of yearly payment of tribute and it was agreed, therefore, that it should be settled every three years.

In 854 A.D. the Bija refused to pay the agreed tribute and raided Egyptian territory. The Muslims reacted by sending an expedition against the Bija which defeated them and Ali Baba, their chief, surrendered. The victorious Muslims dictated a treaty by which they were permitted to work the gold mines in the Bija Country. It was this attraction of gold which brought to the Eastern Desert of the Sudan a succession of Arabian tribes chiefly Rabia and Guhayna who settled among the Bija and married their women. The effect of this Muslim-Arab infiltration was the passing of tribal control to the Arabs and the spread of Islam. Nubia continued to have periods of peace and hostility with the Muslims in Egypt and when al-Mas'udi visited Egypt in the first half of the 10th century there were two Nubian Kingdoms, one in Dongola and the other at Suba near Khartum.

Towards the end of the 10th century the King of Abyssinia asked George II, King of Nubia, to use his influence with the Patriarch of Alexandria to despatch to Abyssinia a properly ordained Abuna (bishop). This request was a success and a new Abuna was sent. In the last two decades of the 10th century Ibn Saleem al-Uswani wrote an account of Nubia, Mukurra, 'Alwa, Bija and the Nile. From his account we know that the Muslims began to encroach on Nubian

Territory from Aswan. They acquired land, converted Nubians into Islam and were practically independent petty kingdoms. South of this Muslim area the king of Nubia, who was known as the Lord of the mountain, was still in control.

Ibn Saleem described the Kingdom of 'Alawa, with its capital Suba, as rich and independent. The King there had more soldiers and horses than the King of Mukurra. In Suba there were fine buildings and churches decorated with gold. In the churches of 'Alwa Greek books which they translated into Nubian were used. Like Abyssinia their bishops were sent to them by the Patriarch of Alexandria. According to Ibn Saleem the Muslims lived in a special quarter in Suba. This indicates that they were a tolerated foreign minority at the end of the 10th century.

The 12th century witnessed the passing of authority in Egypt from the Fatimids to Saladin al-Ayyubi. He sent two expeditions against the Nubians, because the latter seemed to have moved on 'Aswan in support of the Fatimids. Saladin's own brother led the second expedition which resulted in taking Ibrim, pillaging the church, taking prisoners, killing pigs and torturing the bishop. A Muslim embassy to Dongola gave an unfavorable account of the country and described it as extremely poor.

Abu Salih early in the 13th century gave an account of these Nubian lands. According to him the ruler of Maris with capital at Faras wore a turban, two horns and a golden bracelet. In the middle of the 13th century the Mamelukes succeeded the Ayyubites in the rule of Egypt and one of their first acts was to put down an Arab revolt in Upper Egypt. Shortly after Baghdad was sacked by the Mongols and the inevitable result was the displacement of many Arabs, many of whom were distinguished persons. It was a disturbed period in the Near East and most unfavorable to the Arabs. With Arabs already established in the Bija country and acquiring some degree of control in the Northern Sudan the displaced Arabs found new homes in the Sudan. The Christian Kingdom of Dongola which was already on the decline felt the Arab pressure. The Governor of Kus invaded Nubia up to Dongola, because King David failed to pay his tribute. Not strong enough to resist Muslim invasion King David retreated southwards to al-Abwab, but according to Ibn Khaldun he was sent back to Baybars as a prisoner by the ruler of that district. He was kept in prison in Egypt till he died. A large army accompanied by David's nephew defeated the Nubians and the whole northern part became a fief of the ruler of Egypt. There followed a series of murders, ejections and rebellions among the Nubian Kings of Dongola. All through this period of disturbances the kings in Dongola were Christians, but early in the 14th century a Muslim King succeeded to the throne of Dongola. Although Muslim states were established in this way in Nubia there were hostilities between these Muslim rulers and the Mamelukes in Egypt had no control over them. The nomads, who looked upon the Mamelukes as an alien race, trekked southwards into these new territories where they would have more freedom. It was the period of nomad migration, mostly Guhaina, who over-ran the country to the Abyssinian border and Darfur.

The Fung

The establishment of Muslim petty states in the North, the increasing influence and control of Arabs in the Bija land and the migration of nomads for freedom and better pastures during the Mameluke regime in Egypt led to the inevitable result of the ultimate control of Muslim Arabs in the Sudan. Towards the beginning of the 16th century, the remaining Christian kingdom of 'Alwa with a capital at Suba was destroyed by the combined forces of the Fung and the 'Abdallab. The Fung claim descent from Ummayyads, who found their way to the Sudan, probably through Abyssinia, after the destruction of Ummayyad authority in Syria by the Abbassids. There are other theories about their origin. It seems that little was known of the early reigns of the Fung Kings who ruled at Sennar with their 'Abdallab partners at Quarri at the up-stream end of the 6th Cataract.

About the beginning of the 17th Century there flourished in the Fung Kingdom a number of famous Saints including Shaikh Idris, Shaikh Hasan Wad Hisuna, Taj al-Dine al-Bahhari and others. Just at this time when Islam was spreading in al-Jazirah, another Muslim Kingdom was established in Darfur in Western Sudan. The Darfur Kings also worked for the spread of Islamic religious teaching in their dominion.

During the reign of Badi Sid al-Qum early in the 17th Century the Fung after humbling their junior partner, the 'Abdallab, picked a quarrel with their neighbor, Abyssinia. The war that followed was a series of border skirmishes and one major battle in which the Abyssinians came out somewhat the better. During the long reign of Badi Abu Diqin starting in the middle of the 17th century, the Shaiqia of Dongola revolted successfully and this indicated the dwindling control of the Fung over the remote parts of their dominion. In a successful expedition against the little Kingdom of Taqali in the Nuba mountains, Badi brought back a number of prisoners and settled them in villages around Sennar according to the hills from which they had been taken. These villages supplied the Fung Kings with a standing army of Nuba troops. The 18th Century saw the decline of all Sudanese Kingdoms, owing mainly to the deteriorating quality of the monarchs and stagnation resulting from being shut off from outside influences.

When we approach the last decades of the 17th century and the 18th European travellers began to supply us with bits of information about conditions in the Sudan. Poncet, a Frenchman, was sent to Abyssinia by the King of France to establish diplomatic relations. Du Roule, another Frenchman, was sent by his Government on a similar mission. When passing by Sennar, the capital of the Fung, the King there gave him a kind reception. But he displayed a set of distorting mirrors, which gave the impression that he was a magician. He was subsequently detained and eventually murdered. The King of Abyssinia reacted in protest and threatened to divert the Blue Nile. In 1744 the King of Abyssinia led his army in order to conquer Sennar. He marched until he came within sight of Sennar on the Eastern Bank of the Blue Nile, but was forced to retreat by an attack made by a Sennar army led by a Fur Prince who happened to be an exile in Sennar, at the time. The result was the defeat of the Abyssinian army and the capture of an amount of equipment and firearms. The news of this victory spread through the world of Islam. Embassies came to Sennar from some of the Muslim countries and some particularly from Egypt and Morocco came and settled in the Sudan. Kurdufan, situated between the Fung and Fur Kingdoms, was claimed as a vassal state by both, but the Masabat were so firmly established that in practice they were supreme.

King Badi Abu Shelukh, after defeating the Abyssinians, invaded Kurdufan, perhaps at the instigation of his Fur General or in search of horses for his cavalry. The Sennar army was twice repulsed but Shaikh Muhammad Abul Kailik, from the Hamaj, won a victory when appointed Commander of the Fung army. He stayed in Kurdufan as Governor and was reputed to be a good and just ruler. The Sennar nobility who were with Abul Kailik in Kurdufan had some complaints against the King. They succeeded in persuading him to depose the King. Marching from Kurdufan and encamping at al-'Ais (Kawa), he sent for Badi's son Nasir and arranged to declare him King in place of his father. The real power was transferred from the King to the Hamaj Viziers, the descendants of Abul Kailik, up to 1821 when Muhammad Ali's army conquered the country.

For about three centuries the Fung with their junior partners continued to rule that part of the Sudan known to the world as Sennar. It was not a centralized kind of government but rather a loose supervision and supremacy over tribal chiefs. There were occasions when the two partners fought one another and sometimes those tribal or territorial units rebelled against the central authority. Neighboring tribes were in frequent wars over grazing or water. It was in this disunited state of affairs that Muhammad 'Ali of Egypt sent his army for the conquest of the country.*

---

* My authority for this introductory chapter is A. J. Arkell "A History of the Sudan to A.D. 1821," the Athlone Press (London 1955).

THE INDEPENDENT SUDAN

I

THE SUDAN UNDER MUHAMMAD 'ALI OF EGYPT

To consolidate his position in Egypt and to carve out a princi-
pality independent of the Sultan of Turkey, Muhammad 'Ali was
thinking of a strong highly disciplined and trained army. For technical advice on such matters, he had already selected France to give
him guidance, but his problem at the time was the man-power,
which he could recruit. As slave-trade was well-established he could
see for himself the able-bodied black Sudanese who were sold in the
slave markets of Cairo. He heard of their courage, endurance and
loyalty to their masters. They would be the best available material
from which he could man his new modern army.

Furthermore, there were somewhat exaggerated stories of the rich
gold deposits in certain parts of the Sudan in addition to other
products. If this were true, he could utilize these economic resources
to the best advantage of building up his autonomous state in Egypt.
Before indulging, however, in a full-fledged project of conquest he
wished to collect more information about both the economic potentialities of the country and the black Sudanese as a suitable raw
material for the army. He wanted, also, to have a correct assessment
of how strong the rulers of the country were. For this he sent a
special envoy with presents to the King of Sennar ostensibly on a
peaceful mission, but really as a spy to collect information. When
Muhammad 'Ali was in Hedjaz fighting against the Wahhabis, he
met one of the ex-petty kings of the Sudan, who supplied him with
more information of the tribal organization of the country and the
lack of a strong central government.

The Sudan was, also, a focus of his attention for another strategic
reason. Some hundreds of his enemies, the Mamlukes, fled southwards
into the Northern Sudan and established for themselves a little state
in Dongola. They would, certainly, become a permanent menace
against the security of Egypt, so long as they were let loose. They
might proceed still further to the south and destroy the small petty
kingdoms of the Sudan one after the other. There was, therefore,

1

the possibility of the Mamlukes forestalling him in recruiting this raw material of the black Sudanese in their military establishment, with which they might proceed northwards into Egypt in an attempt to restore their lost ground from Muhammad 'Ali.

It was, also, quite possible that he thought of tracing the Nile up to its sources for discovery and control of the tribes that lived on its banks. In this respect he would have been following the practice of the ancient Egyptians. They were greatly interested in the lands of the Sudan south of Aswan and all through their history they extended their influence until there was a time when the northern parts of the Sudan were completely Egyptianized. Interest was lost in the Sudan when Egypt itself was no longer a centre of a big state, but only a province, though rich and important. These were the motives which prompted Muhammad 'Ali to conquer the country.

When the time was ripe for him to start his campaign, Muhammad 'Ali had already gained most valuable experience in warfare under similar conditions. His campaigns in Arabia acquainted him with desert problems of communication. The Sudanese socially and religiously were almost the same as their brothers on the other side of the Red Sea. Fortunately for him Muhammad 'Ali found in his military adviser Muhammad Bey Lazuglu, a most faithful and experienced servant to undertake the fitting out of this expedition to the Sudan. Boats were requisitioned from all parts of Egypt, provisions, arms and ammunition were all prepared. He was aware of the weapon of propaganda which would contribute to his military effort, and might even make actual fighting unnecessary. He should harp on the note of community of race and religion between the people of Egypt and the Sudan. For this purpose tribal chiefs in Egypt were sent with the army in order to persuade their opposite numbers in the Sudan to accept the suzerainty of Muhammad 'Ali without resistance. Learned men in the four schools of Muslim thought accompanied the fighting forces so as to spread the doctrine of the one common religion which would ultimately remove any element of hostility to the newcomers.

Muhammad Bey Lazuglu brought together sufficient forces composed of various elements. They included North Africans, Turks, Albanians and Nomad Arabs. Judged by modern standards at the time it was not an efficient force, being mercenaries of different elements and degrees of training and discipline. But they were quite adequate for the task before them. They possessed firearms which were a great advantage over whatever resistance they might encounter from the Sudanese who would be fighting only with their traditional weapons of spears and swords. All the army with its equipment and provisions were collected at Wadi Halfa and stores of provisions were amassed at some point above the second cataract south of that town. The Mamlukes, who were at Dongola, heard of the approaching army and they had to make up their minds how to meet it. The majority decided to send their Egyptian wives northwards to their relatives, while they themselves trekked still southwards to be out of reach of Muhammad 'Ali's army. They reached Shandi, but losing hope of ever settling in the Sudan they dispersed east and west. Those who decided to go east with a view to crossing the Red Sea and thus reaching the Holy Places in Hedjaz were never heard of. Most probably they were cut down by the Bija tribes in the Eastern Sudan. It is reported that some of those who decided to go west reached Tunisia in North Africa. Those Mamlukes who lost hope of successfully resisting the Pasha went northwards and surrendered to the army.

When all preparations were completed and the army was in a condition to enter into the first phase of its conquest, Muhammad 'Ali appointed his son Isma'il as the commander of the expedition. He was about 25 years of age, intelligent, daring and confident to the degree of failing to consult his very much older and more experienced lieutenants. He was relatively well versed in European Geography and politics, and stammered, because of a natural defect in his jaw. Perhaps this was responsible more than anything else for the many occasions of misunderstanding between him and the Sudanese chiefs, who could not make out what he was saying to them.

Isma'il was served as lieutenants by two experienced officers. 'Abdy Kashif was in the service of Muhammad 'Ali for about fifteen years with a spotlessly clean and faithful record. He was known before joining the expedition as the efficient administrator of Minya Province, and the man who could gain the respect and confidence of the Europeans. The second was Quja Ahmed Agha, who left behind him a record of 25 years of army service. The morale and the organization of the army, however, was not the sort of military establishment which Muhammad 'Ali would like to have as his future force. Most of them were mercenaries serving under monthly contracts. For this particular expedition they were paid six months in advance on condition that they would stay until Dongola was to be conquered. Thereafter there would be fresh contracts for specific periods.

The expedition started from Wadi Halfa southwards into the Mahas country, where rulers surrendered without any resistance whatsoever. Dongola, which was already evacuated by the Mamlukes, was occupied without firing a shot.

The only resistance in this northern part of the Sudan was expected to come from the Shayqiya tribe, who lived in that bend of the Nile south of Dongola and who seemed to have shared with the Mamlukes suzerainty of that territory just before the arrival of the expedition. They were known to be good fighters and boasted of many years of independence. They recognized that they could not maintain their independence against such a force which, though inefficient judged by European standards at the time, was far superior to whatever fighting force they could put in the field. It would be an acceptable formula to them to accept the authority of the conquerors, but at the same time to keep their horses and weapons. For Isma'il, who would very soon be leaving their country southwards to complete his conquest, it was impossible to leave behind him that war-like tribe of the Shayqiya, who might cut his line of communication with Egypt. It was inevitable, therefore, that a trial of strength between the two fighting forces should take place. Although in the ensuing encounters that courageous Sudanese tribe proved their mettle by putting up the strongest resistance, it was a foregone conclusion that the firearms and the artillery of the newcomers should decide the issue against the Shayqiya. They fled southwards to Shandi until the arrival of Isma'il in that area when they preferred to be enlisted in his forces as professional irregular soldiers.

The first stage of conquest was completed by defeating the Shayqiya in Dongola. It was for Isma'il now to proceed southwards to the Ja'alin country with Shandi as center and ultimately to Sennar. While in Dongola boats were the chief means of transport, camels were the only available means for the transport of sodiers and equipment across the desert intervening between the bend of the Nile in Dongola and west of Barbar. Even the heavy guns were carried on wooden poles between two camels. When striking the Nile again, Nasr al-Dine, Mak of Mirafab, Abu Hijil, Mak of Rubatab, and the

Shaikh of the Hassaniyah—all these tribal chiefs surrendered and accepted the authority of Isma'il without any resistance.

Nimir, the celebrated Mak of the Ja'alin at Shandi, however, seemed to have wavered between welcoming the conqueror and resisting. While it was hard on him to subjugate himself and his powerful tribe to the invader, yet he was aware of the futility of any form of resistance. His subsequent attitude towards the conqueror illustrated that state of mind. Instead of showing his submission in a clear form like his colleagues to the north by paying homage in person, he sent his son to meet the Pasha instead. But Isma'il insisted that Nimir should come out of Shandi in person. It was inevitable for the Ja'alin chief to obey the order of the powerful Pasha. He entered the Turkish camp in a solemn ceremony with a handful of body-guard and retinue, wearing his two-horned cap, the sign of chieftainship. Nimir swore allegiance to Isma'il, who confirmed him in his tribe but gave him no sword as he had done to the loyal chiefs like the Kings of Argo and Barbar. This was a clear indication that the Pasha was still in doubt of the loyalty of Nimir.

The army was resting in the Ja'alin country for a while and preparing for the next and what seemed to be the most important and decisive stage of the campaign. Muhammad 'Ali began to worry about what looked to him to be an unnecessary delay. He argued that any time wasted before delivering the final blow would be advantageous to Sennar authorities who were considered at the time to be the toughest enemy. In a letter to his son at this stage Muhammad 'Ali revealed his worries and told his son in strong language that he should show more activity. Before leaving the Ja'alin country southwards Isma'il had to provide for the government of the conquered territory. 'Abdy Kashif was sent back to Dongola and Mohy Bey was appointed as Governor for Barbar and the Ja'alin. Proceeding southwards Isma'il was met by the King of the Abdallab at the western bank of the White Nile near its confluence, and crossing to present-day Khartum he stayed for four days before he resumed his march through the Jazirah on his way to Sennar. No resistance was encountered until Badi, the last King of the Fung met the army outside his capital, Sennar, with complete humiliation and surrender.

How could this lack of any resistance from the Sennar Government be explained? The Fung kings were mere puppets at the time and all power was vested in their viziers the Hamaj. The representative of this group was Muhammad 'Adlan, who was actually organizing a tough resistance to the invading army. He contacted the Ja'alin maks, Magdum Massalam in Kurdufan and the Mak of the 'Abdallab near Khartum for a united front. His son 'Adlan was already sent to the confluence of the Nile as an advance party, when he committed a grievous mistake. Acting under the pernicious influence of his assistant, Arbab Dafa'allah, he had chosen that juncture to write to Shaikh Ahmad al-'Araki dismissing him from the office of the Khalifah of 'Arakiyin fraternity, a high religious post, merely because Shaikh Ahmad happened to be on bad terms with Arab Dafa'allah. Shaikh Ahmad could not bear to be treated in such a high-handed manner. He should meet intrigue with another intrigue. He conspired with Hasan Wad Rajab, the enemy of Muhammad 'Adlan, and both carried out their conspiracy, which was no less a fatal action than the murder of Muhammad 'Adlan himself. The leader of the resistance was thus removed just at the time when Isma'il left the Ja'alin country on his way to Sennar.

It was the plan of Muhammad 'Ali to control all the Sudan including Kurdufan and Darfur. The latter was a well-established kingdom as old as Sennar itself and Kurdufan was at that time tributary to Darfur with Magdum Massalam as Governor. Muhammad Bey, the Defterdar, son-in-law of Muhammad 'Ali, led another expedition into Kurdufan. Although a stiff resistance was put up by the Kurdufan army at Bara north of al-Ubayyid, the Defterdar managed to defeat them mainly because of the use of firearms, which people in the Sudan at that time never used. The conquest of Sennar and Kurdufan completed, it was for Muhammad 'Ali to organize the government of these vast territories so that maximum benefits could be reaped from the conquest.

Orders, instructions, and directions were sent regularly to Isma'il while on his way to Sennar as to the line of action he should take when he had completed the conquest. It was the plan for Isma'il to stay in the capital Sennar and to send lieutenants to the country as far as they could reach looking for booty and able-bodied young Sudanese to man Muhammad 'Ali's new army. An expedition led by Muhammad Sa'id Afandi went to the Dindir area, and another led by Quja Ahmad Agha headed for Jabal Tabi, from which they brought about 1900 prisoners. On their way back to Sennar the Arabs of

Rufa's tribe were raided and the booty comprised 2000 camels, 1000 cows, and about 1600 sheep. All the prisoners and the animals captured were immediately despatched to Egypt. Being anxious to recruit in his army from this first consignment, Muhammad 'Ali gave instructions for selecting the able-bodied young Sudanese for training, the rest of the prisoners either to be used for domestic work or to be sold in the slave markets of Esna, Aswan or Cairo.

Muhammad 'Ali seems to have looked on organizing a government in that vast country of the Sudan and utilizing its economic resources to the best advantage as a task too big for Isma'il to shoulder single-handed. Ibrahim the eldest son should proceed in person to the Sudan and with his younger brother a well-thought-out plan for government and utilization of the country could be implemented.

On arrival at Sennar Ibrahim and Isma'il planned two expeditions, one to be led by the latter to the territories south of Sennar, and the other under Ibrahim to the Dinka land on the Upper White Nile. There was no doubt whatsoever that the objective of these raids was to bring as many able-bodied Sudanese as they could manage to get. Several times Muhammad 'Ali in his letters to his sons and to the first governors-general afterwards referred explicitly to the fact that he had taken all the trouble of conquering the Sudan mainly for suitable man-power for his army. Counting on the impression that there would be no difficulty in obtaining the required number of suitable men, it was the plan of the two brothers before starting their raiding expeditions that as soon as a sufficient number of prisoners was collected, 10,000 young men should be sent immediately. The women and children captured with them would be sent afterwards. It was estimated that, following this procedure, about 40,000 men could be sent to Egypt in this way. The expedition under Ibrahim destined to raid the Dinka had to come back before reaching the White Nile because of the bad health conditions of Ibrahim resulting from illness. Isma'il, however, who had carried out his raid, was not, as successful as it was expected he should be. He managed to obtain only 477 suitable young men.

Notwithstanding this initial disappointment Muhammad 'Ali lost no time in devising and suggesting ways and means by which he would welcome caravans of these young men suitable for a modern army. All sorts of problems and difficulties cropped up. How could they transport this large number across the desert? Camels could not be found in sufficient numbers to carry them. To march on foot would ultimately end in reducing their number through death. He suggested as an alternative the making of a special kind of Nile boats. Camps were erected at Esna and Aswan, his own young Mamlukes were appointed as officers for them, and learned people were appointed as Imams to lead them in prayers after teaching them the elements of Islamic religion. He even went so far as to bargain with his sons about sending reinforcements to the Sudan. For every 3000 black Sudanese he would send 1000 trained soldiers to the Sudan. In order to have complete control on the source of this raw material for his army, Muhammad 'Ali issued instructions that slave-dealers were not allowed to practice their trade outside the Sudan except for his Government. He entered into negotiations with the Sultan of Darfur for trade agreements on slaves and allowed taxes to be collected in kind in the form of able-bodied Sudanese suitable for recruitment.

On his return from the Sudan, Ibrahim submitted a report to his father on conditions there, emphasizing in particular the unsuitability of the climate for Turkish and Albanian troops. He subsequently stated his policy on the distribution of forces over his dominions which included, at the time, in addition to Egypt proper, Arabia and the Sudan. In a letter to the Governor of Jirja he says:[1]

"We have sent a large number of soldiers under the command of our sons and we are still sending them for the purpose of bringing from the Sudan black Sudanese to be employed in Hijaz and similar territories. Our Son, the Governor of Jedda (Ibrahim) has returned from the Sudan and on questioning him, he reported that the Sudan climate would not suit the Turkish soldier and as they are our own race they should be offered the best possible conditions of service by not sending them to outlying places reputed for their severe heat. Their proper place is to be with us in Egypt. This state of affairs makes it imperative that about 4000 soldiers should be recruited from upper Egypt with a view of sending them to the Sudan."

Though Muhammad 'Ali was disappointed, he continued sending instructions for collecting as large a number as possible of this manpower for the army: "We have taken all this trouble not for money, as we have repeatedly written to you, but for obtaining as large a

[1] Book 10 Ma'ia, Corr. 145 dated 25 Jamad Awwal 1237 Hejira Year, Jamhuriya Palace Archives.

number of suitable slaves as possible."[1] In the same month he writes
again to the Sudan saying: "The object of sending you to those
territories with a sufficient force, well equipped, is to obtain slaves,
who would reach Aswan barracks in safety. Slaves suitable for
recruitment are of the same value as precious stones, even more
valuable." Thirteen months have passed by since the conquest of
Sennar without any appreciable results; the number obtained as the
result of raids was comparatively small, great difficulties were encountered in transporting them to Egypt, and death took a heavy
toll on them, whether on the way, or after reaching their camps in
Egypt.

When Isma'il was away on his raiding expedition in Upper Blue
Nile, Muhammad Sa'id Afandi and the head accountant Hana al-
Tawil set to work to levy taxes. The idea of taxation itself was
somewhat foreign to the people and what made it still worse was that
it was too heavy and assessed in money which was scarce, the usual
form of exchange being millet and a kind of coarse cloth locally made
called dammur. Confronted with this unusual situation some of the
people in Sennar area fled to the east, taking refuge in Ethiopia, and
others began to display revolutionary spirit. At this juncture it was
rumored that Isma'il was killed in his raiding expedition, and this
added to the possibility of an open revolt against the new Government. Hanna al-Tawil, feeling the danger in this highly inflammable
atmosphere, left for Shandi, ostensibly for change because of illness,
but really he wished to be away from what would very soon be a
scene of rebellion. Knowing of this situation created by this taxation,
Isma'il hastened to return to Sennar to lead a campaign of appease-
ment in person. He immediately sent messengers on camels to return
the taxation-books which were despatched to Cairo, but at that time
they were out of reach. In spite of this he made a substantial reduction. His measures removed the imminent danger of revolt. Subsequently after this Isma'il made Wad Madani, to the north of Sennar,
his capital because of the latter's unsuitable climate.

It had been almost two years since Isma'il started his Sudan
expedition for conquest. They were spent in fighting and raids under
climatic and living conditions with which he was not familiar. It
was high time that he should take leave back to Cairo, entering it as

---

[1] Muhammad 'Ali to Ismal'il, Book 10, Ma'ia, No. 325, ated 1 al-Qa'ida,
1237 A.H.

a triumphant conqueror in a ceremony similar to that of Ibrahim Pasha when he returned from his successful Arabian campaigns. Leaving Muhammad Sa'id Afandi as his deputy, he proceeded north wards with a body-guard composed of 250 horsemen. Isma'il rode ahead of his guard with personal servants, a physician and a few others, into Shandi, and subsequently a meeting with the two petty kings of the Ja'alin country, Nimir and Masa'ad, was arranged. There is no reliable record of what had passed between them. But it is almost certain that Isma'il asked for exhorbitant demands from the two chiefs. It amounted, according to one version, to £20,000 of cattle, camels, gold, etc., an amount which could not be provided from their limited resources. It seems that Isma'il was determined to take with him to his father some substantial gift. He could not collect anything from Sennar area because of the spirit of revolt reigning there subsequent to taxation. The only area which might supply him with what he wished to take to Cairo was the Ja'alin country. Nimir was taken completely by surprise at the amount he was expected to pay, knowing pretty well the limited resources of his people, and showed his objection in language which displeased the Pasha. Isma'il, a young man of 27, the conqueror of the Sudan and the Son of the great ruler of Egypt, would not tolerate such strong language from a conquered chief, and it was natural under the circumstances that he should respond in an equally strong manner. It was not in words, but by a slap in the face to Nimir with his long pipe. Nimir, on the other hand, the chief of the most illustrious tribe in the Sudan, reached the limit of humiliation by accepting the suzerainty of that young Turk; but now to be slapped in the face in public was going far beyond what he could tolerate. It was inevitable, therefore, that Nimir should retaliate immediately to that insult, and he was already about to draw his sword when his colleague Masa'ad gestured to him to show submission and to postpone the revenge for the night. The conspiracy was planned and executed by burning to death Isma'il and his escort. Although versions of the story differ in details, they were all agreed that the skeleton was exhorbitant demands, insult and revenge. Official records do not throw much light on this incident.

The first government official who got news of the incident was Muhi Bey, Governor of Barbar, who sent the news to Cairo. Isma'il's deputy at Wad Madani sent 300 horsemen to confirm what reached him as a rumor. At the confluence of the two Niles in the present Khartum they knew for certain of the incident and returned to their base. It was the Defterdar in Kurdufan who collected all his available forces and proceeded to the scene of the incident. When reaching the White Nile he started his campaign of revenge on all who happened to be on his way until he reached al-Matammah, the heart of the Ja'alin country. It is estimated that people there suffered at his hands casualties of about 5000 dead. Nimir and Masa'ad, who were by this time to the north of their land, met the Defterdar in battle which raged for hours, and in spite of the valor and courage shown by the Ja'alin youth, it was a victory for the well-equipped Turks. Assured of the collapse of the Ja'alin resistance, the Defterdar returned by the east bank of the Nile and continued his revenge on the inhabitants up to Wad Madani. This first phase of the revenge campaign ended by the Defterdar returning to Kurdufan and Nimir and Musa'ad taking refuge in the Eastern Sudan (Butana), reorganizing their forces to put up another stand to the Turks. After settling his affairs, the Defterdar proceeded again to the east to end the Ja'alin resistance. He met first Nimir in the Butana and then Masa'ad in the Dindir river, and the result of this second and last phase of the campaign was the crushing of his enemies. Nimir resorted to Ethiopia with a few members of his family and the Defterdar sent down to Egypt thousands of the Ja'alin prisoners of war. Muhammad 'Ali gave instructions to sell many of those prisoners in the slave market, but the process was stopped because of the intervention of the foreign consuls.

It was high time that the Defterdar should return to Egypt after pacifying the country, to give place to his successor as governor of Sennar, 'Uthman Bey, who brought with him the first battalions trained and disciplined in the Nizam Jadid. He stayed only about 8 months when he died of tuberculosis. His spell of duty was a continuation of the Defterdar's regime, but he was the first ruler to select Khartum as the future capital of the Sudan. His successor Muhi Bey, the former Governor of Barbar, succeeded to a great extent in restoring the confidence of the inhabitants in the new government after it was severely shaken as the result of the punitive expeditions of the Defterdar and the equally cruel and harsh rule of 'Uthman Bey. These six years of Turkish administration of the Sudan left their very bad effects on the Sudanese. Although the

Turks were, at the time, the leaders of the Muslim world and the Sultan was the religious head of all Islam in his capacity as Khalifah, yet the Sudanese experience in their contact with the Turks was nothing but bloodshed, heavy taxation and cruel methods of rule.

Khurchid Agha's appointment as Governor of Sennar territory ushered in a period of relatively better relations between the rulers and the ruled. He was eminently successful in persuading those people who took refuge in Ethiopia to return to their homes in the Sudan. Although 'Uthman Bey was the first Governor to select Khartum as the capital, it was Khurchid who changed it from a village with a few huts built of straw and skins to a town. He ordered the erection with red bricks of the Mosque, government offices and army barracks. People were encouraged to build permanent homes by giving them free gifts of timber.

It was Muhammad 'Ali's policy executed by Khurchid that the agricultural resources of the country should be explored and developed. For this purpose about a hundred trained Egyptians were sent to the Sudan to train the Sudanese farmers in the best methods of farming. Some Sudanese were sent to Egypt to learn some crafts for which no proper facilities were in existence in the Sudan. Select breeds of sheep, fruit trees, indigo, sugar cane, etc., were all brought to the country from Egypt to experiment with. In spite of the personal supervision of Muhammad 'Ali over the administration in the country and the benevolent rule of Khurchid, evidence of corruption and taking bribes by the ruling class was not lacking, but was not so conspicuous and open as it became later, when the firm hand of Muhammad 'Ali was removed under his successors. Notwithstanding the bitter disappointments which Muhammad 'Ali encountered in finding the adequate number of able-bodied black Sudanese for his new army, he was still hankering after the idea of enlisting in his forces as many as his officials in the Sudan could manage to get. We notice in his correspondence at this time that he used to give instructions for keeping such recruits in the central Sudan for some time to be acclimatized when brought from their southern abodes before sending them finally northwards to Egypt, in addition to taking special care for their food and shelter. Sudanese cattle were exported to Egypt at this time for working the water wheels and camels were sent to Hedjaz for government transport. From the Governor of Sennar Khurchid rose gradually to that of Hakimdar (Governor-General) of all the Sudan.

It was during the second part of Khurchid's rule when he was in control of all the Sudan that the presence of official slavery was revealed to Europe by tourists in the country. Raids for the purpose of bringing Sudanese from their homes were still organized by the Government. Sometimes soldiers, officers and officials were paid their salaries in slaves and taxes were allowed to be paid in human beings also. When representations were made to Muhammad 'Ali by the European powers and more particularly by Britain, on this matter, he issued orders to the Governor-General of the Sudan for the abolition of such forms of official slavery. Official records during this period reveal, also, that the Sudanese were associated with the government of their country as Shaikhs of Khuts; the name of 'Abd-al-Qadir Wad al-Zain of al-Jazirah was mentioned several times.

The exaggerated stories of the abundance of gold in the Sudan were perhaps the second motive for the conquest of the country, the first being the suitable man-power for the army. It was, therefore, quite appropriate for Muhammad 'Ali to think of how to mine scientifically this precious mineral. Among the first consignments of the Sudan produce which Isma'il sent to his father were specimens of earth taken from places known to be rich in gold deposits. Experts on mining were employed and sent to the Sudan and at times a body of experts were holding a series of conferences, which resulted in wide differences of opinion. The Governor-General was especially instructed to proceed to the area of the gold-mines in Fazugli in person and supervise the investigations and conferences which were already in progress. Just at this juncture Khurchid's attention was diverted to the frontiers with Ethiopia which were never properly demarcated. They were no-government land, so to speak, but were controlled by the Shifta (armed bandits).

The Ethiopian hills were refuges for those Sudanese who evaded the payment of heavy taxation, and also sheltered those who flew before the Defterdar's punitive expeditions. Rumors which received very wide publicity stated that a conspiracy between tribesmen on the frontier, refugees, and some Ethiopian chiefs, was staged against the Turkish Government of the Sudan. The time fixed for carrying out the plan was the end of the rainy season, when conspirators would march into the Sudan, fighting the Government forces, and aiming at re-establishing the petty chiefs who ruled the country before the Turks. This plan was believed to be true in Khartum and so Khurchid had to ask for strong reinforcements to be hurried from Cairo. Muhammad 'Ali promptly responded and sent contingents, under Ahmad Pasha, a high-ranking officer equal in status to Khurchid. Meanwhile Khurchid brought together his available forces and led them in person to the Eastern Sudan to be on the look-out lest the conspirators might execute their plan before the arrival of reinforcements. Nothing was done, however, on the Ethiopian side, and it was either a mere rumor without foundation, or the tribesmen were demoralized by the appearance of the Turkish force. Khurchid and Ahmad met at Wad Madani and both returned to Khartum, when Khurchid was permitted to go to Cairo to be cured of an illness from which he was suffering, and Ahmad Pasha was appointed acting Governor-General. A Sudanese chronicler, Shaikh Ahmad, praised the 12 years of Khurchid's rule in high terms as being benevolent and just. After some months as acting Governor-General Ahmad Pasha was confirmed because Khurchid stayed in Egypt and was given an appointment there.

When Ahmad Pasha was confirmed as Governor-General Muhammad 'Ali's army had already been in occupation of Syria for some years, and it seems that he was involved in financial difficulties. This is evidenced by the repeated instructions to Ahmad to send as much as he could of the Sudan gum, and he began to think more seriously of mining Sudan gold in spite of the disappointing reports of experts. He decided to take a journey to the Sudan for the sole purpose of looking into the question of gold in person. It was only after he stayed in Fazugli for about two months and supervized mining operations that he was ultimately convinced that some amount of gold could be mined, but the stories of the large deposits there were extremely exaggerated.

Apart from his benevolent firm administration which in this respect was a continuation of Khurchid's, Ahmad Pasha made a notable annexation by the conquest of the Taka area (Kasalah). He constructed some dams in the Qash to utilize its yearly flow of water for irrigation purposes. After he returned triumphantly from Kasalah, rumors spread far and wide that Ahmad Pasha was planning separating the Sudan from Muhammad 'Ali's dominion to connect it directly with Turkey, with himself as viceroy in the same status as Muhammad 'Ali's in Egypt. Werne, the German traveller who was with Ahmad in Kasalah, recorded that the Governor-General was thinking very seriously of what seemed to be very important matters.

The inference is that he was probably contemplating that hazardous scheme. Muhammad 'Ali seemed to have been rightly worried and naturally asked Ahmad Pasha to proceed to cairo immediately. Feeling that Ahmad was not promptly responding to his orders Muhammad 'Ali sent messages to all provincial governors both in Upper Egypt and the Sudan north of Khartum asking for information about the whereabouts of Ahmad. Suddenly Ahmad Pasha died, when about to embark on boats intending to start his journey to Cairo. His death under such mysterious circumstances caused rumors to spread that Muhammad 'Ali removed him by poison administered to him through one of Ahmad's wives, a slave of Muhammad 'Ali. These rumors of Ahmad's ambition and death were so public in Egypt that Muhammad 'Ali was compelled to announce publicly his appreciation of Ahmad's service and the loss sustained by his death.

But whether these rumors were founded on fact or not, Muhammad 'Ali initiated a radical change in the administration of the Sudan immediately after the death of Ahmad. To avoid the possibility of any strong governor-general nursing the thought of taking the bold and dangerous step of separating the Sudan from Egypt, Muhammad 'Ali decentralized the administration of the Sudan by cancelling the high post of the Governor-General and breaking up the country into provinces directly connected with Cairo Government, very much in the same way as provinces in Egypt proper were administered. Ahmad Pasha al-Minikli was sent as an organizer for the sole purpose of making the new system function. This would mean that he had to allot the security forces to the various provinces according to their requirements and install the new provincial governors with a workable system of co-operation among them. But it was destined for al-Minikli to remain for about three years, proving in the end that the Sudan should be centrally administered. While there, he had to play the role of a governor-general when the frontiers were disturbed by leading his forces against the aggressors. Some provincial governors did not recognize him as Governor-General, particularly that of Khartum, so long as it was the considered policy of Muhammad 'Ali that there was no central authority in the Sudan. Clashes of such nature took place which were detrimental to the smooth running of affairs and at times led to the actual breakdown of authority. Nomadic tribesmen evaded the payment of taxation in telling every provincial authority that they paid it to the

other. The co-operation between the governors which was essential
for the functioning of this new arrangement was lacking.

Compelled by force of circumstances to re-establish the post of
Governor General in the Sudan, Muhammad 'Ali was very particular
about the person who would be selected. Khalid Pasha, a man of
no ambition whatsoever, was appointed. After the annexation of
Kasalah area to the Sudan, administrative difficulties arose about
those tribesmen who moved between the Sudan and the area of
Sawakin and Masawwa'—the two latter were ports under Turkey.
Muhammad 'Ali succeeded in persuading the Sultan to put him in
control of them for Muhammad 'Ali's life on condition that he
should pay a certain percentage of their customs dues to Jedda
treasury. In the last years of Muhammad 'Ali's administration of the
Sudan people in the northern provinces started to migrate to the
Central and Western Sudan, avoiding the exceptionally heavy burden
of taxation. This is evidenced by the number of water-wheels which
were once working and were ultimately deserted.

Muhammad 'Ali's administration of the Sudan was a typical
Turkish one; it was highly centralized, so constituted as to squeeze
the maximum amount of money out of the inhabitants, and requiring them to submit completely to the orders and measures of the
Government. But it was this highly-centralized government which
gave the vast territories of the Sudan for the first time in history
one uniform machinery of government. The country opened to influences of civilization and tourists flocked to it for exploration and
scientific observation. An attempt was made to modernize methods
of agriculture and irrigation, to introduce crafts and light industries,
to increase production generally, and to market the Sudan products
outside. But the curse of his administration was the heavy taxes and
the cruel methods used for their collection. People could not forget
the punitive expeditions of the Defterdar and the atrocities committed by him. Although Muhammad 'Ali, in the end, stopped the
raiding expeditions for slaves and the various forms of official
slavery, officials in the Sudan were busy enriching themselves as
quickly as they possibly could, and in this way the foundation of
corrupt administration was laid by them.

II

THE SUCCESSORS OF MUHAMMAD 'ALI IN THE SUDAN

Abbas I, a grandson of Muhammad 'Ali, became Viceroy in 1848 after the death of his uncle Ibrahim, when his grandfather was still alive but aged and senile. Khalid Pasha was still the Governor-General of the Sudan. It seems the officials took the opportunity of Muhammad 'Ali's old age and became negligent in their duties, and busied themselves with their own personal affairs to become rich in the shortest possible time. It was clear, therefore, to Abbas when he was in power and to his council, that there should be a somewhat radical change in the administration of the Sudan. Khalid Pasha was dismissed after cases of embezzlement were established against him. The status of provincial governors was raised from Kaimkam to that of Miralai and a completely new set of governors was appointed. An ordinance regulating the service in the Sudan was passed by the council. 'Abdel-Latif Pasha, who started the new machinery, was appointed Governor-General. He made changes in the provinces by amalgamating Fazugli and Sennar in one province, and making Dongola and Barbar separate administrative units with the Ja'alin country integrated in the latter. 'Abdel-Latif Pasha took great interest in the development of the town of Khartum. He built the Governor-General's Palace, Khartum Province headquarters, the High Court, and the army barracks—all in red brick. Missionaries were admitted into the Sudan and foreign consulates were established, which were a prelude to increasing trading activities by merchants and firms from Europe and the Levant. 'Abdel-Latiff was greatly embarrassed by these trading companies, who appeared to the people as a government authority. They had in their service armed men. There was evidence that some of them traded in slaves. He made an attempt to protect the inhabitants from profiteering by such merchants. The Kantar of gum was fixed at 60 piastres and the Government was prepared to accept it at this price in lieu of taxes. Penalties were inflicted on buyers and sellers alike in cases of breach of these regulations. Firms and their consuls made a capital issue of

17

these trade restrictions and invoked, through their respective Governments, the privileges of Europeans in the Turkish Empire. The result was the removal of 'Abdel-Latif and the appointment of Rustom Pasha.

'Abbas opened a school in Khartum ostensibly to give schooling facilities to the young of the Sudan, but most probably it was a pretext for banishing out of Egypt such free-thinkers who were not in favor with him, like Rufa'a Rafi' al-Tahtahawi and Bayoumi Afandi. The first thing for Sa'id, when succeeding to 'Abbas, was to close down the school and to recall Rifa'a and others. Work in the gold mines was stopped and the export of cattle to Egypt was also suspended, because it was established economically that these two schemes worked at a loss to the Government.

Muhammad Sa'id Pasha, son of Muhammad 'Ali, succeeded 'Abbas in 1854 after receiving western education and training, which gave him wide horizons and a more humane administration than his predecessors. From the start he had shown special interest and sympathy in Sudanese affairs. It was he who had issued instructions for the formation of a pure Sudanese battalion in his army in Egypt, and the promotion of brilliant Sudanese soldiers to officers' rank. He further instructed his Governor-General of the Sudan to send about 1200 young good-looking Sudanese soldiers to form his own body-guard. Customs dues on merchandise between Egypt and the Sudan were abolished and clear instructions were issued to the Governor-General to visit with severe penalties those traders who dealt in slaves.

'Ali Sirri Pasha was the Governor-General when Sa'id came to power. He was a crying example of those corrupt officials, who accepted bribes and enriched themselves in an open manner. The High Council responsible for appeals of the judiciary submittted a complaint to the Viceroy against his corrupt administration, citing specific cases. This resulted in the dismissal of 'Ali Pasha in disgrace. Shortly after, 'Abd al-Halim Pasha, brother of Sa'id, requested to be appointed as Governor-General for the Sudan, to which Sa'id readily agreed. But he had to return to Egypt after a short spell of duty in the Sudan owing to the outbreak of an epidemic there.

Sa'id decided to travel to the Sudan in person to study its affairs on the spot. When he arrived at Barbar he was showered with a considerable number of petitions addressed to him from all parts of the Sudan and particularly from the northern provinces. It seems that the common complaint in these petitions was the tax and methods of its collection. Sa'id immediately thought of a new policy for that vast territory which would not allow the cruel soldiery to come in direct contact with the people, and would make Cairo rather than Khartum the central authority for the administration of the Sudan. On his way from Barbar to Khartum he began the enforcement of his new policy. The collection of tax, which was substantially reduced, was entrusted to village Shaikhs. These in their turn would either hand over their collections to a higher Sudanese chief of their own choice, or directly to the Province Treasury. The security forces were restricted to keeping the peace and redistributed to province headquarters according to the security needs of the territory. But the same causes which made Muhammad 'Ali's decentralizing policy fall were at work to negative the good intentions of Sa'id. In the last days of Sa'id, when Isma,il was acting viceroy, the policy was reversed and the Governor-General's post was re-instituted.

Isma'il succeeded his uncle Sa'id when the central authority in Khartum was already reinstated by the appointment of Musa Hamdi Pasha as the Governor-General. Musa was familiar with the Sudan, because he had seen service there in various capacities, including, on one occasion, that of assistant to the Governor-General. He was known to be a combination of firm and efficient administrator, but a typical Turk in his extremes of rudeness at times. As soon as he was in Khartum he hastened to hold a meeting in the capital of all the provincial governors with their chiefs and shaikhs, to communicate to them his new policy and to consult them on various aspects of administration. The upshot of that meeting was an agreement on the bases on which taxes should be laid and on how they should be collected. Tax-payers were to be supplied with books in which their total payments were to be written and when instalments were paid the signatures of the recipients were to be shown on the book.

Following his policy of gradually associating the pure Egyptian element with administration in Egypt, Isma'il initiated the same policy in the Sudan. Shaikh Ahmad Abu Sin, chief of the Shukriya tribe between the Blue Nile and the Atbara river, was appointed Governor of a greatly enlarged province of Khartum. He shouldered his responsibility with efficiency and tact which won for him the admiration both of his seniors, and of the people he had to govern. In carrying out his duties he had to deal with a province which had common boundaries with Ethiopia, inhabited by tribes of nomadic Arabs and pagan negroids, and with the cosmopolitan town of Khartum itself. Conflicts and jealousies were not lacking among these tribes and with the tribal chiefs, who would consider themselves of equal status with Ahmad. Yet with such problems and difficulties Ahmad Bey administered his province for about ten years until he died in Egypt when on a visit of duty there.

Musa's next major problem was how to reorganize the army and to make Sudanese troops more and more responsible for the defense and internal security of the Sudan. Two additional Sudanese battalions were raised to make the total ten. Regular Sudanese soldiers who were stationed at the time in Egypt were sent to the Sudan. The need arose for a number of young suitable Sudanese for the new battalions and as replacements for the old who were to be discharged. Arrangements were made with chiefs of the Fazugli, Shuluk, and Dinka tribes for the supply of suitable recruits and the Government was prepared to pay 500 piastres for every young man who would be considered suitable as a soldier. In his correspondence with Musa about this matter, Isma'il made it quite clear that this sum should be considered as a reward to be deducted from these chiefs' taxes for their service, otherwise it would be interpreted as a form of slave-trade. Musa died in Khartum after a spell of duty lasting for three years, which were years of reorganization.

Isma'il thought his Empire was growing, especially after he succeeded in persuading the Sublime Porte to allow the permanent annexation of Sawakin and Masawwa to the Sudan, and that it should be sub-divided into three separate administrative units with the three governors co-operating, Kasalah, Sawakin and Masawwa' to be the first unit, Dongola, Barbar, and Kurdufan to be the second, and that middle territory, including Khartum with al-Jazirah, to be the third. But this administrative change was never executed, because one of those appointed to one of these enlarged provinces declined to go to the Sudan. But still the administration of the vast Sudan merited the appointment of a deputy Governor-General.

Before the new Governor-General's departure from Cairo a mutiny broke out at Kasalah. The mutineers took authority completely into their hands for several days until the arrival of troops from Khartum. Sayyid al-Hasan al-Margani, the most influential religious leader in the area, and probably in the whole of the Sudan, at the time, succeeded in restraining the soldiers from going to excesses and ultimately in facilitating their surrender. The new deputy Governor-General Ja'far Muzhar was instructed to proceed immediately to the scene of the mutiny with sufficient Egyptian forces by the way of Sawakin to restore law and order and enquire into the causes and events leading to the mutiny. His report revealed that the soldiers did not receive sufficient military training, and that for the greater part of their service they were not under the close supervision of their officers, because of their duties in tax-collection. It was also suggested that their leaders were somewhat indiscreet and tactless in dealing with them. The result was that Isma'il disbanded all the Sudanese battalions with the exception of one composed of eight companies. Some of the disbanded soldiers, however, were sent to Egypt to be distributed among the Egyptian battalions. No member of the Dinka tribe or any who was serving in the artillery was to be re-recruited. This Sudanese battalion had to be under strict supervision and would not be allowed to use the big guns.

This serious all-Sudanese mutiny made Isma'il ask for more information about his administration in the Sudan and the reports he received from various quarters directed his attention to the fact that all was not well in that territory, especially the behavior of the officials from the Governor-General downwards. Ja'far Sadiq Pasha, who was appointed Governor-General for only a few months, was recalled; Ja'far Muzhar Pasha, his deputy, was elevated to Governor-General, and Shahin Pasha, minister for war, was sent to Khartum for concerted action with Muzhar. After making a thorough investigation in the administrative machinery, the two high officials laid down what, in their opinion, ought to be the minimum of regulations and changes both in the civil and military set-up. Muzhar's administration, which lasted for about six years, was associated with the development of Khartum town after abandoning the idea of moving the capital to Tuti island. He was known to be a man of culture and learning, which he reflected on the people. But it was he who taxed the waterwheels in the Northern Provinces far beyond their limits in order to see what the Government could actually manage to collect. It was his intention that the average of actual tax collected over three years would be the reasonable figure for taxes. His successors were not made aware of this fact and asked for the whole sum fixed by Muzhar. This started an exodus from these provinces, especially from Dongola, towards the central Sudan and ultimately to the south. It was those people who deserted their water-wheels and looked for a living space where they would not be bothered by this incredible taxation, who in the end formed the best fighting force of al-Zubair as we shall see.

Isma'il made some modifications in his administration of the Sudan. The Eastern Sudan comprising Kasalah, Sawakin, and Masawwa' was made a separate unit with Mumtaz Pasha as Governor, and Barbar was to be administered as private possession of Isma'il with Husain Bey Khalifah as Governor. A further more radical change was introduced. The country was divided into four administrative regions with no central government in the Sudan. They were the East, West, Upper Sudan and Lower Sudan. Mumtaz was moved to Upper Sudan including Khartum, Sennar and Fazugli, and Husain Khalifah was confirmed in Lower Sudan including Barbar and Dongola Provinces. Both governors initiated an agricutural policy of a reformed nature. Canals for flood irrigation in Lower Sudan were dug by Husain and water-wheels and cotton were the main preoccupation of Mumtaz, but the latter was discredited in the end, because he was not aiming in his agricultural development solely to benefit the people and the Government, but also to enrich himself. Mumtaz was suspended and convicted of embezzling government money, and was succeeded by Isma'il Ayyub Pasha as a Governor for Upper Sudan first, and then as Governor-General, when a central Government was re-instituted in Khartum. This first phase of the Khedive's administration of the Sudan should not be closed without mentioning the improvements which he introduced. In the field of education he opened five elementary schools in the headquarters of the provinces and gave substantial grants-in-aid to a number of private mosque-schools. Communications were improved greatly by connecting the main towns of the country with telegraph lines and all with Cairo. Work on a railway line actually started from Wadi Halfa southwards, but had to be stopped later on when Isma'il found himself in financial troubles.

It was in Isma'il's days that the Egyptian empire was built up in Africa. We are, here, concerned with its expansion southwards into Bahr-al-Ghazal and Equatoria and westwards into Darfur. The drive towards the south was closely associated with the humanitarian move of abolishing slavery or at least the slave-trade. In its general perspective this move was part of the humanitarian spirit started in Europe and America in the nineteenth century, after the worst forms of slavery that the world had ever witnessed, on the coast of West Africa, practiced by Europeans, particularly by those who owned plantations in the West Indies and on the mainland of America. In the Sudan domestic slavery was known from time immemorial and people were used and accustomed to slave-labor. Muhammad 'Ali's conquest, as we have seen, was mainly moved by the desire to obtain a sufficient number of able-bodied slaves to be recruited in his army. Raids and expeditions were officially directed to the sources of such human beings. In this man-power hunting firearms were used for the first time for this purpose and this made it the worst and most effective kind of raiding. Private raiders following the example of the new Government, and using the same effective weapon, practiced this abominable hunt and trade. All these raids, whether government-sponsored or private, were in the outskirts of the southern Fung, the Ethiopian borders, the Nuba mountains, and part of the Upper White Nile.

Salim Kaputan's exploration trips on the White Nile opened the way for more trade activities. Ahmad Pasha the Governor-General was himself associated with such activities, and al-Minikli, the organizer, suggested that the Government should monopolize trade in this newly-opened territory, but Muhammad 'Ali did not agree to this line of policy for fear that foreign merchants might invoke the privilege of freedom of trade in the Ottowan Empire. When consulates were established in Khartum in Abbas's time trading companies from Europe and the Levant penetrated still southwards and their number considerably increased. A large number of Sudanese, particularly from Dongola, were enlisted in the services of those companies as crew to the boats or as private armed guards. These traders started illegitimate trading of ivory, ostrich-feathers, etc., but they had gradually learned that trade in slaves was more remunerative. Hunts for obtaining slaves were directed from their zaribas (thorny enclosures) as bases with their well-armed guards. In many cases they used some tribesmen as allies to help in hunting other enemy tribes. Boats began to transport northwards black ivory instead of white. Explorers and travellers passed through these territories when they were subjected to heavy raids by these trading companies. In these circumstances Isma'il was made aware of this deplorable situation and set to work to put an end to it or at least to lessen its bad effects.

It was Musa Hamdi, the first Governor-General under Isma'il, who began the enforcement of measures for the ultimate abolition of the slave-trade by instructions from the Khedive. Special taxes were levied on all people who worked in the boats that sailed up to Upper White Nile and patrols were active to see that no illegitimate trade was practiced. Fashoda was established as a Government Post mainly to supervise traffic on the river. But traders were still in control of the source of slaves and evaded by all means, including bribing the officials, the restrictive measures. European traders under some pressure from their governments sold their zaribas to the Egyptian Government, a step which found great encouragement from Isma'il. As the Government could not conduct legitimate trade in these zaribas they were leased to private compaines, which continued secretly trading in slaves.

It was, however, realized by Isma'il that nothing short of complete annexation of the territories from which slaves were hunted could solve the problem of the slave-trade. This idea fitted in very well with his own ambitious program for building up an African Empire. The first move was in the direction of Bahr-al-Ghazal, the events of which were associated with Zubair. As narrated by himself he received his schooling in Khartum School and went to the south by mere accident. It was his cousin who, contrary to the advice of the family, went in a boat intending to go to Bahr al-Ghazal, the land of hope and fulfillment of ambitions. Hearing of this, Zubair hurriedly overtook the boat some distance south of Khartum in order to persuade his cousin and bring him back. Seeing that the cousin was adamant Zubair swore by the divorce of his wife that he would proceed south in the same boat if the cousin would not change his mind and return to Khartum. Contrary to the expectation of Zubair the cousin also swore by the divorce of his wife that nothing would deter him from continuing the journey. It was under these circumstances that Zubair finally found himself in the land of prospects. He started as a small trader but his intelligence, dash and qualities of leadership led him along the path of riches and influence. It was after Zubair soared to such heights that the Governor of Upper Sudan appointed a certain Shaikh Muhammad al-Bilali at the head of a small expedition to annex Bahr al-Ghazal to the province of Fashoda. The traders interpreted this move as trespass on their ground which they won by their own efforts, and immediately formed themselves into a league, with Zubair as the obvious leader, intending to resist al-Bilali. The encounters that took place ended in the defeat of this expedition and the death of al-Bilali. The immediate reaction of the acting Governor at the time, Adam Pasha al-'Arifi, after ascertaining the facts of the situation was to advise that the Governor of Kurdufan should deal with Zubair as a rebel.

It was perhaps one of the most important decisions for Zubair to take in his life. He should either go on with his resistance to any Government expedition which was bound to be sent, or should try to come to an understanding. He had chosen the second course through the intermediary of Husain Bey Khalifah, the Governor of Barbar. The Khedive pardoned him and even instructed the Governor-General to appoint Zubair a Governor to Bahr al-Ghazal. It was subsequently arranged that he should proceed to Khartum to discuss details of the new province. When Zubair was preparing himself for the departure northwards to Khartum he learned of the raids by the Riziqat tribe of southern Darfur on his province. It was inevitable for him that he should deal with the raiders before he left Bahr al-Ghazal. These events led him ultimately to the conquest of Darfur.

To punish the Riziqat, Zubair outfitted an expedition about 4000 strong, and marched into southern Darfur. Because it was the rainy season, he spent 40 days in travelling what was normally covered in 15 days. Shortage of food was experienced and was responsible for the loss of about 600 of his men. In the encounter that followed Zubair dispersed his enemies and occupied Shaka. Two of the Riziqat chiefs, Munzal and 'Ilayan, fled and took refuge with the Sultan of Darfur, Ibrahim. A series of correspondence continued for a time between Zubair and Ibrahim in which the former insisted that the two refugees should be handed over to him, and the latter was equally adamant that he would not hand over chiefs taking refuge with him and who, furthermore, were his own subjects. In the end Zubair decided to settle the matter by fighting and informed both the Governor-General in Khartum and the Khedive. While Zubair was defeating the Darfurian armies that were sent to meet him, Isma'il Ayyub, the Governor-General, was collecting reinforcements to be marched westwards from Kurdufan, and the Khedive announced to the world that his armies were fighting the Sultan of Darfur because of his activities in the slave-trade. Zubair completed his conquests by inflicting a crushing defeat on the Sultan, who died in the battlefield, and entered al-Fashir, the capital, four days before the arrival of the Governor-General.

The Governor-General took charge immediately, and from the large number of telegrams exchanged between him and the Khedive, the problem of Zubair himself loomed very large. Isma'il Ayyub was very hesitant in entrusting him with any provincial Government, because he was not fit for such a task, in the Governor-General's opinion, in the first place, and also because he (Zubair) might be nursing the idea of declaring his complete independencce of the Khedive, once he was left alone. It was those doubts in the ability of Zubair and the fears of his ambition that made Isma'il Ayyub shower Cairo with a spate of proposals and counter-proposals. Once he would suggest sending Zubair on further conquest to the west, and another time he would be agreeable to giving him part of Darfur to administer. Zubair, however, solved his own problem by asking permission to report in person to the Khedive and to present his complaints. Both Cairo and al-Fashir heaved a sigh of relief and the permission was promptly granted. On arrival in Cairo he was detained under all sorts of pretexts and was never allowed to return to the Sudan until very much later after the reconquest of the country by Kitchener.

To pursue his policy of building up an African Empire and to deal a blow to the slave-trade by annexing those territories which were the hunting-ground for slavers, Isma'il appointed Sir Samuel Baker, the great explorer, as a leader of an expedition for this purpose. Knowing the problems and difficulties of central Africa, Sir Samuel supervised in person the ordering and manufacturing of all equipment that would be needed. For him the task was not just a walk-over. The central Government in Khartum did not readily give the facilities which he needed under instructions from Cairo, and when finally he left Khartum southwards up the White Nile he had to delay for almost a year because he chose the wrong channel in the Sudd area. In Equatoria itself he was strongly resisted by the traders under the leadership of Abu al-Su'ud, who succeeded in instigating the inhabitants, whom he had to liberate, against him. Sir Samuel had to resign in May 1873 after staying in Equatoria for over two years. The net results of his efforts were the establishment of three stations over which the Turkish flag was flying and the soldiers in those garrisons were restricted to a few miles around because the people were still hostile.

Charles Gordon was appointed to Sir Samuel's post after an accidental meeting with Nubar Pasha, the Egyptian prime minister, in the British Embassy in Constantinople. Gordon at once created a most favourable impression on Isma'il by accepting only £2000 salary out of the £10,000 which were paid to Sir Samuel. He surprised all those in authority in both Khartum and Cairo by his wish to take with him as an assistant Abu al-Su'ud, the same man who opposed Sir Samuel. The latter had to ask for his arrest and trial. A number of Europeans were appointed to assist Gordon in various capacities and the obstacles in the river in the Sudd area were removed before his arrival. He was eminently successful in winning the confidence of the people, which went a long way in making him establish more posts and annex more territories to the Egyptian Empire. The move on the part of Mtesa, King of Bugunda, of asking for teachers of Islamic religion from Egypt, which was initiated before Gordon's arrival, culminated under Gordon in the temporary establishment of an Egyptian post in Mtesa's capital at his own request. For some reason or another Mtesa did not maintain that cordial relation with the Egyptian government for long, but very soon turned against the garrison and made its position untenable, until the soldiers were compelled to withdraw under instructions from Gordon. This was a great disappointment to Isma'il and was a means of disturbing the good relations with Gordon. It is suggested that Mtesa knew that there were other stronger powers than the Egyptians and there was more wide-spread religion than Islam, after the arrival in his court of Europeans like Stanley. It was Gordon, also, who thought of connecting the equatorial parts of the Egyptian Empire with the coast of East Africa as a better means of communicating with the outside world than down the Nile with its natural obstacles. Isma'il was fascinated by the idea and fitted out an expedition to East Africa with a view to landing there to penetrate westwards and meet Gordon's, which would start from the lakes eastwards. But the project was frustrated by the intervention of Britain. The net result of Gordon's work in Equatoria was annexing large territories to Isma'il's Empire, making quite creditable explorations and mappings, and establishing good relations with the population there, but he considered himself a failure in the main objective of his mission, i.e. the abolition of the slave-trade. The deep root of slavery, the lack of co-operation among the high officials, not excluding the Governor-General at Khartum, and the vastness of the country, were all elements of frustration to the success of his mission. Under such circumstances he decided not to renew his contract when it had expired, but it seemed that he had given hope to Isma'il when in Cairo that he would return, seeing that the Khedive was keen to have another spell of his services.

In England, after contemplating all possible projects of service, he finally decided to lead an expedition from the coast of East Africa with a view to opening up a route to the lakes. Isma'il had heard from the British consul-general in Cairo that Gordon was not returning to the Sudan, and showed surprise that his friend would not keep his word of honour. This remark had a dramatic effect on Gordon, who immediately decided to keep his word so long as it was believed to be so by Isma'il. On the day of his departure two of his friends advised him to ask from Isma'il the administration of all the Sudan, not Equatoria Province only. On arrival in Cairo Gordon was appointed Governor-General with extraordinary powers to the vast Egyptian Empire which reached its peak at the time.

As a Governor-General under Isma'il Gordon did a lot of trekking in his vast dominion getting in direct contact with the people. His chief pre-occupation, as might be expected, was the slave-trade. He issued strict measures against slave-dealers and drafted regulations which ultimately were the subject-matter of a treaty between Britain and Egypt about the slave-trade. The British navy patrolled the Red Sea vigilantly for any vessels crossing to Arabia with loads of slaves. Although there was a marked improvement, yet the vastness of the area and lack of co-operation of his subordinate officials disappointed Gordon. He started a policy of taking into his confidence chiefs and notables by a lavish award of titles and decorations and the appointment of some in administrative posts. He persuaded a number of Europeans to accept appointments in the Sudan, particularly in Darfur and the southern provinces. Believing that Sulayman al-Zubair, who was in command of his father's troops, was the rallying ground for slave-traders, he followed a policy of humiliation towards him which, in the end, drove him to attack Idris Abter, the Governor of Bahr al-Ghazal. Gordon interpreted this as a rebellion against the Government authority and immediately sent an expedition against him under his friend Gessi, who succeeded in putting it down and executing Sulayman. Gordon acted on the assumption that Zubair, who was at the time in Cairo, was the instigator of that rebellion. His relatives in the Sudan were thrown in prison, his property was confiscated, and orders were even sent to Cairo to arrest Zubair there. Isma'il, however, was not satisfied that there was sufficient evidence to make Zubair associated in any manner with his son's rebellion. Gordon finally resigned when his friend Isma'il abdicated and he saw that he was not wanted. What followed in the Sudan was closely associated with the Mahdist revolution and a general description of the Turkish administration as it was practised both in Egypt and the Sudan would be appropriate.

In general the chief benefits of the régime were the opening up of the country to the outside influences of civilization and the unification of the various parts under one administration. While previously the ties with the outside world had been slender and there was the danger of a static and stagnant society, the conquest opened up the country to foreign elements which spread a higher form of civilization, mostly among the townspeople. At the same time, the centralized administration removed or at least minimized tribal jealousies. The curse of the régime was a whole set of abuses centered round the taxes. They were first and foremost too heavy for the people to bear, and inhuman and cruel methods were employed in their collection. The majority of the administrative service from the Governor-General down to the irregular private soldier used to pocket part of the money or accept bribes for allowing some people to avoid payment.

The reading of the dispatches of the khedives sitting at Cairo leaves no doubt about the nobility of their intentions concerning the welfare of their subjects. Having western education, as Sa'id and Isma'il had, the khedives were on a somewhat higher level than their subordinates on the spot, who were all of the old school and were not educated for modern administration. That was why there was a wide difference between theory and practice, between the decrees issued by the khedives and their application by the governors. A notable example was that of the slave-trade measures in which the rulers on the spot did not believe and so either gave them no support, or applied them half-heartedly, or even connived with the slave-dealers.

The framework of the administration, although there were minor changes from time to time, was in general the same throughout. The country was divided into provinces under mudirs, who appointed nazirs of qisms (heads of districts), who in their turn were assisted by shaikhs of khuts. In the case of the nomadic tribes the chief was the sole head of administration and directly responsible to the mudir. The Turkish law was administered in all civil and criminal cases, but the Muhammadan law regulated questions of marriages, divorces, and inheritance for the Muslims. There were juries in the important towns composed of unpaid ordinary citizens except for the presidents, who in some towns were paid. The same old trade routes carried the products of the country, chiefly ivory, ostrich feathers, and gum. In exchange for these commodities the chief imports were textiles and metal implements.

The administration in the Sudan in organization and tone was nothing but a miniature of the Turkish administration of which it was legally a part. Lord Dufferin, as late as October 1881, writes about the Sultan as being not only at the head of the structure but the chief embodiment and inheritor of the system and a model to be imitated and followed by those farther down the administrative ladder.

He is intelligent, industrious, shrewd, and very fair, but, with all his finesse, extremely naïf in many things and quite ignorant of the ways of the outer world, and of the political forces which govern it. On the other hand, he is so suspicious and mistrustful that he will confide in no one, and has gathered into his own hands all the threads of the administration. Now even if the Empire was in apple-pie order, its affairs would supply work for a dozen ministers, but for a single man to undertake the management of the existing chaos is madness. As a consequence all business is at a standstill, and it is in vain that the ambassadors attempt to get matters settled at the Porte or by the heads of the several departments. The Porte is a *nominis umbra,* and the ministers are less than mere clerks. Moreover, a great part of the Sultan's time and attention is preoccupied with the intrigues and plots which go on at his own palace. Being in continual terror of designs upon his life, he makes it a rule to surround himself with favorites who hate each other, and whose jealousies he is careful to foment; and these petty quarrels going on around him distract his thoughts from greater concerns, so that unspeakable stagnation and confusion reign in all branches of the public service.[1]

This quotation illustrates the atmosphere in the center of authority of the Turkish system of administration. The Governor-General in Khartum and the Governor of the province at his headquarters town both had the same life with the same fears and suspicions, autocratic methods, and distractions from the big issues of the day. There was nothing new in this Turkish system as applied to other parts of the empire because they had been used to it for at least three centuries, but to the Sudan, which was cut off from foreign influences, that form of highly centralized and authoritarian state was a novelty and the people could not develop a digestive system so constituted as to assimilate this new stuff. We have to bear in mind that most of the people in the Sudan, especially those living in the remote parts and the nomads, were never brought completely under authority.

In Egypt, which was the direct sovereign and controlling power in the Sudan, conditions were worsening just at the time when a huge and expansive empire was formed. The history of Isma'il and of his financial policy, which ended in difficulties and ultimate European control and his own abdication, are important factors in the background of the history of this period. In August 1879 we find Tawfiq, son of the Khedive, who had been forced to abdicate, in power in Cairo. Tawfiq had no natural ability and came to power under circumstances that gave him no initiative and would have afforded him no chance of showing his ability if he had had any. Knowing quite well the trend of events that led to the downfall of his father and his own enthronement, he would give no pretext to the powers to molest him and consequently resigned himself meekly to their whims. The hold on the Egyptian administration was further tightened by the dual control established in November

---

[1] Lord Dufferin to Queen Victoria, *The Letters of Queen Victoria,* 2nd ser. (London, 1928), vol. iii, p. 245.

1879 by which the financial control of the country by foreign powers was practically complete.

The opening of the year 1881 witnessed the beginning of that movement in Egypt which aimed first at equality between the officers of the Egyptian army, irrespective of whether they were Turks or Egyptians, in promotion to high ranks, but gradually led to the interference of the army in politics and ultimately ended in a revolution and in the British occupation. In the second half of the same year, 1881, the revolution of al-Mahdi broke out. The whole affair of the army revolution in Egypt was so mismanaged by the Khedive and his advisers that the mutineers scored victory after victory over the authorities in Egypt. The proclamation by al-Mahdi of the revolution in his island of Aba synchronized with the period in Egypt when the misunderstanding between the Khedive and his army was at its peak. While the Governor-General of the Sudan was ineffectively trying to check the movement of al-Mahdi to his mountain retreat in the west, an army mutiny was being staged in Cairo. Certainly the people conducting affairs in the Sudan were not in a mood at this juncture to nip the revolution in the bud. Naturally they were concerned about their families and property in Egypt and about what their position would be after things had been settled in one form or another. Officers and men, hearing of their mutinous comrades in the lower Nile, could hardly have had the heart to fight an insignificant Dervish. When the army leaders gradually assumed the control of affairs in Egypt they objected to any reinforcements being sent to the Sudan as their position would thus be weakened.

The Egyptian soldier at that time, who was entrusted with the task of putting down the rebellion in the Sudan, was in the most miserable condition. According to an English consular agent in upper Egypt in October 1884[1] the fellah in upper Egypt was living wholly on bread made of maize and onion, was stricken with disease, and was sheltered in very unhygienic mud huts. The yield of his land was hardly enough to pay Government taxes and for mere subsistence. He was always at the mercy of the usurer, and

[1] Mustafa Aga to British consular agent at al-Uxur to Her Majesty's agent and consul-general in Cairo enclosed in Baring to Granville, No. 960, Oct. 18, 1884, P.R.O., F.O. 78/3679.

the Mudir gave warning that in default of payment of taxes the land of the fellah would be seized and sold by public auction.

There was a gap that separated the purely Egyptian element and Turco-Circassian one; the latter always held themselves in a position of superiority over the fellah, and being in authority denied the Egyptian the key posts in the civil service and the army. This feeling of enmity between members of the same administration tended to weaken the Government both in the civil service and in the army.

Add to all these points of weakness that the Government soldiers were as Muslims confronted with a difficult task. They were not to put down a rebellion started by an ambitious claimant to power or a discontented subject, but by a man with a mission of religious revival for which the Muslim world had long waited. The soldiers, or some of them at least, found themselves not as neutral spectators but as actual instruments intended to stand in the face of al-Mahdi and to prevent him from fulfilling his mission. The Sudanese elements in the garrisons of the Sudan, and they were many, added to this religious feeling the community of interest with al-Mahdi and his followers. The only men that showed any stubborn resistance were the Negro troops who, even if Muslims, were not imbued with this religious feeling, and were only professional soldiers who fought honestly for the one who paid them. Conclusive evidence of this is to be found in the fact that they fought as well and as gallantly with al-Mahdi as they fought against him after they had surrendered to him at al-Ubayyid and other garrisons. Later, in 1896-98, those of them from the Khalifah's forces, who were taken prisoner by Kitchener's army, transferred their allegiance to the new régime and enlisted in the Egyptian army.

We find, then, in 1881, Egypt under the virtual control of the powers with a mutinous army composed of two hostile elements in the higher ranks and the men mostly drawn from conditions of living that were most miserable. These soldiers were asked to fight a man with a mission expected by the Muslim world, and later on their own country was occupied by a foreign Christian power which had put down a popular movement. A country with its own internal complications of finance, with mutiny in the ranks of its army, with the further complications of a foreign occupation and of ruling over an unwieldy extensive empire—such a country could not be expected to suppress a religious movement at a time when religion was still the most powerful unifying force in the East. The Egyptian Empire at that time was difficult to manage even under more favorable conditions owing to the difficulties of communication and the corruption of the administration. The picture was completed by the disorganization of the whole system and by virtual assumption of authority by a foreign power which disbanded the army and objected to the employment of the newly created one.

The idea in Islam of a Messiah who comes at the end of time to establish the Kingdom of God on earth had been known since the second century of the Muhammadan era. The only reference in the Quran is the return of Isa (Jesus), but al-Mahdi is mentioned in some of the collections of traditions (sayings of the Prophet). They all agree that al-Mahdi would be a descendant of the Prophet, and would fill the earth with justice and equity after injustice and irreligious practices had become widespread. They differ somewhat about the manner and the place from which he is to appear, and about the number of years he will live. Some even go into details of his physical features. There was also a tradition among the Muslims that at the close of every Muhammadan century and the beginning of a new one there would appear a reformer in the Muslim world and names are even given of the various religious leaders who had appeared in previous centuries. The lower the condition of the Muslims became the more expectant they were of the advent of al-Mahdi.

By the eighteenth century the Muslims had sunk to such a depth that Muslim society had lost all signs of health and vigor. The torches of learning that were characteristic of the Muslims in the Middle Ages had either been extinguished altogether, grown dim, or had passed to other hands. The centers of learning confined themselves to uninspired repetition. The people were being oppressed and robbed by their despotic rulers. Initiative was totally lost and everything continued in the routine of the same old methods.[1]

In the realm of religion the same lack of initiative prevailed and learning degenerated into superstitions with the faqirs who wrote amulets and charms in a dominating position. Saints were set up

[1] Lothrop, Stoddard, *The New World of Islam* (New York, 1921), p. 25.

as intermediaries between God and the people, and God became so remote from the ordinary Muslim, and the simple elements of Islam were so obscured by the ambiguities of commentators, that it became the privilege of the few to pardon sin or lead the people to the right way. The ordinary Muslim had to accept what was told him by the religious leader in whom he had confidence. All sorts of irregular practices were rampant, such as wine-drinking and prostitution, and, in short, it looked as if true life had gone of Islam and left nothing but the rigid and lifeless rituals.[1]

It was in the second half of the eighteenth century that a puritan reformer arose in the heart of Arabia in the person of Muhammad IIbn (son) 'Abd al-Wahhab. Nadj was congenial to such a movement in that it was free from the autocratic rule of the Turks, and the environment was still that in which Islam first arose in its simplicity, and was also free from the influence of those influential 'ulama (learned men) who looked upon any departure from the beaten track as a form of heresy. Muhammad was sponsored by the amir (ruler) of Nadj, Sa'ud, who gave the movement political and material support. Although politically the Sultan of Turkey through his vassal Muhammad 'Ali Pasha returned the holy cities of Makkah and Madinah to the orthodox Khalifate, yet the teachings of 'Abd al-Wahhab continued to dominate in Nad and even found adherents in other Muslim countries.

The Wahhabi movement was essentially a puritan reformation advocating the removal of all abuses such as superstitious practices which encumbered the true simplicity of Islam. All the mass of later interpretations and innovations of saint-worship were to be condemned by the reformer. The Quran literally interpreted was to be their sole guide and a strict code of morals was to be observed. An austere life was enforced, and silk clothes and luxurious furnishings and buildings were to be prohibited, and in fine, life was to be as near as possible to that led by the Prophet and his early disciples.[2]

Another thread in the reviving movements in Islam appeared towards the middle of the nineteenth century in the form of better-organized Sufi fraternities. The old fraternities were restricted to religious matters and carried no political significance. The

[1] Ibid.
[2] Ibid., p. 31.

notable example of these new organizations was al-Sanusiya founded by Sayyid Muhammad al-Sanusi. After receiving his education in the religious University of Fas, travelling widely over North Africa preaching the reform of the prevailing religious abuses, and performing his pilgrimage to Makkah, he settled in Tripoli where he built his first zawya (lodge). His impressive personality and organizing ability brought to him a large number of followers, much to the alarm of the Turkish authorities in Tripoli. As a result of strained relations with the authorities he moved to the oasis of Jaghbub in the Libyan desert. The work was carried on by his son al-Sanusi al-Mahdi, who removed his headquarters still farther into the desert to the oasis of al-Juf.

The fraternity exercised great influence in political matters in North Africa and the oasis although it was not openly and officially militant. In nearly every local rising the followers of al-Sanusi took part, but in a private capacity rather than on orders from the head. Al-Sanusi al-Mahdi never established cordial relations with the Sultan of Turkey. With the Christian powers he was equally cautious but he was not essentially fanatical. In fact his attitude was summed up in his remark: 'Turks and Christians: I will break both of them with one and the same stroke.'[1]

The Sanusi program was that of reform achieved gradually and peacefully. It aimed at uniting the African Muslims and then the Muslims in other continents under one theocratic Imamate embracing all true believers, or in other terms at pan-Islamism. While freedom from Christians was their ultimate objective, it was to be preceded by internal consolidation in improving the manners and morals of the people and improving their material conditions. Al-Sanusi persistently continued the policy of covering North Africa with the schools and lodges of the fraternity and converting the Negroes to the south to Islam.

A survey of the Islamic movements in the nineteenth century, however hasty it may be, is not complete without the mention of the pan-Islamic movement headed by Jamal al-Din al-Afaghani. The movement as interpreted by its leader was essentially a defensive one on the part of the Muslim world against the aggression and encroachments of the Christian powers. To Jamal al-Din the powers still hankered after the crusading spirit of Peter the Hermit

[1] Lothrop, Stoddard, op. cit., p. 56.

and he considered that the Muslim states should unite and defend themselves by using Western technique. That is why this movement was sponsored by Sultan 'Abd al-Hamid II, and Jamal al-Din for a time in great favor with him.

Whether al-Mahdi in the Sudan was influenced by these outside movements or not, it is impossible to tell, but in general he like they, attempted to revive religion by a return to the early years of Islam and to take inspiration direct from the fountain of religion the Quran, and from the authentic traditions of the Prophet. Just about that time, i.e. 1880, and onwards we see also the beginning of an Arab movement in Syria with the object of securing home rule from the Turks. Some people therefore began to challenge the authority of the Turk whether on racial or religious grounds, and our Mahdist movement of the Sudan should be conceived in that setting.

III

DECLARATION OF MAHDIISM

About 1840 a boy was born to the boat-builder of the Nile island of Labab, a little to the south of Dongola; he was named Muhammad Ahmad. The family were long known as being descended from the Prophet and, centuries before, were said to have been immigrants from the Kunuz land in lower Nubia, south of Aswan. Dongola ceased to be a suitable place for boat-building as the supply of timber was running short, and the whole family had to trek southwards in search of a more suitable place for the trade. Shandi was the first halting-place, but Karari to the north of Omdurman became the new home for Sayyid 'Abdallah and his family. After the death of the father the sons had to move to Khartum where they might derive more benefit from their trade of boat-building.

It was quite evident that from boyhood Muhammad Ahmad was not inclined to boat-building which normally would have been his future trade. To become a man of letters and learning was the thing for which he was naturally cut out. He began his educational career by attending the Quranic school in Karari, and subsequently in Khartum to which the elder brothers resorted as mentioned before. Ambitious youths who aspired to the heights of religious learning at this time travelled where they could satisfy their desires at the feet of highly esteemed shaikhs of learning. Shaikh al-Amin al-Suwailih to the south of Khartum was one of the rising stars at that time and Muhammad Ahmad attended his classes for some time. Having an insatiable desire to acquire all the learning that could be obtained in the Sudan he travelled farther north to the suburb of Barbar where the mosque school of Shaikh Muhammad al-Dikair[1] was situated and there enrolled as a regular student. That school happened to be one of those which had received grants-in-aid from the Government since the early of Isma'il Pasha's reign. Very soon the new student distinguished himself not so much by the amount of learning he imbibed, but rather in the actual practice of purifying his soul. His were the long noctural

[1] The name was changed by al-Mahdi later into 'al-Khair.'

sittings of meditation and the complete abstention from the com-
forts of life rather than the repetition of the commentaries of
learned men. The story is told that he refused to eat from the
rations given to the students on the pretext that they were extorted
by taxation from the poor people as they were paid for by a
Government grant. He only agreed to eat with his teacher when
the latter assured him that it was the corn of his own farm.

The same insatiable yearning for more learning led him to
another center which had a reputation for religious studies with
special emphasis on the Sufi (Ascetic) aspect. It was the school at
the shrine of the great saint, Shaikh al-Tayyib wad al-Bashir, the
founder of the Sammania fraternity in the Sudan. His grandson,
Shaikh Muhammad Sharif wad Nur al-Dayim, was Khalifah of the
fraternity at that time. There the environment was more to the
liking of Muhammad Ahmad, as it allowed him more time for
meditation, and he was very soon known as the pious young man
who slept but very little by night. At an exceptionally early age
his teacher gave him licence to be a shaikh of the fraternity, and
to accept people to its fold. It was said that he tried business, of
course on a small scale, but failed because he was too honest and
truthful to gain any profit, and in fact it was not suited to his
meditative and retiring nature.

Khartum proved to be lacking in that quietness which he
desired for communion with God, and so in a Dervish-like manner
he went along the White Nile until he came to the island of Aba
near al-Kawwah. That place was not only ideally suited to him,
but attracted the other members of the family, as its huge trees
were just the type suitable for boat-building. He even persuaded his
shaikh, Muhammad Sharif, to establish a lodge for the fraternity,
near al-Kawwah, to which he (Sharif) use to resort for some time
in the year.

It was, and still is, the custom for these fraternities on religious
festivals to flock to the shrine of the saint and to continue religious
dances for at least three days, after which they would disperse to
their homes. Muhammad Ahmad never faltered in his allegiance
to his shaikh, and regularly attended these gatherings at the shrine
of Shaikh al-Tayyib.

Here we come to the widely accepted cause of strained relations
with his shaikh, and although no reliable sources in written form

can be brought forward in evidence, yet the story is quite possible
if one considers the determination and sincerity of purpose of
Muhammad Ahmad. The story goes that on the occasion of the
circumcision of his sons, Shaikh Muhammad Sharif allowed the
women, mainly slave-girls, to dance, and beat tum-tums, which
were considered very abominable by the saint-like religious enthusiasts and certainly by Muhammad Ahmad. The disciple had to
direct the attention of the teacher to this unbecoming practice, and
the response was that Muhammad Ahmad should mind his own
business. It was really a revolution against the accepted custom of
the day for the disciple to give advice to the master in that manner,
as it was the latter who should advise and the former who should
obey orders, or at least not go to the extreme of advising the Shaikh.
It is not surprising, then, that when Muhammad Ahmad persisted in his objection to the practice the teacher excommunicated
him from the fraternity. It was a very hard blow to a pupil who
found spiritual enjoyment in being a member of such a fellowship.
The story continues that many times Muhammad Ahmad went
penitently to his master, but the latter was absolutely adamant and
refused him the grace of returning to the fold. Losing hope of ever
being forgiven by the master he had to seek to continue his connection with his fraternity through another shaikh of it: Shaikh
al-Qurashi of al-Jazirah near al-Masallamiya was the new master,
and in this way Muhammad Ahmad was still considered to be a
member of the fraternity.

    If I am allowed to digress a while from the canons of historical
research and stretch my imagination and live again in the skin of
Muhammad Ahmad at that juncture of his strained relations with
his master, I would see in that episode the start of a spiritual
revolution which culminated in his messianic mission and reform-
ing spirit. The repeated refusal of the master to accept him back
into the fraternity, notwithstanding the humble spirit in which he
approached, perhaps acted on him like a lever to raise his individu-
ality and think for himself instead of following the Shaikh like
a sheep. Once the internal revolution was complete, his eyes would
see quite clearly how conditions were so miserable and how the
world was full of religious abuses; being of a puritan spirit—as
undoubtedly he was—he began to be prepared for the part that
he was about to play as a man with a mission. Perhaps also the repu-

tation that Muhammad Ahmad gained as a saint of the highest order aroused the jealousy of the master and led to strained relations. The whole history of al-Mahdi in its entire details before his movement began, although part of it was recorded as early as January 1883 (Stewart's messages from Khartum),[1] is from hearsay evidence, yet it is in complete harmony with what was known about al-Mahdi in his later life when he was very much in the public eye. One thing which stood out very plainly was that Muhammad Ahmad led a spotlessly clean religious life with no hankering after mundane worldly affairs before he assumed his messianic role.

The aged Shaikh al-Qurashi, the new shaikh of Muhammad Ahmad, died, and the loyal disciple was among the followers who built with their own labor the dome over his grave, and there he made for the first time the acquaintance of 'Abdullahi, his future Khalifa and second in command. Immediately on returning to Aba island, Muhammad Ahmad began to write a number of letters to various religious leaders confiding to them his mission in a vague way. He received in reply some promises of support but the signal was not given for the rising. He made a tour in Kurdufan Province and it was during this tour that certain dignitaries at al-Ubayyid promised him support, and Mak Adam of Taqali mountains a free passage in his dominion because the idea of the flight to the west was foreseen even at that time.

His return from the Kurdufan journey was followed immediately by his circulating letters to religious men declaring this time, in unmistakable language, that he meant business. He openly disclosed to them that he was the 'expected Mahdi,' asked them to flock to his support in his struggle against the forces of evil, and assured them that he was divinely ordained and that there was no doubt whatsoever that victory was his ally. Some of these letters were shown to Muhammad Ra'uf Pasha, the Governor-General, by the recipients and particularly one to Shaikh Muhammad Salih, a religious man of repute in Dongola. Ra'uf is not to be blamed for not taking the matter seriously, because there was no incident in the history of the Sudan which people at that time could recollect in which a Dervish of the type of Muhammad

---

[1] Stewart to Malet, enclosed in Malet to Granville, No. 20, 20 Jan. 1883, P.R.O., F.O. 78/3552.

Ahmad had been a menace to Government authorities of long standing. It is true that there were examples of such people who, in a fit of ecstasy might claim to be men with missions, but the matter would stop there after they had come to their senses. Those who blamed Ra'uf for lack of prompt action were those who are always wise after the event.

Ra'uf's reaction was absolutely normal: It was to send a telegraphic message to the Qadi (religious judge) of al-Kawwah instructing him to go with two learned men to Aba island and see for themselves the truth of the rumors. The order was obeyed and the Qadi confirmed the rumors and sent documentary evidence consisting of copies of Muhammad Ahmad's letters by mail to Khartum.

The next step was to send a peaceful mission to make the man recognize the seriousness of the step he claimed to take and to induce him to abandon such a presumptuous title. Muhammad Bey Abu al-Sa'ud, was, at the time, the assistant Governor-General. He was a man of great experience and had many connections with the people of the Sudan; and for that reason he was selected by Ra'uf to lead the peace mission to Aba island. It was also thought wise that some relatives of Muhammad Ahmad in Khartum and others at al-Fashashuyah should accompany the deputation. On arriving there a conversation took place with no result, and Muhammad Ahmad would not move an inch from his position, but defiantly gave Abu al-Sa'ud to understand that he recognized no authority except his own divinely ordained one.[1]

Nothing remained for the Governor-General, as the chief man responsible for the peace and security of the country, but to send sufficient force to capture Muhammad Ahmad. The report of Abu al-Sa'ud was to the effect that there were about 200 Dervishes with Muhammad Ahmad who might offer resistance. The force collected consisted of two companies of regular troops who were certainly superior in arms and also quite sufficient in number. Thus no doubt was entertained that the matter would be settled. Their instructions were to try peaceable methods first and to apply force

[1] Ra'uf to the Khedive in No. 4 In-Telegram Book, Aug. 14, 1881, 'Abdin Palace Archives, Cairo (the Arabic Department).

only in the last resort. This is conclusive evidence that the move-ment was still considered as probably not a serious one.

Muhammad Ahmad knew only too well that as soon as Abu al-Sa'ud reached Khartum a force would be sent for his capture, and so he set to work immediately to prepare for war. It seemed that his letters to distant places had no effect whatsoever at that time and so he had to rely exclusively on the people who were with him in the island and on the mainland east and west of the White Nile in the immediate neighborhood. The majority of them were from the Dighaim and 'Amarnah tribes and in all they never exceeded 300 men, armed with swords, spears, and some even with sticks. Muhammad Ahmad put the matter clearly to them that it was a holy war and gave them the choice of either freely and of their own will joining him or of returning to their homes. Muhammad Ahmad had lived long enough in that vicinity to be intimately known to them and they saw in him an ideal religious personality on whom they could absolutely rely. So the response was a unani-mous approval of his action and a swearing of allegiance to his cause and leadership. While waiting for the Government troops they had some elementary training of methods of attack and defense. When the steamers carrying troops reached al-Fashashu-yah some of the Dongolese boat-builders there went as quickly as they could to give information to Muhammad Ahmad. It was the fasting month of Ramadan and the news reached Muhammad Ahmad and his supporters while they were performing their nightly prayers. The news gave them warning to be prepared for the fight.

Four flags that were used by his Dervishes were brought and Muhammad Ahmad added to the writing on all of them the words: 'Muhammad al-Mahdi the Khalifah of the Prophet.' And from that memorable night he was known as 'Muhammad al-Mahdi,' which name was engraved on his seal and with which he signed his letters. The story of the battle as reported by Ra'uf Pasha to Cairo[1] tells of the officers going against their instrustions by not trying to send the Qadi of al-Kawwah first on a peaceful mission. Soldiers were disembarked at 3 a.m. and marched straight to the village to

[1] Ra'uf to the Khedive in In-Telegram Book, Aug. 15, 1881, 'Abd. Pal. Arch. Cairo.

find Dervishes more than 200 in number and flying their flags. Orders to fire were not obeyed on the excuse that they were poor Dervishes who should not be killed. But when the poor Dervishes attacked and killed 120 soldiers and six officers the others ran back and took refuge in the steamer where Abu al-Sa'ud was waiting. The battle of Aba was fought on the 12th of August 1881 and on that day al-Mahdi won his first brilliant victory.

If doubt is to be entertained about the sincerity and self-sacrificing spirit of the later followers of al-Mahdi, especially after his great victories, there is no shadow of doubt that those first fighters of Aba were believers in his divine mission. He was not strong enough to bully them, but was a simple Dervish with no arms, and from the very beginning gave them the choice of either joining him in his jihad or sitting back. They chose the first alternative of their own free will, from their previous experience of the sanctity of Huhammad Ahmad. It was this belief in his divine mission that attracted the nucleus of his subsequent troops and followers.

The failure of that first Government expedition, as recorded by Stewart[1] sixteen months later, was mainly due to the disagreement between the two adjutant-majors, both claiming to be in command. One wanted the soldiers to advance at once and attack the village and the other thought it advisable to wait till daylight, while Abu al-Sa'ud remained in the steamer. The result was a failure of united action; part of the soldiers followed the one attack while the rest remained behind with the other. As it was the middle of the rainy season the ground was extremely marshy and the party advanced in a very confused order. They did not know where the village lay in that wooded island; the only man who might have known was Abu al-Sa'ud, who remained in the steamer, and so the adjutant-major asked a villager whom he met to point out to him al-Mahdi's house. The villager replied that he did not know. A conversation then ensued which was ended by one of the soldiers firing his rifle. Immediately after this al-Mahdi and his followers, who were prepared for the attack, turned out, attacked the party, and drove them back to the river with the casualties mentioned before.

After the action at Aba both al-Mahdi and Ra'uf had to prepare

---

[1] Stewart to Malet, enclosed in No. 20, Jan. 20, 1883, P.R.O., F.O. 78/3552.

plans for the future struggle and proceeded accordingly. al-Mahdi's plan seemed to have been thought out long ago and perhaps ever since his Kurdufan tour he had contemplated migration or flight to the west. In the first place it was an imitation of the migration of the Prophet from Makkah to al-Madinah. He proclaimed that he was reviving the mission of Muhammad in a living and similar form, and that he was divinely appointed for the purpose; and he acted on this assumption. Secondly, from the viewpoint of military expediency, Aba was too near Government centers to give him any strategic advantage, and the people in the vicinity, with the exception of that determined group who fought Aba battle, were completely at the mercy of the authorities who might take vengeance on their families if they rallied to the Messiah's standard.

On the morning following the battle he crossed to the mainland on the western side of the river and waited only to allow those of the tribesmen in that neighborhood who chose to go with him time for preparation. It was arranged between 'Asakir Abu Kalam, the chief of the Jimi' tribe, and al-Mahdi that the latter with his followers should not make their way westwards through the former's territory but that individual travellers seeking to join al-Mahdi in his mountain retreat would not be molested by the former. 'Asakir, by this attitude, showed that he was cautious enough not to provoke the wrath of the authorities of whom he was actually an official, but at the same time that as a Muslim he could not openly stand in the way of the 'Expected Mahdi.' al-Mahdi's passage was, then, through the Ahamdah territory to the south of the Jimi'. Here either the chief thought that his land was more remote from the Government centers than the Jimi''s, or he was less cautious than 'Asakir; he not only allowed al-Mahdi a free passage but offered him all the hospitality that he and his people could afford. The march was naturally slow because it was the middle of the rainy season. This was a great advantage in that it solved the problem of water for both men and animals and of fodder for the latter and did not seriously impede the march as the Dervishes were not encumbered with any loads of provisions or ammunition. At the same time it proved a more difficult obstacle for the Government army with their problems of transport and rather heavier equipment.

Mak Adam of Taqali seems to have allowed them, when they

had crossed the plain and come to the fringes of the mountains, to enter his territory but not to come near to where he resided in order not to arouse the suspicion of the Government and accusations of connivance with al-Mahdi. In fact his whole attitude towards the movement was very mysterious, as it appeared at the time and subsequently. While he gave all facilities to al-Mahdi, the Government authorities thought him their ally, even as late as the time of Hicks Pasha's expedition two years later. Anyway, those petty chiefs tributary to him offered their hospitality to al-Mahdi's followers. We shall leave al-Mahdi here quite comfortable in friendly territory, reinforcing his army with more adherents to his cause, and the narrative will switch to Khartum to see what was the reaction of Ra'uf Pasha.

After receiving the news of the Aba disaster Ra'uf Pasha had to make plans to meet the new situation which had assumed proportions quite unexpected. A force was collected from the various garrisons; four companies from Khartum were under orders to proceed to al-Kawwah which was selected as the meeting-place. Instructions were also sent by telegraph to the Governor of Kurdufan to equip and dispatch four companies of regular troops and 200 cavalry of bushbuzuks with the Mudir as commandant of this field force. Three compaines from Fashoda were also ordered to join the campaign.

Muhammad Pasha Sa'id, the commander of that force, arrived at Aba island first and, finding that al-Mahdi was well to the west in the mountains, followed him up to Um Talhah mountains, a part of Taqali range. The report which he submitted to the Governor-General explained that on reaching Um Talhah mountains of Taqali range he became sure of the connivance of Mak Adam with the impostor and of the determination of the people of Taqali to resist. The matter was still further aggravated, in Muhammad Pasha Sa'id's opinion, by the fact that since the conquest of Darfur the Mak had been strengthened by Bahr al-Ghazal and Shaka Gallabah and also because the Mak for a long time had provided a place of refuge to those who fled from parts of Kurdufan to avoid the payment of taxes. In his opinion the subjugation of Taqali required six battalions of infantry and six companies of Shayqiya bashbuzuk. All that he could do was to send the son of Alyas Pasha Um Barir, a merchant dignitary of al-Ubayyid, to advise Mak Adam to capture the impostor and send him to the authorities.[1] So al-Mahdi was left alone to proceed to Qadir mountain. Ra'uf Pasha seems to have accepted this explanation of the situation by the Mudir of Kurdufan as he forwarded the report by telegraph without any comment.

While appreciating from the beginning the great danger from al-Mahdi after his first victory and consequently collecting a force to put an end to it, Ra'uf a week later seems to have had his fears allayed, as he reported to Cairo that tranquility prevailed, and that he had high hopes of settling the problem of the False Prophet for good very shortly. His report was permeated with a tone of confidence and minimized the danger, attributing all the trouble to the Dongolese relatives of al-Mahdi who dealt in slaves. He saw the impossibility of the Sudanese uniting for a common cause because of tribal jealousies; and even the formidable baqqarah, in his opinion, were divided among themselves and would not sink their differences. One thing stood out clearly in those early reports of Ra'uf: that the religious factor in the movement was left out of account and the impression was that the traditional tribal jealousies would prevent the movement from reaching such a degree that it would seriously shake the Government's authority.[2]

The position of al-Mahdi changed materially as a result of his trek to the western mountains. From a simple rebellious subject with a small following armed with primitive weapons, quite accessible to Government garrisons, al-Mahdi's position changed to that of a determined enemy retreating to an extremely difficult mountainous country inhabited by people, whether Nuba or baqqarah, having a history of disobedience and defiance to Government authorities; and all the probabilities indicated that they would ally themselves with him. It was well known that the Taqali mountains had never submitted completely to Government authority and that, the nature of their country being mountainous, the job of dislodging al-Mahdi necessitated an exceptionally strong force. What made the baqqarah tribes of Kurdufan and Darfur ally themselves to al-Mahdi, in addition to their grievances against

---

[1] Ra'uf to the Khedive, Oct. 8, 1881, in Cypher Telegram Book from June 27, 1879, 'Abd. Pal. Arch., Cairo.

[2] Ra'uf to Khedive, Aug. 22, 1881, In-Telegram Book from June 27, 1879, 'Abd. Pal. Arch., Cairo.

the government, was that the principal disciple of al-Mahdi was a baqqari to the core, talking their language and thoroughly conversant with their customs and methods. It was from that initial stage that the movement enlisted on its side the horsemen of the baqqarah, who made very fine cavalry suited and trained for the nature of the country. They were not lacking in qualities of bravery and technique of fighting, as their continual struggle with wild animals and for protection of their life and property through their own arms, made them always fit and ready to enter the field at any moment. They knew how to manipulate the spear and to use the horse to the best advantage in that woody and bushy country of Kurdufan and the Nuba mountains.

After the failure of Muhammad Pasha Sa'id's expedition and the retreat of al-Mahdi to Qadir mountain, Ra'uf thought that it was unnecessary to take any further active measures, that the movement if left alone would collapse of itself, and that al-Mahdi with his adherents would stew in their own juice. Orders were accordingly given to suspend all operations.[1]

So far the authorities concerned with the rising were Ra'uf in Khartum and Muhammad Pasha Sa'id in al-Ubayyid, but the official under whose direct jurisdiction Aba island came had no say in the matter and nothing was heard of him either in the peaceful approaches or in the hostile operations. It was the Mudir of Fashoda, at that time Rashid Bey Ayman, who was the direct ruler of Muhammad Ahmad and his early adherents. How was it that this provincial authority, directly responsible for keeping peace and order, had nothing to do with it at that early stage? The explanation offered by the Governor-General was that Fashoda was not in telegraphic communication with Khartum at the time and the only means of passing information and orders was by steamer, which was obviously slow and would not be effective in dealing with such an urgent matter.[2]

al-Mahdi, after resting in the Taqali range of mountains, resumed his trek southwards, intending to reach Qadir mountain. He encountered some resistance at the Jaradah mountain from a certain Faki Mukhtar, but al-Mahdi managed to defeat him and

---

[1] Stewart to Malet, enclosed in No. 20, Jan. 20, 1883, P.R.O., F.O. 78/3552.
[2] Ra'uf to the Khedive, Aug. 17, 1881, In-Telegram Book from June 27, 1879, 'Abd. Pal. Arch., Cairo.

finally established himself at Qadir mountain. There he resumed the practice of entering a cave for meditation during the best hours of the day, and only appeared in his white clothes on the top of the mountain in the late afternoon when the baqqarah in their encampments around the mountain would see him in that angel-like manner which would add immensely to the spiritual feeling towards him and his mission.

Rashid, the Mudir of Fashoda, asked permission from Khartum to carry out a military expedition against al-Mahdi in his mountain retreat of Qadir, and he thought that the troops under his disposal were quite sufficient to stamp out the movement.[1] Rashid was laboring, like many others in authority at the time, under the impression of the insignificance of the movement and underrated the power of al-Mahdi.[2] Though Ra'uf told him to mind his own business at Fashoda, Rashid disobeyed these orders and could not resist the temptation to be talked of as the hero who suppressed the rising. He set to work in defiance of his superior's orders and brought together a force of 350 soldiers with 70 irregulars and about 1,000 Shuluk tribesmen under their chief, Kaikun Bey. When reminded of the Governor-General's orders and asked by the adjutant-major who was in command of the troops at Fashoda, to write officially about this defiance of authority, the answer was a letter dismissing the major, and the imprisonment of the latter in his house.[3]

Rashid's plan was to take the enemy completely by surprise, and this necessitated forced marches with little rest. The plan would be a great success if the element of surprise were complete, otherwise it would be a certain failure as the soldiers would be utterly exhausted and would hardly be able to bear the attack of an enemy on his own ground and with his vigor unimpaired by forced marches. al-Mahdi knew of the troops marching against him through two independent sources of information; one was the chief of Qadir mountain who used the traditional method of having large fires made at night on top of the mountain by those who

---

[1] Ra'uf to the Khedive, Oct. 6, 1881, In-Telegram Book from June 27, 1879, 'Abd. Pal. Arch., Cairo.

[2] Slatin, Rudolf, *Fire and Sword in the Sudan,* translated from German into English by Wingate, F. R. (London and New York, 1896), p. 140.

[3] Ra'uf to the Khedive, Dec. 17, 1881, In-Telegram Book from June 27, 1879, 'Abd. Pal. Arch., Cairo.

should first see the enemy. These were relayed along the whole range till the news reached the mountain of the chief; the other was Rabhah, a woman from the Kinanah tribe, who walked the whole night to Qadir to tell al-Mahdi, having seen the army in its last stage of the march. Having prepared an ambush on receipt of this information, the Arabs fell on the utterly exhausted enemy and completely annihilated them, except for a few Shuluks who managed to escape to Fashoda to tell the story. The factor of complete surprise on which the whole plan and calculations of Rashid rested was used against him and proved its effectiveness, but to al-Mahdi not to the originator of the idea. So the year 1881 closed with al-Mahdi winning his second round in the conflict, and the prestige and the morale that resulted to him and his troops could hardly be exaggerated. Rumors travelled far and wide in the Sudan that the spiritual power of al-Mahdi was so great that he could turn the bullets into water, and in the fight with Rashid in particular al-Mahdi suffered practically no casualties because the enemy fired no shot owing to the completeness of the surprise.[1] The roads leading to Qadir began to be thronged with new adherents to the cause who had heard of this signally brilliant success. They were naturally at this time mostly from Kurdufan and Darfur provinces and of the baqqarah and the jallabah of the west and south, as the grip of the Government was still tight on al-Jazirah, let alone Barbar, Dongola, and Kasalah provinces.

After Rashid's annihilation the military and political situation became so serious that Ra'uf Pasha was compelled to ask for troops from Egypt or to be allowed to withdraw three battalions from the Abyssinian frontier. The Cairo Government refused both requests at first but eventually allowed him one Negro battalion under Ibrahim Bey Fawzi.[2] These refusals and delays resulted in the loss of most valuable time and prestige, whilst the rebellion gathered strength. al-Mahdi's policy at the time was not to leave his mountain retreat, but to foment trouble by emissaries and letters in other parts of the Sudan.

While the new year 1882 augured well for al-Mahdi after his

---

[1] See Ohrwalder, Joseph, *Ten Years' Captivity in the Mahdi's Camp*, translated from German into English by Wingate, F. R. (London, 1892), p. 9, and also Slatin, op. cit., p. 140.

[2] Stewart to Malet, enclosed in No. 20, Jan. 20, 1883, P.R.O., F.O. 78/3552.

success and he was receiving enthusiastic new adherents, for the Egyptian Government it opened with the joint note of Britain and France.[1] The two governments, after consulation with one another in the last months of 1881, came to the conclusion, chiefly under the initiative of M. Gambetta, that the military ascendancy in Egypt had become so serious as to require a warning. It was in this atmosphere that Ra'uf Pasha asked for reinforcements, and it was quite plain that the Government of Cairo had far greater immediate issues to grapple with than the suppression of an insurrection in a corner of the remote Kurdufan Province. The situation was still further aggravated by the ultimate seizure of power by the military party in February. They had to combat both the Khedive and the powers, which was more than enough work for them, and even if they were able to pay some little attention to Sudan events, they would not part with any section of the army on which the whole strength of their position rested. But the situation became grave in the Sudan and could not be safely neglected. The whole trouble was summarily dismissed as being brought about by the incapacity of the Governor-General. Consequently Ra'uf was recalled and the afairs of the Sudan were in future directed by an officer of ministerial rank for whom a new office was created. 'Abd al-Qadir Pasha Hilmi was appointed to fill the new post, and after a period of about two months it was decided that the minister should proceed himself to Khartum and direct affairs on the spot.

Meanwhile, between the arrival of 'Abd al-Qadir in May and the departure of Ra'uf in February, Geigler Pasha was appointed acting Governor-General. He was a German who had risen rapidly from the post of inspector of the Sudan telegraphs in Gordon's governor-generalship, to head of the department instituted for suppression of slave-trade in Ra'uf's administration, and finally found himself at the head of a government over the vast and expansive Sudan, facing a fanatical religious rising in addition to the already existing complications of the administration. He was one among the handful of those European officials recruited for service in the Sudan by Gordon in the hey-day of his power, when he enjoyed the complete confidence of Isma'il, and was in possession of almost *carte blanche*. Gordon arrived at the policy of employing any Euro-

[1] *Parliamentary Papers* (1882), vol. lxxxii, p. 6.

pean he could get hold of after he finally formed his opinion that no reforms or progress in administration, and especially in the suppression of slave-trade, could be effected with Turkish, Egyptian, or Sudanese officials.

It appeared that Geigler underrated the importance of the rising even more than Ra'uf, being himself a Christian and in utter ignorance of its religious implications. He at once reversed the inactive and the waiting policy of Ra'uf and telegraphed to Cairo saying that it was not at all necessary to send troops from Egypt and that the force in the Sudan was quite sufficient to restore law and order. After some hesitation the Cairo Government allowed him to act as he thought fit. When given permission to act, Geigler instituted censorship on all telegrams sent to Cairo, whether official or private; they could not be transmitted unless they had been passed by him. He himself seems to have sent nothing, as there is no record of reports about the situation in the Sudan sent to the Khedive. He began to form an expedition drawn from Khartum, Kurdufan, and Sennar. That from Khartum was hastily collected and put under the command of Muhammad Bey Sulayman, an officer of twenty-five years' service, who had seen service in Mexico and belonged to the Shayqiya tribe. The Kurdufan portion of the expedition was composed of regular troops, bashbuzuks, and bazinqir or slaves belonging to the Kurdufan tribes, who were still loyal, and this latter section was commanded by 'Abdallah Dafa-'allah. The force from Sennar also included regulars and bashbuzuks and the whole totalled from 3,000 to 3,500.[1] Geigler's plan was, then, to bring together a force composed of all the available material and manpower that he could collect in the Sudan and in one relatively gigantic attempt to strike al-Mahdi in his lair in Qadir.

The chief command of this motley force fell on Yusuf Pasha al-Shallali.[2] Originally with ancestry from lower Nubia, Yusuf was born in Khartum and, on reaching manhood, engaged in trade in the southern provinces. It was at that time the school in which practical lessons of administration and war were taught, the same school from which Zubair Pasha and some leading figures of al-Mahdi's generals had graduated. Yusuf entered the service of the

[1] Stewart to Malet, enclosed in No. 20, Jan. 20, 1883, P.R.O., F.O. 78/3552.
[2] He who comes from Shallal (the first cataract, south of Aswan).

Government in an administrative capacity first and later as second in command to Gessi Pasha, who was dispatched by Gordon to put down the rising of Sulayman al-Zubair in Bahr al-Ghazal. Then he was appointed as Governor of Sennar Province and, at the time when he was entrusted with the command of the expeditionary force, he seems to have been out of employment for some reason. On the 22nd of April all the detachments of the force were collected at Kaka, which was selected as the station from which they would strike westwards to Qadir.

The formation of the Qadir field-force drained the strength of the garrisons so much that secret adherents began to brew trouble, especially in the Sennar area, where only seventy-five regular and thirty-three irregular soldiers were left. The policy pursued by the Government towards the relatives of those prominent figures who fled to al-Mahdi accelerated the pace of discontent among the people; relatives of the fleeing enthusiasts to al-Mahdi were subjected to persecution in order to dissuade people from exposing their families to ill-treatment. It happened just at the time when the Sennar garrison was seriously weakened that 'Amir al-Mikashfi was singled out for all sorts of humiliations and persecutions in order to pay for the crime of his brother Ahmad who had fled to join al-Mahdi at Qadir. Utterly grieved by the injustices inflicted on him, he went to the Rufa'a tribe in the southern al-Jazirah and preached among them allegiance to al-Mahdi and rebellion against the Government. He consequently succeeded in collecting a number of adherents to al-Mahdi's cause, and marched with them on Sennar. 'Amir succeeded in capturing part of the town and the prison, when the Arabs in it were set free, but he was not able to seize the area of the Government offices, which he beseiged. The Mudir of Sennar wired to Khartum asking for assistance. Salih Agha al-Mak, a Shayqi sanjak, volunteered with his 200 irregular troops to proceed to the succour of Sennar. It seems that the route along the Blue Nile was not safe and so he was transported to al-Kawwah on the White Nile and was allowed to take with him 100 bashbuzuks from there. From al-Kawwah he crossed al-Jazirah plain to Sennar by a circuitous route, the direct one being stopped by rebels. Before the arrival of Salih Agha in the vicinity of Sennar, 'Amir renewed his attempt to take the town by assault, but was successfully repulsed by the garrison. When Salih arrived on the

13th of April 'Amir's forces were forming a semi-circle around the town which was on the river front; Salih, with his 300 irregular soldiers, succeeded in driving away the Arabs and raising the siege.

Two days after Salih's success Geigler himself started from Khartum with 300 irregular troops with the intention of reaching Sennar. But on reaching al-Masallamiya it was reported to him that a certain descendant of the Prophet called Sharif Ahmad Taha was about to proclaim for al-Mahdi and rise against the Government on the eastern bank of the Blue Nile opposite al-Masallamiya. Geigler sent Yusuf Agha al-Malik, the head of his bashbuzuk, with fifty soldiers and a few officers to the village of the reported rebel. Yusuf failed, and all his officers and most of his soldiers were killed. Yusuf himself, when he saw that he was defeated, chose to seat himself on his farwah (sheepskin) and order his slave to kill him rather than be disgraced.

Seeing that it would be a risky business if he sent the rest of his irregulars, Geigler telegraphed to the officer commanding in al-Qallabat the Abyssinian frontier to send six compaines of regulars and 100 irregulars to Abu Haraz on the Blue Nile opposite Wad Madani. Pending the arrival of the Qallabat reinforcements Geigler crossed to the east side of the river and made Abu Haraz his headquarters, and entered into communication with Shaikh 'Awad al-Karim Abu Sin, the chief of the Shukriya tribe which lived between the blue Nile and the Atbara river. The Abu Sin family was known to be loyal to the Government and so 'Awad al-Karim collected a number of his tribesmen, some of whom were clad in chain mail. The Qallabat assistance arrived at Abu Haraz under Surur Afandi Rashid, who was instructed by Geigler to launch his attack on the 4th of May. Sharif Ahmad Taha again defeated them with a loss of 210 officers and men killed. The next day Shaikh 'Awad al-Karim arrived at Abu Haraz and joined Geigler. The day following their arrival, the Shukriya, together with Geigler's bashbuzuks, launched an attack on Sharif Ahmad which ended, this time, in the total defeat and killing of the Sharif. This success for the Government, together with the powerful Shukriya tribe declaring against al-Mahdi, saved Khartum and retarded the spread of the rebellion. Had that attack failed also, and had the Shukriya held aloof, there would have been a rising in Khartum itself, and then there would have sprung up a rising throughout the area comprising al-Jazirah and east of the Blue Nile as well as in the districts around Khartum.

After that victory the troops were directed to the Sennar area where, on the 24th of May, an action occurred between the soldiers and some of the rebels at a village called Abu Shukah. Surur Afandi formed his troops in a line facing the wind with the result that under the cover of smoke the Arabs crept close up to his lines. Surur Afandi then fled and his troops retired firing precipitately. The situation was saved by 'Ali Afandi Kashif, the Mudir of Sennar, who rallied the troops, stopped Surur's flight, and ordered an advance. The action was a success as the Arabs were driven into the river, and those who managed to cross were cut down by friendly tribesmen. The irregular troops of the Government lost heavily, but Muhammad Zain, the chief of the rebels, was killed. The remnants of the Arabs retired on Taiqu lake and effected a junction with the main body under 'Amir al-Mikashfi. Geigler now returned to Khartum leaving Salih Agha al-Mak in command of troops in the Sennar area. On June 3 Salih collected four companies of regulars and some irregulars and attacked the Arab concentration at Taiqu which he defeated and dispersed. 'Amir left al-Jazirah and, crossing the White Nile, trekked to al-Mahdi in Kurdufan, and, for the time being, this early rising in al-Jazirah might be considered to have been suppressed.

The material with which 'Amir and Sharif Ahmad started their rebellions was not the same type as the heroes of Aba or as the victors at Qadir. They were nearly all of them nomads who started the affair without the deep religious feeling of those who were intimately connected with al-Mahdi and who fought under the fascination of his captivating personality. Yet they had sufficient courage to keep the embers of rebellion glowing until they were rekindled more vigorously some months later under the leadership of Ahmad al-Mikashfi and others.

Sharif Ahmad Taha, an extremely revered religious chief and a descendant of the Prophet, was representative of those Sufi shaikhs with whom all the villages along the Nile, its two tributaries, and in al-Jazirah were studded. They were absolutely certain that the expected Mahdi would appear one day and fill the earth with justice and equity in place of abuses and injustices. They were only too glad that al-Mahdi had appeared in a person of their class with a marvellous record of sanctity and admirable religious behavior behind him. They were perpetuating the traditions of the early saints of the Fung period to whom we have alluded in the introductory chapter. There was, however, a difference between them in the degree of support which they gave to his cause; undoubtedly some were extremely cautious and still fearful of the Government authority or even hankering after gaining favor, but nevertheless deep in their hearts they welcomed the movement and detested the Government of the Turks who were departing from the true path of Allah. Sharif Ahmad was among the intrepid and fiery class of these shaikhs, and, although awkwardly situated as regards the Government garrisons, and separated by a long distance from Qadir, he chose to throw off allegiance to the Government and declare openly for al-Mahdi.

Before accompanying al-Shallali in his trek westwards to Qadir we will glance at al-Mahdi's position at Qadir after his brilliant success over Rashid. The mere fact that he had annihilated the Rashid expedition almost to a man with practically no casualties on his side and in so sudden and efficient a way that the enemy hardly fired a shot—all this was in itself the greatest of miracles and rallied to his standard people already fascinated by what they had heard about his sanctity and his purely religious past. This time he initiated an efficient system of scouting which brought to him regularly the minutest details of the Government's force. By an agreement with Taifarah, the chief of the Funqur mountain, al-Mahdi's spies waited in that place to take stock of the enemy at their last big stop before reaching Qadir. Rashid's defeat was followed by intensified propaganda in the form of circular letters by al-Mahdi to all parts of the Sudan, and especially to Kurdufan and Sennar, the two places that were already affected. It was at this juncture that the term ansar (helpers) was applied to the adherents of al-Mahdi. So by way of comparison, when there was desertion and faint support to the calls of the war drum in al-Ubayyid on the Government side, the fraternity of ansar was swelled by new adherents who voluntarily sought satisfaction and glory in the jihad or holy war.

al-Shallali's route to Qadir could either be the direct one to Qadir or, still farther south, by Fashoda and then westwards. The first one had the obvious advantage of being a short cut, while the second was a somewhat circuitous route. But the advantage of the short cut depended wholly on the existence of water on the road which he found on inquiry to be scarce at that time. He was, then, compelled to move to Fashoda, and, after a halt of about twelve days, the whole Qadir field-force moved westwards on the 4th of May. At the mountain of Funqur a relatively long halt was made which was considered to be unaccountable in Khartum. In fact it appears that the rainy season was later than usual and, it being the end of the dry season, it would have been a risky affair to move the whole expedition through land scarce in water. Although the beginning of the rainy season would ensure sufficient water, yet it would have the disadvantage of making the march more difficult, which was the case on the last stage of the road.

The stop at Funqur was marked by two important incidents. Taifarah, the chief of the place, went back on his agreement with al-Mahdi and handed over the latter's spies to al-Shallali who made the silly and inhuman mistake of putting them to death by the cruel method of cutting of their limbs one after the other before an assembled crowd of his own soldiers. The calm manner in which they underwent the ordeal and the way in which they showed their deep belief in the divine mission of al-Mahdi by uttering defiant words to the last had a demoralizing effect on the troops. A man who had such a hold on his people that they showed such incredible courage must have something in him, and his mission could only be divinely ordained. The second incident of importance at Funqur was the exchange of religious arguments between al-Shallali and al-Mahdi. Here the two combatants were not evenly matched. While al-Shallali was ignorant of religious matters and seemed to be acting on the advice of a half-learned 'alim, al-Mahdi was fighting a battle on his own chosen ground and was far superior to the advisers of al-Shallali.

On the 21st of May the Qadir force moved from Funqur westwards through very marshy and wooded country. Reaching the vicinity of Qadir in exhaustion and fatigue and morally depressed, they could barely make the semblance of a zaribah[1] as a fortification and fall asleep, before the ansar were on them at the first light of dawn on the 7th of June. Although 'Abdalla Dafa'allah with a

[1] A thorny enclosure.

chosen band of his subordinates made a gallant stand, and although the wife of Taha Abu Sadur, the commander of the irregulars performed the courageous deed of beating the war-drum to rally her fallen husband's men, yet the result was the annihilation of the force. The chief reasons given for that defeat by the Khartum Government were these:

1. The position of the troops was surrounded by dense forests.
2. Owing to their arrival late in the evening of the 6th they could not complete one side of the zaribah.
3. Instead of their picked men being posted at the weakest part, the worst were posted to defend it.
4. Neglect to send out scouts or to reconnoitre the positions of the enemy.
5. Constant quarrelling between Yusuf Pasha al-Shallali and Muhammad Bey Sulayman.
6. The worthless character of the troops. Many hardly understood the use of their weapons.

This crushing blow made the Government position exceedingly critical. Practically, the Government was left defenseless in face of a general insurrection covering a large area. At the time there were no available troops to take the field, no help could be expected from Egypt, and the garrisons were weak and demoralized. The effect of this success on al-Mahdi's ansar amounted almost to that of a miracle. With the news of the victory the story went round that supernatural forces were acting with him in that fire burnt the dead bodies of the soldiers and his name was found clearly written on leaves of trees and eggs.[1]

[1] The story from al-Mahdi's side has been reconstructed from the papers of Sir al-Sayyid 'Abd al-Rahman, the son of al-Mahdi. They consist of reports as recorded from men who took part in the battles narrated. On the Government side the chief source is the report of Major Stewart which he recorded when he first arrived in Khartum and which he seems to have collected from the official records he found in Khartum, supported by verbal reports of officers and soldiers. It was enclosed in a dispatch from Malet to Granville, No. 20, Jan. 20, 1883, P.R.O., F.O. 78/3552. The 'Abdin Palace Archives showed the official communications between the Governor-General in Khartum and the Khedive in Cairo.

IV

'ABD AL-QADIR PASHA'S ADMINISTRATION

'Abd al-Qadir Pasha's arrival in Khartum in May 1882 ushered in a new phase of activity and better management of Sudanese affairs. He was a man of intelligence and determination with an infinitely wider outlook and understanding than his predecessors through his thorough European education. He began by calling up three regular battalions and a number of bashbuzuks from eastern Sudan, altogether some 3,500 men. He then formed two battalions of blacks from slaves voluntarily given to the Government by the merchants and notables of Barbar, Dongola, and Khartum. Some 8,000 to 9,000 bashbuzuks were concentrated from various stations in the Sudan. A thousand recruits, who had just arrived from Bahr al-Ghazal for service, were immediately formed into a battalion. The next step was to issue orders for putting such places as Khartum, Sennar, al-Ubayyid, Bara, al-Kawwah, al-Duwaim, al-Tur'a, al-Khadrah, and Fashoda in a state of defense. As soon as the troops were reasonably organized they were sent in considerable numbers to the various garrisons of the country which were considered to be weak. The people in the country-side had had their faith in the Government noticeably shaken and 'Abd al-Qadir sent proclamations in all directions allaying their fears and telling them that there were no grounds for misgivings; at the end of these circulars he appealed to them to maintain their traditional loyalty to the Government.[1] Since the soldiers, even the regular ones, were shamefully ignorant of the requisite military training, he arranged for a program of training and printed all necessary instructions in a booklet distributed to all officers.

At the end of May 'Abd al-Qadir, while waiting for news of al-Shallili's expedition, thought of trying peaceful means. At that time the head of the 'ulama (learned men) received a letter from al-Mahdi calling on him to accept his (al-Mahdi's) divinely ordained mission. Both 'Abd al-Qadir and the head 'alim agreed

[1] Wingate, F. R., *Mahdiism and the Egyptian Sudan* (London, 1891), p. 19.

59

that the answer should contain an overture for peace together with religious arguments pointing to the weakness of al-Mahdi's position on that ground. It was thought that the letter might have a good effect even if al-Shallali's war operations did not succeed. al-Mahdi was assured forgiveness if he went back on his presumptions and returned to the alleginace of the Government in a penitent manner. It was pointed out to him that the head of the 'ulama would be the intermediary for that peaceful approach.[1]

When news of al-Shallali's annihilation reached him, 'Abd al-Qadir telegraphed the news to Cairo and asked for reinforcements to be sent as quickly as transport could convey them. The reason for demanding fresh troops from Egypt was not only the weakness of the garrisons in number but primarily their lack of training. The sending of untrained soldiers to fight al-Mahdi would result in the latter securing arms and ammunition which would be a great treasure to him. Five days later it seems that 'Abd al-Qadir was pretty certain that reinforcements were unlikely to be sent owing to the troubled condition of Egypt at the time, and he had to be content with 500 rifles and ammunition. 'Urabi Pasha, the Minister for War, replied to 'Abd al-Qadir's demands through the Khedive that there were only enough troops for maintaing internal security and he could only send arms and ammunition.[2] It was a very critical time as on the day (June 17, 1882) on which 'Abd al-Qadir asked for arms, conditions in Egypt had become so serious that 14,000 Christians had already left and 6,000 more were waiting for ships to carry them away. It must be remembered that the bombardment of Alexandria took place less than a month later.

As was to be expected, the victory of al-Mahdi over al-Shallali released a considerable number of Arabs to take the offensive in addition to the increased number of new adherents. The effects of this on al-Jazirah was that Arabs from Kurdufan, with a number of local tribesmen, raised the standard of rebellion in the vicinity of al-Kawwah, which had to be reinforced from Khartum and Sennar. But at that time 'Abd al-Qadir was absorbed in trying to remove al-Mahdi by secret methods, having failed in the peaceful

[1] 'Abd al-Qadir to the Khedive, May 31, 1882, In-Telegram Book from June 27, 1879, 'Abd. Pal. Arch., Cairo.
[2] 'Urabi to the Khedive, June 18, 1882, In-Telegram Book from June 27, 1879, 'Abd. Pal. Arch., Cairo.

overture and seeing the extreme difficulty of carrying on military operations against him when Egypt itself was about to be involved in war against Britain. He mentions in his dispatches that poisoned dates, as a present from a Dervish, were sent to al-Mahdi and that two men had set out with the mission of murdering him. The method which he seems to have considered very important as being most reliable was the dispatch of a dynamite envelope. He asked for such envelopes to be sent from Cairo.[1] It is not surprising that 'Abd al-Qadir received no reply, for the date of his telegram was July 12— the day following the bombardment of Alexandria.

The months following the defeat of al-Shallali up to October were marked by great upheavals in Egypt including war with Britain which ended in the occupation of the country by the latter power. In the Sudan these months were the rainy season and military operations against al-Mahdi in his mountain retreat of Qadir were extremely difficult.

Towards the middle of September 'Abd al-Qadir received information of the repulse at al-Ubayyid of al-Mahdi's formidable attack with severe loss to him. Although he seems to have been at the height of his confidence in the ultimate victory of the Government he again pressed for more reinforcements, asking for four battalions of regular troops and 2,000 Turkish bashbuzuks together with 10,000 Remington rifles, guns, rockets, and other weapons, etc. The reasons advanced by 'Abd al-Qadir for this large reinforcement notwithstanding his apparent confidence in the approaching end of the rising were two; first, that the re-establishment of peace and tranquility in the disturbed areas even after the suppression of the rebellion would require more soldiers; secondly, 'Abd al-Qadir had formed the worst opinion of the Shayqiya bashbuzuks on account of their looting and predatory habits and wished to get rid of them altogether and to replace them by regulars. It seems incredible that 'Abd al-Qadir asked for these reinforcements on the 18th of September, only five days after the battle of Tel el-Kebir, when in actual fact the Egyptian army as such had ceased to exist.[2] Whether this was due to the fact that 'Abd al-Qadir was

---

[1] 'Abd al-Qadir to the Khedive, July 12, 1882, In-Telegram Book from June 27, 1879, 'Abd. Pal. Arch., Cairo.
[2] 'Abd al-Qadir to the Khedive, Sept. 18, 1882, In-Telegram Book from June 27, 1879, 'Abd. Pal. Arch., Cairo.

kept in the dark about events in Egypt or whether he ignored their effect on the situation in the Sudan, it is impossible to decide.

Encouraged by the repulse of al-Mahdi at al-Ubayyid the energetic Governor-General thought of carrying out a war of propaganda. al-Mahdi, in the letters with which he flooded the country and which reached the remotest parts of it, explained with vigour and simplicity his mission and why he had undertaken it. He dwelt at great length on the religious abuses of the day and how the Muslim community had departed from the path of Allah. His was the task of removing all those abuses and reviving in a new form the simple and just practices which characterized the early days of Islam. To refute the arguments of the 'ulama, who might quote traditions (sayings of the Prophet) proving that he was not the expected Messiah, he had to apply all his learning with all the energy and logic he possessed. He first attacked the authenticity of many of these traditions as mere fabrications, which was generally admitted by learned men of that branch of Muslim theology, or at least they were admitted to be of doubtful authenticity. He produced evidence of later saints, such as Ibn 'Arabi and Ibn Idris, to the effect that al-Mahdi would appear in a manner and a place not generally expected. He strengthened his arguments by calling those who did not follow him infidels, since his mission was divinely ordained and assured of ultimate success.

'Abd al-Qadir entrusted the task of writing treatises against the presumption of al-Mahdi to the Grand Qadi (judge), the Mufti, and al-Sayyid Ahmad al-Azhari, one of the learned men. They dwelt on the principle of obeying the authorities and declared that there was no need for such a Messiah as the people were enjoying the peace and good government of the Khedive, and the Governor-General and all Muslims owed allegiance to the Khalifah of Islam in Constantinople. Even if the time were ripe for the advent of the Messiah, the present impostor was not the man expected, as there was nothing in him that conformed to the description they had read in their books. The Mufti added that the idea of al-Mahdi was not universally accepted by Muslim theologians, as it was not mentioned in the Quran, the fountain of Muslim thought. Even in this field al-Mahdi seems to have been far superior to his antagonists.

Ordinary people at that time could not comprehend the high-flown language of the 'ulama and the intricate and ambiguous way in which such arguments were presented to them. The time itself was not opportune for such propaganda on the Government side as Egypt was at its lowest ebb under Christian control and ultimately Christian domination and occupation. al-Mahdi, on the other hand, talked the same language as the village religious shaikhs, who were very influential in matters of religion. al-Mahdi's arguments were forceful and easily understandable. What carried more weight was the fact that he was eminently victorious in all his encounters. As they began to learn more of the past history of al-Mahdi they were favorably impressed with his saintly behavior and they were long schooled in paying their respects and reverence to that class of religious leader.

By October 1882 the Egyptian Government had resumed their functions in Cairo. the Khedive moved from Alexandria and entered the latter city in a manner described by Sir Edward Malet as 'a magnificent sight,' with 'tears in his eyes as he passed through the streets.'¹ According to the information received by the Governor-General the situation in the Sudan had, however, deteriorated when the reinforcements sent to Kurdufan were cut down. The impression formed by him was that the irregular soldiers, who were the only force of note available in Khartum, were utterly demoralized because of al-Mahdi's victories; the native troops, even the regulars, were not to be trusted as they had proved treacherous; blacks from Bahr al-Ghazal were not to be relied upon owing to their lack of training and their high death-rate due to the change of environment. For all these reasons 'Abd al-Qadir pressed for reinforcements from Cairo, otherwise he was in no doubt that the whole Sudan would burst into conflagration and would not be restored to law and order except by very much larger forces.² It was in response to the appeals of 'Abd al-Qadir to relieve the besieged garrisons of Kurdufan that the Government of Cairo set to work to bring together a force in Egypt intended for the Sudan.

Recruiting officers were at once sent to all parts of the country to gather the least compromised non-commissioned officers and

¹ Private letter, Malet to Granville, Oct. 1, 1882, P.R.O., G/D 29/160.
² 'Abd al-Qadir to the Khedive, Oct. 24, 1882, In-Telegram Book from June 27, 1879, 'Abd. Pal. Arch., Cairo.

men from the disbanded army of 'Urabi. A camp was set up in the Barrage, fifteen miles north of Cairo, to which parties were sent as they arrived in Cairo. There was no difficulty with the officers as young officers from school would welcome their enlistment for the service, and for the loyal disbanded ones it was the only means of continuing their past service.[1] By the middle of December the transport of troops was well in hand with some in Khartum and others in the various stages on the way, while others were in camp at the other end. Guns and stores were dispatched before the soldiers and nearly all of them were recieved in Khartum by the end of 1882. Considering the state of affairs in Egypt, the energy and ability shown in collecting and transporting such a large body of troops in face of great difficulties 'reflected a great credit on the Egyptian administration.'[2] Although the Government succeeded in sending the troops, there was a great deal to be said against the morale of the men. The fellaheen soldiers were reluctant and lacking in enthusiasm, and instances of desertion and escape before reaching Suez were noticed.[3] Leaving the force on its way to Khartum via the Sawakin-Barbar road, let us now turn to the attitude of the occupying power to this problem of the Sudan.

As early as the end of September 1882 the British in Egypt came to the conclusion that the Sudan problem had to be tackled. Sir Charles Wilson, who was at this time attached to the British agency as a military adviser submitted a memorandum to Sir Edward Malet on the Sudan.[4] He suggested an agreement with Abyssinia by which Bogos (Eritrea) and al-Qallabat were to be given to the Abyssinian Emperor, Egypt would facilitate the appointment of the Abuna (head of the Abyssinian church), and Masawwa would be made a free port with a prohibition on the importation of arms. Darfur and part of Kurdufan would be given up. To ensure efficiency in administration British officers would

[1] Report by Major Chermside, enclosed in Malet to Granville, No. 803, Nov. 7, 1882, P.R.O., F.O. 78/3443.
[2] Report by Major Chermside, enclosed in Malet to Granville, No. 906, Dec. 20, 1882, P.R.O., F.O. 78/3445.
[3] Report by Major Chermside, enclosed in Malet to Granville, No. 832, Nov. 15, 1882, P.R.O., F.O. 78/3444.
[4] Memorandum by Sir Charles Wilson, enclosed in Malet to Granville, No. 659, Oct. 2, 1882, P.R.O., F.O. 78/3442.

be appointed to the key posts of governor-general, commandant of the army, and a few subordinate posts. To prevent the export of slaves British cruisers would keep watch on the Red Sea and the Arba'in (forty days') road would be guarded at its terminus in Egypt. Owing to lack of information about the state of affairs in the Sudan and to the extremely disturbed state of Muslim society in Turkey, Syria, and Egypt, together with the expectation of the Messiah at the turn of the Muhammadan century, Sir Charles thought it would be desirable to send two British officers to the Sudan to report on the situation as a whole and on what steps should be taken to ensure the pacification of the country. He thought that something of a military nature should be done during the only season suitable for operations, which was approaching. Sir Edward Malet in his covering letter enclosing the memorandum endorsed only the recommendation to send two officers to report.

On the 26th of October Sir Edward Malet telegraphed the substance of a conversation with 'Umar Pasha Lufti, the Minister for War. The latter had informed Malet of the alarming news received from 'Abd al-Qadir Pasha, that the troops which had been sent off to Kurdufan had been cut off and that a force of 10,000 men had been asked for without which Khartum could not be defended. The plan of the Egyptian Government, at this time, was to send Isma'il Pasha Ayyub with General Stone[1] as chief of staff to Khartum in place of 'Abd al-Qadir Pasha. The Government would raise the requisite force, and assured Malet that no danger was to be apprehended from raising such a force, and that trustworthy officers were available.[2]

On the 28th of October Sir Edward Malet sent to the Foreign Office a second memorandum by Wilson[3] on the situation in the Sudan; Malet forwarded it with no comment. According to Wilson the conditions appeared to have become much worse, al-Mahdi seemed to be successful everywhere, and Khartum might fall in a month's time if no reinforcements were dispatched. al-Mahdi's forces were estimated at between 80,000 and 150,000 men. His object was to march on Egypt and after conquering it to proceed

---

[1] An American officer, who was the chief of staff of the Egyptian army, but after the disbanding of that army he was out of employment.

[2] Malet to Granville, No. 740, Oct. 26, 1882, P.R.O., F.O. 78/3442.

[3] Memorandum by Wilson, enclosed in Malet to Granville, No. 744, Oct. 28, 1882, P.R.O., F.O. 78/3442.

to Makkah. The current report was that when Khartum had been taken he would go northwards either down the Nile or to Sawakin on the Red Sea and from thence to Suez. The fall of Khartum would have a very bad political effect in Egypt and it was certain that the population all along the Nile to the north would rally to his standard once he was on the move. People were in such a state of mind after hearing the alarming news that they would accept such a Messiah whose advent was foretold.

The Egyptian Government was not in a position to check the advance of al-Mahdi as their army had been destroyed. The situation called for British assistance, and that speedily, otherwise Khartum would fall, and a large force would have to be sent from Britain. Sir Charles thought that the question divided itself into two; first, the measures to be adopted to save Khartum and second, those which would become necessary in the case of that town's fall. What ought to be done immediately was to get accurate knowledge of what was going on in the Sudan through any European resident in Khartum. The director of telegraphs was to maintain contact with the outlying stations and to ask for information of al-Mahdi's progress. Copies of all telegrams relating to the state of the Sudan received in Cairo should be sent to Her Britannic Majesty's agent and consul-general. If a British force were to operate up the Nile there must be no fear of an armed force in the rear, and to guard against this eventuality more efforts ought to be made to collect arms from the fellaheen and Bedwins. A return of all guns, small arms, and ammunition known to have been sent to the Sudan should be supplied by the Government. Until the country was quite settled the remaining arms of the late Egyptian army ought to be in British hands.

As regards actual operations Sir Charles suggested, in the first instance, sending British officers to Khartum to put the town in a state of defense and report on the situation. The Indian contingent, now on its way back to India, should be stopped at Aden and disembraked at Sawakin in order to operate from there. The two alternatives were either the use of Indian troops in Egyptian pay or Turkish troops. The former was to be preferred as all sorts of political complications might ensue from the employment of the latter. To Sir Charles a force of 5,000 infantry with a due proportion of cavalry and artillery would be sufficient. The arrangements with Abyssinia suggested in his first memorandum were restated.

In the event of the fall of Khartum and the advance of al-Mahdi to the north, the two points at which his advance could be effectively checked were Kurusko and Aswan. At the former he would have reached the place in a disorganized state after the tiring journey across the desert, and at the latter he would have just emerged from the narrow valley at the first cataract.

The same recommendation that British officials should be employed in the two posts of governor-general of the Sudan and commander of the army there was urged. Sir Charles knew of no Egyptian capable enough to deal with the situation. General Gordon would be the best choice if he could be persuaded to take up his old appointment, and he was at this time out of employment. No steps were to be taken by the Egyptian Government except after consultation with the officer commanding the British troops in Egypt, and Sir Charles considered that the best plan might be to put the whole direction of the military operations against al-Mahdi in this officer's hands since the only available troops were British and British officers were to be employed.

The British Government's reply to Wilson's suggestions was telegraphed to Malet on the 30th of October.[1] They definitely refused to permit the stopping of the Indian troops at Aden and rejected the proposal to employ British troops to operate in the Sudan. As to the movement of the Egyptian Government to prepare a force to serve in the Sudan, they would be glad to know the details. 'They would be glad to learn whom it is proposed to place in command, and whether the reconquest of the Sudan is contemplated in case the False Prophet has obtained possession of that district.' They inquired in what capacity Gordon was to be employed and asked their agent to ascertain the opinion of the British commander-in-chief on these matters.

Sir Edward Malet replied to these questions on the 1st of November.[2] He told the Foreign Office that the Egyptian Government intended to appoint 'Ala al-Din Pasha, at that time Governor of the Red Sea provinces, to take command of the forces in the Sudan. He was instructed to proceed at once to Sawakin. They

[1] Granville to Malet, No. 387, Oct. 30, 1882, P.R.O., F.O. 78/3433.
[2] Malet to Granville, No. 768, Nov. 1, 1882, P.R.O., F.O. 78/3443.

hoped to reconquer the Sudan by defeating the False Prophet. As to the employment of Gordon he could only go there as governor-general. But no such suggestion was made by the Egyptian Government and they would certainly not appoint him unless the British Government demanded it. To the appointment of 'Ala al-Din the British Government offered no objection, but still fearing to bear the responsibility for his appointment Granville told Malet: 'in default of fuller information the responsibility in the matter must rest with the Egyptian Government.'[1]

To the officer commanding the British troops in Egypt the insurrection in the Sudan was a matter of direct concern inasmuch as it affected the security of Egypt proper, and now he was asked to give his opinion. On the 3rd of November he drew up a memorandum[2] in which he treated the problem from the military angle. According to his information the Egyptians, out of an army of 26,000 men in the Sudan, had lost 10,000 in the fight against al-Mahdi, and the Governor-General had telegraphed that he could undertake no operations with what remained, having no confidence in them. Lieutenant-General Sir Archibald Alison had good reason to hope that the force in the process of organization by the Government out of the disbanded army would arrest the onward march of al-Mahdi on Egypt. He was asked if he could supply a British officer on active service as a chief of staff to that force. He declined, in the belief that the position of the seconded officer with a force completely and exclusively Egyptian would be anomalous. If this attempt by the Egyptian Government failed, a state of grave danger would arise not only in Egypt but in the whole Muslim world where the advent of a Messiah was expected. If al-Mahdi should ever advance on Egypt he could only efficiently and effectively be arrested in the neighborhood of the first cataract. Sir Archibald's plan in that contingency would be to move a complete division with all his cavalry and field artillery to the first cataract and take the best military position between that place and Edfu and there await the arrival of al-Mahdi. To allow him to advance unmolested to the vicinity of Cairo would give heart to the Muslim population throughout the delta and a

[1] Granville to Malet, No. 393, Nov. 2, 1882, P.R.O., F.O. 78/3433.
[2] Memorandum by Sir Archibald Alison, enclosed in Malet to Granville, No. 787 Confidential, Nov. 4, 1882, P.R.O., F.O. 78/3443.

grievous destruction of life and property would result. Then, surveying the military requirements in Egypt proper, bearing in mind the possibility of meeting al-Mahdi in upper Egypt, he asked for four and a half battalions as reinforcements. If the new Egyptian army under organization by Baker Pasha could be ready before the arrival of al-Mahdi, it would raise both the prestige of the Khedive's Government and the morale of the army itself if an Egyptian army were to check al-Mahdi unaided. Baker Pasha agreed with this plan and suggested the establishment of a powerful advance guard at Kurusko in Nubia with the bulk of his forces below the first cataract with the British army in the rear ready to give support in case assistance were required. Sir Archibald concluded by expressing his entire opposition to the use of British troops in the Sudan whether through Sawakin to Khartum or along the Nile beyond the boundaries of Egypt proper.

With the suggestion, made by Sir Charles Wilson and supported by Sir Edward Malet, of employing British officers to report on the state of affairs in the Sudan, Sir Archibald entirely concurred. The instructions of those officers should be to report on the route between Sawakin and Barbar and thence to Khartum, to ascertain exactly the general situation and examine the defensive capabilities of Khartum itself. They should return from their mission as soon as possible.

On the 4th of November Malet informed the Foreign Office that Baker Pasha had told him that two or three German officers had expressed to him their desire to enter the service of the Egyptian army, especially for the Sudan expedition. In the same dispatch Sir Edward submitted that the Egyptian Government should be allowed, as far as possible to take their own measures in suppressing the revolt 'without aid or advice from Her Majesty's Government'.[1] In his considered opinion the British Government should not interfere and should bear no responsibility in this question, 'lest at some future peroid, should measures taken at our suggestion or in accordance with our advice have proved inefficacious, England would be unavoidably drawn into military operation in the Sudan'.[2] He thought that if the worst fears came true, Egypt would be saved from the advance of al-Mahdi by the British forces stationed there.

[1] Malet to Granville, No. 788, Nov. 4, 1882, P.R.O., F.O. 78/3443.
[2] Ibid.

On the 17th of November, at Granville's invitation, there took place an interview between him and Gordon[1] about the Sudan and Egypt, where the latter had seen over five years' service, first as governor of Equatoria Province and later as governor-general of the whole of Isma'il Pasha's Empire. Gordon, as recorded in a memorandum by Granville, said that the insurrection in the Sudan had been immensely exaggerated. He suggested the appointment of Sir Charles Wilson as governor-general of the Sudan and, in opinion, Wilson would find no more difficulty there than he (Gordon) had. He did not agree to pressing the Khedive to pass an edict against slavery, as it would be extremely unpopular and would be simply a dead letter; on the other hand, the system of registration of slaves should be enforced.

The story of Baker Pasha and his coming to Egypt to organize a newly raised Egyptian army, and how the British Government objected to his being given the high command, is a long one, but it has some connection with the proposal to send him to the Sudan in November 1882 to command the troops there. The objection to giving him the high command of the Egyptian army was only that seconded English officers on the active list would refuse to serve under an officer dismissed from the British army. The employment of the British officers was thought to be essential for the efficient training of the troops.

Granville offered no objection to Baker commanding the Sudan troops. It seemed that when disappointed in losing the command of the new Egyptian army in Egypt, Baker had suggested to Lord Dufferin that he should go to the Sudan to command the troops there.[2] Dufferin himself at that time (November 21st 1882) thought that Egypt should be encouraged to put things in order in the Sudan, and the appointment of Baker, in his opinion, as the high military authority in that troubled country would tend to ease the situation: 'unless a good soldier went there the Egyptians might come to grief, which would greatly complicate matters.'[3] In an interview with the Khedive, Dufferin brought forward the matter of Baker's going to the Sudan. On the Khedive's showing various objections Dufferin did not press the question and the matter was

---

[1] Memorandum by Granville on his conversation with Gordon, Nov. 18, 1882, P.R.O., G/D 29/168.
[2] Dufferin to Granville in a private letter, Nov. 13, 1882, P.R.O., G/D 29/166.
[3] Dufferin to Granville in a private letter, Nov. 13, 1882, P.R.O., G/D 29/166.

dropped.[3] Dufferin used his good offices subsequently to give the command of the Gendarmerie to Baker, a post which he actually filled.

As early as the end of October 1882 the Egyptian Government desired that the newly gathered force intended for the Sudan should have some British officers and, if possible, a British chief of staff.[2] After this request, Malet informed Granville of applications from German and retired British officers to enter the military service of Egypt with the intention of proceeding to the Sudan. Her Majesty's Government adopted the attitude of non-interference, and desired to have nothing whatsoever to do with 'the choice of any officers whom they may wish to employ in the military operation to be undertaken in the Sudan'.[3] The question was reopened early in December when Lord Dufferin reported the request by Sharif Pasha for a first-rate British officer to go to the Sudan as chief of staff. Knowing only too well the attitude of non-interference of the British Government, Dufferin replied that he did not think that that could be done. 'I suppose, however,' he wrote to Granville, 'there would be no objection to the Egyptian Government engaging an English officer retired from the service, if they desired to do so.'[4] The British Government confirmed what Dufferin said to Sharif and entertained 'no objection if the Egyption Government obtained the services of an officer on the retired list.'[5]

Of all the proposals of Sir Charles Wilson the one of which there was general agreement among the British authorities in Egypt was the dispatch of British officers to Khartum to report on the situation. The choice fell on Stewart to be the senior officer heading the mission, and, in the opinion of Alison, two others should accompany him, one an artillery officer and the second an officer of the Royal Engineers. Towards the end of October the Foreign Office informed Malet that they sanctioned Stewart's suggested mission and that he should consult Alison about the advisability of sending other officers with him. Securing approval in principle, Malet and Alison agreed on the two other officers, a measure to which the

[1] Dufferin to Granville in a private telegram, Nov. 25, 1882, P.R.O., G/D 29/166.
[2] Malet to Granville, No. 749, Oct. 28, 1882, P.R.O., F.O. 78/3442.
[3] Granville to Malet, No. 402, Nov. 4, 1882, P.R.O., F.O. 78/3433.
[4] Dufferin to Granville, No. 38, Egypt, Dec. 9, 1882, P.R.O., F.O. 78/3454.
[5] Granville to Dufferin, No. 47, Dec. 14, 1882, P.R.O., F.O. 78/3453.

British Government assented, 'but it made clear that the mission was simply to make inquiries: 'but it must be distinctly understood these gentlemen shall under no circumstances presume to act in any military capacity.[1] This last reservation was included in the reply at the request of Mr. Childers in order to guard against the misunderstanding that Britain was about to undertake any responsibility for the affairs of the Sudan.[2]

Malet and Alison, putting their heads together and noticing the reserved attitude of the Government, decided to dispense with the other two officers and to be content with Stewart alone assisted by M. Messedaglia, an Italian, who had been Governor of Darfur Province under Gordon. It was thought that that gentleman would be of immense value to Stewart because of his knowledge of the language and customs of the country.[3]

The Egyptian authorities both in Egypt and in the Sudan were in complete ignorance of Stewart's mission. The Governor of the eastern Sudan was surprised at his arrival at Sawakin. Stewart inquired about the garrisons of the Red Sea littoral and the distribution of soldiers among them, together with the number of guns and small arms. When he learned that there were many Sudanese soldiers at Masawwa, he advised that it was extremely desirable that they should be sent to the interior of the Sudan and replaced by Egyptians from Cairo. Being unfavourably impressed by the Governor of Sawakin and his deputy, he gave the hint to the Governor of eastern Sudan to dismiss the former and to send the latter, being Sudanese, with the soldiers to the interior of the Sudan to fight. Stewart's idea was to garrison the Red Sea ports with Egyptians brought from Cairo in order to release the Sudanese soldiers who would be dispatched to Khartum to go into action against al-Mahdi.

Arriving at Barbar, Stewart asked the Governor to supply him with lists of the various Arabian tribes wilth the names of their chiefs and the taxes they were to pay. He also asked for the number of sakias (water-wheels) and the amount which was to be collected from them in taxes, and the volume of traffic on the desert roads for the last three years. All this information about Stewart was

---

[1] Granville to Malet, No. 404, Nov. 7, 1882, P.R.O., F.O. 78/3433.
[2] Childers to Granville in a private letter, Nov. 6, 1882, P.R.O., G/D 29/118.
[3] Malet to Granville, No. 836, Nov. 16, 1882, P.R.O., F.O. 78/3444.

telegraphed to the Khedive by 'Abd al-Qadir in Khartum, who had received it by wire from Sawakin and Barbar. 'Abd al-Qadir asked for instructions about the attitude he was to take towards him.[1]

'Abd al-Qadir was told by the Khedive in reply that all that they could gather about Stewart's mission was that he was to report on the impostor, his power, and the tribes giving him support. But the Egyptian Government in Cairo seemed to be at this time not quite certain of the intentions of the British in sending Stewart. It aroused in them all kinds of fear and suspicion, and the more so as Stewart was accompanied by Messedaglia, a man not in the confidence of the Khedive and his Government.

While being told to give all the facilities for getting information asked for by Stewart, 'Abd al-Qadir was instructed to put the two gentlemen under the strictest observation and to report in cypher to Cairo on all their doings and their behavior. All this was to be done in the most secret way and 'Abd al-Qadir had to confide this secret to nobody else and nothing was to be done which would make the two suspect that they were being observed.[2]

The first report sent in cypher to the Khedive, after the arrival of Stewart at Khartum, was to the effect that the latter desired to get a full and intimate knowledge of the Sudan in all its aspects, administrative, military, financial, geographical, and political. He went a step farther than merely collecting information in that he desired to have his advice heard, with a certain amount of insistence, but, when it was pointed out to him by 'Abd al-Qadir that his interference would result in the most unhealthy effect owing to the religious nature of al-Mahdi's movement, he modified his ways a little. Anyway, it seems that 'Abd al-Qadir was converted by Stewart to the idea of employing largely Sudanese troops in the fight owing to their ability to endure the hardships of the climate.[3] It seems also that the fears of the Khedive as regards Stewart's mission were allayed, because very soon afterwards 'Abd al-Qadir was told that on further investigation it was known that the mission contained nothing of a secret nature, and

[1] 'Abd al-Qadir to the Khedive, Dec. 15, 1882, In-Telegram Book from June 27, 1879, 'Abd. Pal. Arch., Cairo.

[2] Khedive to 'Abd al-Qadir, Dec. 16, 1882, Out-Telegram Book, No. 30, 1881-83, 'Abd. Pal. Arch., Cairo.

[3] Abd al-Qadir to the Khedive, Dec. 20, 1882, In-Telegram Book from June 27, 1879, 'Abd. Pal. Arch., Cairo.

of the Sudan and on al-Mahdi's movement. Consequently he was asked to give all the information which Stewart desired, and to burn the previous secret telegrams concerning Stewart.[1]

Not a month had passed after the cessation of hostilities in Egypt before the British Government found themselves immersed in a number of intricate problems with which they had to grapple. They decided to entrust to Lord Dufferin the job of tackling these problems, as he was well aware of the international complications of the question from his experience as British Ambassador in Constantinople. To the British Foreign Office the matter was essentially bound up with the complications arising from international control in Egypt, and in this respect closely connected with the whole Eastern Question.[2]

Although Dufferin's mission was primarily concerned with Egypt, there was, in the first month of the British occupation, alarming news from the Sudan which caused the British Government to instruct Dufferin on the line of policy to follow in Sudan affairs. It was clearly stated to him that 'Her Majesty's Government are not prepared to undertake any expedition into the Sudan,'[3] but would be glad to receive 'full reports from Your Excellency as to the condition of affairs in the Sudan.' What concerned them most in Sudan affairs was the potential danger to Egypt proper. To guard against such a contingency Dufferin was asked, in consultation with the British and Egyptian authorities in Egypt, to indicate the 'nature and extent of the measures' which in his opinion should be taken.

With these general lines of policy about the Sudan, Dufferin could only keep London informed of the news coming from there and consider measures of defense against the spread of the danger to Egypt proper, but he came face to face with the whole Sudan problem when arranging for the organization of the Egyptian army. Before the British occupation the whole Nile valley was treated by the Egyptian Government as one unit from a military and strategic angle, but Dufferin, at an early stage in his investigations, arrived at the conclusion that the two army establishments ought to be

[1] Khedive to 'Abd al-Qadir, Dec. 19, 1882, Out-Telegram Book, No. 30, 1881-83, 'Abd. Pal. Arch., Cairo.
[2] Granville to Malet, No. 386, Oct. 29, 1882, P.R.O., F.O. 78/3433.
[3] Granville to Dufferin, No. 3, Egypt, Nov. 3, 1882, P.R.O., F.O. 78/3453.

separate. Nevertheless, an army for the Sudan had to be provided for. We must remember that the British Government, having just defeated and subsequently disbanded the Egyptian army, was in no mood to create a formidable force which would repeat the movement which they had put down. To them the new army had to perform the humble duty of policing the country and of defending it from the possible attacks of Bedwins.

The first impressions which Lord Dufferin formed about the connection between Egypt and the Sudan were that it (the Sudan) 'has proved a constant drain upon the Egyptian resources,'[1] and that no Egyptian administration, except Gordon's, was known 'to have promoted the happiness of its inhabitants.' It was obviously correct, in his opinion, for the Egyptian Government to abandon Darfur and relieve itself of 'so profitless an encumbrance,' and it might be argued whether it would be advisable for Egypt to get rid of the Sudan as well as Darfur. Notwithstanding the strong reasons for abandoning the Sudan, he saw the great difficulties of persuading any Egyptian Government to 'adopt such a course.' The Sudan was a country with immense possibilities for agriculture if only it could be opened up and a railway laid down both for importing the necessary machinery for cotton and sugar and for transporting the produce to outside markets. Under the circumstances the Khedive and his Government could not be convinced of the desirability of abandoning a country with such possibilities of development. As to the efficient administration of that vast territory, it could be effected if only some person like Gordon could be found to administer it.

Turning to the actual progress of the rebellion, the information received at this time (November 18, 1882) was more reassuring to Egypt than it had been of late, and so long as al-Ubayyid was holding out there was no danger to Khartum. Several battalions had already been sent there. The only misgivings Dufferin entertained were that the Egyptian soldiers would 'perish rapidly[1] in those tropical regions and appear to be of little use for fighting purposes.' This was considered as another reason for separating the two military establishments.

But, in any case, the present crisis had to be met and Dufferin considered that there was at least one notable use in sending forces

[1] Dufferin to Granville, No. 6, Egypt, Nov. 18, 1882, P.R.O., F.O. 78/3454,
[2] In the original draft it was 'die like flies.'

to the Sudan. Egypt, at that time, was teeming with discontented officers, not only of the disbanded army of 'Urabi, but also those who had been dismissed before the disturbances in the time of Isma'il. Although many would ultimately be absorbed in the civil population, yet there would still remain others who would become a source of trouble and danger. To this latter element the army intended for the Sudan would be an attraction. Even if arrangements were made by which an army organization was instituted in the Sudan, supported and paid locally, the Egyptian Government might find it advisable to build up a reserve of black troops with Turkish and Circassian officers. As that would be a safeguard against the danger threatening from the Sudan, Dufferin thought that they should not be hindered from doing so. Already, at this time, a number of Turks and Circassians had been brought into the country to be employed in the police of Cairo and Alexandria, but the project was stopped by Dufferin. It might be convenient to employ them in the army destined for the Sudan.

At the end of January 1883 we see that Dufferin was uneasy about the Sudan, and in his opinion 'the Egyptian soldiers seem perfectly incapable of holding their own against al-Mahdi's men.'[1] The policy of non-interference in the affairs of the Sudan was maintained, as Dufferin wrote privately to Granville saying, 'I have carefully avoided having anything to do with the Sudan business except keeping myself informed of what was happening.'[2] The last thing on record in which Dufferin had to do with the Sudan business was his advice to the head of the newly constituted Sudan Bureau, Ibrahim Bey, when he paid Dufferin a visit. He was favourably impressed by Ibrahim Bey and had no doubt that under his direction the 'present situation of that unfortunate region will improve.'[3] Dufferin conveyed to Ibrahim Bey his own opinion of the causes of the rebellion and of the policy to be followed. He believed that the recent disturbances were attributable to the 'misgovernment and cruel exactions of the local Egyptian authorities at Khartum,' and that al-Mahdi would not have attained any success were it not for the support given him by people thrown into 'despair and misery.' As to the future policy, he suggested that it would be wise for Egypt

[1] Dufferin to Granville in a private letter, Jan. 30, 1883, P.R.O., G/d 29/166.
[2] Ibid.
[3] Dufferin to Granville, No. 93, Apr. 2, 1883, P.R.O., F.O. 78/3567.

to confine its efforts to keeping Sennar and the bordering river banks and in this way the 'annual drain on the Egyptian Treasury would be greatly diminished, if it did not altogether cease.' When efficient administration could be maintained in Sennar, Khartum, and Dongola, the reannexation of the abandoned territory 'would be easily effected at a later period.' This was on the 2nd of April, 1883 and Lord Granville put his big 'G' on the docket under 'approve language.'

While waiting for the full report of Stewart and the recommendations in it, which the British Government had decided to bring to the notice of Egypt, we shall now deal with these proposals which Stewart telegraphed to the British Agent in Cairo. On the 19th of February 1883 he proposed that the Governor-General should be empowered to send orders to the Government authorities in Darfur for the withdrawal of troops and the burning of the stores if hard pressed. That occurred after it was known beyond doubt that al-Ubayyid had fallen and, surprisingly enough, the news he sent was reassuring to the Government notwithstanding the loss of that important centre. He seemed to believe in the rumors of 'great desertions among the rebels and that many of them would join the Egyptian troops if they advanced immediately.' [1]

At the same time, on hearing of the fall of al-Ubayyid, he asked the Government to take care of Dongola. The telegraph line connecting Cairo and Khartum passed through Dongola, and its destruction would put Egypt completely in the dark as to the movements of al-Mahdi. What made things look very serious in Dongola was the rumor that al-Kababish tribe had joined the rebellion and could descend on Dongola Province with considerable forces, and it was probable that the inhabitants would welcome them. Dongola was garrisoned only by about 500 soldiers. [2]

Taking stock of the whole situation in the Sudan, Stewart advised against the immediate sending of the Kurdufan expedition. To him the fall of al-Ubayyid, in addition to the huge stores of war material which had fallen to al-Mahdi, the morale of his troops and the prestige which he had acquired, created a situation which the Egyp-

[1] Malet to Granville, No. 55, Feb. 19, 1883, P.R.O., F.O. 78/3552.
[2] Stewart to Malet, enclosed in Malet to Granville, No. 57, Feb. 20, 1883, P.R.O., F.O. 78/3552.

tian soldiers could not hope to meet. This confirmed the idea that
al-Mahdi was absolutely correct in claiming a divine mission. The
position as it appeared to Stewart, from the point of view of morale,
reduced itself to an irrefutable argument in favor of al-Mahdi:
'Here is a Government well supplied with arms, ammunition, money
and soldiers utterly defeated and paralysed by a poor simple Fakih.
How can such a result happen except by the direct interposition of
God' [1] He therefore doubted very much the advisability of sending
the Kurdufan expedition. From what he was told and knew of the
Government soldiers, to send it 'would be to run a very great risk,
and if the expedition were defeated the probability is that the Sudan
would be lost.' [2] He also advised that Slatin Bey should be ordered
to retreat as best as he could on Bahr al-Ghazal, destroying all
stores. There was the possibility of Khartum being beleaguered, but
he doubted whether 10,000 soldiers would 'allow themselves to be
shut up.' The only disturbing element in the situation was the uncertain loyalty of the troops and their lack of heart in the matter.
We have to remember that the troops collected at Khartum at this
time were the disbanded soldiers of 'Urabi. They had no cause to
fight for, as their own country was occupied by a foreign power, and
they were laboring under the impression that the Khedive had sent
them merely to be slaughtered. What would make their desertion or
easy surrender more probable was their knowledge that al-Mahdi
would spare them and would not kill them. In fact, they might be
comfortably situated if they chose to accept his divine mission and
fight for its cause. The feeling of the people, even those still under
Government jurisdiction, was beyond doubt against the authorities,
and the best evidence of this was the difficulty with which information of al-Mahdi's position could be secured, while the minutest
details of the Government's plans were told to al-Mahdi. 'Altogether,' Stewart wrote, 'the state of affairs is far from being a bright
one and it is really impossible to foretell what may not happen.' [3]
All this was made still worse by the financial stringency in Khartum,
as the 'Treasury is getting rather empty.' [4]

[1] Ibid.
[2] Ibid.
[3] Stewart to Malet, enclosed in Malet to Granville, No. 57, Feb. 20, 1883
P.R.O., F.O. 78/3552.
[4] Stewart to Malet, enclosed in Malet to Granville, No. 88, Mar. 20, 1883,
P.R.O., F.O. 78/3553.

Leaving the political developments in Cairo and the reaction of the British whether in Cairo or London to Sudan affairs, we must now trace the progress of the rebellion and how 'Abd al-Qadir met it. The victory over al-Shallali marked the end of the defensive policy followed by al-Mahdi. al-Ubayyid was singled out as his next objective on the advice of Alyas Pasha Um Barir, a great merchant of that town and a former Mudir of Kurdufan, who had many grievances against the Government in general and against Muhammad Pasha Sa'id, the present Mudir of Kurdufan, in particular. It was reported by Wad al-Badri, an adherent of al-Mahdi, to Father Ohrwalder, who recorded it, that it was the intention of al-Mahdi to go westwards to Dar Firtit and continue his operations there, but Alyas Pasha persuaded him to proceed to al-Ubayyid as the garrison there was comparatively weak and the people were ready to join him.[1] That Alyas Pasha persuaded al-Mahdi to take that step may or may not be true, but certainly the importance of al-Ubayyid could not escape the notice of al-Mahdi who had visited it before the declaration of his mission. It was the mercantile depot for all the produce of all Kurdufan and part of Darfur, and it was the largest or second largest town of the Sudan, with a large number of merchants, both foreign and native. In that respect, therefore, it was the centre of the economic life of all Kurdufan, and its occupation would mean the control of practically the whole province.

For about two months after the annihilation of al-Shallali's expedition, al-Mahdi sent small bodies of troops in all directions to attack and occupy the garrisons and especially those of Kurdufan. As a result, the Kurdufan garrisons fell one after the other; by the end of July the only two places still flying the Turkish flag were al-Ubayyid and Bara. That time of the year, when the rainy season had just set in, was ideally suited to such mobile operations in Kurdufan, as water was in abundance and movement could be free. al-Birkah lake, to the south of al-Ubayyid, in particular, was the scene of battles between the Arabs, who usually concentrated there at that time of the year, and the Government force which had been sent from al-Ubayyid. Although the latter managed to disperse and defeat the Arabs, yet they gathered again as soon as the reinforcements were recalled to al-Ubayyid, and the small garrison left there had to succumb to the superior number of the Arabs.

[1] Ohrwalder, op. cit., p. 10.

By the beginning of August 1882 al-Mahdi seems to have started from Qadir quite slowly owing to the rainy season. In the first week of September the main body of his troops was at Kaba, near al-Ubayyid. al-Mahdi at once sent messengers with letters to the garrison to surrender. Instead of replying to al-Mahdi's summons to surrender by writing back refusing it and showing their determination to fight, the authorities at al-Ubayyid made the mistake of hanging the three messengers on the pretext of their overbearing manner and impolite attitude. The following night the majority of the inhabitants deserted to al-Mahdi: either they were losing confidence in the Government and its ability to stem the rising tide of Mahdiism or they really believed in his divine misson, and, as good Muslims they could not stand in the way of the expected Messiah. Perhaps also they were infuriated by the fact that the Government provided for the protection of the official quarters and left the rest of the town to be pillaged and destroyed.

This brings us to the defensive measures made at al-Ubayyid. When they suspected the intentions of al-Mahdi and his designs on the town, the Government authorities attempted to make a trench and a parapet round all the town, which would be 8 kilometres in length. Seeing the impossibility of manning that length of fortifications, which required at least 20,000 soldiers, they discontinued it and made one which was shorter (2 kilometres) and embraced the official quarters only. The whole garrison, including irregulars, did not exceed 4,000 soldiers, nearly all of them blacks. The soldiers, Government officials, a few loyal inhabitants, and foreigners shut themselves up behind the new short defenses.

A number of about 30,000 warriors, all believing in a religious cause advocated by a leader who so far was eminently victorious, could hardly resist the temptation of attacking the town of al-Ubayyid immediately after the refusal to surrender expressed so cruelly by hanging the messengers. But the operation which al-Mahdi's forces were going to launch was something with which they were not familiar. Previously they used to attack an enemy surrounded by trees and bushes, which gave them the advantage of rushing the square with a comparatively short distance in front of them and thus not giving the defending soldiers a chance to use their fire-arms effectively. The square thus penetrated, the formation of soldiers disorganized, and the advantage of fire-arms cancelled, the sword would win the day. Now they were facing an enemy dug in behind strong fortifications. The great majority of the defending soldiers were the plucky black Sudanese, who would not be disgraced by showing lack of courage.

The story of the fight cannot be better told than by Father Ohrwalder, who, although he was not present in the affair, got the details of it from both sides.

At daybreak the hordes appeared on the rising ground near al-Ubayyid; the defenders heard only the dull roar caused by the mass of voices in the distance, but the clouds of dust prevented them seeing anything; it was only when the fitful gusts of wind blew away the dust that the thousands of horsemen could be seen galloping wildly about and then disappearing again behind the dust. But the noise like approaching thunder became every instant more audible, and soon above the clouds of sand the myriads of flags and banners became visible. Faki al-Mannah, with about 10,000 men, approached from the east, while al-Mahdi's attack was directed on the south-west end of town. The first ditch was soon crossed, and then the Mahdists spread out and completely encircled the town; masses of wild fanatics rolled like waves through the deserted streets; they did not advance through these alone, but hurrying on from house to house, wall to wall, and yard to yard, they reached the ditch of the Mudirieh, and like a torrent suddenly let loose, regardless of every obstacle, with wild shouts they dashed across it and up the ramparts, from which the din of a thousand rifles and the booming of the guns suddenly burst forth; but these wild hordes, utterly fearless of death, cared neither for the deadly Remington nor the thunder of the guns, and still swept forward in ever-increasing numbers.

The poor garrison, utterly powerless to resist such an assault, ran to the tops of the houses and kept up an incessant fire on the masses, which now formed such a crowd that they could scarcely move—indeed the barrels of the rifles from the rapidity of the fire became almost red-hot; and soon the streets and open spaces became literally choked with the bodies of those who had fallen. . . . It was impossible not to admire the reckless bravery of these fanatics who, dancing and shouting, rushed up to the very muzzles of the rifles with nothing but the knotty stick in their hands, only to fall dead one over the other. Numbers of them carried large bundles of Dhurra stalks, which they threw into the ditch, hoping to fill it up and then cross over.[1]

The ansar lost the battle after leaving about 10,000 of their comrades dead and after pressing their attack incessantly for about five hours. They were compelled to retire to Kaba while the soldiers had

[1] Ohrwalder, op. cit., p. 37.

a great feast and general rejoicings. 'Ali Bey Sharif, the Mudir, requested Muhammad Pasha Sa'id, the Governor-General of western Sudan to permit the pursuit of the ansar while they were demoralized after their defeat. Muhammad Pasha refused to allow 'Ali Bey to take this step fearing that al-Mannah, one of the generals of al-Mahdi who was to the north of the town, might seize the opportunity and occupy the town when they had left. Some people have thought that if the garrison had gone out and pursued the retreating Arabs it would have been the end of Mahdiism, but I believe that it would have been the end of the garrison. By going out in the open the soldiers would have given the ansar the opportunity of fighting by their own familiar method of rushing into the midst of soldiers and skilfully using their swords and spears. They might lose heavily in the first onslaught, but in the end those who were utterly reckless would win the day. It was only after this repulse that al-Mahdi sent for the firearms from the Nuba mountains, where they had been left, after having been captured from the previous Government expeditions.

The fight took place on the 4th of September, and the official report reached Khartum on the 17th together with a request from Muhammad Pasha Sa'id for reinforcements. 'Abd al-Qadir thereupon sent a relief expedition composed of two regular battalions and 752 bashbuzuks under 'Ali Bey Lufti. The expedition was attacked and about 1,127 of its members including most of the officers, were killed, while the rest managed to fight their way up to Bara assisted by a sortie from the beseiged garrison.

Having failed in a frontal attack on al-Ubayyid, al-Mahdi determined to lay seige to the town and compel the garrison to surrender. The Arabs, who dispersed after the first shock of defeat, gradually returned, and the towns of al-Ubayyid and Bara were completely surrounded. The garrisons very soon began to suffer from scarcity of food and the usual fever after the rainy season. Seeing that the supplies were getting very low Muhammad Sa'id decided to attempt a sortie, although at the time there were only 1,600 soldiers fit for duty. 'Ali Bey Sharif, however, who was to lead the sortie, called a council of war, which decided not to make the attempt as the force was considered to be insufficient. Small sorties were made after that, and were maintained, mostly with the result of bringing back cattle or corn. The besiegers, on the other hand, established themselves comfortably round the town, some availing themselves of the ruined houses and others building for themselves straw huts, and with patience awaited the inevitable surrender. There was no lack of provisions or men as all the resources of Kurdufan were theirs and every day new adherents to al-Mahdi's cause were received.

The straits to which the garrison was reduced is graphically described by Ohrwalder:[1]

The garrison in al-Ubayyid now began to suffer from the effects of this close siege and blockade. The necessaries of life were failing rapidly; the price of provisions had gone up enormously. The commonest food, known as 'dokhun' (a kind of millet) rose to 150 dollars, and eventually to 500 dollars the Ardab. Meat had almost entirely given out. Our mission brethren in the fort possessed one camel, which was nothing but skin and bone, and which was sold for 1,000 dollars, and two days afterwards the purchaser offered it for sale for 1,500 dollars. Eventually the butcher bought it for 2,000 dollars. A chicken went for 30 dollars; eggs a dollar apiece; a loaf of sugar fifty dollars, and twenty dollars for a pound of coffee. A thimbleful of salt cost a dollar. The above were the prices a month after the close investment had begun. Butter and oil could not be had for any money. The poor began to starve quite at the beginning of the siege, and soon were dying in considerable numbers. A little later, matters came to a terrible pass. All the camels and cattle being finished, donkeys, dogs, mice and even crickets were consumed, as well as cochroaches, which were considered quite tit-bits; while ants, too, were eaten.

And now the deaths by starvation had reached an appalling figure. The dead and dying filled the streets; the space within the fortifications being so limited, there was not room for all people, and in consequence many lay about in the streets and open spaces. The air was poisoned by the number of dead bodies lying unburied, while the ditch was half full of mortifying corpses. Scurvy and dysentery were rife; the air was black with the scores of carrion kites, which feasted on the dead bodies; these ugly birds became so distended by constant gorging that they could not even fly away, and were killed in numbers by the soldiers, who devoured them with avidity.

Later on gum became the only food; there was a quantity of this, but it brought on diarrhoea, and caused the bodies to distend; indeed, numbers died from eating it. The ground was dug up in all directions in search of the white ant's nests; and the food which they had collected for the winter was greedily consumed. Some poor sufferers eked out a miserable existence by living on the undigested food found in the excrement of animals; all sorts

[1] Ohrwalder, op. cit., p. 52.

of leather, shoes and sandals, were boiled and eaten. It was a terrible sight to see these human skeletons—their eyes sunk into the backs of their heads, wandering about in search of food. The Mudir extorted all the corn and money he could from the rich merchants, but of what good was a mere handful of corn to the soldiers? They became desperate, all discipline was at an end and they often broke into the houses by night in search of food.

Even in these conditions, Sa'id Pasha kept up the spirit of the garrison in the hope that the reinforcements would soon relieve them. By the beginning of the year 1883, when winter was making the problem of food still more acute, the garrison of Bara decided to surrender, but fearing the cruelty of the general besieging them, they asked al-Mahdi to send another general to receive their surrender. Consequently 'Abd al-Rahman al-Nujumi was ordered to proceed to Bara, where everything was handed over to him on the 5th of January 1883. Nothing of a cruel nature was committed and the lives of the garrison were spared. This lenient treatment of the surrendering garrison of Bara had a decisive effect on the surrender of al-Ubayyid.

Knowing that the garrison could not continue their stubborn resistance to the forces of hunger, and knowing that no reinforcements were coming, al-Mahdi, on the 13th of January 1883 sent letters to Muhammad Pasha Sa'id, 'Ali Bey Sharif, Iskandar Bey, who were commanding the troops, and all the high-ranking officers pointing out to them that they had held out sufficiently long, that they could not be blamed or accused of treachery, and that if they would surrender, he would guarantee them their lives. Instead of complying with that request they imprisoned the messenger. Receiving no reply and with his own messenger taken prisoner, al-Mahdi ordered his ansar, on the afternoon of the 16th, to advance in force against the garrison, which they did, firing in the air, as they were still hoping that the besieged officers might come to their senses and abandon their hopeless resistance. The garrison replied by firing, also harmlessly, and in the confusion an Arab succeeded in handing a letter to a lieutenant, in which the soldiers and younger officers were informed of the communications that had been sent to their superiors. The recipient of that letter made its contents publicly known with the result that during the night the vast majority of the garrison deserted to al-Mahdi. On the morning of the 17th of January Muhammad Sa'id and other chiefs, findings themselves deserted by their soldiers, had no alternative but to surrender.

al-Mahdi immediately entered the town and went straight to the mosque where he performed the victory prayers. Next he went to Government House where he interviewed Muhammad Sa'id and other officers. He made it clear to them that they would enjoy their freedom only if they gave up all their money and valuables which they denied that they possessed. But, in a careful search in their houses £E.8,000 in gold was found in Sa'id's and £E.7,000 in 'Ali Sharif's and varying sums in nearly all the other houses of officers and Government officials. That threw a shadow of mistrust on them, but otherwise they were leniently treated until some of them, including Sa'id were put to death on a charge of having attempted to communicate with Khartum. When the garrison surrendered, it numbered about 3,500 regulars and irregulars, nearly all blacks. The arms consisted of 5,000 rifles, 5 guns, 1 rocket, and large stores of ammunition. The soldiers, especially the blacks, were recruited into his ansar fraternity, and added greatly to al-Mahdi's fighting strength. It is curious to know that the expedition which was meant to relieve these soldiers was met, when it finally materialized, by that same force as enemies.

The belief was current among the people on the Government side that Muhammad Sa'id Pasha was mainly responsible for all that had occurred. Through his harshness he had antagonized the tribes, through his incapacity and want of courage he had neglected to provision the town when he had the means to do so, and, finally, through his stupidity and want of decision he had lost the opportunity, when it presented itself, for making a sortie. All this may or may not be true, but Muhammad Sa'id was a typical example of the ruling class at that time and he could not do better than he had done.[1]

We have so far narrated the story of al-Mahdi's movements until he finally effected the subjugation of all Kurdufan. We must now take up the story of operations in al-Jazirah, directed from Khartum by the Governor-General himself. It was reported towards the end of September 1883 that Faki al-Silaihabi had collected a force of:

[1] Stewart to Malet, enclosed in Malet to Granville, No. 83, Mar. 13, 1883, P.R.O., F.O. 78/3553.

between 10,000 and 12,000 men and declared for al-Mahdi. This force took up a position which threatened Miraibiah on the White Nile. 'Abd al-Qadir, on receiving this news, instructed that a force should be brought together from the garrisons of al-Duwaim, al-Kawwah, and Miraibiah under the command of Sa'id Bey al-Jimai'abi, and ordered to advance on the Arabs. About October 5 the Government force reached the neighborhood of the Arab's concentration and sustained 800 casualties. The survivors found their way back to their different stations. Faki al-Silaihabi did not follow up his victory because, although victorious, he had suffered heavy losses.

When al-Ubayyid repulsed the attack of the ansar, and there were reports in al-Mahdi's camp that reinforcements were very soon to be dispatched from Khartum to al-Ubayyid, al-Mahdi directed Shaikh 'Abd al-Basit al-Jamri to stir up the smouldering embers of the rebellion on the White Nile in order to prevent the sending of assistance to the beleaguered garrisons of Kurdufan. 'Abd al-Basit advanced close to al-Duwaim with a body of only 400 men hoping to be joined by adherents, but he was disappointed, as his force was not swelled by enthusiasts. Geigler, who happened to be at al-Duwaim, sent a force of 225 picked men against him and on the 11th of November 'Abd al-Basit was defeated and taken as a prisoner to Khartum where he was hanged.

So far all rebellious movements in al-Jazirah and on the two Niles had been started by people who had not seen al-Mahdi but had declared for him in their locality. The rebellion after that date was started afresh by the chief emissary who had been with al-Mahdi in Kurdufan, and who was instructed to come back to al-Jazirah to keep the fire of rebellion burning. Ahmad al-Mikashfi was entrusted with this task. On his way he attacked the garrison of Shat, which was too weak to make effective resistance and so nearly all the soldiers were killed. The next Government post was al-Duwaim, which proved to be too strong for al-Mikashfi, who crossed the White Nile and resumed his journey to Sennar where he was intended to operate.

The start of the rebellious movement in al-Jazirah coincided with the arrival of the first batch of the long-expected reinforcements from Egypt. The immediate problem for 'Abd al-Qadir was how to train these troops. For that purpose he built barracks for them at

Omdurman on the western bank of the White Nile and supervised their instruction in person. They were tested when a body of rebels was reported south of al-Duwaim and a battalion of these newly arrived troops was sent to stop their advance. They did not meet the Arabs as the bimbashi in command showed all sorts of objections to the attack. It was after that incident that 'Abd al-Qadir suggested to the Khedive the employment of the European officers attached in various capacities to the Government service.

Towards the end of the year 1882, after the arrival of the first reinforcements for the Kurdufan garrisons and during a temporary cessation of hostilities in al-Jazirah, 'Abd a-Qadir had to make a plan of campaign. He preferred to advance along the northern road, leading from Omdurman through Gabra to Bara, which was known to be near the powerful and friendly Kababish tribe. A fight was to be expected when approaching Bara and if 'Abd al-Qadir's troops were successful and Bara was relieved, it was more than probable that many of the nominal or enforced adherents of al-Mahdi would begin to fall away. The great difficulty was to find the camels to carry the provisions and ammunition as well as provisions for the famine-stricken garrisons of Bara and al-Ubayyid. In reporting the situation to Malet Stewart declared:

> I would beg to point out how very important it is that the present expedition should prove a success. A failure would probably entail the total loss, if not of the Sudan, of at any rate many provinces. This truth can hardly be brought home with too much force to the Egyptian Government. At the same time I think 'Abd al-Qadir has every right to expect a success. He is taking every reasonable precaution, closely superintends the training of his troops, exerts himself to influence the tribes and natives, and in short appears to be doing his best. He intends personally to take the field. I can only regret that such an active and intelligent man should not be supported by subordinates whom he could trust to carry out his intentions with ordinary intelligence and common sense.[1]

The situation at the beginning of 1883 was far from hopeful. The garrisons which were about to be relieved were reported to be in dire need of food, there were difficulties about the collection of camels, disturbances that should have been suppressed before the start of the expedition broke out afresh in al-Jazirah, and more

[1] Stewart to Malet, enclosed in Malet to Granville, No. 20, Jan. 20, 1883, P.R.O., F.O. 78/3552.

troops ought to have arrived in Khartum from Cairo to protect the town and its environs after the departure of the expedition.[1] Being assured of the presence of Ahmad al-Mikashfi at al-Sabil, near Sennar, 'Abd al-Qadir sent a battalion by steamer to al-Masallamiya to assist in attacking al-Mikashfi. His instructions were for a combined action by that battalion with the four companies at Sennar and the garrison of the irregulars at 'Ibud to the north of al-Sabil. It was reported, after the dispatch of the battalion, that al-Mikashfi had attacked 'Ibud with heavy loss, but that the communications between Sennar and al-Masallamiya were still interrupted and the whole district was declaring for al-Mahdi. Early in the new year 'Abd al-Qadir had shown Stewart his telegram to the Khedive asking for two more regiments to form a reserve at Khartum and stating that, owing to the delay in sending the troops, the rebellion had assumed very large proportions. He begged Stewart to telegraph his request to Malet and Stewart agreed to do so.[2]

'Abd al-Qadir was convinced that the situation in al-Jazirah called for him to take the field in person, and on the 2nd of January he embarked on a steamer intending to go to Sennar. Stewart was hopeful that the expedition would raise the morale of the troops and clear the district between the two Niles. The troops might perhaps learn that the Arabs were not so very formidable and that their religious shaikhs had not the power of making bullets ineffective. 'Abd al-Qadir also, in Stewart's opinion, would have an opportunity of seeing something of the rebels and would learn to place some confidence in his troops. Of the morale and training of the troops arriving from Cairo and of the initiative of officers in the out-stations Stewart gave the following picture:

Besides the gross ignorance of the Egyptian officers nothing is more striking than their want of initiative and their unwillingness to assume any responsibility. Not one of the officers in any of the out-stations will think of attacking unless they have previously sent into Khartum to ask for leave, the result being an enormous loss of valuable time and of many favorable opportunities. It is owing to this cause that the enemy, although there are several strong garrisons along the White and Blue Niles, can move unmolested

[1] Stewart to Malet, enclosed in Malet to Granville, No. 7, Jan. 9, 1883, P.R.O., F.O. 78/3552.
[2] Stewart to Malet, enclosed in Malet to Granville, No. 32, Jan. 30, 1883, P.R.O., F.O. 78/3552.

about the intermediate country and pass almost within gun fire of the forts.
. . . The troops in garrison here are working at elementary drill and tactics
and are making some progress. It is, however, very uphill work, the officers
are so grossly ignorant, and so incapable of grasping the meaning of the
simplest movement. Quite 1/3 of the troops are also ignorant of the use of
the rifle and they would be more formidable adversaries were they simply
armed with sticks. Many have also superstitious ideas of the power of al-
Mahdi and others think the Khedive has simply sent them here to get rid of
them.[1]

On his way southwards 'Abd al-Qadir stopped at al-Masid, where
the family of Wad 'Isa had set up a centre of religious learning.
'Abd al-Qadir asked these shaikhs to use their influence with the
people to remain loyal to the Government, and he put the responsibility for the disturbances on their shoulders, as they could induce
the people to pursue their normal occupations peacefully. At al-
Bashaqra and Wad Rawa, he also interviewed the shaikhs on the
same subject. At Rufa'a he was well received by Shaikh 'Awad al-
Karim Abu Sin, the chief of al-Shukriya tribe with a display of
sword and lance exercises and horsemanship. On reaching the point
opposite al-Masallamiya, 'Abd al-Qadir disembarked and rode to
the town about six miles west of the river. Here also 'Abd al-Qadir
was well received, and he very soon set to work to prepare for the
march to 'Ibud. On the 8th of January the battalion, with some
irregular troops under Salih Bey al-Mak, and some Shukriya horsemen, left for 'Ibud where a small military garrison of 125 irregulars
was stationed.

'Ibud was in the area affected by the rebellion, and only two of
the inhabitants were found, the rest having deserted to a lieutenant
of al-Mikashfi. In the belief that many had been forced to desert,
written pardons from the Governor-General were sent out to them
in order to encourage them to return to their homes. Before the
evening of the same day about fifty had already returned to the village. Reconnaissance carried out along al-Kawwah road revealed
that many of the rebels in the vicinity had dispersed, some returning
to their homes and others going to join the main body of al-Mikashfi.
After he had collected information about the extent of the disaffection, 'Abd al-Qadir realized that the quelling of the disturbances in
al-Jazirah would be more difficult than he had at first thought. He

[1] Ibid.

therefore ordered the battalion stationed at al-Shawwal on the White Nile to march across to 'Ibud and one more battalion to come from Khartum to Sennar. His plan was for the three battalions to march on al-Mikashfi and surround him or to inflict heavy losses. Should the operation succeed the three battalions were then to march on al-Kawwah and either continue their march to al-Ubayyid or wait to rejoin the main expedition.[1]

While 'Abd al-Qadir was at 'Ibud waiting for the concentration of his troops, news reached Khartum that the Hassaniya tribe on the White Nile were in rebellion. A battalion was sent from Khartum on two steamers to pacify the area. The deputy Governor of Khartum Province and some learned men of religion accompanied the soldiers with instructions to enter into communication with the people and to induce them to submit peacefully. The orders given to the battalion were to disembark a little north of the village of al-Qarrasah where the rebels were said to be concentrated and to advance in close order. The soldiers in one of the steamers were disembarked, while the other ran aground and was left behind. A rebel attack was repulsed although the bimbashi commanding the Egyptian troops was killed. Instead of pursuing the rebels, however, they retired to the steamer and the sagh (major), on whom the command devolved, held a council of war which considered that the battalion was insufficient to deal with the enemy and decided to ask for reinforcements from Khartum. On receiving this request Geigler, who was acting for 'Abd al-Qadir, summoned Husain Sirri Pasha, the senior military officer, and drew his attention to this case of cowardice. Husain seems to have made all sorts of excuses for the behavior of the officers of the battalion. Stewart commented on the incident: 'I need hardly point out that unless some very stern measures are taken to show the officers that to retire is more dangerous than to advance, it will be vain to expect a successful ending to the campaign and the Egyptians had much better at once retire to Egypt and thus save both money and lives.'[2]

Husain Sirri appears to have reported the affair to the Khedive

---

[1] Stewart to Malet, enclosed in Malet to Granville, No. 41, Feb. 6, 1883, P.R.O., F.O. 78/3552.

[2] Stewart to Malet, enclosed in Malet to Granville, No. 57, Feb. 20, 1883, P.R.O., F.O. 78/3552.

as a brilliant success. The Khedive naturally congratulated the soldiers and officers, which was an unpleasant surprise for Geigler, who was acting for 'Abd al-Qadir. Further communications between Cairo and Husain Sirri over Geigler's head continued. Husain received a telegram from the Khedive ordering all operations to be suspended and troops to be concentrated in Khartum until the arrival of a colonel from Cairo. When that order was communicated to 'Abd al-Qadir at 'Ibud he replied by telegram that if he withdrew the troops to Khartum the rebellion would certainly extend to the eastern provinces, and that if the expedition did not soon leave for Kurdufan that province would be lost and with it Darfur.[1] The substance of that telegram was also communicated to Stewart in Khartum and he was requested to ask Malet to use his influence to cancel the order. Stewart accordingly telegraphed to Malet, ending his message by saying, 'the state of affairs is very serious and the Khedive should not interfere.'[2] Stewart considered the Khedive's action to be deplorable and likely to result in quarrels between the authorities in Khartum, which would make it impossible to carry out any concerted plan. 'The Khedive must entrust some one here with supreme authority (dictator) and leave him alone. To telegraph what he should do or not do or to correspond with his subordinates over his head is only to make his position quite untenable and to ensure a disastrous termination to the campaign.'[3] When Malet showed Stewart's telegram to Sharif Pasha the latter stated that no such orders had been sent either from the Khedive or himself; the Governor-General had, however, been told that so far 10,000 men had been sent, that no more could be sent, and that he should keep his forces together and not scatter them, lest they should be destroyed piecemeal.

A bimbashi was sent to command the battalion which was awaiting reinforcements at al-Qarrasah. Stewart reported that the orders given by the bimbashi were ill received by the officers, and that when the force finally advanced on the village they were met by only 350 Arabs without fire-arms, but withdrew to the steamers without

[1] Ibid.
[2] Ibid.
[3] Ibid.
[4] Malet to Stewart, enclosed in Malet to Granville, No. 33, Jan. 30, 1883, P.R.O., F.O. 78/3552.

engaging the enemy.[1] A few hours later, reinforcements, in charge
of the qaimaqam who was to take over the command, arrived at
al-Qarrasah by order of the Khedive.

Meanwhile 'Abd al-Qadir was still at 'Ibud awaiting the arrival of
a battalion from Khartum. His intention was to march on Sennar.
He received reports, however, that Sennar was hard pressed by the
rebels under al-Mikashfi, that Karkuj had been taken, and that the
tribe of Rufa'a al-Shariq to the east of the Blue Nile had declared
for al-Mahdi and had attacked 'Ali Kashif and his 200 irregulars at
al-Rahad. It was also reported that al-Sharif al-Hindi had written
to invite 'Awad al-Karim Bey, Shaikh of al-Shukriya tribe, to join
him. In short, the rebellion was rapidly spreading farther east. At
the same time 'Abd al-Qadir received reports that Fadlallah Wad
Kirrif with a party of rebels had invited Faki Musa al-Khanfari,
who was with some rebels near al-Kawwah, to join him and attack
'Abd al-Qadir at 'Ibud. Musa had accepted the invitation and both
leaders were advancing on 'Ibud through the district of Ma'tuq and
forcing all the men to join them.

'Abd al-Qadir had to reconsider his plan and deal with the Ma'tuq
rebels so as not to leave them in his rear in his advance on Sennar.
Believing that many had joined the rebel side under pressure, 'Abd
al-Qadir hoped that Shaikh Hamad al-Nil, a spiritual chief living at
Wad Madani, would persuade them to return to the Government
side. The Shaikh's mission was unsuccessful although he converted
a notable of Ma'tuq, who would give information about the rebels.
The principal rebel leader was Fadlallah Wad Kirrif, whose force
consisted of 10,000 to 12,000 men. A few days later a party of
them attacked and pillaged al-Manaqil.

When the reinforcements had arrived, 'Abd al-Qadir determined
to advance against the main body of the Arabs who were some eight
hours' march distant. Early on the 27th of January he moved on
Ma'Tuq. Before he reached the village the advance party of the
rebels was observed near a small wood, on reaching which 'Abd al-
Qadir halted his troops and formed a square. The Arabs attacked,
passing through the wood with flags flying and loud cries of 'Allah
Dayim Allah Baqi' (Allah is eternal). Instead of pressing the attack
up to the square and then trying to penetrate it, they halted at the

[1] Stewart to Malet, enclosed in Malet to Granville, No. 62. Feb. 26, 1883,
P.R.O., F.O. 78/3552.

near edge of the wood, and Wad Ayyub, a revolted irregular officer, with some blacks, opened fire on the Egyptians. The latter opened heavy fire, and after some minutes the rebels were compelled to retire and cavalry were sent in pursuit after them. It was estimated that the Arabs lost, in wounded and killed, about 600 men. The Arabs then broke into two divisions; one under Wad Kirrif retired to Quz Abu Jim'a south of al-Kawwah, and the other to Ma'tuq village. Against this latter force 'Abd al-Qadir directed all his available cavalry and camel corps, which overtook and totally defeated them, and the remnants rejoined the force at Quz Abu Jim'a. 'Abd al-Qadir then marched to al-Kawwah, where he was met by the two battalions from al-Qarrasah. There were then at al-Kawwah under the command of the Governor-General, five Egyptian battalions exclusive of the garrison.

'Abd al-Qadir left al-Kawwah for Khartum ordering three battalions to march across al-Jazirah to Wad Madani, and the two Qarrasah battalions commanded by the qaimaqam to march out to attack the rebels at Quz Abu Jim'a. 'Abd al-Qadir intended to steam round Khartum to Wad Madani, where he hoped to meet the battalions on the 15th of February and then to advance to the relief of Sennar. But orders from Cairo directed that he should not leave Khartum, and that the relief of Sennar should be entrusted to the miralay commanding the regiment. Stewart commented on the situation:

It is almost unnecessary for me to point out how important it is that the Sennar district should be quieted and how utterly untenable 'Abd al-Qadir's position is when his slightest movement is hampered from Cairo. To attempt to direct the Governor-General's movements from Cairo is absurd and will only lead to disaster, as will also the system of telegraphing to subordinates over the heads of their superiors.[1]

By that time news was received from Kurdufan of a breach between al-Mahdi and the followers of Faki al-Manna Isma'il which, it was believed in Khartum, would before long develop into an open feud which the Government might be able to turn to its own advantage. It was also reported that al-Mahdi's followers had begun to lose faith in his mission. It is curious to note that when this belief was current in Khartum, al-Mahdi was already master of the situa-

P.R.O., F.O. 78/3553.
[1] Stewart to Malet, enclosed in Malet to Granville, No. 71, Mar. 6, 1883,

tion in Kurdufan, having taken al-Ubayyid twenty-two days previously. It was also known in Khartum that 'Ala al-Din was being sent there on a secret mission, supposedly to replace 'Abd al-Qadir. Stewart considered it unwise to change the Governor-General while affairs were still critical.[1]

Meanwhile the Khedive had suggested to 'Abd al-Qadir that the expedition to Kurdufan should be postponed until the rainy season, and at the same time had asked for a report on the condition of Sennar. In his reply 'Abd al-Qadir raised two main objections to the delaying of the expedition. In the first place al-Ubayyid and Bara would probably be unable to hold out until the rainy season, and secondly, although water would be abundant on the road during the rainy season, disease also would be rife. 'The Pasha,' Stewart wrote, 'appears firmly convinced that now or never is the time to send off the expedition and that every day's delay will increase the difficulties tenfold.' [2] 'Abd al-Qadir intended, subject to the Khedive's approval, to start at once with four battalions and the 1,000 camels he had so far collected. He planned to march to Gabra, fortify his advance columns there, and then gradually bring up the remainder of his force. As to Sennar, 'Abd al-Qadir telegraphed that the garrison was 6,000 strong, and insufficiently provisioned. al-Mikashfi was encamped in a neighboring wood on the bank of the Nile and the number of his followers varied from day to day. Unless he was driven off he would induce the other tribes both to the east and to the west of the river to rise. After receiving this report the Khedive agreed that 'Abd al-Qadir should continue with his plan of operations against Sennar and that he should himself lead the troops against al-Mikashfi. At the same time 'Abd al-Qadir suggested that if the march against al-Ubayyid was sanctioned the troops in Khartum should be permitted to march south following the western bank of the White Nile as far as al-Duwaim in order to drive off the insurgents in that region. No reply was received to this suggestion and it appears that the new commanders—'Ala al-Din, Sulayman Niazi, and Hicks—were left to settle the problems of the exepdition to Kurdufan and the pacification of the White Nile region.

'Abd al-Qadir's departure to Sennar was delayed by the absence

---

[1] Ibid.
[2] Stewart to Malet, enclosed in Malet to Granville, No. 83, Mar. 13, 1883, P.R.O., F.O. 78/3553.

of the only available steamer, which had been sent to Wad Madani when 'Abd al-Qadir was instructed to remain in Khartum.

All these delays, orders, counter orders [wrote Stewart] are most perplexing and unfortunate, adding immensely to the difficulties of the situation. It would be greatly to the general advantage if His Highness would abstain from interfering and trying to direct matters from Cairo. It is utterly impossible for him to be as well acquainted with the state of affairs as people are here. If he wants matters to go smoothly he must entrust his agent here with full powers and leave him alone. That a Governor-General engaged in trying to suppress a formidable rebellion should have to ask leave from Cairo to take command of his troops in the field is sufficiently absurd.[1]

When 'Abd al-Qadir had finally left for Sennar, reports were received in Khartum of the activities of the two battalions which had been left in al-Kawwah with orders to attack the rebels at Quz Abu Jim'a. Husain Bey Mazhar, the commander, reported that he had reconnoitred the river-bank from al-Kawwah to Quz Abu Jim'a and, according to his information, the rebels were concentrated in large numbers. He therefore postponed the attack asking for two more battalions with guns, camels, rockets, and cavalry. Stewart commented on the incident:

The real meaning of his report obviously is that both he and his troops are afraid to advance and will not do so on any account whatever. This is but another proof if more were wanting of the utter worthlessness of Egyptian infantry, officered and trained as they are at present. It is almost impossible for me to convey an idea of the contempt with which all classes of people here regard them. Their common nickname is Wad Rif a corruption of Awlad al-Rif, sons of the country, a name used in a contemptuous sense. The negro troops will not associate with them nor will curiously enough the Egyptian officers in command of these troops. We have a considerable number of Egyptian troops encamped at Omdurman opposite Khartum and I am persuaded were the rebels to make a sudden attack that the whole of these troops with Husain Sirri Pasha at their head would instantly be driven into the Nile.[2]

'Abd al-Qadir's operations against Sennar had met with more success. With a regiment of 2,400 men, 600 irregulars, and some irregular and Shukriya cavalry of Shaikh 'Awad al-Karim Abu

---

[1] Stewart to Malet, enclosed in Malet to Granville, No. 83, Mar. 13, 1883, P.R.O., F.O. 78/3553.
[2] Ibid.

Sin, 'Abd al-Qadir had left Wad Madani on the 22nd of February. The force approached a place near the river called Mushra al-Da'i.[1] some eight hours' march from Sennar. That night some Arabs attacked the troops but were repulsed. On the following day the troops improved their position and made a thorough reconnaissance of the neighborhood.

al-Mikashfi, on the other hand, in accordance with al-Mahdi's custom, sent a letter to 'Abd al-Qadir inviting him to surrender to the divine mission and the invincibility of al-Mahdi, and declaring that al-Mikashfi had a special regard for 'Abd al-Qadir and was anxious to save his life. 'Abd al-Qadir paid no attention to this invitation, and in the early morning of the 24th marched on Mushra al-Da'i where al-Mikashfi with some 10,000 to 12,000 ansar was encamped in a forest. 'Abd al-Qadir at once ordered the guns and rockets to be fired, whereupon the ansar left the shelter of the wood and launched their attack on the troops. The attack was delivered with the greatest determination and after severe fighting for about three hours the ansar were dispersed and pursued by 'Abd al-Qadir's cavalry. The loss of the Arabs was estimated at about 2,000 killed, while only twenty-seven of the Egyptian soldiers were slightly wounded. The day following the battle, when it became known that the road was clear, 'Abd al-Qadir moved on to Sennar. The victory had a tranquillizing effect on the villages on the east and west banks of the river in the vicinity of Sennar.[2]

On arrival at Sennar, 'Abd al-Qadir sent out scouts to find out in which direction the main body of rebels had retreated. It was discovered that Ahmad al-Mikashfi, with the bulk of his followers, was encamped at a place called Saqadi Moya, six hours' march west of Sennar. A force of 1,200 irregulars, Shukriya and Abu Ruf friendly Arabs, under the command of Salih Agha al-Mak, was ordered to disperse the rebels. In an engagement of the 4th of March the rebels were totally defeated, losing about 547 killed, including Amir al-Mikashfi, the original leader of the rebellion in the Sennar area. 'Abd al-Qadir next marched south along the western bank of the river to Karkuj and, crossing to the eastern bank, marched north to Khartum, pacifying the country and sup-

[1] Mushra means watering-place on the river.
[2] Stewart to Malet, enclosed in Malet to Granville, No. 101, Mar. 26, 1883, P.R.O., F.O. 78/3553.

pressing a rising led by Sharif al-Hindi between al-Dindir and al-Rahad. These operations ended his term of office in the Sudan. He was superseded by 'Ala al-Din Pasha and recalled to Cairo.[1]

NOTE

The recall of 'Abd al-Qadir Pasha, notwithstanding his successful operations in al-Jazirah, remains a mystery to the present day. An aide-de-camp of the Khedive was especially sent on a secret mission to effect the dismissal of 'Abd al-Qadir and the appointment of 'Ala al-Din. It is suggested that his co-operation with Stewart aroused the suspicion of the Khedive and his ministers.

[1] Stewart to Cartwright, enclosed in Cartwright to Granville, No. 107, Apr. 3, 1883, P.R.O., F.O. 78/3553.

V

HICKS' EXPEDITION

We have seen in the previous chapter how, immediately after the re-establishment of authority in Egypt following the British occupation, the Egyptian Government set to work to prepare a force in response to the demands of 'Abd al-Qadir Pasha. Their first intention was to send Isma'il Ayyub Pasha to succeed 'Abd al-Qadir with General Stone as chief of staff. That plan was dropped and it was decided to send 'Ala al-Din Pasha as commander-in-chief with a British officer as chief of staff leaving 'Abd al-Qadir in charge of the civil administration. When the British government was asked to lend a British officer as chief of staff they declined to do so, but no objection was entertained to the employment of officers on the retired list. Colonel Hicks was chosen to fill the post with a small number of British and other European officers to assist him. All arrangements were made between the officers concerned and the Egyptian Government, most probably through Baker Pasha who was then attempting to raise a new Egyptian army.

Colonel William Hicks entered the Bombay army in 1849 and had taken part in many actions in India. He served as brigade-major during the Abyssinian campaign of 1867-68 and was present at the capture of Magdala, being mentioned in dispatches. In 1880 he was made an honorary colonel, and was appointed to the reserve in the same year.[1] Towards the end of January 1883 we know from Lord Dufferin's correspondence that a 'certain Colonel Hicks,' an ex-Indian officer had arrived in Cairo. At this time Dufferin was very gloomy about the whole question of the Sudan. That 'wretched province' had cost the Egyptians 10,000 soldiers while according to the nearest estimate, about 40,000 of al-Mahdi's men had been killed. It seemed a pity that this 'destruction of human life should be allowed to continue.' Nevertheless, Dufferin carefully avoided becoming involved in the question, and made it clear to the Egyptian Government that Her Majesty's Government would take no responsi-

[1] *The Times,* Nov. 23, 1883.

98

bility for any arrangement made for the Sudan.[1] Dufferin appears to have been impressed by Hicks for he reported to Granville that he was a good man, but again he emphasized that the British Government had nothing to do with the Sudan except to be kept 'informed of what was happening.'[2]

Evidence from Hicks's correspondence from Khartum suggests that he was under the impression that the British Government was concerned with affairs in the Sudan. Hicks, when leaving Cairo, hoped that Baker Pasha would have the entire management of the Egyptian side of the campaign. Still wishing to be informed of the situation in the Sudan, the British Government instructed Stewart to leave his cypher book with Hicks and to request him to forward news.[3] It thus appears that Hicks himself was uncertain of the precise position of Her Majesty's Government and that when he left Cairo he was not told that they wished him to supply information. That Malet asked Stewart to request Hicks to keep the British agent in Cairo informed is clear evidence that Hicks was unaware of British policy towards the Sudan and especially towards the proposed campaign.

The original administrative arrangement made by the Egyptian Government for the campaign had to be modified. While 'Ala al-Din was ordered to go to Sawakin from Masawwa, on the assumption that he was to command the army, with Hicks as his chief of staff, and while he was already at Sawakin waiting to trek to the interior, it was decided to recall 'Abd al-Qadir. 'Ala al-Din's appointment was changed to that of governor-general, and Sulayman Niazi Pasha, an aged general, was appointed to the high command. While 'Abd al-Qadir had gathered all power in his hands at Khartum with the dignified portfolio of a minister, the new arrangement provided for a division of power between the military and civil officers. The situation in the Sudan called for more centralization and more power and discretion for the head at Khartum rather than the division of power. The new machinery was still further complicated by the division of the military command, for Hicks was told that in purely technical military matters his word was supreme.

---

[1] Private letter, Dufferin to Granville, Jan. 22, 1883, P.R.O., G/D 29/166.
[2] Private letter, Dufferin to Granville, Jan. 30, 1883, P.R.O., G/D 29/166.
[3] Stewart to Malet, enclosed in Malet to Granville, No. 88, Mar. 20, 1883, P.R.O., F.O. 78/3553.

In this way the seeds of dissension between the chiefs of the campaign were sown. Added to all this, the three officers appointed were completely new to the country and utterly ignorant of its problems. Stewart in his dispatches deplored very much the recall of 'Abd al-Qadir at a time when he was desperately needed, and spoke in high terms of his ability. 'Abd al-Qadir had just gained experience, and, on the arrival of the new officers at Khartum, was in al-Jazirah leading his troops successfully. Baker in Cairo wanted to extend his own authority in military matters to the Sudan, and he sent telegrams to Hicks exhorting him to see that the soldiers were decently dressed and duly paid, and urging that rebels should be pardoned if they returned to the Government camp. He also directed 'Ala al-Din to send news to him by telegraph.[1]

Baker's telegrams added to the confusion in Khartum, where the situation was already complicated by the undefined positions of 'Ala al-Din and 'Abd al-Qadir. The former was already in Khartum appointed to a high administrative post, while 'Abd al-Qadir was campaigning in al-Jazirah, and his dismissal had not been announced.

The first information telegraphed to Lord Dufferin[2] gave the result of a reconnaissance carried out by Major Farquhar up the White Nile. It reported that people along the west bank of the river were hostile, and that about 45,000 rebels were assembled near Miraibiah and southwards to al-Jabalain in addition to about 1,800 baqqarah cavalry, most of whom were about four hours' march from the bank of the river. The pay of the Government troops was said to be four to six months in arrears, and the troops themselves to be in rags. Some of the soldiers had managed to maintain themselves by selling the grain collected from the deserted rebel villages of Sennar. The main body of al-Mahdi's forces was said to be 100,000 strong, and although dispersed for the time being, it could easily be reassembled. Things seemed to be moving in the right direction in Khartum in Hicks's opinion: 'Ala al-Din had been proclaimed governor-general and could now set to work to make the desired changes among the military officers. The rebels in al-Jazirah had been reinforced from al-Ubayyid and by those who had

---

[1] 'Ala al-Din to the Khedive, Mar. 31, 1883 and Apr. 8, 1883, In-Telegram Book from June 1879, 'Abd. Pal. Arch., Cairo.

[2] Hicks to Dufferin, enclosed in Dufferin to Granville, No. 90, Mar. 26, 1883, P.R.O., F.O. 78/3567.

escaped from 'Abd al-Qadir Pasha's actions in Sennar. Rumors were also reported that Faki al-Manna Isma'il had deserted al-Mahdi. In his first dispatch to Malet, Hicks complained of the state of affairs in the Sudan, declaring that he could get 'no active co-operation and no full information.'[1] His superior officer, Sulayman Niazi, also told the Khedive's chief secretary that the civil authorities in Khartum were not co-operating, especially in obtaining provisions for the army.[2]

Hicks's first concern was to get information about the progress of the revolution and to work out a plan of operations accordingly. It was reported from al-Ubayyid that the surrendering Government officials had been put in the custody of tribal chiefs, and that al-Mahdi had caused the troops who had surrendered to 'swear allegiance to him on the Quran and has given them arms.'[3] Hicks reported that Khartum was full of people 'unfavorable to the Government,' but that the authorities did not apprehend any danger and that the force which had to be left behind was sufficient to meet any contingency. He was delayed by 'insufficient transport and also on account of deficiency of provisions.'

News from the White Nile, however, upset his plan of an early start for Kurdufan. The commanding officer at al-Duwaim reported that a large force of rebels was assembled in the vicinity and reinforcements were urgently required. He considered the rebel force to be formidable because it had a battery of artillery and rockets in addition to rifles. Hicks sent troops to al-Duwaim and accompanied the last batch of reinforcements after asking Malet to inform General Baker and the Egyptian ministers for Foreign Affairs and War of his action.[4]

The next report which Hicks sent was from the White Nile. On arrival at al-Kawwah on the 11th of April he had found that al-Duwaim had not been attacked, but nevertheless he decided to reinforce the garrison. Three chiefs of the district, accompanied by a few followers, tendered their submission to him in person,

[1] Hicks to Malet, enclosed in Baring to Granville, No. 215, Feb. 20, 1884, P.R.O., F.O. 78/3667.
[2] Sulayman to the Khedive, Mar. 19, 1883, In-Telegram Book from June 27, 1879, 'Abd. Pal. Arch., Cairo.
[3] Hicks to Malet, enclosed in Cartwright to Granville, No. 111, Apr. 10, 1883, P.R.O., F.O. 78/3553.
[4] Ibid.

and, as an inducement to future loyalty, Hicks remitted all taxes due by the most influential of these chiefs.[1] His plan was to reconnoitre as far as al-Jabalain, where the rebels were believed to be encamped in force. It was there that he became convinced that the march into Kurdufan should not be risked before the pacification of the disturbed districts of al-Jazirah and the White Nile. He also encountered great difficulty in paying the troops. Although he had brought from Khartum an amount which was considered to be sufficient for the payment of the White Nile garrisons, some of the soldiers' pay was five or six months in arrears, and he had to send a staff officer to Khartum for more money. He commented very unfavorably on the ammunition which the troops were using, and asked for a better kind to be sent from Cairo. His final remark on his first experience of action in the Sudan complained of the 'amount of trouble and vexation I am undergoing, even with this small force. No departments and everything thrown upon Providence.'[2]

On April 14 he sent an official report to the Minister for War[3] in which he disclosed the details of the military operations which he intended to undertake on the White Nile. He planned to proceed up the Nile to the ford of Abu Zaid with a strong detachment, take possession of the ford, which would be held until the arrival of the main body of his army by land, then, after establishing a fortified post at the ford, the whole army would attack the rebels at al-Jabalain. He mentioned the shortage of provisions and money and reported that the bashbuzuks coming from Wad al-Zaki had told their officers that they would not proceed any farther unless they were paid. Finally, he declared that he would endeavor to reach al-Jabalain as quickly as the condition of his force would permit:

I must point out to your Excellency, for his Highness the Khedive's information, that at present I am without sufficient supply of provisions, with an army several months in arrears of pay, with steamers out of repair and too few in number t˜ bring up food, take possession of the ford, patrol

[1] Hicks to Malet, enclosed ˙ˑ Cartwright to Granville, No. 118, Apr. 17, 1883, P.R.O., F.O. 78/3553.
[2] Ibid.
[3] Hicks to Minister for War, closed in Malet to Granville, No. 160, May 15, 1883, P.R.O., F.O. 78/3554.

the river and stop communication between the banks, and I am without store of fuel all of which I have to cut.

Lord Granville, in a dispatch to Cartwright dated May 7, 1883 which was considered to be sufficiently important as to be submitted to Mr. Gladstone, restated the British Government's policy towards the Sudan. They were moved by the messages that they received from Cairo containing telegrams from Hicks to Malet on the subject of military operations in the Sudan. They understood that these messages had been communicated to Malet simply because it was convenient for Hicks to use the cypher left by Stewart. But it was yet once more emphasized that: 'Her Majesty's Government are in no way responsible for the operations in the Sudan, which were undertaken under the authority of the Egyptian Government, or for the appointment or actions of General Hicks.'[1]

In spite of many difficulties Hicks began to carry out his plan. On May 3 he reported to Dufferin a successful action at al-Jabalain in which not only had the rebels been defeated but a number of their chiefs had been killed.[2] On receiving the news of this action from Hicks, Dufferin immediately cabled to Granville calling it 'a decisive victory.'[3] He hoped that the event would lead to the general pacification of the country. The moment itself was considered to be opportune for in a short time the rainy season would set in during which no military operations could be conducted.

From the very island of Aba, where the revolt had first begun, Hicks telegraphed to Dufferin after his victory of al-Jabalain that many of the baqqarah and other chiefs had come to submit and to beg for forgiveness. During the previous days ten chiefs had come to him, and the country around there on both banks of the river was, in his opinion, settled. He was in high hopes that the process of surrender would continue. When meeting the chiefs on the west bank Hicks was not accompanied by soldiers, and that in itself was taken to be a sign of renewed confidence in the Government. The general belief in Government circles was that al-Mahdi would take some action, but in which direction it was only possible to speculate. Elated by victory, Hicks thought that he 'should be in indis-

---

[1] Granville to Cartwright, No. 99, May 7, 1883, P.R.O., F.O. 78/3550.
[2] Hicks to Dufferin, enclosed in Malet to Granville, No. 140, May 9, 1883, P.R.O., F.O. 78/3554.
[3] Dufferin to Granville, No. 48, May 8, 1883, P.R.O., F.O. 78/3567.

putable command.' He wished that his 'orders should be law,' or he feared he would have neither confidence nor success. He requested that his demand should be forwarded to General Baker, after perusal, in order to be shown to the Khedive. He made it clear that he was not influenced by personal motives but by the necessity of the situation.[1]

Malet received this telegram, as Lord Dufferin had already left Egypt, and, remembering his instructions not to interfere in the Sudan business. Malet forwarded the dispatch to Sharif Pasha, instead of to General Baker. He explained to Sharif that although Hicks found it convenient to communicate with Lord Dufferin or with himself, it should not be supposed that they 'endorse in any way the contents of his telegrams.' He thought it unnecessary to repeat that Her Majesty's Government were in no way 'responsible for the operations in the Sudan.' Malet did not stop there, but informed Sharif that the mere sending of a copy of the telegram did not indicate 'expression of opinion with regard to the recommendations contained in it.' But, to guard against prejudicing the case of Hicks, Malet concluded by saying that his remarks were not intended as criticism of General Hicks, 'who appeared to have shown himself to be a very capable officer. They are merely intended to prevent any misunderstanding as to the position of Her Majesty's Government in regard to operations in the Sudan.'[2] Malet seems to have wavered between keeping to the letter of his instructions and endorsing the recommendations of Hicks by hinting that such a capable officer should have his requests complied with. That is presumably why this letter to Sharif was couched in such vague langauge with so much reserve and caution. Sharif, in reply to Malet, declared that he 'entertained no doubt on the point in question.'[3]

With the exception of a number of soldiers of the White Nile garrisons, the whole of Hicks's force returned to Omdurman, since the rainy season had already begun. Meanwhile, preparations had to be made for the big advance into Kurdufan during the rains, when the problem of water on the road would be solved. The most

[1] Hicks to Dufferin, May 13, 1883, enclosed in Malet to Granville, No. 176, May 22, 1883, P.R.O., F.O. 78/3554.

[2] Malet to Sharif, enclosed in Malet to Granville, No. 176, May 22, 1883, P.R.O., F.O. 78/3554.

[3] Sharif to Malet, enclosed in Malet to Granville, No. 192, May 28, 1883, P.R.O., F.O. 78/3554.

important problem for the Kurdufan field-force was to provide a sufficient number of transport camels. The main source for the supply of camels, especially in Kurdufan, was the Kababish land, which was beyond the scope of Government influence, and near enough to al-Mahdi to prevent the inhabitants from co-operating with the Government. Mahmud Ahmadani was engaged in securing camels from Dongola and Barbar, Ahmad al-Tilib from Sennar, and 'Ala al-Din himself was about to set out for the Shukriya tribe.[1]

On the 28th of May Malet telegraphed to Hicks informing him that the Egyptian Government had sent orders to Khartum that no military movement was to be undertaken 'without your advice and consent.' Malet thought that if these orders were executed they would make Hicks 'practically in command.' Sharif had assured Malet that he intended to see that the orders were obeyed. The objection to naming Hicks commander-in-chief was solely because al-Mahdi's movement was a religious one, and the 'nomination of a Christian would fan fanaticism.'[2]

Hicks replied that he quite understood the reason for not appointing him commander-in-chief, but wished that Sulayman Pasha would pay some attention to his orders. He complained of the obstructiveness of Sulayman, and of the great difficulties he encountered in carrying out his plans. He was, even after Sharif's orders, meeting with the same difficulties and considered that the Minister's orders to Sulayman were not 'explicit enough.'[3]

Hicks's optimism soon faded when he returned to Khartum to work out the details of the campaign into Kurdufan. He realized that although al-Mahdi had lost many men in recent engagements he still had a considerable number of supporters which would be increased after harvest. Hicks realized too that his own force was not really adequate to undertake the Kurdufan expedition. There were all sorts of difficulties to contend with: 'Every ounce of food must be taken from here;' the march would be through hostile country inhabited by powerful tribes; garrisons would have to be left behind to guard the lines of communications and the depots; convoys would

---

[1] 'Ala al-Din to the Khedive, May 27, 1883, In-Telegram Book from June 27, 'Abd. Pal. Arch., Cairo.

[2] Malet to Hicks, May 28, 1883, enclosed in Baring to Granville, No. 215, Feb. 20, 1884, P.R.O., F.O. 78/3667.

[3] Hicks to Malet, May 31, 1883, enclosed in Baring to Granville, No. 215, Feb. 20, 1884, P.R.O., F.O. 78/3667.

require escorts; the force available at the time was only 6,000 strong
and would be diminished by sickness after the rainy season; all
garrisons on the Blue Nile would have to be kept at full strength
although the White Nile garrisons could be reduced, and, since
Khartum was full of rebels, some troops would have to be left there.
In the end only 5,000 infantry would be available and, of these,
2,000 would be needed to keep open lines of communication leaving
3,000 infantry for the attacking force. Hicks, considering that he
required at least 10,000 men, asked whether the Egyptian Government could spare any more soldiers. He thought that no risk should
be taken, as defeat would not only mean the loss of Kurdufan and
Darfur, but also of Sennar and possibly of Khartum. He estimated
the cost of the coming six months' operations at roughly £120,000. [1]

Sir Edward Malet could not pass such an alarming dispatch to
the Egyptian Government while merely repeating the British Government's refusal to take any responsibility for the Sudan campaign.
Malet was aware of the increased burden which the military operations had added to the cost of the Sudan administration which, even
in peace-time, was a drain on Egyptian finances. It was impossible for
the Egyptian treasury to meet the Governor-General's frequent demands for money for the operations in the Sudan, and the campaign
ran a considerable risk of failure unless it were conducted on a
large scale and the army were well provisioned and supplied. In such
circumstances Malet asked Granville 'whether General Hicks should
be instructed to confine himself to maintaining the present supremacy
of the Khedive in the regions between the Blue and White Niles.'[2]
He informed Granville that he had, as requested, given Sharif Pasha
a copy of General Hicks's telegram but 'without any comment or expression of opinion upon its contents.'

The papers about financial demands for the Sudan and Hicks's
demands for reinforcements, entailing more expenditure, together
with Malet's covering dispatch containing the implied suggestion that
Hicks should be stopped from advancing into Kurdufan—all these
were considered by Granville who, with characteristic vagueness
wrote: 'I do not think the Home Government have committed themselves further than they said. Malet was getting on too rapidly but

---

[1] Hicks to Malet, June 3, 1883, enclosed in Malet to Granville, No. 210,
June 5, 1883, P.R.O., F.O. 78/3555.
[2] Malet to Granville, No. 210, June 5, 1883, P.R.O., F.O. 78/3555.

our telegram and Sharif's answer seem to have put that right.' [1] The correspondence was then passed to Mr. Childers, Chancellor of the Exchequer, who declared that he did not like the 'look of these papers.' He considered Egypt and the Sudan to be financially separate, although Egypt made an annual contribuion of £E.100,000 to the Sudan. He recollected that the British Government's general opinion was that they had no 'interest in keeping up the dependency of the Sudan on Egypt.' They had declined to allow any officers or men to serve in the Sudan, although officers were sent there to collect information. Mr. Childers thought they had gradually gone beyond their original intention as they apparently recognized 'the *employment* of English officers there, and this heavy drain of the Sudan operations on Egyptian finance.' It was difficult to see how 'we should retrace our steps,' but he was quite certain that the Government should order the 'discontinuance of telegraphic communication between Sir E. Malet and General Hicks.' He sensed danger in Malet's telegram, which implied 'that (directly or indirctly) we are to give General Hicks instructions based on his representation to Sir E. Malet.'

The real issue was evaded by both Granville and Childers. The former did not wish to give a categorical answer as to whether or not the expedition should go on, and the latter could give no advice on the financial question. The results of that hesitant and vacillating policy were embodied in a telegram to Malet: 'Your telegram No. 37, reinforcements for Sudan. Report as early as possible decision of Egyption Government taking care to offer no advice but pointing out that it is clear that the Egyptian Government should make up their minds what their policy is to be, and should consider carefully the financial side of the question.' [2]

On the following day Malet cabled the decision of the council of ministers in Cairo. Reinforcements were ordered to proceed to the Sudan; four companies amounting to 400 men were ordered from Dongola; two companies in Egypt, about 200 men previously destined for Harrar were to go to Khartum instead. About 600 bashbuzuks were also to be sent from Cairo; the artillery was increased by the dispatch of one mountain battery with seventy men;

[1] Minutes on Malet to Granville, No. 179, May 24, 1883, P.R.O., F.O. 78/3554.
[2] Granville to Malet, No. 32, June 11, 1883, P.R.O., F.O. 78/3561.

and the numbers further increased by 1,800 old soldiers formerly with the army, who had been rejected by General Baker because of slight physical defects. The costs to the end of the year for transport' pay, and rations would amount to £40,000. The Egyptian Government considered that the efforts and expenditure already made and the success secured by General Hicks would be lost if reinforcements were not sent. Malet wrote that in his opinion 'this view appears to be reasonable.'[1] Some days later Malet reported that the Governor-General of the Sudan had been informed of the Egyptian Government's decision to provide the money for the estimated maintenance of the army in addition to the £40,000, but at the same time the Governor was instructed to try to meet the non-military expenses of the administration from the revenues of the Sudan.[2]

Hicks had, from the first, been a little dubious of the type of soldier which would form the major part of any reinforcements which could be sent to him. He had told Sir Evelyn Wood on the 8th of June that he had asked for 5,000 soldiers who could only, as far as he knew, be collected by 'dragging from their homes and fields unwilling men and sending them away in chains.'[3] He also had misgivings about the type of officers that would be sent. He declared that he would be content with four battalions from Wood's army and hoped to return them within six months. Nothing came of this suggestion that Hicks should be reinforced from Wood's army, since it was not intended for major operations outside Egypt proper, but it is clear evidence that General Hicks was aware how little reliance could be placed in the motley force which the Egyptian Government collected for him.

It is curious to see how General Hicks fluctuated between pessimism and optimism. On the 13th of May he wrote confidently from Aba island after his victory at al-Jabalain asking to be placed in sole command. On the 3rd of June he pressed for reinforcements, saying that it was hopeless to attempt to defeat al-Mahdi without them. On the 6th of June he went so far as to advise the abandonment of Kurdufan expedition altogether. On the 18th of June,

[1] Malet to Granville, No. 232, June 12, 1883, P.R.O., F.O. 78/3555.
[2] Malet to Granville, No. 245, June 21, 1883, P.R.O., F.O. 78/3555.
[3] Hicks to Wood, June 8, 1883, enclosed in Baring to Granville, No. 285, Feb. 20, 1884, P.R.O., F.O. 78/3667.

without any reason for his optimism, he telegraphed to Baker Pasha that he was prepared to undertake the campaign with the force available, the risks are as I said in case of a mishap, but I think this is not all probable.' [1] He informed Baker that he had strengthened the fortifications of Khartum in such a way as to 'render the place impregnable to such forces as the rebels could bring.' He planned to march into Kurdufan along the Bara road, establishing depots at Kajmar and Bara. He had previously disliked the idea of marching into a hostile country, but he now thought the 'rebels will join us as we advance, and I have no doubt the captured soldiers now with al-Mahdi will do so.'

Towards the end of June Hicks became a little uneasy about his position and asked Malet whether Sharif had sent orders to Khartum and whether any steps had been taken to support him. If his orders were not to be obeyed he considered that it was pointless for him to stay there, and in that case he begged to be recalled. [2]

Although he was informed that orders had been sent to Khartum to pay attention to his advice on military matters, Hicks waited for eighteen days and then repeated his complaints to General Baker, naming Sulayman Niazi as the chief obstacle. Hicks believed that Cairo had ceased to support him after the departure of Lord Dufferin. He asked Baker to effect his recall as he could not 'undertake the responsibility, with my ideas so diametrically opposed as they are to Sulayman Pasha's.' [3] Malet replied that he 'hoped to get Sulayman recalled or forced into obedience.' [4] But Hicks was impatient, and before receiving this message he wired to Malet on the 23rd of July informing him that he had just sent his resignation to the War Office in Cairo. It was, he maintained, a step he had taken with regret, but he could not undertake the projected campaign under the same circumstances as the last one. In Hicks's opinion Sulayman Pasha had understood the orders

[1] Hicks to Baker, June 18, 1883, enclosed in Malet to Granville, No. 254, June 23, 1883, P.R.O., F.O. 78/3555.

[2] Hicks to Malet, June 28, 1883, enclosed in Malet to Granville, No. 275, July 2, 1883, P.R.O., F.O. 78/3555.

[3] Hicks to Baker, July 16, 1883, enclosed in Malet to Granville, No. 324, July 21, 1883, P.R.O., F.O. 78/3556.

[4] Malet to Hicks, July 22, 1883, enclosed in Baring to Granville, No. 215, Feb. 20, 1884, P.R.O., F.O. 78/3667.

from Cairo to mean obedience to Hicks's view after he, Sulayman, had approved them.[1] Malet hastened to confide to Hicks secretly that it had been decided to recall Sulayman, but no announcement was to be made before the decision had been officially communicated. Malet hoped 'that this concession being made, you will find your task easier and your way clear. 'Ala al-Din will be nominal commander-in-chief.'[2] Assured of Sulayman's recall, Hicks insisted that clear instructions should be sent, stating that he should not be further obstructed.[3]

By the beginning of August Hicks again became pessimistic although his unco-operative chief had been removed. Al-Mahdi was kept well informed of all that went on, and his spies were always in Khartum, while no information was procured by the Government, not even about water-supplies on the road. Hicks was told that more than half the Government employees and clerks supported al-Mahdi and that in the event of a reverse to his expedition, the danger to Khartum would begin with trouble from Government officials.[4] He therefore repeated yet again his request for definite and clear orders that his word in military affairs should be supreme.[5]

When the telegram from the private cabinet of the Khedive appointing 'Ala al-Din commanding officer reached Khartum, Hicks was not satisfied with it. It contained no definite and clear instruction but simply 'hoped for the continuation of the concord and union with General Hicks Pasha.' In Hicks's opinion[6] he was in exactly the same position as before. He admitted that 'Ala al-Din would not be obstructive, but past experience warned him against plunging into another campaign under the same conditions. The only reasonable objection to putting him in command lay in the religious element of the rebellion, and that had 'so far disappeared.' He declared

[1] Hicks to Malet, July 23, 1883, enclosed in Baring to Granville, No. 215, Feb. 20, 1884, P.R.O., F.O. 78/3667.
[2] Malet to Hicks, July 23, 1883, enclosed in Baring to Granville, No. 215, Feb. 20, 1884, P.R.O., F.O. 78/3667.
[3] Hicks to Malet, July 31, 1883, enclosed in Baring to Granville, No. 215, Feb. 20, 1884, P.R.O., F.O., 78/3667.
[4] Hicks to Malet, Aug. 1, 1883, enclosed in Malet to Granville, No. 343, Aug. 8, 1883, P.R.O., F.O. 78/3556.
[5] Ibid.
[6] Hicks to Malet, Aug. 3, 1883, enclosed in Baring to Granville, No. 215, Feb. 20, 1884, P.R.O., F.O. 78/3667.

that he would avail himself of 'Ala al-Din's assistance and experience, and 'should wish him to accompany the forces,' but he insisted that in military matters he should be supreme and that a step in rank should be given him.[1]

Her Majesty's Government were not slow to notice the continuation of correspondence between Hicks and Malet, and decided to disclaim yet again all responsibility for the Sudan campaign. In a dispatch to Malet[2] seen by Gladstone, Granville remarked on General Hicks's repeated communications with him about 'the financial difficulties which he meets with in the Sudan, under the impression that you will exert your influence with the Egyptian Government to induce them to give favorable consideration to his wishes.' Malet was reminded that Her Majesty's Government assumed 'no responsibility whatever in regard to the conduct of affairs in the Sudan,' and that it was desirable that Hicks should understand that position although they would be glad to 'receive information as to the progress of the Campaign.' It was, however, their considered policy to 'abstain as much as possible from interference with the action of the Egyptian Government in that quarter.'

While still pressing for the supreme command, Hicks began to plan the Kurdufan campaign. The immediate problem was how to pay the troops. He asked Sir Evelyn Wood to impress on the 'war minister the necessity for seeing that money is sent me for the payment of troops.'[3] Everywhere the pay of the soldiers was seriously in arrears and their condition most miserable. At Fazughli they lacked both food and clothes, and were unable to obtain supplies from the villages because the country was swarming with rebels. It was hardly surprising that they showed signs of insubordination. Hicks could not see how the Fazughil garrison could be supplied, as the town could not be reached by steamer. He planned to withdraw the garrison to Karkuj, but according to information given by the Mudir, who had escaped from Fazughli in a small boat, the troops were 'reduced to the last extremities' and by the time relief reached them they would either be dead of starvation or have joined the rebels. The staff officer sent to Sennar reported that the irregular

[1] Ibid.
[2] Granville to Malet, No. 187, Aug. 8, 1883, P.R.O., F.O. 78/3551.
[3] Hicks to Wood, Aug. 5, 1883, enclosed in Malet to Granville, No. 347, Aug. 13, 1883, P.R.O., F.O. 78/3556.

troops there had 'positively refused to go where ordered, in consequence of not having been paid.' On the Blue Nile in general there there was no grain. A steamer had been asked for to bring grain from Khartum while Hicks required more steamers to bring up reinforcements and supplies for the Kurdufan expedition. The officer thought it quite probable that the Arabs would rise again after the season when the fear of disease would be lessened, the grain would have been harvested, and they would be free to move where they wanted. He viewed the situation with misgivings, for when the Kurdufan expedition had gone there would remain in Sennar, to keep law and order, an army without money and transport. 'It is almost impossible to contend against all these adverse conditions.'

Meanwhile, Hicks had obtained information about the movements of al-Mahdi's troops. Several ansar leaders had been sent from Kurdufan to al-Jazirah to stir up the tribes, who were prepared to rebel. According to a report four of these tribes had already assembled to divide the Government force and delay its march into Kurdufan. To meet this threat, Hicks sent a small force by river from Sennar to Wad Madani and then inland to 'Ibud, where the rebels were believed to be gathered in force. A column mounted on camels was also sent to al-Kawwah to make a demonstration towards al-Jabalain, Saqadi Moya, or al-Masallamiya, from which places similar reports had been received. These two columns were considered sufficient to check the rising, which might, however, break out again as soon as 'we leave for Kurdufan.'[1]

Three days later Hicks reported that, according to his latest information, the chief who was supposed to be stirring up the tribes had been brought to al-Kawwah and had denied the accusation. The two columns were, however, to be sent out on reconnaissance. The irregular troops were very discontented 'on account of their long arrears of pay,' and with the money at the disposal of the Government their demands could not be satisfied as they should be paid out of the Sudan revenues. In the end he asked for money to be sent from Cairo for the payment of the irregular troops.[2] Three days later, the cloud of anxiety appears to have lifted from the sky

[1] Hicks to Malet, Aug. 7, 1883, enclosed in Malet to Granville, No. 347, Aug. 13, 1883, P.R.O., F.O. 78/3556.
[2] Hicks to Malet, Aug. 10, 1883, enclosed in Malet to Granville, No. 347, Aug. 13, 1883, P.R.O., F.O. 78/3556.

of al-Jazirah for Hicks reported: 'The Province of Sennar remains quite.'[1] He countermanded the orders for the movement of the al-Kawwah column, but the force from Sennar was ordered to set out and to halt at Wad Madani. By now 'Ala al-Din had arrived from the east after buying camels for the expedition, and Hicks spoke highly of him as a man of energy.

On the 19th of August Hicks wired to Malet that the Khedive had appointed him supreme commander of the Sudan forces. Hicks further declared that he had little fear of 'any increase of fanaticism,'[2] and added: ' 'Ala al-Din and I will get on very well.' In accordance with his instructions, Malet attempted to make absolutely clear to Hicks the British Government's policy of non-interference in the affairs of the Sudan. On Hicks's appointment to the supreme command Malet therefore congratulated him but at the same time pointed out that his appointment was 'spontaneous on the part of the Egyptian Government.'[3] Malet declared that he was willing to transmit to the Egyptian Government telegrams from Khartum, but that he was debarred by his instructions from suggesting any course of action. It was the policy of Her Majesty's Government to abstain as much as possible from interference in the Sudan.

The last report from Hicks before he started from Khartum on the Kurdufan campaign reveals his anxiety about the road between Barbar and Sawakin. But Malet believed, on the basis of reports received in Cairo, that the disturbances in that part of the Sudan had been suppressed. Hicks expected to come against great difficulties in supplying his force with water, but believed the arrangements made would 'prove successful.'[4] The general impression at that time was that al-Mahdi was 'no longer believed in.'

The private letters of Mr. Frank Power, *The Times* correspondent in Khartum, provide an unofficial estimate of the situation there before Hicks's departure. Power intended to accompany the expedition but was detained at Khartum by ill health. Even at the beginning of August Power spoke of 'the False Prophet in posses-

[1] Hicks to Malet, Aug. 13, 1883, enclosed in Baring to Granville, No. 215, Feb. 20, 1884, P.R.O., F.O. 78/3667.
[2] Hicks to Malet, Aug. 19, 1883, enclosed in Baring to Granville, No. 215, Feb. 20, 1884, P.R.O., F.O. 78/3667.
[3] Malet to Hicks, Aug. 18, 1883, enclosed in Malet to Granville, No. 355, Aug. 20, 1883, P.R.O., F.O. 78/3556.
[4] Malet to Granville, No. 403, Sept. 10, 1883, P.R.O., F.O. 78/3557.

sion of the country ten miles from this city.'[1] At the beginning of
September, just a week before the expedition started, he wrote to
a friend that in three days Hicks's force would 'march on a campaign that even the most sanguine look forward to with the greatest
gloom. We have here 9,000 infantry that fifty good men would
rout in ten minutes, and 1,000 cavalry (bashbuzuk) that have
never learned even to ride, and these with a few Nordenfeldt guns,
are to beat the 69,000 men al-Mahdi has got together.'[2] Power expressed lack of confidence in the Egyptian troops, whom he considered not worth the ammunition they would throw away. The
black troops were to be left to guard Khartum because the Arabs
and the townspeople fear them.[3] In Power's opinion the people
in Khartum belived al-Mahdi to be a true prophet because he
answered to the description in the religious books, 'and even our
officers and men (a cowardly, beggarly mob) believe that he is a
prophet, and are less than half-hearted in the business, so that the
ruffianly though brave bashbuzuks and the niggers are the only
men to be relied on.'[4] 'I pity Hicks,' Power wrote, 'he is an able,
good, and energetic man, but he has to do with wretched Egyptians, who take a pleasure in being incompetent, thwarting one,
delaying, and lying.'[5]

The whole force paraded at Omdurman on the 8th of September
1883: it was composed of 7,000 infantry, 500 cavalry, 400 mounted
bashbuzuks with 10 mountain guns, 100 cuirassiers, 2,000 camp
followers, and about 5,500 transport camels.[6] '*Ala al-Din Pasha,
the Governor-General, who to accompany the expedition in his
capacity as chief political and administrative officer, was by that
time already on the White Nile inspecting the garrisons there, procuring guides, and choosing the route. Hicks and 'Ala al-Din were
in communication while the expedition was marching to al-Duwaim,
and they were both satisfied with its progress. It took them eight
days to reach al-Duwaim where Hicks was welcomed by 'Ala al-Din.
The day following their arrival at al-Duwaim, differences and

---

[1] Power, Frank, *Letters from Khartum* (London, 1885), p. 18.
[2] Ibid., p. 20.
[3] Ibid., p. 21.
[4] Ibid., p. 22.
[5] Ibid., p. 24.
[6] Wingate, F. R., *Mahdiism and the Egyptian Sudan*, p. 77.

lack of harmony among the high-ranking officers began to tell on the efficiency of the expedition. Rajab Bey Siddiq had been in charge of the camp since the troops had left Omdurman, but he apparently thought that Husain Pasha Muzhar, a more senior officer, would take over once the force reached al-Duwaim. As a result of this misunderstanding as to who was responsible, the transport camels were kept without food for twenty-three hours, while all around the camp grass was plentiful, and it was only after 'Ala al-Din had reported the situation to Hicks that Rajab Bey was reprimanded and freed the camels to graze.

On the 23rd of September Hicks and 'Ala al-Din discussed the route to be taken, the places where military posts were to be established, and those at which the army was to halt. It was agreed that the longer, southern route via al-Rahad should be followed owing to the abundance of water for that huge assembly of men and animals.

A battalion, commanded by Rajab Bey, was sent to Shat, the first halt after al-Duwaim, to prepare the camping ground and to see that the wells were cleared. When he sent word that everything was ready, the whole army moved. The entry into Shat took place in great disorder, the men not knowing their companies or battalions, and the animals mingled with the soldiers. Such was the confusion that the expedition would most surely have come to an end had there been even a small group of determined Arabs in the vicinity. Husain Pasha Muzhar was very loud in his criticism of Hicks's management of the expedition, attributing all the confusion to his orders. Hicks and Husain met in the tent of the Governor-General to remove the misunderstanding. Hicks made it clear that he alone was to give orders, and that Husain Pasha was merely his deputy. In any case, Husain should have made his criticisms confidentially to Hicks. Hicks further maintained that the disorderly manner in which the army had entered was directly against his orders, and that mistakes had been made in the transmission of his orders. Hicks was so enraged at Husain's accusation of ignorance that he thought that either he or Husain would have to return to Khartum. Finally, however, 'Abbas Afandi Hilmi, assistant to 'Ala al-Din, apologized on behalf of Husain, explaining that he had not meant to criticize the orders but desired that the officers should understand beforehand how they were to proceed.

It was then agreed that no orders were to be issued until the Governor-General and the senior officers had been consulted. This discord between the foreign commander-in-chief and the most senior Egyptian officer at the very beginning of the march did not augur well for the efficient management of the expedition, and although outwardly everything was settled, yet the rift continued to exist.

Another unfortunate incident also took place at Shat. A soldier of 'Ali Bey Lufti's force which had been sent by 'Abd al-Qadir Pasha to assist the al-Ubayyid and Bara garrisons was taken prisoner by the Arabs and became one of al-Mahdi's followers. When the troops were camping at al-Duwaim he came to 'Ala al-Din pretending desertion from the enemy, and gave information about al-Mahdi which was in complete accord with that already known, thus proving his sincerity. In Shat he went out with another soldier to graze the camels and then fled, taking with him a swift camel, a rifle, and ammunition, together with the clothes and money given him as reward for his loyalty and service. He knew everything about the army and had witnessed the discord between Hicks and Husain Muzhar, and he most certainly gave al-Mahdi most valuable information about the expedition sent against him.

On the march between Shat and Zuraiqa, the next station, it was noticed that the villages were deserted. Moreover, a fresh misunderstanding arose between Hicks and Husain about the manner in which the force was to proceed. In addition there was the difficulty of surface water in ponds. It was reported that the Arabs had driven their cattle in to these ponds in the path of the army, and had left very little water in them. This made it necessary for scouting parties with guides to precede the army to ascertain the quantity of water before the whole force marched.

Hicks had planned to secure his line of communication by establishing posts of 200 men each in strongly fortified positions at twelve places between al-Duwaim and al-Ubayyid. About 1,000 camels were to be bought, and biscuits and ammuition could be transported from post to post to the front. Depots were to be formed in these posts, and in case of a reverse, a line of retreat would be secured and the soldiers could fall back on these fortified posts. In Shat, which was the first halt, a post was established but on the march after Shat it became clear to 'Ala al-Din that the army was passing through hostile country, and that posts could only be effective if the inhabitants co-operated.'Ala al-Din considered that once these posts were left behind they would be in a state of siege and would ultimately fall to the enemy as they would be too weak to offer resistance, and even if they could beat back the attacks no line of communication would remain. They would, in effect, weaken the striking force of the army. I am naturally very averse,' said Hicks, 'to this, but if, as His Excellency assures me, it is a fact that the posts will not be supplied from the base at al-Duwaim and supplies will not be forwarded through them, I should, in garrisoning these posts, be only weakening my fighting force without gaining any advantage.'[1] Hicks was convinced that the matter at least required discussion. He requested that the members should record their opinion.

Husain Pasha Muzhar wished to retain post up to half-way between al-Duwaim and al-Ubayyid suggesting that these posts should be garrisoned by troops sent from Khartum and Cairo. Hicks commented that time would not allow for the arrival of troops from Cairo, and that Khartum was already held by a very weak force. Rajab Bey Siddiq and 'Abbas Afandi thought that posts should not be set up. Farquhar, chief of staff, agreed with this opinion. It was believed that after the fall of al-Ubayyid and the success of the expedition, a small force would be able to establish the line of communication with al-Duwaim without difficulty.[2]

'Abbas Afandi recorded in his diary a more detailed discussion than that reported by Hicks. According to 'Abbas's account Husain Pasha insisted on the retention of the posts, demanding troops from Khartum to garrison these posts, as he believed they had been specially sent from Cairo for that purpose. 'Abbas also recorded that Hicks stated that he was in favor of establishing the posts, but that when the Governor-General, who was familiar with the land, emphasized the undesirability of retaining them, Hicks called the council to order to show that the decision was based on the opinion of the men most competent to judge. When 'Ala al-Din had given the reasons for his opinion he left Hicks to decide the issue. The incident at Shat and the discussion about the establish-

[1] Report by Hicks to the Minister of War in Cairo, Oct. 3, 1883, enclosed in Baring to Granville, No. 565, Nov. 28, 1883, P.R.O., F.O. 78/3559.
[2] Report by Hicks to the Minister of War in Cairo, Oct. 3, 1883, enclosed in Baring to Granville, No. 565, Nov. 28, 1883, P.R.O., F.O. 78/3559.

ment of posts made it quite clear that Hicks and Husain were not at all in agreement, and this discord between the two did much to weaken the efficiency of the expedition.

On penetrating deep into Kurdufan the expedition found the villages not only deserted but burnt, and the few old people who remained told them that the inhabitants knew about the arrival of the Turks, and that as they could not offer effective resistance, they had fled. So far, however, the army had not met any armed rebels. It was only when they were marching towards Nawarbi on the 8th of October that they encountered for the first time some hostile activity. A guide, familiar with the country, was sent out with two others to search for water. On arriving at a brook they were attacked by Arabs and the guide was seriously wounded. The significance of the incident lies in the fact that the army became aware of the presence of the Arabs for the first time, and they had, therefore, to be more cautious in their march.

On the last stage of the march before reaching the big khur (watercourse) known as the 'Nile' there was a great shortage of water and the army was in such a terrible state of thirst and confusion that any attack from the enemy might well have ended the expedition or at least have seriously weakened its striking power. On the day following the wounding of the guide, all the other guides were gathered together and asked what they knew of the water supply in the immediate neighborhood. They all seem to have agreed that water was plentiful. Some misunderstanding about the order of march arose in the early morning between Hicks and Farquhar, which eventually ended in further discord between 'Ala al-Din and Hicks. When the march was resumed, in the confidence that water was near and plentiful, the army marched for hours without seeing any sign of water. The little water the soldiers had in their water-skins was soon consumed and the soldiers began to think that the guides had misled them. The soldiers became completely out of hand and all attempts to restore order failed. Their thirst was aggravated by their having eaten heavily of the lubia (a Sudanese kind of bean) which requires a large quantity of water. Regardless of the efforts of Hicks, 'Ala al-Din, and the other senior officers, soldiers dispersed in search of water. Water-melons lessened the thirst of some soldiers, but the final relief came when ducks were seen hovering over a large pool of about fifteen minutes' march ahead. Attempts to regularize the taking of water failed, and there were further accusations of mismanagement between Hicks and Husain. Eventually the army reached the big khur and the difficulty of water-supplies was overcome. The difficulty illustrates, however, the lack of real discipline in the army and how the discord between Hicks and Husain was increased by each successive difficulty. Some historians have considered that the major disagreement was between 'Ala al-Din and Hicks, and that 'Ala al-Din not only failed to co-operate but actually sabotaged Hicks's scheme. According to 'Abbas Afandi's dairy, 'Ala al-Din sometimes disagreed with Hicks, but in the end always left the final decision to Hicks as commander-in-chief. The disagreement between Hicks and Husain Muzhar, on the other hand, was open and outspoken. But to pin every failure on to this discord between Hicks and Muzhar would be to disregard other factors. Nearly all the officers were strangers to the country, and lacked experience in this kind of expedition and in leading an army which was inclined to mutiny. In addition, the army was encumbered with huge numbers of baggage camels, and the soldiers had not all received the same kind of military training.

The Corban Bairam (a Muslim religious festival) occurred after their terrible ordeal of thirst. The Governor-General celebrated the occasion as though he were in Khartum, and it was taken by the soldiers to be a favorable augury for their coming encounter with al-Mahdi. While resting, 'Ala al-Din, Hicks, and 'Abbas Afandi discussed the causes of the rebellion and the utter ignorance of the Egyptian Government of conditions in the Sudan. They also discussed what ought to be done with al-Mahdi when they had captured him, whether he should be put to death or spared until orders had been received from the Khedive. 'Ala al-Din thought of using a woman they had picked up on the way as a messenger to the chiefs of the tribes in the neighborhood. A proclamation signed by 'Ala al-Din and Hicks was written and sent out, asking these chiefs to rally to the cause of the Government and telling them of the huge expedition that would surely put an end to the rebellion.

The leaders of the expedition also discussed the general situation. They were naturally alarmed that they could get no news whatsoever from al-Mahdi's side and could not establish communication with Khartum. Neither soldier nor camp-follower could be induced by al-Duwaim and certainly none would venture westwards to al-

Ubayyid to get information: it was quite clear that all the places behind them were under enemy control and that the expedition was isolated. Farquhar suggested that an attempt should be made to communicate with Alyas Pasha Um Barir at al-Ubayyid in the hope of preventing the escape of al-Mahdi, offering as a reward the promise of high rank and 20,000-30,000 dollars. Their main concern at this time was not the prospect of defeat, for they were fairly confident of their superiority, but that al-Mahdi might escape with his Ansar from al-Ubayyid. But it was no easy matter to communicate with Alyas Pasha. It is curious to note that they had hopes of attracting Alyas to their side, for his son was one of al-Mahdi's generals. 'Ala al-Din related the story of the man who left Khartum for al-Ubayyid disguised as a merchant, taking from the Government 10,000 dollars with the intention of giving them to any person who would kill al-Mahdi. The man duly arrived at al-Ubayyid and sent back a message to Khartum that he was only waiting an opportunity of finding a man to do the job. Nothing more was heard of him. The opposition of al-Mahdi's followers began to go beyond merely inciting the inhabitants to desert and cutting the army's line of retreat. They began to make attacks by night, and were beaten back by shells and bullets. Some of the soldiers who attempted to go, unarmed, some distance from the camp to gather melons were attacked and killed by Arabs hiding in the standing crops. Orders were afterwards issued that no soldiers were to leave the zaribah without arms. The rapid loss of camels through lack of care by the men was, at this time, also causing concern. 'Ala al-Din reminded Hicks of the seriousness of the position, which Hicks admitted, but he could do nothing, for his orders in that respect were simply ignored. Feeling that some of the officers were fomenting discontent among the men, Hicks intended to dismiss them, but news of his intention led to signs of disobedience among a large number of officers. It was also known by that time that, owing to the neglect of the artillery officers, the Krupp guns were not functioning.

While on the march, it occurred to Colonel Farquhar to use his compass instead of guides, whom he believed to be misleading the army. Instead of following the road round a jungle he ordered the army to plunge into it and take a short cut to the other side. The passage through the jungle proved to be so arduous that many hours were spent in penetrating it, and there was much grumbling among the soldiers. It was rumored, among the officers as well as among the men, that it was the intention of the English to destroy the army. The army finally encamped on a hill surrounded by inflammable dry grass. Believing the guides to be traitors, Hicks seems to have ordered their close supervision, but his order was misinterpreted, and they were in fact imprisoned. This infuriated 'Ala al-Din, who had employed the guides and whose confidence in them remained unshaken. He protested vehemently to Hicks, who said that he had not intended them to be imprisoned, but merely to be kept under observation, and he ordered their release. 'Abbas Afandi commented on Hicks's behaviour in this incident, saying: 'How clever are they to find excuses and liberate themselves from the responsibility of their acts.' High-ranking Egyptian officers considered that Hicks wished to attribute all the trouble resulting from the penetration of the jungle to the guides, and not to Farquhar's reliance on his compass, knowing only too well how indignant the men were against the Englishman's guidance.

About the 21st of October the army came to a khur, on the edge of which the camp was pitched. It was soon known that the Arabs were established on the opposite bank, for they began to fire incessantly on the square. They availed themselves of the bushy and wooded nature of the land which concealed them. In order not to waste ammunition their fire was returned only occasionally But it became clear that they ought to be dislodged from their position if the army were to have a rest for the night. It was decided to send a battalion to the other side of the khur to encamp in an open space and keep watch on them. Fortunately, the Arabs withdrew of their own accord. The following day, the Arabs, hiding behind trees, directed their fire against the army. A small number of soldiers were killed, but Arab casualties could not be estimated.

Leaving the last station before coming to al-Rahad, Hicks's army was constantly harassed by the Arabs. Nevertheless, the morale of the army rose very high when they knew that a large number of dead bodies of the Arabs had been seen, while their casualties were very light. Before the army reached al-Rahad, al-Mahdi flooded the square with copies of a proclamation calling on the soldiers to surrender to him and not to attempt to stand against his divinely ordained mission relying only on their guns and powder. He related how the Turks who had been killed by

him had pleaded with Allah, that he, al-Mahdi, had killed them
without warning, but how Allah had revealed that they had been
duly and properly warned. He requested the soldiers not to accept
a similar fate but to surrender and be spared. Certainly the High
Command saw that copies of this proclamation were collected and
burned, but enough were read by the officers and men. al-Mahdi's
warning came at a most inopportune moment, for the soldiers were
elated by the number of casualties they had inflicted on the Arabs
on the previous day.

On reaching al-Rahad Hicks's army found that water was plentiful but not sufficient to last the army indefinitely. A fort was begun
on high ground in the middle of the zaribah in order to mount the
guns. It occurred to Hicks at al-Rahad that a guide ought to be
sent to Mak Adam of the Taqali mountains with a letter requesting
him to meet the expedition with horsemen as he had promised.
'Ala al-Din objected to this on the grounds that the guide could
not be spared, that if he were sent he would most probably be
killed by the Arabs, and that Mak Adam could not be relied on as
his past record and that of his family showed much disobedience
and defiance to the Government. His position was that of a vassal
who paid tribute to the authorities, but who received presents in
excess of the tribute paid. In 'Ala al-Din's opinion Adam would
already have joined the expedition had he really meant to fulfil his
promise. The idea of communicating with Adam was therefore
abandoned, and the discussion turned to the route to be taken from
al-Rahad to al-Ubayyid. It was generally agreed that the army
should march to 'Alluba, taking two days' supply of water, to
Kazqail also with two days' supply of water, and finally to Mulbas,
where a camp site would be selected and further arrangements made.

As the whole force approached al-Ubayyid, 'Ala al-Din considered that they were in desperate need of information about
al-Mahdi. He therefore planned to send one or more regiments to
capture some Arabs from the neighboring villages in the hope
of securing information from them. Hicks and Farquhar entirely
agreed with the plan. Hicks would have led the sortie himself had
the soldiers been Englishmen, but it was natural, in the circumstances, that an Egyptian officer should command them, and the
most senior officer, Husain Pasha Muzhar was chosen. The raid
was carried out but Husain reported that he had met nobody and

the plan consequently failed, leaving the expedition in the same state of ignorance about al-Mahdi's movements and conditions as before. For about two days there was a marked absence of harassing and skirmishing by the ansar, and the commanders were most anxious to know the reason for this.

It was suggested, in the last stages of the expedition, that the army should feed on the corn in order to conserve the biscuits for the future. An Egyptian officer set an example to his men, who had objected, by eating corn himself. Both 'Ala al-Din and Hicks were so pleased with his conduct that he was promoted to a higher rank.

Arabs were observed occupying the zaribah recently vacated by the army and the exchange of fire was resumed. It was feared that these Arabs were the vanguard of al-Mahdi's force for it was noticed that they were new rebels and not the old group, who had harassed them all along the march. It was also after al-Rahad that the behavior of 'Abd al-Rahman Bannaqa began to be suspected. He was a merchant whose father had been with al-Mahdi ever since the approach of the latter to al-Ubayyid. He had been made to accompany the expedition to use his good offices with his father and thereby to facilitate the task of the expedition. But now evidence was forthcoming that he might endanger rather than assist the expedition, and he was therefore put in chains and imprisoned. 'Abbas Afandi's diary ends abruptly on the 1st of November 1883 with the very important incident of the return of one of their guides who had been captured by the ansar and had managed to escape, knowing everything about al-Mahdi's movements and condition. No details of his information are given and it appears that all were busy preparing for the coming encounter with al-Mahdi.[1]

al-Mahdi, however, was well informed of events in Khartum. He knew of 'Abd al-Qadir's recall and of the collection of a large force to be sent westwards to fight him. He had heard of the success of Hicks's army on the White Nile but it had no demoralizing effect on him or his followers in the west. When the news reached al-Ubayyid that the long-awaited force had begun to march from Omdurman, al-Mahdi began his preparations to meet it. His first act was to issue a proclamation to all his generals to be read to

[1] This is the story of Hicks's expedition from its departure from al-Duwaim as summarized from 'Abbas Afandi's diary which is preserved in Newbold Library Archives, University College of Khartum.

the soldiers. It repeated his previous utterances about the divine nature of his mission, his assurance of ultimate victory and the virtues of the holy war and the promised paradise. Next he quitted al-Ubayyid and pitched his tent under a large tree outside in earnest of his intention to abandon the life of comparative ease and comfort. His example was very soon followed by the khalifahs, generals, and finally by the whole body of his ansar. Couriers were sent in all directions asking people to join his force, which they did willingly. Every day witnessed the enlargement of his camp by new straw huts. Detachments of ansar were also sent to collect the people and the result of these efforts was that whole tribes streamed to al-Ubayyid. Manoeuvres and reviews were held daily, and the horses were accustomed to the noise of battle. Ohrwalder, who gives this account, also recorded that al-Mahdi instilled great enthusiasm into the masses, and 'we began to have some fear for Hicks.'[1]

al-Mahdi's general plan was to wait for the army in the neighborhood of al-Ubayyid, letting his enemies undertake all the difficulties of the road between the White Nile and al-Ubayyid. The inhabitants on the route were to be dissuaded from co-operating or giving any form of assistance to them, and forces of his ansar were to harass the enemy and cut their line of retreat. To conduct this operation, al-Mahdi selected three of his generals, 'Abd al-Halim Masaad, Hajj Muhammad Abu Qarja, and 'Umar alyas Um Barir. They were instructed not to appear in the open and never to engage in close conflict with the advancing army, but to withdraw before them filling up the wells in front and cutting their line of retreat. They were also to encourage the villagers to join al-Mahdi. Their success is described in 'Abbas Afandi's diary: all villages were deserted and only occasionally could the advancing army pick up a woman or an old man who would only say that the people had deserted to al-Mahdi.

The whole of Hicks's army was completely in the dark until they came to al-Rahad a few days before the final encounter. Then, one of their captured guides escaped from al-Mahdi's camp and for the first time described the situation there. Whole tribes of Jim'a and Ahamda under their chiefs had quitted their dar (territory) and either joined the harassing column or the main body of ansar

[1] Ohrwalder, op. cit., p. 76.

encamped outside al-Ubayyid. The expedition was virtually in a state of moving siege after two or three halts from al-Duwaim: communications with Khartum were completely cut and no one could be persuaded by any reward to carry a message back to al-Duwaim let alone to go westwards to secure information from al-Ubayyid.

'Abd al-Halim Musaad sent his clerk back to al-Ubayyid to report to al-Mahdi and to ask that he might be allowed to fight the advancing enemy. al-Mahdi ordered him to carry out the previous instructions until al-Rahad had been reached, when the next move would be decided on. With his reply al-Mahdi sent thousands of copies of his proclamation[1] to be put in the way of the expedition. From al-Rahad 'Abd al-Halim rode to al-Ubayyid leaving his skirmishers behind in order to report and receive fresh instructions.[2]

After 'Alluba, where 'Abbas Afandi's diary ends, we have to rely entirely on the accounts given by survivors of Hicks's expedition such as Muhammad Nur al-Barudi, who made his statement about nine years after the event, or on Father Ohrwalder and Slatin who recorded their accounts more than ten years later. It appears that al-Mahdi had decided to meet the enemy either at al-Rahad itself or beyond it, before they could reach al-Ubayyid. From his camp outside the town he dispatched the main body of his troops to al-Rahad and subsequently he and the reserve set out for al-Birkah. Possibly al-Mahdi guessed that Hicks would make for al-Birkah for water before advancing on al-Ubayyid: he therefore decided to occupy the pool with the reserve while sending the main body to encounter them on the way. It was at 'Alluba that the ansar gathered in force and the black troops of al-Mahdi under Abu Anja, hidden by trees, began to harass the expedition. A march to Kazqail was attempted but was forced to halt at Shikan on an open space surrounded by a forest. The ring of the ansar grew thicker, water was running short, and the band was ordered to play incessantly to keep up the morale of the soldiers. On the night of November 4, Abu Anja's blacks fired on the troops throughout the night, allowing them no sleep.

---

[1] *Vide supra*, p. 102.
[2] Statement by Hasan Muhammad Habashi, the clerk of 'Abd al-Halim given to the intelligence branch of the Egyptian army, preserved in Newbold Library Archives, Khartum.

On the morning of the 5th the expedition was formed into three squares at points of a triangle with the cavalry to the left and right, and an attempt to march in that formation was being made, when al-Mahdi ordered a general attack. Each of the three squares was surrounded, and three heaps of dead bodies of human beings and animals was the result of the encounter, including those of Hicks, 'Ala al-Din, and all officers, while those who tried to escape lay dead away from the squares.[1] There were only about 250 survivors who had either been slightly wounded or had hidden among the dead bodies until al-Mahdi had ordered the survivors to be spared.

The pitiful condition of the expedition during its last four days is described in the notes and diaries of Herlth, Farquhar, and O'Donovan, all Europeans, the first two officers, and the third a newspaper correspondent. These notes and diaries were read by Slatin and Ohrwalder after the affair, but the impressions taken from them were recorded from memory nine years later in the case of Ohrwalder and thirteen years later in the case of Slatin. In detail, therefore, their accounts may not be accurate, although the general picture is probably true enough.[2] The main defects of the expedition were the low morale of the troops, who had no faith in their cause, and the discord between the Turco-Egyptian element and the Europeans among the Officers. The camels were badly looked after and many died on the way, while the rest suffered from terrible wounds made by the rubbing of wooden saddles on their backs. Notwithstanding this suffering, the camels had to add to their heavy burdens those of their dying colleagues. Many of the horses died before the army reached al-Rahad. Farquhar criticized the military mistakes of Hicks, and blamed him for taking such an army and plunging it into the forests of Kurdufan. According to Muhammad Nur al-Barudi, Hicks's cook, no serious conflict took place between 'Ala al-Din and Hicks except on two occasions, when there were differences of opinion. But it was

[1] Statement by Hasan Muhammad Habashi, (Newbold Library Archives, Khartum).

The three heaps of bones were seen by Lupton and Muhammad 'Abdallah some months after the battle when they were brought as prisoners from Bahr al-Ghazal to al-Ubayyid (Newbold Library Archives, Khartum).

[2] The diaries of the Europeans in Hick's army were most probably destroyed by the Mahdiya after being read by Slatin and Ohrwalder.

observed that they were not friends and that their relationship was a purely formal one.

The crushing defeat of Hicks drew attention to the seriousness of the revolution in the Sudan. Previously it had been considered a private matter to be suppressed by the Khedive, and the British Government had been content to be informed of events without intervening. The Muslim would now begin to pin its hopes on the success of this religious movement, and even the leaders of the pan-Islamic movement, Jamal al-Din al-Afaghani and Muhammad 'Abdu, thought of it as a genuine religious revival long awaited by the Islamic world.

In England Parliament was not in session, but when it first met there was no subject more widely discussed than the British attitude towards Hicks's expedition. The Opposition censured the Government for its aloofness. It was in answer to criticism of their policy in Egypt, and more especially in the Sudan, that the ministers, in Parliament, in memoirs, and in private letters defended their policy.

Sir Charles Dilke, alone among his colleagues, admitted that they 'foresaw the failure of the Hicks expedition, and should perhaps have done better had we more distinctly told the Egyptian Government that they must stop it and give up the Sudan, holding Khartoum only; but to say this is to be wise after the event.' [1] Mr. Childers thought that they had made a grave mistake in not forbidding Hicks's employment by Egypt after having refused officers on the active list permission to go to the Sudan. 'The Foreign Office seems to have slid into this without consulting others. At least I was party in November, 1882 to the prohibition, and was alarmed to find in May a number of officers in the Sudan and Dufferin corresponding with Hicks.' [2]

In answer to statements in the press that the expedition was a forlorn hope from the outset and doomed to destruction, Lord Dufferin described the conditions in Egypt and the Sudan up to

---

[1] Gwynne, S. L., and Tuckwell, Gertrude M., *The Life of the Rt. Hon. Sir Charles W. Dilke, Bart., M.P.*, (London, 1917), vol. i, p. 552.

[2] Childers to Viscount Halifax, Jan. 14, 1884, in Childers, S., *The Life and Correspondence of the Right Hon. Hugh C. E. Childers 1827-1896* (London, 1901), vol. ii, p. 180.

the time when he left Cairo in May 1883, defending the Egyptian Government's decision to send the expedition.[1] Lord Selborne's impression at the time when the expedition was in preparation was that the Khedive should be allowed to go on with it if it could be done without too great a strain on Egyptian resources. The British Government saw difficulties in requiring the Khedive to give up a large and important territory without proved necessity. Moreover, there were weighty reasons for the opinion that it would be for the benefit of Egypt and civilzation if Egypt could manage to hold the whole or part of the Sudan. The abuses of administration might be reformed by European influence if the Sudan remained under Egypt, but there would be no influence if it passed under a new Arab dominion; there was nothing to show that such new dominion would be less oppressive than that of the Khedive. The Arabs, in the absence of Egyptian authority, would do all they could to revive the slave-trade. Their command of the Nile above the cataracts would be a standing menace to Egypt, especially if the British troops were to be withdrawn from Egypt. Commercial intercourse with Nubia was essential to upper Egypt.

Access by the White Nile to the great equatorial regions, which recent discoveries and explorations had done so much to open, and by means of which the influence of Christianity and civilization might gradually be extended to Central Africa, would be cut off, if a hostile fanatical power stood in the way.[2]

The Earl of Derby told the House of Lords that a disaster like that which had occurred to Hicks's expedition was not within the bounds of reasonable expectation, but admitted that they had no means of estimating the full force of Arab fanaticism.

There has been nothing like it, I will not say since the days of the prophet, and his immediate successors, but certainly since the Wahhabi movement in Arabia. Is it anything new that great popular movements should take the world by surprise? Who foresaw the European revolution of 1848? Who predicted the Indian mutiny? Who expected that 1871 Paris would be all but destroyed by its own inhabitants? [3]

[1] Dufferin to Granville, Dec. 14, 1883, *Parl. Pap.* (1884), vol. lxxxviii, p. 143.
[2] Palmer, Roundell, Earl of Selborne, *Memorials* (London, 1898), vol. ii, p. 134.
[3] *Hansard,* 3rd ser., vol. 284, col. 642.

Lord Edmond Fitzmaurice struck the same note as Lord Derby.

Probably since Pharaoh's host perished in the Red Sea, there had been no disaster so sudden and so overwhelming, no such complete destruction of a host, as the destruction and disappearance, we might almost say, of General Hicks's Army in the wastes of Kurdufan. How, in the spirit of common fairness, could Her Majesty's Government be expected to foresee such a disaster as that? [1]

[1] Ibid., col. 1044.

VI

ABANDONMENT OF THE SUDAN

The first real problem in the Egyptian question for Sir Evelyn Baring to contend with on his appointment as British consul-general in Cairo in September 1883 was a complete surprise to all parties concerned, the Egyptian Government, Her Majesty's Government, and Baring; the problem was the complete annihilation of Hicks's army and the indisputable victory of al-Mahdi. There could be no better evidence of the surprise than the negotiations already in progress between Cairo and London about the reduction of the British garrison in Egypt in general and its withdrawal from Cairo to Alexandria. If there had been any reasonable doubt about the seriousness of the Sudan situation, that step would hardly have been contemplated.

Towards the end of September 1883 Sir Evelyn Baring reported the substance of a conversation with Sharif Pasha[1] about the plan for the Sudan after the 'issue of General Hicks' military operations.' The plan included the abandonment of the direct administration of Darfur by making it a tributary state, the appointment of a commission of three persons of whom one might possibly be a European, to reorganize the administration, and, thirdly, the construction of a railway. In accordance with previous instructions to Malet, Baring had been 'very cautious' in his language about the Sudan and had 'abstained from giving any advice.' The Foreign Office approved his reserve but he was 'authorized to support the scheme for a railway from Sawakin to Barbar.'[2]

Baring himself was not opposed to the project if the promoters of the scheme, who would be granted the concession, could be trusted to fulfil their engagements.[3] There was considerable opposition to the scheme in Cairo political circles, chiefly by 'Ali Pasha Mubarak, Minister of Public Works, but Baring thought that it might possibly be overcome. Baring could not take any active step

---

[1] Baring to Granville, No. 43, Sept. 28, 1883, P.R.O., F.O. 78/3557.
[2] Granville to Baring, No. 247, Oct. 3, 1883, P.R.O., F.O. 78/3551.
[3] Baring to Granville, No. 445, Oct. 7 1883, P.R.O., F.O. 78/3558.

in the matter until he was in possession of more complete and satisfactory assurances of the ability of the promoters to carry out their project.

The railway was given international importance because of the rivalry and opposition of France. The French were planning to make a free port on the Red Sea in order to attract the trade of Abyssinia and the upper Nile to it.[1] Baring advised the Egyptian Government that the proposed railway, in addition to its obvious advantages, would counteract French designs.

While Hicks was marching westwards from the Nile, Cairo was the scene of negotiations for the reduction of British forces in Egypt and of preparation of plans for the Sudan. But all these ended suddenly. On the 17th of November 1883 Baring reported to Granville privately that the affairs of the Sudan were assuming great importance, as from the long silence of Hicks it appeared that he was in difficulties.[2] Next day Baring wrote officially to Granville that from information received from Khartum by the French Consul-General in Cairo, it appeared that General Hicks with his army was surrounded and suffering from lack of provisions.[3] On the following day (19th) Baring explained in a long official telegram the difficulties of Egypt in the Sudan and the probable defeat of Hicks.[4] The authority of the Egyptian Government in the eastern Sudan was limited to the coast of the Red Sea and even there it was seriously threatened. In the west, although no definite confirmation of Hicks's difficulties had been received, he had not been heard of since the 27th of September. He had only two months' provisions when he started, and the Egyptian Government was becoming anxious and was evidently expecting bad news. Geigler Pasha, whom Baring had interviewed, considered that Khartum would probably fall if Hicks was defeated. Financially, the Egyptian Government was incapable of fitting out another expedition, and their manpower had been almost drained by the last one. The only armed forces were the newly raised army of Sir Evelyn Wood and the Gendarmerie of General Baker. Egypt would, therefore, lose the whole of the Sudan if the news of Hicks's defeat were confirmed

[1] Baring to Granville, No. 452, Oct. 9, 1883, P.R.O., F.O. 78/3558.
[2] Baring to Granville, Private, Nov. 17, 1883, P.R.O., G/D 29/161.
[3] Baring to Granville, No. 525, Nov. 18, 1883, P.R.O., F.O. 78/3559.
[4] Baring to Granville, No. 529, Nov. 19, 1883, P.R.O., F.O. 78/3559.

132   THE INDEPENDENT SUDAN

unless outside assistance could be given. If the Government were to
withdraw from the Sudan it would not be easy to say where the
rebel movement could be effectively stemmed.

Sir Evelyn Baring learned, in conversation with Sharif Pasha,
that the latter would request the British Government to send
British or Indian troops to the Sudan. Sharif remarked casually
that England would not, he supposed, like to see Turkish troops
called in to reconquer the Sudan. In order to be prepared for such
probable requests, Baring asked Granville for instructions on the
attitude to adopt towards Turkish intervention, and whether he
was to tell Sharif that in no circumstances would the assistance
of either British or Indian troops be given. The two alternatives
of Turkish intervention or evacuating the Sudan would be very
distasteful to the Egyptian Government and it could not be told
which they would dislike the more. 'My own opinion is that, once
General Hicks's army is defeated, it would be wiser for the Egyptian
Government to accept the fact and withdraw to whatever position
on the Nile they can be sure of defending.' ¹ This policy would
certainly afford an impulse to the slave-trade. 'But they will not
readily be persuaded to adopt this plan.' Baring thought it would
be most undesirable to have recourse to Turkish assistance. Sharif
might ask for the employment of Wood's army, and Baring was
of opinion that it should be retained in Egypt proper, especially in
view of the partial withdrawal of the British troops. The most that
could be done, in Baring's opinion, was to assist the Egyptian
Government to obtain the services of some English officers not on
the active list. Baring concluded by asking for instructions, declaring: 'It will be difficult for me to maintain an attitude of such
complete reserve as to give no advice whatever on these questions.'
The last statement is most significant, as it urges a departure from
the attitude that Her Majesty's Government had hitherto maintained. In all matters of the Sudan they had been persistently
advocating the policy of non-interference in and the disclaiming
of responsibility for the Sudan problems. Now for the first time,
the man on the spot found himself almost compelled to offer advice.

On the next day, Baring was instructed that Her Majesty's
Government could not lend English or Indian troops. He was

¹ Baring to Granville, No. 529, Nov. 19, 1883, P.R.O., F.O. 78/3559.

told not to encourage British officers to volunteer for the Egyptian service. The invitation of the Turkish troops into the Sudan would not be to the advantage of Egypt. Finally, Granville instructed him: 'If consulted recommend abandonment of the Sudan within certain limits.'[1]

When by November 22 it was reasonably clear that the news of Hicks's destruction was true, the first concern of the British Government was whether that disaster would endanger Egypt proper. Baring, in consequence, was instructed to look into this matter in consultation with Stephenson and Wood, and to report on the measures which they considered ought to be taken.[2] Baring replied that 'it would be premature to say what effect the complete defeat of the Egyptian army in the Sudan'[3] would have on the general situation in Egypt, but to guard against possible dangers he advised that the withdrawal of troops from Cairo should not be hastened. Orders were given to the naval commander-in-chief, East India Station, to maintain the authority of Egypt on the Red Sea coast.[4] British interest in the coast of the Red Sea was quite obvious.

In a private letter to Granville, Baring submitted the reasons for taking a more active part in the affairs of the Sudan. He thought that the garrison in Egypt should be maintained at its present strength. He fully understood the policy of not being drawn into the affairs of the Sudan and could see no reason why it should not be maintained. But it was clear to him that it was impossible to 'separate the Egyptian question from the Sudan question altogether. If the whole of the valley of the Nile is to be abandoned down to Wadi Halfa the political and military situation here will become one of very great difficulty.'[5] To him the reconquering of any of the provinces south of Khartum was out of the question, and local opinion in Khartum and the best military opinion in Cairo considered that Khartum itself could not be held.

One problem, at this time, was how to open the Barbar-Sawakin route for the withdrawal of the garrisons of Khartum, the outlying stations, and the civilians, both European and Egyptian. That route

---

[1] Granville to Baring, No. 99, Nov. 20, 1883, P.R.O., F.O. 78/3561.
[2] Granville to Baring, No. 297, Nov. 22, 1883, P.R.O., F.O. 78/3551.
[3] Baring to Granville, No. 538, Nov. 22, 1883, P.R.O., F.O. 78/3559.
[4] Granville to Baring, No. 298, Nov. 22, 1883, P.R.O., F.O. 78/3551.
[5] Baring to Granville, Private, Nov. 22, 1883, P.R.O., G/D 29/161.

was held by the rebels, and it was planned to send Baker to Sawakin in command of 2,000 Gendarmerie to open the road.

The general opinion in Cairo among the authorities, whether British or Egyptian, was that the withdrawal from Cairo and the reduction of the British troops in Egypt should be postponed, although the effect of al-Mahdi's victory in the Sudan could not yet be estimated. Sharif and the Khedive were particularly concerned with the danger which might result from the religious influence that al-Mahdi's success might have over the fanatical portion of the population, especially in upper Egypt. Baring himself was not yet in a position to give a definite opinion, but Stephenson and Wood inclined to think that, as a precaution, the garrison should be maintained at its present strength until the situation became clearer.[1]

Lord Wolseley, as adjutant-general and the commander of the successful operations in Egypt a little more than a year previously, was unlikely to be neutral in such an important question threatening the security of Egypt. He submitted a memorandum[2] to his minister Lord Hartington on the 23rd of November outlining the measures which he thought should be taken. He considered that a well-disciplined force, under British officers, stationed, for example, at Aswan would give heart to the people of upper Egypt. Khartum, Barbar, and Sawakin should be immediately reinforced and British officers put in command. He opposed withdrawal from the Sudan, firstly because of the difficulty of carrying out the operation in such a vast country, and secondly because Egypt would not voluntarily give up any territory east of the White Nile, which she had held for sixty years, and it would be unwise to advise her to do so. To give up Darfur, Kurdufan, and Fashoda, west of the White Nile, and make peace with al-Mahdi on those conditions would be a very reasonable measure, but the great bend made by the Nile from Khartum to al-Dabbah should be retained by Egypt.

In Cairo, Sharif Pasha, having hinted at Turkish intervention, made definite proposals to recruit soldiers in Turkey. The Egyptian Government therefore intended to ask permission from the

---

[1] Baring to Granville, Private, Nov. 23, 1883, P.R.O., G/D 29/161.
[2] Memorandum by Wolseley, enclosed in Hartington to Granville, Private, Nov. 23, 1883, P.R.O., G/D 29/133.

Porte, and requested Baring to inquire whether the British Government would support the application.[1] Baring, in forwarding the proposal, recommended it for support. Sharif seemed to have doubts about the approval of the British Government, for on the next day he intimated to Baring that if difficulties arose in Turkey, it would be possible to recruit Turks from Albania and Thessaly.[2] General Baker suggested recruitment from Cyprus, but Baring thought that the objections to recruitment in Turkey would also apply to Cyprus. Sharif assured Baring that application to the Porte would not be made until the answer of the British Government had been received.

Gladstone commented on this suggestion: 'I do not quite know why they should not recruit in Egypt where the people made good soldiers.'[3] This shows that Gladstone had not read Stewart's reports from Khartum on the inefficiency of the soldiers and officers there and that he was unaware of the real reasons of the annihilation of Hicks's expedition. He thought that if it were necessary to support the application the troops should be used to defend Egypt and not to reconquer the Sudan. Gladstone added that it was a 'thorny prospect, and the known bad faith of the Sultan might probably render anything of the kind impracticable.'[4]

Since no official reply appeared to be forthcoming from the British Government, Sharif impressed on Baring the urgency of the matter. Baring reported Sharif's reminder, commenting that in normal circumstances he would have agreed with Lord Dufferin on the undesirability of employing mercenaries. But in present conditions he had to recognize that 'their employment is well nigh unavoidable.'[5] Personally he preferred the recruitment of Turks in northern Greece. This reminder crossed with Granville's reply.

Granville agreed with Baring in objecting to recruitment in Cyprus, but raised no objection to Egypt's obtaining permission of the Sultan to recruit in Turkey. Yet again, the British Government disclaimed all responsibility for operations in the Sudan and responsibility was left to 'rest with the Egyptian Government relying on their own resources. We think that the restricting of the

[1] Baring to Granville, No. 539, Nov. 22, 1883, P.R.O., F.O. 78/3559.
[2] Baring to Granville, No. 543, Nov. 23, 1883, P.R.O., F.O. 78/3559.
[3] Gladstone to Granville, Private, Nov. 24, 1883, P.R.O., G/D 29/127.
[4] Gladstone to Granville, Private, Nov. 25, 1883, B.M. Add. MS. 44547.
[5] Baring to Granville, No. 556, Nov. 26, 1883, P.R.O., F.O. 78/3559.

operations as proposed by the Egyptian Government to defensive operations seems to be reasonable.'[1]

In reply to Granville's dispatch Baring declared that it was fully understood by the Egyptian Government that they must meet the expenses of the Sudan from their own resources and that the whole responsibility of operations in the Sudan was still theirs. He further reported that the Egyptian Government hoped that reports of the disaster would not be confirmed or might have been greatly exaggerated. After second thoughts they preferred to wait for definite news before asking the Porte for leave to recruit in Turkey. They thought it possible that, in answer to their request, the Sultan might send his own troops to the Sudan. Baring added that Stephenson, Wood, and himself were awaiting confirmation of the disaster before advising the strengthening of Wood's army by the addition of some Turkish battalions under British officers, not for service in the Sudan but for the defense of Egypt proper.[2]

This suggestion of introducing Turks into the Egyptian army, with British officers, somewhat perplexed Granville. The proposal seemed open to objection, and even if the Sultan consented he might well insist upon a much larger force under his own officers. 'In any case the recommendation should hardly come from Baring or Stephenson.'[3] Granville requested Gladstone's opinion on a matter which he considered, 'very ticklish either way.' Granville did not understand how Turkish troops were to be employed, and he telegraphed Baring asking whether it meant the Sultan's troops or Turks drilled and officered by Englishmen.[4] Baring telegraphed that it was intended that the Egyptian Government should recruit Turks on her own behalf, and that they should be officered by Englishmen.[5] Finally, Granville wrote privately to Baring[6] apologizing for his mistake in thinking that it was proposed to employ Turkish regiments. He had no objection to recruitment if it could be done without impossible conditions. He personally doubted if the Sultan would grant permission. The whole question of supporting the application was left to the discretion of Lord Dufferin

[1] Granville to Baring, No. 105, Nov. 25, 1883, P.R.O., F.O. 78/3561.
[2] Baring to Grandville, No. 561, Nov. 26, 1883, P.R.O., F.O. 78/3559.
[3] Granville to Gladstone, Private, Nov. 27, 1883, B.M. Add. MS. 44176.
[4] Granville to Baring, No. 112, Nov. 29, 1883, P.R.O., F.O. 78/3561.
[5] Baring to Granville, No. 573, Dec. 1, 1883, P.R.O., F.O. 78/3560.
[6] Granville to Baring, Private, Dec. 7, 1883, P.R.O., G/D 29/199.

in Constantinople. Events, however, took another turn and the question of recruitment by Egypt in Turkey was never raised.

While awaiting a reply to their proposal to recruit troops in Turkey, the Egyptian Government decided to hold Khartum and reopen communications between Barbar and Sawakin. All efforts and resources at their disposal were to be concentrated on these two objectives. It was hoped to concentrate all available forces in the Sudan in Khartum by withdrawing the garrisons of Darfur, Bahr al-Ghazal, and Fashoda. The troops on the White Nile were believed to be already falling back on Khartum. Sennar was to be held, for the time being, in order to provision Khartum. It was intended to dispatch a force of 2,000 Gendarmerie and 6,000 Bedwins to re-establish communications between Sawakin and Barbar. In the absence of the Gendarmerie, Egypt would be policed by Wood's army.

Baring added that according to several telegrams received from Khartum it was the general opinion of the people there that the town could not possibly be held, and that it would be necessary to retire to Barbar. Baring expressed no opinion whether the measures intended to be carried out by the Egyptian Government should be sanctioned.[1]

By the 24th of November the British authorities in Cairo, Stephenson, Wood, and Baring had given their considered opinion about the British garrison in Egypt. They recommended the maintenance of the British force in Egypt at its present strength and the postponement of the withdrawal of the British garrison from Cairo. They thought that the movement in the Sudan was a source of danger, especially if Khartum fell, which was not improbable. In support of this opinion Baring reported that both Sharif and the Khedive had expressed their desire for the postponement of the British withdrawal from Cairo as they feared 'a serious religious movement the limits of which it is at present impossible to define.' [2]

It is interesting to leave official circles and see the attitude of public opinion in England as represented by *The Times* towards this question of abandonment. *The Times* definitely approved the abandonment of Kurdufan and Darfur and the retention of Khartum and the Nile valley. 'It would not be easy for any ruler

[1] Baring to Granville, No. 542, Nov. 23, 1883, P.R.O., F.O. 78/3559.
[2] Baring to Granville, No. 547, Nov. 24, 1883, P.R.O., F.O. 78/3559.

responsible for the welfare of Egypt to permit Khartum to fall under the domination of al-Mahdi. Khartum is the center of an important commerce, and belongs to Egypt geographically, strategically, and commercially as truly as Cairo itself.'[1]

The British Government was hardly in a position to decide what advice they should tender to the Egyptian Government. They had been told that plans were being made in Cairo for holding Khartum and reopening the Barbar-Sawakin route. Baring, however, had expressed no opinion on the advisability of attempting to hold Khartum. He had in fact confused them by reporting that it was believed to be impossible to hold Khartum. The Government's chief military adviser, Lord Wolseley, had recommended active measures in the Sudan to preserve the Nile valley for Egypt while abandoning the south and west.

Gladstone was unable to decide what degree of weight was to be attached to these telegrams from Khartum.[2] To him the vital question was whether or not the town could be held. If it could not would it be desirable 'to make the attempt with the expectation of failure?' He thought the whole thing depended on considerations unknown to them, such as the form withdrawal would take and the military advantage that would be given to the enemy by the evacuation. With these queries unanswered he would prefer defensive operations until they had further information on which to base a judgment.

So far a week had been spent in hesitation, and no straightforward reply had been sent to the proposals made by the Egyptian Government. However, a telegram from a reliable source in Khartum was at last received in Cairo. Colonel de Coetlogon, an English officer of Hicks's expedition who had been left behind in Khartum, telegraphed to Sir Evelyn Wood.[3] De Coetlogon declared that Khartum and Sennar could not be held for more than two months as food supplies would then be consumed. He recommended a retreat on Barbar at once, and that the route between Sawakin and Barbar should be opened, expeditions setting out simultaneously from both places. He thought that only very strong reinforcements

[1] *The Times,* Nov. 24, 1883.
[2] Remarks by Gladstone, enclosed in Granville to Baring, No. 105, Nov. 25, 1883, P.R.O., F.O. 78/3561.
[3] De Coetlogon to Wood, Nov. 25, 1883, enclosed in Baring to Granville, No. 560, Nov. 26, 1883, P.R.O., F.O. 78/3559.

could reach Khartum and only by land, and there would be no supplies for them in Khartum. River transport was unreliable as the strategic position of al-Sabaloqa George afforded a good place from which to stop the transport. The river at that point was narrow and shallow and towing steamers, of which there were only two, were necessary. In any case, in a month the state of the river would make transport by steamer very difficult. 'Again, I say, the only way of saving what remains is to attempt a general retreat on Barbar; this is the real state of affairs here and I beg you to impress it on His Highness the Khedive.' Until the receipt of his telegram the authorities in Cairo and London had been ignorant of the difficulties, but now a reliable person had set out information from which they could judge the situation.

The telegram was so alarming that a meeting of Stephenson, Baker, and Wood was urgently called in Baring's house to consider the situation. Baring reported that 'they were unanimously of opinion that the Egyptian Government will find it impossible, with the forces at its disposal, to hold the Sudan,'[1] and that it would eventually be necessary to fall back on Egypt proper after withdrawing the garrisons. Khartum should be held long enough to allow the more distant posts and isolated garrisons to be withdrawn. They also thought it desirable that the Egyptian Government should act from Sawakin and give as much support as possible from there.

From his experience as ex-Viceroy of India and because as First Lord of the Admiralty he was concerned with the Red Sea coast, Lord Northbrook expressed his opinion on the Sudan question. He thought that it was possible to employ Indian troops and that it was impossible to abandon all concern for Egypt's position in Khartum.[2] Northbrook's opinion startled Gladstone a great deal for to him it indicated 'a great movement of his [Northbrook's] mind since the last cabinet.'[3] Gladstone at this juncture seems to have been convinced that the British force should be kept in Egypt until the danger was over, but the idea of engaging 'in warfare to recover the Sudan is quite another matter.' Even at the end

[1] Baring to Granville, No. 553, Nov. 26, 1883 ,P.R.O., F.O. 78/3559.
[2] Northbrook to Granville, Private, enclosed in Granville to Gladstone, Nov. 28, 1883, B.M. Add. MS. 44176.
[3] Gladstone to Granville, Private, Nov. 29, 1883, B.M. Add. MS. 44547.

of November the British Government was not prepared to commit themselves 'in the Sudan, beyond giving maritime assistance'[1] to the ports of the Red Sea. It was, however, decided not to withdraw the British garrison from Cairo.

For another week there was no fresh development in British policy towards the Sudan, and even up to December 7 it persisted in the policy of non-intervention, but Lord Granville was beginning to feel that such an attitude could not be maintained much longer. He told Baring that as a British Government they were right not to 'take the responsibility of directing measures for objects of a doubtful value,' and they were equally right in not taking the responsibility for preventing Egypt from defending a vast territory which she did not wish to give up. They were also right in not taking upon themselves the duty of repairing that great disaster. 'But we are resting on the edge of a knife. It is almost impossible that such events should not react upon Egypt proper.'[2] Essentially, however, the policy of non-interference was maintained, and from Cairo Baring, in a long dispatch surveying the whole question, declared: 'I venture to express a hope that Her Majesty's Government will adhere steadfastly to the policy of non-interference in the affairs of the Sudan.'[3]

On December 10 Baring telegraphed to Granville privately explaining that he did not ask for fresh instructions because he thought it useless to do so until events had developed in such a way as to enable him to recommend a definite line of action. However, it was clear to him that more definite instructions ought to be sent him on the Government's policy towards the Sudan. In his opinion the Egyptian Government was drifting along without any definite plan and would continue to do so until they were advised on the course most favorable to their interests. It was absolutely essential to make a decision either to hold to Khartum and the country to the north of it or to retire to Wadi Halfa.[4] The Egyptian Government thought that every effort and sacrifice ought to be made to maintain the Khedive's authority as far south as Khartum. Baring doubted the ability of the Khedive's Govern-

[1] Granville to Baring, Private, Nov. 30, 1883, P.R.O., G/D 29/199.
[2] Granville to Baring, Private, Dec. 7, 1883, P.R.O., G/D 29/199.
[3] Baring to Granville, No. 577, Dec. 3, 1883, P.R.O., F.O. 78/3560.
[4] Baring to Granville, Private, Dec. 10, 1883, P.R.O., G/D 29/161.

ment to govern efficiently even that restricted territory, but at the same time was unwilling to urge the abandonment of the whole country south of Wadi Halfa. Baring therefore submitted three suggestions for the holding of Khartum.

The first was to send English or Indian troops to maintain order. He personally thought it to be the worst solution possible, and he would spare no efforts to prevent it as he did not like any measure which involved the British Government in assuming responsibility outside Egypt proper. The second course was to deny British or Turkish help and leave the Egyptians to their own resources. If that course were adopted the Egyptians would probably lose Khartum and the whole country up to Wadi Halfa and become engulfed in the rebellion. The idea of having al-Mahdi on the frontiers of Egypt proper was detested by the Egyptians and they would rather call in the Sultan. Considered on its own merits, this course would be open to objection. It would make the task of administering Egypt very much more difficult and would necessitate both the increase of the British garrison there and the postponement of their ultimate withdrawal.

The third course was to call in the troops of the Sultan. Sharif would like this if he could feel sure that the Turks would depart after pacifying the country. The objections to this, in Baring's opinion, were obvious, but he could not see anything better. 'We can hardly refuse aid ourselves and at the same time object to the Egyptian Government calling in the Sultan.' To Baring the choice was between evils. 'I dislike exceedingly the idea of Turkish interference, but can you suggest a lesser evil?'

Baring decided to send this dispatch privately in case an official telegram should embarrass the Government. He asked for an early expression of opinion. Granville sent copies of the telegram to Gladstone, Northbrook, Hartington, and Harcourt.

Gladstone's reaction indicated his preference for the abandonment of the Sudan as far as Wadi Halfa. He thought it impossible, however, to make a definite judgment 'without some knowledge of the condition of the country between that place and Khartum; its military position, and the point of easy defense; its civil conditions and the power of easy and steady government.'[1] He asked Granville to consider carefully the possibility of Turkish interven-

[1] Gladstone to Granville, Private, Dec. 11, 1883, P.R.O., G/D 29/127.

tion and thought there was force in Baring's argument that 'we cannot well forbid Sharif to apply to the Turk while we refuse him aid ourselves.'

The basis of the discussion on the telegram that should be sent to Baring in reply was most probably a memorandum drawn up by Lord Northbrook.[1] He thought that it was beyond the strength of Egypt to hold Khartum, that Britain was not able to do so, and that the Turks could not do so without ruining the Ottoman Empire. From a financial point of view it seemed to be clearly out of the question for Egypt to pay the cost of the operation and neither England nor Turkey was willing to do so. Her Majesty's Government in Northbrook's view, was responsible for defending Egypt from some point like Wadi Halfa—if al-Mahdi advanced—and it was in the interests of Great Britain that the Red Sea ports should be held by Egypt. Northbrook could see no serious objection to the temporary garrisoning of the Red Sea ports from India. In addition to the military and financial difficulties if Turkey were asked to assist, 'the Egyptian Government could not refuse to admit Turkish troops into Lower Egypt (which would probably under present conditions be the best base of operations), and this would make our position in Egypt untenable.' In conclusion, Northbrook declared that he would 'prefer the deliberate abandonment of the attempt to govern the Sudan from Egypt, the withdrawal of Egyptian troops to such a point as may be decided upon with our consent, coupled with the assurance that we will protect Egypt, for a specified time, within these limits.'

On December 12th a telegram based on Northbrook's memorandum was drafted by Granville and approved by Hartington, Northbrook, and Dilke. Calingford, who was not present at the meeting, saw the 'thing in the same sense.'[2] The draft was then sent to Gladstone who approved it with minor amendments. The telegram was then wired privately to Baring as a reply to his of the 10th.[3]

The telegram declared that the British Government had no intention of sending English or Indian troops, but raised no objection to the use of Turkish troops, based on Sawakin, if they were paid

---

[1] Mallet, Sir Bernard, *Thomas George, Earl of Northbrook, A Memoir* (London, 1908), p. 174.

[2] Granville to Gladstone, Private, Dec. 12, 1883, B.M. Add. MS. 44176.

[3] Granville to Baring, Private, Dec. 13, 1883, P.R.O., G/D 29/199.

by the Sultan. It was doubted whether the Sultan would accept such conditions. No expenditure on the Sudan was to be sanctioned except for carrying out the retreat. The Egyptian Government was advised to make an early decision to abandon all the country south of Wadi Halfa. England was willing to maintain order in Egypt proper, defend it against agression and protect the Red Sea ports Objection was made to the employment of Zubair, who had been named to command the troops in the eastern Sudan under Baker Pasha.

Baring asked permission to use the substance of this telegram in conversation with Sharif Pasha. Baring believed the policy to be 'the best of which the circumstances will admit,'[1] but extremely difficult to carry out. He was inclined not to interfere with the appointment of Zubair and inquired whether he might use his discretion in this matter. Baring foresaw that a decision to abandon the Sudan would bring about the resignation of Sharif, and suggested that in that event he should advise the Khedive to send for Nubar. Granville, in reply, left both these matters to Baring's discretion.[2]

Meanwhile, Baring had an interview with Sharif who told him that a council of ministers, presided over by the Khedive, had been held and had decided to place themselves 'in the hands of Her Majesty's Government.'[3] The ministers thought it best to ask the Sultan for help and wished the British Government to undertake the negotiations with the Sultan. They insisted, however, on the withdrawal of Turkish troops once they were no longer required. The chief Egyptian objection to the use of British or Indian troops was that the religious movement in the Sudan might gain more ground by the interference of Christians. Sharif asked Baring for an early reply. Thus on the same day Cairo and London were asking each other to 'arrive at an early decision,' but in opposite directions; Cairo was interested in rescuing the Sudan with Turkish assistance and London was asking Cairo to give up the Sudan.

On December 16th Baring informed Sharif verbally of the substance of the British Government's telegram of December 13th. Sharif saw 'considerable objections to the adoption of this policy', but said he would consider the matter further and would commu-

[1] Baring to Granville, Private, Dec. 14, 1883, P.R.O., G/D 29/161.
[2] Granville to Baring, Private, Dec. 15, 1883, P.R.O., G/D 29/161.
[3] Baring to Granville, No. 597, Dec. 12, 1883, P.R.O., F.O. 78/3560.

nicate to Baring the views of the Egyptian Government in a written memorandum.[1] Baring supplemented his official communication with a private telegram to Granville, saying that Sharif disliked 'intensely' the policy of abandonment, and it was very dubtful whether any amount of persuasion would induce him to accept it. So far nothing had been said about resignation, but Baring gathered that Egypt would probably decide to hold the Nile valley to Khartum and give up the ports of the Red Sea, which Sharif considered as of more interest to England than to Egypt. Sharif foresaw further danger to the independence of his country, for this policy would certainly necessitate an increased British garrison entailing increased expenditure and the maintenance of British garrisons in Egypt for a longer period.

Baring admitted the validity of these arguments whilst pointing out to Sharif that the best hope of preserving the independence of Egypt was to abandon the Sudan. To allay Sharif's fears, Baring suggested that Granville should send him a telegram which he could show to Sharif saying that Her Majesty's Government would not change their declared policy in respect to Egypt proper. Although the British garrisons might be reinforced and the occupation prolonged, it was the wish of the British Government to withdraw altogether as soon as circumstances permitted. Further, the best hope of maintaining the autonomy of Egypt 'in fact, as well as in name' was for her to abandan her extended empire and devote herself to the good government of Egypt proper.[2]

Baring guessed that Sharif and other Egyptians thought the advice to abandon the Sudan was merely a snare to render permanent the presence of the British in Egypt. Baring could not give any pledge beyond the one which he had recommended to Granville since circumstances might compel 'us to eat our words.' He thought that the situation might necessitate 'an increase rather than a diminution in the amount of interference before the policy of withdrawal will be at all possible.'

On December, in a private letter to Granville,[3] Baring again emphasized that the policy of withdrawal from the Sudan was so distasteful to the Egyptian Government that he doubted if anything

[1] Baring to Granville, No. 615, Dec. 16, 1883, P.R.O., F.O. 78/3560.
[2] Baring to Granville, Private, Dec 16 1883, P.R.O., G/D 29/161.
[3] Baring to Granville, Private, Dec 17, 1883, P.R.O., G/D 29/161.

would avail but 'the very strongest language, and possibly a change of ministry.' The crux of the matter lay in financial and administrative ability: the Egyptian Government was unable to govern the Sudan and Egyptian politicians could not grasp that 'very unpalatable truth.'

Granville consulted Gladstone who recommended that Baring should be supplied with the telegram which he had requested.[1] Gladstone was surprised that all the talk was about holding or surrendering this or that territory, while nothing was said about 'establishing peace. Is it wholly impossible that al-Mahdi who has no quarrel with us (unless as Christians) might be disposed to accept us as mediators.' While making this proposal Gladstone admitted that very little was known of the disposition and the power of al-Mahdi. But he thought that a peaceful approach might be made by the Egyptians in such a way 'that policy and self respect taken together may require. Pity that Sharif should after all suspect us, but pity also, if he resigns.'

By December 20 the British Government was better informed of the situation in the Sudan.[2] Baring was, therefore, authorized to inform Sharif that Her Majesty's Government 'adhere entirely to the policy which they have laid down with regard to Egyptian affairs'[3] and which had been interrupted by the destruction of Hicks's army. They considered that 'ineffectual efforts on the part of the Egyptian Government to secure their position in the Sudan would only endanger its success.' They adhered to their previous advice on Egyptian policy in the Sudan.

On December 22 Baring received the note promised by Sharif giving the arguments of the Egyptian Government against the abandonment of the Sudan.[4] The first objection to such a policy was a legal one. By the firman of August 7, 1879 the Khedive was not permitted to alienate any territory. Even if Egypt exercised absolute right to dispose of the Sudan there would be harmful consequences. The position at the time, Sharif argued, was that Egypt was already maintaining law and order in all parts of the Sudan with the exception of Kurdufan Province. If the policy of

[1] Gladstone to Granville, Private. Dec. 18, 1883, B.M Add MS. 44547.
[2] Granville to Baring, No. 329, Dec. 20, 1883, P.R.O., F.O. 78/3551.
[3] Granville to Baring, No. 331, Dec. 20, 1883, P.R.O., F.O. 78/3551.
[4] *Parl. Pap.* (1884), vol. lxxxviii, p. 153.

abandonment were to be implemented it would mean abandoning to insurrection eastern Sudan, the provinces of Barbar and Dongola, and the whole of the Nile valley from its sources to a point to be defined as the southern frontier of Egypt. The False Prophet would find himself master of these vast territories, and the tribes that remained loyal, as well as those that were wavering, such as al-Kababish, would swell the rebel force. Thus Egypt would have contributed to the prestige of al-Mahdi who would then directly threaten her with his fanatical hordes at a time when she would be reduced to her narrowest limits. Another source of danger would be the Bedwins surrounding the Nile valley in Egypt, who, following their instincts of pillage and encouraged by the prospects of looting, would not remain indifferent to al-Mahdi's appeals. The loyal tribes, such as al-Ababdah and al-Bishariyin, would be a permanent source of anxiety to the Government. Egypt, thus deprived of her natural frontiers and vulnerable on all sides, would need for her security a large army which she could not afford to maintain. On the other hand, the retention of the Sudan, under good administration, would allow her to recruit easily and cheaply in these territories and would also allow her to make the Sudan bear part of the expenses for an army to preserve order in Egypt as well as in the Sudan. Up to the time of the conquest of the Sudan by Muhammad 'Ali, Egypt had been constantly compelled to take offensive action in order to avoid the incursions of the tribes of the upper Nile. 'His Highness's Government could not, therefore, adopt the decision to abandon territory which they regard as necessary for the safety and even existence of Egypt.'

Moreover, Sharif declared, it was due to the efforts of Egypt that the regions as far south as the lakes had been opened to the outside world; this was in spite of criticisms directed against Egyptian administration in the Sudan. It was because of Egyptian conquests that European houses of commerce were able to establish themselves there, that scientific and exploring expeditions were undertaken, and that Christian missions were able to settle. It could not be denied that Egypt had restricted the slave-trade as far as possible, and that al-Mahdi had found ready support from those who had benefited from that trade.

For all these reasons Sharif thought that Egypt should continue her civilizing work in the Sudan and provide for the protection of

Egypt and the re-establishing of her authority there. All that was needed to accomplish this was a force of 10,000 men. This force would be used in the first instance to open up the road between Sawakin and Barbar, and then to form a garrison for a fixed period until the Khedive's Government could organize and concentrate a force to replace it. There was no intention of undertaking a new expedition into Kurdufan, and efforts would be confined to holding Khartum and maintaining security in the eastern Sudan with the ultimate object of commanding the course of the Nile.

Taking into consideration the religious nature of the insurrection it was thought that Turkey would be the best source for such temporary assistance. The Sublime Porte ought not to refuse such aid, for Egypt had supplied similar assistance to Turkey in the Crimea, Serbia, Crete, and Bulgaria. The Sultan would, further, be interested in suppressing the rebellion to prevent its spreading to Tripoli and Arabia. 'In any case the Government of His Highness are particularly desirous that any arrangements in the subject should be confirmed by an understanding with Great Britain, whether Her Majesty's Government consent to negotiate on behalf of Egypt or whether the latter should come to a direct understanding with the Sublime Porte.'

Commenting on that memorandum[1] Baring said he was sure any negotiations with the Porte with a view to making Turkey pay the expenses of an expedition would be doomed to failure. 'My own opinion is that the policy recommended by Her Majesty's Government is the best of which the very difficult circumstances of the case admit.' He thought that the position was not so alarming as appeared to be believed in England. According to information dissension had already arisen between the tribes supporting al-Mahdi and some of the most important were opposed to him. 'It is quite possible that by a judicious expenditure of money, and by good management, the Government of the Khedive may succeed in maintaining its authority northwards from Khartum.' They would, however, only be able to hold the country with great difficulty, and Baring believed them to be incapable of giving it proper government. On the other hand, Khedivial authority would receive a 'very serious blow' by the abandonment of the Sudan, and Sharif's argument about the Bedwins was 'very forcible.'

[1] Baring to Granville, No. 642, Dec. 22, 1883, P.R.O., F.O. 78/3560.

Baring thought that the unavoidable corollary of the policy of abandonment would be the prolonged occupation of Egypt by British troops. He therefore suggested that this fact should be recognized by the British Government and that Egypt should be told that the British occupation would last 'from five to ten years,' by which time the Egyptian Government might be expected to have provided for the defense of the country. Another important fact was the increased expenditure since the abandonment of the Sudan would necessitate a considerable increase in the Egyptian army.

Baring was certain that no amount of persuasion would make the present Egyptian ministers accept the policy of abandonment. In this case the Khedive would have to be told that if his ministers refused to carry out the policy, others who were prepared to do so should be named. Baring was not quite sure whether ministers who would be both willing to carry out the policy and capable of doing so were to be found. Consequently, Baring thought that the British Government ought to be prepared to meet the possible necessity of appointing temporary English ministers. He would regret very much the change of ministry, and thought that the loss of Sharif would be 'very detrimental to the country,' but it would be 'almost inevitable' if the policy had to be carried out. In conclusion, Baring said: 'It would also be necessary to send an English officer of high authority to Khartum with full powers to withdraw all the garrisons in the Sudan and to make the best arrangements possible for the future government of that country.'

In view of the importance of the decision to be made, he recommended that the Government should not answer his telegram until they had seen Mr. Cross, Under-Secretary at the India Office, who had spent two months in Cairo and was due to arrive in England on Christmas Eve. Cross would be able to give a true picture of the situation.[1] At the same time he suggested that he should go to England for a short while, although he recognized the objections to his leaving Cairo at that time. He asked for leave to proceed to England because he doubted his ability to 'pull together through the present difficulties without a personal consultation.' Granville preferred to wait for Cross, as the 'inconvenience of your absence from Cairo seems to counterbalance

[1] Baring to Granville, Private, Dec. 22, 1883, P.R.O., G/D 29/161.

obvious advantages.'¹ In a private letter of December 23 Baring expressed his confusion of mind: 'I must confess that I do not see my way clear either about the Sudan, the financial question or the Egyptian question generally. I expect that we are all in for stormy time of it both here and in parliament.'²

When Baring's long telegram was circulated to the ministers in London it naturally aroused much comment. Mr. Gladstone at once put down his impressions. His first remark was that England ought not to 'press at once for abandonment.'³ He thought that no opposition should be made to Turkish intervention. He suggested that the Egyptian Government should assume that the expenditure would be borne by Turkey, and if compelled to retreat from this ground, should fix a reasonable sum and then discuss the fixing of the geographical limits of the intervention and press the anti-slave policy on the Sultan. Once the pacification was accomplished the withdrawal of Turkish troops should be regulated. It was quite clear, therefore, that Gladstone was prepared to allow Turkey to interfere in the Sudan on certain conditions. Gladstone's suggestion that abandonment should not be insisted on did not convince Granville, who thought that the limits to be imposed on Turkish intervention would make it possible for the Turks to accept.⁴

Northbrook had been 'greatly troubled' about the British position in Egypt and the Sudan and set out his opinions in a memorandum.⁵ From reading books by Sir Samuel Baker and General Gordon, and Colonel Stewart's report, he was convinced that Egyptian rule over the Sudan had been 'a great evil to the people of that country.' In spite of the declarations of several khedives against the slave-trade, the officials on the spot encouraged it. He doubted very much whether Tawfiq really wished to discourage it. Ra'uf Pasha, who succeeded Gordon as a governor-general, was twice dismissed by the latter. Ra'uf's first act had been to get rid of Gessi, who had checked the slave-trade in Bahr al-Ghazal. Zubair Pasha, who was just being sent with Baker Pasha to Sawakin, was only a 'few years ago the greatest slave dealer of the Sudan.'

¹ Granville to Baring, Private, Dec. 23, 1883, P.R.O., G/D 29/161.
² Baring to Granville, Private, Dec. 23, 1883, P.R.O., G/D 29/161.
³ Gladstone to Granville, Private, Dec. 24, 1883, P.R.O., G/D 29/127.
⁴ Granville to Hartington, Private, Dec. 28, 1883, P.R.O., G/D 29/133.
⁵ Northbrook to Granville, Private, Dec. 24, 1883, P.R.O., G/D 29/139.

He trusted that the Khedive would not be allowed to spend 'a sixpence on supporting Zubair Pasha.' al-Mahdi, who was reported to favor the slave-trade, could hardly be 'worse than the Egyptian rulers of the Sudan.' He thought it impossible to check local slave dealings in central Africa, but they ought to be able to do something to check the export of slaves which was 'so terrible in its incidents.'

Northbrook recommended that Egypt should be protected against a possible attack by al-Mahdi. English officers might be sent at any rate to Wadi Halfa and Aswan. Among their duties they should take care that no slaves came down the Nile or by the caravan routes parallel to the Nile. Secondly, the British Government should do all they could to prevent the export of slaves from the Red Sea ports, which they undertook to protect.

When it was known that a decision was to be postponed until Granville had seen Cross, Northbrook was tempted to write more. He thought that the state of affairs described in the telegrams was very critical and required speedy action.[1] He repeated his conviction that the policy of withdrawal from the whole of the Sudan was the correct one and that no expedition with English or Indian troops into the Sudan should be contemplated. In addition, he did not think it advisable to encourage the Porte to govern the whole of the Sudan or to send an expedition against al-Mahdi, but suggested that Red Sea ports might be given to Turkey. He saw great difficulty, however, in carrying out this policy in view of the possible resignation of Sharif and possible abdication of the Khedive.

In preparation for his interview with Cross, Granville reviewed all Baring's dispatches on the Sudan, deducing that Baring was in agreement with the policy of abandonment but saw the many difficulties it would entail, and especially the prolongation of the military occupation of Egypt. Granville could not see how the occupation could end 'until Egypt has recovered somewhat from the blow.'[2] The main question was how to hasten that recovery. 'It takes away somewhat of the position of a man if he has to sell his racers and hunters, but if he cannot afford to keep them, the

---

[1] Northbrook to Granville, Private, Dec. 28, 1883, P.R.O., G/D 29/139.
[2] Granville to Baring, Private, Dec. 28, 1883, P.R.O., G/D 29/199.

sooner they go to Tattersalls the better.'¹ Granville hoped that
Baring would be able to persuade Sharif not to resign and, if he
insisted on doing so, that Nubar would take office or, as a last
resort, 'some plausible Egyptian who with Clifford Lloyd as a
double, would work the coach for a time.' Granville thought that
the appointment of English ministers should be avoided. It is thus
clear that before he saw Cross, Granville definitely favored abandonment even if it entailed the resignation of Sharif and any Egyptian
ministry.

The eagerly awaited interview with Cross took place on December 29 and Granville recorded the conversation.² According to
Cross, Baring agreed with the Government that the abandonment
of the Sudan was the 'best and only practicable policy,' but Cross
could not tell whether Baring's opinion had been modified by the
better news coming from Khartum. While Baring admitted that
this policy was the only feasible one, there were difficulties in
enforcing it on the Egyptians. The Egyptian Government was
aware that they could not regain the Sudan by their own resources,
and that the British would not undertake the task, but they were
equally aware that if they agreed to withdraw without exhausting
all possible resources they would be for ever 'disgraced in the
opinion of the governing class of their countrymen and of the
Muhammadan world.' Cross said that Baring thought it better for
Britain rather than Egypt to ask the Turks to intervene. Baring did
not believe that a British application to the Turks would succeed,
but the refusal would have the advantage of relieving the Egyptians
of some of their difficulties and would remove those of Britain.
Egypt strongly disapproved any suggestion that Britain should
hand back the Sudan to the Turks.

When Granville asked Cross whether the abandonment of the
Sudan would be unpopular with the masses in Egypt, the latter
answered, 'that their first prayer was plenty of water, and their
second, to be saved from being sent to the Sudan. It was among
the influential and political classes that the loss of the Sudan was
unpopular.' The idea of the Bakers (Sir Samuel and Baker Pasha)

¹ Ibid.
² Memorandum on Cross's interview, by Granville, Dec. 29, 1883, P.R.O.,
G/D 29/146.

that Khartum was the key to Cairo was not at all accepted by Sir Evelyn Wood and General Stephenson. Colonel Watson, who had been with Colonel Gordon in the Sudan also took the latter view and believed that the inhabitants of the Sudan only wished 'to be left alone.' There was an English engineer in Egypt who thought there was a danger of the Nile being diverted from its course to the ruin of Egypt, but Cross thought it 'to be chimerical.'

Cross thought that while the Egyptian authorities were absolutely docile after Tel el-Kebir, they were beginning to be more difficult to manage. Ministers and provincial governors were saying that it would be quite logical, if the English were remaining, for them to undertake the care and responsibility of those 'foolish reforms,' for there was little point in their being enforced if the Egyptians were to be left to themselves. In answer to Granville's question whether the Egyptian Government would like the withdrawal of the British troops, Cross said that they 'would do anything to avoid it, and he agreed with me [Granville] that if we insisted upon any ministers or governors being dismissed, who did not follow the advice which we gave while we are occupying the country, it would be successful.'

The last two days of the year 1883 and the New Year's Day of 1884 brought alarming news to Baring from the Sudan. Mr. Power from Khartum and General Baker and Consul Baker from Sawakin informed him of the situation. Power reported that the general impression was growing in Khartum, among the Europeans and the loyal population, that they were 'either forgotten or abandoned'[1] by the Cairo Government. The state of affairs, in his opinion, was 'very desperate.' The latest news about the rebellion, about twenty-three days old, was that al-Mahdi was assembling a great force to march on the capital, and it was known that al-Ubayyid was only eleven days' journey from Khartum. The number of soldiers al-Mahdi could muster in the field was unknown, but the Government had a total force of 3,000 to hold a line of earthworks four miles long. On the fortifications were mounted some old bronze guns and one Krupp field-piece. In Power's opinion 3,000 soldiers could not even properly man the walls, and no reserve or relief was left to be moved to any threatened point in case of attack. Also no guard

[1] Power to Baring, Dec. 30, 1883, enclosed in Baring to Granville, No. 2, Jan. 1, 1884, P.R.O., F.O. 78/3665.

could be left in the city, which would be at the mercy of 'an undisguisedly rebel population.' The Government of Khartum was not strong enough to seize the well-known 'ringleaders or agents of al-Mahdi.'

This state of affairs, Power considered, was well known to the Cairo Government, but already about forty days had elapsed and they had not heard of a relief column. It seemed that people in Khartum were expecting Baker and Zubair to come to their relief. Power mentioned that Cairo had told them that Zubair and his Bedwins had left Cairo and that Baker had left for Sawakin via Suez. Power feared that 'in three days this town may be in the hands of the rebels'. He maintained that if Khartum fell Egypt would be the next victim, as al-Mahdi had announced his intention of sweeping across the Suez Canal into Arabia, and the people from Khartum to Asyut would be in arms to join him as he advanced. The people in Khartum, even those who pretended to be loyal to the Khedive, believed in the divine mission of al-Mahdi. Although Power testified to the indefatigable efforts of Ibrahim Haydar Pasha and Colonel de Coetlogon, yet he considered the odds to be against any successful resistance if al-Mahdi were to deliver a determined attack.

From Sawakin, Consul Baker sent a letter to Granville, on the 26th of December 1883, through Baring, expressing the opinion that the force there was 'totally inadequate'[1] for the task of dispersing the rebels around Sawakin and at the same time opening the road to Barbar. An intercepted letter from 'Uthman Diqna to the garrison of Tūkar stated that al-Mahdi intended shortly to proceed into Egypt and called upon the garrison to surrender. Throughout the letter a spirit of hostility was manifested to the Turks. General Baker, in a long letter to Baring, described the situation in the eastern Sudan and the impressions he had formed on his arrival. Although most of the letter[2] dealt with his suggestions for an understanding with Abyssinia and the route between Kasalah and Masawwa, yet his opinion of the inability of Egypt to hold the Sudan unaided made Baring more anxious to have definite instructions from Granville.

[1] Baring to Granville, No. 4, Jan. 1, 1884, P.R.O., F.O. 78/3665.
[2] Baker Pasha to Baring, Dec. 27, 1883, enclosed in Baring to Granville, No. 6, Jan. 2, 1884, P.R.O., F.O. 78/3665.

On New Year's Day 1884, therefore, Baring telegraphed to London asking that the Government's answer to his dispatch of the 22nd of December should not 'be delayed much longer. If the Egyptian Government is left to itself, I feel no doubt whatever that they will lose the whole of the Sudan.' If it had been decided no to give Indian or British assistance, it would be advisable for the Egyptian Government to decide at once to retire to Egypt proper. Stephenson and Wood when again consulted, concurred in this opinion. On the other hand, the present Egyptian Government lacked the energy and administrative ability necessary to carry out the abandonment, even if they readily accepted it. Baring once again repeated that its adoption would render the task of governing Egypt and organizing her defence far more difficult than before. 'If the policy of abandonment is carried out Her Majesty's Government should certainly be prepared to exercise a far more direct interference in the Government of Egypt than has hitherto been contemplated.' [1]

Before receiving this request Granville had already decided on the course to be submitted for Cabinet approval. The resolution to send no British or Indian troops was to be maintained.[2] He raised no objection to the employment of Turkish troops on condition that they did not increase the pecuniary difficulties of Egypt, and were to have their base at Sawakin. It was known that the Turks were most unlikely to agree to sending troops to the Sudan, and if they agreed it would be on conditions unacceptable to Egypt, and negotiations would indefinitely postpone the date of a decision which ought to be made at once.

Granville proposed to recommend the abandonment of the Sudan and the cessation of military operations there except for the rescue of outlying garrisons. The defence of Egypt at Aswan or Wadi Halfa, the maintenance of order in Egypt proper, and the defence of the ports of the Red Sea would be the duty of Her Majesty's Government. Secret instructions were to be sent to Baring empowering him to insist on being obeyed, and to secure the dismissal of ministers and governors of provinces who would pay no attention to the advice given by the occupying power.

[1] Baring to Granville, No. 7, Jan. 1, 1884, P.R.O., F.O. 78/3665.
[2] Granville to the Queen, Jan. 1, 1884, P.R.O., G/D 29/43.

Instructions to take measures against slavery by closing the markets were also to form part of the new policy.

On January 2nd Sharif called on Baring and expressed his anxiety for an answer to his note of some ten days earlier. In the course of conversation Baring gathered that Sharif had modified his views on the situation, and he therefore requested him to draw up a further note. Sharif prepared the note and submitted it to Baring on the same day.[1]

Sharif said that the news received from Baker Pasha indicated that the Egyptian forces at Sawakin could not cope with the insurrection in the eastern Sudan. If they were not to have any assistance from Her Majesty's Government they would be compelled to apply immediately to the Porte for 10,000 soldiers to be sent to Sawakin. If the Sultan did not comply with this request, they were determined to hand back to Turkey the shores of the Red Sea and eastern Sudan. Egypt would return to the frontiers of Muhammad 'Ali's time, and the Government would be able to concentrate in the Nile valley about 15,000 soldiers, which, Sharif thought, would be sufficient to maintain order in that restricted area. 'I earnestly beg you to submit these views to Her Majesty's Government in the name of His Highness and of his Government, and to request an early reply, which will put an end to our present state of uncertainty—uncertainty which exhausts us by increasing every day the difficulties we have to overcome.'

Baring 'entirely disbelieved'[2] that any Egypptian force could be collected to hold the valley of the Nile from Khartum downwards. In fact it was too late, for Baring had already asked for definite instructions owing to the alarming news from the Sudan, and Granville had actually prepared the instructions which included abandonment as a cardinal point, and was awaiting only the sanction of the Cabinet.

On January 4th the instructions were sent. Baring was informed that the conclusions reached on the question of the Sudan could not be modified. Britain raised no objection to the Khedive's application to the Porte to send troops to Sawakin provided that it would not increase the 'expenditure falling on the Egyptian Treasury or cause the Egyptian Government to delay coming to

[1] *Parl. Pap.* (1884), vol. lxxxviii, p. 181.
[2] Baring to Granville, No. 11, Jan. 2, 1884, P.R.O., F.O. 78/3665.

a decision as to the movements of their troops from the interior of the Sudan.'[1] No objection was raised to the handing back to the Porte of the Red Sea ports and eastern Sudan, if Turkey declined to send troops to the Sudan. Baring was further instructed to impress upon the Egyptian Government the great importance of their deciding on a policy without delay. It should be urged on the Khedive and his ministers with utmost earnestness that 'all military operations excepting those for the rescue of outlying garrisons should cease in the Sudan.' Assistance would certainly be given by the British naval forces for the protection of the Red Sea ports, and Egypt proper would be defended at Aswan or Wadi Halfa.

It was one thing to make clear Her Majesty's Government's policy on the Sudan and quite another thing to persuade the Egyptian Government under Sharif to accept it willingly and continue in office. Baring, in both private and official correspondence, had kept Granville well informed of the trend of Egyptian politics. Her Majesty's Government had, therefore, to consider how far their advice should be interpreted as a command in matters of importance if it meant the resignation of the Egyptian ministers. They had to give Baring a clear line of policy on this matter. From his interview with Cross, Granville knew that the mass of Egyptian people was indifferent to the abandonment of the Sudan and the only class that resented it was the ruling one. He also knew that there would be no evil consequences if the British Government insisted on being obeyed in matters of importance. Baring was therefore instructed that in matters in which the administration and safety of Egypt 'were at stake,'[2] it ought to be clearly understood that the advice tendered to the Khedive was to be followed as long as the 'provisional occupation of the country by English troops continues.' They certainly gave full consideration to the views of the Egyptian Government before giving advice. Ministers and governors of provinces were clearly to understand that responsibility, which for the time rested on Britain, obliged her to insist on the policy which she recommended, and it would be necessary that 'those ministers and governors who do not follow this course, should cease to hold their offices.' The British Government could

[1] Granville to Baring, No. 5, Jan. 4, 1884, P.R.O., F.O. 78/3662.
[2] Granville to Baring, No. 6, Secret, Jan. 4, 1884, P.R.O., F.O. 28/3662.

not contemplate the appointment of British ministers except with the greatest reluctance. They felt confident that in the event of a change of ministry Egyptians, whether already of the rank of minister, or occupying less prominent positions, would be found to carry out the policy of the Khedive based on the advice of Her Majesty's Government. Baring was assured, when making his representations on these questions, of 'the full support' of the British Government.

Surprisingly enough all the discussion of the Sudan question was concentrated on matters of policy alone. Argument was centered around the advisability or otherwise of the Egyptian Government's abandoning the Sudan or making a stand somewhere, the part Turkey should play, and whether Aswan or Wadi Halfa should mark the southernmost limits of Egypt proper. The difficulties of the retreat itself were either neglected altogether or their importance was minimized. But the man with an eye on the practical military aspect of the situation did not fall into that error. Lord Wolseley, Adjutant-General, on the day on which Baring received definite instructions to impose the abandonment policy, submitted a memorandum on the Sudan to Hartington suggesting that it should be forwarded to Granville.[1]

Wolseley emphasized the necessity for sending immediate orders to the English colonel, de Coetlogon, at Khartum, to effect the retreat of the garrison, after withdrawing, the scattered garrisons on the White Nile and possibly Sennar. He was to decide by which route the withdrawal should be made and was to be given the fullest particulars about conditions at Sawakin and its neighborhood, and along the Barbar—Sawakin road. Wolseley thought that it would be safest to keep to the Nile, and that the best soldiers from Wood's army should assist by occupying Wadi Halfa and that advance posts should be establised near the third cataract. Arrangements ought to be made with Abyssinia for withdrawing the troops from Kasalah and the garrisons on the Abyssinian side. The garrisons of western Sudan would have to make the best terms possible with the enemy and if they could march out and reach the Nile in Dongola they might do so. Communication with the Equatorial provinces would not be possible and there would be no alternative but to leave the forces there to their own resources

[1] Wolseley to Hartington, Jan. 4, 1884, P.R.O., G/D 29/170.

to make the best terms possible with the enemy. Anyway it was highly probable, in Wolseley's opinion, that al-Mahdi would leave them unmolested for the time being. If the Turks were to be allowed to occupy the ports of the Red Sea they should be restricted to those south of the line of latitude parallel to Wadi Halfa. He urged the Government to consider the details of the retreat: 'I need scarcely add that a retreat is always one of the most difficult of military operations and its dangers are immensely increased and intensified when it has to be carried out in face of an Eastern foe.' Yet Granville seems either to have tired of the question of the Sudan thinking that definite orders to evacuate relieved him of responsibility or to have thought it to be the responsibility of the Egyptian Government. Ultimately, it was the lack of appreciation of the practical difficulties of the situation, by the British Government and mainly by Granville, that complicated the question of the Sudan.

On January 6th Baring called on Sharif Pasha and handed him a letter explaining the views of Her Majesty's Government on the question of the Sudan. He then called on the Khedive and left with him a copy of the letter. The letter contained the purport of the final instructions he had received from the Foreign Office together with a review of the history of previous communications and conversations between him and Sharif from the 16th of December 1883. The letter ended by stating the final views of the British Government as being in favor of the concentration of Egyptian troops in the Sudan, but that they desired 'the withdrawal of the forces from the interior of the Sudan, including Khartum. I am instructed to insist on this point.' [1] In the course of conversation both with Sharif and with the Khedive, Baring informed them of his instructions to demand the acceptance of the British Government's advice in important matters affecting the safety of Egypt, and added that 'ministers must carry out that advice or forfeit office.' [2]

On the day on which he presented the letters to Sharif and the Khedive, Baring reported privately to Granville that he had endeavored to persuade Sharif not to resign but 'I do not think

[1] Baring to Sharif, Jan. 6, 1884, enclosed in Baring to Granville, No. 21, Jan. 6, 1884, P.R.O., F.O. 78/3665.
[2] Baring to Granville, No. 21, Jan. 6, 1884, P.R.O., F.O. 78/3665.

I have succeeded.'¹ There was also some talk of the Khedive's abdication but Baring did not think, from conversation with him, that there was any intention of his doing so.

Sharif had been determined to resign ever since the question of the Sudan became acute and Britain began to interfere more seriously in the matter. He was, however, kept in office longer than he really wished by his colleagues who spared no effort to hold on to their portfolios. They often dissuaded Sharif from resigning and endeavored to identify the Khedive with the cause of the ministry to such an extent that British insistence on the dismissal of the ministry would also mean the abdication of the Khedive. Thus, rumors were circulated that the Khedive was in complete agreement with his ministers and he would rather abdicate than disagree with them.² It was in this atmosphere that Baring viewed the future with misgiving and thought of the probability of employing English ministers because, to him, there was only very faint hope of finding Egyptians willing to co-operate.

The whole situation was changed by the unofficial efforts of Mr. Moberly Bell. *The Times* correspondent in Cairo. After Hicks's defeat Bell had favored Egypt's holding Khartum. After an interview with Baring, however, Bell completely changed his opinion. Some years later, Bell wrote, of his interview, to Baring:

. . . I remember perfectly well all the first part of our talk, in which you laid stress on the point that Egypt's interest in Khartum was to prevent it falling into other European hands, but that so long as there was no danger of that, the Sudanese might stew in their own juice, as there was no alternative. This made the most impression on me, because it converted me to your own view, as to which I had been rather sitting on the fence.³

Completely convinced by Baring's arguments, Bell set to work to convert the authorities, particularly the Khedive, to the policy of abandonment, and to persuade some Egyptians to take office, acting on British advice. When he first saw the Khedive he was shown a memorandum which was to be sent to the council of ministers, embodying His Highness's views. It had been drafted by Tigrane Pasha and suggested that England might provide a

¹ Baring to Granville, Private, Jan. 6, 1884, P.R.O., G/D 29/162.
² *The times,* Jan. 8, 1884.
³ E. H. C. Moberly Bell (his daughter), *The Life and Letters of C.F. Moberly Bell* (London, 1927), p. 91.

second line of defense at Dongola and that Egypt ought to hold Khartum. The Khedive gave Bell a positive assurance that no minister would accept office and give up Khartum, not even Nubar. From Tawfiq Bell went to Nubar and told him part of his conversation with the Khedive. Nubar considered that there was no question of abandoning the Sudan, because the Sudan had already abandoned Egypt. Bell inferred that Nubar might be ready to accept office. Bell's subsequent efforts are not recorded, but in a private letter, written after the crisis had passed, Bell stated that he was very much behind the scenes in all the events, and asserted that he had prevented the Khedive from 'making a fool of himself.' [1] The Khedive's change of attitude astonished Baring and the Egyptian ministers who 'thought that they had got him under their thumb.'

As was expected, Sharif decided to tender his resignation to the Khedive on the evening of January 7,[2] and on the 8th Baring officially reported that he had had an interview with the Khedive on the subject on the same day.[3] Baring was informed in that interview that the resignation of the ministers had been accepted, and that the Khedive 'accepted cordially the policy of abandonment of the whole of the Sudan,' which he believed to be the best in the interests of the country 'on mature reflection.' He further added that he 'had thorough confidence that any advice given by Her Majesty's Government would be in the true interest of Egypt.'

Riaz Pasha was asked to take office but declined, and Nubar readily agreed to form a ministry He entirely concurred 'in the wisdom of abandoning the Sudan,' [4] but he wished to retain possession of Sawakin. Baring wired privately to Granville after the storm had been successfully weathered, reporting most favorably on the Khedive's conduct. 'He is in very good humor and has beraved exceedingly well.' [5] Baring asked for 'something pleasant' to show the Khedive. 'He will do anything he is told.' There was a sigh of relief in the Foreign Office when native ministers, accepting the policy of abandonment, had been found. Granville

---

[1] Ibid., p. 92.
[2] Baring to Granville, No. 26, Jan. 7, 1884, P.R.O., F.O. 78/3665.
[3] Baring to Granville, No. 27, Jan. 8, 1884, P.R.O., F.O. 78/3665.
[4] Baring to Granville, No. 30, Jan. 8, 1884, P.R.O., F.O. 78/3665.
[5] Baring to Granville, Private, Jan. 8, 1884, P.R.O., G/D 29/162.

approved Baring's proceedings and received the information with 'much satisfaction.' [1]

In his letter of resignation Sharif stated that he considered it essential to protect Egypt and maintain tranquility by holding the Nile valley including Khartum. The eastern Sudan could be handed back to Turkey if circumstances made it necessary. He told how the British Government had insisted on abandonment and on the acceptance of their advice on important matters. He believed that to accept such a situation would interfere with the independence of His Highness's Government as well as with the responsibility of the ministers to His Highness. It would also alter the provisions of the rescript of August 28, 1878.[2] In spite of its confidential nature Tawfiq showed Sharif's letter of resignation to Baring who forwarded a translation of it to the Foreign Office. Pauncefote, Permanent Under-Secretary, minuted the dispatch: 'The letter is interesting as showing that one of the grounds of resignation is that the action of Her Majesty's Government interferes with the independence of the Khedive's Government.'

Once the policy of abandonment had been decided on and accepted, Her Majesty's Government had to take all necessary measures to defend Egypt from possible attack by al-Mahdi. It was unanimously agreed among the military authorities in Cairo that Aswan should be the place to check the advance from the south.[3] Sir Evelyn Wood in a memorandum[4] outlined the general line of military policy. He thought, for strategical and political reasons, that Aswan should be garrisoned, and that later, advance posts for observation should be established at Kurusko and possibly at Wadi Halfa. He urged that these measures should be taken before the intention to abandon Khartum was made known. When al-Mahdi began to march on Egypt it would be necessary to place a field force at Aswan and from there to defend the Nile valley between Wadi Halfa and al-Uxur. It might also be necessary, later, to place a field force in the vicinity of Asyut and to form a general reserve in Cairo. In estimating the forces required Wood thought

[1] Granville to Baring, No. 20, Jan. 9, 1884, P.R.O., F.O. 78/3662.
[2] Sharif's letter of resignation, enclosing in Baring to Granville, No. 38, Jan. 10, 1884, P.R.O., F.O. 78/3665.
[3] Baring to Granville, No. 25, Jan. 7, 1884, P.R.O., 78/3665.
[4] Memorandum by Sir Evelyn Wood enclosed in ibid.

it would depend on such factors as the state of public feeling and the strength of the Egyptian army even after its increase. His general idea was to station the Egyptian army at Aswan, with advance observation posts, and with the field-force at Asyut and the reserve at Cairo composed of British troops. British troops were to be posted at Asyut to command the roads leading to Cairo and to give moral support to the Egyptians at the frontier. Wood concluded by: 'but it will be in any case desirable to let the Khedive's army try conclusions with the invaders of Egypt before British troops are called upon for action.'

Stephenson concurred with Wood in the plan to move a portion of the Egyptian army towards the frontier at short notice when Khartum was threatened and before it was evacuated. He did not advise sending a force to any great distance beyond Aswan except for observational purposes. He thought that in the event of a reverse it would inspire the enemy and would excite religious feeling throughout Egypt and in all probability would produce a bad effect among the Egyptian troops.

On the day of Sharif's resignation news from Khartum received by the Khedive from Colonel de Coetlogon was somewhat alarming.[1] De Coetlogon expressed not only his own opinion in his picture of the situation, but both Husain Sirri Pasha, the deputy Governor-General, and Ibrahim Haydar Pasha, the commandant of the troops, concurred in his report. There were only two alternatives in their opinion: either to reinforce Khartum with a large force immediately, or to order the retreat of both the Sennar and the Khartum garrisons on Barbar. One-third of the Khartum garrison was so demoralized as to be a danger, and could not be used even to suppress the disloyal inhabitants. These men were, therefore, to be classed with the rebels. Even if it was decided to send reinforcements it would take them about two months to be assembled at Khartum and by that time retreat would be impossible. De Coetlogon therefore urged the Khedive to give 'an immediate order for retreat.' He maintained that even if the forces at the disposal of the Government were twice their actual size, Khartum could not hold out against the whole country which was beyond any doubt 'one and all against' them. That retreat would be a choice of the

---

[1] De Coetlogon to Khedive, Jan. 7, 1884, enclosed in Baring to Granville, No. 35, Jan. 9, 1884, P.R.O., F.O. 78/3665.

lesser evil, as undoubtedly Sennar and Khartum would be lost, but His Highness's army, or at least the greater part of it, would be saved from destruction. The difficulties of the retreat itself could not be underestimated, but if it were ordered at once it could be effected with comparative safety. 'It is unpleasant for me,' de Coetlogon concluded, 'to have to urge this course on your Highness, but I consider I should fail in my duty to you if I did not place the true situation before you.' Forwarding this letter to London, when Nubar had accepted office and the ministerial crisis was over, Baring remarked that if any doubts remained as to the necessity of adopting the abandonment policy they should be 'entirely removed' by that 'unanimous expression of opinion' by the chief Government officials in Khartum. He further stated that preliminary instructions had been given to prepare for a retreat. When the new Minister of War arrived he would issue more definite orders.

The prophecies of de Coetlogon and the others began very soon to be realized. On the 9th of January Power reported to *The Times*[1] that the telegraph line between Khartum and Sennar had been cut and that it was reported that some 5,000 of the rebels were harassing the country at a few hours' distance from the capital. al-Mahdi's brother-in-law was leading the revolt in al-Jazirah and the Shayqiya, who formed one-third of the garrison, were disaffected. The following day Power reported that the Mudir of Khartum had returned from his short trip towards al-Jazirah and had found the telegraph poles pulled down all along the way from the capital to Sennar. His intelligence confirmed that all the shaikhs had declared for al-Mahdi. A native was arrested in Khartum trying to buy large quantities of gun-powder and percussion caps. Power once more reported the untrustworthiness of about half the garrison and the general grumbling among the soldiers because their pay was much in arrears.

On the 11th of January Baring reported to London[2] that the Governor of Khartum had been authorized to make preparations for sending to Barbar women, children, and all those of the civil population who were able to leave Khartum, with orders to assemble the outlying garrisons. The gravity of the situation and the opinions

---

[1] *The Times,* Jan. 11, 1884.
[2] Baring to Granville, No. 44, Jan. 11, 1884, P.R.O., F.O. 78/3665.

formed by the residents of Khartum were expressed much better in a private letter by Power to his mother. 'They have done nothing for us yet from Cairo. They are leaving it all to fate and the rebels around us are growing stronger.'[1] By the 14th of January Power reported that all the people on both sides of the Blue Nile between Khartum and Sennar had declared for al-Mahdi, and communication with the latter town was cut off. Steamers carrying dispatches and soldiers to Sennar had returned having proceeded only a short distance beyond Khartum.[2]

The ministers in Cairo laid down the details of the withdrawal six days after they had taken office. It was decided that 'Abd al-Qadir, the Minister of War, should proceed in person to Khartum 'to superintend the withdrawal of the garrison'[3] from the Sudan. It was recognized that the operation would be one of great difficulty, for in addition to the troops a large number of civil employees, women, and children would have to be evacuated. It was also known that a considerable portion of the civil population would wish to leave the country. The decision to put the high command in the hands of 'Abd al-Qadir Pasha was considered to be the best possible. He knew the country and was a brave and competent officer. Further difficulties of the task were explained by Baring in a private letter to Granville.[4] They included the great distance to be traversed, the scarcity of provisions, the impossibility of sending steamers up the Nile at that time of the year, and the unreliability of the tribes along the Nile valley. Baring also envisaged the financial difficulties and the amount of money which might be spent on the retreat, although it would, of course, be less than would be spent in the attempt to keep the Sudan.

On January 16 Nubar Pasha, after a lengthy consultation with 'Abd al-Qadir Pasha, Wood, Stephenson, and Baring, sent telegrams to the sub-Governor of Khartum with orders to carry out the policy of abandonment. The sub-Governor was instructed to communicate with Sennar by all possible means and to inform the authorities there to withdraw on Khartum bringing the civil servants and such people who wished to leave in addition to the

[1] Power, Frank. *Letters From Khartum*, p. 72.
[2] *The Times, Jan.* 15, 1884.
[3] Baring to Granville, No. 52, Jan. 14, 1884, P.R.O., F.O. 78/3665.
[4] Baring to Granville, Private, Jan. 14, 1884, P.R.O., G/D 29/162.

garrison. Khartum would be held for the time being in order to facilitate that withdrawal. He was also ordered to communicate with the Bahr al-Ghazal and Equatorial authorities, informing them of the situation, and that no reinforcement would be sent to them. Their course of action was left entirely to their discretion.[1]

The next day these instructions were slightly modified. The sub-Governor was ordered to leave to the discretion of the senior authority in Sennar the decision to withdraw to Khartum along the Blue Nile or along the Abyssinian frontier via Kasalah to Masawwa. The sub-Governor of Khartum was to be informed which route was being taken. As to Bahr al-Ghazal and Equatoria, according to Mr. Bohndorf who had recently arrived at Khartum, the only available route would, in his opinion, be via Zanzibar. Finally, he was instructed to send an estimate to the authorities in Cairo of the number of people wishing to leave Khartum.[2]

Nubar sent a third lengthy telegram giving more detailed instructions for the withdrawal of the Khartum garrison and people. By that time the Cairo authorities had received Baker Pasha's suggestion for withdrawal to the east via Abu Haraz, Kasalah, and Masawwa. The authorities at Khartum were told that Cairo would give no opinion on that suggestion, but would rather leave the decision to them whether to try and beat the rebels on the Blue Nile and withdraw to Abu Haraz or whether to go northwards as previously arranged. In deciding on the course to adopt they should, however, take into consideration that it might be impossible to open the Sawakin-Barbar route and that the Nile route would be the only one available. Nevertheless, they were instructed to send north all the civil servants and non-combatants who might wish to leave and for whom transport could be found. It was desirable that such food as could be spared should be carried with them as Barbar Province might be short of food. Non-combatants should be left to proceed by themselves if no risk would be incurred, but if there was any danger, such soliders as would secure their safe conduct were to be employed, remembering that Khartum itself should be held until the withdrawal of

[1] Nubar to sub-Governor, Khartum, Jan. 16, 1884, enclosed in Baring to Granville, No. 79, Jan. 19, 1884, P.R.O., F.O. 78/3665.

[2] Nubar to sub-Governor, Khartum, Jan. 17, 1884, enclosed in Baring to Granville, No. 79, Jan. 19, 1884, P.R.O., F.O. 78/3665.

the Sennar garrison. Husain Pasha Khalifah, the Mudir of Barbar, was told to induce the Bedwins to furnish camels and supplies on payment, and to do the same between Khartum and Barbar. Although it was the Khedive's wish to withdraw non-combatants at once, the people on the spot were to do their utmost to prevent panic and disorder.[1] These were the last orders about the evacuation of Khartum which the Egyptian Government sent to the Khartum authorities.

It was clear, then, that although the evacuation of the Khartum garrison and of those civilians who wished to go, was sanctioned, yet it was thought desirable to delay it until the withdrawal of the Sennar garrison to Khartum or to Masawwa via Kasalah. The postponement, therefore, of the retreat from Khartum, until it was later made impossible, was due mainly to associating it with the withdrawal from Sennar.

[1] Nubar to sub-Governor, Khartum, Jan. 18, 1884, enclosed in Baring to Granville, No. 79, Jan. 19, 1884, P.R.O., F.O., 78/3665.

VII

GORDON'S MISSION

It was only natural that Gordan's name should appear in official correspondence as soon as the British settled in Egypt after Tel el-Kebir, and especially when there was news of the rebellion in the Sudan. Gordon was the greatest of the few Englishmen who had real experience of Sudanese affairs. He had spent more than five years of his life there, first as governor of Equatoria Province, and later as governor-general over all the vast expanse of the Sudan, and was entrusted with immense power and confidence by Khedive Isma'il. His intimate knowledge and great experience was due not only to his having been governor-general, but to the many months he had spent trekking through the remote parts of his dominion.

Sir Charles Wilson's second memorandum on the question of the Sudan in October 1882 suggested Gordon as the most suitable man to reduce the country to order in a few months, if he could be persuaded to take up his old appointment of governor-general.[1] The Foreign Office asked Malet how Gordon could be employed. Malet replied, pointing out that it was Wilson's suggestion and not that of the Egyptian Government, who had no intention of employing him unless pressed to do so.[2] There the matter rested for the time being.

On the 17th of November 1882 Sir Harry Verney wrote to Granville suggesting the employment of Gordon in the Sudan: 'He has always exercised a very remarkable influence over wild, uncontrollable, uncivilized peoples.' Sir Harry urged that Gordon should be immediately approached as he was likely to go to Palestine unless work was offered him by the Government.[3] On the day on which Verney wrote to Granville the latter discussed Egyptian problems with Gordon. Gordon thought that a force of 8,000 men with English officers on the active list, without Baker

[1] Memorandum by Sir Charles Wilson, Oct. 28, 1882, enclosed in Malet to Granville, No. 744, Oct. 28, 1882, P.R.O., F.O. 78/3442.
[2] Malet to Granville, No. 750, Nov. 1, 1882, P.R.O., F.O. 78/3442.
[3] Sir Harry Verney to Granville, Nov. 17, 1882, P.R.O., G/D 29/168.

Pasha, would be the best form for an Egyptian army. The Egyptian police, in his opinion, had always been very good. To him the insurrection in the Sudan 'had been immensely exaggerated.' The proper thing to do, he advised, was to appoint Sir Charles Wilson as governor-general and he would find no more difficulties than he (Gordon) had. About slavery his advice centers round introducing the system of registration, but not pressing the Khedive to issue an edict against it, as it would be exceedingly unpopular and would be a dead letter.[1]

Towards the end of the same month, the possibility of Gordon's going to the Sudan was still being discussed. Northbrook wrote to Granville doubting very much whether Gordon would go to the Sudan again and whether it would 'be wise to try him.'[2] He restated Gordon's idea that Sir Charles Wilson would be the best man. In December of the same year, when the Queen was shown all the papers connected with the Sudan, she expressed her anxiety about it. Although she did not wish that Englishmen should go there, yet she believed that Baker or Gordon might settle the revolt in two months.[3] The year closed without the Government's appointing an Englishman to the Sudan and it was thought best to send Stewart to report on the whole question.

The suggestion of employing Gordon was not raised again until after the annihilation of Hicks's army. The suggestion came from Colonel Bevan Edwards in a letter to Sir A. Clarke, who was to forward it to the Government with his comments. Edwards thought that the only man capable of dealing with the question of the Sudan was Charles Gordon.[4] He thought it unlikely that Gordon would accept work directly under the Khedive, but might perhaps go if asked to assist the Khedive, working directly under the Government at home. 'His name alone would do wonders, but no time should be lost.' He should be given supreme power with the local rank of Lieutenant-General in the British army. Edwards even suggested putting at Gordon's disposal a division from India

---

[1] Memorandum by Granville on his conversation with Gordon, Nov. 18, 1882, P.R.O., G/D 29/168.

[2] Northbrook to Granville, Nov. 23, 1882, P.R.O., G/D 29/138.

[3] Ponsonby to Granville, Dec. 24, 1882. Also Ponsonby to Sanderson on the same day, P.R.O., G/D 29/41.

[4] Childers, S., The Life and Correspondence of the Right Hon. Hugh C. E. Childers 1827-1896, vol. i, p. 176.

composed of two European and four or five native battalions. 'By making Gordon supreme, he will settle the matter for them in a way that no one else would.' If an announcement were made that British troops would not be withdrawn, but would be reinforced, if necessary, and that Gordon was appointed with authority to ask for a contingent from India, all would be well in the Sudan.

Clarke, in forwarding the letter to Childers, Chancellor of the Exchequer, added that if England were to intervene his advice would be to 'place the whole affair without reserve in Gordon's hands. If the Mahdi is a prophet, Gordon in the Sudan is a greater . . .' On receiving the suggestion from Childers, Granville replied expressing his approval of the idea and saying that, pending consultation with Gladstone, it would be wired to Baring.[1] Granville then telegraphed to Gladstone asking him whether he had any objection to Gordon's being employed in the Sudan.[2] 'He has immense name in Egypt. He is popular at home.' When Gladstone raised no objection Granville telegraphed to Baring asking whether Gordon, if willing to go, would be of any use to him or to the Egyptian Government, and 'if so in what capacity?'[3] Baring replied immediately declaring that the Egyptian Government was 'much averse to employing General Gordon'[4] because the movement in the Sudan was a religious one; the appointment of a Christian to such a post of command would result in alienating those tribes who had remained loyal to the Government. Baring considered it best to 'leave the whole responsibility of the affairs of the Sudan to the Egyptian Government,' and not to press the subject any further.

When the employment of Gordon in the Sudan was again suggested, it had been decided to abandon the Sudan, and Gordon himself had been appointed to the Congo in the service of the King of the Belgians. When the negotiations with the King were complete, Gordon asked permission of the British Government to take up service in a foreign country. The Secretary of State for War consulted the Foreign Office on both the principle and that specific case. The Foreign Office thought that permission

[1] Granville to Childers, Nov. 27, 1883, P.R.O., G/D 29/118.
[2] Granville to Gladstone, Nov. 27, 1883, B.M. Add. MS. 44176.
[3] Granville to Baring, No. 117, Dec. 1, 1883, P.R.O., F.O. 78/3561.
[4] Baring to Granville, No. 576, Dec. 2, 1883, P.R.O., F.O. 78/3560.

should be refused as it might involve Britain in international complications.[1] Granville agreed but consulted Gladstone, who replied that he had 'no means to judge. Certainly no cause to dissent.'[2] Granville finally replied to Hartington that he disapproved of an officer on full pay 'being connected with this non-descript association.'[3] Harrington accordingly telegraphed to Gordon, who was in Palestine; 'The Secretary of State declines to sanction the arrangement.'[4] When it was received by Gordon, the message read 'decides' in place of 'declines.' Gordon therefore went to Belgium and completed his arrangements with the King. On the War Office ruling set forth in their telegram, Gordon would lose his British rank and pension if he enlisted in the service of the King of the Belgians.

Feeling that it was unfair for his brother to lose his pension, Sir Henry Gordon wrote to Granville's secretary drawing attention to the War Office decision.[5] In reply he was told that the question was primarily one which concerned the War Office, and it had not as yet come before the Foreign Secretary.[6] This was not true, and Granville himself admitted that he had given wrong information, because he had forgotten about Gordon and the Congo.[7]

When Lord Hartington heard that Gordon had accepted employment under the King of the Belgians contrary to the Government's decision, he decided to advise Gordon privately to resign his commission and to retire without pension under the administrative regulations.[8] If he declined to retire, he would have to be removed. Granville, while admitting the soundness of the principle that a general on full pay should not accept such employment, thought the penalty too severe and that it would be awkward to quarrel with 'so deservedly popular a man.'[9] Granville mentioned in this letter to Hartington that Baring had been asked whether Gordon would be of use to Egypt. So far, the mistake in the telegram sent to Gordon had not been discovered.

[1] Paunefote's opinion, Oct. 16, 1883, P.R.O., G/D 29/168.
[2] Gladstone's minute on ibid.
[3] Granville to Gladstone, Jan. 14, 1884, P.R.O., G/D 29/128. This letter reviews the whole problem.
[4] Ibid.
[5] Sir Henry Gordon to Sanderson, Jan. 4, 1884, P.R.O., G/D 29/168.
[6] Sanderson to Sir Henry Gordon, Jan. 7, 1884, P.R.O., G/D 29/168.
[7] Granville to Hartington, Jan. 9, 1884, P.R.O., G/D 29/134.
[8] Hartington to Granville, Jan. 8, 1884, P.R.O., G/D 29/134.
[9] Granville to Hartington, Jan. 9, 1884, P.R.O., G/D 29/134.

Gordon's Mission 171

Hartington saw in the new ministry in Egypt a way out of his difficulties about Gordon. Nubar Pasha was known to be a friend of Gordon and might be more willing than Sharif to employ him.[1] Wolseley thought Gordon's employment would be most desirable, but it was known that Baring did not like him.

By now Hartington had received Gordon's resignation and found no possible compromise between accepting it and approving his employment. An officer on full pay, in his opinion, ought to be at the disposal of the Government which possessed the right to his services and might require them at any moment. If he were allowed to accept other employment it was because it was sanctioned by the Government as being of advantage to the public service. The present circumstances might have changed Baring's opinion about Gordon's employment in Egypt and Hartington wondered whether it was worth while asking Baring again. He believed that people thought 'highly of the value he would be of there.' Gordon's resignation could not be accepted until the Foreign Office had replied. Hartington thought that while Gordon was unlikely to create difficulties, for he understood the necessity of resignation, it would not be generally understood and would be unpopular.[2]

Acting on Hartington's suggestion, therefore, Granville telegraphed on the same day to Baring again suggesting that Gordon or Sir Charles Wilson should be employed by the Egyptian Government. Baring again replied in the negative.[3] The position, therefore, was that the British Government were uncomfortable about Gordon's employment in the Congo, public opinion was clamoring for him to be sent to the Sudan, while the Egyptian Government, through Baring, definitely refused his services. Meanwhile, Gordon had written to his friend Wolseley announcing his arrival at Southampton and his impending departure for West Africa, and requesting him to help him in the matter of his pension. Wolseley wired to him to come and see him at the War Office on the 15th of January.[4]

Notwithstanding Baring's refusal, the weight of opinion in favor of Gordon's employment in the Sudan was so great that the

[1] Hartington to Granville, Jan. 10, 1884, P.R.O., G/D 29/134.
[2] Hartington to Granville, Jan. 10, 1884, P.R.O., G/D 29/134.
[3] Baring to Granville, No. 43, Jan. 11, 1884, P.R.O., F.O. 78/3665.
[4] Maurice, Sir F., and Arthur, Sir George, *The Life of Lord Wolseley* (London, 1924), p. 172.

Government decided to find out from Gordon himself whether he would be willing to go to the Sudan if it were possible to employ him there. It was arranged that it should be made known whether Gordon had simply refused or had asked for a considerable force, such as he had mentioned in 'rather a foolish letter' [1] in *The Times* of that day. If Gordon believed that he could, by his personal influence, induce the tribes to 'escort the Khartum garrison and inhabitants to Sawakin a little pressure on Baring might be advisable.' Granville very much deprecated the destruction of 'these poor people.' which would certainly be a great disaster and if it happened would create a great sensation both at home and abroad. Hartington and Granville further agreed that if Gordon refused to go to Egypt, the objection to his service in the Congo would be withdrawn. It might be explained that they had sufficient grounds for objecting, but that as Gordon had made his agreement with the King of the Belgians on the assumption that the War Office approved, he might be allowed to retain his rank for it would be a pity to lose such a distinguished officer. Only then was the mistake in the telegram discovered.

At the meeting between Wolseley and Gordon, Wolseley persuaded Gordon to give up the Congo plan of which he, Wolseley, had never approved. Gordon was told then that the Government 'wanted to evacuate the Sudan' [2] and the situation there was thoroughly discussed. In reply to Wolseley's question as to what he would do if he had the direction of affairs, Gordon stated that he would send himself out direct to Sawakin without passing through Cairo. Then he set on paper the terms on which he would be willing to go. He could not give definite advice to the Government until he had seen the situation for himself. It is curious to note that his behavior when he was employed was the reverse of his declaration. Elaborate plans and suggestions were formulated as soon as he left Charing Cross station and when he actually arrived at Khartum batches of correspondence indicated his plans for dealing with the Sudan problem. Gordon thought it possible that he might ask the Government 'to appoint him governor-general of the Sudan' with some expenditure of money, or alternatively that he might recom-

[1] Granville to Gladstone, Jan. 14, 1884, P.R.O., G/D 29/128.
[2] Maurice and Arthur, loc. cit.

mend absolute and immediate withdrawal.[1] But he could give no
final opinion until he had seen things for himself. In a note of the
meeting, Hartington pressed the urgency of the matter.

Gordon himself drew up the following plan:

1. To proceed to Sawakin and report on military situation of Sudan and
   return. Under Baring for orders and to communicate through him
   better be under flying seal.
2. Government not indebted beyond money and £3 per diem travelling
   expenses.
3. Notify public.
4. Nubar and Baring to be notified as to give all assistance, telegraph
   and etc.
5. Admiral Hewett to give me an account up to £500 and to be accounted
   for.
6. Letter to me saying leave is given me to go to Congo after my mission
   to Sawakin.
7. I understand Her Majesty's Government only wish me to report and
   in no way bound to me.
8. Telegraph Egypt to Government to send Ibrahim Bey Fawzi to meet
   me at Suez with a writer to attend on me.[1]

It remained now for Granville to approve the substance of that
arrangement and to ask Baring for his opinion. In a private telegram Granville told Baring that he had heard indirectly that
Gordon was ready to go straight to Sawakin without passing
through Cairo 'on the following [rather vague] terms.'[3] His mission
was to report to Her Majesty's Government on the military situation of the Sudan and to return without any further engagement.
He could receive instructions through Baring and would communicate through him under flying seal. It was for both Nubar and
Baring to give Gordon every assistance and facilities and he (Gordon) would like Ibrahim Fawzi to meet him at Suez with a writer.
'[He might be of use in informing you and us of the situation. It
would be popular at home, but there may be countervailing objections.] Tell me your [real] opinion [with or without consultation
with Nubar].'[4]

[1] Note by Hartington, Jan. 15, 1884, B.M. Add. MS. 44147.
[2] Note by Hartington, Jan. 15, 1884, B.M. Add MS. 44147.
[3] Granville to Baring, Jan. 15, 1884, P.R.O., G/D 29/200.
[4] This private telegram was redrafted, omitting all the words in brackets, and
made into an official dispatch on Jan. 26, 1884. Granville to Baring, No. 31B,
Jan. 15, 1884, P.R.O., F.O. 78/3662.

When Gladstone was shown this telegram to Baring he 'found no fault' with it, but made several comments all dealing with the avoidance of taking any responsibility for Sudanese affairs.[1] He thought that while Gordon's opinion would be of great value the Government should be careful in any instructions which were to be given him. Gladstone feared that Gordon might 'shift the center of gravity' of responsibility for the Sudan on to Britain. Gordon should not be the judge, in Gladstone's view, of the advice given and should not commit the Government by 'advice officially given.' He saw the extreme difficulty of rejecting his advice after sending him. It should, therefore, be made clear to Gordon that he was not the agent of Her Majesty's Government for the purpose of 'advising on that point.'

Granville took great pains drafting his private telegram to Baring about the employment of Gordon, for Baring had twice refused his services. Granville emphasized the popularity at home of such an appointment and Gordon's willingness to proceed immediately to Sawakin, but at the same time he did not wish to impose Gordon on Baring. Granville was, therefore, greatly relieved to receive an official telegram from Baring saying that the Egyptian Government would 'feel greatly obliged'[2] if Her Majesty's Government would select a well-qualified British officer to go to Khartum and conduct the evacuation. That officer would be given supreme power. Originally 'Abd al-Qadir Pasha, the Minister of War, had been appointed to conduct the withdrawal, but he had declined after disagreeing on points of detail, but the telegrams crossed. It is worth noting that the Egyptian Government had specifically asked for a British officer to conduct the retreat of the garrisons and the inhabitants who wished to leave the Sudan. Gordon, on the other hand, had suggested to Wolseley that he should be appointed to report on the situation, and Gladstone had interpreted this to mean that it would not involve the British Government in Sudanese affairs or commit them to a line of action. If he were to be under the orders of the Egyptian Government, there was no point in the mission which he had suggested. It would have been logical to have cancelled that mission altogether and let Gordon go ahead with the practical task of evacuating the Egyp-

---

[1] Gladstone to Granville, Jan. 16, 1884, P.R.O., G/D 29/127.
[2] Baring to Glanville, No. 58, Jan. 16, 1884, P.R.O., F.O. 78/3665.

tians from the Sudan. It was Granville's attempt to combine the two which introduced an element of vagueness at the very start.

In a private telegram Baring declared that 'Gordon would be the best man' if he would 'pledge himself' to carry out the policy of withdrawal from the Sudan. Baring also emphasized the importance of impressing on Gordon that he was to take his instructions from the British representative in Cairo and to report to him.[1] Baring told Granville that he would have Gordon rather than anyone else, on condition that there was 'a perfectly clear understanding' with him as to his position and the policy which he was to carry out. Failing Gordon, Baring said he would prefer Sir Charles Wilson, though the Khedive did not like him, and, failing Wilson, Stewart. 'Whoever goes,' concludes Baring, 'should be distinctly warned that he will undertake a service of danger and difficulty.'

The ministers, especially Hartington and Granville, were thus relieved of their troubles both with Gordon's proposed Congo appointment and with the Sudan. In a private letter to Baring, Granville expressed his pleasure at Baring's approval of Gordon, and maintained that he might possibly be of great use to Baring and that his appointment would be popular with 'many classes in this country.' Baring was also told that Gordon had praised him very highly and had expressed a wish to be placed entirely under him. Gordon at first wished to be allowed to report in favor of retention of the Sudan should it appear more desirable than an early avacuation. 'But he now perfectly understands that our decision in final.'[2] At that time, Gordon did not wish to see the Khedive, although he spoke well of Nubar. It was feared in London that friction might arise between Baker and Gordon. Should that happen, Baring was instructed to devise something to put Gordon in the more commanding position. Baring was asked to discuss the slavery question with Gordon. 'I shall be curious,' Granville concluded, 'to get your first telegram after the interview.'

When the details of Gordon's mission had been arranged and he was on his way to Egypt, Baring wrote privately to Granville expressing his views on the subject.[3] He considered the mission

[1] Baring to Granville, Jan. 16, 1884, P.R.O., G/D 29/162.
[2] Granville to Baring, Jan. 18, 1884, P.R.O., G/D 29/200.
[3] Baring to Granville, Jan. 21, 1884, P.R.O., G/D 29/162.

to be an experiment, and that it was impossible to say beforehand how it would turn out. It was satisfactory that Gordon should be under his instructions, but Baring doubted very much whether 'a man who habitually consults the prophet Isaiah when he is in difficulty' would be prepared to obey the orders of anyone. Baring thought that Gordon might clash with Baker, and, moreover, that he might not be able to reach Khartum if he insisted on going via Sawakin. Moreover he ought to see the Khedive, and his dislike for him was 'rather silly,' Baring believed that Gordon would be of great use if he went to Khartum to organize the retreat and to establish some sort of rough government under the tribal chiefs. Gordon would be able to establish a government, if he did not press the slave question too hard. In Baring's opinion, effective abolition of slavery could only be attained by the occupation of the country by the British army. Baring hoped to be able to draw up a plan with Gordon, which would be in harmony with the Government's policy.

On January 18 Gordon was summoned to a hurriedly called meeting with some Cabinet ministers. Gladstone, who was at Hawarden, was informed of the meeting by Granville who telegraphed: 'As Gordon was ready to start to-night, Hartington, Northbrook, Dilke and I settled that he should go accompanied by Colonel Stewart. He has instructions.'[1] Gladstone wired back his 'concurrence'[2] in their action. Baring was notified officially of Gordon's instructions and that he would proceed that night to Egypt accompanied by Lieutenant-Colonel Stewart to 'report to Her Majesty's Government on the state of affairs in the Sudan.'[3] It was confirmed that he would be under Baring's instructions and would perform 'such other duties beyond those specified in my despatch' as might be entrusted to him by the Egyptian Government through Baring. Baring was further asked to make arrangements for meeting Gordon at Ismailia, as he was anxious not to go through Cairo, and to discuss with him whether he should go direct to Sawakin, or go himself to Khartum via the Nile or dispatch Colonel Stewart there.

Baring also received a letter from Northbrook reporting the

[1] Granville to Gladstone, Jan. 18, 1884, P.R.O., G/D 29/128.
[2] Gladstone to Granville, Jan. 19, 1884, P.R.O., G/D 29/128.
[3] Granville to Baring, No. 40, Jan. 18, 1884, P.R.O., F.O. 78/3662.

decision of the meeting that Gordon should leave that night for Sawakin, 'to report on the best way of withdrawing garrisons, settling the country, and to perform such other duties as may be entrusted to him by the Khedive's Government through you.'[1] According to Northbrook, Gordon did not believe in the great power of al-Mahdi, or that tribes would not go beyond their own confines, and he could not see why the garrison should not escape. 'He did not seem at all anxious to retain the Sudan and agreed heartily to accept the policy of withdrawal.'

Sir Charles Dilke wrote that he had suddenly been summoned to a meeting at the War Office with Hartington, Granville, Northbrook, and Gordon. Gordon stated that the danger at Khartum was 'grossly exaggerated' and that the two Englishmen there had 'lost their heads.'[2] He would be able to bring away the garrisons without difficulty. The decision as recorded by Dilke was for Gordon to go to Sawakin 'to collect information and report on the situation in the Sudan.' It was also understood that if he found himself able to do so he should go to Barbar. Lord Selborne, a member of the Cabinet who was not present at that meeting, wrote that although he was not consulted about Gordon's mission, nobody objected to it and he did not suppose that any objection would have been raised at the time if all the ministers had been consulted. Gordon seemed to be the 'right man in the right place; and we thought that, if there was anything which could usefully be done, he would find the way to do it.'[3] Gordon's record of the meeting declared that the ministers asked whether he was prepared to evacuate the Sudan and that he had agreed to do so.[4]

After the meeting, Hartington made a note of eight points raised by Gordon. They dealt with matters of pay and expenses for him and Stewart, the cypher to be supplied to him for communication with Baring, and a confirmation that he might go to the Congo after completing his mission in the Sudan and might remain on the active list. Other points dealt with arrangements for Ibrahim Fawzi and a writer to meet him at Suez, also for him to pass

[1] Mallet, Sir Bernard, *Thomas George, Earl of Nothbrook, A Memoir*, p. 177.
[2] Gwynn, S. L., and Tuckwell, Gertrude M., *The Life of the Rt. Hon. Sir Charles W. Dilke, Bart., M.P.*, vol. ii, p. 29.
[3] Palmer, Roundell, Earl of Selborne, *Memorials*, vol. ii, p. 137.
[4] Allen, Bernard M., *Gordon and the Sudan* (London, 1931), p. 229.

directly through the canal to Sawakin, and for Baring to meet him at Ismailia. In the last, and most important point, Gordon stated: 'I wish the appointment to be announced in Egypt that I am on my way to Khartum to settle future settlement of Sudan to the best advantage of the people.'[1] It was left to Granville to see that Gordon's eighth point was carried into effect.

Gordon's final instructions were drawn up in the Foreign Office and handed to him on the day of the meeting, January 18, the day on which he left England. They provided for Gordon to proceed to Egypt at once to report to Her Majesty's Government on the military situation in the Sudan and on the measures which it might be advisable to take for the security of the Egyptian garrisons still occupying positions in that country, and for the safety of the European population in Khartum. He was also requested to consider and report upon the best methods of carrying out the evacuation of the interior of the Sudan and upon the manner in which the safety and good administration of the Red Sea ports could best be secured. He was also asked to pay special consideration to the steps that might usefully be taken to counteract the possible stimulus which it was feared might be given to the slave-trade by the policy of the withdrawal of Egyptian authority from the interior. It was definitely mentioned in these instructions that he should consider himself working under the instructions of the British Consul-General in Cairo through whom his reports should be forwarded under a flying seal. He was also 'to perform such other duties as the Egyptian Government' might desire to entrust to him, which were to be communicated to him by Baring. The question of his going direct to Sawakin was left for him to arrange with Baring.[2]

Gordon's appointment to the Sudan was received with satisfaction by the British Government, by the Queen, and by public opinion. Her Majesty was 'much relieved'[3] to hear that Gordon was going to Egypt, but she wondered whether it might not be 'too late.' She trusted that he would be put in communication with Sir Evelyn Wood. The press received the news with the greatest approval, and *The Times* considered it 'a welcome sur-

[1] Hartington to Granville, Jan. 18, 1884, P.R.O., G/D 29/134.
[2] Granville to Baring, General Gordon No. 1, Jan. 18, 1884, P.R.O., F.O. 78/3696.
[3] Queen to Granville, Jan. 18, 1884, P.R.O., G/D 29/43.

prise'[1] to learn of Gordon's departure not for the Congo but for Egypt. He was called 'the Englishman best acquainted with the affairs of the Sudan.' Some Cabinet ministers, together with Wolseley, saw Gordon off from Charing Cross station. At the last moment, when the train was leaving, Wolseley asked Gordon whether he had any money. After searching through his pockets he could produce only a few shillings, and Wolseley therefore insisted that Gordon should take his watch and chain.[2]

It is interesting to see the part played by the English Press in sending Gordon to the Sudan. The influence of the press should not, however, be over-estimated. Since October 1882 the name of Gordon was constantly brought to the notice of the Government. Early in 1884 there appeared in *The Times* a letter from Sir Samuel Baker suggesting Gordon's appointment as High Commissioner for the Sudan. At the same time Gordon received a letter from Baker urging him to communicate his views on the Sudan to the press. Gordon replied that his inner voice warned him against doing that and that he would not 'go to the Sudan for I feel it is too late.'[3] On January 5 *The Times* expressed regret that the Foreign Office should make Gordon resign his commission in the army, which would lose one of its best officers.

On January 8 the editor of the *Pall Mall Gazette* interviewed Gordon, who, after some hesitation, gave his opinion on the Sudan, declaring his opposition to evacuation, which was most difficult to execute. On the 9th the same paper published an account of the interview and demanded that Gordon should be sent to the Sudan with absolute power. On the 10th the *Morning Advertiser* expressed the fear that disaster and massacre might ensue from the withdrawal from Khartum and urged the Government to take action. On the 11th the *Pall Mall Gazette* returned to the question, having heard that Gordon was to be forced to resign his commission instead of being sent to the Sudan. 'The ablest leader of irregular forces in the world is now no longer in the service of the Queen.' On the 12th the *Morning Advertiser* stated that all England had been looking for the employment of Gordon in the Sudan.

[1] *The Times,* Jan. 19, 1884.
[2] Maurice and Arthur, op. cit., p. 176.
[3] Allen, op. cit., p. 211.

Since the first mention of Gordon in connection with revolt in
the Sudan, those putting forward his name had intended that he
should be given power and authority to deal with the problem
and not merely instruction to report on it. It was also understood
that Gordon himself disapproved of the policy of withdrawal from
the Sudan mainly because of the physical difficulties and the
demoralizing effect it might have on the retreating soldiers. He
had made this point clear in his interview with the *Pall Mall
Gazette* on January 8, as also in his discussions with members
of the Government. The Egyptian Government's request for a
British officer specifically to conduct the evacuation was quite
clear and definite. And yet, in spite of the views which he had
expressed, Gordon readily accepted the policy of evacuation as
laid down in his instructions from Granville. Gordon, although
assured and mindful of the difficulties of the situation, had changed
his mind, accepted the policy, and declared his readiness to execute
it. Granville, on the other hand, was fully aware that if the request
of the Egyptian Government was approved, it meant that Gordon
would go to Khartum and simply conduct the evacuation. There
was, then, little point in his reporting on the situation if he was
going to carry out a definite policy which had already been decided
on. Yet, his instructions contained elaborate sentences on his task
of reporting on the situation while declaring that the Egyptian
Government and Baring were left to instruct him on any further
duties which he might be called upon to undertake.

Gordon wished to avoid Cairo in order to avoid seeing the
Khedive. He was under the impression that the latter did not like
him, and only six days before his departure he wrote to Sir A.
Clarke saying: 'As to Tawfiq I could never serve him, for he would
never forgive my letter.'[1] Baring telegraphed to the Foreign Office
expressing his satisfaction that Gordon and Stewart were on their
way to Egypt, but he was of the opinion that it would be useless
for them to proceed to Sawakin as General Baker was doing all
that could be done there. He thought it best for them to come to
Cairo, and after discussing matters to go to Khartum.[2] Baring,
moreover, was so anxious that Gordon should visit Cairo that he

[1] Vetch, R.H., *Life of Lieut. General The Hon. Sir Andrew Clarke* (London,
1905), p. 264.
[2] Baring to Granville, No. 76, Jan. 19, 1884, P.R.O., F.O. 78/3665.

telegraphed privately to Granville urging that it was 'absolutely essential.'[1] Cairo was the only possible route to Khartum and 'so marked an act of disrespect to the Khedive would harm and increase the difficulties of the situation.' It was also necessary for Gordon to discuss his plans with Nubar, Wood, and himself. Baring was also anxious for it to be made clear to Gordon that he was not to carry out the policy set forth in his interview with the *Pall Mall Gazette*, for otherwise Baring anticipated 'a good deal of trouble.'

A message was accordingly telegraphed to Gordon through the British Consul at Port Said instructing him to go to Cairo. Granville in a private telegram told Baring that his views about Gordon would be supported and that it was felt that Gordon would carry out the Government policy and 'not that announced in *Pall Mall*.'[2] Graham, who was known to be a friend of Gordon, was asked to write to him urging that he should visit Cairo. Graham appealed to Gordon to 'throw over all personal feeling.'[3] if he had any, and act 'with straightforward directness.' Graham tried to persuade Gordon that Gordon had no personal aims in the matter and, therefore, that his personal feelings should not be allowed to interfere. His object was to go to Khartum, and Cairo was the more direct route. To travel through Cairo would give him the advantage of seeing Baring and Nubar and of making the arrangements for his 'great enterprise, in which we all so earnestly wish you success.'

As soon as Gordon had left England for Egypt misunderstandings arose among the ministers about the character of his mission. Sir Charles Dilke wrote to Granville stating that he was alarmed at Gordon's hints to the newspapers. He had heard nothing of 'his going to Khartum, or anywhere except to Sawakin.'[4] Dilke feared that if Gordon went up towards Khartum and was carried off to be held to ransom, an enormous force would have to be sent after him if he 'should go without instructions.' Childers asked Granville about the nature of Gordon's mission. He particularly wanted information about Gordon's relations with the Egyptian authorities. 'Is he to be under Evelyn Wood, or under Baring i.e. who will

[1] Baring to Granville, Jan. 19, 1884, P.R.O., G/ 29/162.
[2] Granville to Baring, Jan. 20, 1884, P.R.O., G/D 29/200.
[3] Vetch, R. H., *Life, Letters, and Diaries of Lieut.-General Sir Gerald Graham* (Edinburgh and London, 1901), p. 253.
[4] Dilke to Granville, Jan. 21, 1884, P.R.O., G/D 29/122.

be responsible?' Granville's reply stated that Gordon wished to be under the orders of General Stephenson, 'acting upon instructions from Baring.' [1]

Gordon set to work as soon as he left Charing Cross station and the next day he enclosed with a letter to Granville copies of eight telegrams which he intended should be sent to Baring.[2] The first telegram dealt with a draft proclamation to the people of the Sudan to be issued by the Khedive before Gordon's arrival. In it Tawfiq was to say that the immense distances separating the Sudan from Egypt had given rise to disturbance culminating in a revolt against his authority. The cost of the revolt in both money and blood had been great. For that reason he considered restoring their independence to the various sultans of the country. Gordon, who had previously been known as governor-general, would be his representative to arrange with them the evacuation of the country. As the British Government was also interested in their welfare they had appointed Gordon as their commissioner for the same purpose. 'General Gordon is hereby appointed Governor General for the time necessary to accomplish the evacuation.' The proposed proclamation ended by appealing to the people to lay down their arms and to endeavor peacefully to form their future government.

The second proclamation was intended to emanate from Gordon himself to the people of the Sudan. It informed them that Her Majesty's Government and the Khedive had asked him to arrange with them the withdrawal of the Khedivial troops and the future government of their country. He had accepted the post of governor-general of the Sudan for the time necessary to accomplish that end. He trusted that they would receive him honorably, as he was coming with a sincere desire to aid them in restoring their independence. It was therefore pointless to continue hostilities against the Khedivial troops. Finally, he trusted that they would 'remain quiet.'

The third and fourth proclamations were addressed to the shaikhs of tribes in the eastern Sudan, and to the tribes themselves near Sawakin. Gordon appealed to the first to meet him at Sawakin in order to discuss with them the future government of the Sudan

---

[1] Childers, op. cit., vol. ii, p. 178.
[2] Gordon to Granville, Jan. 19, 1884, P.R.O., F.O. 78/3696.

and to the second to allow the garrisons to be withdrawn without bloodshed. The other telegrams concerned the appointment of a member of the Darfur reigning family as Sultan of Darfur, the question of his ex-private secretary in the Sudan, the recruitment of black troops for the Egyptian army, and measures for preventing Zubair from sending emissaries or letters to the Sudan.

While still on his way to Egypt, Gordon, in a private letter to Northbrook expressed his view of the question of the Sudan. He believed that there would be no point in reconquering the Sudan without the guarantee of future good government. British policy in Egypt, in his opinion, brought back the old oppression without such a guarantee. 'It is wonderful that the wretched despised Sudan has forced our hand, and that we are now really going to benefit the people of Egypt.' [1] To Gordon the decision to evacuate the Sudan was a good one as no good future government would be guaranteed to the Sudanese. He considered purely as academic such questions as whether the British had acted correctly in allowing Hicks to command the expedition and in allowing the Egyptian Government to spend money on the expedition. He was glad that these events had happened as nothing short of 'the Sudan explosion' would have awakened the British to their responsibilities in lower Egypt. He believed that the slave-trade would continue so long as Tawfiq himself kept slaves. It could only be stopped from the Congo. He estimated that the evacuation would cost £100,000, which was to be paid by Egypt.

By the 22nd of January these suggested proclamations and decrees had been discussed in Cabinet, and it was decided to authorize Baring to make the arrangements suggested, or to await Gordon's arrival in Egypt and to discuss them with him then.[2] The Cabinet's decision was based on the fact that the Government had not sufficient local knowledge to enable them to form an opinion of the practicability of these suggestions. Dilke recorded that the full Cabinet approved Gordon's mission on that day when his suggestions were before them. 'Mr. Gladstone did not object although strongly opposed to our undertaking responsibility in the Sudan because Gordon still spoke in every sentence of conducting the evacuation.' [3]

[1] Gordon to Northbrook, Jan. 20, 1884, G/D 29/139.
[2] Granville to Baring, No. 43A, Jan. 22, 1884, P.R.O., F.O. 78/3662.
[3] Gwynn and Tuckwell, op. cit., vol. ii, p. 30.

184184 THE INDEPENDENT SUDAN

While the Cabinet in London were discussing his suggestions, Gordon was drafting an elaborate memorandum on S.S. *Tanjore*.[1] He first stated that Her Majesty's Government had come to the 'irrevocable decision' to secure to the people of the Sudan a just future government. Consequently, it had been determined to 'restore to these peoples their independence.' To achieve this Her Majesty's Government had decided to send him to the Sudan to arrange for the evacuation of those countries and for the safe removal of the Egyptian Government's employees and troops. His plan was that the restoration of the country should be made to the petty sultans who ruled the country at the time of Muhammad 'Ali's conquests and whose families still existed. al-Mahdi was to be ignored at this stage of the settlement, but when the sultans had assumed power they might accept al-Mahdi's suzerainty or not, according to their own wishes. Gordon himself thought that the sultans would probably hold on to their independence, for they would not benefit by acknowledging the sovereignty of al-Mahdi. There would then be two factions: the sultans on the one side trying to assert their independence, and al-Mahdi's party trying to control them. To give the arsenals and the war equipment to al-Mahdi in that case would be a mistake, and they ought to be handed to the sultans in whose states they were situated. Gordon thought it most difficult to decide to whom arsenals in such towns as Khartum, Kasalah, and Dongola should be handed. Those towns had no families of long standing. He thought it best, therefore, to postpone the decision about these towns until the inhabitants had made known their wishes.

If this supposition of the opposition of the petty sultans to the supremacy of al-Mahdi were correct, there could be little doubt that al-Mahdi would endeavor to assert his authority by force and that he would consequently oppose any evacuation of Government employees and troops. Gordon thought that the bulk of al-Mahdi's forces would probably refuse to cross the Nile with him and leave their own country. The section of his army which might follow him anywhere would principally consist of the black soldiers who had deserted and, in Gordon's estimate, al-Mahdi would in this case have between three and four thousand men. These black troops, if offered fair terms, would desert to the Government side.

[1] Memorandum by Gordon for Baring, at sea, S.S. *Tanjore*, Jan. 22, 1884, P.R.O., F.O. 78/3696.

A situation might therefore arise in which the sultans accepting territory would refuse the supremacy of al-Mahdi, who would try to impose his will on them by force. If al-Mahdi's black troops then deserted him, he would be considerably weakened. What was to be done if al-Mahdi, even in that weakened state, were to attack the evacuating columns?

In trying to answer this question Gordon assumed that the soldiers would resist the attack and would not allow themselves to be slaughtered. Their resistance might result in a victory over al-Mahdi. In such a case it would only be reasonable to allow them to follow up their success to such an extent as would allow them to complete their march in safety. It would be difficult to obtain instructions from Her Majesty's Government on this matter, but Gordon called their attention to it. The decision was clear that the country was to be evacuated with as little fighting as possible. As no definite line of action could be decided on beforehand, Gordon declared that he would carry out the evacuation as far as possible according to the wishes of the British Government, avoiding as far as possible, all fighting. 'I would, however, hope that Her Majesty's Government will give me their support and consideration should I be unable to fulfil all their expectations.'

Gordon's objection to Zubair was that he was a first-class general and a man of great capacity and he 'would in no time eat up all the petty Sultans and consolidate a vast state as his ambition is endless.' Gordon, therefore, wished him to be kept away, as his restoration 'would be not alone unjust but might open the Turco-Arabic question.' The sultans, when left to themselves, would perhaps fight among themselves and some might try to dominate the others, but it would be an easy task for Zubair to overcome the different states and to form a large independent one.

Though it was not his duty to express an opinion on the Sudan policy pursued by Her Majesty's Government, yet he maintained that it would be iniquitous to conquer the Sudanese and then hand them back to their old oppressors, the Egyptians, without any guarantee of good government. It was evident to Gordon that good government could not be secured without inordinate expenditure of men and money. To him

the Sudan is a useless possession ever was so and ever will be so. Larger than Germany, France and Spain together and mostly barren it cannot be governed except by a dictator who may be good or bad. It had and will cause constant revolts. No one who has ever lived in the Sudan can escape the reflection 'what a useless possession is this land.' Few men also can stand its fearful monotony and deadly climate.

Gordon referred to Sa'id Pasha's horror at the misery of the people when he visited the country, and to his declaration that he would be no party to such oppression. These arguments had led Gordon to the logical conclusion that Her Majesty's Government was fully justified in recommending the evacuation of the Sudan, since the sacrifices necessary for securing good government would be far too great for such an attempt to be made. Her Majesty's Government would 'leave them as God has placed them, they are not forced to fight among themselves and they will no longer be oppressed by men coming from lands so remote as Circasia, Kurdistan and Anatolia.'

When the steamer reached Port Said, Gordon received a telegram from the Foreign Office, through the British Consul at Port Said, telling him that Baring had given sound reason why he should go to Cairo, and it was hoped that he would do so.[1] He received also a letter from his friend General Graham, and another from Baring, while Wood met him in person. Against this formidable array of opinion, both private and official, Gordon had to go to Cairo. He asked Wood in a beseeching tone—'Must I see the Khedive?' and Wood replied that it would be essential to do so.[2]

On January 25th, his first morning in Cairo, Gordon, accompanied by Sir Evelyn Wood, saw the Khedive. Gordon apologized for his former brusque behavior and the interview was most successful.[3] Immediately after this interview a meeting was held in Baring's house to discuss the details of the action to be taken in the Sudan. There were present Baring, Wood, Gordon, Nubar, and Stewart. A number of points were discussed and decisions were reached on them. A credit of £E.100,000 was to be put at Gordon's disposal. The evacuation was to be gradual. Two firmans were to be issued appointing Gordon Governor-General of the Sudan, and in one of them the evacuation would be mentioned. Baker Pasha was to be named Governor-General of eastern Sudan, including the

---

[1] *Parl. Pap.* (1884), vol. lxxxviii, p. 196.
[2] *The Letters of Queen Victoria*, 2nd ser. (London, 1928), vol. iii, p. 476.
[3] Stewart's diary, enclosed in Baring to Granville, No. 171, Feb. 11, 1884, P.R.O., F.O. 78/3667.

coastline from Ras al-Haya to Masawwa, and inland so as to include Tukar, Sinkat, and Bogos in Eritrea. An officer from Aden, unaccompanied by any Egyptian official, was to proceed to Harrar to report. Gordon's suggested proclamations were accepted. A member of Darfur's ruling family was to be selected to accompany Gordon. Other financial matters were also decided. On the next day another meeting was held, and the Egyptian Government's instructions to Gordon were read and approved. At Gordon's request an interview took place between him and Zubair.[1]

While Gordon was on his way to Egypt the Khartum authorities had been instructed to arrange for the retreat of the Sennar garrison on Khartum, and then for the evacuation of both garrisons to Barbar. When, however, the time came for the retreat to be begun, difficulties became evident. De Coetlogon reported on the 20th of January that forces of rebels were assembling on both the Blue and the White Niles and in al-Jazirah between them. The low level of the Blue Nile prevented large steamers from going to Sennar and only two small ones could be used. All wood for fuel had to be carried on board as nothing could be obtained en route, and both banks of the river were held by the rebels.[2] The mere announcement in Khartum of the proposed evacuation had a demoralizing effect. Authorities in Khartum maintained that they would wait until the withdrawal of the Sennar garrison, when they would be strong enough to hold Khartum, as long as food lasted, in the face of any force that might be sent against them. By that time it was estimated that between 10,000 and 15,000 civilians wished to leave Khartum.[3]

While Gordon was conferring with the authorities in Cairo, two steamers were sent to destroy a bridge of boats known to have been made by the rebels. The water being too shallow, the steamers were unable to reach the bridge and returned. One of them was attacked with great fury by Arabs wading out to her, but the rocket tube and the mountain gun on her and the bullets of soldiers beat off the attack.[4]

To satisfy Granville's curiosity Baring wrote privately, giving a

[1] Ibid.
[2] De Coetlogon to Fraser, Jan. 20, 1884, enclosed in Baring to Granville, No. 83, Jan. 21, 1884, P.R.O., F.O. 78/3666.
[3] Baring to Granville, No. 90, Jan. 21, 1884, P.R.O., F.O. 78/3666.
[4] *The Times*, Jan. 28, 1884.

picture of Gordon.[1] 'What a curious creature he is! He is certainly half cracked but it is impossible not to be charmed by the simplicity and honesty of his character.' There had been no difficulty in persuading him to visit Cairo and he had not raised the least objection to visiting the Khedive, to whom he apologized for having written disagreeable things about him. The Khedive was delighted, and had signed all the proclamations put before him without making any difficulty. Gordon spoke very hopefully of finishing his task in three or four months. 'He wishes particularly to impress on me that he entirely agreed in the policy of abandoning the Sudan. Nothing could be more friendly and conciliatory than his conduct to everyone.' Baring expressed his pleasure at Gordon's appointment, and his only fear was that Gordon was 'terribly flighty, and changes his opinions very rapidly.'

After the first meeting in Cairo both Baring and Nubar thought it desirable to give Gordon further written instructions supplementing those which he had received in London. The draft was prepared by Baring and read to Gordon who expressed 'his entire concurrence'[2] with its content. The only amendment which he suggested was that the policy of abandoning the Sudan, with which he agreed, 'should on no account be changed.' The instructions were officially approved and endorsed by Granville.

Baring, in his letter to Gordon containing the new instructions, referred to the original ones from London which provided that Gordon was 'authorized and instructed' to perform such duties as the Egyptian Government might desire to entrust to him, which would be communicated to him by Baring. The new instructions, therefore, derived their legality from the original ones. Gordon's attention was drawn to two points in these instructions. The first was the measures which it would be advisable to take for the security of the Egyptian garrisons still holding positions in the Sudan and for the safety of the European population in Khartum. The second dealt with the best means of carrying out the evacuation of the interior of the country. The number of Europeans in Khartum was believed to be very small, but it was estimated that between 10,000 and 15,000 people would wish to move northwards from Khartum when the garrison was withdrawn. The Egyptian

[1] Baring to Granville, Jan. 28, 1884, P.R.O., G/D 29/162.
[2] Baring to Granville, No. 100, Jan. 28, 1884, P.R.O., F.O. 78/3666.

Government hoped that no effort would be spared to ensure the retreat of these people and of the Egyptian garrisons without loss of life.

No detailed instructions were necessary for effecting the retreat and everything would be left to Gordon's discretion. At one time the situation in Khartum had appeared to be critical, but later it improved and gave rise to no anxiety. The orders for immediate retreat were therefore delayed until Gordon's arrival there. The main end was the evacuation of the Sudan—a policy adopted by the Egyptian Government on the advice of Her Majesty's Government, to which Gordon had agreed. He was therefore to restore the country to the petty sultans, who existed at the time of Muhammad 'Ali, and was to endeavor to form a confederation of these sultans. He was to retain the troops for such a period as he might think necessary in order that the evacuation of the country might be accomplished with the least possible risk to life and property. A credit of £100,000 was opened for him, and he was told that further funds would be supplied after the exhaustion of that sum. 'In undertaking the difficult task which lies before you,' the letter concluded, 'you may feel assured that no effort will be wanting on the part of the Cairo authorities, whether English or Egyptian, to afford you all the cooperation and support in their power.' Gordon apparently left Cairo without officially giving his assent. He therefore wrote from upper Egypt acknowledging receipt of the instructions and saying that he fully understood their purport and would act accordingly 'as far as circumstances will admit, while keeping in view that the evacuation of the Sudan is the object of Her Majesty's Government.' [1] The instructions from Cairo did not mention any instructions to report on the situation, for the Egyptian Government had asked specifically for a man to conduct the evacuation.

The task of evacuating Khartum was made more difficult by including the civilian inhabitants who wished to leave. The original instructions from London spoke only of the troops and the Europeans, who were very few in number. Gordon himself in his memorandum of the 22nd of January spoke of the troops and employees who would certainly not amount to such a large num-

---

[1] Gordon to Baring, Jan. 28, 1884, enclosed in Baring to Granville, No. 119, Feb. 4, 1884, P.R.O., F.O. 78/3666.

ber. This is an important point, because the safe evacuation of those civilians in Khartum was really an impossible task to perform in the circumstances and it was Gordon's determination to withdraw them to the north in accordance with his instructions that prolonged his stay unnecessarily in Khartum.

Gordon, even when in Cairo and in a better position to estimate the importance of the revolution in the Sudan, was under the illusion that it had little or no religious significance. General Graham, who was in close touch with Gordon during his stay in Cairo, states that Gordon thought that al-Mahdi was 'a mere figurehead,'[1] and that he could not take the offensive as his followers would not advance beyond their tribal frontiers. Perhaps that was the biggest misconception from which Gordon suffered.

On the 26th of January Gordon, Stewart, and the new Sultan of Darfur, accompanied by Graham and his aid-de-camp, left Cairo by steamer southwards. While on the way Gordon was very active in drawing up plans even for Egypt itself, as he suggested that the desert roads between the Nile and the Red Sea in Egypt should be guarded against the slave caravans. Gordon first planned to crush the Hadandawa, who were blockading Sawakin, and he asked for five British officers to assist him. Both Graham and Stewart tried to dissuade him from sending this plan of operations to Cairo, but they only made him nervous and irritable. Gordon was very much worried about the position of Slatin in Darfur. He declared himself willing to offer to al-Mahdi £10,000 for the safe conduct of the Darfur garrison to Khartum, and declared that he would write to al-Mahdi saying that there was no reason why they should not be at peace with al-Mahdi as Governor of Kurdufan and Gordon as Governor of Khartum.[2]

At Aswan Gordon entered into telegraphic communication with Husain Khalifah, the Governor of Barbar. Husain thought that people would flock to Gordon as soon as he came among them. There would, he thought, be no fear of al-Mahdi, who was the nephew of an old servant of Gordon's and that he, Husain, would

---

[1] Graham, Lt.-Gen. Sir Gerald, *Last Words with Gordon* (London, 1887), p. 4.

[2] Stewart's diary, enclosed in Baring to Granville, No. 171, Feb. 11, 1884, P.R.O., F.O. 78/3667.

soon be able to open communication with Sawakin. This pleased Gordon so much that he discarded his plan of operations and cancelled his request for five British officers.

When Graham parted from Gordon he was charged to tell Baring that he (Gordon) would dismiss first the higher Egyptian officials and then the lower ones, replacing them at the same time by Sudanese. Then he would form a Sudanese army. In due course the time for sending back the Egyptian troops would come when the Khedive's firman severing the connection between Egypt and the Sudan would be produced. The troops would be given the choice of going back to Egypt or staying in the Sudan under the new Sudanese Government.[1]

Graham recognized the gigantic task confronting Gordon, even if al-Mahdi gave him no trouble. He would have to construct a government and an army out of purely native materials, because Gordon was determined to send back all the Egyptians. Graham thought that organization would hold together as long as Gordon was there, but once he had gone there would be 'deluge, anarchy and slavery.'[2] When he had completed his mission in the Sudan, Gordon proposed to proceed to the Congo. Graham thought it was inadvisable to announce the withdrawal of the troops and Gordon's proposed departure from Khartum. If people were told that the troops were to be withdrawn, that a native government would be established, and that Gordon himself would leave, the country would ultimately be delivered over to anarchy. All his appointments, his enactments, and his remission of taxation would be of no value if he were to leave. The scheme would only work, in Graham's opinion, if a federation of chiefs could be made with Gordon remaining as a dictator and another European succeeding him if he should leave.

While still at Aswan, Gordon thought out the high appointments to his new native government. 'Awad al-Karim Bey Abu Sin, the chief of the Shukriya tribe and Sa'id Bey Husain al-Jamaabi, an old adherent of Zubair, would be made pashas. Ibrahim Bey Fawzi, although an Egyptian, would be made a pasha also and a commandant of the troops. Fawzi was to be employed mainly to

---

[1] Graham, op. cit., p. 32.
[2] Ibid., p. 28.

keep him fully informed of the state of public opinion. Stewart would be Gordon's deputy and would replace him should anything happen to Gordon.[1]

Taking stock of what he had heard on his journey, Gordon formed the opinion that for the present al-Mahdi would not attack Khartum. That was why he thought the English officers would not be needed. The revolt at Sawakin was due, in his opinion, to the oppression and venality of the Sawakin and Barbar officials. He anticipated no danger during his journey to Khartum. His reasons for the above conclusions were, firstly that Husain Pasha Khalifah would not have accepted the post of Governor of Barbar and Dongola if he had known that the Government would be overthrown. In the second place, there were no rebels in the vicinity of Khartum, Barbar, and the country between them, as the telegraph line was intact and caravans had recently passed that way without molestation. In the third place, Gordon received an overwhelming number of telegrams from notables in Dongola and Barbar asking for employment. They would not have done so had there been any danger of the Government's being overthrown. In addition it had been reported that al-Mahdi had no bazinqir (slave soldiers) among his troops and so it was improbable that he would proceed to Bahr al-Ghazal and Equatoria for the purpose of slave-hunting. The available evidence tended to show that the rebellion was 'almost entirely due to the oppression, venality and folly of the so-called Egyptian Government.'[2] There was also a report, which might or might not be true, that al-Mahdi's followers had settled down to their normal occupations.

Gordon asked Stewart to comment on these arguments and conclusions. Stewart was inclined to admit that there was a considerable force in his first three points. He thought it probable that the danger of attack on Khartum had been greatly exaggerated. But it should be noticed that the Blue Nile which was the source of Khartum's food supplies had been closed by the rebels. According to credible evidence the town had only sufficient food for three months. It was also very likely that al-Mahdi would not assume

---

[1] Stewart's diary, enclosed in Baring to Granville, No. 171, Feb. 11, 1884, P.R.O., F.O. 78/3667.
[2] Ibid.

the offensive, but would wait until Khartum was forced to submit through hunger. This had been his plan for capturing al-Ubayyid. In any case, Stewart thought that as they proceeded on their journey they would be in a better position to form an opinion since they would have become better acquainted with the true state of affairs and with the feeling of the people.

From Kurusko in Egypt, on the Nile, Gordon's party plunged into the desert, full of hope after his telegraphic communication with Husain Khalifah. His last messages from upper Egypt to Baring directed that all his correspondence might be published.[1] Gordon's desire that all his correspondence might be published was responsible to a great extent for the vagueness and misinterpretation of his dispatches. He seemed to have been concerned more with the impression that they might create on public opinion than with convincing arguments that might persuade the Government to comply with his demands.

It is interesting to return now to London to see how Gordon's mission was interpreted. When the question of sending Gordon to the Sudan arose Parliament was in recess. The majority of the ministers themselves understood only the broad principles of Gordon's mission. When Gordon left Charing Cross station he began to evolve very elaborate plans which he sent back to London for approval. In Cairo the long discussion with the authorities produced still further details to those plans and a number of proclamations, instructions, and suggestions. While on his way from Cairo to Khartum, Gordon sent back to Baring and Nubar from almost every halting-place all sorts of suggestions and ideas embracing topics which were often entirely unconnected with his mission. It was against this background that Parliament met, with the Opposition asking many questions about Gordon's mission, Sudan policy, and the Egyptian problem in general.

In an attempt to clarify some aspects of Gordon's mission the Foreign Office asked Baring about the proclamations which Gordon had taken with him from Cairo. Baring stated that Gordon had been provided with two documents to use at his own discretion.[2] In one of them the evacuation of the Sudan was specifically alluded

---

[1] Baring to Granville, No. 149, Feb. 9, 1884, P.R.O., F.O. 78/3666.
[2] Baring tc Granville, No. 113. Feb. 1, 1884, P.R.O., F.O. 78/3666.

to, while the other contained vaguer references to the intentions
of the Government. Gordon's original suggestions [1] were the basis
of those proclamations. Baring confirmed that Gordon fully understood that he was going up to Khartum for the purpose of carrying
out the policy of evacuation and that he had expressed his fullest
concurrence in the wisdom of that policy. Baring emphasized that
the instructions had been drafted at the request and with the
fullest approval of Gordon himself. It was, however, thought
desirable to leave Gordon the widest discretionary power in carrying out the instructions and in publishing the proclamations at
Khartum. When Baring received the first batch of letters and telegrams from Gordon in upper Egypt, he wrote privately to Granville
remarking that 'some of them are rather wild.' [2] but that it did not
matter. Baring stated that he would do everything to support
Gordon and meet his wishes.

On the 5th of February Parliament met, and the speech from
the throne referred to Gordon's mission: 'I have also dispatched
Major-General Gordon to report on the best means of giving
effect to the resolution of the Khedive to withdraw from the
interior of the Sudan and have permitted him to act in the execution of the measure.' [3] Salisbury remarked that Gordon was unsuitable for carrying out such a policy: a soldier who had spent his
life advancing and striking hard blows at the enemy was hardly the
right man to conduct a retreat from the Sudan. [4]

Meanwhile, Baring had received further letters from Gordon
which alarmed him slightly. Stewart wrote very privately to Baring
that Gordon was 'in a state of great nervous excitement and
irritability, and that he fires off telegrams and letters without
thinking much of what he is doing. He is, in fact, terribly change-
able.' [5] In spite of that, Stewart stated that Gordon was sound so
far as the main lines of policy were concerned.

A discussion in the House of Commons about the nature of
Gordon's appointment took place on the 7th of February. Members
of the Opposition asked whether Gordon was in the service of the
Khedive. Lord Hartington answering for the Government stated:

[1] *Vide supra*, p. 162.
[2] Baring to Granville, Feb. 4, 1884, P.R.O., G/D 29/162.
[3] *Hansard*, 3rd ser., vol. 284, col. 4.
[4] Ibid., col. 20.
[5] Baring to Granville, Feb. 5, 1884, P.R.O., G/D 29/162.

'The Khedive, I believe, has appointed General Gordon governor general of the Sudan. The mission upon which General Gordon was sent is a mission upon which he was sent by Her Majesty's Government.'[1] When it was further pointed out that it was very confusing that the Khedive should have appointed him and at the same time left him outside his employment, no reply was given. In the early days of this session the question of giving material aid to Gordon was also raised. Gladstone in reply, stated that from the information they had received, the Government were not justified in adopting any measure of any kind; they would be guided by the information in their possession and would endeavor to form the best judgment they could. Mr. Ashmead Barlett commented on this above statement with the prophetic remark 'when it is too late.'[2]

By the 8th of February Granville seemed to be alarmed at Gordon's changeability and worried for his safety. Northbrook thought that Gordon would say all the foolish things that passed through his head but that 'his judgment is excellent.'[3] Granville feared that if bad news arrived about Gordon it might turn the Liberal party out of office.

Emerging from the desert and striking the Nile at Abu Hamad, Gordon was well received by the people who crowded round him in great number 'to kiss his hand and hear what he had to say.'[4] Gordon made a speech to the effect that he was not going to make war on al-Mahdi, that he would grant pardon to all offenders, and that taxes would be reduced by one-half, with the remittance of arrears. He ended his speech by announcing that the country would, in future, be governed by the Sudanese, and invited them to send influential people to Khartum for that purpose. Although the people hearing the speech seemed to be greatly pleased, Stewart doubted very much whether they thoroughly appreciated it. Gordon was so favorably impressed at Abu Hamad that he sent a telegram to Baring and Nubar saying that there should not be the 'slightest anxiety about the Sudan.' He trusted that with the help of God, order would be restored in the Sudan in a month.

[1] *Hansard,* 3rd ser., vol. 284, col. 99.
[2] Ibid.
[3] Granville to Baring, Feb. 8, 1884, P.R.O., G/D 29/200.
[4] Stewart's diary, enclosed in Baring to Granville, No. 255, Mar. 3, 1884, P.R.O., F.O. 78/3668.

and that Muhammad Ahmad would renounce his claim to be al-Mahdi. Gordon pointed out that it was Ra'uf who had given al-Mahdi that title.[1]

Before leaving Abu Hamad for Barbar, Gordon sent by ordinary mail an elaborate memorandum embodying his ideas about the future government of the Sudan.[2] He inferred from the number of telegrams which he had received, asking for employment, and from other signs of loyalty and confidence in the Government, that the country was far less disturbed than had been reported. He thought it probable that the mass of civil employees would refuse to leave the Sudan even if dismissed. His first concern when he arrived at Khartum would be to send to Cairo the families of all dead employees and soldiers, and then attend to the pacification of the country and the reopening of communications. These he considered to be his immediate objectives, and he wished Baring to consider the next stages.

The country, in Gordon's view, had long been accustomed to a system of government which provided law-courts, posts, and telegraphs and other controlling and directing departments. To disturb or abolish such a system at a moment's notice would result in complete anarchy. Gordon maintained that even when the administration had been completely 'Sudanized,' Egyptian troops evacuated, and the firman severing the connection had been read there would ensue a period of 'violent and protracted commotion' which might be detrimental to Egypt because of the long and intimate connection between the two countries. Gordon therefore proposed that Egypt should continue to be the suzerain power, nominating the governor-general and the mudirs, and acting as a supreme court of appeal. The controlling influence was to be strictly moral and not to exceed the tendering of advice. 'In spite of all that has occurred, I feel satisfied that the prestige of the Cairo Government except in so far as the conduct of its troops in the field is concerned, is not seriously shaken,' People still looked to the Cairo Government as emanating from the Khalifah of the Muslims in Turkey and they would be horrified at complete separation. He would, therefore, 'earnestly beg that evacuation,

[1] Gordon to Baring, Feb. 8, 1884, enclosed in Baring to Granville, No. 163, Feb. 11, 1884, P.R.O., F.O. 78/3667.
[2] Gordon to Baring, Feb. 8, 1884, enclosed in Baring to Granville, No. 225, Feb. 25, 1884, P.R.O., F.O. 78/3667.

but not abandonment' be the policy and that the firman should be changed to one recognizing moral control and suzerainty.

Gordon asked Stewart to comment on this memorandum. Stewart agreed with Gordon that anarchy and bloodshed would result if the policy of abandonment were to be carried out in its entirety, but Gordon's program depended 'a great deal on the policy which the British Government intended to follow in Egypt. If they intended to evacuate Egypt and cease to have a directing and influencing voice in her affairs, then he decidedly favored the abandonment of the Sudan. In that case if Egypt were given even nominal control over the Sudan, it would mean more interference and an ultimate return to 'misgovernment, oppression, venality and Cairene intrigue.'[1] If, on the other hand, Britain retained her influence in Egyptian affairs he thought that Gordon's suggested program could be followed with 'considerable advantage.' Although Stewart did not agree that the prestige of Cairo was not greatly diminished, he thought that what remained of it would be quite sufficient to curb the forces of disorder, adding: 'whether, or for how long such an influence may last, it is impossible to say.'

The reactions of Baring and Granville to this memorandum have little significance for it was not received in Cairo until the 25th of February and had already been superseded by Gordon's telegram from Khartum on the day of his arrival there, February 18th. Nevertheless it gives an indication of Gordon's state of mind. It also confirmed the earlier impression of Gordon's changeability and inconsistency and in that way contributed to the lack of confidence in his plans and policy.

Leaving Abu Hamad for Barbar, Gordon had many interviews with the leading personalities of the Rubatab district. Before reaching Barbar he ordered a letter to be written to al-Mahdi appointing him the Sultan of Kurdufan and saying that as Gordon was Governor of Khartum there was no necessity for war between them. al-Mahdi was also told that when he became Sultan he should free the European prisoners, encourage trade with Khartum, and allow the telegraph line to al-Ubayyid to be replaced, as it was of great use. 'The General's idea,' says Stewart, 'in sending this letter is to sow dissension among al-Mahdi's followers, and to quiet the Fakis and religious fanatics throughout the country as

[1]Stewart's remarks enclosed in ibid.

far as possible.' [1] That letter, with an order to issue a similar proclamation at Barbar, was forwarded to Husain Khalifah who was
instructed to wrap it in silk and send it to al-Mahdi. Stewart
thought that the letter would at least cause the Kababish tribe to
leave al-Mahdi and join the Government side. Husain Pasha
Khalifah thought that al-Mahdi cared only for religion and that
now he was recognized as Sultan his position in the country would
be much stronger.

Husain Khalifah met Gordon on the steamer at Qinainita.
Husain told Gordon that the Sudan did not want independence
but simply to get rid of the Turks. This provided still further
evidence for Gordon that some controlling or directing power was
necessary to give moral support to the native rulers.

All the way to Barbar Gordon was warmly received and when
he actually entered that town a considerable crowd of people from
the villages had joined the party. The usual guard of honor and
official receptions greeted Gordon at Barbar. Gordon spent the
night at Barbar and early next morning Stewart recorded in his
diary: 'I was called up at 5 a.m. by General Gordon, who having
pondered deeply all night, had come to the decision of opening
the Pandora Box and openly proclaiming the divorce of the Sudan
from Egypt.' [2] Gordon planned to form a local militia and to
appoint Sudanese officials to every important post. When the
Governor and the Qadi (religious judge) made their appearance
that morning, Gordon produced for them the secret firman declaring the separation of the Sudan from Egypt. A committee acting
as a provisional government and consisting of six of the most
influential notables of the province was therefore appointed. It
was announced that henceforward the province was independent
of Cairo but subject to General Gordon as 'Governor-General and
Commissioner of the British Government.' [3] This proclamation
was affixed to the gate and caused great excitement, but as far as
Stewart could judge, the people seemed to approve.

Gordon was overwhelmed with petitions, while a deputation of
Arabs from Dongola complained of their mudir by yelling. Also
a deputation of the notables inquired whether Gordon's program

[1] Stewart's diary, loc. cit.
[2] Ibid.
[3] Ibid.

included the Slavery Treaty. 'General Gordon, knowing the utter futility of saying, "Yes" replied "No" and published a proclamation to this effect.' [1] Stewart commented that it was probable that this proclamation interested and pleased the people more than anything else. The proclamation aroused a great stir in London but the Government, convinced by the exigencies of the situation and by Baring's explanation, succeeded in gaining the approval of both public opinion and Parliament.

An official assembly of the leading men of the province, with the Mudir at their head, was held, and Gordon made a speech and showed them the secret firman. The document caused the most profound astonishment and from their speeches it appears that they were delighted. Stewart and Gordon attempted to find out the real opinion of those present, and they were told that the proclamation had been a mistake and that the 'probable effect will be to lead those who heard the firman to conclude that all the concessions made by General Gordon viz. half tax, were made merely with a view of getting the troops out of the country without danger and to leave the people to stew in their own juice.' [2] Stewart thought it very difficult to judge the matter, but he would have preferred to follow Nubar's advice which was that the announcement of the firman should be delayed until the situation was clearer and could be better judged.

By that time Gordon had become convinced that there would be no difficulty in maintaining law and order without incurring responsibility if the British Government would agree to name a governor-general for the Sudan. He was confident that if this plan were not sanctioned, bloodshed and misery would follow. This opinion differed from that which Gordon had experssed in the memorandum which he wrote at Abu Hamad.[3] Now he thought that the moral support should be provided by Great Britain while previously he had thought that it ought to be provided by the Egyptian Government.

Meanwhile, Khartum itself was remarkably quiet. In general, it was a matter of surprise to Power and others that the townspeople had remained quiet for so long. It was thought at the time

[1] Ibid.
[2] Ibid.
[3] *Vide supra*, p. 174.

that they were probably waiting for the rebels outside to come nearer in order to co-operate with them. As a result of the energetic measures and precautions taken by Muhammad Bey Nushi, the acting Chief of Police, Power began to have no fear. These precautions, in Power's opinion, were the real reason for the quiet state of the town.[1]

Whenever people collected on the way from Barbar to Khartum the circulars announcing the cancellation of slave liberation, the reduction of taxes, and self-government were distributed. It became clear to Gordon and Stewart that the people always welcomed with joy the circular cancelling the liberation of slaves and paid comparatively little attention to the others including that announceing self-government.[2]

By the 12th of February both Cairo and London were relieved of their anxiety about Gordon's safety, having heard that he had arrived safely at Barbar. Gordon's messages from upper Egypt were received in Cairo and their substance was telegraphed to London. Baring wrote privately to Granville saying that he was 'very favorably impressed with all Gordon's messages,'[3] but advising that, in considering Gordon's messages, attention should be paid to his ideas, which were excellent, but undue importance should not be attached to his words.

In Parliament Gordon's mission and its vagueness invoked heated discussion. Sir Michael Hicks-Beach stated that the Government was involving Gordon in a very hazardous mission. He was expected to tame a fanatical leader and his followers, who had defeated two Egyptian armies led by English officers, to withdraw 27,000 men in the teeth of that enemy, to set up members of the old reigning families in the various districts of the Sudan as rival powers to al-Mahdi, and to hand over the arsenals to these powers. He was to do all that by personal influence aided by nothing except an unlimited amount of money from an empty Egyptian treasury.[4] If those new rulers were very soon to submit to al-Mahdi there was no point in setting them up and if they were going to rival al-Mahdi, Her Majesty's Government was preparing the Sudan for a civil

[1] Power to Baring, Feb. 12, 1884, enclosed in Baring to Granville, No. 267, Mar. 5, 1884, P.R.O., F.O. 73/3668.
[2] Stewart's diary, loc cit.
[3] Baring to Granville, Feb. 12, 1384, P.R.O., G/D 29/162.
[4] *Hansard*, 3rd ser., vol. 284, col. 1110.

war similar to that for which they had prepared Zululand. Supposing that the result were not favorable to Gordon, was the Government going to send an expedition for his support? Or were they going to 'leave him to shift for himself?' Hicks-Beach hoped that the Government would make up their minds on that question.

The character of Gordon's task was by this time completely changed. It had originally been the intention of the British Government to send him to Sawakin to report on the situation and possibly to use his influence with the Arabs to open the Barbar–Sawakin road, and thus facilitate the Egyptian evacuation of the Sudan. Gordon had, however, become the officer responsible for the actual withdrawal of the Egyptian garrisons and civilians from the Sudan and for the establishment of a Sudanese Government. The difficulties of his task had not been ignored. The statements of Baring and Gordon show that both these men were fully aware of the dangers inherent in the situation. It also appears that the Conservative opposition were more fully alive to the difficulties of the evacuation than the Government, despite the fact that since the annihilation of Hicks's expedition, dispatches and other correspondence from Egypt had stressed the dangers of the operation. Gordon was, for the most part, left to take the initiative, while the authorities in Cairo and London were left to approve, disapprove, or modify his policy as they saw fit. The British Government, at least, was later to pay a heavy price in popularity for the vagueness of their instructions to Gordon and their inability to grasp the seriousness of the situation in the Sudan.

VIII

EXPEDITIONS TO THE EASTERN SUDAN

The rising for the cause of al-Mahdi in eastern Sudan was closely connected with two personalities—'Uthman Diqna and Shaikh al-Tahir al-Mujzub. 'Uthman belonged to a famous Sawakin family which was descended by marriage from Kurdish and Hadandawa stock. As was usual with nearly all inhabitants of Sawakin, the Diqna family earned their living by trading with the outside world, particularly with Arabia. At that time the slave-trade provided a very lucrative occupation. 'Uthman and his brothers were unfortunate in having a consignment of some eighty-six slaves seized by the British warship *Wild Swan* which patrolled the Red Sea in an attempt to stop traffic in slaves.[1] Moreover, through the pressure of the British Consul in Jadda on the Turkish authorities, their shops were also searched and their goods confiscated.

'Uthman was embittered and indignant against both the British and the Turks, and had to start business again, mainly in Sena and in supplying the gin factory of Mr. Alyas Dabbas with water. Hearing of 'Urabi's revolt in Egypt, 'Uthman apparently attempted to create trouble for the Government by starting seditious activities in Sawakin. The influential notables of the town and the authorities agreed, however, that it was not to their advantage, being an unfortified port, to incur the wrath of Britain who could destroy the town with one man-of-war. They therefore decided to expel 'Uthman who subsequently made his way to the interior and established headquarters at Barbar.

Although he was considered to be a danger to the safety of Sawakin, he frequented the town and even attempted to rouse the people against the Government. No measures were taken against him, mainly because of the influence of Shaikh al-Tahir al-Majzub who was his friend and the head of his religious fraternity. When he returned to Barbar he heard of the successes of al-Mahdi at Aba and Qadir and at the siege of al-Ubayyid. One of his brothers had already joined al-Mahdi and had died while the

[1] Wylde, A. B., *'83 to '87 in the Sudan* (London, 1888), vol. i, p. 21.

Mahdists were still besieging al-Ubayyid. We do not know exactly when 'Uthman trekked to the west to join the revolution, but he was with al-Mahdi when the latter was celebrating the surrender of al-Ubayyid.[1]

After the fall of al-Ubayyid, the main subject of discussion among al-Mahdi's generals was how to stop the reinforcements that were pouring into Khartum via the Sawakin–Barbar road. They had already heard that a large number of soldiers and a large amount of material had been collected in Khartum to be used against the movement in Kurdufan. It was, then, an obvious course to attempt to destroy their enemy's source of reinforcement. It was there that 'Uthman Diqna took upon himself the task of cutting the line of communication between the Red Sea and Barbar.

al-Mahdi subsequently appointed him commander-in-chief of the eastern Sudan, giving him letters of recommendation to the chiefs of tribes, to Shaikh al-Tahir al-Majzub the spiritual leader, and even to the Government authorities at Sawakin. al-Mahdi could not have chosen a more suitable man for this operation. 'Uthman was well acquainted with the country around Sawakin, and harbored grievances against the British, the Turks and the inhabitants of Sawakin. He was intimately connected with Shaikh al-Tahir, the most influential spiritual leader of that region, who exercised undisputed control over the Hadandawa, the most powerful tribe in the vicinity of Sawakin.

As soon as 'Uthman left Barbar for the east he began to preach for al-Mahdi. He met with no success at first, as al-Mahdi's center of activity was too remote from that neighborhood for him to have any influence on the people who were not impressed with 'Uthman's qualifications as a religious leader. Moreover, 'Uthman himself was not well known except in the immediate neighborhood of Sinkat and Sawakin. When he came to the headquarters of Shaikh al-Tahir a dramatic opportunity gave the movement a start which compensated for the remoteness of al-Mahdi and the lack of spiritual qualities in 'Uthman.

Shaikh al-Tahir was a member of the Majazib family who had been renowned for their sanctity and religious learning since the time of the Fung dynasty. They lived at al-Damar near the junction of the Atbara river with the main channel of the Nile. Their

[1] Jackson, H. C., *Osman Diqna* (London, 1926), p. 23.

spiritual influence was dominant all along the Nile among the illustrious and famous Ja'alin tribes. al-Tahir, however, had centered his religious activities at Sawakin and among the Hadandawa tribes in the neighborhood. Although that eastern portion of the Sudan was claimed by the Marghani fraternity as their sphere of spiritual influence, yet at that time they had lost their hold on the Hadandawa tribes, and Shaikh al-Tahir was their acknowledged spiritual guide who lived among them and who was near at hand, while the members of the Marghani family lived in the towns, especially at Kasalah.

It was the custom at the time, and still is in some places in the Sudan, for such a religious dignitary as Shaikh al-Tahir to seat himself on a chair or an 'anqarib (Sudanese bed) and for all other people to assemble round him, sitting on the ground. 'Uthman arrived at the headquarters of al-Tahir when the latter was attending such a state assembly. Normally, 'Uthman, being a follower of the Shaikh would have approached very humbly, kissing the Shaikh's hand, and squatting on the ground with the other followers. But on this occasion he went boldly up to al-Tahir and handed him the letter addressed to him from al-Mahdi. Immediately after reading the letter, al-Tahir kissed it and put it on his head which was a sign of great respect for the author of the letter. Very soon Shaikh al-Tahir retired to a room with 'Uthman and shortly afterwards came out dressed in Dervish fashion, having cast aside the rich silk clothes which he had been wearing not long before. He then seated 'Uthman in his place and crouched under his feet as a humble follower.[1] The change of the Shaikh's attitude had a hypnotic and dramatic effect on all present, who most certainly carried news of the event to all their friends and fellow tribesmen who had not been present. It is hardly surprising, then, that all followers of Shaikh al-Tahir should espouse the cause of al-Mahdi who had had such an astonishing effect on their spiritual leader. The Hadandawa, like many tribesmen in the Sudan, had been long schooled in obeying their spiritual leaders in matters of religion.[2]

The first report of 'Uthman's hostile activity came from the Governor of Sawakin who reported that an emissary from al-Mahdi, called 'Uthman Diqna, was already preaching the cause of the Mahdiya among the Bishariyin and Amarar on the Barbar road.

[1] Jackson, op. cit., p. 27.
[2] Ibid.

To put an end to the menace the Governor of Sawakin himself, Tawfiq Bey, proceeded forthwith to Sinkat to capture 'Uthman before the rising became too serious.[1] The second report of the rising in the east was telegraphed to the Governor-General when he was in the Shukriya country buying camels in preparation for the Kurdufan expedition. 'Uthman seems to have succeeded in persuading some camel-men to desert with their camels between Sawakin and Barbar, thus making the road unreliable for Government transport, for it became clear that the people who usually undertook transport would not co-operate with the authorities as they had previously done.[2]

When 'Ala al-Din arrived at Khartum he received a telegram from Sawakin giving him details of the first encounter between al-Mahdi's emissary and the Government troops at Sinkat.[3] On the 5th of August 1884 'Uthman appeared before Sinkat with 1,500 men after refusing the repeated summons sent him by Tawfiq Bey. 'Uthman immediately demanded, in the name of al-Mahdi, that the towns of Sinkat and Sawakin should be handed over to him with all their contents including arms and money and even the keys of the houses in Sinkat belonging to people at Sawakin. When the demand was refused 'Uthman attacked these houses of the Sawakin people which were scattered over the plain around Sinkat. The inhabitants, assisted by the garrison led by Tawfiq Bey, resisted the attack and finally succeeded in beating it off although the Arabs at one time penetrated into the barracks. The fight lasted for an hour, at the end of which 'Uthman himself was seriously wounded and about sixty-five of his followers killed. On the Government side seven soldiers and six inhabitants were killed. The Arabs returned to Arkawit and although nothing was known about their future plans, it was believed that they would renew their attack on either Sinkat or Sawakin. Takfiq Bey therefore asked for more troops, particularly from Masawwa, in order to meet a further attack by 'Uthman's force.[4] 'Ala al-Din supported

[1] Governor-General to Khedive, Aug. 3, 1883, In-Telegram Book from June 27, 1879, 'Abd. Pal. Arch., Cairo.
[2] Governor-General to Khedive, Aug. 6, 1883, In-Telegram Book from June 27, 1879, 'Abd. Pal. Arch., Cairo.
[3] Governor-General to Khedive, Aug. 13, 1883, In-Telegram Book from June 27, 1879, 'Abd. Pal. Arch., Cairo.
[4] Consul Moncrieff to Malet, Aug. 13, 1883, enclosed in Malet to Granville, No. 359, Aug. 20, 1883, P.R.O., F.O. 78/3557.

Tawfiq Bey's request for more troops for the new eastern front, demanding the strengthening of the garrisons there owing to the importance of the Sawakin-Barbar road which was then used for military transport to the interior of the Sudan.[1]

Although 'Uthman received a set-back in his first encounter, the neighboring tribesmen did not appear to be impressed by the Government's victory. Tawfiq Bey, however, decided to take the offensive and to attack 'Uthman in his retreat at Arkawit. On the way an attack was made on Tawfiq's force, but was successfully repulsed. After the Government's second victory, 'Uthman appeared to them to have been abandoned by his followers.

On October 18 a force of 150 gendarmes were making their way in loose order from Sawakin to Sinkat, as reinforcements, when they were ambushed by the Arabs in a pass. The attack was so sudden that panic ensued, and the officers lost control of the soldiers, each man attempting to save his own life. The whole force was thereupon cut to pieces. This incident encouraged the rebels and demoralized the Government soldiers.

It was intended after this incident to send another force of 150 men to reinforce the 600 already at Sinkat with Tawfiq. The authorities still considered that 'Uthman's power was not really formidable and that the failure of the soldiers was due to their cowardice and lack of discipline. If the new reinforcement would

behave better or have better fortune than their predecessors, he (Tawfiq) will, I hope, have a sufficient force to make Sinkat safe, and bring Diqna to a decisive fight. The latter is said not to have more than 500 to 600 men with him lately and might be quickly suppressed, if the Fellah troops would fight. Hitherto, however, only the excellent black troops, and some Bashbuzuks have done real work and there appears to be a great want of such officers as might persuade the Fellah to his duty.[2]

At the beginning of November it was reported to Sawakin that Tukar was threatened by the rebels. That town was the granary for the Red Sea coastal towns and its capture by the rebels would react most unfavorably on the food supplies of the towns along that coast. Mahmud Pasha Tahir, the new commander of troops at Sawakin, favored the sending of an expedition to reinforce the

[1] Governor-General to Khedive, Aug. 20, 1883, 'Abd. Pal. Arch., Cairo.
[2] Moncrieff to Baring, Oct. 25, 1883, enclosed in Baring to Granville, No. 489, Nov. 1, 1883, P.R.O., F.O. 78/3559.

town and prevent its falling into the enemy's hands, and then the rescue of Sinkat could be attempted. Consul Moncrieff seems to have supported Mahmud Tahir against the cautious Sulayman Pasha Niazi, the Governor-General of eastern Sudan. Sulayman's opinion of the nature and strength of the rebellion had completely changed. While at the beginning he thought too light of it, he maintained later that it was very much more formidable than it appeared and that 10,000 Turkish troops would be required to pacify the eastern Sudan. Yet he was aware that there was practically no Egyptian army besides Wood's new recruits, who could not be hazarded so early. Above all, Sulayman stressed that the Government knew very little about conditions in the interior. Moncrieff estimated the rebel force collected around Sawakin, Sinkat, and Tūkar at 7,000 men, 'but the greater part are cowardly.' [1]

Mahmud Tahir prevailed over the cautious attitude of Sulayman and took about 500 soldiers to Tirinkitat, the landing-place for Tūkar. Consul Moncrieff accompanied the party on his own authority without instructions from his Government. Both Mahmud Tahir and Moncrieff were newcomers to the country and were still ignorant of the forces behind the rebellion in the Sudan. They thought of it only as a combat between well-armed soldiers and a band of badly organized and undisciplined natives. Mahmud Pasha thought that the three towns of Sinkat, Tūkar, and Sawakin would hold their own if their garrisons were reinforced with a further 1,000 men, with a supply of money to buy camels for their own transport so that they need not rely on hired camels. This information was sent by Moncrieff to Baring a few minutes before the march of Mahmud's force from Tirinkitat to Tūkar. Moncrieff emphasized the desirability that the reinforcements sent to the eastern Sudan should be 'as good as possible and well *officered. I* think they will fight, if led, we ought to see today.' [2]

On landing, Mahmud Pasha formed his soldiers into a square and marched towards Tūkar. When they were half-way there they saw the rebels, almost 600 in number, occupying the wells of al-Taib, and flying a number of flags. Mahmud at once ordered his men, who were drawn up in a square, to fire. Regardless of

---

[1] Moncrieff to Baring, Nov. 4, 1883, enclosed in Baring to Granville, No. 527, Nov. 19, 1883, P.R.O., F.O. 78/3559.
[2] Ibid.

the losses they had sustained from this fire, the Arabs attacked and succeeded in penetrating the square. Panic broke out, and the soldiers fled in all directions. A number of officers, consul Moncrieff, and four Greek merchants were killed in the fray. Only thirty of the 120 soldiers who were killed fell in battle, all the rest being cut down in flight.¹ The rest of the troops made for the sea with Mahmud Tahir at their head and managed to take the steamship back to Sawakin. Mahmud never left the ship on his return to the town, although Sulayman Pasha persuaded him to come near to the shore, as it was his duty to live on shore near his soldiers.²

After consultation between Sulayman Pasha and Mahmud Pasha, the former left Sawakin for Masawwa to bring four companies of black soldiers for the relief of both Sinkat and Tūkar. The general belief among the senior officers at Sawakin was that no reliance could be placed on the type of Egyptian soldiers who were stationed there. In the first place they were old people, brought to Sawakin in chains as if they were criminals. Secondly, they were hampered by their wives and children. Thirdly, most of them had been with 'Urabi Pasha and they were under the impression that they were being sent to Sawakin as prisoners. They were, therefore, not fit to fight at all. As soon as the four companies of black troops arrived, Mahmud Pasha would hasten to the relief of Tūkar and Sinkat.³ The death of Moncrieff made it necessary for the British Government to protect British subjects in Sawakin, and for that purpose Her Majesty's Ship *Ranger* was dispatched from Aden to Sawakin.⁴

While the authorities were waiting for the black troops to come from Masawwa, the rebels were making unsuccessful attacks on Sawakin, but there was no doubt whatsoever that the town was in a state of siege and that, although these attacks were bloodless, yet they were annoying to the inhabitants, demoralizing to the troops, and in general greatly weakened the Government's influ-

¹ Izzet Effendi to Baker Pasha, Nov. 10, 1883, enclosed in Baring to Granville, No. 572, Nov. 30, 1883, P.R.O., F.O. 78/3559.
² Brewster to Baring, Nov. 15, 1883, enclosed in Baring to Granville, No. 536, Nov. 22, 1883, P.R.O., F.O. 78/3559.
³ Izzet Effendi to Baker Pasha, Nov. 10, 1883, enclosed in Baring to Granville, No. 572, Nov. 30, 1883, P.R.O., F.O. 78/3559.
⁴ Baring to Granville, No. 509, Nov. 13, 1883, P.R.O., F.O. 78/3559.

ence. An expedition to punish the rebels in the plain between Sawakin and the mountains was fitted out after the arrival of the black troops from Masawwa on the 2nd of December. The force consisted of 20 cavalry and 2 staff officers, 500 picked black troops including 13 officers, and 200 bashbuzuks and Egyptian soldiers with 2 officers and a mountain gun.[1] They were attacked by the rebels some twenty-four miles from Sawakin, just short of Tamanib on the Sinkat road, on broken ground at the foot of the mountains. The attacking force of the Arabs was composed of 3,000 able-bodied Hadandawa, who penetrated the square and threw the troops into disorder. The blacks fought back to back but they could not resist such an overwhelming number of determined fighters, fighting with spears and swords—weapons with which they were familiar. Practically the whole expedition was annihilated except a few soldiers who managed to escape to Sawakin to tell the story. Mahmud Tahir had sent the force under Qasim Bey, without transport or support, and he had remained behind.

There has been something nearly akin to crime in the behavior of Sulayman Pasha Niazi, Governor-General of the Eastern Sudan, and Mahmud Tahir the general, in the way they have behaved. They ignored all the local influence, have quarrelled with the camel Shaikhs, who do the whole of the transport, have not accepted their services, they have not tried to conciliate any of the men that might have been won over, and they have lost the confidence of every one, and now simply through fear of the rebels, many of the men that ought to have been helping the Government have been forced to join the rebels, as the Government gave them no protection.[2]

Baring, in forwarding this information from Wylde, who was a merchant at Sawakin, mentioned that 'it is impossible to acquit the Egyptian Government at Cairo of blame in this matter.' He had spoken to Sharif Pasha in the strongest terms about the conduct of Tahir Pasha in the incident in which Moncrieff had died. The Egyptian Government had decided to recall Tahir Pasha and try him by court martial at Cairo.

'Uthman Diqna had won his second brilliant success, which raised the morale of his followers and at the same time attracted to him still more adherents from the wavering tribesmen. It was

[1] Wylde to Baring, Dec. 4, 1883, enclosed in Baring to Granville, No. 592, Dec. 10, 1883, P.R.O., F.O. 78/3560.
[2] Ibid.

evident after the second defeat that the chances of sending relief to Sinkat from the remaining troops at Sawakin were very remote. Moreover, Tawfiq Bey and his band of determined black troops experienced great difficulty in obtaining food in that cold weather.

'Uthman Diqna's victories were attributed, in Cairo, to the inefficiency of the Egyptian command and their military mistakes. It was also thought that 'Uthman, with his ill-armed Hadandawa, far away from the center of spiritual inspiration, would not prove so formidable an enemy as he had appeared to be in the minor battles. The Egyptian Government in the Sawakin area had however to contend with difficulties of transport. It was essential that 'Uthman's rising should be suppressed because he was operating along a vital link in communications with the interior and the best and easiest approach to Khartum. The authorities in Cairo therefore had no alternative but to attempt to clear the road by suppressing 'Uthman's rising. The destruction of Hicks's army made it even more necessary to make this attempt without delay.

The young army raised by Wood would have been, in ordinary circumstances, the proper force to undertake this task. At this time, however, it was extremely improbable that it would be sent to the Sudan. The British Government was adamant that it should not be sent on active service beyond the boundaries of Egypt proper. The army collected for service in the Sudan a year before and further augmented at Hicks's request had almost exhausted Egyptian manpower. Nothing was left to stem the rising tide of rebellion in the eastern Sudan except Baker Pasha's Gendarmerie.

To compensate for his disappointment at being refused the command of the new regular army, Baker had been given the command of the Gendarmerie. This force was intended to preserve internal peace and to act as a police force, leaving the suppression of the more serious risings in Egypt itself to the army. Baker set out to organize the force with that end in view, but he emphasized the military side of their training rather than the civilian aspect, for he himself had been a soldier. He had to build up a force to keep law and order among the fellaheen in the semi-urban districts of the small towns and in the large towns of Cairo, Alexandria, and Port Said. It was, therefore, necessary for the force to be, both in personnel and in training, of a varied character. Whilst the bulk of the force should naturally be composed of Egyptians, he had to take into account that the population of the big towns included numbers of Maltese, Greeks, and Italians, commonly known as the Levantine element.[1] To have a police force which could deal with that element, Baker had to include among his recruits men drawn from it. He also wished to include Turks in his force who would be useful in cases where he could not rely on the Egyptians. The duties of the force also varied from detective work in the big towns to mounted patrols in the rural areas.

On the 24th of November 1883 Baring telegraphed privately to Lord Granville[2] that there was some idea of sending a force under Baker Pasha to open the Sawakin-Barbar road. Baring considered that it was the best course for the Egyptian Government to take, for it might 'dispense as it likes of the Gendarmerie but not of Wood's army.' It was thought at the time that Baker's objective would not be confined to opening the route to Barbar by suppressing the rebels near Sawakin, but that he would also lend support to the garrisons of the interior alarmed by the annihilation of Hicks's army.[3] This was borne out by evidence in Power's letters that Baker's force was expected to go to Khartum.[4] 'We hope Baker Pasha and his army will be here in six weeks to our relief.' Power expected the arrival of Baker with a number of European officers at Khartum to cause some stir: 'We are looking out anxiously for it,' he reported.

Baker's final instructions before leaving Cairo assigned to him the command of the operations aiming at the 'pacification of the region lying between Barbar and Sawakin, and the maintenance of communications between these two points.' While he was to attain his objective by arms should the rebels resist, he was to 'use every means of conciliation and diplomacy, with a view to secure the obedience and submission of the Shaikhs of the different tribes before having recourse to force.'[5] Baker was also informed that the black battalions recruited and commanded by Zubair Pasha would be added to his Gendarmerie. Zubair would be placed directly

---

[1] Sartorius, Ernestine, *Three Months in the Sudan* (London, 1885), p. 72.
[2] Private telegram Baring to Granville, Nov. 24, 1883, P.R.O., G/D 29/161.
[3] De Coetlogon to Wood, Nov. 25, 1883, enclosed in Baring to Granville, No. 560, Nov. 26, 1883, P.R.O., F.O. 78/3559.
[4] Power, op. cit., pp. 54, 57.
[5] *Parl. Pap.* (1884), vol. lxxxviii, p. 169.

under Baker's command and might use his influence with the tribes. As soon as he arrived Baker was to be in supreme control of all parts of the Sudan which he could reach. The Khedive also wrote privately to Baker, asking him to 'act with the greatest prudence on account of the insufficiency of the forces placed under your command.'[1] He was advised not to begin hazardous military operations until the reinforcements commanded by Zubair Pasha had arrived. While waiting for these troops he was to devote his time and energy to 'raising the tone and courage of the soldiers, and assuring the safety and defense of the town of Sawakin.'

It is quite worth noting that Baker's instructions, both the official and the private, were couched in extremely cautious language and were very vague. Baring explained the vagueness of these instructions in answer to criticism from the London press.[2] It was clear to Baker and to others with some knowledge of the situation that with his original force Baker could do very little, and in consequence 'should not run any serious risk of further disaster.' Baring thought it was only fair to Baker that the responsibility of adopting a cautious line of action 'should devolve not on him but on the Egyptian Government.' Baker entirely agreed with these instructions, which in fact he had drafted, and he expressed his gratitude to Baring for helping him to obtain written instructions. It must, moreover, be remembered that the expedition was fitted out while the disaster to Hicks's force was still fresh in Egyptian memory.

Zubair's appointment as a commander in the Sudan was first made known to the British public in The Times of December 1, 1883. The reports of Moberly Bell, The Times correspondent in Egypt, were not correct in some details. He portrayed Zubair as a rebel against the Government who had been defeated by Gordon and Gessi, and when taken prisoner to Cairo had been released by the Khedive. Certainly Bell had confused Zubair with his son, Sulayman, who had been killed by Gessi during Gordon's governor-generalship. Five days later Bell collected more accurate information about Zubair, reporting that it had been suggested that Zubair should be appointed Governor of Kurdufan and Darfur. As he was a notorious slave-dealer there were obvious

[1] Ibid., p. 170.
[2] Private letter, Baring to Granville, Jan. 22, 1884, P.R.O., G/D 29/162.

objections to that course, but it had to 'be remembered that the surrender of these provinces to which Egypt may now be considered resigned, implies the necessary continuation of slave dealing there.' [1] To Bell the abolition of slavery was more likely to be achieved by the suppression of the markets in Egypt proper rather than by 'interference in a country which would never be effectual without a reconquest of that country.'

Two days before Bell's message appeared in *The Times*, the British and Foreign Anti-Slavery Society addressed the Foreign Secretary in very strong terms against Zubair's appointment. Granville minuted their memorandum: 'Reply that Her Majesty's Government have received no official confirmation to this report, but that they do not consider it desirable to interfere with the measures which the Egyptian Government may be disposed to adopt in the Sudan.' [2]

On the 9th of December Baring sent an official dispatch about Zubair. He told Granville that Zubair had been 'intimately connected with the slave trade.' Baring thought that in normal circumstances Zubair's appointment would have been objectionable and that it would have been his duty to have remonstrated against it. But at that time it was neither necessary nor desirable to interfere with the discretion of the Egyptian Government. Despite his faults Zubair was believed to possess 'great energy and resolution.' The Egyptian Government was anxious to employ him to command the Bedwins in Baker's army and to conduct the negotiations with the tribes along the Barbar-Sawakin road and elsewhere. Baker, who was to lead the expedition, was also anxious to have Zubair's services. Baring pointed out that since responsibility for the conduct of affairs in the Sudan had been left entirely to the Egyptian Government, it would have been illogical 'to have objected to that Government using its own discretion on such a point, as the employment of Zubair Pasha.' [3] But the British Government objected later, and Nubar's administration had to stop Zubair from being sent to the Sudan.

The appearance of the Egyptian element in Baker's troops on

---

[1] *The Times*, Dec. 6, 1883.
[2] Minutes by Granville on a memorandum by the British and Foreign Anti-Slavery Society, Dec. 4, 1883, P.R.O., F.O. 78/4194.
[3] Baring to Granville, No. 587, Dec. 1883, P.R.O., F.O. 78/4194.

parade could not have been finer. Individually, they were big, strong, and powerful, hardly any of them being less than 5 feet 9 inches in height; almost all of them had been non-commissioned officers in the late 'Urabi army, which accounts for their proficiency in drill. But beneath this fine appearance there lurked a spirit of mutiny and reluctance to fight. This spirit had already found expression in desertion; about 280 out of 800 had escaped from the train on the way to Suez. The Turkish element in the Gendarmerie hid their reluctance to fight until the last moment when they were called to parade before the Khedive at 'Abdin Palace; mutiny suddenly broke out and they collectively refused to go. After some time, one-third of them were induced to set out. The Turkish troops agreed that they had joined the service on the clear understanding that they were to be employed only in Egypt proper and were not to be sent to the Sudan.[1]

The troops finally departed amidst the loud lamentations of their relatives. The scene was so disagreeably demoralizing that General Baker ordered the train to move before the time appointed, and General Sartorius, who was to have travelled with the troops, missed the train.[2] Baker himself was unavoidably delayed in Cairo in order to make arrangements for transport.[3]

On arrival at Sawakin, Sartorius found the town short of both food and fodder, and he had to face the problem of sending provisions for the beleaguered garrison of Sinkat. He reported that notwithstanding the scarcity of provisions in Sawakin he was making arrangements to send fifteen days' rations to Sinkat. The rebels were about nine miles from Sawakin and said to be gathered in strength, but he thought that their numbers could not exceed 6,000 men.[4]

Sartorius finally decided that he could not provision Sinkat with the soldiers at his disposal, and would therefore try to bribe friendly Arabs to deliver to the garrison the provisions which he had collected. If he failed to induce the Arabs to carry out this plan, he would order the troops to march to the relief of Sinkat. If it were necessary to march, Sartorius asked Baker's approval for ordering

[1] Memorandum by Baker Pasha, enclosed in Baring to Granville, No. 601, Dec. 12, 1883, P.R.O., F.O. 78/3560.
[2] Sartorius, op. cit., p. 33.
[3] The Times, Dec. 10, 1883.
[4] Baring to Granville, No. 605, Dec. 14, 1883, P.R.O., F.O. 78/3560.

up the black troops from Masawwa and replacing them by Egyptians.[1] He asked Baker to allow the European volunteers to join him at Sawakin at once, as the 'business is a very serious one, and will require every man.'

Before Sartorius's arrival Colonel Harrington had built an inner line of defenses round Sawakin, making a surprise attack from the mainland impossible. These defensive measures and the arrival of Sartorius allayed the panic of the inhabitants, but this was counterbalanced by the alarming behavior of the irregulars who had arrived.[2]

The aged Sulayman Niazi Pasha, who had been removed from Khartum as a result of Hicks's demands, was at that time Governor-General of the Red Sea. Sartorius had not been long in Sawakin before he quarrelled with Sulayman over measures which he, Sartorius, thought necessary. He reported all instances of Sulayman's apathy or obstructiveness, not excluding those told to him by Mr. Wylde, the English merchant at Sawakin, and Captain Darwall of H.M.S. *Ranger*. The cowardly behavior of Mahmud Pasha, the commander of the troops, was also reported. As a result of these complaints, Sulayman and Mahmud were recalled, and on his arrival, Baker took over supreme command.

After he had been only five days at Sawakin,[3] General Sartorius drew up the details of his plan to relieve Sinkat. A force of more than 2,000, drawn from the motley army assembled at Sawakin, was to escort a convoy of provisions to Sinkat. The road was carefully studied and some strategic positions on it were to be fortified and manned in order to keep intact the line of retreat for the return journey. Shaikh Mahmud 'Ali was to march with his friendly Arabs in front and on the flanks as scouts, but always separate from the troops to prevent treachery. On reaching Sinkat the provisions were to be left for the soldiers, and the women and children to be withdrawn to Sawakin. Sartorius received no reply when he submitted this proposal to Baker who apparently thought that the decision could be postponed until his arrival at Sawakin.

[1] Sartorius to Baker, Dec. 8, 1883, enclosed in Baring to Granville, No. 606, Dec. 14, 1883, P.R.O., F.O. 78/3560.

[2] Wylde to Baring, Dec. 10, 1883, enclosed in Baring to Granville, No. 610, Dec. 15, 1883, P.R.O., F.O. 78/3560.

[3] Sartorius to Baker, enclosed in Baring to Granville, No. 637, Dec. 20, 1883, P.R.O., F.O. 78/3560.

In the absence of any British consul after the death of Moncrieff, Mr. Wylde supplied Baring with news. On the 16th of December Wylde reported[1] that according to information brought by a spy, who had penetrated the garrison of Sinkat and had met Tawfiq Bey, the town had sufficient provisions to hold out for another six weeks. While he had been there the Arabs had attacked the town but had been repulsed. There was a marked tendency among the tribes to desert from the Government, and Shaikh Mahmud 'Ali, the contractor of the Barbar road, reported that his tribe was dwindling daily. They complained that the Government would not support them, but Wylde thought that they would simply drift to the stronger side. Wylde considered that Egyptian influence had fallen off because of the mismanagement of affairs by the Turkish pashas. Events might have favored the Government and 'Uthman's rising might have been suppressed had the ideas of Tawfiq Bey been carried out. Wylde ventured to suggest the appointment of Christian governors to the chief districts and of a Christian governor-general: from his experience with the natives they would be happier and quieter under Christian rulers.

On the 18th of December an enormous crowd, composed of nearly all the Europeans in Cairo and a number of Egyptians, assembled at the station to bid Baker Pasha farewell. Bell spoke of the popularity of Baker Pasha and the 'hopelessness of his mission.'[2] Bell's last remark is very significant because it indicates that well-informed circles looked upon Baker's adventures as hopeless even before the policy of the abandonment of the Sudan had been forced on Egypt.

On arrival at Sawakin Baker hastened to send Baring his impressions on the affairs of Sawakin and on the Sudan question in general.[3] He found in Sawakin harbor three men-of-war including the flagship *Euryalus* with Admiral Hewett on board. They occupied good positions for the defense of the town. The defenses on the land side had been very much strengthened by Sartorius though they were not yet complete. These two defensive measures having been taken there was no fear for the safety of the town.

---

[1] Wylde to Baring, Dec. 16, 1883, enclosed in Baring to Granville, No. 639, Dec. 21, 1883, P.R.O., F.O. 78/3560.

[2] *The Times*, Dec. 19, 1883.

[3] Baker to Baring, Dec. 27, 1883, enclosed in Baring to Granville, No. 6, Jan. 2, 1884, P.R.O., F.O. 78/3665.

News had been received from Tawfiq that he could hold Sinkat until the 23rd of January. Reports from Tūkar, however, were not so satisfactory: the garrison was well provided with food but was short of ammunition, and the morale of the troops was not so high as at Sinkat. Making allowances for exaggeration, Baker estimated the number of rebels around Sawakin at 20,000 men. The friendly Arabs were so small in number that they would be practically valueless, even if they definitely gave their support to the Government. All the great tribes had either already joined the rebels or were awaiting the turn of events. Baker thought that the whole movement had been misunderstood by the authorities in Cairo. He no longer doubted that 'we are face to face with a most formidable fanatical religious movement, which is organized and directed with considerable skill, and which is spreading rapidly over the whole country.' The once despised Arab tribes had changed their character. 'They have now become desperate fanatics with a complete contempt for death and each man is inspired with the courage of an Indian Faqer.'

In the absence of reliable information on the state of affairs on the Barbar-Sawakin road there was reason to believe that the southern Bishariyin were all in revolt. The only district remaining quiet was Kasalah. Assuming that Kasalah would remain tranquil, Baker drew up a plan to open the road from Khartum to Masawwa in case it should be decided to abandon the Sudan and withdraw the garrisons of the interior. The only difficulty was presented by the Abyssinians between Kasalah and Masawwa, and Baker hoped to visit Masawwa to make temporary arrangements with Ras Alula about the safety of the road. He suggested that a Christian Egyptian accompanied by a British agent should immediately be sent from Cairo to Masawwa with power to make a long-term agreement with Abyssinia.

Assuming that he could succeed in getting 800 black troops from Masawwa and the neighboring garrisons, and that Zubair would arrive with some 1,200 new black recruits, Baker thought that he could outmaneuver the enemy and beat them. To him to 'attempt to force the difficult defiles between this [Sawakin] and Sinkat would be a most hazardous enterprise with a very small chance of success.' Baker was certain that Egypt would be compelled to abandon the Sudan if not assisted by English or Turkish troops.

He was, however, equally sure that 'the most serious danger will threaten Egypt in the future if this formidable movement is allowed to acquire further prestige by the abandonment of the Sudan provinces while England is in occupation of Egypt.'

By the 5th of January 1884 Baker had returned to Sawakin from Masawwa, and on the 8th he wrote a long letter[1] to Baring elaborating a plan of operations to be carried out with black troops and friendly Arabs from the eastern Sudan. He thought that this project would enable Egypt to hold her own in the Sudan without outside assistance. In forwarding this letter, and another from Baker, to Granville, Baring described them as 'two interesting letters,' for on the day on which Baker wrote to Baring Nubar accepted office on the understanding that the Sudan was to be abandoned by Egypt. When Baring forwarded the letters, Gordon was already on his way to carry out that policy.

The new policy of abandonment accepted by Nubar's ministry made it necessary to send Baker fresh instructions. He was now instructed to cancel that part of his orders giving him discretion to open the Sawakin-Barbar road west of Sinkat. He was not to attempt to do so. If he found it absolutely necessary to relieve the beleaguered garrisons of Tūkar and Sinkat by the use of force, he might do so provided that his force was sufficient and that he could 'reasonably count on success.'[2] The enforced submission of soldiers holding out in those two places would be considered 'very painful to His Highness the Khedive,' but such sacrifice would be better than 'that you and your troops should attempt a task which you cannot reckon fairly to be within your power.' No effort was to be spared to open the Barbar-Sawakin road by diplomatic means.

The troops under Baker's command hardly provided the best material for the struggle against 'Uthman Diqna. They were mutinous before they left Cairo, and to guard against the desertions, which were noticed while troops were being transported to Suez, some soldiers were put in leg-irons.[3] On board the ship to

---

[1] Baker to Baring, Jan. 8, 1884, enclosed in Baring to Granville, No. 81, Jan. 19, 1884, P.R.O., F.O. 78/3665.

[2] Instructions from the Khedive to Baker, Jan. 9, 1884, enclosed in Baring to Granville, No. 47, Jan. 11, 1884, P.R.O., F.O. 78/3665.

[3] Ware, J. R., and Mann, R. K., *The Life and Times of Colonel Fred Burnaby* (London, 1885), p. 269.

Sawakin, frequent quarrels took place between the Egyptian and the Sudanese officers, and Colonel Burnaby heard one of the latter unhesitatingly saying that he would take the first opportunity of deserting to al-Mahdi.[1] No notice was taken and the officer was allowed to go on 'spreading sedition to the best of his ability among the men.'

In Sawakin the bashbuzuks refused to drill until General Sartorius forced them to do so by flogging. The Governor-General, Sulayman Pasha, remonstrated, telling Sartorius that they should not be forced to drill. Sulayman considered that since they were volunteers they ought to be asked to drill and if they refused to do so they should not be forced.[2] When practicing drill movements the soldiers did not appear to understand how to form a square. Many of the irregulars had had no experience of drill until they reached Sawakin, and they could not have more than a month's training in all, which obviously was not enough.[3] Zubair's blacks had even less experience of drill, and the old soldiers were as undisciplined as the new recruits. The men from Masawwa had a little experience of military training. 'It is to be hoped,' says Mrs. Sartorius, 'the enemy will not fight, and will be kept off by the look of the men when in large body together.'

There was also further evidence of the unfitness of Baker's force. The black troops, who had been given three months' pay in advance, had almost spent their last penny many days before they were ordered to fight. They had, moreover, brought with them from Egypt a large number of children and women.[4] They thus found themselves on active service with only their ration of dry biscuits, which they detested, and on which their families also had to exist. They were, therefore, discontented with their rations, and had to fight without the hope of any reward afterwards. It was not, therefore, surprising that they had no heart in the matter, no cause to fight for, and no incentive to do so. The last batch of Zubair's blacks shared these disabilities, in addition to which their total lack of training was such that they were hardly able to march and they did not know how to fix their bayonets. Their officers were lieutenants and sub-lieutenants who had been many years on the

[1] Ibid.
[2] Sartorius, op. cit., p. 129.
[3] Ibid., p. 155.
[4] Ibid., p. 210.

retired list and not one was fit to drill a company. Signs of disobedience were already noticeable among these soldiers and they were brought to reason by flogging in the same way as the irregular Albanians.[1]

The Egyptian soldiers in the force were told exaggerated stories of the tribes. They would not have volunteered for the Gendarmerie had they known that they were to be sent to the Sudan. That was definitely a breach of faith as far as they were concerned. They had been led to believe that they were to undertake police work in Egypt proper, and that the most dangerous duty that they might be called upon to do would be to chastise the wretched Bedwins surrounding the delta.[2] It must be remembered that they were drawn mostly from the fellaheen, who were fanatically religious, and they could not accept the idea of fighting a man with a religious mission. Those in Hicks's army who had attempted to resist al-Mahdi, had been practically annihilated. Moreover, they were ignorant of the cause for which they were fighting, for their own country was occupied by a foreign infidel power.

Some of the men of Baker's force showed reluctance to sleep out of the town in Sawakin. When the murmur of discontent became so loud that the officers could not hide it from the commander, they reported the story to Baker.[3] The commander took a firm stand telling them: 'Any man or officer who leaves the zaribah and comes into Sawakin without order, will be shot within ten minutes of his arrival. I shall not try him by court-martial; he will simply be shot.' This warning had the desired effect, but it was a clear indication of the low state of morale of the troops. During the embarkation for the journey to Tirinkitat, careful watch was kept on the men to prevent their returning to Sawakin and avoiding the impending battle.

Baker's expedition had been fitted out on the assumption that the Sudan would not be abandoned. Zubair's personal assistance was refused at the last minute and it was believed that his recruits, whether Bedwins or blacks, could only understand his language and would refuse to be led by any other officer. In addition it had been hoped that Zubair's influence would be successfully brought

---

[1] Ibid., p. 209.
[2] Wylde, op. cit., vol. i, p. 29.
[3] Sartorius, op. cit., p. 205.

to bear on those tribes who, while wavering in their loyalty to the Government, had not yet joined al-Mahdi. The bad effect of the announcement of the abandonment of the Sudan was soon seen: the friendly Arabs who were about to go to the rescue of Sinkat were dissuaded from doing so. Moreover, immediately on hearing of the new policy, the Qadi of Sawakin deserted to 'Uthman Diqna leaving a letter behind him excusing his behavior. He declared that although the Government was determined to give up the Sudan, he was an inhabitant of that country, and could not go away. He would be among the first to feel the revenge of the rebels. He was, therefore, determined to try to make his peace with them.[1]

To counteract the religious propaganda of the rebels it was arranged that a member of the great Marghani family, which was revered and respected in the Sawakin area, should preach there. A member of that family who was residing in Egypt therefore went to Sawakin before Baker's arrival. There, in the Marghani mosque, he preached a sermon which aroused a great deal of enthusiasm for the Government's cause. He told General Sartorius that everything would end satisfactorily and that the tribes would see the folly of their ways. But the townspeople of Sawakin already supported the Government and did not need persuasion. It was, on the other hand, a matter of great urgency that the plucky and determined Hadandawa tribe should be weaned from the Mahdist cause. In this respect the Marghani utterly failed and the spiritual leadership in that area was indisputably held by Shaikh al-Tahir al-Majzub.

When he considered the situation of the two garrisons of Sinkat and Tūkar it was quite clear to Baker that the former was in the worst position, for it faced starvation while the Tūkar garrison suffered only from a shortage of ammunition. Baker decided to go to the relief of Tūkar first, merely because he was not able to relieve Sinkat. He thought that the pressure on Sinkat might be lessened by an attack on the enemy at Tūkar. On January 18, 1884, the day on which Gordon left London for the Sudan, Baker began the embarkation of his troops for Tirinkitat whence he intended to march on Tūkar. Mr. Wylde recorded after a conversation with Baker that the latter had been urged by the Egyptian Government

[1]Ibid., p. 202.

to act at once, although people in Sawakin thought that he ought to wait until the arrival of more black troops from Harrar.[1] Confidence in the other troops was already shaken and it was thought there would be more hope of success if the black troops were reinforced.

All the force together with the stores and animals was disembarked on a little island separated from the mainland by shallow water. A fort three miles inland on the mainland was thrown up as a base; the island was useless for this purpose owing to difficulty of access. By 6:30 in the morning of February 4 a force of 3,500 men was ready to move. The morning was very dull and misty, with heavy rain from time to time. Halts to close the ranks were frequent.[2] The mist and rain made visibility poor, and made it necessary to proceed cautiously. When for the first time the enemy was seen at the wells of al-Taib, Colonel Ahmad Kamal ordered the square to be formed and this first operation was performed well, in a short time. The Cairo and Alexandria battalions were no sooner in their places than they began firing furiously into the air so rapidly that in less than a quarter of a minute the place was completely covered with smoke. No orders could be heard and the confusion spread to the other contingents, who also began firing aimlessly. The Arabs were approaching from all sides but they were still far enough away to allow for the restoration of order. However, before order could be restored, the Cairo and Alexandria battalions surged inwards carrying away a part of the Turkish troops and completely routing the Masawwa blacks. Baker Pasha in his official report said: 'On the square being only threatened by a small force of enemy, certainly less than 1,000 strong, Egyptian troops threw down their arms and ran, carrying away black troops with them, allowing themselves to be killed without the slightest resistance.'[3] More than 2,000 of Baker's force were killed and the rest managed to escape to Tirinkitat. The remaining troops were embarked and returned to Sawakin.

On receiving Baker's report, Baring telegraphed to Consul Baker at Sawakin to tell General Baker that he, Baring, was sure that

[1] Wylde, op. cit., p. 53.
[2] Sartorius, op. cit., p. 334.
[3] Baker to Baring, Feb. 6, 1884, enclosed in Baring to Granville, No. 131, Feb. 6, 1884, P.R.O., F.O. 78/3666.

Baker had done all that could be done and that 'he has my entire
confidence, and that I shall continue to do all I can to help and
support him.'[1] Granville approved Baring's telegram.

Wylde declared that General Baker attributed his defeat to the
badness of his material and his not having had enough time to
train his men. He thought that he would have been in a better
position had he used the blacks alone and fought in another formation.[2] In fact the weather on that particular day was unfavorable
to Baker's force, but by that time the Arabs had gained considerable experience in penetrating the soldiers' formation. A spy had
once reported that the Arabs were certain that they would never
fail in their attacks on the Egyptians. They had only to wait till
the soldiers had fired enough shots to have covered themselves
with smoke, and then they could rush without danger into the
square.[3]

Meanwhile, in Sinkat Tawfiq Bey was heroically holding his
own and quite confident of maintaining his position as long as he
had provisions. The news of Hicks's defeat was taken to Sinkat by
Diqna's messenger, who summoned Tawfiq and the garrison to
surrender. Tawfiq's memorable answer was that 'his life was the
Khedive's, his honor his own, and his daughter Effendina [the
Khedive] had promised to look after. Therefore he intended to
defend the place to the last.'[4]

By the time the advanced party of Baker's force under Sartorius
had reached Sawakin the food situation in Sinkat had become
difficult. Sartorius had planned to dump provisions in Sinkat
and to withdraw the women and children. On Baker's arrival in
Sawakin the matter was more carefully considered. It was then
decided that Sinkat should not be relieved as it would be madness
to march the troops through broken and mountainous country. It
was, moreover, hoped that a successful action in the direction of
Tūkar might lend moral support to Tawfiq and encourage Mahmud 'Ali, the Shaikh of the friendly Arabs, to advance on Sinkat.[5]
The last letter from Tawfiq, while breathing 'so much determination and pluck,' conveyed the impression that only a miracle could

[1] Baring to Granville, No. 131, Feb. 6, 1884, P.R.O., F.O. 78/3666.
[2] Wylde, op. cit., p. 108.
[3] Sartorius, op. cit., p. 168.
[4] Ibid., p. 64.
[5] Ibid., p. 210.

save him. The authorities at Sawakin therefore gave Tawfiq discretion to make terms with the rebels or take any measures he might think best.

Tawfiq, however, was determined that on no account would he surrender or accept any terms from the rebels. 'When every cat, dog, rat or fourfooted animal was gone,' [1] any kind of leather, bones, insects, and leaves of trees were served as food. Then starvation was reached and no help had reached them. Tawfiq held a council which decided to make an attempt to reach Sawakin rather than to surrender and be butchered in cold blood. The plan was prepared at night; everything that might be of use to the rebels was destroyed or thrown into the wells; defenses were destroyed and guns were spiked. Then about 700 persons left the place, the troops leading and the women and children following, protected by other troops. When they had marched little more than a mile they were overtaken by the Arabs and the engagement commenced. The defenders of Sinkat were overpowered and, though they fought gallantly, they were massacred to a man. Many of the women and children were also killed, but the remainder were taken prisoner. 'In the annals of the Sudan there never has been a more perfect hero than Tawfiq Bey, and his memory will last and be told in the hill side and the camp fire among the Sudan warriors long after the present generation has passed away.' [2] The disaster of Sinkat made a deep impression on the inhabitants of Sawakin, for there was hardly a family that had not lost a relative.

When Baker's defeat produced panic in Sawakin, the British Government instructed Admiral Hewett to take over the supreme civil and military command of the town, for they had pledged themselves to the Egyptian Government to protect the Red Sea ports. The Cabinet met twice on February 6 and decided to send marines to Sawakin. The two chief military advisers to the Government, the Duke of Cambridge and Lord Wolseley, considered that a British expedition should be sent to Sawakin to chastise any Arab force which might invest the town.[3]

Acting on that advice and urged on by the press and even by Liberal members of Parliament, Hartington, Dilke, and Chamber-

[1] Wylde, op. cit., p. 127.
[2] Wylde, loc. cit.
[3] Gwynn and Tuckwell, op. cit., vol. ii, p. 35.

lain proposed that the suggestion should be considered. Hartington, as Secretary of State for War, consulted Gladstone, who thought that the measure would 'alter fundamentally the whole *basis* of our position as to the Sudan.'[1] It would entail operations against Sinkat and Tūkar and to Gladstone 'chastising' meant following Arab horsemen a great way. Nevertheless, Gladstone was prepared, if his colleagues wished, to discuss the question in Cabinet. Hartington, Dilke, and Chamberlain felt that their own party in the House of Commons was hankering after an expedition, but both Gladstone and Granville appear to have been unaware of any such feeling. Before giving a decision, however, it was thought expedient to send a carefully worded telegram to Gordon, who was at the time between Abu Hamad and Barbar, asking him whether a military expedition to Sawakin to chastise the Arabs would be desirable from his point of view.[2] On February 8 a Cabinet meeting was held at which five ministers, including Hartington, favored the sending of the proposed telegram to Gordon, while Gladstone and Granville opposed it. No decision was reached at that meeting.[3]

Soon after the meeting Gladstone wrote to the Queen explaining that the Cabinet saw many objections to the proposed expedition to Sawakin. The Queen, however, thought that a blow '*must* be struck, or we shall *never* be able to convince the Muhammadans that they have not beaten us. These are wild Arabs and they would not stand against *regular* good troops at all. The *Queen trusts* Lord Wolseley's plan will be considered, and our *whole position remembered.*'[4] She pointed out that both the defeated expeditions had been commanded by Englishmen, although the troops were Egyptians. Baker's defeat had been preceded by Hicks's annihilation which, the Queen declared, '*must* lower us in the eyes of all the world, and most particularly of India.' Her Majesty asked for a demonstration of strength and determination: 'we must not let this fine and fruitful country, with its peaceful inhabitants, be left a prey to murder and rapine and utter confusion. It must be a *disgrace* to the British name, and the country will *not* stand it.'

[1] Gladstone to Granville, B.M. Add. M.S. 44547, Feb. 7, 1884.
[2] Hartington to Granville, Feb. 7, 1884, P.R.O., G/D 29/144.
[3] Gwynn and Tuckwell, loc. cit.
[4] The Queen to Mr. Gladstone, Feb. 9, 1884, *The Letters of Queen Victoria*, 2nd ser., vol. iii, p. 477.

By February 10 Gordon arrived at Barbar and was once more in telegraphic communication with Cairo. He believed that the people who had defeated Baker would not leave their tribal limits and would remain in the vicinity of the garrisons in the east. He suggested that a fresh force of black troops should be formed at Sawakin, and that a proclamation signed by Baker or Wood should be made to the rebels, that no operations would be started against them until they had refused the terms, which he, Gordon, was authorized to offer. In Gordon's opinion the garrisons of Tūkar and Sinkat might be considered lost.[1] Gordon thought that the only thing which might be done would be to invite the principal shaikhs to meet him in council at Khartum and make arrangements for the independence of the Sudan.[2] On the same day Gordon telegraphed to Cairo suggesting that 3,000 Turkish troops could do more than any other force to suppress the rising at Sawakin, for 'it would be sufficient for the Padisha's troops to appear to cause a collapse of all fanatical feeling.'[3]

Gordon's reply to the question as to whether British troops should be sent to Sawakin was not absolutely clear. 'As to sending forces to Sawakin to assist withdrawal I would care more for the rumor of such an intervention than for the forces. What would have the greatest effect would be the rumor of English intervention.'[4] When forwarding Gordon's reply to Granville, Baring expressed his opinion that the arrival of the marines would produce the effect which Gordon desired, but that he, Baring, was altogether opposed to the landing of troops except for the protection of the town. He reported that all these questions had been fully discussed in Cairo, and many objections had been raised to conducting military operations in the interior, one of the greatest difficulties being the lack of water.

On the 11th of February a heated discussion about the relief of Sinkat and Tūkar took place in the House of Commons. On the

[1] Gordon to Baring, Feb. 11, 1884, enclosed in Baring to Granville, No. 179, Feb. 12, 1884, P.R.O., F.O. 78/3667.

[2] Gordon to Baring, Feb. 11, 1884, enclosed in Baring to Granville, No. 182, Feb. 12, 1884, P.R.O., F.O. 78/3667.

[3] Gordon to Baring, Feb. 11, 1884, enclosed in Baring to Granville, No. 181, Feb. 12, 1884, P.R.O., F.O. 78/3667.

[4] Gordon to Baring, Feb. 11, 1884, enclosed in Baring to Granville, No. 178, Feb. 12, 1884, P.R.O., F.O. 78/3667.

following day a meeting of the Cabinet was held and the decision to send an expedition to Sawakin was made in spite of Gladstone's opposition.[1] The fall of Sinkat aroused immense feeling and contributed to the Cabinet's decision. When presenting to Parliament the papers on that expedition, Granville omitted Baring's unfavorable opinion of the expedition. Informing Baring of this omission, in a private letter, Granville emphasized the strong popular feeling in favor of the expedition. 'You might as well try to stop a mule in a snaffle bridle, as check the feeling here on the subject.'[2]

Informing the Queen of the Cabinet's decision, Gladstone wrote: 'The Cabinet was of opinion that a force should at once be collected at Sawakin, with the object—if possible—of relieving the garrison of Tūkar if it should hold out, and of taking any measure necessary for the defense of the Ports.'[3] The Queen approved the decision 'to act with energy at last. May it not be too late to save other lives! The fall of Sinkat is terrible.'[4]

On the same day General Stephenson, the commanding officer in Cairo, was instructed to organize a force, selecting his three best battalions with other necessary arms, with a view to sending them to Sawakin. Major-General Sir G. Graham would command it.[5] Granville informed Baring of the decision and asked him to render every assistance to Stephenson in carrying out his instructions. Baring was instructed to arrange with the Egyptian Government for cavalry horses, camel battery, and the equipment required for the expedition to be obtained from Wood's army.[6] Admiral Hewett was informed[7] that a force sufficient for the relief of Tūkar might be expected to collect at Sawakin on the 19th of February and that he should make an announcement to this effect. An attempt to inform the beleaguered garrison that they would be relieved by British troops was to be made by a native messenger. But it was also to be made clear that the attempt to rescue that garrison was

[1] Gwynn and Tuckwell, op. cit., vol. ii, p. 37.
[2] Granville to Baring, Feb. 15, 1884, P.R.O., G/D 29/2C0.
[3] Gladstone to the Queen, Feb. 12, 1884, *The Letters of Queen Victoria*, 2nd ser., vol. iii, p. 477.
[4] The Queen to Gladstone, Feb. 12, 1884, ibid., p. 478.
[5] Colvile, H. E., *History of the Sudan Campaign* (London, 1899), Part II, p. 21.
[6] Granville to Baring, No. 90, Feb. 12, 1884, P.R.O., F.O. 78/3662.
[7] Granville to Baring, No. 91, Feb. 12, 1884, P.R.O., F.O. 78/3662.

not intended to interfere with the British Government's decision that the Sudan should be evacuated.[1] Baring intended to permit a battalion of the newly raised Egyptian army to go to Sawakin, but the British Government refused to sanction the employment of Wood's army outside the confines of Egypt proper.[2]

Seven days after the sanctioning of the expedition to Sawakin the House of Commons debated an Opposition motion condemning the Government's policy in the Sudan as vacillating. The Opposition reviewed the British policy in the Sudan from the time of the occupation of Egypt. It was avowedly a policy of non-interference in the affairs of the Sudan, giving the Egyptian Government which was unfit to govern its own country almost a free hand there. Every stage in the Government's policy was subjected to severe criticism. Hartington replying for the Government went on to declare that England had no interests in the Sudan nor were there any European interests which would justify the employment of British forces or the expenditure of British resources in an expedition to restore Egyptian authority over that vast part of Africa.[3]

Not long after the fall of Sinkat, news reached Sawakin that the Tūkar garrison was arranging to capitulate. The authorities at Sawakin did not consider that the situation called for the surrender of the Tūkar garrison, for there was no question of starvation as in the case of Sinkat. It could only be explained by the fact that the garrison was not led by a man like Tawfiq Bey, and that the majority of the garrison were Egyptian convicts and old soldiers, lacking the character of the men of the Sinkat garrison. Before General Graham's arrival it was definitely known that the garrison had capitulated and that the inhabitants had been spared.[4]

Wylde was the first man to meet Graham on his arrival at Sawakin, and to break to him the news of the fall of Tūkar, which Graham received badly, for his mission was its relief.[5] It would be very difficult to restrain a soldier from fighting when all his men and equipment had been concentrated in the field and when he had already planned his formation for the attack as Graham had

[1] Granville to Baring, No. 92, Feb. 12, 1884, P.R.O., F.O. 78/3662.
[2] Granville to Baring, No. 95, Feb. 14, 1884, P.R.O., F.O. 78/3662.
[3] *Hansard*, 3rd ser., vol. 284, col. 1433.
[4] Wylde, op. cit., vol. i, p. 128.
[5] Ibid., p. 130.

actually done on board ship before arrival.¹ Public opinion in
England called for a fight with 'Uthman Diqna although Tūkar
had surrendered. It was felt that Graham should strike a blow
at Diqna in order to check the progress of the insurrection and
destroy his prestige.² When Graham suggested to the British
Government that he should go on with his campaign they therefore allowed him to do so. On the other hand, there were members
of Parliament who objected in the strongest terms to any operations
against 'Uthman Diqna. The expedition had been sent to Sawakin
in the interests of humanity. It was understood that there was no
intention of occupying any territory except Sawakin and even then
only temporarily. There was, however, a strong feeling that Tūkar
ought to be relieved so as not to share the fate of Sinkat. But with
the fall of Tūkar there could be no reasonable object in fighting
the Sudanese except the desire for prestige and military glory. It
could not be reconciled with the peaceful policy of Gordon, who
was supposed to be negotiating with al-Mahdi and trying to put
and end to the war by leaving the Sudanese independent of the
Egyptian rule.³ How did the Government, asked Randolph
Churchill, reconcile the facts that 'Uthman was to be slaughtered
and al-Mahdi was to be rewarded? It made one shudder, said
Sir Wilfrid Lawson, to read articles crying out for slaughter and
blood for the prestige of this country. Wylde, the English business
man at Sawakin, thought the policy a bullying one, and, as the
Sudan was to be abandoned, there was no point in fighting.⁴

Graham's whole expeditionary force was taken by ship and disembarked at the same harbor of Tirinkitat where Baker and
Tahir Pasha had made their landings, with the intention of reaching Tūkar and relieving it. As Gordon had expressed a desire that
before the attack was made the chiefs should be invited to meet
Gordon at Khartum to confer with him on the future of the Sudan,
Graham was instructed to send a warning to this effect. Accordingly, Graham wrote a proclamation requiring the shaikhs of tribes
between Tirinkitat and Tūkar, in the name of the British Government, to disperse their fighting men before daybreak on the

¹ Vetch, R. H., *Life, Letters, and Diaries of Lieut.-General Sir Gerald Graham*, p. 266.
² *The Times*, Feb. 25, 1884.
³ *Hansard*, 3rd ser., vol. 284, col. 1891.
⁴ Wylde, loc. cit.

following day or take the consequences. Instead of fighting the British troops, they should send delegates to Gordon at Khartum. 'The English Government is not at war with the Arabs, but is determined to disperse the force now in arms in this neighborhood and near Sawakin.'[1] It was too illogical for the Arabs to accept, and the required answer was not given.

The order to advance was given and the rebels were found to be occupying al-Taib wells, where they had mounted the Krupp guns captured from Baker. A severe battle raged for three hours, at the end of which Graham was victorious, and the Arabs lost more than one-third of their force. Graham's casualties were 34 men killed and 155 wounded. *The Times* correspondent, who accompanied the expedition, gave this account of the action:

Inch by inch the rebels had fought the ground for three and a half hours, with a courage that only fanaticism could give, and no higher praise can be given to our men that they met a worthy enemy. That naked savages should have held their own against troops splendidly trained and disciplined and armed with the best arms existing, makes it easier to understand General Baker's defeat. It is regrettable to be obliged to fight such an enemy for such an ally.[2]

After the battle, the march to Tūkar was resumed, and the town was reached without further fighting. Many of the inhabitants of Tūkar accompanied the army on its return to Tirinkitat on the 4th of March. The whole force with the people from Tūkar embarked for Sawakin, where the concentration of troops was found adequate for the time being.[3]

On hearing of the victory, Gordon sent Graham a telegram in Arabic conveying not only his own congratulations but those of Stewart, Power, and the inhabitants of Khartum. 'I also send my regards to all the British troops and hope very soon the entire Sudan may be pacified and contentment reign among the people as formerly.'[4] Gordon was moved to send that telegram in Arabic, I think, by his desire to impress on the people of Khartum and through them on the rest of the Sudan, that British troops were

[1] Colvile, op. cit., Part II, p. 22.
[2] *The Times,* Mar. 3, 1884.
[3] Colvile, op. cit., Part II, p. 23.
[4] Vetch, op. cit., p. 269.

in action. By that time Gordon had reached the conclusion that his peaceful policy could only be enforced by a show of power.

On the 2nd of March Admiral Hewett had recommended that an attack should be made upon 'Uthman Diqna. It is to be noticed that by that date Graham was still at Tūkar. This shows that the military authorities at Sawakin considered that although the Arabs had lost heavily, their power was not broken and that the victory should be followed up in order to break up their forces completely. The whole question, in Baring's opinion, depended upon whether 'Uthman in fact still threatened Sawakin and whether it would be possible to deliver a decisive blow at a short distance from Sawakin. Obviously those in Sawakin would be best able to decide. It would, however, be of great advantage to strike the blow, as otherwise a considerable garrison of English troops would have to be left at Sawakin. Baring thought that the best plan would be to concentrate the force at Sawakin and for Graham to obtain information about 'Uthman's intentions and position. 'I would not eventually allow an advance unless General Graham feels tolerably confident that he can bring on a decisive engagement near Sawakin.' [1] He thought that both following 'Uthman Diqna far into the interior and advancing and retiring without engaging him should be avoided. Of course it should be made clear that any military operations carried out on that front were solely to protect Sawakin and were not an attempt at conquering the eastern Sudan. General Stephenson was in complete agreement with Baring's recommendations.[2]

Her Majesty's Government agreed that Hewett and Graham should call the rebel chiefs to go to Sawakin and tender their submission. Failing that, the British force would advance on 'Uthman's camp to disperse the tribes assembled there.[3] Graham accordingly advanced, on March 13, on Tamay wells, where the rebels were known to be in force. Although the troops were surprised and thrown into disorder at the beginning, yet they resumed order and kept up a steady fire on the Arabs until they had driven them away into the hills leaving behind about 2,000 dead. The whole Arab

[1] Baring to Granville, No. 253, Mar. 3, 1884, P.R.O., F.O. 78/3668.
[2] Ibid.
[3] Granville to Baring, No. 147, Mar. 7, 1884, P.R.O., F.O. 78/3662.

force was estimated at 12,000 men. The British loss was 5 officers and 104 men killed, and 8 officers and 104 men wounded.[1] Immediately after the engagement, and before the return of troops to Sawakin, Admiral Hewett telegraphed that the losses were heavy, although the troops had been successful. In order to prepare for any eventuality he asked for reinforcements from Cairo and Aden.[2] On the same day, Baker, the British Consul at Sawakin, also reported heavy losses which were 'generally attributed to the vacillation of General Graham, who is said to have needlessly changed the formation of his troops during the enemy's attack, thus creating great confusion.'[3]

The situation after the second battle was that 'Uthman Diqna had been twice defeated, with the loss of more than 4,000 of his followers, and yet there was no sign of his submission. He simply retreated to the mountains, still with a considerable number of adherents, and still showing a determination to harass the vicinity of Sawakin. Graham thought that a third blow might see the end of 'Uthman. He therefore telegraphed to the Secretary of State for War asking for permission to advance on Sinkat. Baring and Chermside, military adviser to the Residency in Cairo, both agreed that this advance should be sanctioned as it would facilitate the negotiations with the tribes. By that time, Gordon had reported from Khartum that the tribes between Barbar and Khartum were in a state of unrest and might endanger his own safety. Baring thought it necessary not only to open the Sawakin-Barbar road, but also to come to terms with the tribes between Barbar and Khartum, otherwise the question of sending an expedition to Khartum to bring away Gordon would very likely arise.[4] The proposed operation against Sinkat had been approved by the British Government, but they would not authorize a move in the direction of Barbar until they had been informed of the military conditions and were satisfied that it was necessary for Gordon's safety. Their information suggested that it would not be safe to send a small body of cavalry as proposed, and that it was impossible to send a large force.[5] Graham's plan was to make even a mock

[1] Colvile, op. cit., Part II, p. 24.
[2] Baring to Granville, No. 215, Mar. 13, 1884, P.R.O., F.O. 78/3669.
[3] Baker to Granville, Confidential, Mar. 13, 1884, P.R.O., F.O. 78/3669.
[4] Baring to Granville, No. 315, Mar. 16, 1884, P.R.O., F.O. 78/3668.
[5] Granville to Baring, No. 146, Mar. 16, 1884, P.R.O., F.O. 78/3669.

demonstration on the Barbar road, although he was quite sure that his troops needed rest. His aim was to impress on the rebels that the troops were to remain and were not leaving the country as was rumored, and that they were able to move anywhere. His military plan was to order a strong battalion with a regiment of cavalry to advance on Hendub and reconnoiter along the Barbar road.[1]

Gladstone was much worried by Graham's proposal which he thought involved too great a risk. He was astonished that the victories had brought no substantial results.[2] Hartington therefore telegraphed to Graham telling him to be more cautious. Baring was averse to the sending of a small force and saw great difficulties in sending a large one. Moreover, it was known that the heat would soon become intolerable for English troops.[3]

The Government's decision about the Sawakin theatre of operations was transmitted to Baring who was to forward it to Graham. Graham was to be instructed to supply rations to Mahmud 'Ali, the friendly chief, and to distribute some money among the shaikhs who had submitted as an inducement to others to follow their example. It was to be impressed on these shaikhs that the Government's object was the opening of the Sawakin-Barbar road. It had been suggested that the road might be divided into sections, and that the shaikhs of the district traversed by each section might be made responsible for keeping his portion open by paying him a subsidy. Graham's plan provided for the joint action of the British troops and the friendly tribes, but the British Government doubted the wisdom of this plan. However, they gave discretion to Graham and Hewett on that point. 'They, however, deprecate the despatch of an expedition against 'Uthman Diqna with whom they would be disposed to recommend, if possible, treating on the basis of his submission and rendering himself answerable for the safety of Barbar Road and the protection of traders and other travellers.' The details of instructions to be sent to Graham were left to Baring's discretion.[4]

[1] Colvile, loc. cit.
[2] Minutes by Gladstone on a telegram from Graham to Hartington, Mar. 17, 1884, B.M. Add. MS. 44147.
[3] Private letter, Baring to Granville, Mar. 18, 1884, P.R.O., G/D 29/162.
[4] Granville to Baring, No. 178, Mar. 21, 1884, P.R.O., F.O. 78/3662.

On receiving these instructions, Baring telegraphed on the same day to Graham transmitting the various suggestions contained in them.[1] Graham replied that it was impossible for him to enter into communication with 'Uthman Diqna. 'Uthman considered all these attempts to come to an understanding with him as a sign of weakness and they would provide very effective propaganda among his adherents. Graham, therefore, made up his mind to move on Taminaib and attack 'Uthman immediately before the beginning of the hot weather. It was likely, in Graham's opinion, that 'Uthman, after his defeat, would be willing to submit.[2]

Gladstone showed great uneasiness about the prospect of a third battle with 'Uthman. He observed to Granville that the communication giving discretion to Graham ought to have been submitted to the Cabinet. 'The first was fought with the belief that it was to be final. So was the second. Now all that is said is that after a third "he may possibly be prepared to submit." Are we to be drawn into series of these actions without limit?' Gladstone admitted that it would not be possible to instruct Graham to fight no more, but he ought to be more cautious and ought not to carry out war operations unnecessarily.[3]

On the 27th of March Graham's force occupied the village of Taminaib after the rebels had evacuated it. He did not encounter 'Uthman's forces, and after burning the village returned to Sawakin.[4] On the same day the Cabinet met in London to decide whether an advance should be made with a small force along the Barbar road to Barbar itself. The question had been raised on March 5 when Graham, foreseeing the result of his success, telegraphed to Stephenson suggesting that Gordon should be asked whether he would recommend an advance along the Barbar road and if he agreed how far he would be prepared to co-operate. Gordon welcomed the idea, especially since he knew that an emissary sent by al-Mahdi was attempting to raise the people of Shandi. If this attempt succeeded, Khartum would be cut off, and therefore he thought that the success near Sawakin should be

[1] Baring to Graham, Mar. 21, 1884, enclosed in Baring to Granville, No. 33ᵗ. Mar. 21, 1884, P.R.O., F.O. 78/3669.

[2] Hewett to Baring, Mar. 22, 1884, enclosed in Baring to Granville, No. 3· ?, Mar. 22, 1884, P.R.O., F.O. 78/3669.

[3] Gladstone to Granville, Mar. 23, 1884, B.M. Add. MS. 44547.

[4] Colvile, op. cit., Part II, p. 25.

followed up by the sending of a small force to Barbar. Stephenson, however, did not support Graham, fearing the great difficulty of scarce water. Nevertheless, Graham entrusted one of his senior officers with the preparation of a scheme for the Mounted troops to advance on Barbar. Stephenson and Wood later expressed their opinion that the undertaking was not impossible, but that a very great risk was involved.[1]

Gladstone was not present at the Cabinet meeting which discussed the advance on Barbar. There was a heated discussion among the members who were present. Harcourt insisted that a definite answer should be given that in no circumstances should an expedition be sent to Khartum. The Lord Chancellor was equally strong in the opposite direction. There was every shade of opinion between these two extremes, but the majority were against committing the Government. Finally, a telegram was drafted. Graham was told that the Government had no intention of sending British troops to Barbar. The operations in which he was engaged should be limited to the pacification of the area round Sawakin and to restoring communication with Barbar, if possible by peaceful means and particularly by the influence of the friendly tribes. Graham's own reports about the effect of heat on the troops strengthened the Government's desire that the operations round Sawakin should be brought to an early conclusion and 'preparations made for the immediate embarkation of the bulk of force.' [2]

Graham complied with these instructions and replied that he considered his active operations were completed and he would soon report the manner in which he proposed to deal with the friendly tribes for opening up the road to Barbar.[3] On the 3rd of April General Graham embarked with his staff for Suez and the operations by British troops in the vicinity of Sawakin were officially terminated. Thus ended these warlike operations which had been carried out for no purpose, and had resulted in the slaughter of 4,000 Arabs for no reason other than that they were adherents of al-Mahdi, to whom, curiously enough, Gordon had offered the crown of Kurdufan.

[1] Colvile, loc. cit.
[2] Granville to Gladstone, Mar. 27, 1884, B.M. Add. MS. 44176.
[3] Baring to Granville, No. 366, Mar. 27, 1884, P.R.O., F.O. 78/3669.

IX

GORDON'S POLICY

At 9:30 a.m. on February 18, 1884 Gordon's steamer arrived at the landing-stage of the Governor-General's palace in Khartum. An array of officials and officers in gorgeous uniforms, and crowds of inhabitants received him. Shaking hands with a select few, the Governor-General passed through lines of soldiers to the reception hall. After a short meeting with the officials, Gordon proceeded to the courtyard where, before a gathering of the people, the firman appointing him Governor-General was read. Gordon then made a speech. He expressed sympathy with the people for the miserable condition into which the Sudan had drifted, and appealed to them to help him to redress their wrongs. 'I have come here alone without troops, and we must ask Allah to look after the Sudan, if no one else can.' [1] He told them that he had halved their taxes and that he would not interfere with their owning slaves. Old records of taxes were taken to the public square where, with the whips and instruments for bastinadoing, they were burnt. In this dramatic way Gordon meant to bid farewell to the old régime.

Power described the general satisfaction in Khartum first at Gordon's proclamations and then at his arrival. Two days before the arrival of Gordon's steamer, his proclamations had been made public and acclaimed with satisfaction. In trying to ascertain the feeling of the people Power reported this statement from an intelligent Arab: 'Gordon Pasha will be received as a friend of the Arabs and blacks. His coming means no more Turks with their baksheesh and kourbash. But he should have come a year ago: it is now too late.' [2] On his way from the province headquarters to the palace about 1,000 people had pressed forward kissing Gordon's hands and feet, and calling 'Sultan,' 'Father,' and 'Savior.' [3] Power also asserted that since it had been known that Gordon was coming the

[1] Stewart's diary, enclosed in Baring to Granville, No. 296, Mar. 11, 1884, P.R.O., F.O. 78/3668.
[2] *The Times,* Feb. 16, 1884.
[3] *The Times,* Feb. 19, 1884.

mood of the people had so changed that fears of disturbances in the town had become remote.

Up to now Gordon's program had gone smoothly and with his safe arrival at Khartum and his hearty welcome everything seemed to augur well for the future. Notwithstanding, both the London and Cairo governments felt suspicious of Gordon's strange behavior, his changeability, and his temperament. But all that had been brushed aside by the success which he had so far met with.

On the very day of his arrival Gordon drew up a scheme based on the employment of Zubair as his successor as governor-general of the Sudan. No aspect of the question of Egypt and the Sudan aroused so much discussion as Zubair and so it may therefore be desirable to give an outline of his career.

Zubair began as an ordinary merchant in Bahr al-Ghazal, but he acquired wealth and power and very soon occupied a dominating position among the merchants in these regions. The Government at Khartum decided to make good their claim to sovereignty over Bahr al-Ghazal, and for this reason sent a small expedition under Shaikh Muhammad al-Bilali to annex the country. The league of merchants there regarded this movement as an infringement of their rights, and, with Zubair at their head, resisted the invading army. In two encounters the Government's army was utterly defeated and al-Bilali was killed. It was a period of confusion among the central authority at Khartum. Mumtaz Pasha, the Governor, was in prison, accused of embezzlement, and a Sudanese officer, Adam Pasha al-Arifi, was acting at Khartum pending the arrival of the new Governor. Adam Pasha recommended that if any action was to be taken it should be from Kurdufan rather than from Khartum.

Zubair wrote to Khartum and to the Khedive through Husain Bey Khalifah, Governor of Barbar and Dongola, expressing his loyalty and saying that the situation in Bahr al-Ghazal had arisen from the mistakes of the late commander of the Government army. The Khedive pardoned Zubair and appointed him Governor of Bahr al-Ghazal, on terms to be arranged with the Governor of Khartum.

While preparing to go to Khartum, Zubair quarrelled with the Rizaiqat tribe in southern Darfur and became involved in a war with the Sultan of Darfur. The Government of Khartum decided to assist Zubair and Isma'il Ayyub Pasha, the new Governor-General, marched into Darfur from the east. Zubair defeated the Sultan's armies and entered al-Fashir, the capital, four days before Isma'il's arrival.

Isma'il Ayyub took command and after completing the pacification of the country he organized its administration. In all his plans Isma'il tended to deprive Zubair of his conquests and to restrict his authority to the original province of Bahr al-Ghazal. Although Zubair manifested his loyalty to the Khedivial Government, the ruling class in both the Sudan and Egypt were extremely suspicious of him and feared that he would declare his independence if he were put in possession of the vast territories of Bahr al-Ghazal and Darfur.

Zubair, for his part, thought that it was the policy of Isma'il Ayyub alone to deprive him of his conquests and decided to go to Cairo to present his case to the Khedive. The Khedive granted his request, but detained him in Cairo, not allowing him to return to the Sudan until the outbreak of the revolution.

Although Zubair was thus removed, his bazinqir (slave soldiers) under his son Sulayman, still remained a menace. While Gordon was Governor-General of the Sudan Sulayman attacked a rival who had been appointed Governor of Bahr al-Ghazal. Gordon considered this a rebellion against the Government, and an expedition under the Italian Gessi suppressed Sulayman's revolt. Gordon thought that Zubair, although in Cairo, had been a party to the revolt. He therefore took measures against Zubair's property and relatives in the Sudan and demanded Zubair's trial. The Khedive, however, did not agree with Gordon but Zubair felt that he had good reason to hate Gordon.

Gordon proposed that Zubair should be deported to Cyprus, but the Foreign Office had replied that he could not be sent, since the Government had no power to detain him there. However, they instructed Baring to watch Zubair.[1]

It is typical of Gordon that he changed his attitude towards Zubair the moment he saw him in Sharif Pasha's house in Cairo. Instead of advocating his exile, Gordon went to the other extreme of taking Zubair with him to Khartum wishing to make him his

[1] Granville to Gordon, c/o British Consul, Port Said, No. 1, Jan. 23, 1884, P.R.O., F.O. 78/4194.

successor as governor-general. An interview between the two men was arranged and took place on January 26.

In a memorandum, written before the interview, Gordon stated that he would risk taking Zubair and would bear the responsibility for doing so, believing that Zubair's return would hasten the end of al-Mahdi. Gordon maintained that only Zubair could prevent war in the Sudan after the Egyptian evacuation. Zubair would be accepted by all and in two months would end al-Mahdi's rule. 'My duty is to obey the orders of Her Majesty's Government that is to evacuate the Sudan as soon as possible *vis-à-vis* the safety of the Egyptian employees. To do this I want no Zubair. But if the Addenda is made that I leave a satisfactory settlement of affairs the Zubair becomes a *sine-qua-non*.' [1] He thought that if Zubair bore him no malice he would take him 'as a humanly certain settler of al-Mahdi and of those in revolt.' He therefore intended to take Zubair if Nubar and Baring after the interview felt the same mystic feeling as he had felt on meeting Zubair at Sharif Pasha's house. 'In this affair my desire, I own, would be to take Zubair, I cannot exactly say why, but I feel towards him thus; I feel sure that his going would settle the Sudan affairs to the benefit of H.M.G. and the Egyptian Government, and I would bear the responsibility of recommending him.' [2]

At the interview there was much argument: Gordon maintained that Zubair had instigated his son to revolt and Zubair complained that Gordon had treated him unjustly. After the interview, Gordon, Nubar, and Baring discussed Zubair. Finally, at Gordon's suggestion, Zubair was told that he would be allowed to remain in Cairo but the Government's treatment of him would depend upon the safe return of Gordon from the Sudan. [3]

When seeing Gordon and Stewart off to the Sudan, Baring told Gordon that if on his arrival at Khartum he thought it necessary to send for Zubair, he, Baring, would endeavor to facilitate his departure. [4] From Kurusko Stewart wrote privately to Baring that Gordon was still hankering after Zubair and that it was highly probable that he would ask for him. Stewart doubted very much

[1] Gordon's memorandum on his relation with Zubair, Jan. 25, 1884, enclosed in a private letter from Baring to Granville, Jan. 28, 1884, P.R.O., G/D 29/162.
[2] Ibid.
[3] Baring to Granville, No. 99, Jan. 28, 1884, P.R.O., F.O. 78/3666.
[4] Allen, B. M., *Gordon and the Sudan*, p. 251.

the wisdom of sending Zubair and thought it to be 'a dangerous experiment.' It was quite possible, in Stewart's view, that the influence attributed to Zubair might be exaggerated, as his bazinqir had ceased to exist.[1] At Abu Hamad Gordon wrote to Baring: 'With respect to Zubair, he is the only man who is fit for Governor-General of the Sudan if we wish it to be quiet.'[2]

Baring himself favored the sending of Zubair. 'I have always,' he wrote to Granville, 'thought and still think, that there was a good deal in the idea of sending Zubair to the Sudan. I do not believe—and in this Gordon entirely agrees with me—that it would affect the question of slavery in one way or the other.'[3] But Baring thought that it was out of the question to send him immediately. There would be a great risk that he would either murder Gordon or cause him to be murdered.

In his memorandum of January 18 Gordon referred to his Abu Hamad memorandum in which he had stated the necessity for setting up a Sudanese government. The head of that government could, however, do nothing unless he were supported by an outside government. The protecting power would have to be chosen from Great Britain, Egypt, or Turkey. It would be only nominal sovereignty without expenditure of money or troops and without responsibility. Turkey and Egypt were equally unsuitable for the task, and Gordon therefore concluded that the British Government would have to give a commission to his successor without incurring any responsibility. An analogy could be drawn from the situation in Afghanistan where the Amir was given moral support by Britain and in his case even subsidy which would not be required in the Sudan.[4]

Gordon therefore recommended that Her Majesty's Government should select a man, give him a commission, and promise him moral support but nothing more. If it were argued that Britain was countenancing a man set over a slave state, similar situations might be cited in Afghanistan and Socotra. Gordon went on to show the advantages to Britain of such an action. With the inevitable collapse of the Turkish Empire nominal control of such a large

---

[1] Cromer, the Earl of, *Modern Egypt* (London, 1908), vol. i, p. 481.
[2] Ibid.
[3] Baring to Granville, Jan 28, 1884, P.R.O., G/D 29/162.
[4] Gordon to Baring, Feb. 18, 1884, enclosed in Baring to Granville, No. 209, Feb. 19, 1884, P.R.O., F.O. 78/4194.

Arab-speaking land as the Sudan could be of great importance to Her Majesty's Government. Also the British hold on Egypt would be strengthened by such a protectorate. Gordon also emphasized that the Khedive's Government should be plainly told that all questions concerning Egypt's relations with the Sudan were to be dealt with through Her Majesty's Government.

'As for the man, Her Majesty's Government should select one above all others, namely Zubair.' He was the only man with the ability to rule that country and would be acceptable to all. He should be made a K.C.M.G. and be given presents. The terms of his appointment Gordon suggested should be:

1. Engagement not to go into equatorial or Bahr al-Ghazal Provinces, and which I should evacuate.
2. Engagement not to go into Darfur.
3. Engagement, on payment of £200 annually, to telegraph height of Nile to Cairo.
4. Engagement to remain at peace with Abyssinia.
5. Engagement not to levy duties beyond 4 per cent. on imports or exports (of course he would not have Sawakin or Masawwa).
6. Engagement not to pursue anyone who was engaged in suppressing his son's revolt.
7. Engagement to pay the pensions granted by the Egyptian Government to old employees.
   To the above may be added other clauses as may seem fit.

In a postscript Gordon explicitly stated that the choice of his successor ought not to be left to a council of notables.

Gordon asked Stewart to give his opinion. Stewart maintained that the policy urged by Gordon would greatly facilitate their retirement from the Sudan. The Turco-Arabian question was, he thought, a question requiring serious consideration, and he was unwilling to pass judgment on the appointment of Zubair. It was probable that anyone nominated as governor-general would be accepted for a time.[1]

In forwarding Gordon's memorandum, Baring supported the principle and the choice of Zubair.[2] But he agreed with Stewart that there was no necessity to decide at once. Knowing that the

---

[1] Stewart's remarks enclosed in Gordon to Baring, Feb. 18, 1884, enclosed in Baring to Granville, No. 209, Feb. 19, 1884, P.R.O., F.O. 78/4194.

[2] Baring to Granville, No. 209, Feb. 19, 1884, P.R.O., F.O. 78/4194.

main objection to Zubair would be his notoriety as a salve-trader, he told the Foreign Office that he had discussed the question of the slave-trade with Gordon in Cairo, and they had both agreed that Zubair's presence or absence would not affect the question one way or the other. He also agreed with Gordon that Zubair's residence in Cairo had greatly modified his character and that he could now understand European power. Baring said that he would prefer to deal with a man like Zubair rather than with al-Mahdi. But he would be altogethher opposed to having Gordon and Zubair together at Khartum. As soon as Gordon had arranged for the withdrawal of the garrisons and the rest of the Egyptian element, he ought to leave Khartum and shortly afterwards Zubair would start from Cairo to replace him. Baring was convinced from the interview between the two men in Cairo that Zubair felt a bitter hatred against Gordon and he would, therefore, be opposed to putting Gordon in his power.

Referring to the terms of Zubair's appointment suggested by Gordon, Baring stressed that they should be put in the plainest language and in writing, as Zubair was extremely untruthful and would pervert the meaning of words to suit his own purpose. He would not understand 'moral support' and would not attach any importance to it unless it had material backing. Of the effect of his appointment upon public opinion in England Her Majesty's Government could judge for themselves, but apart from that Baring saw no reason why Zubair should not be proclaimed ruler of the Sudan with British approval. It should be made clear to Zubair in writing that he would have to rely solely upon his own resources to maintain his position. It might be arranged for him to receive a moderate sum of money from the Egyptian Government at first. He should, however, communicate with the Egyptian Government through Her Majesty's representative in Cairo, as Gordon had suggested. The detailed terms of appointment which Gordon had drawn up should Baring thought, be considered further. Baring concluded by saying that he had no idea whether Zubair would accept the position which it was proposed to offer him.

On the very day on which they received these communications from Gordon and Baring, the British Government was closely questioned in Parliament about Gordon's proclamations on slavery.

Its substance had appeared in the press, but the Government put off the question on the pretext that the actual text of the proclamation had not yet been received.[1]

Gladstone thought that there were a number of 'conclusive objections'[2] to England's becoming the ruler of the Sudan. The most important question, in Gladstone's opinion, was that of the appointing authority. 'The fact that Baring takes no notice of them whatever shows perhaps that he is overdone, perhaps that he weighs a question of the widest character in *local* scales, perhaps both.' The withdrawal of the Egyptians would leave the Turks in undisputable possession of the country *de jure*, but Gordon took no account of that. Gladstone referred to a letter from Gordon to Northbrook in which the former had pronounced against British intervention. 'I do not absolutely see why the Khedive should not propose to Turkey the nomination of a proper person with Sultan's authority and in case of hesitation arrange with the man provisionally and leave him to make good his ground.'

Granville's first reaction was that, for parliamentary purposes, the Government would do better without telegraphic communication with Gordon. He expected that the Cabinet would be against Zubair as a great slave-dealer and a good general.[3] Dilke stated that if they countenanced the appointment of Zubair 'Foster, supported by the anti-slavery society and the conservatives, would at once have upset us in the House of Commons and reversed policy.'[4]

The Cabinet finally came to this decision, which Granville himself recorded: 'There are the gravest objections to the appointment of a successor to General Gordon by our authority. We do not, as yet, see the necessity of going beyond Gordon's memorandum of 22nd ultimo by making a special provision for the Government of the country. Public opinion here would not tolerate Zubair.'[5]

Gordon's first step in effecting the withdrawal was the separation of the white troops, who were to be sent across the White Nile to Omdurman and later sent to Egypt under their commander

[1] *Hansard*, 3rd ser., vol. 284, cols. 1344 and 1440.
[2] Gladstone to Granville, Feb. 20, 1884, B.M. Add. MS. 44547.
[3] Granville to Baring, Private, Feb. 21, 1884, P.R.O., G/D 29/200.
[4] Gwynn and Tuckwell, op. cit., vol. ii. p. 33.
[5] Granville to Baring, No. 109, Feb. 1884, P.R.O., F.O. 78/4194.

Ibrahim Pasha Hayder. The Sudanese black troops were put under the command of Faraj Pasha al-Zaini and the bashbuzuks under Sa'id Pasha al-Jimaabi. Gordon's plan was to evacuate the white troops first, then the white-brown, leaving the Sudanese to manage their own affairs.[1]

Gordon thought that a peaceful policy towards al-Mahdi's emissaries would succeed. He ordered three gates in the ramparts to be opened to allow people to enter, and the soldiers were warned not to molest the incomers. A long letter in Arabic was written to Shaikh al-Basir, the most powerful emissary of al-Mahdi in al-Jazirah. The advantages offered by Gordon were set forth and included the reduction of taxes, permission to possess slaves, and Sudanese self-government. Verses from the Quran were quoted to prove the sinfulness of Muslims killing one another. It concluded with an invitation to Shaikh al-Basir to come and see Gordon. People in Khartum who knew the situation better believed that Gordon's peaceful policy would not succeed, and so both Faraj Pasha and Sa'id Pasha made representation to Gordon to keep the Egyptian troops and not to send them immediately. Gordon replied with abuse, which vexed them very much. Gordon told Sa'id Pasha that he should send for Zubair if he were afraid, and called Faraj Pasha a woman.[2]

Naturally Gordon was anxious to receive news about al-Mahdi's movements in Kurdufan. On February 22 a man coming from al-Ubayyid brought the first information. al-Mahdi's force was estimated at 12,000 men, mostly Sudanese, armed with rifles, with some Egyptians armed with lances. Before Gordon's arrival al-Mahdi had ordered two chiefs with a number of Arabs to march on Khartum but the advance was stopped when it was known that Gordon was coming because the Arabs thought that he was bringing English troops. The Arabs would not march on Khartum as they feared the steamers on the river. It became apparent also that some of the tribes were not over-friendly with al-Mahdi who had deprived them of the booty they had taken from Hicks's expedition. Many of the Arabs questioned al-Mahdi's right to his title.

[1] Stewart's diary, enclosed in Baring to Granville, No. 317, Mar. 17, 1884, P.R.O., F.O. 78/3669.
[2] Ibid.

Another report from Kurdufan stated that al-Mahdi was becoming more unpopular as he oppressed the people more. According to this report, al-Mahdi's ambition was to secure a safe place of retreat in the Taqali mountains. It confirmed a previous report that the Kababish were friendly to Gordon. Still later reports added that the population of al-Ubayyid did not like al-Mahdi, for they suffered from the looting of his adherents.

On the other hand, the wealthy people of Khartum waited on Gordon imploring him not to send away the troops, for they were in great fear of the revolution. Messengers came from Salih Bey al-Mak who was beseiged in al-Jazirah reporting that the whole country was in insurrection, and that Gordon's proclamations were not worth the paper on which they were written. It was reported also that Shaikh al-Jmam of Jar al-Nabi, a village on the White Nile, and Faki 'Ali from Suba, a village on the Blue Nile, had collected some men and asked Shaikh al-Ubaid to allow them to march on Fadasi to fight Salih Bey. Another report stated that Faki Mudawwi with some followers had taken up a position at Sabil about three to four hours' march from Khartum and was preventing people from going to the capital. An appeal was received from Shaikh 'Awad al-Karim Abu Sin, chief of the Shukriya tribe, that if reinforcements were not hurried to Salih Bey and to him, he would be compelled to join the rebellion as his own son had declared for al-Mahdi, taking with him many of the Shukriya.[1]

Power gives an interesting account of Gordon's prestige in Khartum at this time. He stated that Gordon was a dictator and that al-Mahdi had gone down before him. 'It is wonderful that one man could have such an influence on 200,000 people. He is, indeed, I believe, the greatest and best man of this century.'[2]

Such was Gordon's personal prestige in Khartum when he received the Government's reply to his second memorandum. Baring telegraphed that the British Government refused to accept his recommendations, and remarked that the views which he had expressed in his memorandum written from Abu Hamad, were inconsistent with those set out in his memorandum from Khartum.

---

[1] Stewart's Diary, enclosed in Baring to Granville, No. 317, Mar. 17, 1884;, P.R.O., F.O. 78/3669.

[2] Power, Frank, *Letters from Khartum* (London, 1885), p. 97.

To Baring, however, the important thing was to find a man, or several men, who would take over the Government of the country south of Wadi Halfa, especially that of Khartum. 'In view of the objections entertained in England against Zubair, can you suggest any other names?'[1]

With the reports of al-Mahdi's unpopularity in Kurdufan and the activities of his emissaries in the vicinity of Khartum fresh in his memory, Gordon replied to Baring. He was convinced that his peaceful mission could not be realized, and all sections of population, including the military section, had implored him to postpone the evacuation of the troops. He could suggest no other man, and Zubair only could settle the question. 'You must remember that when evacuation is carried out Mahdi will come down here and by agents will not let Egypt be quiet.'[2] He maintained that his first duty was the evacuation, and his second the establishment of a Sudanese government. The first he hoped to accomplish, but the second was a more difficult task and concerned Egypt more than himself. 'If Egypt is to be quiet Mahdi must be smashed up. Mahdi is most unpopular and with care and time could be smashed.' He then asked for another £100,000, a force of 200 Indian troops to be sent to Wadi Halfa, and an officer, ostensibly to find quarters for the troops in Dongola but really to get information. These measures were necessary if al-Mahdi were to be destroyed. 'I repeat that evacuation is possible but you will feel effect in Egypt and will be forced to enter into a far more serious affair in order to guard Egypt. At present it would be comparatively easy to destroy Mahdi.'[3]

Baring repeated Gordon's reply to London together with his Abu Hamad memorandum and some other suggestions about the recruitment of troops and subsidies for their maintenance. Baring remarked that there were obvious inconsistencies in Gordon's proposals, but a question of principle of a most serious nature had been raised, which he would commend to the earnest attention of Her Majesty's Government. The alternatives were either to evacuate the Sudan making no provision for establishing a government or to take such measures as circumstances would admit, to set up

[1] Baring to Gordon, Feb. 23, 1884, enclosed in Baring to Granville, No. 240, Feb. 28, 1884, P.R.O., F.O. 78/3667.
[2] Gordon to Baring, Feb. 26, 1884, enclosed in Baring to Granville, No. 240, Feb. 28, 1884, P.R.O., F.O. 78/3667.
[3] Ibid.

some form of government. Gordon was undoubtedly in favor of the latter and Baring entirely agreed with him. The attempt might not succeed but Baring was strongly of opinion that it should be tried. 'It will be a most serious matter from every point of view, political, military and financial, if complete anarchy reigns south of Wadi Halfa and anarchy will certainly ensue when Gordon comes away if some measures be not taken beforehand to prevent it.' [1]

Referring to Gordon's memorandum of January 22, on which the British Government seemed to have laid great stress, Baring said that he regarded it as a preliminary sketch of the policy to be pursued and even then Gordon had alluded to the difficulty of dealing with those towns where there were no families of old standing. No moral or material support should be given by the British Government to the ruler of the Sudan, and it was unimportant whether he was nominally appointed on the authority of Her Majesty's Government or not. 'Whatever may be said, Her Majesty's Government is really responsible for any arrangements now made in the Sudan and I do not think it possible to shake off that responsibility.' If it were not intended to assume responsibility then, 'Gordon and the Egyptian Government should be left free to act as they think best.' [2]

Baring had no doubt about the best course to be pursued. Zubair should be allowed to succeed Gordon with a sum of money to start with and an annual subsidy for five years of, say, £50,000, conditional on good behavior. That would permit Zubair to maintain a moderate military force and the arrangement would prove, in the end, to be economical for the Egyptian Government. The chief difficulty lay in the choice of the man. It would be useless to send a man with no local influence. The objections to Zubair were obvious, though overrated. 'But I believe Gordon is quite right in saying that he is the only possible man. I know of no other. Nubar Pasha is strongly in favor of sending him.'

Baring further declared that it would lead to harm if attempts were made to settle Egyptian questions in the light of opinion in England instead of on the advice of responsible authorities in Cairo and the Sudan.

Meanwhile the situation in Khartum had deteriorated. Rumors

---

[1] Baring to Granville, No. 178, Feb. 28, 1884, P.R.O., F.O. 78/4194.
[2] Baring to Granville, No. 178, Feb. 28, 1884, P.R.O., F.O. 78/4194.

of all sorts about the activities of al-Mahdi's emissaries were spread in town. There was fear of a rising in the town. Six hundred Egyptian troops were ordered back to Khartum from Omdurman ostensibly for expeditions up the Blue and White Niles but really to guard against possible incidents.[1] It now became clear to Gordon that the weakness lay in his peaceful overtures. He therefore issued a further proclamation to all the inhabitants of the Sudan.[2] He referred to his announcements when he first arrived at Khartum in which he had promised good treatment and justice to all natives. Now that it was clear that such advice had had no effect on some people he was compelled, contrary to his inclination, to have recourse to severe measures: 'so much so that the troops of the British Government are now on their way and in a few days will be at Khartum.'[3] Anyone persisting in rebellious conduct would therefore get the treatment he deserved. Those people who so far had not joined the rebellion should abstain from holding intercourse with the rebels or they would share their punishment. 'I am watching these things closely, and you should not think that I am ignorant of what is going on.' The war which was being carried on would end in the ruin and destruction of the country. This proclamation, which Gordon certainly meant to be of a purely local importance and a threat to the people, perplexed Gladstone. He feared that it might involve the Government in difficulties if it became known. 'Gordon assumes a license of language to which we can hardly make ourselves parties.'[4]

Stewart went on a steamer up the White Nile on a mission of peace. During his absence Gordon sent a number of telegrams to Baring giving the latest news and fresh suggestions. The state of affairs at Khartum, according to Gordon, was that one-third of the population, excited by the emissaries of al-Mahdi, was terrorizing the two-thrids. Instead of supporting the latter the policy was to evacuate the Egyptian soldiers and leave them helpless.[5] He

---

[1] Stewart's diary, enclosed in Baring to Granville, No. 239, Mar. 22, 1884, P.R.O., F.O. 78/3669.

[2] Gordon's proclamation, Feb. 27, 1884, enclosed in Baring to Granville, No. 237, Feb. 27, 1884, P.R.O., F.O. 78/3667.

[3] Ibid.

[4] Gladstone to Granville, Feb. 27, 1884, B.M. Add. MS. 44547.

[5] Gordon to Baring, Feb. 27, 1884, enclosed in Baring to Granville, No. 248, Mar. 2, 1884, P.R.O., F.O. 78/3667.

thought that if the fellaheen soldiers were to be evacuated within a few days the town would send for al-Mahdi and offer him submission, not from love of him but because they would be without other hope. Thus the evacuation of the Sudan would be impossible until the Government could assert its authority. They could hold out for a time and force back the tide of rebellion, but gradually that position would become untenable and money would run out. The only evacuation that could be effected would be that of the sick, and Gordon asked whether partial evacuation would meet the authorities' wishes. If not, Indian troops should start at once from Wadi Halfa.

By the tenth day after his arrival in Khartum, therefore, Gordon had become convinced that the hasty evacuation of the Egyptian troops and employees would mean the handing over of the country to al-Mahdi, and he thought that the only way to carry out the evacuation would be by a display of force and the assertion of governmental authority. It is interesting to remember that he had replied with abuse to the two pashas when they had implored him to postpone the sending away of the Egyptian troops very shortly after his arrival at Khartum.

Gordon was convinced that al-Mahdi's emissaries and supporters in the vicinity could be bribed to join the Government side, and he asked permission to use this method and asked whether the extra funds could be found.[1] Gordon also repeated his suggestion that 200 British troops should be sent to Wadi Halfa, adjutants should be sent to inspect Dongola, and that the Sawakin-Barbar road should be opened up by Indian Muslim troops if the Government wished to intervene.[2] He thought that these measures would cause an immediate collapse of the revolt. 'Whether you think it worth while to do this or not, you are, of course, the best judge. I can only tell you the *modus operandi* of an expeditious intervention. If you decide against this, you may probably have to decide between Zubair and al-Mahdi with £100,000.'

Baring was most confused by Gordon's telegrams. He called his proposals 'hopelessly bewildering and contradictory,'[3] attributing

[1] Gordon to Baring, Feb. 28, 1884, enclosed in Baring to Granville, No. 248, Mar. 2, 1884, P.R.O., F.O. 78/3667.
[2] Gordon to Baring, Feb. 29, 1884, enclosed in Baring to Granville, No. 248, Mar. 2, 1884, P.R.O., F.O. 78/3667.
[3] Baring to Granville, Private, Feb. 29, 1884, P.R.O., G/D 29/162.

them to the absence of Stewart on the White Nile. This was not to be interpreted as a loss of confidence in Gordon, but it was difficult to know what he really meant and still more difficult to judge what was worthy of attention and what was 'more or less nonsense.' Baring thought there would be no use in forwarding all telegrams for instructions as the difficulty would be greater in London than in Cairo. He asked for full authority to do the best he could in conformity with the general policy of the Government. Baring received the discretion he had asked for but Granville added that when there was time, the Government would like to know his reasons.[1]

Granville told Baring privately that Zubair was unpalatable to them, but at the same time a flat refusal against the opinion of their advisers 'on the spot' would be undesirable. 'We have,' Granville says, 'a cabinet meeting and although there would have been much reluctance, if we have been obliged to answer at once categorically about Zubair, yet we should probably have yielded to your, Gordon's and Nubar's opinion. If you persist in it, I am certain it will be carefully considered.'[2] The Cabinet felt that there had been a change of front about the withdrawal from the Sudan. Granville believed that Zubair was the only man strong enough to cope with al-Mahdi. But could it be guaranteed that his official income would be sufficient to prevent him from returning to his former lucrative trade or to prevent his joining al-Mahdi?

Officially and confidentially Granville informed Baring that the Government was considering the proposal to send Zubair as Gordon's successor. They feared, however, that Zubair might become a source of increased danger to Egypt, either through an alliance with al-Mahdi, with whom he was already supposed to have some connection, or in some other manner. In the second place there was no assurance that he would prevent or even discourage the slave-trade bearing in mind his reputation as a slave-dealer. In the third place it was impossible to overlook the danger in which Gordon might be placed if they were both in the same region at a time when Zubair would have supreme control. Baring was asked for his comments on these points.[3] There appeared to

[1] Draft reply by Granville under ibid.
[2] Granville to Baring, Private, Feb. 29, 1884, P.R.O., G/D 29/200.
[3] Granville to Baring, No. 131A Confidential, Feb. 29, 1884, P.R.O., F.O. 78/4194.

be no hurry, for both communications were sent by ordinary mail.

In replying to Gordon's bewildering telegrams Baring told Gordon that he was most anxious to help him in every way, but that he did not understand exactly what Gordon wanted. Baring therefore suggested that Gordon should reconsider the whole question carefully and should then state his recommendations in one telegram so that if necessary instructions might be obtained from the Government.

If I understand rightly, your main ideas are as follows: first, you wish the policy of eventually evacuating the Sudan including Khartum, to be firmly maintained; secondly, you see clearly that anarchy may ensue on the withdrawal of the Egyptian Government, which may affect Egypt proper; thirdly, you see special objections to the immediate withdrawal of all Egyptian employees. The remedy which you recommend to prevent anarchy, so far as is possible is to hand over the Government to Zubair, as your successor, who would receive, for a time at least, a subsidy from the Egyptian Government, in order to enable him to maintain an armed force.[1]

Baring could not understand Gordon's attitude to the Egyptian employees. He pointed out the inconsistency between the Abu Hamad memorandum, in which Gordon had suggested that the Egyptian Government should maintain some influence, and subsequent communications in which interference from Cairo was condemned. Baring saw no objection to any Egyptian employee remaining if he wished to do so and if Zubair or whoever took over the government wished to retain his services. Gordon himself was best judge of the suggestion to entice al-Mahdi's troops from their allegiance by money. Baring was not prepared to risk the sending of a small force of 200 men to Wadi Halfa, but he had authority to send British detachments to upper Egypt. In any event, however, they would not be allowed south of Aswan. Baring did not like the suggestion that on officer should be sent to Dongola, because there was no intention of sending troops there. He was also not prepared to recommend the opening of the Sawakin-Barbar road by Indian Muslim troops. 'Now Graham has gained a victory could not Husain Khalifah open the road?' Although it was not desirable to spend money on the Sudan, yet Gordon could have more money if he had already spent the £100,000, and if he

---

[1] Baring to Gordon, Mar. 2, 1884, enclosed in Baring to Granville, No. 248, Mar. 2, 1884, P.R.O., F.O. 78/3667.

was in real need. He should, however, bear in mind that the Sudan was to be evacuated in order to relieve the over-taxed people of Egypt, for the Sudan had been a constant drain on the Egyptian treasury.

Before making a final decision Her Majesty's Government requested more information about the urgency of the immediate appointment of a successor to Gordon. They trusted that Gordon might remain for a time in Khartum and if it were found necessary to make an arrangement in that respect the Government would consider the matter carefully. They also thought that if such an appointment were made it might be advantageous if it received the Sultan's confirmation.[1] Baring told Gordon that he might 'regard the question of Zubair as still under discussion, and not finally settled,'[2] and transmitted to him the substance of the reply from London.

Stewart's voyage on the White Nile convinced him that the country beyond about fifteen to twenty miles south of Khartum was in a disturbed state. In a private letter to Baring he stated that the attitude of the natives was threatening, and that they might have been fired at had they attempted to land. Stewart also thought that al-Mahdi was simply waiting to see whether Gordon was supported by British troops. Once he was convinced that there were no British soldiers he would advance. For that reason Stewart would approve of Graham's pushing on to Barbar after having defeated 'Uthman Diqna. Unless such a move were made there could be no hope of withdrawing the garrisons of Sennar, at any rate for the next two months until the rise of the Blue Nile.

The prestige of the Government has now greatly declined, confidence in it is everywhere shaken, people see that we have no force at our command and that we are inclined to give up the Sudan. I heartily approve of the policy of giving up this useless and unprofitable country but I think we are in honor bound to withdraw the garrisons and others in safety, hence the necessity of an advance on Barbar.[3]

Stewart thought that the choice of the future ruler of the Sudan

---

[1] Granville to Baring, No. 132, Mar. 1, 1884, P.R.O., F.O. 78/3662.
[2] Baring to Gordon, Mar. 2, 1884, enclosed in Baring to Granville, No. 248, Mar. 2, 1884, P.R.O., F.O. 78/3667.
[3] Stewart to Baring, Mar. 1, 1884, enclosed in Baring to Granville, No. 340, Confidential, Mar 22, 1884, P.R.O., F.O. 78/3669.

lay between Zubair and al-Mahdi. Politically and socially the former was to be preferred. To have a religious ruler in the Sudan would be of great disadvantage to the British in Egypt, not to speak of the probable consequences in other parts of the Arab world. 'If once we establish Zubair here and gave him something to start upon, we might let matters slide and act on the Darwinian theory "survival of the fittest." ' Stewart was anxious to know what possible answer he might give to the question asked by the natives: 'What are we to do in the event of the rebels marching on us? We are not strong enough to resist them and hence we shall be obliged to join them in self-defense.' It seemed to Stewart that the only class of people who would suffer from the withdrawal were the rich merchants, both Arab and Greek. He had no sympathy for them and grudged any British money spent in their support. 'Let them make their own terms and get out of the mess as best they can.'

The villagers and the nomads with their own peculiar organizations would probably 'fight and squabble amongst themselves' but that would be their own affair. All the towns were simply collections of mud huts which if burnt one day could be rebuilt the next. Stewart concluded that no one would be more glad than he when the whole miserable business was over and when 'we have seen our last of the Sudan. The country is only intended by nature for nomad tribes and a few settled Arabs along the banks of the Nile. It annoys me greatly to see blood and treasure wasted on it.' [1]

Gordon received Baring's remarks on his twelve telegrams, and wrote back still maintaining the policy of eventually evacuating the Sudan including Khartum. Then he restated his case for the appointment of Zubair, subsidized by the Egyptian Government. Gordon declared that he had no alternative but to stay in Khartum because the matter had 'passed out of my hands.' [2] Referring to the sending of 200 soldiers to Wadi Halfa, it was not the number that was important but the prestige, which he needed. 'I am sure the revolt will collapse if I can say that I have British troops at my back.' Zubair would see to the bribing of al-Mahdi's troops. Gor-

[1] Stewart to Baring Mar 1, 1884, enclosed in Baring to Granville, No. 340, Confidential, Mar. 22, 1884, P.R.O., F.O. 78/3669.
[2] Gordon to Baring, Mar. 4, 1884, enclosed in Baring to Granville, No. 263, Mar. 4, 1884, P.R.O., F.O. 78/4194.

don himself would do his best to see that Husain Pasha Khalifah opened the Sawakin-Barbar road. As to the expenditure of money, he recognized the financial difficulties of Egypt and promised not to be extravagant.

It was reported from Kurdufan that al-Mahdi feared the Bedwins round al-Ubayyid, and was therefore trying to stir up the people round Khartum in order to besiege the town and starve it out. Gordon therefore maintained that it was impossible to withdraw the Egyptian employees from Khartum without risking the capture of the town by al-Mahdi's emissaries. If that happened all hope of saving the Egyptian employees at Kasalah, Sennar, Bahr al-Ghazal, and Equatoria would be lost. Dongola and Barbar would then fall.

I am strongly against any permanent retention of the Sudan, but I think we ought to leave it with decency, and give the respectable people a man to lead them, around whom they can rally, and we ought to support that man by money and by opening road to Barbar. Pray do not consider me in any way to advocate retention of Sudan, I am quite averse to it, but you must see that you could not recall me nor could I possibly obey until the Cairo employees get out from all the places.[1]

He had appointed men to different places and by doing so he had involved them with al-Mahdi. 'How could I look the world in the face if I abandoned them and fled?' Gordon stated that it might have been a mistake to send him to the Sudan but having done so he had no option but to organize the evacuation because 'if I was mean enough to escape I have no power to do so.'

Baring replied that there was no intention of recalling him, but on the contrary a recent dispatch from the Foreign Office authorized him to remain. Baring pointed out that what he really wanted was a reply which he could send to London about the questoin of Gordon's successor. If Zubair were to be recommended, the question had better stand over for a little while, as it would be dangerous to have both him and Zubair there at the same time.[2]

Gordon replied, not in one telegram, but in many, maintaining that it was absolutely necessary for Zubair to stay with him for four months. He did not believe that there was the slightest fear

---

[1] Gordon to Baring, Mar. 3, 1884, enclosed in Baring to Granville, No. 254, Mar. 3, 1884, P.R.O., F.O. 78/3667.

[2] Baring to Gordon, Mar. 3, 1884, enclosed in Baring to Granville, No. 254, Mar. 3, 1884, P.R.O., F.O. 78/3667.

of their quarrelling, for Zubair would know that the subsidy depended on Gordon's safety. 'To do any good we must be together, and that without delay.'[1] Gordon stressed the fact that the weakness of his position arose from his being a foreigner, a Christian, and peacefully inclined. It was only by sending Zubair that such prejudices could be removed. The situation was not yet serious, but it might become so if Zubair's appointment were to be delayed.

In a telegram to Baring, Stewart restated Gordon's reasons for urging the immediate appointment of Zubair.[2]

On receiving the telegrams from Gordon and Stewart urging the immediate dispatch of Zubair, Baring wrote to Granville saying that he had carefully reconsidered the whole question and still thought that Zubair should be allowed to succeed Gordon. 'I do not think that anything would be gained by postponing a decision on this point; on the contrary I would say that delay would be injurious.'[3] Baring was no longer inclined to object to Zubair's going at once to Khartum, but he could express no final opinion until he had seen Zubair. The main issue would still have to be decided by Her Majesty's Government, whether Zubair were to be allowed to return to the Sudan or not. Baring intended to wait for an answer on that point before taking action.

On the same day as he had telegraphed to Baring, Stewart wrote to him privately. This letter throws light on Gordon's character and at the same time describes the state of affairs in the Sudan. Stewart maintained that the only way to end the conflict in the Sudan was to appoint Zubair as Gordon's successor. The chances were that they could hold out until the rise of the Blue Nile, when the Sennar garrison would be withdrawn. By that time communications with the Equator might be established and those who wanted to leave would be on their way. 'All this will not, however, have solved the difficulty of our final evacuation. Even if we could sneak away I am convinced Gordon is the last man in the world who would do so. There is no one here we can appoint who would stand for a day, hence I see no option but Zubair, with a small

[1] Gordan to Baring, Mar. 3, 1884, enclosed in Baring to Granville, No. 263, Mar. 4, 1884, P.R.O., F.O. 78/4194.

[2] Stewart to Baring, Mar. 4, 1884, enclosed in Baring to Granville, No. 265, Mar. 4, 1884, P.R.O., F.O. 78/4194.

[3] Baring to Granville, No. 263, Mar. 4, 1884, P R.O., F.O. 78/4194.

subsidy.'[1] Although there was an element of risk, it was the best solution in the circumstances.

Stewart remarked that Gordon's telegrams were inconsistent. This was because Gordon telegraphed directly an idea struck him, and there was no use in trying to stop him. 'Were I you, I should always wait for a few days before acting unless the subject matter is so evident that there can be no doubt of it.'[2]

Stewart advised that the troops at Sawakin should not be sent away as it would prejudice their position in Khartum. 'The Government, having sent Gordon up here will have to support him, and I am convinced from what I know of him that he will never leave the Sudan until he has established some sort of tolerably stable government. I must also add that, I think, he is perfectly right in the view he takes.'

March 7 was a black day in Khartum. Messengers of al-Mahdi were very active as it was expected that Shaikh al-Ubaid, a most influential religious shaikh living near Khartum, would decide whether or not to join al-Mahdi.[3] His decision would very soon be known by telegraph. If the telegraph did not work it would be certain that the country between Khartum and Barbar was in rebellion. Stewart thought it most important 'to follow up the success near Sawakin by sending a small force up to Barbar. The Home Government should not delay in sending Zubair. He has great influence with his tribe between Barbar and Khartum. He might come up with the British force to Barbar.'[4]

Fearing that the telegraph line might soon be cut, Gordon wired a stream of telegrams to Cairo for four successive days. In one he advised if they were hemmed in and an expedition had to be sent to their relief, that Indian Muslim troops should be sent.[5] It was expected that the tribes around Khartum would try to cut off supplies and cut the telegraph line without launching a direct

---

[1] Stewart to Baring, Mar. 4, 1884, P.R.O., G/D 29/162.
[2] Ibid.
[3] Gordon to Baring, Mar. 7, 1884, enclosed in Baring to Granville, No. 274, Mar. 8, 1884, P.R.O., F.O. 78/3668.
[4] Stewart to Baring, Mar. 7, 1884, enclosed in Baring to Granville, No. 274, Mar. 8, 1884, P.R.O., F.O. 78/3668.
[5] Gordon to Baring, Mar. 8, 1884, enclosed in Baring to Granville, No. 285, Mar. 9, 1884, P.R.O., F.O. 78/3668.

attack. Provisions in Khartum were sufficient for six months.[1] Gordon recommended that in face of the storm that was likely to break on them, Wood's army should be utilized in a move on Dongola and thence to Barbar. 'The route is safe and camels plenty.'[2] It was reported that there was difference of opinion between Shaikh al-Ubaid and his son as to whether they should proclaim immediately for al-Mahdi or not. For Khartum itself, Gordon had no fear, as he did not think the rebels would attack but would cut the roads.

Meanwhile, Her Majesty's Government had no information to make them change their impression of Zubair, which had been formed, among other things, from Gordon's and Stewart's memoranda of the 22nd of January, written on board the S.S. *Tanjore*. 'Unless these impressions could be removed,' wrote Granville to Baring, 'we should not be able to make ourselves responsible for sending Zubair to Khartum.'[3] They asked about the progress made so far for the extrication of the garrisons and how soon it might be hoped that the whole or the principal part of the garrisons would have been withdrawn. They also asked how the appointment of Zubair was to be reconciled with the policy of evacuation. 'Have you dropped idea of consulting chiefs?' Just before receiving the telegram which Baring had sent him on the basis of Granville's dispatch, Gordon was in one of his spiritual moods when he firmly believed that providence would extricate him from his troubles. 'Be assured that whatever is decided by H.M.G. in re Zubair, I honestly accept it as I should look on it as ruled by a Higher Power, and it will be sure to come right. As I have been inconsistent about Zubair it is my fault, and I should bear the blame, if Zubair is sent, and should put up with inconvenience if he is not.'[4]

Gordon replied to the second refusal to appoint Zubair that the question of extricating the garrisons was bound up with Zubair. He could see no possible way of accomplishing their evacuation

---

[1] Gordon to Baring, Mar. 8, 1884, enclosed in Baring to Granville, No. 285, Mar. 9, 1884, P.R.O., F.O. 78/3668.

[2] Ibid.

[3] Granville to Baring, No. 137, Mar. 5, 1889, P.R.O., F.O. 78/4194.

[4] Gordon to Baring, Mar. 6, 1884, enclosed in Baring to Granville, No. 278, Mar. 8, 1884, P.R.O., F.O. 78/4194.

except through Zubair who, being a native of the country, could rally the people around him as they would know that he intended to remain in the Sudan. He did not see a contradiction between giving a subsidy to Zubair for two years and the policy of complete evacuation. It would be only giving him a lump sum in two instalments under the conditions which had already been agreed upon. Zubair's appointment would make no difference to slave-holding in the Sudan, because the treaty of 1877 was impossible to put into practice. The evacuation of Bahr al-Ghazal and Equatoria would prevent slave-hunting. If, after two years of the subsidy, Zubair attempted to take these districts, pressure might be applied to him from Sawakin. 'I feel sure that Zubair will be so occupied with the Sudan proper, and with consolidating his position, that he will not have time to devote to those provinces.' [1] As far as Egyptian security was concerned, Zubair's residence in Egypt should have made him understand British power and his being a merchant would rather lead him to seek the closest alliance with Egypt.

Little progress had been made in the extrication of the garrisons: all the sick men and the women and children of those killed in Kurdufan had been sent from Khartum. Gordon then described the position of the other garrisons and again restated his case for the appointment of Zubair. 'If you do not send Zubair, you have no chance of getting the garrisons away; this is a heavy argument in favor of sending him.'[2] There would be no possibility of dividing the country between other chiefs, as none of them could stand for a day against al-Mahdi's agents, and Husain Pasha Khalifah would also fall. The chiefs would find great difficulty in gathering in Khartum as they were already defending their lands against the rebels. There was not the slightest chance that Zubair would make common cause with al-Mahdi for he was far more powerful than al-Mahdi. 'al-Mahdi's power is that of a Pope, Zubair's will be that of a Sultan. They could never combine. Zubair is fifty times al-Mahdi's match.'[3] Gordon thought that Zubair would become superior to al-Mahdi possessed neither of these bair would become superior to al-Mahdi, for he was of a good

[1] Gordon to Baring, Mar. 8, 1884, enclosed in Baring to Granville, No. 282, Mar. 9, 1884, P.R.O., F.O. 78/4194.
[2] Ibid.
[3] Ibid.

family and well known while al-Mahdi possessed neither of these advantages and besides was a fanatic. 'I daresay Zubair who hates the tribes did stir up the fires of revolt in hopes that he would be sent up to quell it. It is the irony of fate that he will get his wish if he is sent up.'

Baring in forwarding this information to Granville maintained that the policy of sending Zubair with a subsidy was in complete harmony with that of evacuation. 'It is in principle the same policy as India adopts towards Afghanistan and the tribes in frontier.'[1] Slavery might receive a stimulus from the abandonment of the Sudan, but the dispatch of Zubair would not affect it in one way or the other. On that subject there was no middle course. Baring also believed that Zubair might be made a bulwark against al-Mahdi in spite of the risk that he might constitute a danger to Egypt. This danger was small, and it would be preferable to take this risk rather than incur certain 'disadvantages of retiring without making any arrangements for the future government of the country, which would then necessarily fall in the power of al-Mahdi.'[2]

Baring urged that an early decision should be made and showed much uneasiness at Gordon's telegrams. 'He evidently thinks that there is considerable risk of his being hemmed in at Khartum, and contemplates the dispatch of British troops to release his. So far as I can judge, he exercises little or no influence outside Khartum, and though he was at first hailed as a deliverer, his influence is sure to decline as time goes on.'[3]

When the possibility of appointing Zubair became known in Britain, the Anti-Slavery Society addressed a note to Lord Granville declaring that the committee were 'unanimous in the feeling that countenance in any shape of such an individual by the British Government would be a degradation for England, and a scandal to Europe.'[4] The committee could not speak for the retention or otherwise of Khartum, but they earnestly hoped that if arrangements had to be made for setting up an independent rule there, provision would be made to secure the country from a reign of anarchy and barbarism and from that of a slave-trader. 'As yet,

---

[1] Baring to Granville, No. 206, Mar. 9, 1884, P.R.O., F.O. 78/4194.
[2] Ibid.
[3] Baring to Granville, No. 206, Mar. 9, 1884, P.R.O., F.O. 78/4194.
[4] Chairman of the Anti-Slavery Society to Granville, Mar. 10, 1884, P.R.O. F.O. 78/4194.

however, the Committee are unable to believe that Her Majesty's Government will thus stultify that anti-slavery policy which has so long been the high distinction of England, or that they thus discharge a trust which they have undertaken on behalf of the British people and of Europe.'[1]

Gladstone was taken ill on March 10 but was able to take part in any necessary conversations. 'They press us very hard in point of time as to Zubair,' he wrote to Granville. 'Would it be possible to propose to Gordon that he should retain his position and responsibility for a fixed time say 12 months or even 6, with liberty to the persons he should employ to cooperate with him or come under him? Of course this would mean Zubair.'[2] Next day Gladstone elaborated his suggestion. He added, however, that if this suggestion were not approved there was nothin left but the alternatives of 'accepting Gordon's proposal as to Zubair pure and simple, or of breaking with him and procuring his recall.'[3] Finally, Granville telegraphed to Baring telling him that the arguments against Zubair were not answered. The British Government agreed, however, to the employment of any other Muhammadan assistance and to the supply of any reasonable sum of money which Gordon might require. They were not prepared to send troops to Barbar and, as the withdrawal of the garrisons might take a considerable time, they would not force Gordon's hand although they still attached great importance to early evacuation. They would 'propose to extend his appointment for any reasonable time required for the objects of his mission.'[4]

By March 12 the temporary interruption of telegraphic communication had been overcome and Baring received a number of telegrams from Gordon dated March 9 and 10. In one of them it was mentioned that Stewart would proceed to Barbar and thence to Dongola to return with Wood's army.[5] On the same day Gordon recognized the difficulty of sending the retreating refugees under Stewart unless the Barbar-Sawakin road was open, as the group

[1] Ibid.
[2] Gladstone to Granville, Mar. 10, 1884, P.R.O., G/D 29/128.
[3] Gladstone to Granville, Mar. 11, 1884, P.R.O., G/D 29/128.
[4] Granville to Baring, No. 149, Mar. 11, 1884, P.R.O., F.O. 78/4194.
[5] Gordon to Baring, Mar. 9, 1884, enclosed in Baring to Granville, No. 304, Mar. 13, 1884, P.R.O., F.O. 78/3668.

would be augmented by Husain Khalifah and his company. Gordon also maintained that he had the written authority from the King of the Belgians to take over the provinces of Equatoria and Bahr al-Ghazal together with the financial responsibilities.[1]

The consuls in Khartum were somewhat worried about the situation in the town, and in reply to their questions Gordon told them that Khartum was not directly menaced, but he would help them to go to Barbar if they wished to do so although the road there was threatened. Gordon expected that the exodus of foreigners would have a bad effect, since it would be interpreted to mean that assistance was unlikely to reach Khartum. He therefore asked what should be done to neutralize the ill effects of their departure. 'You know exactly the position of the different garrisons as far as I can explain it, and that there is no probability of the people rallying round me, or of paying any attention to my proclamations.'[2]

If the proposal to divert British troops to Barbar and to install Zubair in the Sudan were accepted, it would be worth while to hold on to Khartum. If, on the other hand, neither of these was to be done, there would be no point in holding on to Khartum, because it would be impossible to help the other garrisons and would mean sacrificing the whole of the troops and employees. 'In this latter case your instructions to me had better be that I should evacuate Khartum and, with all the employees and troops remove the seat of Government to Barbar.'[3] That step would mean that all the outlying places were to be sacrificed except Barbar and Dongola. 'You must give a prompt reply to this, or even the retreat to Barbar may not be in my power in a few days; and even if carried out at once the retreat will be of extreme difficulty.'[4]

Ten minutes later Gordon elaborated a scheme for the retreat if it were decided to abandon Khartum irrespective of the outlying garrisons. He would send the Cairo employees and the white troops down to Barbar with Stewart to await orders from Cairo. He would then ask Her Majesty's Government to accept his resignation of his commission and would take all the steamers and stores up to Bahr

[1] Ibid.
[2] Ibid.
[3] Ibid.
[4] Gordon to Baring, Mar. 9, 1884, enclosed in Baring to Granville, No. 304, Mar. 13, 1884, P.R.O., F.O. 78/3668.

al-Ghazal and Equatoria, which provinces would be considered as being under the jurisdiction of the King of the Belgians.[1]

Next morning Gordon telegraphed that he considered that the position at the time required Zubair to be sent with a British division to Barbar. 'Zubair's value naturally diminishes in degree as the tribes take up sides with al-Mahdi, and thus involve themselves.'[2] He again asked whether he might send Stewart and Power to Barbar as they could be of no use if 'you decide on the immediate evacuation of Khartum.'

Two hours later Gordon, expecting the line to be cut, considered what should be done in that emergency. Husain Khalifah was instructed to send scouts out and to go himself to meet the forces that might be advancing from Sawakin at Obak. Three steamers which could pass the cataracts would be ordered to remain at Barbar. If any force came from Sawakin, Husain Khalifah was to send up all the black troops from Barbar to Khartum. Gordon would send down to Barbar all the white troops. There was no doubt that the wavering tribes between Khartum and Barbar were not reassured by the evacuation of some people. 'If I could have given any hope to the people as to the future government, probably, things might have been better. It is evident that no one will throw in his fortunes with a departing government.'[3] In forwarding these telegrams Baring told the Foreign Office that he had instructed Gordon to hold on to Khartum until he, Baring, could communicate further with Her Majesty's Government and also that Gordon should on no account proceed to Bahr al-Ghazal and Equatoria.[4]

Her Majesty's Government replied on the same day. They repeated their refusal to appoint Zubair and permit the diversion at Barbara. They were prepared to allow Gordon to stay in Khartum for any length of time if his early departure would diminish the chances of establishing a government there.[5] The Queen commented on this telegram: 'Having placed your entire confidence in Gordon have you now decided to throw over his advice and that of Baring and risk loss of all garrisons?'[6]

[1] Ibid.
[2] Gordon to Baring, Mar. 10, 1884, enclosed in Baring to Granville, No. 304, Mar. 13, 1884, P.R.O., F.O. 78/3668.
[3] Ibid.
[4] Baring to Granville, No. 304, Mar. 13, 1884, P.R.O., F.O. 78/3668.
[5] Granville to Baring, No. 142, Mar. 13, 1884, P.R.O., F.O. 78/4194.
[6] Queen to Granville, Mar. 14, 1884, P.R.O., G/D 29/43.

Realizing that their refusal might react unfavorably on Baring, Granville tried to explain in a private letter the real reasons why they objected to Zubair. There had been two Cabinet meetings at which Gladstone had not been present and there had been a difference of opinion about the appointment of Zubair, but the 'unanimous opinion of the commoners in the Cabinet was that no liberal or conservative Government could appoint Zubair.'[1] The difficulties of sending troops to Barbar were very great and might result in still greater difficulties. 'If Gordon can save the garrisons of Khartum, Barbar and of Dongola it will be in itself a great feat.'[2]

Baring was still prepared to fight it out to the bitter end. He telegraphed to Granville that the instructions contained in Granville's last dispatch would lead to such very serious consequences, that he would hesitate, even if the line were working, to communicate them to Gordon before again ascertaining that the question had been fully considered in all its bearings. Gordon's idea of staying for an indefinite period in Khartum was so vague that it might lend itself to various interpretations. It might mean that he would be succeeded by a governor-general working under instructions from Cairo. This would mean the reversal of the policy of abandonment. It would lead either to the Egyptian Government's governing the Sudan again unaided or to a succession of English governors-general, probably with other British officials. That would ultimately involve the British Government in becoming virtually responsible for the Sudan. Baring hoped that Her Majesty's Government would not adopt such a policy. If it was intended to extend Gordon's period of office for a few months, then Baring could assure them that delay would not facilitate his task, but, on the contrary, would rather increase the difficulty of establishing a settled government. The evacuation to Barbar of the Khartum garrison alone would be most difficult to execute. It would involve the sacrificing of nearly all the other garrisons and Baring thought that the retreat could not be carried out 'without great personal risk to Gordon and Stewart.'[3]

'The ultimate effect,' Baring maintained, 'will be that Khartum must fall to al-Mahdi whose powers will thus be immensely increased and the policy of creating a bulwark between Egypt and

[1] Granville to Baring, Mar. 14, 1884, P.R.O., G/D 29/200.
[2] Ibid.
[3] Baring to Granville, No. 217, Mar. 14, 1884, P.R.O., F.O. 78/4194.

al-Mahdi which I cannot but think is the only wise course to follow, will have to be finally abandoned.'[1] Baring begged Granville not to attach too much importance to the contradictions in Gordon's telegrams. His main contentions appeared to be perfectly clear and reasonable. 'They are first, that the two questions of withdrawing the garrisons and of arranging for the future government of the country cannot be separated. Secondly, that it is most undesirable, even if it be possible, for him to withdraw without having some prominent man to take his place.'[2]

Baring regretted that no man other than Zubair could be found to succeed Gordon. He was very much aware of the great difficulties which would have to be encountered in Britain by Zubair's appointment although he believed that British opinions on that point were based on an incorrect appreciation of the facts. 'But the real question is not whether the appointment of Zubair is objectionable but whether any other practicable and less objectionable alternative can be suggested. I can suggest none.' He would not again have pressed for Zubair, if he could have seen any less objectionable way out of the very difficult position. 'On the other hand, I should not be doing my duty if I did not lay before Her Majesty's Government the grave dangers which will result from, and the objections which may be urged against the alternatives set forth in your Lordship's telegram under reply.'[3]

When this telegram was considered by the Cabinet, Gladstone was still in bed. In a letter to Granville he recorded what seemed to him to be the four possible solutions of the question. The first was for Gordon to remain in Khartum in the hope of organizing a government. The second was that Gordon should depart from Khartum at once. In that case he would not absolutely oppose the sending of the cavalry to Barbar, although he disliked it, provided that the military authorities would declare it possible and necessary to Gordon's safety. The third solution would be to send Zubair provided that Baring was in favor of doing so and was satisfied that Gordon still desired it. Fourthly, there was the possibility of negotiations with al-Mahdi, which seemed to Gladstone to be improbable, but he would not exclude it altogether and would give a

[1] Ibid
[2] Ibid.
[3] Ibid.

general discretion for any course of action to be taken in the Sudan only, and 'independent of us.'[1]

The Cabinet reconsidered the question, but, after a full consideration of the 'weighty arguments' of Baring and Gordon they saw no reason to change the instructions of the 13th. Their objection to Zubair remained the same. The discretion allowed to Gordon to remain was interpreted as applying only to the time necessary for evacuating the garrison and for affording the prospect of a settled government. If both Baring and Gordon agreed that the difficulty of establishing a settled government would increase rather than diminish with time, there could be no advantage in Gordon's remaining. He should then take steps for the evacuation of Khartum following the instructions of the 13th and should exercise his discretion about the disposal of the steamers and stores.[2] The Queen, when shown that telegram, approved it, but she still felt that her Government would 'incur fearful responsibility in refusing their constantly repeated advice.'[3]

Baring repeated the Government's telegram to Gordon, adding that he should regard the idea of sending Zubair as having been finally abandoned, and that 'he must act as well as he can up to the instructions contained in these telegrams.'[4] This was telegraphed to Barbar and from there was to be taken by steamer to Khartum.

Graham's proposal to send a force to Barbar, which both Gordon and Stewart had approved, was also rejected by the British Government, until it should be found necessary for Gordon's safety and until military considerations clearly demanded it. At that time it was not safe to send a small body of cavalry as proposed, and it would be impossible to send a large force.[5] Baring agreed with the Government's decision on this point. Moreover, after some time, the heat would become 'well nigh intolerable for English troops.'[6]

On the day on which the final rejection of Zubair was sent from London to Cairo, Baring received telegrams from Gordon dated the 10th of March. He stated that through the weakness of the Govern-

---

[1] Gladstone to Granville, Mar. 16, 1884, B.M. Add. MS. 44176.
[2] Granville to Baring, No. 162, Mar. 16, 1884, P.R.O., F.O. 78/4194.
[3] Queen to Granville, Mar. 17, 1884, P.R.O., G/D 29/43.
[4] Baring to Granville, No. 226, Mar. 18, 1884, P.R.O., F.O. 78/4194.
[5] Granville to Baring, No. 146, Mar. 16, 1884, P.R.O., F.O. 78/3669.
[6] Gordon to Baring, Mar. 10, 1884, enclosed in Baring to Granville, No. 316, Mar. 16, 1884, P.R.O., F.O. 78/3668.

ment many had joined the rebels. 'All news confirms what I have already told you, viz. that we shall before long be blockaded. The utility of Zubair is greatly diminished owing to our weakness which has forced the loyal to join our enemy.' [1] He also advised that in the event of an expedition being sent to Barbar, speed was of the greatest importance. A small advance guard at Barbar would keep quiet the riverain tribes between Khartum and Barbar, and would reassure the population of the towns.[2] Gordon also informed Baring that the enemy was reported to be four hours' distant on the Blue Nile, but that so far there was no panic in the town.[3]

[1] Gordon to Baring, Mar. 11, 1884, enclosed in Baring to Granville, No. 316, Mar. 16, 1884, P.R.O., F.O. 78/3668.
[2] Ibid.
[3] Baring to Granville, Private, Mar. 18, 1884, P.R.O., G/D 29/162.

X

GORDON'S RELIEF

On the 19th of March a note of alarm was sounded from Barbar, Khartum being out of communication by telegraph line. Both Husain Pasha Khalifah (the Mudir) and Mr. Cuzzi (Gordon's agent at Barbar) spoke in strong language of the impending danger. Rumors were current at Barbar that certain Arab chiefs were trying to close the road to Kurusko. It was also rumored that some of 'Uthman Diqna's Arabs had already gone to cut that one line of retreat. 'If this were true, thousands and thousands of persons would be massacred, and the Sudan would be cut off from all communication.'[1] If Britain were not prepared to hold the Sudan it would nevertheless be necessary to send troops to protect the retreat of thousands of men, women, and children. If millions were spent for nothing, some millions might be spent to save thousands of lives. Britain, who had shown generosity on previous occasions would not withdraw at that critical moment. 'At any rate troops are indispensable and that quickly. Otherwise everything will be lost.'[2]

Wolseley thought that some measures to support Gordon ought to be taken. He proposed sending a portion of Wood's army to Wadi Halfa to give moral support and also proposed that six British officers should proceed to Barbar to await Gordon's instructions. If possible they should be selected from those serving in the Egyptian army who would have acquired a knowledge of Arabic and experience in handling the natives. Hartington thought it desirable to get Baring's opinion on these points.[3] The Foreign Office therefore telegraphed Baring asking him for his opinion.[4]

In reply, after consulting Wood and Stephenson, Baring reported that Gordon would not be helped by moving the Egyptian troops

[1] Translation from Italian, Cuzzi to Baring, Mar. 19, 1884, enclosed in Baring to Granville, No. 333, Mar. 19, 1884, P.R.O., F.O. 78/3669.
[2] Ibid.
[3] Wolseley to Granville, Private, Mar. 22, 1884, P.R.O., G/D 29/170.
[4] Granville to Baring, No. 179, Mar. 22, 1884, P.R.O., F.O. 78/3662.

up to Wadi Halfa. If any movement had to be made it should be to Kurusko which was on the direct road to Barbar. There would be no point, however, in sending them beyond Aswan unless it was the intention to push on to Barbar. As to the British officers, it was stated that those who had joined Wood's army recently had no knowledge of Arabic, and to take six of his trained officers would be detrimental to the efficiency of the Egyptian army. A fuller answer could not be given unless more precise information was given about the objects for which it was proposed to send the officers.[1]

Gordon's position seems to have been not only the concern of the authorities in Cairo and London, but also of his fellow officers, who read avidly all the news from Khartum. Being aware of the difficulties that Gordon would encounter, they were of opinion that some military assistance would be necessary to extricate him. Among these officers was General Sir John Adye, officer commanding in Gibralter. In a letter to Childers he expressed great uneasiness about Gordon's position at Khartum. Although Her Majesty's Government was anxious to avoid, as far as possible, taking any responsibility for the Sudan, circumstances would force them to interfere as 'now Gordon is at Khartum appointed by us, and Graham has also been acting on the Red Sea coast under our orders.'[2] He maintained that Britain could not leave the matter there. The Government would be compelled to go still farther though unwillingly.

In his opinion the results of Graham's victories should be followed up by opening the road to Barbar. This would mean sending out materials for a railway at once, making the Arab chiefs responsible for its safety, and employing their tribesmen whom Sir John thought would be on Britain's side. The railway would be only 200 miles in length and most of it, he presumed, would be easy to construct. When once this railway was completed the difficulty of holding Khartum would soon cease to exist. Small armed steamers would be sent in sections to be assembled in Barbar and to ply between that town and Khartum. He thought that very large subsidies would

[1] Baring to Granville, No. 345, Mar. 23, 1884, P.R.O., F.O. 78/3669.
[2] Childers, S., *Life and Correspondence of the Right Hon. Hugh C. E. Childers 1827-1896*, vol. ii, p. 181.

not be required to induce the tribes between Sawakin and Barbar to ensure the safety of the road after Graham's victories. Once the railway and the telegraph had been laid their protection would be simple.

Baring also reviewed the situation in the Sudan in a dispatch to Granville. The Government's instructions to Gordon, dated the 13th and the 16th of March, had been forwarded to Gordon but no reply had yet been received. Baring believed that in the existing conditions Gordon would not be able to carry out these instructions. 'The question now is how to get General Gordon and Colonel Stewart away from Khartum.'[1] In considering that question it should be remembered that they would not willingly come back without bringing with them the garrison of Khartum and the Government officials. He believed that Graham's success would result in the opening up of the road to Barbar, but no action at or near Sawakin could exert much influence over the tribes between Barbar and Khartum.

Unless any unforeseen events should occur and change the situation, only two solutions appeared to be possible. The first would be to trust that Gordon would be able to maintain himself at Khartum until the autumn when, because of increased supplies of water, operations along the Sawakin–Barbar road would be made easier. The alternative would be to send a portion of Graham's army from Sawakin to Barbar with instructions to open up communications with Khartum. There would be difficulty in reaching Barbar, but once the road was open, small detachments could be sent. 'General Gordon is evidently expecting help from Sawakin, and he has ordered messengers to be sent along the road from Barbar to ascertain whether any English force is advancing.'[2]

Baring therefore recommended that an effort should be made to assist Gordon from Sawakin if it were militarily possible. Stephenson and Wood, while admitting the great risk to the health of the troops and the 'extraordinary military risks,' considered the undertaking to be possible. They thought that Graham should be further consulted. It was considered by the authorities in Cairo that in spite of all the difficulties attending operations from Sawakin they were yet more

[1] Baring to Granville, No. 350, Mar. 24, 1884, P.R.O., F.O. 78/3669.
[2] Ibid.

practicable than any operations from Kurusko and along the Nile. 'If any thing is to be done no time should be lost, as each week increases the difficulty as regards climate.'

In a private letter to Granville written on the same day, Baring expressed himself more strongly on the situation. 'Certainly of all the difficult positions the English Government—not to speak of their perplexed representative—has ever been in, I do not think it would be easy to find any thing in the past to equal the difficulty of this Egyptian-Sudan situation.'[1] He regretted every day more and more that Zubair had not been sent a month previously. 'If he had been sent we should be in a very different position now. I think you will eventually be driven by the force of circumstances to come back to the idea of sending him, or else eventually to undertake the government of the Sudan.'[2] The latter, in Baring's opinion, would be the worst possible solution of existing difficulties.

Dismissing the question of Zubair and the hope of any settled government for the time being, Baring declared that he had been 'torturing' his 'brains all the week to think of some possible solution of the most pressing and immediate difficulties.' He was quite sure that Gordon would not be able to obey the instructions which had been sent to him, and it was most important to consider how to get him out of the trap in which he was caught. 'As matters have turned out I blame myself for ever having consented to his going.' He declared that he was not influenced by the opinions of the English press. 'I do not think we can leave him stranded at Khartum if from the military point of view it is at all possible to help him.' Although it was understood that the difficulties of a military expedition to Barbar were great and of a serious nature, yet it was not impossible, and he thought 'as a choice of evils that it ought to be done.'[3]

The British Government refused to sanction the expedition to Barbar on the grounds that the dangers of the climate of the Sudan at that time of the year were great and also because of the risk from a military point of view. They wished to communicate this decision to Gordon in order that he might adopt measures in accordance with it. 'Her Majesty's Government desire to leave

---

[1] Baring to Granville, Mar. 24, 1884, P.R.O., G/D 29/162.
[2] Ibid.
[3] Ibid.

full discretion to General Gordon to remain at Khartum if he thinks it necessary, or to retire by the southern or any other route which may be found available.' [1]

Why they reached that decision was explained in a note from Granville to the Queen enclosing this telegram for approval. Granville, Hartington, and Northbrook had had a long discussion in the morning with Wolseley and Wilson, and in the evening they had considered Baring's proposal. They had observed that the sending of the troops was contrary to Baring's previous advice. It was believed to be impossible for the tribes to take Khartum by assault, and the garrison had six months' provisions. Even if it were desirable to expose more British troops the operations would be easier when the water was high.[2] The Queen approved the draft telegram, but once again regretted 'that nothing can be done.' [3]

The Government, however, conceded less important points. They approved an earlier request for two officers to be sent to Barbar to act as liaison between Graham and Chermside on the one side and Gordon on the other. It was also stated that the object in dispatching units of the Egyptian army to Wadi Halfa was to assist General Gordon in any military operations which he might have to undertake.[4]

Baring was not satisfied and replied that he was not sure whether it would be possible for him to communicate this decision to Gordon and he submitted the case again for Granville's consideration. He wished Her Majesty's Government to place themselves in Gordon's and Stewart's position. 'These officers have been sent on a most difficult and dangerous mission by Her Majesty's Government. Their proposal that Zubair Pasha should be sent to Khartum, which, if it had been acted on some weeks ago, would, without doubt, have entirely altered the situation, was rejected; and the consequences which they foresaw have ensued.' [5]

If Gordon and Stewart received the instructions contained in that telegram they would understand that they, with all who were with them, were to be abandoned by the British Government.

[1] Granville to Baring, No. 182, Mar. 25, 1884, P.R.O., F.O. 78/3662.
[2] Granville to the Queen, Mar. 25, 1884, P.R.O., G/D 29/43.
[3] The Queen to Granville, Mar. 25, 1884, P.R.O., G/D 29/43.
[4] Granville to Baring, No. 184, Mar. 26, 1884, P.R.O., F.O. 78/3662.
[5] Baring to Granville, No. 362, Mar. 26, 1884, P.R.O., F.O. 78/3669.

Colonel de Coetlogon's information stated that so long as the rebels held the banks of the Nile around the sixth cataract it would be impossible for boats to pass down the river. It would be impossible for Gordon to cut his way through by land. De Coetlogon ridiculed the idea of Gordon's retreating with the Khartum garrison and employees and others to the Equator and it was quite certain that 'General Gordon and Colonel Stewart will refuse to come away alone.'[1]

Baring maintained that it would be possible to help Gordon even during the summer if Indian troops were employed and money was not spared. But if it were finally decided to give no immediate help, Gordon should be told to maintain his position at Khartum during the summer and then if he were still besieged an expedition should be sent as early as possible to relieve him. That would give him hope and its announcement would prevent the defection of the tribes who might still be wavering. 'No one can regret more than I do the necessity of sending British or Indian troops to the Sudan, but having sent General Gordon to Khartum, it appears to me that it is our bounden duty both as a matter of humanity and policy not to abandon him.'[2]

Granville's reply contained not only a refusal to send a force to Barbar immediately but a refusal to promise to send it in the autumn. The Cabinet still thought that they were not justified in dispatching a British force to Barbar and repeated that Gordon had full discretion to remain at Khartum or to retire by the southern or any other route which might be available. They were not prepared to alter their previous instructions which Baring was told to communicate to Gordon as soon as possible. They were, moreover, not prepared to add to those instructions until they had received further information as to 'General Gordon's actual conditions and prospects as to security, and also if possible as to his plans of proceeding and wishes in the present position of affairs in the Sudan.'[3]

When the original draft of this telegram was shown to the Queen she remarked that she 'cannot say she likes this telegram.' She observed that the first sentence was unnecessarily 'curt and harsh,'

[1] Baring to Granville, No. 362, Mar. 26, 1884, P.R.O., F.O. 78/3669.
[2] Ibid.
[3] Granville to Baring, No. 191 Secret, Mar. 28, 1884, P.R.O., F.O. 78/3662.

and suggested that it should be amended to: 'Have given your telegram our most serious consideration and with the greatest wish to assist General Gordon do not see how we can alter our instructions of the 25th.' [1] She amended the wording of the opening sentence, not because it expressed her own feelings but because she thought it would convey what she understood to be the opinion of the Government in terms which would not lead Baring and Gordon to 'suppose that their suggestions and appeals are treated with contempt.' [2] The telegram was duly changed.

'You shot a heavy cannon ball,' wrote Granville privately to Baring, 'your last protest as to our instructions to Gordon.' [3] Although Baring's proposals were a complete reversal of their policy, the Government quite understood his feelings. They could not pledge themselves to a promise to Gordon to send a military expedition to Khartum in the autumn. They hoped that Graham's victory might have outweighed the bad effects of Baker's defeat. Their military advisers assured them that unless the garrison rebelled against Gordon the Arabs could not take Khartum. They felt that Gordon was in no immediate danger because he had provisions for six months. 'The only new incident as affecting the original views with which Gordon set out, and upon which we consented to send him, was the restriction upon Zubair's joining him, the objections to which were chiefly furnished by you and by him.' [4] Granville also conveyed the opinion of Sir Henry Gordon, the brother of General Gordon. He had stated that he was not in the least alarmed for his brother 'who has extricated himself from more dangerous positions than the present.' He was not at all sorry that Zubair was prevented from going to his brother. 'His chief anxiety is that his brother should think we do not believe that he has sufficient discretion as to forming a government, which may prevent anarchy.' [5]

Sir Charles Wilson, however, took a very different view. On March 28, 1884 he drew up a memorandum maintaining that Gordon was in a most difficult position at Khartum and that if there were no very grave objections his requests ought to be

[1] Ponsonby to Granville, Mar. 28, 1884, P.R.O., G/D 29/43.
[2] Ibid.
[3] Granville to Baring, Mar. 28, 1884, P.R.O., G/D 29/200.
[4] Ibid.
[5] Ibid.

granted. Wilson thought it better that troops should be sent to Wadi Halfa rather than to Kurusko, for Wadi Halfa was on the road by the riverside. Moreover, Gordon, who knew the country better than anyone else, had suggested Wadi Halfa. Wilson declared that Dongola was a very important town and should be carefully watched. He supported Gordon's proposal for sending a British officer ostensibly to look for camping places. The officer would be badly needed in Dongola as it had been reported that the Mudir of Dongola was in communication with al-Mahdi. Wilson concluded, 'I think matters in the Sudan are too serious to allow this communication to go on without some british control.' [1]

By the end of March it was clear in both Cairo and London that no immediate action was to be taken to improve Gordon's position. 'The only thing we can now do about Gordon is to sit still and see what the future will bring forth. I do not believe that he is in very immediate danger.' [2] Baring believed that if al-Mahdi chose to advance he would not do so until the autumn when the wells would be full, and it was to be hoped that by that time inter-tribal quarrels might weaken his forces. Baring considered that the publicity which Gordon had given to Zubair was most unfortunate. Baring became anxious about Zubair's behavior after he knew that he was not to be sent to Khartum. Although Zubair was being watched, yet Baring asked to be authorized to spend about £100 from the secret-service fund to obtain information about his movements.[3]

Attempts were being made to effect the opening of the Sawakin-Barbar road through the friendly Ababdah tribe who controlled the road from Abu Hamad to Kurusko. Major Kitchener of the Egyptian army was instructed to enter into negotiations with the Ababdah tribe with a view to their operating on the Barbar-Sawakin road. He was also instructed to communicate with the son of Husain Pasha Khalifah, who was not far from Aswan, in an attempt to collect some Bedwins to accompany Kitchener to Barbar via Kurusko.[4] But these attempts were doomed to failure

---

[1] Memorandum by Sir Charles Wilson, Mar. 28, 1884, P.R.O., G/D 29/170.
[2] Baring to Granville, Private, Mar. 31, 1884, P.R.O., G/D 29/162.
[3] Baring to Granville, Apr. 2, 1884, P.R.O., G/D 29/162.
[4] Baring to Granville, No. 410, Apr. 11, 1884, P.R.O., F.O. 78/3670.

as the Ababdah had no interest in entering into bloody wars with the Hadandawa.

The parliamentary session which opened in February 1884 was characterized by great interest in the Egyptian question and particularly policy towards the Sudan and Gordon's position. On the 3rd of April both Gladstone and Hartington made statements in the House of Commons on the Government's policy in the Sudan and their attitude to Gordon. Gladstone stated that Gordon had been sent from England by Her Majesty's Government and under their authority 'to ascertain the best means of executing the evacuation of the Sudan.'[1] The House was already aware that when he arrived in Egypt he received from the Egyptian Government executive powers to be exercised in the name and on the authority of the Egyptian Government, 'although they are powers with regard to which Her Majesty's Government feel both great interest and responsibility.' Gordon had moreover been instructed to use his own discretion about withdrawing from the Sudan and he was under no orders requiring him to remain in that country. Her Majesty's Government believed that Gordon was able to leave the Sudan if he wished to do so.

Gladstone concluded his speech:

This is the 17th night on which the House has been introduced to an Egyptian debate. I want to know whether that is a course which is beneficial to the country? As the Head of Her Majesty's Government I enter my protest against that course. I say there is no precedent for it. There is not in all the annals of parliament anything in the slightest degree resembling the conduct that has been pursued by the opposition, and by the Leader of the opposition, with respect to these Egyptian transactions—you have had your discussion for 17 nights out of the two months which the House has, as yet, been able to give to the affairs of the Empire.[2]

Hartington, on the same night, stated that the Government's information led them to believe that al-Mahdi did not possess outstanding military ability although it could not be disputed that he exercised considerable authority over the tribes in certain districts of the country and had attained several successes over the

[1] *Hansard,* 3rd ser., vol. 284, col. 1510.
[2] Ibid

troops sent against him. Nevertheless, he had not shown any great capacity for following up his victories.[1]

News received on the 7th of April from the Mudir of Barbar stated that the number of rebels surrounding Khartum was increasing, that all the population south of Shandi had already joined the revolt, and that those north of Shandi were ready to join at any moment. Later, it was reported that communication between the rebels and the Bishariyin Arabs, with the object of besieging Barbar and cutting off communication with Kurusko, were believed to be taking place.[2]

In spite of their aversion to committing themselves to an autumn campaign, the military authorities were making all the preliminary preparations for a campaign to relieve Gordon in case it was thought necessary. The military advisers were not agreed as to the road to be used. Wolseley favored the river road from the north, and Sir Charles Wilson preferred the Sawakin road. Hartington considered that it should be announced that an expedition was being prepared as it would 'have a healthy effect on the situation.'[2]

Wolseley suggested that a telegram should be sent to Gordon *en clair* through Husain Khalifah, saying that as soon as the climate permitted the movement of British troops, an expeditionary force would be sent to Khartum. In cypher Gordon should be told that he might calculate on being relieved before the 15th of November next.[4]

Gladstone was averse to sending an expedition of English troops except 'in the last and sad necessity of its being the only available means of rescuing him.'[5] Gladstone also suggested sending a carefully prepared questionnaire to Gordon about his future situation and plans. This Gladstone thought necessary because Gordon had taken little notice of any general questions which had been put to him. Hartington was doubtful whether Gordon would reply in time for the Government to make up their

[1] Ibid.
[2] Baring to Granville, No. 393, Apr. 7, 1884, P.R.O., F.O. 78/3670.
[3] Hartington to Gladstone, Apr. 11, 1884, B.M. Add. MS. 44147.
[4] Holland, Bernard, *Life of Specer Compton, 8th Duke of Devonshire* (London, 1911), vol. i, p. 443.
[5] Gladstone to Hartington, Apr. 13, 1884, B.M. Add. MS. 44547.

mind. Communications with Khartum were so bad that it was not known whether Gordon had received any messages from Cairo since the 10th of March. 'I think it is now clear enough that whether he has a right to do so or not he expects help in some shape or another, and it is also, I think clear that he will not be asked to leave Khartum without some such help.' [1] Hartington was of opinion that it was time that Her Majesty's Government decided what they proposed to do about Gordon and Egypt. His impression was that the Government was hoping to get a message from Gordon saying that he would not require British troops and that he would effect the evacuation of the Sudan in some other way. 'This is rather a broken reed to lean on, and in my opinion was finally shattered by his last telegram.' [2]

Northbrook was of opinion that Gordon should be ordered to leave Khartum, leaving the main part of the garrison behind him. Hartington, however, remarked that Gordon would not obey such orders and would certainly be supported by public opinion. 'In fact I think the first thing we have to do is to decide whether we intend to leave Gordon to his fate, because, if we do not, the sooner we begin to make preparations the better.' [3] Hartington also maintained that if Her Majesty's Government were compelled to send an expedition at all, they should reconsider their decision to abandon the eastern Sudan. 'I doubt whether we were right at first in accepting Baring's opinion that it was impossible for Egypt to hold it. Events go to show that it would have been easier to hold it than to get out of it.' It would not probably be necessary to restore Egyptian Government there but to 'replace it with some sort of independent government under our protection.' [4]

Hartington agreed with his principal adviser, Lord Wolseley, on these matters. Wolseley proposed to telegraph to Gordon:

If authority were given you to announce publicly and positively that you and another English officer after you, were to remain to govern Sudan east of White Nile for benefit of Sudan people independent of Egypt and its employees, eighty or one hundred thousand pounds per annum being allowed you for a few years, could you start a government with any chance of success?

[1] Hartington to Granville, Apr. 15, 1884, P.R.O., G/D 29/134.
[2] Hartington to Granville, Apr. 16, 1884, P.R.O., G/D 29/134.
[3] Ibid.
[4] Ibid.

Would influential men join you? And would such a move relieve your present difficulties and render despatch of British troops to Khartum in autumn unnecessary.[1]

If Gordon were to reply in the affirmative, Wolseley suggested that his proposal should immediately be implemented. Meanwhile Baring had raised the question of Gordon's relief. He maintained that he had no wish to urge an expedition to Khartum unless, after very full consideration, it was clear that there was no alternative. 'No one can entertain stronger objections than I do to the despatch of a force to Khartum,'[2] but as Hartington had declared in the House of Commons, the British Government was responsible for Gordon's safety.

Baring's aim was to set out the actual situation as far as it could be ascertained, without making any definite proposal. He admitted the difficulty of giving positive advice on such a difficult situation. In his most recent telegrams Gordon had mentioned that for two months he would be as safe in Khartum as in Cairo. Baring was not quite sure what this statement meant. If Gordon meant that he could not hold out for more than two months it would be impossible for an expedition to reach Khartum by the end of May. In previous telegrams Gordon had stated that he had provisions for six months and that, if al-Mahdi advanced on Khartum, he would probably not do so before September or October. Baring had asked Gordon to explain this point more fully but owing to the difficulty of communicating with Khartum it would be a considerable time before an answer was received.

Meanwhile it appeared that the Government might find themselves obliged to relieve Gordon. In that eventuality all the authorities whom Baring had consulted were of opinion that if operations were to be undertaken by the Nile route 'no time should be lost in making preparations, so as to be ready to move directly the water rises.'[3] Gordon might be able to extricate himself and in that case the preparations would simply be useless. 'On the other hand, unless they are undertaken now, it may be that when the necessity for moving arises so long a delay will ensue as to frustrate the objects of the expedition.'

[1] Wolseley's proposal, enclosed in ibid.
[2] Baring to Granville, No. 422, 14, 1884, P.R.O., F.O. 78/3671.
[3] Baring to Granville, No. 422, Apr. 14, 1884, P.R.O., F.O. 78/3671.

Baring therefore thought that the Government should consider whether to order the naval and military authorities to take some preliminary steps to be ready to move when the need arose. 'It would be better, I think, to run the risk of incurring some unnecessary expenditure rather than to find ourselves unable to seize the opportunity of moving when the favorable moment arises.' [1]

Cuzzi again reported alarming news from Barbar. Both Husain Khalifah and Cuzzi repeated their request for English troops. Khartum was completely blockaded and both banks of the river between that town and Barbar were lined by rebels. 'Troops must be sent at once if you want to save General Gordon, Colonel Stewart and Mr. Power, with thousands and thousands of persons who will meet with the end which befell the troops under General Hicks in Kurdufan. It is impossible that Europe should stand by a cold spectator of such a slaughter.' [2]

Messages from Gordon had by this time reached Cairo. The only thing that Gordon feared was that al-Mahdi would send his captured guns to his followers who were investing Khartum. 'If he does we are completely done, for the steamers would be as earthen pots before them.' [3] Gordon reported that Khartum was quiet and that there was plenty of food.

Gordon considered himself free to act according to circumstances and he declared that he would hold on to Khartum as long as he could and would 'endeavor to suppress the rebellion and that if he cannot do so he will retire to the Equator.' [4] Gordon had also directed both Stewart and Power to go to Barbar as soon as it was possible to send steamers down the river. But they had preferred to proceed south with Gordon as the road to Barbar was blockaded and, if opened, the road from there to Sawakin was closed. [5]

Having lost hope of having Zubair sent to him, Gordon made a new suggestion which he telegraphed to Sir Samuel Baker. He suggested that an appeal should be made to British and American millionaires for £300,000 for engaging 3,000 Turkish troops from

[1] Ibid.
[2] Cuzzi to Baring, Apr. 15, 1884 enclosed in Baring to Granville, No. 430, Apr. 16, 1884, P.R.O., F.O. 78/3671.
[3] Gordon to Baring, Apr. 3, 1884, enclosed in Baring to Granville, No. 428, Apr. 16, 1884, P.R.O., F.O. 78/3671.
[4] Baring to Granville, No. 429, Apr. 16, 1884, P.R.O., F.O. 78/3671.
[5] Stewart and Power to Baring undated, enclosed in ibid.

the Sultan and sending them to the Sudan. In his opinion this would settle the Sudan and al-Mahdi for ever. 'For my part I think you would agree with me. I do not see the fun of being caught here to walk about the streets for years as a dervish with sandalled feet, not that (D.V.) I will ever be taken alive; it would be the climax of meanness after I had borrowed money from the people here, had called on them to sell their grain at a low price etc. to go and abandon them.' [1]

The confusion and anxiety in which the British Government found themselves was described by Granville in a private letter to Baring. 'The misfortune during the last 2 years has been that we hardly ever had anything but bad alternatives to choose from. The objections to whatever was decided were pretty sure to have the best of it. If we can get out of the enormous Sudanese difficulty, I do not see why Egypt proper should not get into at least as promising a condition as that which you described when you first took the mission.' [2]

On April 21 Baring left for England for consultation with the Government about the financial difficulties of Egypt, which would be the subject of a conference in London. Before he left, however, he forwarded to London 'a most distressing telegram' [3] from Husain Pasha Khalifah at Barbar, for it was believed that telegraphic communications with that town might be cut at any moment. At the same time Baring forwarded a telegram from Gordon acknowledging the receipt of the Government's decision not to send troops from Sawakin to Barbar. Gordon complained bitterly that it was not sent in cypher, because it would throw the people of Barbar and probably those of Khartum into panic. Gordon referred Baring to the previous occasions when his, Gordon's, attention had been directed to the danger of uncyphered telegrams.

After the lectures you have read me about indiscreet uncyphered telegrams I am astonished at this and I cannot reconcile your action in again fighting 'Uthman Diqna after the relief of Tūkar and your telegram to Cuzzi saying it is not intended to advance British troops to Barbar. Had you telegraphed this to me in cypher, I would see some use in it, but why you should un-

---

[1] Gordon to Baring, Apr. 8, 1884, enclosed in Baring to Granville, No. 440, Apr. 18, 1884, P.R.O., F.O. 78/3671.
[2] Granville to Baring, Apr. 18, 1884, P.R.O., G/D 29/200.
[3] Baring to Granville, No. 451, Apr. 21, 1884, P.R.O., F.O. 78/3671.

necessarily throw dismay into Barbar, I do not understand, seeing that Barbar is our line of retreat.[1]

Gordon concluded by saying that Khartum was quiet and that the telegram had not even given 'us a twitter.' Baring defended his action, saying that Gordon had repeatedly asked him not to send telegrams in cypher as it was unnecessary, but in spite of that he, Baring, continued to send them in cypher. As Cuzzi at Barbar had no cypher, Baring was obliged to send the telegram in question *en clair*. Baring intended to tell Cuzzi clearly that there were no troops advancing from Sawakin as the latter repeatedly asked to be informed of the whereabouts of the British troops and when they would be sent. Baring thought it unfair to leave the people at Barbar under the wrong impression.[2]

In fact Gordon had asked for telegrams to be sent *en clair* in order to raise the morale of the people. But he had believed that the telegrams would announce the sending of reinforcements and especially of British troops. He even went so far as to suggest the sending of such good news even if it were false. But one of Gordon's main troubles was that he did not put his arguments quite clearly and even sometimes threw out suggestions without giving arguments in their support.

Egerton was appointed to act as consul-general during Baring's absence. His first communication from Granville instructed him to consult Stephenson, Wood, and Nubar about the position of Barbar which seemed to be in imminent danger. Egerton was instructed to report whether any step could be taken by negotiation or otherwise for its relief.[3] Just before the authorities met in Cairo to reply to this communication, Husain Khalifah made yet a further appeal for the immediate dispatch of troops 'as the only chance of saving the town from falling into the hands of the rebels.'[4] He reported that an emissary of al-Mahdi was raising the population of the southern part of the province and that the villages were joining him. A party of rebels to the west of the town were only awaiting his approach before attacking Barbar.

[1] Gordon to Baring, Apr. 7, 1884, enclosed in Baring to Granville, No. 452, Apr. 21, 1884, P.R.O., F.O. 78/3671.
[2] Baring to Granville, No. 452, Apr. 21, 1884, P.R.O., F.O. 78/3671.
[3] Granville to Egerton, No. 218, Apr. 21, 1884, P.R.O., F.O. 78/3663.
[4] Husain Khalifah to the Egyptian Government, enclosed in Egerton to Granville, No. 459, Apr. 23, 1884, P.R.O., F.O. 78/3671.

Acting on this information, Nubar, Stephenson, and Wood were unanimous that negotiations without a force to back them were useless. Nubar, however, suggested that the two Egyptian battalions stationed at Aswan, together with 500 Ababdah Arabs should be sent to Barbar as soon as the Ababdah could be collected. Both Stephenson and Wood, on the other hand, were strongly opposed to sending the Egyptian soldiers alone, and discussed the possibility of sending a mixed force of British and Egyptian troops. Egerton reported: 'The only thing that can be done towards the immediate safety of Barbar is to give the assurances that material assistance will be afforded by England as soon as practicable.' [1]

Gladstone maintained that they ought not to act in the Sudan by other than pacific means except to ensure the safety of Gordon and his party. If it became necessary to send military assistance it should be made quite clear to Gordon and others that it was being sent only to take him away from Khartum. A message should therefore be sent to Gordon, by any means possible, instructing him to keep Her Majesty's Government informed not only of the immediate but of any prospective danger at Khartum, and to advise them on the force necessary to effect his removal. He should be informed that the Government would not be party to supplying him with Turkish troops, and that if he preferred to stay in Khartum he should state to them the cause and the intention of his doing so. [2] The Cabinet approved Gladstone's memorandum and a dispatch was accordingly drafted to Egerton on the lines of this memorandum. [3]

Hartington was decidedly against the course taken. 'I look on the decision as one practically to do nothing and make no preparations, and this I cannot acquiesce in.' [4] In a letter to Stephenson, Hartington wrote that the general opinion of the Cabinet was that Her Majesty's Government was responsible only for the safety of Gordon and his immediate suite. It would not accept responsibility for the garrison or any part of the population of Khartum

---

[1] Egerton to Granville, No. 460, Apr. 23, 1884, P.R.O., F.O. 78/3671.
[2] Memorandum on Gordon's relief by Gladstone, Apr. 23, 1884, P.R.O., G/D 29/128.
[3] Granville to Egerton, No. 218A, Apr. 23, 1884, P.R.O., F.O. 78/3663.
[4] Holland, op. cit., vol. i, p. 448.

or other places in the Sudan and for this reason the word 'removal' had been used in the telegram to Gordon. Hartington believed that Gordon would not accept this interpretation.[1]

Egerton sent copies of this telegram to Gordon through Barbar, Dongola, Sawakin, and Masawwa. Cuzzi, however, replied that there was no chance of a messenger reaching Khartum as the previous one had returned because the road was completely blocked.[2]

The authorities in Egypt recommended an attempt to relieve Barbar or at least to stop the spread of the rebellion to the north of that town. They suggested that majors Kitchener and Rundle should proceed at once to Abu Hamad with 500 Fuqara Ababdah in an attempt to keep Abu Hijil, the chief of the Rubatab, loyal to the Government. The supply of water would give much difficulty if an expedition were sent by the Kurusko route, and the danger would be increased if Abu Hamad were in enemy hands. 'Personally,' Egerton wrote, 'I now strongly recommend this action as something may thus be done or be found possible to do to hinder the tide of rebellion, which not from its strength but from not meeting the slightest hindrance is becoming threatening to Upper Egypt.'[3] The use of regular troops at that time of the year was out of the question because of the climate.

Baring's departure from Cairo and the preoccupation of Her Majesty's Government with the conference on Egyptian finance diverted attention from Sudan affairs. The Cabinet were awaiting the information which they had asked Gordon to give before they could reach a decision. In the meantime Gladstone seemed to have found something reasonable in Gordon's proposal for the employment of the Turkish assistance. Gladstone contemplated the handing over of the Sudan difficulties to the Sultan by allowing Gordon to make arrangements directly with him without reference to London. It was only an idea on Gladstone's part and was never discussed seriously.[4] In Cairo it was clear that the announcement of an expedition to the Sudan in Egypt would certainly be of great advantage and would steady the waverers if it was decided to send

[1] Ibid.
[2] Cuzzi to Egerton, Apr. 25, 1884, enclosed in Egerton to Granville, No. 464, Apr. 25, 1884, P.R.O., F.O. 78/3671.
[3] Egerton to Granville, No. 481, May 1, 1884, P.R.O., F.O. 78/3672.
[4] Gladstone to Granville, May 8, 1884, P.R.O., G/D 29/128.

it. On the other hand, it would not be prudent to publish the news if no expedition were to be sent.[1]

Just at the time when it was thought that the Sudan might best be left until Gordon had replied to the telegram, trouble began to brew on a new front. The Mudir of Dongola reported that the messenger sent with the telegram to Gordon had returned stating that Khartum was invested by the rebels. Other messengers had been sent in the hope of being able to reach the town. The Mudir also asked the Egyptian Government to send him reinforcements. It was decided to send an Egyptian battalion from Aswan to Wadi Halfa and Kurusko. This, it was hoped, would have the double effect of lending moral support to Dongola and contributing towards the safety of the British naval officers who had been sent to survey the Nile beyond Wadi Halfa.[2]

A vote of censure was proposed in the House of Commons on May 12 by Sir Michael Hicks-Beach, who moved the motion 'that this House regrets to find that the course pursued by Her Majesty's Government has not tended to promote the success of General Gordon's mission and that even such steps as may be necessary to secured his personal safety are still delayed.'[1,3]

Gladstone, replying for the Government, said that the Egyptian question, of which the Sudan was only a part, presented a remarkable combination unexampled in his experience. It was of secondary importance as far as the interests of England were concerned and commanded little notice or attention and yet it had been attended with difficulties, 'such as no Government, to my knowledge, has ever been called upon to encounter.'[4] If the Government were to take severe measures, in Mr. Gladstone's opinion, 'it would be a war, a war of conquest against a people struggling to be free. ["No, no!"] Yes these are people struggling to be free, and they are struggling rightly to be free.' He declared that Her Majesty's Government was determined not to undertake the reconquest of the Sudan and not to place England in conflict with a people fighting for their liberty. 'This question thus difficult we have had to carry on from day to day under the pressure of parliamentary action, of parliamentary interposition in every form, by questions,

[1] Egerton to Granville, No. 488, May 5, 1884, P.R.O., F.O. 78/3672.
[2] Egerton to Granville, No. 505, May 10, 1884, P.R.O., F.O. 78/3672.
[3] Hansard, 3rd ser., vol. 288, col. 31.
[4] Hansard, 3rd ser., vol. 288, col. 58.

by demands for information, by votes of censure, made and attempted about once in three weeks in defiance of all precedents and customs of Parliament.'[1] Gladstone restated the natural difficulties to be encountered in a country which Gordon had described as terrible, a country in the conquest of which Cambyses, the Persian Emperor, failed 2,000 years ago, while he succeeded in putting down the rival empire of Egypt. 'The gentleman advises us to carry the line of conquest by British and Christian arms among the Muhammadan people struggling for their liberty in the Sudan.'

Hartington repeated the circumstances in which Gordon had been sent to the Sudan. Gordon at the time was the only man with real influence in that country. Gordon appeared to be of opinion that it would be possible, by sending himself without the support of any military force, to accompany the withdrawal of the garrisons. In the conversation which he had with members of the Cabinet before he undertook his mission he said: 'that in his opinion the danger of massacre of the garrisons was greatly exaggerated, that the power of al-Mahdi was greatly exaggerated, and that it was probable that no opposition would be offered to the peaceful withdrawal of the Egyptian officials and such portions of the garrisons as might desire to leave.'[2]

Gordon had even gone so far as to express the opinion that probably the greater number of the Egyptian population would not desire to leave, that the majority of the troops would join al-Mahdi, and those who would desire to be withdrawn could be removed without any great difficulty or great risk of massacre. It was quite possible that Gordon had overrated his influence and underestimated the power of al-Mahdi, but on the basis of the evidence in their possession the Government still hoped that he could accomplish his mission as he had planned. It had been believed before Graham's expedition had been sent out that the moral effect of such an expedition would be so great that there would be no fighting at all, 'but the moral effect was not even to save the garrison of Tūkar. The siege was continued, and the garrison surrendered.'[3]

Sir Charles Dilke declared: 'General Gordon was not only sent

[1] Ibid.
[2] Ibid., col. 227.
[3] Ibid., col. 232.

on a pacific mission, but he was sent at his own suggestion, with instructions that were drawn up by himself.'[1] Dilke stated that he had met Gordon on the day he left London and he appeared to be confident of the success of his mission.

It is one of the curious difficulties under which we labor—as it would be a difficulty to any Government—that up to this moment we do not know, and we have not the evidence before us from which to deduce, the reasons which prevented that pacific policy being carried out. We do not know how it is that as regards certain garrisons al-Mahdi has been unwilling to come to a friendly arrangement and to let them leave the Sudan—that is a matter on which we have no information at this time.[2]

Once in Khartum Gordon suddenly changed his views about the character of his mission, and he had 'told us he was now sending out troops to show his force, and in a telegram later in the same day he said that an expedition would start immediately to attack the rebels in the vicinity.'[3] He had also issued a proclamation to the people saying that he was compelled to resort to severe measures and that those who persisted in disobedience would be harshly treated. Dilke concluded that they were completely in the dark as to the cause of this sudden change. The evidence which the Government possessed indicated that there was no immediate danger to Khartum. In the division on the motion the Government's majority was only twenty-eight.

Meanwhile, a second alarm had been sounded from Dongola, giving warning that there was a serious rising in the district of Marawi. The number of the insurgents actually under arms was estimated at 10,000, and they were apparently only awaiting an emissary of al-Mahdi called al-Hiday before advancing north-wards. Another message received from the director of Sudan telegraphs reported that the wires had been destroyed by insurgents between al-Dabbah and Marawi, and between Marawi and Barbar. He also reported that the road from Barbar to Kurusko was no longer safe as the last refugees who left Barbar had been pillaged and massacred by the tribes along the road. Alarm was still further intensified by a telegraphic petition from the officers of

[1] Ibid., col. 284.
[2] Ibid.
[3] Ibid., col. 285.

the garrison at Dongola declaring that they were too few in number to be expected to offer effective resistance to the large masses of rebels. They therefore asked for reinforcements.[1]

Nubar and Wood asked Egerton to request the British Government to give an opinion on whether the Mudir of Dongola should be instructed to make the best terms he could for his own safety and that of the people of Dongola. It was hoped in Cairo that if an expedition for Gordon's relief were promised later, the Mudir of Dongola might be able to offer some resistance to the rebellion.[2] Granville, however, replied that the Mudir should be allowed to make the best terms he could with the rebels, if they advanced, as no pledge of future action could be given.[3]

The British Government was most anxious to get a reply from Gordon. Granville asked Egerton whether, by liberal expenditure of money, he thought he could ensure a message being delivered to Gordon through the influence of Zubair, Husain Khalifah, or anyone else.[4] Egerton replied that he did not think that even the offer of money could ensure the transmission of a message to Gordon. The main obstacle to communication seemed to be in the vicinity of Khartum. However, an arrangement had been made with a man selected by Zubair. Granville approved this action and instructed that the messenger's departure should be delayed until a further message had been sent from London.[5]

The next day Egerton received the following message to add to the Government's previous telegram to Gordon:

As the original plan for the evacuation of the Sudan has been dropped, and as aggressive operations cannot be undertaken with the countenance of Her Majesty's Government, General Gordon is enjoined to consider either to report upon, or, if possible to adopt at the first proper moment measures for his own removal and for that of the Egyptians at Khartum, who have served him faithfully including their wives and children, by whatever route he may consider best having special regard to his own safety and that of the other British subjects.[6]

Gordon was further authorized to make free use of money or

[1] Egerton to Granville, No. 517, May 12, 1884, P.R.O., F.O. 78/3673.
[2] Egerton to Granville, No. 518, May 12, 1884, P.R.O., F.O. 78/3673.
[3] Granville to Egerton, No. 249A, May 13, 1884, P.R.O., F.O. 78/3663.
[4] Granville to Egerton, No. 252A, May 15, 1884, P.R.O., F.O. 78/3663.
[5] Granville to Egerton, No. 265, May 16, 1884, P.R.O., F.O. 78/3663.
[6] Granville to Egerton, No. 266, May 17, 1884, P.R.O., F.O. 78/3663.

promises of rewards at his discretion to these Egyptians. For example, he might assign to Egyptian soldiers at Khartum sums of money for themselves and for persons brought with them, granting so much a head. He might also pay the tribes in the neighborhood to escort them. If Gordon had dispatched any person or agents to other places, he might spend any money required for the purpose of recalling them or securing their safety. The substance of this message, particularly the extract quoted, was suggested by Gladstone, who was anxious for a reply to the Government's telegram of April 23.[1]

The rebels, whom Husain Khalifah had reported in his last messages to be collecting in the southern part of the province marched northwards under an old teacher of al-Mahdi, Shaikh Muhammad al-Khair, and laid siege to Barbar. After some days of blockade the ansar assaulted the town and captured it, taking Husain Khalifah and others prisoner. Kitchener, who was in upper Egypt, confirmed its fall.[2]

Information had meanwhile been received in Cairo from various sources that the Mudir of Dongola was playing a double game and was in communication with al-Mahdi. Suspicion of the Mudir's intentions prevented the Egyptian Government from sending him the money and rifles he had demanded.[3] The dispatch of troops to Wadi Halfa, however, apparently convinced the Mudir that the Government was becoming the stronger side. He quite wisely kept secret the instructions permitting him to make terms with the rebels, for he had hopes of restoring order in the southern part of his province with the troops at his disposal. Nubar, Stephenson, and Wood decided to send him the arms which had been held up at Wadi Halfa, and Egerton, although at first opposed to taking such a risk, acquiesced in face of the arguments advanced.[4]

On the 27th of May the Mudir reported that he had defeated the rebel Shayqiya and forced their leader to seek a distant refuge. Many of the rebels had surrenderd and he had granted them a full pardon. He was so elated by his victory that he suggested the reconquest of the Sudan. 'As it is now time for the Government

[1] Gladstone to Granville, May 17, 1884, B.M. Add. MS. 44176.
[2] Kitchener to Wood, June 10, enclosed in Egerton to Granville, No. 624A, June 11, 1884, F.O. 78/3675.
[3] Egerton to Granville, No. 539, May 18, 1884, P.R.O., F.O. 78/3673.
[4] Egerton to Granville, No. 557, May 22, 1884, P.R.O., F.O. 78/3673.

once more to take possession of the Sudan, I repeat my solicitations for 7,000 men with all munitions of war and to be sent via Dongola in order that the Sudan may not be lost.'[1] There followed an exchange of views between Cairo and London on the advisability of starting negotiations with the Kababish tribe in the hope of their facilitating Gordon's escape. It was, in the end, decided to send Major Kitchener to Dongola for that purpose.[2]

The Mudir of Dongola had asked for reinforcements and for ammunition and arms, but his request could not be granted. However, he was given permission to evacuate the province if he felt that it was necessary. The Mudir very much regretted this order, considering Dongola to possess a most important position strategically. However, he declared that he would comply with the order although, in his opinion, it would entail the loss of Egypt.[3]

Influenced by the alarming news from Dongola, Nubar and the War Minister urged on Egerton the necessity of sending one or two Egyptian battalions to save Dongola, the loss of which would not only entail great trouble throughout the country from al-Mahdi's emissaries, but also guerilla war with the Bedwins. Egerton answered that the arrangements for military action for the defense of Egypt had been decided upon some months previously, and that he had received no military opinion which modified these arrangements.[4] Egerton himself, however, favored the retention of Dongola, the loss of which he thought would be a misfortune, since it would bring al-Mahdi's emissaries into Egypt. 'My personal view has always been that it should be held for the present, till Gordon can get out, but such is not the opinion of the military authorities and their program will have to be carried out.'[5]

Baring, who was then in London, disagreed with Egerton, for he knew of no way of holding Dongola with any degree of confidence except by sending English troops, a measure to which he was opposed. 'Of course in saying this I leave out of account the

[1] Mudir of Dongola to Nubar, May 29, 1884, enclosed in Egerton to Granville, No. 597, June 3, 1884, P.R.O., F.O. 78/3674.
[2] Pauncefote to Egerton, No. 360, July 25, 1884, P.R.O., F.O. 78/3664.
[3] Egerton to Granville, No. 680, July 7, 1884. P.R.O., F.O. 78/3676.
[4] Egerton to Granville, No. 688, July 7, 1884. P.R.O., F.O. 78/3676.
[5] Egerton to Baring, Private, July 7, 1884, P.R.O., G/D 29/163.

290 THE INDEPENDENT SUDAN

question of an expedition to bring away Gordon, which involves other considerations.'[1] To hold Dongola permanently, in Baring's opinion, would be inconsistent with the policy which had been quite clearly laid down. Consequently neither British nor Egyptian troops should be sent to Dongola. Baring was not quite clear what the Egyptian Government meant by attempting to save Dongola by means of the Kababish tribe. 'It would be quite consistent with Egyptian character and with the past conduct of the Khedive and his advisers since the defeat of Hicks, that, having accepted in principle the evacuation of the whole of the Sudan, they should in detail advocate action which is not in harmony with the policy of evacuation.'[2] Baring thought, therefore, that the Egyptians should be made to understand clearly that the British Government would not allow any action, either by military aid or by the expenditure of money, which aimed at maintaining Egyptian authority at Dongola.

When Northbrook was shown Baring's comments he agreed that it should be made clear to Nubar that the Egyptian Government would not be allowed to hold Dongola. But any arrangements for establishing the Mudir or the chief of the Kababish or any other component authority at Dongola, independent of Egypt, would be consistent with British policy, and, in Northbrook's opinion, much to the advantage of Egypt. He also remarked that the use of the term 'rebel' was in itself a clear indication that the 'governing chaps in Egypt are hankering after the Sudan, at any rate the Eastern Sudan.'[3]

On the 21st of July Egerton telegraphed to London the news that the Mudir of Dongola had received a letter from Gordon asking the strength and whereabouts of the relief expedition. The Mudir asked to be instructed what reply he should give to Gordon. The genuineness of this message purporting to come from Gordon was questioned, since it might have been a move on the part of the Mudir to find out the plans for the relief of Gordon in order to plan his course accordingly. On the other hand, it was difficult to believe that the Mudir would have had the audacity to send such a telegram to the Khedive unless there were good foundations for

[1] Remarks by Baring, July 14, 1884, on ibid.
[2] Ibid.
[3] Northbrook's remarks on ibid.

it.[1] Egerton's conclusion, after consulting many officials, including Nubar, was that the telegram was genuine. The Egyptian Government's impression of the Mudir was that in public he was acting a part, because of his weakness, but that at heart was really loyal to the Khedive.[2]

Towards the end of July reports reached Cairo that the Mudir of Dongola had won a brilliant victory over al-Hiday, the emissary of al-Mahdi, in the southern district of the province.[3] Nubar and Wood thought that as a result of that victory the Mudir should be given a subsidy to maintain his position in Dongola. Egerton considered the Mudir to be a very unsatisfactory and independent subordinate. He could only be employed if a detachment were to be sent beyond the second cataract so that he might feel sufficiently supported to attempt Gordon's rescue in conjunction with the Kababish. 'Otherwise I consider him to be a self-willed man who is playing with two weak superiors in the Khedive and Nubar Pasha.'[4] The retention of Dongola was, at this time, supported by the chief military authority in Cairo. Stephenson thought its retention, pending the decision as to the expedition, to be very important.[5]

With Kitchener's arrival in Dongola the veil of mystery covering the situation in the Sudan was lifted. Kitchener's first impressions of the Mudir were favorable. The Mudir's last battle against the ansar was a victory of great importance and the people of Dongola supported him.[6]

The next day Kitchener was in a position to report on the feeling of the inhabitants and the demands of the Mudir for dealing with the situation there. He considered that the state of the province was critical. The inhabitants spoke a different language from the Arab followers of al-Mahdi. The province was rich and populous and the loyalty of the people was illustrated by their having willingly sent men to the Government side for the last battle. As far as Kitchener could judge the people there had less sympathy with al-Mahdi than the people of upper Egypt. Although the

[1] Egerton to Granville, No. 720, July 21, 1884, P.R.O., F.O. 78/3676.
[2] Egerton to Granville, No. 721, July 21, 1884, P.R.O., F.O. 78/3676.
[3] Egerton to Granville, No. 742, July 27, 1884, P.R.O., F.O. 78/3676.
[4] Egerton to Granville, Private, July 30, 1884, P.R.O., G/D 29/163.
[5] Egerton to Granville, Private, July 31, 1884, P.R.O., G/D 29/163.
[6] Kitchener to Wood, enclosed in Egerton to Granville, No. 758, Aug. 2, 1884, P.R.O., F.O. 78/3677.

Mudir had been ordered three times to evacuate the town, yet he could not comply with the orders, and he asked how he could leave the people, who believed in him and in the Egyptian Government, to their fate.

In the opinion of the Mudir, Dongola was the gate of Egypt. al-Mahdi could easily penetrate into Egypt if he took possession of Dongola and followed the watercourse. But without Dongola he could only reach Egypt by the desert route, for which sufficient transport could not be provided. Both the people and the Mudir implored that at least one or two battalions of soldiers might be sent, which action would have an excellent effect. Armed steamers were also considered to be necessary and the Mudir undertook to provide men for bringing them across the cataracts. 'I would strongly recommend that some force may be sent here. Please inform me if any is likely to come.' [1]

In the light of Nubar's previous suggestion to subsidize the Mudir of Dongola and Kitchener's first favorable impressions of him, the British Government harbored the hope that he might be employed to play the role which Gordon had suggested for Zubair. Gladstone thought that some Egyptian money could be well and economically spent on such a project if it could be made to work. Kitchener was on the spot and Northbrook, who would very soon be in Cairo, could implement the move. 'It is of such immense importance to solve the Gordon problem and only through this is a chance. Yet no chance should be neglected.' [2]

An official dispatch was accordingly sent to Egerton instructing him to ask Kitchener whether the Mudir could hold his own at Dongola as an independent ruler with an annual allowance after Gordon had left Khartum and evacuated the garrison. He might draw that allowance so long as he remained friendly to Egypt and facilitated trade in the same manner as Gordon had proposed that Zubair should do. [3]

Kitchener opposed the scheme. The war-cry of al-Mahdi was 'Death to the Turkish oppression,' and the Mudir was a Turk to the core and was surrounded by Turks. Trade could not flourish under Turkish rule. Kitchener reported that the Mudir had so far

[1] Kitchener to Wood, Aug. 3, 1884, enclosed in Egerton to Granville, No. 772, Aug. 5, 1884, P.R.O., F.O. 78/3677.
[2] Gladstone to Northbrook, Aug. 12, 1884, P.R.O., G/D 29/128.
[3] Pauncefote to Egerton, No. 384, Aug. 15, 1884, P.R.O., F.O. 78/3664.

told him several lies and tried to deceive him. He was a confirmed intriguer. 'English are liked and respected and I feel sure an Englishman could rule here under the circumstances you describe and maintain order. I would not mind guaranteeing to do so under certain conditions.' [1]

al-Mahdi in Kurdufan was for a time under the impression that Mustafa Pasha Yawir, the Mudir of Dongola, was his own amir and not that of the Government. This was a result of an exchange of letters between al-Mahdi and the Mudir. But having heard of the battle between the Government troops and his ansar in Dongola, al-Mahdi began to doubt the expressions of loyalty manifested by the Mudir. He therefore sent Mahmud al-Hajj Ahmad from Kurdufan with some ansar to take charge of the province. In a letter to the Mudir, al-Mahdi instructed him to serve the cause of the Mahdiya at first in a subordinate position, and then, when his loyalty had been tested, he would be promoted to a more responsible position. The Mudir met the combined forces of Mahmud al-Majj Ahmad and al-Hiday and defeated them. Both Mahdist leaders died in the action and the letter of al-Mahdi to the Mudir was found on the body of Mahmud.[2] This finally removed anxiety from Dongola and paved the way for the relief expedition based on Dongola to operate in the Sudan.

Hartington, as Secretary for War, took up the question of relieving General Gordon. He asked Gladstone on July 1 to hold a Cabinet meeting to consider military preparations for the Sudan before the Cabinet's attention was again absorbed by the conference on Egyptian finances and the Franchise Bill. 'I really do not feel that I know the mind and intention of the Government in respect of the relief of General Gordon and I also feel that the Government, and especially I as responsible for the military department may at any moment be placed in a most painful position from the want of some clear indication of what the policy of the Government is.' [3] Hartington thought that any day they might receive news from Khartum which would prove the necessity of

[1] Kitchener to Egerton, Aug. 19, 1884, enclosed in Egerton to Granville, No. 814, Aug. 20, 1884, P.R.O., F.O. 78/3677.
[2] Telegram from the Mudir, Sept. 8, 1884, enclosed in Baring to Granville, No. 871, Sept 10, 1884, P.R.O., F.O. 78/3678. Translation of al-Mahdi's letter also enclosed in the above.
[3] Hartington to Gladstone, July 1, 1884, B.M. Add. MS. 44147.

an expedition for Gordon's release. Also the time was approaching when the climate would permit military operations, but nothing could be done because of lack of preparation. 'I am anxious that the Cabinet should at least share the responsibility of this position with me and to ascertain if I can the circumstances if any under which they would consider an expedition necessary.'[1] Hartington was unfortunate, and complained: 'I got five minutes at the fag end, and was as usual put off.'[2]

A fortnight later Hartington submitted a memorandum after a meeting with Northbrook, Baring, and Wolseley. It was the unanimous opinion of the meeting that nothing could be decided as regards Dongola or the other military question unless the Cabinet would decide whether or not to send an expedition to bring away Gordon and the Egyptian garrison from Khartum. Almost three months had passed since a message had been received from Gordon. Messages had been sent to him from Cairo but, although fifty days had passed, no reply had been received. It was impossible to believe that Gordon and Stewart found any opportunity for sending messages of which they did not avail themselves. Their silence, it was believed, pointed to the fact that Khartum was invested by a more fanatical enemy than had been anticipated. 'This impossibility of transmitting a message is almost unprecedented in the East.'[3] It was also believed that a peaceful withdrawal from Khartum, even if Gordon was willing to take that course, was not open to him. 'The Cabinet must decide whether he is to be left to his fate or to be rescued by force.'

The operations on the Sawakin-Barbar road had ceased to be of practical value because of the delay in making a decision. The proposed railway could only be constructed in the cool months of the year and then only for a short portion of the distance. It was also to be expected that severe battles would be fought at the two ends of the road, and the difficulty of the supply of water at the Barbar end had to be remembered. Further, the alarm caused by the advance of the rebellion necessitated the movements of troops,

[1] Ibid.
[2] Hartington to Granville, July 15, 1884, Fitzmaurice, Lord Edmond, *The Life of Lord Granville* (London, 1905), vol. ii, p. 390.
[3] Memorandum by Hartington, enclosed in Hartington to Granville, July 15, 1884, P.R.O., G/D 29/134.

both British and Egyptian, to upper Egypt and operations on the Sawakin front would have no effect on tranquillizing upper Egypt. Despite the difficulties of river transport, Wolseley considered that a force six or seven thousand strong collected at Wadi Halfa on October 1st could reach Khartum in three months. If it were decided to send such an expedition it would be worth while to keep Dongola out of the hands of rebels. If not, Hartington agreed with Northbrook and Baring that the Egyptian Government should be made to understand that it was to be completely abandoned. 'But the first and indispensable condition of forming any opinion on any of the military questions in Egypt is a decision whether Gordon is to be rescued or abandoned, and I submit that there is no reason for any delay in coming to a decision on this.' [1] In his letter to Granville enclosing this memorandum, Hartington declared: 'I cannot be responsible for the military policy in Egypt under such conditions.'

Gladstone recorded on July 16, in his Cabinet memoranda, that there had been much discussion about the Sudan expedition, but that there was a difference of opinion. It was favored by Hartington and Selborne with Dodson, Calingford, Northbrook, and Granville lukewarm. 'I was disappointed with the Cabinet of today in regard to an expedition for or towards Khartum.' [2]

Wolseley was anxious about the delay in the preparations and thought that if an advance were decided on, immediate preparations were essential. 'My military experience tells me that in all such affairs the worst course to pursue is to shirk the question and to imagine you dispose of it by shutting your eyes and trying to ignore or forget it.' [3] The ministers, in Wolseley's opinion, had given assurances to Parliament that they were responsible for the safety of Gordon and Stewart. 'Is it wise, is it honest, to refuse to look the difficulties of the position straight in the face, to refuse to make the necessary preparations now when you have time to do so, in fact to postpone their consideration to a period when all preparations will be in vain?' [4] Wolseley concluded his memorandum to

[1] Memorandum by Hartington, enclosed in Hartington to Granville, July 15, 1884, P.R.O., G/D 29/134.
[2] Cabinet memoranda, July 16, 1884, B.M. Add. MS. 44645.
[3] Memorandum by Wolseley, July 23, 1884, Holland, op. cit., vol. i, p. 468.
[4] Ibid.

Hartington by asserting that it was not wise to ignore or even make light of the danger in which Gordon found himself.

Supplied with these arguments and warnings by his chief military adviser, Hartington, in conjunction with Selborne, who also felt strongly on this matter, circulated a memorandum to the members of the Cabinet. Hartington wished to bring the subject once more to the consideration of the Cabinet before Parliament was prorogued. He repeated what he had already submitted about the military aspect of the problem, and stated that plans had been drawn up for an expedition up the Nile.[1]

Selborne dwelt at great length on Gordon's action. Gordon, in his opinion, should not be considered at fault by attempting to leave behind a settled government at Khartum. That was, beyond all doubt, desirable for the security and tranquiltiy of Egypt. That Gordon had had to meet force with force was not in itself conclusive evidence that he sought to accomplish his objects by other than peaceful means.

His language about 'crushing al-Mahdi', etc. is perfectly intelligible if he was attacked or threatened by al-Mahdi's followers, without imputing to him any such purpose. It is surely premature (to say the least) to treat him as having disobeyed or disregarded the orders or messages latterly sent to him, until we really know what he has actually done, and why he has done it, and whether those orders and messages were received by him or not.[2]

Selborne expressed his aversion to sending an unnecessary and costly expedition but he was equally averse to acting towards 'a public servant, in whose reputation and safety all England, and (I might almost say) the world, is interested—who has accepted at our instance a mission of extraordinary difficulty—as if we had no real sense of responsibilities which we have publicly acknowledged, as if something (of which I can see no evidence at all) had happened to absolve us from these responsibilities.'[3]

Hartington told Granville in a letter that Gladstone's mind was made up and that nothing was to be done. 'This is a conclusion which I do not think it is possible for me to accept. I, with you

---

[1] Memorandum to the Cabinet by Hartington, July 29, 1884, in Holland, op. cit., vol. i, p. 472.
[2] Memorandum by Lord Selborne, July 29, 1884, in Palmer, Roundell, Earl of Selborne, Memorials, vol. ii, p. 143.
[3] Ibid.

and Northbrook are more responsible than any other members of
the Cabinet for sending out Gordon, but I consider that I had the
largest share of the responsibility.'[1] He maintained that he had
given assurances in the debate on the vote of censure which, in
his opinion, had certainly affected the division. 'I think this is a
different set of questions from the numerous ones on which I have
differed from the Cabinet. It is a question of personal honor and
good faith, and I do not see how I can yield upon it.'[2]

Granville sent Hartington's letter to Gladstone, who wrote
back most privately saying that he intended to give much time to
collecting evidence as to Gordon's position, but that the receipt
of Hartington's letter had diverted him. The letter, in Gladstone's
view, created a very formidable state of things at a moment when
'we have already on our hands a domestic crisis of the first class
likely to last for months, and a foreign crisis of the first class,
morally certain however, to be decided or developed in a few days.
It is a difficult but paramount duty for each one of us to ask himself what he can contribute towards meeting the present exigency.'[3]
He could not be a party to the proposed dispatch as a first step to
sending a brigade to Dongola. He did not think that the evidence
of Gordon's position required or justified military preparations for
the contingency of a military expedition. But there were, however,
prepartions of various kinds which could be made, and which
would entail expenditure of money but would not involve a change
of policy. 'To these I have never offered an insuperable objection,
and the adoption of them might be, at the worst, a smaller evil than
the evils with which we are threatened in other forms.'[4] He hoped
that nothing would be done to accelerate 'a Gordon crisis' until
the next week, in order to see what the conference on Egyptian
finance would produce.

The only record of Granville's reply to Hartington is this: 'I
agree with you that these declarations commit us to a certain
degree, but not as far as I gather you believe.'[5] Joseph Chamberlain wrote a minute against what was called an expedition or full

---

[1] Hartington to Granville, July 31, 1884, B.M. Add. MS. 44147.
[2] Hartington to Granville, July 31, 1884, B.M. Add. MS. 44147.
[3] Gladstone to Granville, Aug. 1, 1884, B.M. Add. MS. 44147.
[4] Ibid.
[5] Granville to Hartington, Aug. 1, 1884, Holland, op. cit., vol. i, p. 447.

preparations for an expedition. He was of opinion that the information they possessed was not sufficient to justify it. He hoped for more information and wished if necessary to strengthen Kitchener's force by 1,000 men to enable him to communicate with Khartum and obtain information on which further action might be based.[1]

Both Hartington and Selborne made it clear that they would at once resign if preparations were not made. The compromise reached, however, between the minority supporting Hartington and the majority which accepted Gladstone's view, was that no expedition was to be sent immediately to Dongola, but that Parliament would be asked for a grant of £300,000 in order to enable Her Majesty's Government to undertake operations for the relief of Gordon if it became necessary.[2]

Gladstone introduced the vote for £300,000 in Parliament by referring to the very considerable embarrassment caused by the lack of communications with Gordon. This state of affairs had perplexed the Government for four months. As the parliamentary recess was approaching, Her Majesty's Government therefore decided to take precautions in case an emergency should arise during the recess. 'That is the main and proper object of the vote of censure [laughter]—I mean the vote of credit.'[3]

In reply to remarks made by a member in the House of Commons about Gordon's disobeying his instructions, Hartington said that there was no proof whatever of such disobedience although rumors which reached London from time to time appeared to report actions which were inconsistent with Gordon's instructions and were difficult to understand. Explanations, however, had been demanded. There was no proof that Gordon had departed in any way from the original object of his mission. Hartington admitted that they had heard lately that Gordon was engaged in active operations. 'How much of that is true or not, it is impossible to say. But it is quite reasonable and very probable that the only means that General Gordon might find for maintaining his own position at Khartum, and withdrawing the garrison, was to assume offensive operations.'[4] It was probable that Gordon, before retiring from

[1] Ibid., p. 477.
[2] Ibid., p. 478.
[3] *Hansard,* 3rd ser., vol. 291, col. 1759.
[4] Ibid., col. 1787.

Khartum, might desire to establish some form of settled government. 'That, in the opinion of Her Majesty's Government, would be exceeding his instructions ["Oh"]. His mission, and his primary object, were to evacuate the Sudan. Certainly no instructions were ever given to general Gordon to establish a settled form of government.'⁴ But at the same time there was not the slightest doubt, in Hartington's opinion, that he had undertaken a most beneficial work.

The Government obtained their vote of credit by an overwhelming majority, only fourteen members dissenting.

¹ Ibid.

XI

THE RELIEF EXPEDITION

Having secured the parliamentary vote for an expedition if it were found necessary, Hartington wrote officially to Stephenson, the officer commanding in Egypt. He told Stephenson that after comparing the two routes via Sawakin and the Nile, it had been decided to choose the latter if an expedition were sent to save Gordon. Water transport was considered to be the safest and most economical, if not the only practicable means, when all circumstances had been fully considered.

The first step, in Hartington's view, would be to convey by water to Dongola a brigade of all arms. The plan provided for the return of the troops to Egypt proper before the end of the approaching winter season. Wolseley was the general who used a certain kind of boat in the Red River campaign. This was a success and Wolseley thought that it would be successful in the Nile as conditions appeared to him to be similar. Stephenson was, however, opposed to the use of the specially designed boats suggested by Wolseley. He was supported in that view by the naval officer charged with the survey of the cataracts, and who reported that transport could be found in local native boats and steamers.

Despite this opposition Hartington believed that the project was capable of being carried out.[1]

One of the reasons why the Nile route was chosen was that the inhabitants of upper Egypt were becoming increasingly sympathetic towards al-Mahdi's cause, on religious grounds, and troops had to be moved in order to nip in the bud any insurrectionary movement. Ever since the crushing defeat of Hicks's army al-Mahdi's prestige had been rising. In all his proclamations he stated that he was fighting against the Turks who corrupted religion, and that he was not an enemy to Egypt. He claimed universal allegiance to his cause which was that of all Muslims.[2]

[1] Secretary of State for War to General Officer Commanding in Egypt, No. 7700/77, Aug. 15, 1884, P.R.O., W.O. 32/124.
[2] *The Times,* Nov. 26, 1883.

Towards the end of 1883 Baring had reported that information from several sources indicated that belief in the divine mission of al-Mahdi was 'gaining ground in Egypt proper.' [1] When Gordon was on his way to the Sudan, Baring pressed for permission to move British troops to upper Egypt. To him the population of that part was more turbulent than that of the delta, and English officers in the Egyptian police declared that with the means at their disposal they could not be responsible for public security knowing that emissaries of al-Mahdi had been sent to upper Egypt. All reports showed that there was fanatical excitement among the population and if any disturbance should take place, the Coptic population would be the object of attack by the Muslims. [2] Mr. Clifford Lloyd, the British adviser to the Ministry of Interior, stated in a memorandum that a large portion of the population of upper Egypt was in sympathy with al-Mahdi especially the ancient Arab families. The repeated victories of al-Mahdi and the presence of his emissaries 'have created a dangerous feeling of expectation' [3] among the people.

An American missionary, who had been in the country for twenty-eight years, reported the fears of the Coptic inhabitants, who asserted to him that the state of fanaticism was in some respects worse than the worst days of 'Urabi. All the Muslim officials were intently watching al-Mahdi's movements and 'longing for the day when he will drive the English out of the country. Then will follow the day of reckoning with the Christian dogs who gloried over the fall of 'Urabi.' [4] Clifford Lloyd read this letter to Nubar, who considered that there was much truth in it. 'I may add that all my information bears out the accuracy of the general remarks made.' [5] The Khedive was so much alarmed by the state of feeling for al-Mahdi that he suggested the appointment of Ra'uf Pasha as inspector-General in upper Egypt in order to oppose the influence of al-Mahdi's emissaries. [6]

[1] Baring to Granville, No. 602, Dec. 13, 1883, P.R.O., F.O. 78/3560.
[2] Baring to Granville, No. 216, Feb. 20, 1884, P.R.O., F.O. 78/3667.
[3] Memorandum by Clifford Lloyd, enclosed in Baring to Granville, No. 228, Feb. 26, 1884, P.R.O., F.O. 78/3668.
[4] John Hogg to Clifford Lloyd, Feb. 29, 1884, enclosed in Baring to Granville, No. 264, Mar. 4, 1884, P.R.O., F.O. 78/3668.
[5] Clifford Lloyd to Baring, enclosed in Baring to Granville, No. 264, Mar. 4, 1884, P.R.O., 78/3668.
[6] Egerton to Granville, No. 484, May 3, 1884, P.R.O., F.O. 78/3672.

However, before actually moving the troops beyond Aswan Hartington asked Gladstone's approval. The Prime Minister considered it a matter of great political importance that could not be decided without reference to other members of the Cabinet. Gladstone seemed still reluctant about the expedition and still seemed to hanker after other schemes which might solve the problem without an actual advance of troops. He mentioned that Gordon might make his way to Dongola if he thought fit but that it was questionable whether he (Gordon) would do so. Again Gladstone mentioned the employment of the Mudir of Dongola as a second Zubair 'to take over Khartum, so putting an end to this most perplexing and distressing affair.' [1]

Another distressing factor, in Gladstone's opinion, was the renewal of correspondence between Gordon and the Mudir of Dongola without any communication having been made to the British Government. Granville believed that Gordon had received the Government messages and did not choose to answer them. 'If the time has come when a decision must be taken whether to go to Dongola or not, then I think the Cabinet should know what forces you propose to send there and most of all for what purpose it is to go.' [2] Gladstone preferred to achieve the rescue of Gordon by financial and possible material means rather than by the advance of a British force. He associated with a British expedition 'the very serious danger of stirring a religious war.' He even doubted the success of such a British force as 'surely it is singular to note that our force, gallant as it was, could not get rid of Othman Diqna.' [3] Gladstone asked Hartington to work out a plan, in consultation with Northbrook, as he considered it quite unfair to the Cabinet to take steps in advance without a plan, so that they might know what they were about and 'be assured that they were not about to become unawares the slaves of Gordon's (probably) rebellious ideas.' [4]

Hartington replied that Granville did not object to the movement on Dongola but hoped it would not commit Her Majesty's Government to an expedition to Khartum. Northbrook had agreed

---

[1] Gladstone to Hartington, Aug. 19, 1884, B.M. Add. MS. 44147.
[2] Ibid.
[3] Ibid.
[4] Ibid.

to the movement long ago and there was nothing to indicate that he had changed his opinion. 'It is, however, obvious that the longer the orders for such an advance are delayed, the longer it will be before it can be commenced and before its advantages (if there are advantages) can be secured.' [1] As to its purpose, Hartington referred Gladstone to previous telegrams from Egerton, in one of which he had advised the movement of troops to Dongola 'with a view of giving a hand to Gordon for escape via al-Dabbah and Dongola.' [2] The object appeared to be, in Hartington's opinion, to give confidence and support to the Mudir of Dongola, who proved to be loyal and powerful and also to have influence with the Kababish tribe who held the road to within three days' journey to Khartum. 'Whether Gordon can make his way to Dongola, or whether being able he will do it must be a matter of pure conjecture, but it is quite certain that his ability to do it will be increased by anything which strengthened the Mudir, and which tends to secure the support of the Kababish.' [3] There was no conclusive evidence that Gordon was ignoring the Government's orders and public opinion would not be satisfied with an action based on that supposition unless it proved to be accurate.

Hartington agreed that all possible use should be made of the Mudir of Dongola, but although he might be very useful in Dongola, there was no reason to suppose that he had any influence at Khartum. Kitchener's last reports about him were not encouraging and Northbrook, before leaving London, was distinctly of opinion that no use could be made of him at Khartum. Hartington did not share Gladstone's fears of raising a religious war by sending troops to Dongola, as the Mudir himself had asked for them and Kitchener seemed to have been well received by the people there. As to the inability of the British soldiers to dispose of 'Uthman Diqna, Hartington admitted that 'Uthman's forces were fanatical but he believed that they were crushed. It was only the hurried departure of the troops that had set Diqna up again. 'I feel quite certain that with your, Granville's and Northbrook's consent, the Cabinet would not object to despatch a moderate force as now proposed to Dongola.' Chamberlain had advocated more than once

[1] Hartington to Gladstone, Aug. 20, 1884, B.M. Add. MS. 44147.
[2] Egerton to Granville, No. 780, Aug. 6, 1884, P.R.O., F.O. 78/3677.
[3] Hartington to Gladstone, Aug. 20, 1884, B.M. Add. MS. 44147.

the sending of a small force to support Kitchener. Hartington knew of no one who dissented except Harcourt who objected to everything, even to the vote of credit and the preparations. 'If when the Cabinet is scattered all over the country, I have to wait in the case of every decision of any importance to collect the opinions of ministers subject perhaps in the case of difference to the delay of summoning the Cabinet, I despair of acquitting myself of the responsibility which will be placed on me by my colleagues and parliament.' Hartington told Gladstone that he had already taken a great responsibility in authorizing preparations on meagre instructions from the Cabinet and that he had spent and would spend a great deal of money. 'But what is more important perhaps is that they are preparations of such a character as will make it appear almost absurd not to send the expedition when they are complete, except on the clearest proof that Gordon's position does not require it.' [1]

After writing this letter to Gladstone, Hartington met Dilke, who agreed with the terms of the letter and gave his opinion that if Gladstone consented no one would object. As to Harcourt it was understood that 'though objecting to any expedition for the relief of General Gordon he had waived that objection and would not oppose any measures of this character.' [2] Hartington disclosed that there was a good deal of difference between the War Office in London and Stephenson in Cairo about the plan of operations. He hoped that when the officers leaving England arrived in Cairo these differences of opinion might be removed. 'But what I hope I may receive tomorrow is authority from you to send forward such a limited force from Wadi Halfa to Dongola as we and Stephenson may consider safe. I believe that in this step lies the best chance of averting the necessity of sending a considerable expedition.' [3]

The differences between the War Office and Stephenson reached such a proportion that it was considered by Hartington and his miltary advisers not advisable to entrust such a very important expedition to a man who did not believe in the efficiency of the plan decided. 'We are at cross purposes,' wrote Hartington to Gladstone, 'here and in Egypt as to the plan of operation on which

[1] Hartington to Gladstone, Aug. 20, 1884, B.M. Add. MS. 44147.
[2] Ibid.
[3] Ibid.

preparations are based.'[1] He asked Gladstone whether he might be allowed to send Wolseley to take command in Egypt as he was responsible for the plan which had been adopted. Hartington feared the risk of failure by putting the command in 'unwilling hands.' Wolseley had the advantage of having been in touch with the Secretary of State for the last months about the details of the relief and he was well acquainted with the Government's policy of reluctance to send an expedition except in case of absolute necessity. 'Firmly believe that this would offer best chance of avoiding serious expedition and of success if it must be undertaken.' Wolseley's position would be that of 'General commanding troops in Egypt and not necessarily in command of an expedition.'[2]

'I feel strongly,' wrote Granville to Hartington, 'the difficulty of your position and should be loath to make objection to anything you think necessary.'[3] Granville doubted whether Gladstone would consent to the immediate dispatch of Wolseley. He feared that it might be interpreted as an absolute decision to send the expedition. War would be the most exciting game of skill and chance to attract a successful soldier, and Granville feared that Wolseley, once in Egypt, would advocate an expedition. However, Granville had no doubt that 'if Wolseley goes out there will either be an expedition or the moral effect of his appointment will make one unnecessary. But the latter advantage is neutralized by my doubts as to Gordon availing himself of a fair opportunity of coming away.'[4] However, Granville and Northbrook consented to appoint Wolseley to the High Command in Egypt.[5] Hartington felt the necessity of announcing it in such a way as to avoid creating the impression that an expedition was actually decided on, and at the same time to guard against unnecessarily wounding the 'susceptibilities of Stephenson and the officers in Egypt.'[6]

As the British Government had decided to send a force to Dongola, Egerton's proposal to inform Gordon of the preparations for his relief was approved. Egerton was instructed to inform Gordon that steps were being taken for his relief in case of neces-

[1] Hartington to Gladstone, Aug. 22, 1884, B.M. Add. MS. 44147.
[2] Ibid.
[3] Granville to Hartington, Aug. 23, 1884, P.R.O., G/D 29/134.
[4] Ibid.
[5] Hartington to Gladstone, Aug. 22, 1884, B.M. Add. MS. 44147
[6] Ibid.

sity. At the same time he was instructed to demand of Gordon what causes prevented him from replying to the British Government's messages.[1]

Towards the end of August, five messages from Gordon written in Arabic on small slips of paper were received in Dongola. They all contained the same sentence: 'We are all well, and can hold out 4 months.'[2] In reply, Egerton authorized Kitchener to inform Gordon that 'steamers are being passed over second cataract and that we wish to be informed exactly through Dongola when he experts to be in difficulties as to provisions and ammunition.'[3]

On his arrival at Cairo to take over command, Wolseley asked for a considerable addition to his force. He considered this addition to be essential for the success of the expedition if it should have to be undertaken. As this demand had apparently been made with the concurrence of Northbrook, who was also in Egypt, it was decided to comply with it.[4] On the second anniversary of his victory at Tel el-Kebir, Wolseley wrote from Cairo to his wife conveying his first impressions of how his future campaign might end.

This day two years ago, thank God, ended brilliantly. I can remember my feeling of growing anxiety all through the hours from 1 a.m. until I stood on the bridge at Tel-al-Kebir, with a defeated army flying from us in all directions. If I am equally blessed I ought to shake hands with Gordon near Khartum, about the 31st January next.[5]

In one of his telegrams Gordon mentioned that he had instructed Stewart to go to Barbar and burn the town, but Baring in Cairo, without reference to London, instructed Kitchener to inform Stewart by the first possible opportunity not to allow Barbar to be burnt.[6] Gladstone commented: 'The Gordon telegram in Baring's 588 beats everything I have ever seen. I called him at the outset inspired and mad, but the madness is now uppermost . . . we are in danger of becoming simply ridiculous in our communica-

[1] Pauncefote to Egerton, No. 386, Aug. 20, 1884, P.R.O., F.O. 78/3664.
[2] Egerton to Granville, No. 840, Aug. 29, 1884, P.R.O., F.O. 78/3677.
[3] Egerton to Kitchener, Aug. 30, 1884, enclosed in Egerton to Granville, No. 845, Aug. 30, 1884, P.R.O., F.O. 78/3677.
[4] Hartington to Gladstone, Sept. 12, 1884, B.M. Add. MS. 44147.
[5] Wolseley, Garnet J., The Letters of Lord and Lady Wolseley, edited by Sir George Arthur (London, 1922), p. 119.
[6] Baring to Granville, No. 891, Sept. 20, 1884, P.R.O., F.O. 78/3678.

tion with him.'[1] The two main telegrams of April and May were, in Gladstone's opinion, the basis of Her Majesty's Government's policy and Gordon had to conform to that policy or else he should be made to understand 'he will cease in any manner to represent the British Government.'

As instructed from London, Baring informed Gordon, through Kitchener, that he would be expected to obey Wolseley's orders. The Khedive was also asked to limit Gordon's powers to Governor-General of Khartum, Sennar, and the immediate neighborhood of Barbar. Gordon was also told not to send any expedition for the relief of garrisons up the White Nile without further instructions.[2] In order to avoid any misunderstanding, Baring proposed that the Khedive should furnish Wolseley with a firman giving him full civil and political powers so that he would virtually supersede Gordon. The firman would be kept secret and Wolseley would only use it in case of necessity.[3] The Khedive also supplied Wolseley with another firman addressed to the people of the Sudan asking them to obey Wolseley and submit to his will without any opposition.[4]

Wolseley's first instructions were verbal and of a negative character: 'He is *not* to undertake an expedition except in case of absolute necessity; he is *not* to send more than a small force beyond Wadi Halfa, and *not* to send any force at all beyond Dongola without instructions from the Government.'[5] Hartington was of opinion that the object of the expedition, if it should take place, would be 'to enable General Gordon and Colonel Stewart with the Egyptian garrison of Khartum to leave that place if it should appear that they cannot do so by any other means.'[6] Hartington entertained the idea that if the operations were successfully accomplished it would be desirable and necessary to hold Khartum, Barbar, and Dongola. 'I have for some time thought that our decision to abandon these places was a mistake.'

Wolseley's instructions, however, as they finally materialized

[1] Gladstone to Granville, Sept. 19, 1884, P.R.O., G/D 29/128.
[2] Baring to Granville, No. 894, Sept. 21, 1884, P.R.O., F.O. 78/3678.
[3] Baring to Granville, Sept. 25, 1884, P.R.O., G/D 29/163.
[4] Khedive's firman, Sept. 26, 1884, enclosed in Baring to Granville, No. 920, Confidential, Sept. 29, 1884, P.R.O., F.O. 78/3678.
[5] Hartington to Granville, Sept. 16, 1884, P.R.O., G/D 29/134.
[6] Ibid.

were drafted by Northbrook, Wolseley, and Baring in consultation in Cairo.[1] It was made clear that the primary object of the expedition up the valley of the Nile was to bring away Gordon and Stewart from Khartum. Once that object was achieved no offensive operations of any kind were to be undertaken. It was desired that the operations should be as limited as possible and Wolseley should not proceed southwards unless it was absolutely necessary to attain his primary object. Wolseley was instructed to enter into communication with Gordon and Stewart, who were placed under his orders, and supreme political and civil power would be conferred upon him south of Aswan. Wolseley was reminded that the policy of Her Majesty's Government was that Egyptian rule in the Sudan should cease.

The garrisons of the eastern Sudan, Darfur, Bahr al-Ghazal, and Equatoria were considered outside Wolseley's jurisdiction and he should not send troops south of Khartum to secure the retreat of the Sennar garrison. He had to use his best endeavors 'to ensure the safe retreat of the Egyptian troops which constitute the Khartum garrison, and of such of the civil employees of Khartum, together with their families, as may wish to return to Egypt.'[2] The Egyptian Government, however, would be prepared to pay a reasonable subsidy to any chief or a number of chiefs 'who would be sufficiently powerful to maintain order along the valley of the Nile from Wadi Halfa to Khartum.' If any such chief or chiefs could be found to accept the subsidy, it would be on condition that he or they should remain at peace with Egypt and should repel any raids on Egyptian territory. These chiefs would also be required to prevent and discourage by all possible means any expeditions for the sale and capture of slaves and to encourage legitimate trade with Egypt. Wolseley was authorized to conclude any agreements necessary to fulfill those general conditions.

It had been recognized when drafting the instructions that the main difficulty in the establishment of a Sudanese government lay in finding an individual or a number of individuals with sufficient authority to maintain order. The widest discretion was left to

---

[1] Draft of instructions to General Lord Wolseley, enclosed in Baring to Granville, No. 896, Sept. 21, 1884, P.R.O., F.O. 78/3678.

[2] Draft of instructions to General Lord Wolseley, enclosed in Baring to Granville, No. 896, Sept. 21, 1884, P.R.O., F.O. 78/3678.

Wolseley in this respect, but his attention was drawn to the fact that Her Majesty's Government could not withdraw their objection to the employment of Zubair. Those who were found willing to be placed in authority south of Wadi Halfa should clearly understand that they would have to rely solely on their own strength in order to maintain their position. 'Beyond the adoption of this measure neither Her Majesty's Government nor the Egyptian Government are prepared to assume any responsibility whatever for the government of the Nile Valley south of Wadi Halfa.' [1] When the draft instructions were shown to Gladstone he readily approved them except that he did not like absolutely to exclude Zubair.

While instructions and firmans were being issued to Wolseley in Cairo and London, letters and news from the Sudan and from Gordon were arriving in Dongola. The Mudir of Dongola telegraphed to Cairo that according to a Mahdist prisoner, Zubair was in communication with al-Mahdi. Zubair was alleged to have told al-Mahdi all about the policy to abandon the Sudan and urged him to march on Dongola and complete the conquest of the Sudan as quickly as he could.[2] It was after the receipt of this report that Zubair's movements were carefully watched; the shadow of suspicion and doubt fell on him, and he was arrested and deported to Gibraltar some months later.

It was only on September 20 that Gordon's reply to Her Majesty's Government's first dispatch of April 23 was received. He referred to his opinions on the subject as expressed in his previous telegrams. He added that on the very day on which he had written that dispatch his soldiers had killed Ibrahim, son of al-Shaikh al-'Ubaid and had slain his followers to the north of Khartum. He also hoped to defeat the rebels to the west of Khartum after which there would be no Arabs left in the vicinity. He reported rumors that al-Mahdi was coming, but so far he had not appeared. The condition of the garrison at Khartum was satisfactory and it had provisions for five months.[3] In a later dispatch

[1] Ibid.
[2] Mudir of Dongola to the Khedive, received in Cairo Sept. 17, 1884, enclosed in Baring to Granville, No. 882, Sept. 19, 1884, P.R.O., F.O. 78/3678.
[3] Gordon to the Khedive, Nubar, and Baring, undated but received in Cairo Sept. 20, 1884, enclosed in Baring to Granville No. 890, Sept. 20, 1884, P.R.O., F.O. 78/3678.

he reported that the senior Egyptian officers were being sent to Barbar with a view to continuing their journey northwards. The Egyptian troops at Khartum would also proceed to Barbar under Hasan Bey al-Bahnasawi and would remain there until the reinforcements about which he had written to Cairo reached Barbar. He had also ordered the retreat on Khartum of the Egyptian battalions from Sennar, and they in their turn would be sent on to Barbar: 'I do not wish harm to happen to any of the Egyptian officers or soldiers in the war, the Sudanese troops are, however, accustomed to fighting in the Sudan.' [1] Gordan wished that negotiations with the Sublime Porte might proceed so that the necessary assistance might quickly be sent to the Sudan 'so as to render it possible to extinguish the flame of this false Mutamahdi before it becomes difficult.' He requested the Khedive to award certain promotions and decorations to the Egyptian colonels.

A long petition signed by twenty-four superior military officers and eighteen civil employees at Khartum was also received in Cairo. They described the desperate situation on Gordon's arrival and how through his energy and efficient guidance they had been spared the horrors of hunger and destruction. But that could not go on forever, and without aid from outside they would certainly succumb to the inevitable and be destroyed. They reminded the Khedive of the pretensions of al-Mahdi, which were not restricted to the Sudan but embraced all the Turkish dominion, of which he was contemplating the total annihilation by war. 'Therefore we appeal to your Highness and show you the true state of our calamities, imploring your mercy to deliver us from this great and universal misfortune.' [2]

Gordon's reply to the second important dispatch of the British Government (May 5) was received in Cairo on September 28. He announced that he hoped to open the road to Sennar in a few days and that in general he was satisfied with the conduct of the troops and people. 'My retreat is impossible, unless I abandon the civil employees and their families. The feeling of the soldiers is against

[1] Gordon to the Khedive, undated, enclosed in Baring to Granville, No. 892, Sept. 20, 1884, P.R.O., F.O. 78/3678.
[2] Petition by forty-two officers and employees of Khartum to the Khedive, Aug. 19, 1884, enclosed in Baring to Granville, No. 895, Sept. 21, 1884, P.R.O., F.O. 78/3678.

this.'[1] If he could succeed in opening up the Blue Nile he would be strong enough to retake Barbar if Dongola held out. As the money sent for him had been captured at Barbar, he required a further sum of £200,000 to be sent via Kasalah.

I will not leave Khartum till suitably replaced and if Europeans wish to go to the Equator I will give them steamers. Before abandoning the Sudan I must remove the Egyptian population; even if the road was open, the people would not let me leave without them unless a government was established. My stay is indefinite unless you send al-Zubair with an annual subsidy or let the Sultan have the Sudan back.[2]

'I shall send Stewart,' wrote Gordon, '[who though he does all I can possibly wish him to do, and is a good honest fellow, yet his heart is not in the matter and he does not like the people as I do.]'[3] Gordon believed that Equatoria and Bahr al-Ghazal could be relieved later, and Darfur might be thought of it when it was known whether the garrison still held out. He would evacuate Sennar, if it were possible, although he doubted it, and he thought that the moral effect of evacuating it would be fatal to his future plans besides adding to the difficulties of feeding the refugees. 'I repeat I have no wish to retain this country, my sole desire is to restore the prestige of the Government in order to get out garrisons and to put some ephemeral government in position in order to get away.'[4] Baring considered these letters from Gordon to be more rational than anything he had written since his arrival at Khartum.[5]

When Northbrook was on a tour of the Nile on board the *Zinat al-Bahrain*, he wrote a long private letter to Gordon. He told Gordon that he had come on a mission to try and settle the finances of Egypt after the deadlock brought about by the failure of the London conference. It was not within his province to propose any change in the policy towards the Sudan. 'The expedition under

[1] Letters from Gordon, dated July 30 and 31, received by Commodore Molyneux at Sawakin, enclosed in Baring to Granville, No. 915, Sept. 28, 1884, P.R.O., F.O. 78/3678.

[2] Ibid.

[3] Gordon to Baring, July 31, 1884, enclosed in Baring to Granville, No. 925, Oct. 5, 1884, P.R.O., F.O. 78/3679. The words in brackets were omitted when the letter was published.

[4] Ibid.

[5] Baring to Granville, Private, Oct. 5, 1884, P.R.O., G/D 29/163.

Lord Wolseley, who has free powers, military and political, is not sent for the purpose of defeating al-Mahdi, but only of enabling you and the Egyptian garrison of Khartum with the civil employés there and their families, within reasonable limits to return to Egypt.'¹ Northbrook hoped that, owing to the favorable turn which affairs had taken, the expedition would not have to go to Khartum.

Gordon's gallant stand in defense of Khartum for five weary months had won for him the admiration of all, particularly of the Queen, who commanded Northbrook to convey to Gordon 'her hearty congratulations and sympathy.' He was also commanded by Her Majesty to confer on Gordon the Grand Cross of the Bath as a mark of her appreciation of his distinguished services. As Gordon had expressed on previous occasions his disinclination to accept any honor, Northbrook told him that the honor was not coming from the Government but direct from the sovereign, and therefore, as a soldier and a loyal subject, Gordon should not feel any scruple in accepting it. It was, in Northbrook's opinion, of paramount importance that some sort of government should be established in the Sudan.

Northbrook went on to put forward the arguments against the employment of Zubair. The suggestion had met with general disapproval in England because of the fear felt for Gordon's safety, of the possible danger to Egypt in putting such a formidable man on the frontiers, and of the effect his rule might have in reviving the slave-raids. When the news of the proposed employment of Zubair had been telegraphed to *The Times* by Power it was at once denounced by Salisbury, by Forster, and by the Anti-Slavery Society. 'Even if the Government had supported it, it would inevitably have been condemned by a vote in parliament.' Northbrook's own opinion was decidedly against Zubair in whom he had no confidence. Some of the considerations affecting the British Government's decision at the time were that Gordon's life would not be safe from Zubair, and that al-Mahdi's power was thought to be diminishing. The idea of 'an army marching upon Egypt from the Sudan had proved to be a bugbear' and conditions were telling against slave-hunters. On the other hand, Zubair's conduct was not free from suspicion. It was hard to believe, in Northbrook's view, that he had no hand in the rising of the tribes

¹ Northbrook to Gordon, Oct. 8, 1884, P.R.O., G/D 29/140.

between Barbar and Khartum. The Mudir of Dongola reported that a letter had been sent by Zubair to al-Mahdi instigating the latter to attack Dongola. It was also rumored, but not proved, that Zubair would make exorbitant demands on the Egyptian Goverment if he were asked to go to Khartum. These considerations as a whole would have made it extremely undesirable to employ Zubair, but if there was no other possible solution for the government of the Sudan, his employment was not 'entirely out of the question.'

Northbrook could not understand Gordon's suggestions for a large force of Turkish troops to be sent to the Sudan. The Sultan was quite helpless, and was a victim of hesitation and suspicions. He also had no money and it was certain that the British Government would not give him any for that purpose. 'The English Government would rather leave the Sudan alone than help the Turks to conquer it.' The Mudir of Dongola seemed to be a possible man to undertake the government of the country, as he acted courageously and straightforwardly, but Gordon knew the man better than any of them. 'The plan which we should like to see carried out is that some ruler should be placed at Khartum, who might hold also Barbar and Dongola, or separate rulers for each district; that he, or they, should receive a moderate subsidy from Egypt on condition of keeping peace, opening trade and abstaining from the slavery trade; I do not mean domestic slavery but the slave raids and the slave caravans.' Colonel Chermside was working on those lines through al-Sayyid Muhammad 'Uthman, a religious shaikh, and through the Beni Amir tribe, for the government of Kasalah, with a fair prospect of success. 'To conclude I feel sure you will do your utmost to devise in conjunction with Lord Wolseley a settlement of our difficulties and the sooner it is made the better.'[1] Gordon never received this letter which was captured by al-Mahdi's followers from the messenger who carried it.[2]

In consultation with Northbrook it was decided in Cairo that Lord Wolseley should start for upper Egypt. Wolseley's plan was to go to al-Dabbah or Um Bakul on the river in Dongola Province,

[1] Northbrook to Gordon, Oct. 8, 1884, P.R.O., G/D 29/140.
[2] Wolseley to Baring, Nov. 29, 1884, enclosed in Baring to Granville, No. 1084, Nov. 29, 1884, P.R.O., F.O. 78/3680.

from which places roads cross the desert to Khartum and Shandi. If all went well Wolseley planned to take 1,000 or 1,500 men on camels into Khartum, 'capture and bring him [Gordon] back with me. If I can do this and we have no fighting, I ought to be in Hill Street before April Fool's Day.'[1]

On arrival at Wadi Halfa Wolseley reviewed all the news from the Sudan as set out in Gordon's dispatches.[2] On September 16 an undated telegram from Gordon addressed to the Seal Keeper of the Khedive was received in Cairo. Gordon stated that he would not announce to the people in Khartum the firman leaving the government of the Sudan to its people owing to complications which had occurred before his arrival. The probability was that the announcement would result in the people joining al-Mahdi. 'I am satisfied,' wrote Gordon, 'that if this firman were read to them, they would understand that the Government of the Turks had ceased, and that there was now no government here except that of al-Mahdi.' The rebellion of the people of al-Jazirah, in Gordon's opinion, had resulted from their hearing at the beginning, of the Government's intention to evacuate the Sudan.

Gordon maintained that on his arrival the reports of the intended evacuation gained in belief but that, disregarding them, he had published notices declaring that his aim was the establishment of peace and safety, that the laws were to remain as they were, and that a military force would come to maintain order.

If it were still intended [Gordon wrote] as before, to leave the Sudan and to withdraw the soldiers and employés and were this intention known to the false Mahdi, then, without doubt, he would have started from Kurdufan and come to Khartum with so large a force that resistance would have been impossible. They would have made raids, they would have pillaged, and Khartum with its employés, its arms and ammunition would have been captured as fell to the lot of the Mudirieh of Barbar.

But when it was rumored that the Sudan would not be abandoned and that troops were coming to Khartum, al-Mahdi had not moved from his position. Gordon hoped that on the arrival of the troops at Khartum the rising in al-Jazirah would be suppressed and order would be restored. He maintained that 'the Nile route is now the most important object, and the prosperity of Egypt can only result

---

[1] Wolseley to his wife, Sept. 20, 1884, Wolseley, op. cit., p. 120.
[2] Wolseley to Hartington, No. 7700/550, Oct. 5, 1884, P.R.O., W.O. 32/124

from the restoration of peace in the Sudan.' Gordon's plan was to send troops to retake Barbar in order to re-establish communications with Dongola and Egypt.

In a succeeding telegram[1] Gordon stated that he was prevented from carrying out the policy of withdrawal by the insurrection of the Arabs and the interruption of the communications and that was why he had asked for reinforcements, the delay of which had caused the fall of Barbar. 'It is right,' he said, 'that I should have been sent to Khartum with only seven followers after the destruction of Hicks Pasha's army, and that no attention should have been paid to me until the communications had been cut? . . . Having now so often promised the people of Khartum that assistance would come, we have become like liars in their eyes.' Gordon doubted very much whether the Sudan could be held by Sudanese troops alone and thought the best plan would be to negotiate with the Sublime Porte for the dispatch of Turkish troops, giving them £200,000 for expenses.

Here I am in Khartum a hostage and a guardian! I trust as long as I remain, and the Sultan's troops arrive, the people of the Sudan will be unable to resist them, that no shot will be fired, and that peace and order will return. It is impossible to leave Khartum unless a regular government is established on the part of some power. . . . Perhaps the British Government will be displeased at the advice which I have given. The people of the Sudan are also displeased with me on account of my fighting against them, and of their not attaining their object in following the False Mahdi.

In a telegram dated Khartum, August 24,[2] Gordon outlined his plan for the evacuation of the Sudan. The first step, in his opinion, was to send English troops to the Sudan and for Zubair to be appointed at a yearly salary of £6,000. On the arrival of the English troops the Egyptian soldiers would return to Egypt. If the Sultan would then send 2,000 men the Sudan would be handed over to him. 'If no part of this scheme is carried out,' Gordon maintained, 'and if the rebels attack the people and kill them, you will be responsible for their lives and their salaries.'

From Wadi Halfa Wolseley also took up the question of appointing the Mudir of Dongola as governor of Khartum. He suggested

[1] Undated.
[2] Gordon to the Khedive, Aug. 24, 1884, in Wolseley to Hartington, No. 7700/550, Oct. 5, 1884, P.R.O., W.O. 32/124.

that the Mudir should be appointed ruler of Khartum on certain conditions, for five years, after which the terms would be reviewed. In Wolseley's opinion the Mudir should be given an annual subsidy of £100,000 with all the steamers south of Hannik and plenty of arms and ammunition. He would govern Khartum, Barbar, Abu Hamad, and Dongola as an independent ruler under the suzerainty of the Khedive, paying no tribute and collecting his own revenue. It would also be essential for him to prevent and discourage the slave-trade and to keep the trade routes open.[1] These proposals were discussed in Cairo by Northbrook, Baring, and Nubar, who approved them, except that the subsidy should be £100,000 for the first year and £50,000 for subsequent years, because of the financial embarrassment of the Egyptian Government. Wolseley was authorized to open negotiations on this basis, but his attention was then directed to Muhammad 'Ali Pasha, whom Gordon had mentioned as the only person fit to succeed him.[2]

It seems that the British Foreign Office objected to the suzerainty of the Khedive over the Governor of the Sudan and asked whether some pacific arrangements might not be entered into. Wolseley replied that al-Mahdi could make no treaty, for he must either fight or cease to be a Mahdi. Wolseley urged that it was high time to appoint a new governor to Khartum in order to enable Gordon, and anyone wishing to do so, to leave Khartum and to withdraw the British troops, leaving the new governor to fight as best he could if attacked by al-Mahdi.[3] In his covering letter to Wolseley's reply, Baring stated that the only considerable objection to the Mudir was that being a Circassian he might be unpopular in the Sudan and would be inclined to lean too much on Egypt. Baring maintained, however, that they really had very little choice. 'It is essential to install some governor at Khartum and we must take whoever has the best chance of success, without paying much attention to minor objections.'[4] As to the Khedive's suzerainty, Baring thought that the use of the word should be

<hr />

[1] Wolseley to Baring, Oct. 22, 1884, enclosed in Baring to Granville, No. 974, Oct. 1884, P.R.O., F.O. 78/3679.

[2] Baring to Wolseley, Oct. 23, 1884, enclosed in Baring to Granville, No. 974, Oct. 23, 1884, P.R.O., F.O. 78/3679.

[3] Wolseley to Baring, Oct. 27, 1884, enclosed in Baring to Granville, No. 985, Oct. 28, 1884, P.R.O., F.O. 78/3679.

[4] Baring to Granville, No. 985, Oct. 28, 1884, P.R.O., F.O. 78/3679.

avoided as it would create difficulties. 'Abd al-Qadir Pasha, the Egyptian Minister for War, who could speak with authority on the Sudan, thought that the more the name and prestige of the Khedive were used by the new governor, the greater would be the chances of maintaining his authority. This view, in Baring's opinion, contradicted the idea that any connection with Egypt would be unpopular in the Sudan. 'It is difficult for anyone not on the spot to state positively which of these two lines of arguments should prevail. I would, therefore, propose to state the facts to Lord Wolseley, and leave him a wide latitude to decide, after local enquiry and negotiation with the Mudir.'

On November 3 Wolseley arrived at Dongola and was officially and ceremonially received by the Mudir. On the next day the Khedivial firman addressed to the Mudir, 'ulama (learned men), judges, notables, merchants, and shaikhs of Bedwins was publicly read. The Khedive informed these people that Wolseley had arrived in the Sudan as commander of the British troops to carry out whatever military operations might be required. The firman appealed to all to obey Wolseley's orders and submit to his will. After the march past of the troops, Wolseley rose and installed His Excellency the Mudir, Mustafa Yawir Pasha, A Knight of the Order of St. Michael and St. George, in the name of the Queen. The Mudir was told that Her Majesty had been graciously pleased to confer that high distinction on him in appreciation of the services he had rendered to the Khedive and to his country, and for the ability he had shown in leading his troops against the followers of al-Mahdi.[1]

The next day Wolseley telegraphed to Cairo that in a few days he would send Sir Herbert Stewart with 300 mounted infantry to Um Bakul, which was considered to be a better place than al-Dabbah for a supply depot. Wolseley expected to be able to concentrate the whole of his force at Um Bakul by the end of the year, which was later than he had previously estimated. The steamers had broken down between Asyut and Wadi Halfa, because of the difficulties of securing coal and the scarcity of native labor. Wolseley had decided not to make any arrangement with the Mudir until he had consulted Gordon. Husain Pasha Khalifah

---

[1] Wolseley to Baring, Nov. 6, 1884, enclosed in Baring to Granville, No. 1047, Nov. 18, 1884, P.R.O., F.O. 78/3680.

seemed to be a possible rival to the Mudir as Governor of Khartum.[1]

In a letter to his wife, Wolseley revealed that things had not been going as well as he would have wished. Owing to many delays he could not expect to reach Shandi until at least a month later than he had calculated upon. The operations would consequently be retarded and, therefore it would be well into the hot weather before they returned to Cairo. 'However, perhaps I may be able to avoid moving up the Nile beyond al-Dabbah or Um-Bakul, and may, from that neighborhood, be able to push on camels across the desert direct to Khartum.'[2]

Waiting at Dongola for about twenty-two days, Wolseley was a little depressed about the progress of supplies to the front and the slowness of his whalers on the river. However, he found consolation in religion, feeling sure that God would find him a way out of his difficulties. 'He has been with me in all my previous expeditions, and when things have looked blackest, much darker than they do at this moment, He has come to my assistance and shown a way out of my difficulties.'[3] Failure to attain his objective would be exaggerated by his enemies at home and would be 'more dreadful than it would be to one who would be merely regarded as having failed to accomplish a very difficult or impossible task.'

On November 14 Wolseley received a long letter from Gordon dated November 4. Gordon acknowledged the receipt of a letter from Wolseley in cypher, which could not be decyphered since Stewart (who had left Khartum by steamer for Dongola)[4] had taken the cypher. He told Wolseley that five steamers with nine guns had been sent from Khartum to await his orders at al-Matammah. 'We can hold out forty days with ease; after that it will be difficult.' Gordon reported that al-Mahdi was eight miles away. Although they had occasional fights with the Arabs, it had been rumored that al-Mahdi would not fight during the month of Muharram. Gordon warned Wolseley not to send any more private letters as it was too great a risk and there was no use in writing in cypher because Gordon had no cypher and al-Mahdi knew everything. 'I should take the road from Um Bakul to al-Matammah,

---

[1] Baring to Granville, No. 1005, Nov. 4, 1884, P.R.O., F.O. 78/3680.
[2] Wolseley, op. cit., p. 128, Nov. 5, 1884.
[3] Ibid., p. 131, Nov. 25, 1884.
[4] Stewart, Power, and some Greeks from Khartum were killed by al-Manasir between Abu Hamad and Marawi.

where my steamers wait for you.'[1] The pay of the soldiers in Khartum was only half a month in arrears, and paper money had been issued. Wolseley was warned not to bring any Egyptian soldiers to Khartum. 'Mark my words, you will not get out of the Sudan for a year unless you make convention with the Sultan to take over the Government with a subsidy of £200,000 a year. This was why I sent Stewart down, though when he started from Khartum I despaired of your coming. If you make convention you can leave in January 1885.'

Wolseley, however, had sent another letter to Gordon a week before he received the news of the loss of the cypher. He told Gordon that a considerable force would be concentrated around Um Bakul or al-Dabbah about Christmas time. Wolseley would like to avoid taking that large force, if possible, round by Abu Hamad, Barbar, and Shandi. He would prefer moving across the desert to Shandi if it were safe to cross with about 1,500 British soldiers on camels. Gordon was also asked to suggest anyone, excepting Zubair, who could hold his own at Khartum with a subsidy of £100,000 during the first year and £50,000 for four years thereafter together with all the arms and steamers in the Sudan and a liberal allowance of ammunition. 'The Government of Dongola, Barbar and Khartum to be handed over to him and he to be responsible for keeping open the trade routes, and protecting of frontiers of Egypt from invasion and to discountenance the slave trade.'[2] The only two men whom Wolseley could suggest were Husain Pasha Khalifah and the Mudir of Dongola. The former had behaved well until he was abandoned and virtually told to make his own terms. If Gordon thought him suitable he could be contacted and offered the appointment. The Mudir was a man of power, energy, courage, and ability, but he was a Circassian and would lean much on his Turkish and bashbuzuk followers. In Wolseley's opinion a native of the Sudan was much to be preferred, but failing that Wolseley would recommend the Mudir if he would accept the terms. 'Could Muhammad 'Ali, who you mentioned in your letters as being with you, undertake the position

[1] Gordon to Wolseley, Nov. 4, 1884, enclosed in Baring to Granville, No. 1036, Nov. 15, 1884, P.R.O., F.O. 78/3680.
[2] Wolseley to Gordon, Nov. 7, 1884, enclosed in Baring to Granville, No. 1070, Nov. 25, 1884, P.R.O., F.O. 78/3680.

with any prospect of success?' The war seemed to Wolseley to be aimed at ridding the country of foreigners rather than setting up al-Mahdi. Therefore, if Husain Pasha or Muhammad 'Ali Pasha could be installed in Khartum, it was quite probable that Muhammad Ahmad would be glad to settle down as Sultan of Kurdufan, the position which Gordon had originally offered to him.

Under the impression that Slatin, although a prisoner, was a friend of al-Mahdi, Wolseley wrote to him[1] saying that a considerable force was beginning to move and would soon reach al-Dabbah. 'My men are all English soldiers and your knowledge of the world will tell you that no matter how many or how large the armies which Muhammad Ahmad could bring against us we should sweep them aside and destroy them with ease.' Wolseley would be glad to give peace to Muhammad Ahmad and recognize him as Sultan of Kurdufan upon his surrendering all his European and fellaheen prisoners. He wished very much to avoid all further bloodshed and his object upon reaching Khartum would be to establish a strong native government there. 'If you are a true friend of Muhammad Ahmad, advise him to settle down as Sultan of Kurdufan while he can do so as his pretensions to be a Mahdi are now laughed at everywhere.'[2]

When Wolseley knew that his letters could not be decyphered, he wrote to Gordon en clair. 'I shall have an army between al-Dabbah and Um Bakul on a date which you can fix by counting 283 days on from this year's anniversary of the date of your commission as Major General.'[3] Wolseley was too careful to give the number of his soldiers, but he emphasized that it was strong enough 'to wipe Muhammad Ahmad and all his followers off the face of the earth.' 'The more men he brings to meet me the better, as the greater will be the number we shall kill. My soldiers hope he will fight as they like war and will be disappointed if after coming so far from Home, they have no chance of killing Muhammad Ahmad.' Wolseley himself had seen so much bloodshed during his life that personally he would prefer to settle this matter peacefully. He would pardon Muhammad Ahmad and would

[1] Wolseley to Slatin, Nov. 7, 1884, enclosed in Baring to Granville, No. 1070, Nov. 25, 1884, P.R.O., F.O. 78/3680.
[2] Ibid.
[3] Wolseley to Gordon, Nov. 17, 1884, enclosed in Baring to Granville, No. 1119, Dec. 9, 1884, P.R.O., F.O. 78/3681.

install him as independent and hereditary Sultan of Kurdufan. He would establish a strong native local governor at Khartum, who should become hereditary ruler of the provinces of Dongola, Barbar, and Khartum, and be independent of Egypt after Gordon had left the Sudan. If Muhammad Ahmad would not accept peace, Wolseley would let his soldiers have their wish to fight. They were the flower of the army, and they were already on the river or marching along its banks towards Dongola. 'Can you recommend a good man of the Sudan to rule in Khartum as I have already described, receiving a subsidy for no use recommending the black gentlemen in Cairo as Government would not have him, and as he has been a traitor to us ever since you left Cairo?'[1]

The entry of December 14, 1884 was the last in Gordon's journal and also the last day on which he wrote letters and messages which were received in Dongola and Cairo. A messenger from Khartum arrived in Dongola on the last day of 1884 carrying on a piece of paper, the size of a postage stamp, the following: 'Khartum all right. 14/12/84 C. G. Gordon.'[2] But Gordon had also entrusted the messenger with a verbal message to Wolseley. Khartum was besieged on three fronts, Omdurman, al-Halfaya, and Hillat Khujali, and fighting was going on day and night. The Arabs would not take Khartum except by starving the garrison out. Wolseley was told not to scatter his troops as the enemy troops were numerous. 'Bring plenty of troops if you can. . . . We want you to come quickly. You should come by al-Matammah or Barbar. Make by these two roads. Do not leave Barbar in your rear. Keep enemy in your front, and when you have taken Barbar send me word from Barbar.' Gordon warned Wolseley to do all that without allowing rumors of his approach to spread.

By the same messenger Gordon conveyed a gloomy picture in a letter to Colonel Watson: 'The game is up, and send Mrs. Watson, you and Graham my adieux. We may expect a catastrophe in the town on or after 10 days' time. This would not have happened (if it does happen) if our people had taken better precautions as to informing me of their movements, but this is spilt milk.'[3]

[1] Ibid.
[2] Wolseley to Baring, Dec. 31, 1884, enclosed in Baring to Granville, No. 1, Secret, Jan. 1, 1885, P.R.O., F.O. 78/3799.
[3] Gordon to Watson, Dec. 14, 1884, enclosed in Baring to Granville, No. 182, Feb. 25, 1885, P.R.O., F.O. 78/3801.

Gordon's message made Wolseley change his plan. He decided to take Barbar by river before moving on Khartum. In the meantime he would establish a post at al-Matammah in order to communicate with Gordon. This would necessitate an expedition on camels across the desert from the Nile in Dongola Province to al-Matammah. From the latter place Khartum could be reached by steamers, and the exact position would be learned and they would be able if 'he [Gordon] were *in extremis*, before the infantry arrived, by river, to push forward with the Camel Corps to help him at all hazards.'[1]

Just at this time, when Wolseley was preparing his plan in accordance with the information and advice received from Gordon, Baring asked him whether he was sufficiently confident of success to be able to dispense with a demonstration from Sawakin. Baring's opinion was that a check to Wolseley would be very serious and that the demonstration from Sawakin would reduce the possibility of such a check. Baring thought that the question of extra expenditure was not important so long as it would ensure the success of the expedition. Wolseley replied that he felt very confident of success if Khartum could hold out until boats with troops could reach its vicinity. If circumstances made it necessary to push on with the desert column to Khartum, the operations near Sawakin could have no effect on the position near Khartum. Wolseley, however, thought that operations at Sawakin could contribute towards final success. He did not believe that al-Hadandawa would fight again against British troops, and he thought that there would be no peace in eastern Sudan until 'Uthman Diqna had been decisively defeated.[2]

Hartington could not understand how a force at Sawakin could materially assist Wolseley, as it would be sent from England and would not land at Sawakin until some six or eight weeks later.[3] Gladstone objected to a Sawakin expedition and was averse from trying conclusions with 'Uthman Diqna once again. 'We have already performed once, of course with loss and with frightful slaughter of most gallant Arabs in two bloody battles, this operation of pacifying the Eastern Sudan, and I am very loath to have

---

[1] Wolseley to Baring, Jan. 2, 1885, enclosed in Baring to Granville, No. 10, Confidential, Jan. 2, 1885, P.R.O., F.O. 78/3799.
[2] Ibid.
[3] Hartington to Baring, Private, Jan. 5, 1885, enclosed in Baring to Granville, No. 23, Secret, Jan. 8, 1885, P.R.O., F.O. 78/3799.

another such pacification and quite unable to see how it is to be better or more effective.'[1]

Baring advocated an expedition to Sawakin in the hope that it might pacify the eastern Sudan, and would materially help Wolseley. Considering the very difficult and dangerous nature of the enterprise and the gravity of the issue at stake, Baring thought that every possible eventuality should be guarded against. He considered the worst thing that could happen would be a repulse to Wolseley's forces.[2]

Wolseley thought that he would be helped by the sending of all available men-of-war to Sawakin, to anchor there, rather than by the sending of a military expedition. The sailors might land frequently and exercise with guns outside the works, and as many marines as possible should be in red coats. It should be made known to and believed by all that an attack on the tribes was being prepared. If that belief spread to 'Uthman Diqna's camp, it would prevent him from sending help to Barbar.[3] 'In war there is no such thing as certainty, but with God's help I shall have a great success. I never felt more confident in any previous operation,—a confidence that I know is shared by all about me.'[4]

At a Cabinet meeting, however, at which Gladstone was not present, all the ministers present except Childers and Trevelyan agreed to send to Sawakin an expedition for war operations.[5] Graham was again chosen to command the expedition.

On December 30, 1884 the first convoy of the desert column marched off from Kurti to Jakdul. On January 8, 1885 Sir H. Stewart the commander of the desert column, left Kurti with the main body of his troops. He had been ordered to establish posts at Jakdul and Abu Tlaih and to occupy al-Matammah. He was then to return to Jakdul leaving Sir Charles Wilson in command at al-Matammah. It was Wolseley's original intention to lead this desert column himself to al-Matammah and if necessary to Khar-

[1] Gladstone to Hartington, Jan. 6, 1885, P.R.O., G/D 29/129.
[2] Baring to Wolseley, Jan. 6, 1885, enclosed in Baring to Granville, No. 23, Secret, Jan. 8, 1885, P.R.O., F.O. 78/3799.
[3] Wolseley to Baring, Jan. 6, 1885, enclosed in Baring to Granville, No. 23, Secret, Jan. 8, 1885, P.R.O., F.O. 78/3799.
[4] Wolseley to Baring, Jan. 7, 1885, enclosed in Baring to Granville, No. 23, Secret, Jan. 8, 1885, P.R.O., F.O. 78/3799.
[5] Childers to Gladstone, Jan. 7, 1885, B.M. Add. MS. 44132.

tum. Gordon's message warning him not to leave Barbar in the
rear, however, made him change the plan and order the desert
column to have as its objective only the establishment of communication with Gordon.

Sir Charles Wilson was instructed to accompany the column.
He was to enter into friendly relations with the Hassaniya tribe
and to induce them to carry supplies for the army across the desert
and to sell them sheep, cattle, and other supplies. As soon as
al-Matammah had been occupied, he was to send political information to Kurti by Stewart's messengers. When the naval officers
accompanying the column were ready to start in the steamers for
Khartum, he was to take with him on board a small detachment of
infantry to Khartum. He was to march these soldiers through the
town in order to show that the British troops were near at hand.
He was to remain in Khartum long enough to confer fully with
Gordon and was then to return with his soldiers in the same
steamers to al-Matammah, leaving only three officers to assist
Gordon. After his return to al-Matammah Wilson was to rejoin
Wolseley's headquarters as soon as possible.

It is clear from these instructions to Wilson that Wolseley
thought it quite possible that when al-Mahdi realized that British
soldiers were approaching Khartum, he would retreat and the
siege would be raised. Then Khartum would become the political
center, but Barbar would be the military objective. Only a few
troops would be sent to Khartum in red coats on steamers, and
they would impress on the inhabitants that they owed their safety
to the presence of the British army. The siege of Khartum having
been thus raised, all military arrangements would be made for
the occupation of Barbar and for marching eastwards across the
desert to Ariab on the Sawakin road.[1]

In framing these instructions Wolseley assumed three things.
In the first place he believed that the presence of the British troops
in their red coats, however few they might be, would frighten
al-Mahdi from Khartum. Secondly, he did not consider the
possibility of resistance to the colummn before it reached the river
at al-Matammah. Thirdly, he assumed that the only possible way
for al-Mahdi to take Khartum was by starving the garrison and the
inhabitants into surrender and not by direct assault.

[1] Colvile, H. E., *History of the Sudan Campaign*, Part II, p. 3.

al-Mahdi, however, had a different plan. His main purpose in delaying the attack on Khartum was his hope that the town would capitulate without bloodshed as had happened at al-Ubayyid. But the attack could no longer be delayed if there was any possibility of relief arriving to the beleaguered garrison.

When the desert column approached Abu Tlaih wells, the scouts reported the presence of the ansar. The troops moved very cautiously and halted about 3½ miles from the wells. Seeing that the ansar appeared to be in considerable force and that it was too late to fight, Stewart ordered a zaribah to be made as protection. During the night the ansar showed much activity and made prepartions for the fight.[1] After serving out breakfast under hot fire from the ansar, Stewart gave the orders to march in square formation and take the offensive. On the march the square was subjected to heavy firing, which necessitated frequent halts. When the skirmishers, who were outside the square, were about 200 yards from the ansar flags, the square was halted to allow the rear to close up, and at that moment the ansar rose from a ravine in which they were hidden. 'It was a beautiful and striking sight, such a one as Fitz James must have seen when Roderick Dhu's men rose out of the heather; nothing could be more applicable than Scott's description. How they managed to conceal their horses I know not, but they did so very effectually.'[2] The ansar were following their own peculiar method of attack at an even, quick pace and the skirmishers of the British troops had only just time to get into the square before the ansar were upon it.

Wilson relates that when the ansar commenced their advance he had a feeling of pity mixed with admiration for them, as he thought all would be shot in a few minutes. It was not believed that men in close formation could advance for 200 to 400 yards over bare ground in the face of fire from such precision weapons as Martini-Henrys. His feeling was changed to that of wonder when they advanced and the fire had so little effect. But when they were within eighty yards of the square the fire began to take its toll and dead bodies rose in huge piles. Still those who remained advanced, and wheeled right to envelope the rear of the square.

[1] Colvile, H. E., *History of the Sudan Campaign,* Part II, p. 15.
[2] Wilson, Sir Charles, *From Korti to Khartum* (London, 1886), p. 26.

I remember thinking, 'by Jove, they will be into the square!' and almost the next moment I saw a fine old Shaikh on horse back plant his banner in the centre of the square, behind the camels. He was at once shot down, falling on his banner. He turned out to be Musa, Amir of Dighaim Arabs, from Kurdufan. I had noticed him in the advance, with his banner in one hand and a book of prayers in the other, and never saw anything finer. The old man never swerved to the right or left, and never ceased chanting his prayers until he had planted his banner in our square. If any man deserved a place in the Moslem paradise he did.[1]

Although the square was penetrated at one point, the troops closed the gap and killed all the enemy who had penetrated. The ansar then retreated and the re-formed square advanced on the wells, leaving the stores behind in the zaribah.

On the resumed march from the wells to the river, the troops were repeatedly harassed by the ansar, but they managed to reach the river near al-Matammah. Making arrangements for the wounded, who included Sir Herbert Stewart, and leaving the bulk of the soldiers in fortified positions, Wilson, on whom the command devolved, embarked in Gordon's steamers for Khartum with twenty-four British soldiers and black troops. Surmounting all the difficulties of the river, they at last came within sight of Khartum, but instead of being heartily welcomed, they received showers of bullets from both banks of the river. Although they were told by people on the banks that Khartum had fallen, they thought they ought to make sure for themselves. They were reasonably convinced when they were met by this hostility and by the absence of the Egyptian flag on Government House. The return journey was beset with difficulties from the river and from the ansar.

Since March 12, 1884 Khartum had been besieged and hostile activity had never ceased. In the first stage the siege had been left to the emissaries of al-Mahdi in the neighborhood of the town, chief among whom was Shaikh al-'Ubaid Wad Badur. Then Hajj Muhammad Abu Qarja was dispatched by al-Mahdi with 2,000 men from Kurdufan to be the commander-in-chief. In the third stage 'Abd al-Rahman Wad al-Nujumi conducted the operations of the siege with still more troops and guns. Gordon on his part made use of every material to strengthen his fortifications. He availed himself of the rise of the Nile to send his steamers to Sennar to get

[1] Ibid., p. 28.

grain and to reassure the garrison there. Sorties were frequently made in which sometimes the besieged garrison gained successes but sometimes they were terribly defeated.

The large number of ansar collected at al-Ubayyid with al-Mahdi seems to have been too large for the water-supply of the town and it became inevitable that al-Mahdi's camp should move to al-Rahad where there was plenty of water. At the end of the rainy season of 1884, when there were no problems of water and fodder, al-Mahdi began his movement eastwards towards the Nile. The number of his followers increased as they proceeded, and when they reached Omdurman their numbers, including those already besieging Khartum, exceeded 100,000.

al-Mahdi immediately entered into communication with Gordon suggesting that he should surrender. In one of these letters al-Mahdi actually promised Gordon a safe conduct to the north to join the British expeditionary force. Gordon's replies were defiant and showed his determination to resist any attack, saying that British troops would very soon arrive. In the early stages of the siege the assault of Khartum was a difficult military operation for the ansar, but by the middle of January conditions rendered such an attack possible. Famine in the town had begun to tell on the spirit and morale of the soldiers, the fortifications could not be kept in a state of repair as the soldiers were enfeebled by shortage of food; as the Nile was at its lowest level the ditch and the ramparts could not be extended to the water's edge and the ansar could outflank the fortifications on the White Nile side. Above all, such a large number of enthusiasts with their spiritual leader in their midst could have surmounted almost any obstacle.

When the news of the encounter with the British troops at Abu Tlaih was heard in al-Mahdi's camp, it was evident that their advent at Khartum would make the capitulation of the town very doubtful. There was no alternative left to al-Mahdi but to attempt to take it by force.

At dawn on January 26 the ansar launched their attack. The fortifications yielded to the first assault and great slaughter ensued, Gordon himself being killed. Slatin asserts that al-Mahdi never wished Gordon to be killed, but he contemplated exchanging him for 'Urabi.[1] It was only two days after the capture of Khartum and

---

[1] Slatin, op. cit., p. 344.

the death of Gordon that Wilson's steamers appeared before the town.[1]

Wilson stated that the sight at that moment was very grand:

the masses of the enemy with their fluttering banners near Khartum; the long rows of riflemen in the shelter trenches at Omdurman; the numerous groups of men on Tuti; the bursting shells, and the water torn up by hundreds of bullets and occasional heavier shot,—made an impression never to be forgotten. Looking out over the stormy scene, it seemed almost impossible that we should escape.[2]

When the desert column plunged into the interior Wolseley became most anxious about the result. On January 15 he wrote to his wife saying that he expected that the next fortnight would be the most trying time. He thought that Wilson with Gordon's steamers would be in Khartum on the 20th and would be back at al-Matammah on the 27th.[3] On January 21 Wolseley received the news of the battle of Abu Tlaih, which was a success, although the losses were heavy and the commanding officer had been wounded. 'One or two more such tussles will finish the whole business but it shows us that we are not to have a walk-over and that al-Mahdi means to fight hard.'[4]

When telegraphing the news of the fall of Khartum on February 4, Wolseley asked for fresh instructions as the object of his mission was no longer possible. He could, if the Government wished, advance on Khartum and defeat al-Mahdi, but operations under the new conditions were much more difficult than before. The season was somewhat late, and the hot weather would very soon prove a most formidable enemy.[5]

In London the news caused such a shock that the Queen sent telegrams *en clair* to her ministers stating that the catastrophe might have been prevented and 'many precious lives saved by

---

[1] For the story of Khartum's siege and fall see (a) Gordon, Major-General C. G., *The Journals cf Gordon at Khartum* (London, 1885,) (b) Report by a Committee of Egyptian officers under Mahammad Nushi Pasha, *Sudan Notes and Records* (Khartum, 1930), vol. xiii, p. 1.

[2] Wilson, op. cit., p. 147.

[3] Ibid., p. 155.

[4] Ibid., p. 159.

[5] Wolseley to Secretary of State for War, No. 44, Feb. 4, 1885, P.R.O., W.O. 33/34, Part II, p. 224.

earlier action.' [1] Gladstone took a very serious view of his being telegraphed *en clair* and was considering whether he could remain in office having been condemned by the Queen in such a manner.[2]

Wolseley was immediately instructed that the objects of his mission were: '1. Safety of Gordon, if alive, which must be assumed till we are certain of his death. 2. To check advance of al-Mahdi in districts now undisturbed.' [3] The Government was of opinion that a hazardous operation at that time was not essential to the attainment of these objects. They were, however, prepared to send Wolseley any reinforcement.

Wolseley thought these instructions vague, as they gave no information about the policy the Government wished him to follow in the Sudan. If it was their intention that he should proceed to Khartum during the next cold season and overthrow al-Mahdi's power, Barbar and Abu Hamad should be captured. If, on the other hand, no move to Khartum was contemplated it would be unwise to capture Barbar, but the capture of Abu Hamad would be necessary for checking the advance of al-Mahdi.[4]

Hartington replied that the Government's policy aimed at over-throwing the power of al-Mahdi at Khartum and that Wolseley was to decide when to attack, and when and where reinforcements would be required.[5] It appears that this bold policy was dictated by the strong feeling of the British people who objected to Britain's being beaten.[6] 'To my extreme astonishment,' Wolseley wrote to his wife, 'the Cabinet have determined to fight it out with al-Mahdi.' [7]

It was Wolseley's plan, after receiving these instructions, to hold Barbar and Abu Hamad before advancing on a large scale in the coming autumn, but reports, which he received from the commanders of the desert and the river columns made him change his plan and concentrate all his force in Dongola Province.

[1] *The Letters of Queen Victoria*, 2nd ser. (London, 1928), p. 597.
[2] Ibid., p. 603.
[3] Secretary of State for War to Wolseley, No. 122, Feb. 6, 1885, P.R.O., W.O. 33/34, Part 2, p. 227.
[4] Wolseley to Secretary of State for War, No. 50, Feb. 6, 1885, ibid.
[5] Secretary of State for War, No. 117, Feb. 7, 1885, ibid., p. 229.
[6] Holland, Bernard, *Life of Spencer Compton, 8th Duke of Devonshire,* vol. ii, p. 13.
[7] Wolseley, op. cit., p. 167.

The initial excitement which had moved the Government to decide on beating al-Mahdi had by this time cooled down and trouble with Russia was brewing in Afghanistan. In reply to the incessant demands of Wolseley to be given the position of governor-general of the Sudan, the Government therefore replied that the position with Russia in Afghanistan was critical and it would be inexpedient to make comprehensive declarations of future policy in the Sudan.[1] Wolseley retorted that he would be extremely disappointed if he had to return without capturing Khartum. 'I am anxious that as a nation we should get out of the Sudan altogether but we must get out of it with honor, and we cannot do that unless we go to Khartum.'[2]

Although as a general Wolseley wished to go to Khartum and win a victory, he was so weary of life in Dongola that he wished that those at home who criticized his actions might experience the climate of the Sudan. 'I wish that old crocodile, Gladstone, could be condemned to spend the ensuing summer at Dongola.'[3]

The Government, however, relieved him of the necessity of spending the summer in Dongola, and he was asked to proceed to Cairo. His impression, at that time, was that he would not return, as he doubted whether the Government would carry out the advance on Khartum if forced into war with Russia.[4]

The idea that there was no justification for embarking on a costly war in the Sudan was gaining ground, apart from the trouble with Russia. It was emphatically declared by the Government that although it was intended to capture Khartum, the town would ultimately be evacuated. It was, therefore, obvious that a campaign would serve no purpose.[5] This idea was reinforced by a private letter from Wolseley to a liberal member of parliament who passed it on to the Cabinet. 'This Sudan war,' wrote Wolseley, 'will be the most serious since Waterloo.'[6] As an Englishman Wolseley deeply deplored the necessity of seeing Great Britain embark on an 'enterprise of which I cannot forsee the end.' He

[1] Granville to Baring, No. 77, Secret, Mar. 13, 1885, P.R.O., F.O. 78/3812.
[2] Wolseley, op. cit., Mar. 17, 1885, p. 207.
[3] Ibid., Mar. 22, 1885, p. 209.
[4] Ibid., Mar. 29, 1885, p. 211.
[5] Holland, op. cit., vol. ii, p. 27.
[6] Maurice, Sir F., and Arthur, Sir George, *The Life of Lord Wolseley* (London, 1924), p. 230.

would prefer to spend money on coaling stations and arms, which would consolidate the empire. Gladstone considered the letter to be an extraordinary one and blamed Wolseley for not giving them the smallest idea of his real opinions. Gladstone, therefore, suggested that before having a Cabinet meeting they should wait until they had heard from Wolseley 'all his mind.' [1]

Acting on Gladstone's suggestion Hartington told Wolseley that he already doubted whether the country would willingly go on with the expedition. Many members of the Government disliked it and had only accepted it, because it was thought that to retire in face of the successes of al-Mahdi would endanger the security of Egypt, and because on Wolseley's authority they believed that the overthrow of al-Mahdi would not be a difficult task. But Wolseley's present opinion would strengthen the hands of members of the Government who 'detested the enterprise from its very commencement.' [2] He asked Wolseley to make a full report of his views and requirements.

Further support against an advance on Khartum came from Baring who in a very long lettter analyzed the various factors of the situation and came to the conclusion that Britain should undertake no military operations and should come to terms with Turkey over the Sudan. [3]

On his arrival at Cairo from Dongola, Wolseley immediately gave the views and requirements asked for by Hartington. He urged that the campaign should go on until al-Mahdi had been overthrown and for that purpose he asked for twelve extra battalions. He thought that until al-Mahdi was defeated there would always be difficulties. A retreat would be interpreted by the people in the East as a defeat and disgrace. 'I urge the destruction of al-Mahdi at Khartum from no motive of revenge, but putting aside all question of national honor, because it is an indispensable measure if you mean to remain some years in Egypt.' [4] It seems that Wolseley wished to avoid responsibility for the policy of retreat. In a letter to his wife earlier he said, 'I say this lest the Government should give out that I advise retreat. I disgust Glad-

[1] Gladstone to Harrington, Apr. 2, 1885, B.M. Add. MS. 44148.
[2] Holland, op. cit., vol. ii, p. 28.
[3] Baring to Granville, Private, Apr. 3, 1885, P.R.O., G/D 29/165.
[4] Wolseley to the Secretary of State for War (Wolseley) No. 202, Apr. 12, 1885, P.R.O., W.O. 32/265.

stone and Co. so much that it is necessary I should be always on my guard.'[1] The Government, however, especially after receiving Baring's long letter, were convinced of the advisability of avoiding war in the Sudan, but they disagreed with Baring's proposal to hand over the Sudan to Turkey.[2]

It was not an easy task for a parliamentary government to reverse their policy in two months and to justify this change publicly. In February 1885 the Government had declared that they would advance on Khartum for four reasons. In the first place there were people in Khartum to whom Gordon held himself bound in honor and it was the Government's duty to go to their assistance. Secondly, the advance would make it possible to establish in the Sudan an ordered government friendly to Egypt. Thirdly, the slave-trade would be checked. Fourthly, the possession of Khartum would, without further extension of operations, help to relieve the garrisons still holding out. The two months that had passed had thrown new light on all four points. Firstly, there was no evidence that any of the population had felt bound to Gordon or had suffered on his account. Secondly, there had been no news of anarchy at Khartum and it was not established that the country was governed worse than it would be under Turkish or Egyptian rule. Thirdly, it was not believed that the possession of Khartum would be of any great value as regards the slave-trade. Fourthly, it was not certain that the possession of Khartum would relieve the garrisons without military operations. On the major question of the consequences of al-Mahdi's successes on Egypt and the East it might be observed that he had attempted to march to the north but had speedily abandoned the attempt even in the first flush of victory. It should also be realized that the conflict was 'not with the arms of an enemy, but with nature, in respect of climate, distance and supply.'[3]

In a letter to Wolseley, Hartington maintained that the decision to give up the Khartum expedition had come sooner than he expected. He felt that the facts on which the decision to advance had been based in February, had materially altered and that there was 'really no sufficient object to be gained by an enterprise of

[1] Wolseley, op. cit., Mar. 21, 1885, p. 208.
[2] Granville to Baring, Private, Apr. 15, 1885, P.R.O., G/D 29/201.
[3] Gladstone's memorandum to the Cabinet, Apr. 15, 1885, B.M. Add. MS. 44769.

such magnitude as we gradually began to realize that this was going to be.'[1] There were no friends of the British among the population even in Dongola. It was, moreover, feared that after the conquest of Khartum the Government might be committed to a policy of permanent occupation which they would not countenance under any circumstances. It was also certain that they could not go on with the Sudan expedition if they were going to fight Russia.

Wolseley wished that the announcement to abandon the advance on Khartum should be made in such a way as not to make it clear that al-Mahdi would not be fought. In Wolseley's opinion al-Mahdi might disappear at any moment, either being killed or handed over to the British by his enemies. The definite announcement that there would be no advance on Khartum would discourage al-Mahdi's enemies and would make every native in the Sudan side with al-Mahdi.[2] Baring hoped that the Government would not be in a hurry to retire from Dongola. 'If we hold on for a while and say nothing about retiring, we may be able to get away without doing much harm for there seems a real probability that internal dissensions and want of trade are helping to smash al-Mahdi.'[3]

Granville told Baring that there was no intention of permanently occupying Dongola, but it was understood that its evacuation would take time. In the meantime the Government would like some information about the possibility of a settled government in Dongola, subsidized by Egypt as indicated in Wolseley's instructions, and also of the possibility of finding a company to take over the railways and the steamers. They also wished to have the reports of Kitchener and Wilson on the political situation, with the comments of both Wolseley and Baring.[4] Baring replied that it was the unanimous opinion of all civil and military authorities in Egypt that the evacuation of Dongola should not be hastened, and he forwarded a number of suggestions for establishing a settled government there.[5]

Hartington was inclined to act on the advice of the Govern-

---

[1] Hartington to Wolseley, Apr. 17, 1885, Holland, op. cit., vol. ii, p. 33.
[2] Wolseley to the Secretary of State for War, Secret, 21 Apr. 1885, P.R.O., W.O. 32/265.
[3] Baring to Granville, Private, Apr. 22, 1885, P.R.O., G/D 29/165.
[4] Granville to Baring, Private, Apr. 28, 1885, P.R.O., G/D 29/201.
[5] Baring to Granville, No. 378, May 3, 1885, P.R.O., F.O. 78/3803.

ment's officials in Egypt and to postpone the evacuation, but when the question was discussed in Cabinet he was supported only by Selborne, Northbrook, and Calingford. The members of the Cabinet who sat in the House of Commons were almost all of them of the opposite opinion, and were supported by Granville, Derby, and Kimberly.[1]

On June 8 Gladstone's Government was defeated in the House of Commons in a division on supplies necessary to meet war charges. The Cabinet assembled the following day and decided to resign. Salisbury then formed a Conservative Cabinet. Very soon after taking office, Salisbury sent a personal telegram to Wolseley announcing that he had succeeded Gladstone. This telegram had the most heartening effect on Wolseley. 'How different,' he wrote to his wife, 'from the party just retired, from whom I have not had a line of thanks.'[2]

Officially, Wolseley was asked by the new Government about the number of troops at Dongola and how far north the retreat had reached.[3] Wolseley's reply described the distribution of troops north of Dongola and suggested that there would be no serious difficulty in reoccupying positions which they recently held. Wolseley ordered the rearguard not to leave Dongola.[4] This reply seemed to be hopeful, but the Government thought that before reversing the decision of their predecessors they should be in possession of Wolseley's views of the whole situation.[5] Wolseley maintained that the best course would be to continue with the autumn campaign as originally planned and to fight and defeat al-Mahdi on his own ground. There would be no peace, in Wolseley's opinion, so long as al-Mahdi's power was intact. Even if he ultimately advanced on Egypt and was defeated at the frontier, to him it would only mean the loss of a few thousand followers. His supply of men was unlimited, while his recurring attacks would drain both the Egyptian army and the exchequer.[6] Pending the

---

[1] Holland, op. cit., vol. ii, p. 36.

[2] Wolseley, op. cit., p. 218.

[3] Secretary of State for War to Wolseley, No. 321, June 26, 1885, P.R.O., W.O. 33/44, Part II, p. 413.

[4] Wolseley to Secretary of State for War (Wolseley, No. 324), June 26, 1885, P.R.O., W.O. 33/44, Part II, p. 413.

[5] Secretary of State for War to Wolseley, No. 322, June 26, 1885, P.R.O., W.O. 33/34, Part II, p. 413.

[6] Wolseley to Secretary of State for War (Wolseley, No. 325), June 27, 1885, P.R.O., W.O. 33/34, Part II, p. 414.

Cabinet's final decision Wolseley was instructed to hold on to Dongola and to report on the strength required to retain it apart from any advance in the autumn.[1]

When Buller, who was conducting the retirement, was informed of the decision to hold Dongola he replied that the difficulties were so great that it would be better to continue to retire.[2] 'Of course it is possible to reoccupy Dongola, but it cannot be done without what will be really a new expedition. I believe that Dongola Province is exhausted of grain, and that, whenever our present store runs out, we shall have to bring everything from Egypt for the next six months.'[3] Buller's report decided the Government to continue the policy of evacuation to such a point as would provide for the security of Egypt,[4] and the Sudan had to be finally abandoned.

On June 22 the hero of the story died in his new capital Buq'at al-Mahdi or Omdurman a little to the north of the fort known by this name.[5] He had completed the conquest of Kurdufan and central Sudan in person, while emissaries conquered for him the provinces of al-Taka (Kasalah), Barbar, Darfur, Bahr al-Ghazal, and part of Equatoria. Sennar and Kasalah towns were, however, still holding out, and were to be conquered by his successor, al-Khalifah 'Abdullahi. Sawakin was never conquered by the Mahdists. al-Mahdi's death was premature, for he had contemplated extensive conquests. There followed the administration of the Sudan by 'Abdullahi, Khalifat al-Mahdi.

[1] Secretary of State for War to Wolseley, No. 328, June 27, 1885, P.R.O., W.O. 33/34, Part II, 415.

[2] Wolseley to Secretary of State for War (Wolseley, No. 331), June 29, 1885, P.R.O., W.O. 33/34, Part II, p. 415.

[3] Wolseley to Secretary of State for War (Wolseley, No. 332), June 29, 1885, P.R.O., W.O. 33/34, Part II, p. 416.

[4] Secretary of State for War to Wolseley, No. 343, July 1, 1885, P.R.O., W.O. 33/44, Part II, p. 449.

[5] Wingate, op. cit., p. 228.

XII

ADMINISTRATION OF KHALIFAH 'ABDULLAHI, 1885-1898 A.D.

Khalifah 'Abdullahi was already firmly seated in the saddle before the premature death of al-Mahdi. Coming from the Ta'isha tribe of southern Darfur, 'Abdullahi was the son of Sayyid Muhammad, who was an acknowledged religious man of the saintly type. Various versions state that it was the father who prophesied to the son the glorious future that lay in wait for him. 'Abdullahi joined al-Mahdi some time before the latter declared his mission in an open way. From the start he was taken into complete confidence and it was not at all a surprise that 'Abdullahi became the first lieutenant of the expected Mahdi. The Khalifah's papers show clearly that in all such questions as the army, the treasury and the day-to-day administration 'Abdullahi was in command even when the movement was restricted to Kurdufan and Darfur alone. On various occasions when the ambition of his relatives, the Ashraf, and their reluctance to obey 'Abdullahi, were exhibited, al-Mahdi made public announcements in his sermons or wrote it in circulars that 'Abdullahi was his Khalifah and obedience to him was obedience to al-Mahdi himself. That was the position when al-Mahdi died, about five months after the conquest of Khartum, in Omdurman, his new capital. 'Abdullahi immediately issued a circular in which he quoted extracts of Abu Bakr after the death of the prophet Muhammad: "Those who worshipped Muhammad should know that he is now dead." He referred to the glorious achievements of the Muslims after the death of the prophet and appealed to them to follow in the footsteps of their ancestors and to achieve the same degree of success. He harped on the same note in his letters to the 'Amils (provincial governors).

The immediate problems before him were how to watch the British who were retreating from Dongola, and to subjugate both Sennar and Kasalah towns, which were still holding out. Preparations for the invasion of Egypt came next. al-Mahdi had already sent

Husain Khalifah, the ex-Governor of Barbar, to Upper Egypt as an emissary. Letters were sent to the chiefs of tribes there, particularly the 'Ababdah. It was his (Mahdi's) intention that the army of invasion should be led by Khalifah Muhammad Sharif, his cousin. Troops started from Omdurman to Barbar and then ultimately to Dongola as a base for launching the big attack. Abd al-Rahman al-Nujumi led this advance party to be followed by the rear-guard and then Sharif would proceed to take command. But after some months it became evident to all observers that there were clouds in the sky and the jealousy of the Ashraf did not seem to have abated in spite of all those clear words of al-Mahdi that 'Abdullahi was his undoubted successor.

In his letters to his most trusted general and friend, Hamdan Abu 'Anja, 'Abdullahi revealed that the 'Ashraf were hankering after control over al-Jazirah and Kurdufan. There was pressure on him from his own people to send his relative Yunis al-Dikaim to take charge of Kurdufan after sending its present governor to Dongola. But 'Abdullahi thought that Yunis was not tactful and might commit indiscretions which might arouse feeling against him, especially in the expected coming of Muhammad Khalid from Darfur through Kurdufan. To forestall the Ashraf he told Abu 'Anja that he would send Yunis to al-Jazirah with a view to settling all the western troops there. He instructed Abu 'Anja also not to send anything to Beit al-Mal (Central Treasury) under Ahmad Sulayman, who was believed to be favoring Awlad al-Balad (Riverian people) and against Awlad al-'Arab (Western people). Ahmad ultimately found himself in trouble with the Khalifah and subsequently dismissed and imprisoned. Western troops who were with Muhammad abd al-Karim in the siege of Sennar complained of him and that widened still further the gap between 'Abdullahi and the Ashraf.

The idea of allowing Sharif to lead the army of invasion seemed to have been dropped and the Khalifah sent circulars to the troops, inhabitants of Dongola, Mahas and Nubia, informing them of the appointment of al-Nujumi and asking their help and actual participation in that jihad (religious war). The black troops who were relatively well-trained and disciplined were gathered from the various flags and put under the command of the Khalifah's own brother Ya'qub. His two colleagues, 'Ali Wad Hilu and Sharif, were thus deprived of a very important source of power. But the Ashraf had a powerful force still under the command of Muhammad Khalid, Governor of Darfur. He was instructed by al-Mahdi himself and ·Abdullahi before their move from Kurdufan to Khartum to come and join them in the march. But it seemed that there was great difficulty in finding a successor in Darfur powerful enough and loyal to the cause of the Mahdiyah to be entrusted with the government of the province. After the death of al-Mahdi Khalid received a number of letters from the Khalifah and a letter from the principal leaders residing at Omdurman to come over and renew his oath of allegiance to the Khalifah and visit the tomb of al-Mahdi. The delay that occurred gave some anxiety to 'Abdullahi, but Khalid moved and Abu 'Anja received a series of instructions on how to deal with forces under Khalid. At first it was for the division of the black troops among the three flags, then for handing them all to Abu ·Anja and finally for handing over everything. These reflect develop-ments which were taking place in the capital and this final stage coincided with the last phase in the process of concentrating all the Mahdiya power in his hands.

By now 'Abdullahi was safe from any possibility of a serious split in the Mahdiya power, but had to occupy himself almost in-cessantly in suppressing internal territorial or tribal revolts or in wars with Ethiopia and Egypt. It was known very early in the Mahdiya movement that Salih Fadlallah, chief of the Kababish tribe, was not an obedient servant to the cause of the movement. Despite messages of good will the Khalifah never trusted him. Then it was proved beyond any doubt that he had contacts with Egypt, evi-denced by the confiscation of weapons and ammunition coming from there to him. The instructions of the Khalifah to 'Uthman Adam, who succeeded Abu 'Anja in Kurdufan, were clear that under no pretext whatsoever should the campaign against Salih be relaxed. After an economic blockade to the Kababish Dar (territory) ·Uthman Adam launched an attack of about 10,000 men, which ensured the subjugation of the tribe and the end of Salih. Kurdufan nad afterwards an uninterrupted period of peace. The rebels in the Nuba mountains were already reasonably subjugated by Abu 'Anja. The source of future trouble for the Mahdiya seemed to be Darfur. Those descendants of the Sultans there proved to be disloyal, al-though they were tried as rulers in a restricted part of the Province. The withdrawal of the forces under Muhammid Khalid from the

Province made the Fur nurse the hope of rebelling to regain their independence. It was inevitable, therefore, that the garrison of the Western Sudan should be moved from al-Ubayyid to al-Fashir. Accordingly 'Uthman Adam was instructed to move there.

In the East frontier skirmishes with Ethiopia led to actual full-fledged wars and 'Abdullahi had to resort to his most trusted general to deal with the situation. Abu 'Anja was instructed to move with western troops and jehadiya (black soldiers) to Omdurman and to enter the town in a manner that would impress the disloyal and the jealous people, with the formidable power of the Mahdiyah under the Khalifah. He was subsequently sent to Qadarif to take command and repel any incursions in Sudanese territory. The Emperor of Ethiopia entered into correspondence with Abu 'Anja with a view to settling their outstanding problems and combining together to meet the Europeans who were the common enemy. Abu 'Anja, strictly interpreting the Mahdist creed, rejected any compromise short of complete surrender and belief in the movement. In the wars which followed Abu 'Anja carried his troops well into the Ethiopian territory and was eminently successful. The Emperor had to react to this danger by mobilizing all his forces and to launch a counter-attack led by him in person. But Abu 'Anja died and in him the Khalifah lost his ablest general.

Ahmad'Ali, a relative of the Khalifah, and who was deputy to Abu 'Anja, was appointed acting area commandant, but it seems that jealousies among the leaders there sprang up to the surface in a manner that might ultimately lead to chaos. al-Nur 'Anqara, one of the high-ranking officers there, wrote to Omdurman giving warning that there was danger of a split in the army owing to these jealousies. 'Abdullahi resorted to the appointment of commissions in such circumstances, and one was duly sent to the Eastern Frontier under his chief justice (the Kadi of Islam), Ahmad 'Ali.[1] Their terms of reference were not clear in the correspondence, but the Khalifah wrote to Ahmad 'Ali the acting commandant to accept the decision of the commission with grace if it was not in his favor. Shortly after the arrival it was announced that Zaki Tamal was to succeed Abu 'Anja. It was the same man who was first unfavorably reported to the Khalifah by Ahmad 'Ali immediately after the death of Abu

[1] Not to be confused with the other Ahmad 'Ali who was the acting commandant.

'Anja. Now he was the leader and Ahmad 'Ali was to be his subordinate. Although the latter had repeatedly shown in writing that he would co-operate with Zaki, the jealousy between the two had never died out as we shall presently see.

It was for Zaki to meet that big offensive launched against the Mahdiyah forces and carried into Sudanese territory led by Emperor John in person. The battle that ensued was one of the fiercest in which the Sudanese were outnumbered by the Ethiopians. But the death of the Emperor in the battlefield turned the scales to the side of the Mahdiyah and ended in the victory of the Sudanese. Among the spoils of war which were carried to Omdurman was the golden crown of John. Zaki was entrusted with missions which took him many months away from his command in the East. His rival, Ahmad 'Ali, resumed his intrigues against him. Both Zaki and Ahmad were recalled to Omdurman for consultation and investigation. In the end Ahmad 'Ali succeeded in making both the Khalifah and his brother Ya'qub believe in the allegations of the ambition and even unsound mind of Zaki which ultimately ended in his execution. It is stated by some authorities that the Khalifah repented his sentence against Zaki. This example of jealousies among the leaders in the outlying provinces was one of the chief problems of the Khalifah's administration. In certain cases it meant lack of co-operation not only between two persons, but also between groups or tribes, and that is why he had to handle such situations very carefully, usually by such neutral commissions of enquiry composed of wise and respected men.

On the Egyptian front things were not progressing satisfactorily. The authorities in Barbar, who were to send fighters from the Ja'alin territory, were encountering difficulties because the majority of the people did not have their heart in the matter and were reluctant to part with their homes and families, although they were allowed to take wives and children with them. In Dongola itself there was complete lack of co-operation between al-Nujumi and his deputy Masa'ad Qaidum, a relative of the Khalifah. This faction had behind it the rivalry between the Riverian group and the Western group and the bone of contention seemed to be the treasury and who had to control it. Things did not improve even after the recall to Omdurman of both Nujumi and Masa'ad. The matter was partly solved by the appointment of Yunis al-Dikaim over all. Subsequently after this Nujumi led his ill-fated expedition into Egypt and died in the battlefield. Jealousies and lack of co-operation started afresh in Dongola, strangely enough, this time, between Yunis and Masa'ad, which reached such proportions that the Khalifah had to resort to his usual wise practice of the Commission. Muhammad Khalid, the ex-Governor of Darfur, succeeded Yunis for some months, but accusations were very soon reported to Omdurman against him that he was in contact with the Egyptians.

Kasalah and Sawakin were considered at first separate administrative units. But very soon it was recognized that Sawakin area with its large number of fighters sitting at the gates of that town which was in enemy hands could not be supported by the revenue of that desert area. The army there had to be provisioned from the nearest area which could supply grain and it was Kasalah. For this reason and because of the tribal movements in both territories it was decided to amalgamate the two into one administrative province. 'Uthman Diqna the celebrated warrior was in command on the Sawakin front and Muhammad 'Uthman Abu Qarja was in Kasalah. The troops of Diqna complained against his administration of the treasury, however much they liked his command in the field. Taking all these factors into consideration, the Khalifah distributed power between the two, giving Abu Qarja control of the treasury and the day-to-day administration, leaving to Diqna the military command. This did not work either because of the differences between the two leaders or their followers, who were Bija tribesmen in the case of the latter and mainly Danaqla in the case of the former. This was a clear case for sending a Commission to investigate on the spot and recommend a workable system. The Commission under Muhammad Khalid found Diqna willing even to be relieved of his command and to be reduced to an ordinary soldier, while they encountered some difficulties with Abu Qarja. These jealousies and differences between the two men were ended only after the removal of Abu Qarja who fell into disfavor and was ultimately deported to Bahr al-Jabal in the southern Sudan. Musa'ad Gaidum was again instrumental in putting the loyalty of Abu Qarja under a cloud when he was appointed to Kasalah.

al-Jazirah, the granary of the Sudan in the staple food of grain, was used as provisioning stores for the army stationed at Omdurman. All taxes collected in kind were floated on Nile boats down to the

capital, under the able and efficient administration of Ahmad al-
Sunni. This brings us to the policy of the Khalifah aimed at the
mass migration of all the western tribes known as Baqqara (cattle-
owners) from their abodes in Kurdufan and Darfur. It is maintained
by some that he initiated the policy only when his conflict with the
Ashraf was open. This might have accelerated the process but documentary evidence establishes beyond any doubt that as far back
as the days of al-Ubayyid 'Abdullahi entered into correspondence
with Muhammad Khalid, then governor of Darfur, with a view to
persuading and encouraging those Baqqara tribesmen to come over
to the Mahdi and honor themselves by joining his cause. Many of
them, however, showed great reluctance to leave their homesteads
and some even attempted desertion from Omdurman later on under
the Khalifah. The detrimental effect of all this on the economic life
of the country could not be exaggerated. Animal owners and breeders
were concentrated either in the capital or on the frontiers as standing army, and peasants in Kurdufan and the northern provinces
were to leave their homes as producers of grain and join the fighting
forces. It was not surprising, therefore, that there was a famine in
the fourth year of his reign when there was an exceptionally low
rainfall. It was estimated that the people who died as the result of
that famine exceeded those who died in the wars of the Mahdyia.

  I tried in the preceding pages to mention some of the problems
with which the Khalifah was confronted when he was left alone in
control of a popular religious movement spreading over vast territories. Although he was put in a very advantageous position at the
start by gaining experience and actually in authority during the lifetime of al-Mahdi, yet the premature death of the leader left
'Abdullahi laboring under enormous disadvantages and disabilities.
The movement was a religious one taking its inspiration from the
personality and achievements of al-Mahdi. People were promised
more successes and conquests outside the Sudan and the teachings
of al-Mahdi aimed at the denunciation of this world and leading
a simple and puritan life. His successor must maintain this standard
of puritanism and fulfill the promises of conquests. He could not
relax the discipline nor could he confine himself within the boundaries of the Sudan.

  In trying to prove a worthy successor to his Imam and keep the
torch of the Mahdiya burning, he, however, lacked the religiously

inspiring personality of al-Mahdi. The factions and differences between the Westerners and the Nile people which were temporarily sunk under the fascinating personality of al-Mahdi had to come up to the surface after his death. The Ashraf, relatives of al-Mahdi, under the leadership of Khalifah Sharif, resented the concentration of power in the hands of 'Abdullahi and the misunderstanding had reached such proportions as to amount to actual disobedience and defiance of 'Abdullahi's authority. Seeing that promises of more glorious conquests were not fulfilled, and particularly after the disaster to al-Nujumi's attempt to invade Egypt, religious fanaticism among many lost its glamor. The austere life imposed on the people, which was in accordance with the extreme puritanism of Islam as interpreted by al-Mahdi, was too much for such people, who were either unbelievers in the movement from the start, or lost their belief after the death of al-Mahdi. It is to be noted that for the first time in the history of the Sudan a purely Sudanese government established such a centralized administration in all this vast territory. We have already seen how jealousies among his own governors and people in command were sources of frequent worries for him and in consequence detrimental to good and efficient government. With all the above disadvantages and disabilities he managed to give the country a fairly good administration which was only ended by an outside power with which his military machine could not cope, as we shall see in the next chapters.

XIII

GUARDING THE NILE VALLEY AGAINST ITALY

The immediate concern of the British Government after abandoning the Sudan was how to defend Egypt proper from any possibility of Mahdist aggression. They were, however, somewhat relieved on hearing of the death of al-Mahdi, but no idea of the reconquest of the Sudan was entertained at the time, however weak the Khalifah's power might be. The question was whether to allow trade connections to be resumed. Business concerns that used to trade with the Sudan petitioned the Egyptian Government as early as July 1886 requesting the opening up of trade with the country. They were told by Baring that the question had been under consideration by both the Egyptian and the British governments and that they (the merchants) should convey to the Sudanese the fact that trade would depend on how peaceful they would be.[1] As any connection with the Sudan was inevitably governed by military considerations Baring sent a memorandum by Sir Frederick Stephenson on the subject to the British Government. Stephenson suggested that Wadi Halfa, Kurusko, Aswan, and some oases should be made the only stations for the levying of dues and for preventing the export of contraband which included all war material.[2]

The desirability or otherwise of imposing a duty on goods arriving from the Sudan by the Nile valley was carefully considered. Although the Egyptian Government ceased to exercise any authority over the Sudan except for some parts of the Red Sea coast, yet Baring thought that from a technical point of view 'the Province still forms part of the Ottoman dominions.'[3] The foreign exporter at Alexandria would contend that he had a right to receive back any duty levied at Wadi Halfa or Kurusko save the 1 per cent, which was allowed by treaty. 'Under these circumstances

[1] Baring to Rosebery, No. 313, July 10, 1886, P.R.O., F.O. 78/3928.
[2] Stephenson's memorandum, enclosed in Baring to Earl of Iddesleigh, No. 20, Jan. 9, 1887, P.R.O., F.O. 78/4039.
[3] Baring to Secretary of State for Foreign Affairs, No. 68, Jan. 27, 1887, P.R.O., F.O. 78/4039.

344

and having regard also to the desirability of encouraging trade and the difficulty of stopping smuggling it has been thought wiser on the whole not to levy any duty.' [1] Fear of protest from Turkey also confirmed Baring in his decision not to levy any duty on goods coming from the Sudan. On the mere rumor that a duty of 8 per cent, was about to be levied on Sudanese goods Mukhtar Pasha at once made representations on the subject, but found out that the rumor was untrue. 'Though the Sudan Provinces are not *de facto* they still are *de jure* a portion of the Egyptian dominions.' [2]

When the Conservative Government under Salisbury came to power in 1885 they thought that the Egyptian question might well be solved by co-operation with Turkey. With this in view they sent Sir Henry Wolff to Constantinople. A convention was signed there on October 24, 1885 between the Porte and Her Majesty's Government by which two commissioners, one British and the other Turkish, were sent to Cairo. What concerns us here is the proposal concerning the Sudan. In Article II of the convention it was provided that the Ottoman Commissioner was to discuss with the Khedive 'upon the best means of tranquilizing the Sudan by pacific measures.' [3] This was probably based on the Turkish idea that the Muslims in the Sudan would not reject the suzerainty of the Khalifah at Constantinople. It was thought desirable that the religious aspect should be left to the two Muslim countries to settle by negotiation with the Mahdiya. Yusuf Shuhdi Pasha was sent to the frontier at Wadi Halfa in order to try direct negotiations with the Mahdists. To knowledgeable people this was doomed to failure, as al-Mahdi and his successor openly denounced the leadership of the Constantinople Khalifah. Their views about both Egypt and Turkey were that religion there was corrupt and al-Mahdi's mission was originally a movement for the purification of religion in all Muslim countries. Anyway, it was an attempt to come to terms with the Sudan, but it ended in failure.

On the Sawakin frontier Colonel Kitchener, who was a governor there, favored very strict conditions controlling the opening up of trade with the interior. Baring was, however, against such

---

[1] Baring to Secretary of State for Foreign Affairs, No. 68, Jan. 27, 1887, P.R.O., F.O. 78/4039.
[2] Baring to Salisbury, No. 100, Feb. 10, 1887, P.R.O., F.O. 78/4040.
[3] Cromer, the Earl of, *Modern Egypt,* vol. ii, p. 61.

restrictions and thought that the less interference by the Government in trade, the better. The only thing to be guarded against was the traffic arms.[1] In a private letter to Baring when on leave Kitchener thought that the opening up of trade without stringent restrictions would alienate the friendly Arabs who had given up Mahdiism and who were prepared to help the Government in the surrender of Tūkar. Baring was not convinced by Kitchener's arguments, but was willing to let Kitchener pursue this policy for a little while until his own return from leave. If there was no change in the situation at Sawakin and if Kitchener persisted in his opposition, it would be desirable to send someone else in his place.[2]

On his return from leave Baring took up the question of trade between Sawakin and the interior, and secured the British Government's approval. Then Baring sent the following telegram to Kitchener at Sawakin: 'It has been decided to abandon completely the policy of delaying the opening of trade until Tūkar submits. Draw up at once and send to me a plan for opening trade fully with only such restrictions as are necessary for Custom House purposes etc. to prevent the importation of arms and ammunition.'[3] Kitchener yielded and remained at Sawakin to execute the above order.

An attempt was being made by a British company to secure a monopoly of trade with the eastern Sudan based on Sawakin along the lines of the East India Company. British officials on the spot, like Baring and Kitchener, pointed out the obstacles in front of the company, but the real opposition was forthcoming from Riyaz Pasha, the Egyptian Premier. Riyaz emphasized that the Mahdist movement was essentially religious. He believed that no influence other than religious could be exercised on the Sudanese at that time. The British company would not meet with the smallest success and nobody could aspire to exert any influence unless he was of great weight in the Muhammadan religious world.[4] The project was finally abandoned chiefly because of the strong objection of Riyaz and also on account of the failure of actual attempts

[1] Baring to Salisbury, No. 100, Feb. 10, 1887, P.R.O., F.O. 78/4040.
[2] Private letter from Kitchener to Baring and the latter's comments on it, May 28, 1887, P.R.O., F.O. 78/4046.
[3] Baring to Kitchener, enclosed in Baring to Salisbury, No. 470, Oct. 9, 1887, P.R.O., F.O. 78/4048.
[4] Baring to Salisbury, No. 380, Dec. 8, 1888, P.R.O., F.O. 78/4149.

made by Mr. Fox, the representative of the company at Sawakin. It was also proved beyond any doubt that any agreement or compromise with the Khalifah was impossible, after he had sent letters to Queen Victoria, the Sultan, and the Khedive calling on them to follow the teachings of Mahdiism.

Although the British policy of evacuating Dongola in 1885 was final, and the international situation did not call for any revision of it, yet as early as 1886 and 1887 the idea of restoring the lost provinces was the subject of discussion or of requests by some of the Sudanese themselves. A petition presented by a brother of Alyas Pasha um Barir, with notables and some tribal shaikhs in Kurdufan as signatories, asked in a beseeching tone for the help of the Egyptian Government in the restoration of the old régime.[1] Salih Bey, of the Kababish tribe, in a letter to Jawdat Bey, ex-sub-Mudir of Dongola, wondered at the dilatoriness of the Government and he asserted that all the tribes were awaiting the coming up of the Government.[2]

Even the English press in 1888 made frequent allusions to the desirability of undertaking the reconquest of Dongola. Riyaz Pasha was known to be inclined in this direction. In a letter to *The Times* Sir Samuel Baker advocated operations in the Sudan of an extended nature. Baring had noted all these tendencies, but he was not approached in any way by either the Khedive or Riyaz Pasha. The latter advocated an advance on Dongola, but he recognized the impossibility of assuming the offensive at that time. The military authorities were of opinion that it would be useless to regain Dongola unless an advance were made on Barbar and probably to Khartum. Baring himself was doubtful of a secure frontier even with the capture of Khartum. 'Plausible and even valid reasons would not be wanting to show the desirability of an extension of territory towards Sennar on the one hand and Kurdufan on the other.'[3]

The difficulties confronting the Egyptian Government, in Baring's opinion, were those which were inevitable in the case of a civilized government living in 'close proximity to a number of

---

[1] Translation of an Arabic petition, enclosed in Baring to Salisbury, No. 82, Feb. 4, 1887, P.R.O., F.O. 78/4040.
[2] Salih to Jawdat, enclosed in Baring to Salisbury, No. 184, Mar. 27, 1887, P.R.O., 78/4042.
[3] Baring to Salisbury, No. 318, Oct. 9, 1888, P.R.O., F.O. 78/4147.

barbarous tribes as neighbor.' These problems were similar in nature to those experienced by the British Government in India and the Russian Government in central Asia. In such a case Baring maintained that it could not be said with any degree of certainty that the possession of any spot would secure tranquility of the frontier. It might have the effect of shifting the difficulties a stage farther from the center. It was only natural, in Baring's opinion, that people like Sir Samuel Baker, who were responsible for the extensions of the Khedive's dominion in central Africa would feel grievously disappointed at the collapse of their policy. But Baring maintained that 'the task undertaken by the late Khedive was far beyond the military strength and administrative capacity of the Egyptian Government. It was hardly possible that it could have been carried to a successful issue. Sooner or later the whole fabric must have inevitably been overthrown at the hands of the Mahdi or of some such leader.' [1]

To Baring there were only two alternatives; either to remain on the defensive at Wadi Halfa and Sawakin or to undertake operations which might ultimately lead to the reconquest of the whole or the greater part of the Sudan. This latter course would unavoidably involve military operations on a large scale and would seriously embarrass Egyptian finances. Even after the conquest there would arise difficulties in the exercising of an effective European control over the conquered territories. 'There is but little guarantee that the Egyptian Government of the Sudan would be more successful in the future than it was in the past.' Baring concluded by emphasizing a defensive policy, with which the officer commanding in Egypt agreed, and abandoned altogether any idea of offensive operations. The British Government approved of Baring's policy.[2]

The attempts of the British company to secure a concession in the eastern Sudan were interpreted by the Porte to mean handing over Sawakin to that company. Consequently the Grand Vizier wrote to the Khedive informing him of the decision of the Sublime Porte to take over the administration of Sawakin and asked the Khedive to indicate the means by which the change-over could be carried out.[3] The Foreign Office replied that as long as the

[1] Ibid.
[2] Salisbury to Baring, No. 211, Oct. 30, 1888, P.R.O., F.O. 78/4141.
[3] French translation of a letter from the Grand Vizier to the Khedive, enclosed in Baring to Salisbury, No. 383, Secret, Dec. 14, 1888, P.R.O., F.O. 78/4149.

Egyptian Government retained Sawakin the British authorities practically commanded there and could be answerable for the defense of the place. Turkey herself was considered by the British Government to be so weak that no reliance could be placed on her to hold Sawakin. It was likely that the Mahdiya would gain possession of the place if it were evacuated by the British and Egyptian and occupied by Turkish troops. Baring was instructed to let the Khedive reply that there was no ground for the suspicion that Sawakin and the adjacent territory were likely to be handed over to an English company, and that both Her Majesty's Government and the Egyptian Government had 'incurred a responsibility in respect of the defense of Sawakin which they do not feel justified under present circumstances in renouncing.' [1]

Towards the close of 1888 a suggestion was initiated by the military authorities in Cairo for entering into negotiations with the Dervishes in the eastern Sudan. The British Government showed no objection in principle to such a course but first wanted to know what was to be offered to the Dervishes and what arrangement they would be asked to agree to. Her Majesty's Government, however, retained their objection to any military advance into the interior from Sawakin.[2] Baring saw a great difficulty in negotiating with the tribes because there was nothing to offer them. Again in the question of operations on the Sawakin front the British press advocated activity, but Baring maintained a defensive policy and considered that all they could do was to attempt to form a coalition of tribesmen against the Dervishes. The evidence that he had at that time was that the tribes disliked the Dervishes very much more than the Egyptian rule.[3]

High hopes were pinned to the rising of Abu Jummaiza in Darfur against Khalifah 'Abdullahi. The leader of the revolt was believed to be an emissary of Sanusi of Cyrenaica. According to Major Wingate's reports, the Khalifah was in such fear of this movement that he was contemplating flight from Omdurman and it was even reported that he had already left. Wingate could not establish connection between the rising and Sanusi, but he had no doubt that Sanusi was morally responsible for the movement, which was being carried out entirely in his name. Wingate ventured

[1] Salisbury to Baring, No. 251, Dec. 25, 1888, P.R.O., F.O. 78/4141.
[2] Salisbury to Baring, No. 250, Dec. 24, 1888, P.R.O., F.O. 78/4141.
[3] Baring to Salisbury, No. 33, Jan. 15, 1889, P.R.O., F.O. 78/4234.

to recommend that an overture on the part of the Egyptian Government to Sanusi should be made as soon as Abu Jummaiza should have succeeded in ousting the Khalifah's régime.[1] Consulting Muhammadan authorities Baring thought that any Government established under the influence of Sanusi in the Sudan would be superior to the Mahdiya. It was highly probable that Sanusi's Government in the Sudan would be friendly to Egypt, if left alone and not attacked.[2] These high hopes, however, did not persist for long. Colonel Schaeffer, the head of the Slavery Department in Egypt, who seemed to have more trustworthy sources of information, maintained that the movement was a purely local rebellion against the Dervishes. In Schaeffer's opinion there was nothing which pointed to a religious crusade against the Mahdiya by the followers of Sanusi.[3] A month later Baring reported in the following terms: 'I may, however, say that the information I have received from several quarters goes to show that the importance of Sanusi movement has been a good deal exaggerated.' [4] Abu Jummaiza was actually defeated by the Khalifah's general and he himself died of smallpox.

In July 1889 attention was switched once more to the eastern Sudan. There was a general drought throughout the country in the neighborhood of Sawakin, causing great mortality among the flocks and herds upon which the inhabitants depended for their living.[5] Colonel Holled Smith, the military governor of Sawakin, in agreement with the Sirdar of the Egyptian army advocated subsidizing the Arabs with a view to their assisting in driving away the Dervishes from the environs of Sawakin and ultimately in retaking Tūkar. Mr. Barnham, the British Consul at Sawakin, however, was opposed to this policy. He maintained that tribal jealousies were too great to admit of any combination of the Arabs which would be sufficiently powerful to overthrow 'Uthman Diqna unaided. The friendly Arabs, in Barham's opinion, would be only too glad to see the last of 'Uthman, but they would ask for protec-

---

[1] Major Wingate's report, enclosed in Baring to Salisbury, No. 179, Secret, Apr. 9, 1889, P.R.O., F.O. 78/4239.
[2] Baring to Salisbury, No. 179, Secret, Apr. 9, 1889, P.R.O., F.O. 78/4239.
[3] Baring to Salisbury, No. 184, Apr. 13, 1889, P.R.O., F.O. 78/4239.
[4] Baring to Salisbury, No. 232, May 12, 1889, P.R.O., F.O. 78/4240.
[5] Colonel Holled Smith to Sir Francis Grenfell, enclosed in Baring to Salisbury, No. 238, May 28, 1889, P.R.O., F.O. 78/4240.

tion from others against him. 'The real feeling of the tribes is that they would gladly accept the protection of any one, who would fight their battles for them and leave them to trade in peace.'[1] He, therefore, considered any money given to the Arabs as simply squandered. It seemed that Barnham's opinion won the day as Holled Smith was instructed from Cairo not to incur any further expenditure, to give no more assistance in the way of food and arms to the tribes, and not to renew his promises to the shaikhs without authority from Cairo.[2]

In the same year (1889) in which high hopes were entertained, for a time, that Sanusi might cause the overthrow of the Mahdiya, Khalifah 'abdullahi sent his troops under Amir 'Abd al-Rahman al-Nujumi to invade Egypt. The idea of invasion of Egypt was a cardinal point in al-Mahdi's program, as his mission was for the Muslims and not for the Sudanese alone. It was alleged that al-Mahdi projected that invasion immediately after the fall of Khartum and intended to lead his army in person. But as certain garrisons like Sennar and Kasalah were still holding out, the project was delayed until the complete pacification of the Sudan. After the death of al-Mahdi the Khalifah required some time to consolidate his power before he would go on with al-Mahdi's program. Before the order to march on Egypt 'Abd al-Rahman al-Nujumi was appointed to the chief command of Dongola Province and with his headquarters at Dongola town, he was to make his preparations.

On the Egyptian side it became evident that some special measures were necessary to ensure the tranquillity of the southern frontiers. The Dervishes were displaying renewed activity and frontier tribes owing allegiance to the Egyptian Government were becoming very difficult to control. 'However the raids and frontier disturbances which take place from time to time have met with considerable sympathy, if not assistance, from the riverain population between Aswan and Wadi Halfa.'[3] Under these circumstances Sir Francis Grenfell, Sirdar of the Egyptian army, recommended the division of Esneh Province into two. The southern portion

[1] Barnham's report, enclosed in Clarke to Salisbury, No. 302, Confidential, July 17, 1889, P.R.O., F.O. 78/4241.
[2] Clarke to Salisbury, No. 340, Sept. 11, 1889, P.R.O., F.O. 78/4242.
[3] Baring to Salisbury, No. 128, Mar. 18, 1887, P.R.O., F.O. 78/4044.

from Aswan to Wadi Halfa would be placed under the command-
dant of the frontier at Wadi Halfa with a sub-Mudir at Aswan to
conduct the civil work. It was also thought necessary to reinforce
the frontier post. For this purpose a decision was made to send
more Egyptian and black battalions to Wadi Halfa.[1]

When it became clear that Nujumi had moved from Dongola
northwards the British officer commanding in Egypt thought that
the Egyptian force at Wadi Halfa under the command of Colonel
Wodehouse was in a difficult position. Not very much reliance
could be placed upon the fellaheen regiments which, at that time,
alone constituted the force. In his opinion, British support should
be ready in case of need, in view of which the officer commanding
suggested to the Secretary of State for War that the British force
in Egypt should be augmented by two British battalions.[2]

All the Egyptian army was concentrated at Wadi Halfa and
Aswan waiting to stop the advance of Nujumi, who received his
first check at Argin on the west bank of the Nile opposite Wadi
Halfa. In spite of heavy casualties Nujumi proceeded on his way
northwards. The intelligence of the Egyptian army told of the
terrible plight of the Dervishes. Numbers of them deserted and
there were many stragglers. The army was encumbered with a
large number of women and children. Nujumi himself in a letter
to the Khalifah described the shortage in food and ammunition
and the non-co-operation of the inhabitants through whose land
they passed. Notwithstanding all these difficulties and handicaps
Nujumi was determined to fight and fulfil his mission. In a reply
to General Grenfell's letter to surrender he said: 'I cannot stop
now; take my advice and surrender. Remember Hicks and Gordon
and what little good their armies availed them.'[3] At Tuski Nujumi
was met by Grenfell's forces and in spite of the valor and courage
with which the ansar fought, the issue was decided in favor of
the disciplined army and modern arms and equipment. The ansar
force was estimated to be 3,000 fighting men with large numbers
of camp followers.[4] The serious threat to Egypt from the Mahdiya

[1] Baring to Salisbury, No. 497, Oct. 27, 1887, P.R.O., F.O. 78/4048.
[2] Clarke to Salisbury, No. 287, July 10, 1889, P.R.O., F.O. 78/4241.
[3] Translation of a letter from Nujumi to Grenfell, enclosed in Clarke to
Salisbury, No. 304, July 20, 1889, P.R.O., F.O. 78/4241.
[4] Grenfell to General Officer Commanding in Egypt, enclosed in Clarke to
Salisbury, No. 331, Aug. 26, 1889, P.R.O. F.O. 78/4242.

was averted and the ability of the new Egyptian army was tested. Grenfell reported on the army under his command as follows:

In conclusion it is my pleasant duty to bring to your notice the excellent conduct of the Egyptian troops on the occasion of the action of Tuski. The conduct of the black troops has been tested on previous occasions but the conduct of the purely Egyptian troops who were brought into close contact, in line formation, with large number of Dervishes, was most satisfactory.[1]

After the repulse of Nujumi's invasion and the securing of the southern frontier Baring made a tour of inspection in upper Egypt. He spoke in high terms of the discipline and efficiency of the Egyptian army due to the British officers. The information he received about the Sudan was that the inhabitants were sick of Dervish rule and oppression.

But however unpopular the Dervish rule may be with certain classes, the most warlike tribes remain generally faithful to the Mahdist cause. These are notably the Ja'alin and the baggara. The former, however, are said to be wavering more specially since the death of Wad al-Nujumi. Some of their leading men recently made overtures to Colonel Wodehouse and the best authorities on frontier matters think that before long it may perhaps be possible to detach the Ja'alin from the Mahdist cause.[2]

Although the Dervish rule was unpopular and the defection of the Ja'alin possible, yet there was no prospect of the Mahdiya being overthrown by reason of internal dissensions.

In Baring's opinion any advance of Dongola save as a first step towards the reconquest of the Sudan was undesirable. It would only mean the exchange of a frontier which was already secure for one which certainly appeared to be relatively weak, the operation itself could not be undertaken by the Egyptian army at its strength at the time, and there were obvious reasons which would prevent Her Majesty's Government from employing British troops to assist in the undertaking. All in all, there was no good reason to move the frontier from Wadi Halfa to Dongola. Even if the conquest of Dongola with a view to the ultimate restoration of the Sudan were deemed necessary, the financial difficulties would be almost prohibitive. Such an undertaking, in Baring's view, would

---

[1] Grenfell to Clarke, enclosed in Clarke to Salisbury, No. 331, Aug. 26, 1889, P.R.O., F.O. 78/4242.

[2] Baring to Salisbury, No. 401, Dec. 11, 1889, P.R.O., F.O. 78/4243.

354   THE INDEPENDENT SUDAN

involve not only a very heavy temporary expenditure but also a large annual increase in the cost of the Egyptian army which would have to be strengthened. The Egyptian finances, which had at last been put on a tolerably sound footing, would be again disorganized and as a result 'a whole crop of local and international difficulties would spring up afresh.'[1] Baring again emphasized that the government of the Sudan, when conquered, would present difficulties. The employment of British officials would not be possible owing to climatic and other difficulties. On the other hand, 'I look in vain for any sufficiently numerous staff of trained Egyptian administrators to undertake the government of the country without the most serious risk of again relapsing into the misgovernment which was probably the main original cause of the Sudan rebellion.'[2] Baring finally strongly urged that on no account should the reconquest of the Sudan be contemplated.

In May 1889 the Treaty of Occiali was concluded between Italy and King Menelek, by which the Italians formed the impression that Abyssinia was put under their protection at least as regards foreign affairs. In November of the same year a copy of it was unofficially and secretly transmitted to the British Government.[3] With the consolidation of their position as regards Abyssinia, the Italians seemed to have embarked upon a program of expansion which would perhaps sooner or later disturb the *status quo* in the eastern Sudan.

By this time England was no longer in the comfortable position in which she had been when she was almost the workshop of the whole world. In addition to the goods which she used to export to the European countries she sent out industrial machinery and in this way she undoubtedly helped to equip other continental nations with the means of production. These nations took over not only their own home markets, but eventually entered into competition with Britain in the world markets. Both Germany and France temporarily settled their national problems and a good deal of energy was released for industrial activity. By the middle of the 80's Germany was already a first-class industrial country. Like the majority of the continental states, she had abandoned the doctrine of free

[1] Ibid.
[2] Ibid.
[3] Kimberly to Baring, No. 274, Secret, Nov. 11, 1889, P.R.O., F.O. 78/4234.

trade and adopted a policy of protecting her new industries. The competition was not restricted to the production of goods and to outside markets but extended to the employment of capital in the less developed areas.

This economic rivalry resulted in the French economic theorists declaring in favor of acquisition of colonies for future saftey and thus they dragged the Germans after them. There was a widely accepted idea on the Continent that Britain attained her greatness through acquisition of colonies. Jules Ferry stressed the necessity of colonies not only for new markets but for new fields of investment: 'Colonies are for rich countries one of the most lucrative methods of investing capital. . . . I say that France, which is glutted with capital and which has exported considerable quantities, has an interest in looking at this side of the colonial question. . . . It is the same question as that of outlets for our manufactures.' [1]

The Germans and the French, then, had to indulge in colonial expansion by taking over territories in Africa and Asia. The effect on Britain was that she had to keep what she already had and not be left behind in the race for colonies. The British, therefore, entered upon the policy of taking over large blocks of territory not for immediate development, but merely to prevent them from falling into the hands of competitors. The fact that stood out very clearly was that economic control was not possible without political control. Respect for the principle of free trade began to decline and it was quite clear that it would be foolish to continue with it while all the world turned protectionist. In spite of the new tendencies that ultimately made free trade unworkable, Gladstone and the older leaders of the Liberal party were still sticking to the teachings of Cobden. But among the younger members of the party there was realization of the new situation. Joseph Chamberlain broke away from the Liberal party in 1886 and with others formed the Unionist party which eventually joined the Conservatives in forming a government. He believed that England should try to extend her influence in Africa, that trade would follow the flag, and that empire was commerce—commerce without which the home country could not exist. Another representative of this

[1] Langer, Professor William L., *The Diplomacy of Imperialism 1890-1902* (New York and London, 1935), vol. i, p. 74.

new tendency among the Liberal leaders was Lord Rosebery, who did not break with his party, but remained to convert the greater part of it to a forward colonial policy. In a speech at Leeds in 1888 he declared: 'The other powers are beginning a career of colonial aggrandisement. We formerly did not have in our foreign affairs to trouble ourselves much with colonial questions, because we had a monopoly of colonies. That monopoly has ceased.'[1] In November 1889 Lord Salisbury, as Prime Minister, told his audience: 'Africa is the subject which occupies the Foreign Office more than any other.'[2]

This was the sort of atmosphere in which Baring sent a very important dispatch to Lord Salisbury explaining the situation in the Nile valley resulting from Italian activities in the eastern Sudan.[3] Before forwarding his dispatch he had collected reports and memoranda from the authorities at Sawakin. It seems that Lord Salisbury held, with reference to former Egyptian territory in the eastern Sudan, the view that it would be very difficult to keep other people out of savage territory which they were unable to occupy. Baring fully recognized the force of this observation, but he pointed out that the case of the Sudan was not quite analogous to that of other savage territories: 'de jure, although not de facto, the Sudan constitutes part of the Ottoman dominions. The Khedive pays tribute to the Porte on account of the Sudan.'[4] In Baring's view the Italians evidently wanted to obtain possession of Kasalah and if no arrangements were made as to the limits of the territory which was to be under their direct rule, it was more than probable that they would, after a short while, endeavor to extend westwards. This would inevitably lead them to the valley of the Nile, either at Khartum or at some point near Khartum.

Baring ventured to think that it was essential in Egyptian interests to avert any such calamity, for it was no exaggeration 'to say that the establishment of a civilized Power in the Nile Valley would be a calamity to Egypt.' The only danger that could be apprehended from the Mahdist Government was interference with the regular supply of the Nile, on which the whole well-being and agricultural

[1] Ibid.
[2] Cecil, Lady Gwendolen, *Life of Robert, Marquis of Salisbury* (London, 1932) vol. iv, p. 254.
[3] Baring to Salisbury, No. 405, Dec. 15, 1889, P.R.O., F.O. 78/4243.
[4] Ibid.

life of Egypt depended. But 'the savage tribes who now rule in the Sudan do not possess the resources or the engineering skill to do any real harm to Egypt. The case would be very different were a civilized European power established on the Nile Valley. Such a power would, as Col. Moncrieff very truly said "have Egypt in its grip." They would so reduce the water supply as to ruin the country.'

To Baring the question could not be easily dismissed as of mere local interest to the Egyptians and their Government: 'Whatever power holds the Upper Nile Valley must, by the mere force of its geographical situation, dominate Egypt.' This would mean that a British interest of great magnitude was involved in that question. 'I have never denied, nor do I now deny, that the abandonment of the Sudan was very much to be regretted, that the country naturally belongs to Egypt and that the Government which rules the Delta of the Nile should also hold the banks of the river, if not to its source, at all events for a long way up its course.' Baring thought that they were beginning to see daylight. There was a prospect that in the course of the next few years the Sudan might be brought back to Egypt, perhaps by peaceful means or at a very small expenditure of blood and money. Any attempt to take immediate action would, however, be altogether premature. He was of opinion that a stigma attached to the British in that the Sudan was lost to Egypt during their occupation. To remove it, the greater portion if not the whole of the Sudan should be brought back to Egyptian rule—'not indeed the Egyptian rule of former times—but to an improved Egyptian domination acting under English control and guidance.'

If the Italians were to be allowed to establish themselves in the Sudan, the probability of carrying out this program would be greatly diminished, and

it will go down to history that the English Government found Egypt extending from Alexandria to the sources of the Nile and left it shorn of half its territory and dominated by an European Power, which, though now friendly, may at some future time be hostile, occupying the headwaters of the river on which the whole life of the country depends. I confess I cannot look forward to the possibility of any such consummation without the greatest regret.

Baring observed that when the Italians first established them-

358 THE INDEPENDENT SUDAN

selves at Masawwa, they were aided by the friendly attitude of the English Government of the day. It was quite clear that Abyssinia would eventually fall under Italian domination and it was never contemplated that their ambition would drive them to extend seriously in the direction of the Sudan.

I cannot help thinking that looking at all the circumstances of the case, we have a very fair right to demand and even to insist that the Italians should look to Abyssinia as the legitimate field for their colonial enterprise and that they should do nothing which will seriously affect the broad lines of English policy in Egypt. . . . I submit that it would be paying too high a price, even for Italian friendship, to make any serious sacrifice on a point of this importance.

Even if the occupation of Kasalah were not a first move westwards there would be objections to it. The possession of Kasalah secures the domination of the Atbara, a very important affluent of the Nile. Also the presence of Italians in Kasalah would bring under their domination the Shukriyah and the Hadandawah tribes and this would lead to an establishment of a protectorate over their territory and could be notified by the Italians to Britain under the Congo act. The general conclusions of Baring were: 'that it is most desirable to come to an early settlement with the Italian Government as to its territorial limits; that the first essential basis of any such arrangement is to exclude the possibility of the Italians establishing themselves in the Nile Valley or at Kasalah.' Salisbury's reaction was that he was completely convinced by the arguments advanced for the inviolability of the valley of the Nile and its affluents, but he refused to be disturbed at the prospect of Italian competition on the coast of the Red Sea.[1]

In March 1890 Baring received reports from the British authorities at Sawakin that the Italians were active and that there was a possibility of an early advance on Kasalah by them. 'As regards the question of an Egyptian advance upon Tūkar the subject is one of great importance and has for some time engaged my most serious attention and I may perhaps at an early date have to address your Lordship in reference to this matter.'[2] Baring began even to think of the administration which he thought should

[1] Cecil, op. cit., vol. iv, p. 326.
[2] Baring to Salisbury, No. 85, Mar. 13, 1890, P.R.O., F.O. 78/4308.

be set up in the Sudan. He certainly deplored a purely Egyptian administration and the ideal arrangement, in his opinion, would be that 'the English officers of the Egyptian Army must be given the chief civil control over the newly acquired provinces. Under them a very small number of natives may be employed. This system has worked admirably in the frontier Provinces which extend from below Aswan to Wady Halfa.'[1] Of the two alternative routes for the reconquest of the Sudan Baring preferred the advance on Tūkar mainly because of the Italian activities there.

Although he was prepared to understand the argument for Kasalah, which commanded an affluent of the Nile, Lord Salisbury was not at all prepared to yield in the case of Tūkar. He could not understand the doctrine of the military authorities which advocated that the possession of the territory round Sawakin could protect the flank of Wadi Halfa, which was 300 miles off. 'Tūkar has nothing to do with the Nile Valley.'[2] In principle Salisbury showed his dislike of following military advice and feared that they would drag the Government into entanglements.

When once you have permitted a military advance the extent of that military advance scarcely remains within your discretion. It is always open to the military authorities to discover in the immediate vicinity of the area to which your orders confine them, some danger against which it is absolutely necessary to guard, some strategic position, whose invaluable qualities will repay ten times any risk or cost that its occupation may involve. You have no means of arguing against them. They are upon their own territory and can set down your opposition to civilian ignorance, and so step by step the imperious exactions of military necessity will lead you on into the desert.[3]

As far as he could see matters, Salisbury was of opinion that no military activities should be initiated on the Red Sea until it was decided to advance to Barbar and ultimately to Khartum. To him the object should be the establishment of authority in the Nile valley and then only as pure luxury to extend dominion to the Red Sea. 'But I confess I look with apprehension upon a reversal of the process, because I think it is only by a forced process of reasoning that the Eastern Sudan, draining into the Red Sea, is

[1] Baring to Salisbury, No. 87, Mar. 15, 1890, P.R.O., F.O. 78/4308.
[2] Salisbury to Baring, Mar. 28, 1890, Cecil, op. cit., p. 327.
[3] Ibid.

represented as essential to the safety of Egypt.'[1]

After the return of Sir Francis Grenfell, Sirdar of the Egyptian army, from a tour in upper Egypt, Baring discussed the Sudan question with him. It was clear to both Grenfell and Baring that no positive opinion could be given as regards the Dongola front without knowing the result of the reconnaissance which had to be undertaken. Grefell deprecated any sudden advance on Dongola because of the difficulty of obtaining supplies.

> After hearing all he has to say I have come to the conclusion that, in so far as Dongola is concerned, it would not at present be desirable to depart from a policy of expectation. As I have already explained, if action can be delayed for a while, the Egyptian Government will be better prepared than at present to meet the strain, and in all probability the task will be easier.[2]

But in the case of Tūkar Baring was still adamant. He and Grenfell had come to the conclusion that the occupation of Tūkar was desirable. Four days later Baring pressed for permission to allow the advance on Tūkar. 'Indeed if the Egyptian Government does not move, the Italians will probably be invited to do so.'[3] This appeal was rejected and the correspondence about Tūkar continued for a time privately between Baring and Salisbury.

In a private letter Baring thought that the Italians should be kept away from the walls of Sawakin and 'I am beginning to doubt whether anything short of action will stop them.'[4] He considered the Nile valley as the most important to guard, but he did not like to see the Italian soldiers running all over the eastern Sudan, bringing under their influence the tribes between Sawakin and Barbar. 'The Sawakin-Barbar route, rather than the Nile valley, must eventually be the commercial route for the Sudan.'[5] In his eagerness to avoid military operations Lord Salisbury thought of settling this boundary question peacefully with Italy. With Count Tornielli he drafted a demarcation of spheres of influence, with Tūkar on the Egyptian side. When the draft was sent to Cairo, it was criticized in a number of details. Salisbury's attention

---

[1] Ibid.
[2] Baring to Salisbury, No. 102, Confidential, Mar. 23, 1890, P.R.O., F.O. 78/4309.
[3] Baring to Salisbury, No. 109, Mar. 27, 1890, P.R.O., F.O. 78/4309.
[4] Baring to Salisbury, Private, Apr. 4, 1890, Cecil, op. cit., p. 328.
[5] Ibid.

was, however, distracted by other issues. The British chartered companies in Africa, proposals and counter-proposals with Lisbon and Cape Town, and the expected French jealousy—all were questions that required both his time and energy. With the objections to his proposed draft of demarcation with Italy emanating from Cairo and already preoccupied with issues of major importance elsewhere, Salisbury was convinced that it would be useless to attempt a settlement with Count Tornielli in London. At the same time to attempt a settlement between officials at Sawakin and Masawwa was equally doomed to failure. The only alternative open to Salisbury was to wait until Baring was on leave in England and allow him to conduct negotiations with the Italian legation in London.

In a private letter to Baring Salisbury raised a new question. He thought that it should be made clear whether a British or an Egyptian interest was involved. If it were to be proved beyond any doubt that it was a British one, the whole responsibility of decision would be vested in the British Government.[1] Baring did not allow this distinction to be made. He maintained that as there was no possibility of evacuating Egypt for a long time to come, he attached little importance to the distinction between British and Egyptian interests. Anyway, the proposal that Baring should be the negotiator on the British side was slightly modified. Instead of carrying out the talks in London with the Italian Ambassador, Baring was to pass through Rome when going back to Cairo from leave.

Salisbury instructed Baring to insist on the command of all the affluents of the Nile so far as Egypt formerly possessed them. As to the Red Sea, Salisbury did not clearly understand the British interest or that of her ward Egypt there although he did not counsel unlimited concessions. Baring was instructed also not to sanction the tribal theory, which advocated that the exercise of authority over a portion of a tribe would automatically put all the rest of it under the power ruling the portion. 'Actual right over the soil itself proved by the exercise upon it of the functions of a ruler is the only title we could accept.'[2] If it was not possible to persuade the Italians to keep their hands off the affluents of the Nile, it would be better to stop the negotiations and to send a note to the

[1] Salisbury to Baring, Apr. 25, 1890, Cecil, op. cit., p. 329.
[2] Salisbury to Baring, Aug. 31, 1890, ibid., p. 330.

Italians making it clear what British claims were. 'I do not think England will lose by delay. Italy is pursuing a policy which is financially impossible. Sooner or later she must recede from it and then she will not be so particular about frontiers. I dare say things will go on as they do now as long as Crispi is at the head of affairs. But he is 71.' [1] The meeting between Baring and Crispi took place at Naples and the views were so divergent that it was impossible to bridge them. Crispi did not accept the theory of the Egyptian claim to her former dominions in the Nile valley.

With the failure of negotiations with Italy and his return to Cairo, Baring began to receive reports from the Red Sea that made him return to the charge about Tūkar. He showed his unwillingness to return to a subject which was fully considered at the beginning of the year. But he found that a very strong opinion was persistent among both the British and the Egyptian military authorities as to the advisability of occupying Tūkar. Baring agreed with Grenfell that the occupation of Tūkar could be easily carried out without any increase in the strength of the army and at a very small cost. 'I would venture to ask your Lordship to reconsider the matter.' [2] Salisbury argued that operations on so small a scale would simply result in destructive attacks on the Arabs and held that they would serve no purpose if they were not part of large-scale operations for the reconquest of the Sudan. In the face of objections raised by his chief, Baring thought of defining the restricted objective of the Tūkar campaign. To him the taking of Tūkar would make things more comfortable at Sawakin, would assist in the fight against the Red Sea slave-trade, and would be the easiest of achievements.[3] After more exchanges of letters Salisbury gave in and sanctioned the advance on Tūkar which was duly occupied in February 1891. Although the military authorities gave it as their opinion that the advance would not meet with resistance yet in actual fact the Dervishes proved to be stronger than was estimated. In a letter to Salisbury, Baring made the following confession: 'If I had known how strong the Dervishes were, I should certainly have hesitated to recommend the advance.' [4]

In February 1891 Signor Crispi fell from power in Italy. He

---

[1] Ibid.
[2] Baring to Salisbury, No. 298, Nov. 7, 1890, P.R.O., F.O. 78/4309.
[3] Baring to Salisbury, Nov. 28, 1890, Cecil, op. cit., p. 333.
[4] Ibid., p. 334.

was defeated in the Chamber chiefly on his reckless and extravagant colonial policy. Di Rudini, his successor, showed a more
accommodating spirit. African negotiations between Italy and
Britain were brought to a successful conclusion. An agreement was
signed before the summer of 1891 and the cardinal point in it
was the recognition by Italy of the Egyptian claims in the Sudan
including Kasalah. On this understanding the British raised no
objection to the temporary occupation of Kasalah by the Italians
should their warfare with the common Dervish enemy require it.
The occupation of Tūkar and the recognition by Italy of the
Egyptian claims in the Sudan removed the element of uncertainty
from the Sudan question for the time being.

The Liberals formed a government in 1892 with Lord Rosebery
as a leading figure. His imperialistic tendency was already in
evidence as far back as 1887 and he had by this time succeeded in
converting his chief, Gladstone, to the idea of the permanent
occupation of Egypt. The first issue in the Egyptian problem
with which he had to contend was a protest by Tigrane Pasha, the
Egyptian Foreign Minister, to the acting British Consul-General
in Cairo about the activities of the British East Africa Company.
He took the opportunity, when in conversation respecting repatria-
tion of Egyptian refugees from the former Equatorial Province,
to reserve the territorial rights of Egypt over all these portions of
the Sudan up to and inclusive of Wadelai, which had been occupied
and administered by Egyptian authorities before the Mahdiya.
'There was the question whether a state could properly claim, to
the exclusion or detriment of others, the ownership of territories,
in which it could not enforce and had desisted from all attempt at
enforcing its authority.' [1] This argument advanced by Hardinge
was in clear contradiction to the one used by Baring for guarding
the Nile valley against Italian encroachment. Sir Thomas Sanderson, the Permanent Under-Secretary of State for Foreign Affairs,
approved Hardinge's language.[2]

In February 1894 the Italians suggested that there should be
close co-operation between the authorities at Sawakin and Masawwa
against 'Uthman Diqna and the Dervishes.[3] A week later the
Italians elaborated a concerted plan of action by which any attack

[1] Hardinge to Rosenbery, No. 138, Aug. 22, 1892, P.R.O., F.O. 78/4452.
[2] Sanderson to Hardinge, No. 135, Sept. 19, 1892, P.R.O., F.O. 78/4448.
[3] Rosebery to Clare Ford, No. 43, Feb. 14, 1894, P.R.O., F.O. 78/4986.

by the Dervishes would bring an automatic movement of forces to the same place by both parties in order to threaten the Dervishes. Lord Rosebery replied to Count Tornielli on this subject that the question was essentially of a military nature, and being a civilian he could offer no opinion but he would telegraph the plan to Lord Cromer.[1] The Italians were not content with the approaches that were made by their Ambassador in London, but they sent to Cairo Count Samminiatelli with the particular purpose of devising a plan by which there could be an intercommunication of news between the Italian military authorities at Masawwa and the Egyptian authorities at Sawakin and Cairo. Baring was of opinion that there would not be the least difficulty in meeting the wishes of the Italians on this point. In the course of conversation with Cromer, the Italian envoy remarked that the presence of the Dervishes at Kasalah was very embarrassing to the Italian Government and under the arrangement of April 15, 1891 Italy had the right to occupy Kasalah temporarily. Samminiatelli asked Cromer how this would be received by Britain. Cromer replied that it would not be welcome. In discussing with Major Wingate details of the proposed co-operation, the Italian envoy proposed that the Italian and Egyptian forces should act in concert and make a combined attack on Kasalah. The Egyptian troops would then remain to garrison the town and the Italians would retire. That would make possible the reduction of the Italian garrison in Eritrea. It seems that the Italians wanted a compromise between reduction of the military expenditure on their colony and the bad effect on the Italian public of evacuating all or part of it. They thought that a strong garrison of Egyptian troops in Kasalah would make this compromise possible. The military authorities in Cairo objected to the proposal and Cromer agreed with them. Cromer deprecated any measure that would lead to the opening of the Sudan question in any serious manner at that time. 'The Egyptian Government has neither the men nor the money to undertake such an operation as the reoccupation of Kasalah.'[2] It was possible, in Cromer's opinion, that the Italians might exercise the right of temporary occupation if their proposal of concerted action was rejected. 'But I trust they may be dissuaded from doing so. I cannot help

[1] Rosebery to Clare Ford, No. 45, Feb. 21, 1894, P.R.O., F.O. 78/4986.
[2] Cromer to Rosebery, No. 35, Feb. 25, 1894, P.R.O., F.O. 78/4986.

doubting whether any real military necessity for a forward movement exists. Moreover, my impression is that any such movement would be costly to the Italian Government, and possibly lead them into military operations of some magnitude.'[1]

Ten days later the Italian envoy again called on Cromer and told him that the Ras of Tigre had made an offer to the Italian authorities at Masawwa to co-operate with them against Kasalah. Samminiatelli strongly urged the desirability of an Egyptian occupation of Kasalah. He showed the difficulty of the Italian command there, whose hands might be forced by the military authorities at Masawwa and public opinion in Italy. 'I discouraged the idea but informed him that I would communicate his views to your Lordship.'[2] Lord Rosebery instructed the British Ambassador in Rome to discourage the plan if it were mentioned to him. 'Our military authorities are altogether opposed to the scheme which they consider would involve too great a strain on the military resources of Egypt.'[3] Towards the end of March the Italians were still making their inquiries about their proposal for concerted action to meet attacks by the Dervishes. The British Government was still opposed to any plan for an attack on Kasalah, but they asked Cromer whether there was not something to be said for co-operation for defensive purposes.[4] After consulting Colonel Kitchener Cromer replied that for various military reasons it would be impossible to arrange any concerted action for purely defensive purposes. 'All that can be done is that each side should keep the other fully informed of anything which may be learned as regards Dervish movements and intentions. But any action had better be independent.'[5] Kimberly conveyed to the Italian Ambassador the objections offered by Cromer and the suggestion of interchange of information about Dervish activities and intentions.[6]

Attention on the Sudan was directed from another quarter; this time from some of the Sudanese themselves. When 'Abdallah

[1] Ibid.
[2] Cromer to Rosebery, No. 35 (Tel.), Confidential, Mar. 7, 1894, P.R.O., F.O. 78/4986.
[3] Rosebery to Clare Ford, No. 5, Mar. 7, 1894, P.R.O., F.O. 78/4986.
[4] Kimberly to Cromer, No. 19, Mar. 29, 1894, P.R.O., F.O. 78/4986.
[5] Cromer to Kimberly, No. 43, Mar. 30, 1894, P.R.O., F.O. 78/4986.
[6] Kimberly to Count Tornielli, Apr. 11, 1894, P.R.O., F.O. 78/4986.

Wad Sa'ad had succeeded to the chieftainship of the powerful tribes of the Ja'alin in the Sudan, he immediately sent a relative of his to negotiate with Kitchener. 'Abdallah asked that there should be pardon for past offenses, that the chieftainship of the Ja'alin should remain in the hands of 'Abdallah and his family, that there should be remuneration for expenses incurred in hostilities with the Khalifah, and that when the Ja'alin besieged the baqqarah at Omdurman, troops should be sent to give moral support to the Ja'alin. Kitchener had no doubt that there was a very wide and growing feeling of discontent at the Khalifah's rule. 'Abdallah's relative hoped that after bringing about the overthrow of the Khalifa's forces, 'the tribes will demand British administrators and not natives, either Egyptian or Turks.'[1] It was impossible for Kitchener to say what importance should be given to this overture and what might be the result, but he thought 'the Ja'alin were once a very powerful tribe and are certainly very clever, unscrupulous and brave.'[2]

Cromer commented that the Egyptian Government had long been in possession of information as to the unpopularity of the rule of the Khalifah, whose authority at the time depended solely on the support of his formidable baqqarah tribes. His own views on the conquest of the Sudan were that no premature movement on the part of the Egyptian Government for the recovery of authority in the Sudan should be countenanced. 'At the same time the ultimate necessity of opening up communications with these regions and of re-establishing the reign of law and order in the Sudan is an object which Egypt cannot abandon.'[3] The rebels on the borders would constitute a menace and source of permanent inconvenience. 'While on the other hand the rapid development of affairs in central Africa and the zeal with which a forward movement is being organized in certain quarters into all those territories which are not yet placed under the control of a civilized Government make it the more desirable that the eventual re-establishment of Egyptian authority at Khartoum should not be too long postponed.'[4] Cromer thought that there was no risk in spending

---

[1] Memorandum by Kitchener, June 19, 1894, enclosed in Cromer to Kimberly, No. 91, Secret, June 20, 1894, P.R.O., F.O. 78/4575.
[2] Ibid.
[3] Cromer to Kimberly, No. 91, Secret, June 20, 1894, P.R.O., F.O. 78/4575.
[4] Ibid.

a certain amount of money for this purpose, but at the same time he recorded that he had little faith in the realization of the projects entertained by the Ja'alin. Nothing had come of similar projects before. The action taken by Cromer in authorizing expenditure was approved by the British Government.[1]

Losing hope of ever achieving concerted action with the Egyptian authorities at Sawakin, the Italians finally decided to take the risk by themselves and succeeded in occupying Kasalah. To allay any fears or misunderstanding with Britain the Italian Foreign Minister in a private letter to the British Ambassador at Rome stated that 'this military operation on the part of the Italian forces does not prejudice any territorial question. It preserves Masawwa and Sawakin from fresh attacks and for the moment places Italy in a position co-occupant with England of Egyptian territory in virtue of interests which are common to both countries.'[2] Britain was somewhat alarmed by the Italian occupation of Kasalah but wished her to give official and public assurance that she intended strictly to observe the engagements under the protocol of April 1891 about the eventual evacuation of Kasalah whenever Egypt should be in a position to resume possession. It was thought that this procedure would have a good effect in Egypt and Constantinople.[3] It was therefore clear that the danger to the Nile valley from the Italian quarter was averted by a protocol. Cromer was convinced that the Khalifah's rule in the Sudan was unpopular, but that the conquest was premature.

[1] Foreign Office to Rodd, No. 98, Secret, July 10, 1894, P.R.O., F.O. 78/4573.
[2] Clare Ford to Kimberly, No. 50, Confidential, July 20, 1894, P.R.O., F.O. 78/4986.
[3] Kimberly to Clare Ford, No. 48, July 23, 1894, P.R.O., F.O. 78/4986.

XIV

GUARDING THE NILE VALLEY
AGAINST FRANCE

Britain successfully guarded the Nile valley by concluding agreements with Italy and Germany concerning spheres of influence. Belgium was also given a territory on the upper Nile on lease only. But the one nation which did not recognize these agreements, and which was going to give trouble to Britain, was France. Ever since the British occupation of Egypt France had been diametrically opposed to any action that might lead to the consolidation of British authority in Egypt. After it was known that British diplomacy was directed towards keeping the Nile valley as a British sphere of influence, France started plans by which she might challenge British authority and embarrass her position in Egypt. The plan was to send an expedition from their possessions in Central Africa eastwards to Bahr al-Ghazal and ultimately to plant the French flag on the upper Nile.

The French were greatly encouraged and assisted in this respect by their countryman, M. Prompt, who was an engineer in the Egyptian Service. Prompt gave an address in January 1893 to the Egyptian Institute on certain problems of Nile hydrography. In this lecture he surveyed all the feasible Nile dams at the outlets of the lakes and at the confluence of the Sūbāt and the White Nile, which would increase the water supply to Egypt. With reservoirs behind them these dams would store large quantities of water for use during the summer. M. Prompt went on to speculate on the damage that might be done to Egyptian agriculture if these reservoirs were not properly used. If water in them were not let out in time the supply to Egypt would be halved. If they were thrown open suddenly there would be disaster to Egyptian civilization. These arguments confirmed the fears of Baring when he wrote his famous dispatch of December 1889 on Italian activities.

M. Prompt's ideas had a very disquieting effect on the British public. This was evidenced by a letter of Sir Samuel Baker to a friend in May 1893: 'If we settle at the headquarters of the Nile we

368

command Egypt, and a barrage at a narrow pass, where the Nile
cuts through a rocky defile only eighty yards in width below the
exit from the Albert Nyanza, would raise the level of the great
reservoir of the Nile by fifty feet and entirely control the water
supply of Egypt.' [1]

The French Government, under the initiative of M. Delcassé,
the Colonial Under-Secretary, were already thinking of a plan to
embarrass the British position in Egypt and it so happened that
M. Carnot, the President of the French Republic, was an old
school friend of M. Prompt. On May 5, 1893 the people concerned
with this plan were summoned to the Elysée Palace by the President: M. Delcassé under whose guidance the project was to be
implemented, M. Monteil, a French explorer, who was to head
the expedition, and M. Prompt, who was the expert to advise on
the strategic position on the upper Nile. It was agreed that an
expedition, which should plant the French flag at Fashoda, should
be fitted out. The occupation of Fashoda by a French force would
forestall any Belgian designs on the upper Nile and at the same
time would frighten the British in Egypt by the threat to the water
supply. Monteil was instructed to proceed at once. Starting from
upper Ubangi he would push on to the east with a considerable
force. His objective would be the occupation of Fashoda, which
commanded the main channel of the Nile and the two affluents of
Bahr al-Ghazal and the Sūbāt. Preparations were being made with
great energy and vigor. But an obstacle appeared suddenly from
an unexpected quarter. The Belgians, who were already busy
consolidating their position in those same regions that were to be
traversed by the French, threatened to use force to stop the
French expedition. The French then thought of trying to reach an
agreement with the Belgians by negotiation. The French Governor
in Ubangi counselled caution and the French Government were
inclined in that direction, because their relations with Italy were

[1] Langer, William, *The Diplomacy of Imperialism*, vol. i, p. 127.
It is the best book dealing with these colonial affairs in this period. For the
French official attitude and successive decisions my authority is M. Pierre
Renouvin in an article entitled 'Les Origines de l'expédition de Fachoda'
published in *Revue Historique* (Paris), issue of Oct.-Dec. 1948. It is the first
time that knowledge acquired from official documents has been summarized.
Unless otherwise indicated in this chapter these two sources between them
supply the material for my story.

already tense and naturally they did not wish to add more complications. Preparations for the advance on the Nile were therefore temporarily stopped. Monteil was sent on a mission to Berlin about Anglo-German arrangements in the Cameroons, which were considered to be prejudicial to French interests. The Germans seemed to be prepared to allow compensation to the French in other spheres. An agreement was signed on March 15, 1894 which gave France freedom to extend to the east as far as she could go. After his return from Berlin Monteil urged his Government to resume action.

He pointed out that British expansion from Uganda would ultimately lead to control by them of the upper Nile and would therefore frustrate the French plan. The only obstacle to the whole French scheme, Monteil argued, was the opposition of the Congo Government which could be settled by negotiation. In April 1894 French delegates went to Brussels to negotiate, but the negotiations were an utter failure. The Belgians insisted on the offers made to them by the French in 1892 which the French were no longer in a position to offer in 1894.

Losing hope of an agreement with the Belgians and strongly desirous of the expedition, the French resumed their plan of advance. This time the initiative came from M. François Deloncle, one of the active Colonialists in the French Chamber even before the return of Monteil from Berlin. Deloncle approached Chaillé Long, the American who had seen service in Egypt and Equatoria under Gordon, with a view to persuading him to head a mission from the Ubangi to the White Nile. Long held the opinion that the plan was absurd and reiterated a project which he had suggested to the French Government some years ago. It was Long's view that the Abyssinians should be induced to attack and defeat the Mahdiya Government in the Sudan, after which the Abyssinian Emperor would be proclaimed Sultan of the Sudan under the protection of France. It seemed that Deloncle was impressed with the idea, but when this scheme was discussed by the Prime Minister in a conference, it was observed that it was too daring and might possibly lead to conflict with Italy.

Guided by the writings of Captain Lugard the British Government, who had been hesitating about Uganda, proclaimed a protectorate over it as a step towards the security of the Nile valley against the French designs. Just at the time, when the Franco-German agreement became known, the British Government was disturbed by the rumors of a Belgian advance towards the Nile in the neighborhood of Wadelai. Colonei Colvile, Commissioner in Uganda, was directed to send out one of his subordinates to the Nile valley and to investigate the truth of the Belgian rumor. Captain Owen, who was sent by Colvile, did reach Wadelai, found it abandoned, planted the British flag, and as usual concluded treaties with the chiefs of the place.

But Britain thought that the Belgian threat should be averted by peaceful means. Towards the end of March 1894 Rennel Rodd was sent to Brussels. It was agreed that the Belgians should hold the left bank of the Nile from Lake Albert to Fashoda as lease-holders under Britain. Although the arrangement met with the opposition of the Little Englanders in the Liberal party, and although the attempts to modify it with King Leopold had failed, yet it was finally signed in May 1894. French indignation knew no bounds, as they themselves were, at the time, carrying out negotiations with Leopold. This episode took place at a time when the French were in one of their Cabinet crises. But the Colonialist group of the Chamber kept the embers of indignation glowing in the interval between the old and the new cabinets.

After the new French Government had had time to understand the problem an important debate took place in the French Chamber. M. Etienne, leader of the Colonial group, gave a historical survey of colonial affairs emphasizing the sharp practice of England in Africa. He was followed by M. Deloncle, who explained the British policy as aiming at the protection of the Nile basin ever since Prompt's revelations had become known. For fear of another power threatening the water-supply to Egypt, Britain had been more anxious than ever to get control of the Nile valley and hold Egypt at her mercy. M. Hanotaux, the Foreign Minister, speaking for the Government recalled the efforts of the French to reach an understanding with King Leopold. Then he entered into discussion of the rights of Turkey and Egypt, which had been included in the firman of investiture of the new Khedive in 1892 and which had received the approval of Europe. In his opinion Britain was giving away a territory to which she had no title. He concluded that France would not allow treaties to be torn up in that way. In their protest against this Anglo-Belgian agreement France was supported by Germany for reasons connected with a lease of territory by the Congo State to Britain, which was not far away from German East Africa.

The British response to this French protest was that France had no right to interfere. The Belgians, on their side also, maintained that Bahr al-Ghazal was not among the territories in dispute between them and the French. However, inside the British Cabinet there was divergence of opinion. Sir William Harcourt, who opposed the treaty from the start, objected to any measure that might give provocation to France. The Germans demanded the abrogation of the article that gave Belgian territory on lease to Britain. They exercised pressure on the Brussels Government until Leopold became frightened. The British Foreign Office allowed him to suppress the objectionable article, which was duly done on June 22, 1894. Rosebery thought that once the Germans were satisfied on this point they would gladly co-operate to oppose French activities. But as things turned out there was no divergence between Germany and France in African affairs, but rather a co-operation. On the other hand, the arrangement between Belgium and Britain on Bahr al-Ghazal put Belgium in an awkward position with France, who took the matter seriously. The Paris Government was determined to stop the Belgian advance at all costs.

It was decided to send out Monteil immediately to drive the Belgians out of the territory north of latitude 4° N. and to push on to the Nile. This plan had to be supplemented by an expedition pushing on from Abyssinia to bring supplies from the Sūbāt. Getting wind of this renewed French activity Britain gave a warning through their Ambassador, Lord Dufferin, who said to M. Hanotaux on June 29, 1894: 'If you make another Mizon mission in these parts, there will be a most serious conflict between the two countries.' [1] Notwithstanding this warning the French Chamber voted the necessary expenditure for the defense of French interests in Africa and Monteil was appointed Commissioner for the upper Ubangi.

On July 13, 1894 Monteil received new instructions from Delcassé, who at that time became Minister for the Colonies. These instructions counselled caution in relations with the Belgians and

---

[1] Renouvin, op. cit., p. 183.

also ordered Monteil to watch 'scrupulously that the forces placed under your orders should abstain from penetrating into the Nile Basin, so that the question of the Egyptian Sudan should remain entirely and completely reserved.' This stipulation was demanded by M. Hanotaux, the Foreign Minister, to avoid precipitation of a conflict with the British. The day previous to receiving his instructions from Delcassé, Monteil was received by Hanotaux who recorded the conversation in a note: 'He gave me a formal undertaking, which was in any case in accordance with his instructions, never to send troops or even one man to the Nile Basin.' This restricted objective of Monteil's mission seemed to aim only at bringing pressure to bear on the Congo Independent State for the purpose of success in negotiations. On July 16 Monteil left Marseilles and thus the French Government showed their determination to go on with her plan, while at the same time they thought that they could induce Leopold to yield to the French pressure. He was forced to sign an agreement with the French on August 14 which was a compromise. Leopold gave up the idea of occupying the Bahr al-Ghazal region, but the French raised no objection to allowing him the lease of a restricted territory on the Nile which was provided for by the Anglo-Congolese arrangement. The essence of the agreement was that the road to the Nile was left open to the French. As the negotiations reached such a satisfactory conclusion the French were not in a hurry and therefore sent counter orders to Monteil on August 22. It meant that the mission to reach Fashoda was abandoned for a time, because Hanotaux put a brake on the colonial group. It cannot be ascertained whether Hanotaux was guided in this policy by Lord Dufferin's warning, but it looks as if he thought it desirable to try an amicable arrangement with Britain.

Four months later the project of the march to the Nile reappeared, this time in the form of a mission to be led by Liotard. What circumstances aroused interest in the project? In the course of discussion between the British and the French concerning the Anglo-Belgian arrangements in Bahr al-Ghazal, Lord Dufferin alluded to the possibility of Franco-British discussions on all African questions. It was in September 1894 that these talks were initiated between Hanotaux and Sir Eric Phipps, the British chargé d'affaires in Paris. In a first talk they reviewed all points of conflict in Africa and then concentrated on the upper Nile question. Hanotaux declared that he was ready 'to recognize a British sphere of influence in the part that is not Egypt' provided that France should receive compensation. Phipps suggested that France should undertake for the time being not to engage in any project 'beyond the demarcation line of the Nile Basin and the Congo Basin.' At the same time England would promise not to undertake anything on the upper Nile north of Uganda. Hanotaux seemed to be disposed to accept this suggestion as it would be a 'mutual provisional abstention' which would make future negotiation possible. But it came up against opposition both in France and Britain.

The Director of Political Affairs at the Colonial Office in Paris notified Manotaux in this sense: 'The Colonial Ministry, upon reflection, would not adhere to overtures made by Mr. Phipps on the mutual stoppage of expansion on the Upper Nile.' Subsequently M. Delcassé, in two talks with Hanotaux, confirmed the point of view held by the Colonial Office. It was rumored at that time that a British mission under Colonel Colvile in Uganda was preparing to make for the middle Nile. It was believed by the French Colonial Office that M. Liotard, who had just been appointed High Commissioner in upper Ubangi, could arrive on the Nile before Colvile. The whole question, as it appeared to the French Colonial Office, was a race for the Nile, in which they were in a better position than the British and therefore they would be the losers in any arrangement for mutual abstention.

The British, on their side also, did not view this Phipps-Hanotaux proposal with favor. They were not yet aware of this French opposition. On October 20 the British Government sent orders to Phipps to interrupt the conversations until the return of Dufferin who was on leave. On his return to Paris Dufferin made it clear to the French Government that the British Cabinet did not accept the proposal of 'mutual provisional abstention' suggested by Phipps and he stated that the boundary of British influence in the Nile valley starting from Uganda extended to the north as far as Fashoda. Hanotaux, on his part, replied that the French Government would not, therefore, undertake not to extend the French sphere of influence 'beyond the Congo Basin.'

From that moment it was evident that the French would resume their projected advance towards the Nile. Hanotaux, who had previously put the brake on the Colonialists, would no longer resist them. A note by him bearing the remarks 'deliberated in council November 17, 1894' says:

The council decided, upon the observations of M. Delcassé and in accordance with the information which I supplied on the progress of the negotiations concerning the Upper Nile, that we could not but leave the negotiations concerning this region in abeyance, but that the Colonial Administration must take the necessary precautions, so that the occupation of the regions in question should be accomplished as far as possible before the Colvile Mission take possession. M. Delcassé said that M. Liotard, who left on October 25, thought he could reach the Nile in approximately a year.

In a letter to Delcassé dated December 5 Hanotaux repeated the contents of this note and wished to be kept informed of the progress of the Liotard mission. Thus a new mission under Liotard was set in motion. What were Liotard's new instructions? M. Renouvin states that he was unable to find the text of these instructions in the archives of the Colonial Ministry.

This French ministerial decision did not remain entirely secret. The British Government got wind of the French attitude by several indications. In January 1895 there appeared in the French press under the pen-name of 'Harry Alis' an article by M. Percher, a journalist, who was at the same time the secretary-general of a committee for French Africa. He stated that France should take up a position on the Nile so as to prevent further British encroachments. In February 1895 De Brazza, Governor of the French Congo, in an interview he gave at Algiers, stated that access to the upper Nile was the only way to settle the Egyptian question in accordance with French interests. The French agreement with the Congo state assured France access to the Nile valley. Later on in the same month during the debate on the Colonial Budget in the French Chamber, Deputy F. Deloncle, the mouthpiece of the colonial circles, revealed what he considered to be the aim of the occupation of upper Ubangi and the upper Nile. He maintained that the occupation of these unhealthy regions would not aim at permanent colonization. 'Today having opened for ourselves access to the Upper Nile, we are in a good position to take our rivals in the rear, thus providing our diplomacy with new elements for negotiation, which I consider to be indispensable within a short time, with a view to bringing about at last the much-promised evacuation of the Khedive's territories.' The French policy, therefore, as interpreted by Deloncle, aimed at bringing pressure to bear on Britain to carry out the evacuation of Egypt by occupying a strategic position on the upper Nile. In this way French policy returned to the first aim initiated by Delcassé and sponsored and encouraged by President Carnot.

On March 5, 1895 *The Times* sounded the alarm that 'there can be now no doubt that the advanced Colonial spirits of France will not rest until the tricolor is planted upon the Upper Nile, unless they are forestalled by enterprise from another direction.' The question was raised in the House of Commons on March 11. It was the opinion of the members that the whole Nile valley was in the British sphere of influence and that Britain would not tolerate any other occupation there. But the statement which raised a storm was made by Sir Edward Grey, the Parliamentary Under-Secretary of State for Foreign Affairs in reply to a question on March 28, 1895. He stated that the spheres of influence of both Egypt and Britain covered the whole of the Nile valley. As to the rumors of a French expedition with instructions to enter the Nile valley, Sir Edward maintained that they had no reason to suppose that these rumors ought to be given credence:

I will go further and say that, after all I have explained about the claims we consider we have under past agreements, and the claims which we consider Egypt may have in the Nile valley, and adding that the fact that our claims and the view of the Government with regard to them are fully and clearly known to the French Government—I cannot think it is possible that these rumors deserve credence, because the advance of a French Expedition under secret instructions right from the other side of Africa, into a territory over which our claims have been known for so long, would be not merely an inconsistent and unexpected act, but it must be perfectly well known to the French Government that it would be an unfriendly act, and would be so viewed by England.[1]

Baron de Courcel, the French Ambassador in London, described Grey's declaration as 'a haughty statement' in a dispatch to Hanotaux. In de Courcel's opinion a direct blow had been struck at France with the almost unanimous assent of Parliament. He

[1] *Hansard*, 4th ser., vol. 32 (1895), cols. 405-7.

thought that the British resorted to the raising of a diplomatic barrier because they were not in a position to occupy the Nile valley before the possible arrival of the French mission. In the view of the Ambassador Britain had seized upon the opportunity, when Russia was absorbed in Far Eastern affairs and France was engaged in the Madagascar campaign. The Ambassador's reply, as recorded in the French Archives, was immediate: 'You are provoking us,' said he to Lord Kimberly, 'just as if we were obliged to bear anything. Of course, if you are after us, we shall be there; but we do not wish you to be after us.' According to the French version of the conversation between de Courcel and Kimberly on April 1, 1895 the latter was reported to have said that Grey's statement did not amount to an effective taking of possession. It only expressed Britain's claim. The question of the upper Nile was still in abeyance. The sole aim of the British Cabinet had been to 'secure itself against the consequences of an occupation of disputed territories by a French expedition' while the discussion was going on. 'Tell M. Hanotaux to go by our actions rather than by our words, because the latter are always reparable.' Kimberly's tone was meant to be conciliatory. But de Courcel's opinion was that the British at bottom had not given up anything. 'We must, therefore,' wrote de Courcel to Hanotaux, 'not exaggerate the practical importance of the mitigation arising from Lord Kimberly's explanations. In truth, his carefully guarded language has not in any effective sense compromised the dominant position conquered for Britain by statements of Sir Edward Grey.' The most that France could be granted by Britain would be the partition of Bahr al-Ghazal to which Kimberly had made a discreet allusion; all in all, in de Courcel's opinion, there was no question of Britain's allowing France access to the Nile.

According to Kimberly's record of conversation de Courcel had no instructions from Hanotaux to speak on the subject; he had only heard from him privately. But he could not conceal from Kimberly the bad impression which would be created by this British statement, and feared that it would have a prejudicial effect on the relations between the two countries. De Courcel maintained that while the negotiation was still pending, the British declared that they could not admit the question of their rights in the territory which was the subject of discussion. Kimberly replied that from the British point of view it was exactly for this reason they had 'ground for complaint if, while the negotiation was still pending, a French expedition entered the territory, which was the subject of discussion. I hoped, however, that we should receive from the French Government an assurance that these rumors were unfounded.'[1] De Courcel said that there was no news about the expedition in those parts and he, therefore, did not see how it would be possible for the French Government to give assurances while 'they were in ignorance of the actual facts.' Kimberly told de Courcel that on their part the British had not advanced beyond Unyoro, where they were engaged in war with the natives for the protection of Uganda. 'I attached much more importance to action than to words, and I hoped that the French Government would be guided by the same principle.' De Courcel said that he could not but regard the declaration as amounting to a 'prise en possession' on the British part of the whole basin of the upper Nile. Kimberly replied that he could not see that the reiteration of a claim to a sphere of influence over the Nile basin, which they had already made fully known to the French Government, could be regarded as a 'prise en possession.' 'I would remind him also, that we had stated in explicit terms that we did not ignore the claims of Egypt, and had assured the French Government that, if Egypt should hereafter be able to reoccupy the territories in the Sudan formerly under her rule, we should recognize her right to their possession.'

Although the members of the British Government maintained their solidarity in public, yet Grey's declaration aroused a mild storm in the British Cabinet. Harcourt saw no excuse for the deliberate tirade. Lord Rosebery admitted that Grey's declaration was too strong to please some members of the Cabinet. The first reaction of Hanotaux to the declaration was that he did not take the threat seriously: 'I think there is a great deal of home politics in it . . . I know that it has to be taken with a pinch of salt.' He formed the impression, however, that the British Government meant to create confusion between the rights of Egypt in the Nile valley and those of Britain. Later on, when he learned about

---

[1] Temperly, Harold, and Penson, Lillian M., *Foundations of British Foreign Policy* (Cambridge, 1938), pp. 504-5.

the remarks of Kimberly, he saw in them a substantial mitigation of Grey's statement.

Assuming that Liotard's expedition might arrive at the upper Nile earlier than the British pushing down from Uganda and knowing the effect of this on the British, Hanotaux took the opportunity of making a suggestion that would be favorable to the French position

I would wish it to be well understood that, in the minds of the two Governments, the missions in the disputed territories, if they do not bear the character of military expeditions, are considered on both sides as not involving the policy of the two countries, and that they will have no effect other than clarifying the negotiations, while leaving the respective positions and the questions under debate intact.

It should be understood that Liotard, who was supposed to head or organize the mission was a civilian high commissioner. So his mission, in Hanotaux's interpretation, could not be considered a military one. Kimberly was not disposed to accept this suggestion without examination. Following his new line of policy Hanotaux made a speech in the Senate on April 5 whose tone was generally moderate. But he affirmed France's right to send missions into regions not owned by another European power. 'Between two great nations,' he said, 'there can be neither aggression, nor injunction.' In his opinion no one could claim to shackle the initiative of brave men who wished to go in search of new countries. It is clear from the above that Hanotaux meant to interpret Liotard's mission as an example of the 'initiative of brave men.' Then he added: 'when the time comes to decide the final destiny of these distant lands, I for one think that while securing respect for the rights of the Sultan and the Khedive, while reserving for each that which belongs to him according to his works, two great nations will be able to find the proper formulae to reconcile their interests.' The day after this speech Kimberly expressed the wish to resume negotiations but things remained on the diplomatic plane. In spite of the mitigation introduced by Kimberly, Baron de Courcel was still of opinion that the danger of conflict was imminent. He thought that Liotard's mission was on its way to the Nile and would very soon be there. With this understanding he told Kimberly on April 1 that the French Government could not reply that a French mission 'will not one day appear on the banks of the Nile, in spite of us and in spite of you, because it is beyond the reach of our directions.' The Ambassador then added: 'What would be our position on either side?'

Hanotaux's moderate tone and Kimberly's mitigation and wish to resume negotiations did not alter the situation caused by Grey's declaration. From this time both the British and the French were preparing to follow their own policies. On the British side the London Chamber of Commerce passed a resolution on April 10 emphasizing the need to 'assume control of the Nile valley from Uganda to Fashoda.' They thought that the situation called for immediate action on the construction of the Mombasa railway. Colonel Colvile, Commissioner in Uganda, was reported to hold the opinion that there were no obstacles in the way of the British advance in the Nile valley. England could take it if she wanted. It was only a matter of Government orders. This East African British railroad had its own history. It was recognized by Isma'il Pasha, acting on the advice of his representatives in the southern Sudan that the connection of the equatorial lakes with the outside world should be through a railway to the coast of East Africa rather than down the Nile. When England became interested in those regions and curbed the activities of Isma'il, they held the same view. The opposition of Sir William Harcourt to this project, however, led Rosebery to postpone the project for some time, but on May 27, 1895, moved by the French activities and meeting the wishes of the public represented by the London Chamber of Commerce, Rosebery was able to report to the Queen that the Government had decided on the immediate construction of the Uganda railway. Although the Liberal Cabinet resigned in June, yet Rosebery's successor, Lord Salisbury, who was known to be a warm protagonist of the project, secured 'parliamentary vote of £20,000' for it on August 20. Thus it was clear that British activity in the race for the upper Nile was based on Uganda.

But there was the other alternative of the advance from Egypt. In April 1895 in a private letter Rosebery put certain questions to Cromer: 'Was the Egyptian Government at all interested in, or disquieted by the threatened advance of France in the direction of the Upper Nile? Had the Egyptian Government shown any recent desire to move towards Dongola? Would it be difficult for the French to undertake an advance into Bahr al-Ghazal, and what would be the nature of their difficulties?' Cromer replied that the Egyptian ministers were a great deal disturbed by the advance of the French on the upper Nile. It was the topic of discussion in the native press. Military authorities in Cairo were of opinion that there would be no difficulty for the French in occupying Bahr al-Ghazal. Cromer was certain that the Egytians favored the reconquest of the Sudan and of Khartum in particular. The only reason why the Egyptian ministers were not outspoken in this matter was that they knew Cromer himself to be opposed to the idea. He, then, restated what he held persistently as regards the reconquest of the Sudan: 'I have always been so afraid of the soldiers and others getting the bit in their teeth and running away with one that I have persistently put forward the objections to the adoption of a forward policy. . . . The Sudan is worth a good deal to Egypt, but it is not worth bankruptcy and extremely oppressive taxation.' It was admitted by Cromer, however, that the presence of the French in the upper Nile would alter the situation and might prematurely force their hands. In the light of the new situation Cromer proceeded to discuss the whole Egyptian question in its international aspect:

In all Egyptian matters we have for the last twelve years been continually moving round in a circle and we always arrive at the same conclusion— namely, that we must either yield to the French and make the best terms we can with them, which, under the given conditions, must almost of necessity be very bad terms for us, or, if we take any decisive step on our own account, we risk a very serious quarrel with France.

It was, therefore, in Cromer's opinion, for the Government to choose between these two alternatives, weighing the advantages and disadvantages of each. But he wished to put his opinion resulting from his intimate knowledge of the Egyptian question at the disposal of his chief:

Eleven years ago I said that the ultimate solution of the Egyptian question would depend on the relative naval strength of England and France. At the time no one believed me. I hold to that opinion more strongly than ever now. The force of circumstances much more than the faults of any ministry or of any individual has driven us into a situation which renders war a not improbable solution of the whole mess. . . . I wish the works of Gibraltar were finished.

Cromer maintained the the policy of evacuating Egypt was not feasible, and practically impossible of execution. This would mean that the vital interests of Egypt should be guarded: 'It is obvious that if any civilized power holds the waters of the Upper Nile, it may in the end be in a position to exercise a predominating influence on the future of Egypt. I cannot, therefore, help thinking that it will not be possible or desirable to maintain a purely passive attitude much longer.' [1] He stated that if the British did not move backwards they would sooner or later move forwards. 'The only question, if this view be allowed to obtain, is, when and how we shall move forward?'

On the French side it turned out that Liotard was not on the point of reaching the Nile. He was marking time in upper Ubangi for lack of equipment and money. In May 1895 Monteil and some of his assistants appeared in Paris after carrying out the mission to which he was diverted on the Ivory Coast. Marchand was one of those assistants. It seemed that Marchand was particularly impressed with the project of reaching the Nile, which was revealed to him by his chief. He immediately indulged in extensive propaganda for the project and began to make official contacts.

On September 21, 1895 M. Chautemps, the Colonial Minister, wrote to his colleague the Foreign Minister saying that he had asked Captain Marchand to study the possible extension of the French influence 'particularly in the direction of the Nile' and to work out a plan for a mission. 'I have ordered Captain Marchand,' Chautemps wrote to Hanotaux, 'to explain to you personally the various features of this plan, and I shall be obliged to you, if you will see him for the purpose, and request you to let me know after the interview what you think of this question, which affects general policy even more than purely colonial interests.' Hanotaux, it will be recalled, had in November 1894 agreed to the plan of the Liotard mission, but since that date Grey's warning had intervened. What was his reaction this time? It is recorded that he saw Marchand. The only trace of this talk is an undated note in the hand of a cabinet attaché. In it Marchand proposed to reach the

[1] Temperly and Penson, loc. cit.

Congo-Nile watershed and enter Bahr al-Ghazal. How this conversation ended and what attitude Hanotaux held is not known. Anyway, the fall of the Ribot Cabinet which occurred on November 1 postponed the project. But Marchand himself stated in an interview given to the *Matin* that Hanotaux was ready to sanction the project. In the new Cabinet of Leon Bourgeois, the Colonial Minister was Quieysse, who was urged by his department to write to his colleague at the Quai d'Orsay about Marchand's project. It seemed that Marchand was asked to write a supplementary note dated November 10 which, according to the author's testimony, was the chief document.

In this note Marchand urged that they should devote all their efforts and all their resources to the extension of French influence towards the Nile, since their position had been consolidated by the Franco-Congolese convention of August 14, 1894 on the upper Ubangi. He was of opinion that this program would necessitate the intervention of the French Foreign Office, since it might at a given moment create an international political incident. It would not be logical to aim at the annexation of the Egyptian Sudan because France supported the rights of the Khedive against the British claim in the Nile valley. But the realization of the French project would have the effect of collective pledges to restore to Egypt the territories that formed the Egyptian Sudan. In this way Britain would be compelled to agree to a European conference where the question of the Nile valley would be discussed and decided on an international level. It was also to be hoped that 'the question of the evacuation of Egypt would quite naturally flow from that of the Egyptian Sudan.' To achieve this result it would be sufficient to send to the Nile a mission of a non-military character which would only plant the flag if it should meet a rival mission. 'No conflict could in any case and under any pretext arise from such meeting.' The leader of each mission would take note of the presence of the other and the whole matter would be dealt with between the respective governments. It was clear, therefore, that Marchand's project was meant to be only an instrument for ultimately bringing about the abandonment of Egypt by Great Britain.

On November 21st, during a sitting of the council of ministers, the Colonial Minister handed to his colleague Berthelot, the

Foreign Minister, a note requesting an immediate order for the Marchand mission. The following day the Colonial Office wrote to the Foreign Office requesting the letter for the mission as soon as the Foreign Minister was able to sign it. On November 30 the letter was signed by the Foreign Minister. It summarized Quieysse's opinion and Marchand's supplementary note of November 10. The object of this non-military mission was to try to reach the Nile. Its presence would put France in a position 'to intervene usefully in settling the question of the Egyptian Sudan.' Berthelot concluded: 'as far as I am concerned, I can only give complete adherence to the project in question.' However, this decision, which was termed urgent, was not actually carried out for about three months. The archives do not give any indication why it was delayed. But according to Marchand it was Quieysse, who held back the mission.

It was on February 24th, 1896 that the Colonial Minister finally drafted the instructions for Marchand and Liotard. Instructions to Liotard kept in the archives recalled the mission to upper Ubangi, which had been changed at the end of 1894 to secure 'access to the Egyptian Sudan,' and which had the same goal as the new project of Marchand. Although the two projects had the same goal, yet they envisaged different methods. Liotard had concluded alliances with the Sultan of Rafai and Zemio in the M'Bomu Zone and intended to rely on them in his advance on Bahr al-Ghazal, occupied at the time by the Mahdists. Marchand, on the contrary, wanted to spare the Mahdists. It was evident that the two projects should be brought in harmony in order to ensure unity of action. The Minister, therefore, decided to place Marchand under the direction of Liotard, whose task was to reconcile the two methods and decide the line of action. But it was the task of Marchand to advance towards the Nile valley. 'I must,' wrote the Minister to Liotard, 'call your special attention to the importance, which the Government attaches to the realization of M. Marchand's program, if not in its entirety, then at least in its main lines, and that it insists that the raid which he intended to attempt should be carried out.'

All the above describes the French and the British activities in their race towads the Nile, but there were also the Belgians. It will be recalled that Leopold was frustrated in his plans for penetration into the Sudan both by pressure from the French and by being deserted by the British. His policy was directed towards establishing contact with the French, who proved to be a force to reckon with. In September 1895 the Belgian King arrived in Paris in order to discuss colonial matters with the French Government, the new President, M. Felix Faure, being an old friend of his. It seemed that a course of common action was decided upon. On his return he began preparations for a large expedition with the object of reaching the Nile and occupying the Lado-Enclave, the only part of the British lease which the French recognized in their agreement with the Congo Free State of August 1894. This expedition was supposed to co-operate as closely as possible with Marchand's mission, which was to advance to the north of them.

At the same time Leopold tried to reach an understanding with Britain. He appeared in London in October 1895 and conferred with Lord Salisbury. He proposed that the Khedive of Egypt should give over to him (Leopold) on lease the whole of the Nile valley from Khartum up towards the Nyanza lake, to a point where the British claims began. Salisbury gave no encouragement to this proposal, fearing that France and possibly other powers would try to establish themselves in the Nile valley. Not losing hope Leopold returned to London in December, hoping to threaten England by his close relations with the French. What he asked from England was that she should give up her conflict with France by fixing a date for the evacuation of Egypt, and should persuade the Khedive to make a concession of the Sudan above Khartum to him (Leopold). In return for all this, Britain would have a free hand for annexations in China and, in case the Ottoman Empire should fall to pieces, England would have Egypt back again. Salisbury's reaction to these fantastic schemes was that Leopold did not mean them seriously. However, he felt the necessity for keeping quiet until England could construct the Uganda railway by which troops could be brought to the area.

In January 1896 Leopold appeared for the third time in London, still pressing for the lease of the Sudan above Khartum. When he had completed the subjugation of the Sudanese he would put them at the disposal of Britain. They could be used to occupy Armenia. This was too much for Salisbury, who wrote to the Queen remarking that the idea struck him as being so curious that he 'hastened to give the conversation another turn,' lest he should be betrayed 'into some disrespectful commentary.' The Queen agreed that the account of the King's visit was 'quite preposterous. It really seems as if he had taken leave of his senses.'

It seems that Salisbury was of opinion that the question of the Nile would sooner or later have to be decided even by force and that he should let negotiations or attempts at reaching a solution drag on until Britain was in a position to have military backing in these African affairs. This is the only explanation of Britain's permitting negotiations in January and February 1896 to drag on first with Leopold and then with the French although it was clear that any proposal giving a European power influence in the Nile valley would not be tolerated by Britain. Salisbury was anxious to appease the French for the time being so as to discourage them from undertaking any hostile action. The whole matter, in Salisbury's opinion, was to be postponed as far as possible until Britain could act with more vigor. But as matters turned out the British were not allowed to choose their own time to make their influence in the Nile valley effective, as will be seen in the next chapter.

XV

DONGOLA CAMPAIGN

By 1896 it became clear to the British that the French threat to their sphere of influence was imminent and that something more effective than reliance on treaties was necessary. However, they were not as yet prepared to make their claims and those of Egypt effective. In the north it was evident that Egypt was not in a financial position to enable her to advance into the Sudan. In the south the British position in the lakes area was still isolated and the railway connection with the east coast of Africa was not yet made. However, they were compelled to go into action in March 1896 on the pretext of giving assistance to the Italians.

This brings us to the origins of the Italo-Abyssinian conflict which precipitated war between them. Ever since the evacuation of the Sudan in 1885 the British looked with favor on the planting of the Italian flag on the Red Sea coast. The Italians were fortunate in that they made friends with Menelek, King of Shoa, but they were at loggerheads with John, King of Kings. For this reason they supplied Menelek with war equipment. To the common relief of both Menelek and the Italians the Sudanese removed John, who lost his life in battle with the army of Khalifah 'Abdullahi. The road was, therefore, open for Menelek to assume control all through Abyssinia and to succeed John. Recognizing the debt he owed to the Italians and at the same time realizing the necessity of establishing close relations with one of the great European powers, Menelek concluded with the Italians the Treaty of Uccialli in May 1899. By this treaty Menelek abandoned to Italy part of north-east Abyssinia, thus allowing them access to the inland plateau. The significant part of the treaty was not the territorial gain to the Italians, but the provisions of Article XVII which, according to the Italian interpretation, gave Italy what amounted to a protectorate over Abyssinia. The British recognized the whole of Abyssinia as an Italian sphere of influence in their agreement of 1891. Menelek, however, did not agree to this Italian interpretation as in his Amharic copy of the treaty it was written that he 'might

387

make use of' the Italian Government in his dealings with other
powers. It was the French who had drawn his attention to this
Italian allegation. He formally denounced the treaty in 1893. At the
same time he was preparing for war by collecting rifles and ammunition probably through French and Russian agencies. In 1895 war
was declared between Menelek and Italy, which culminated in the
disastrous defeat of the Italians at the battle of Adua on March 1,
1896.

While war was going on the possibility of alliance between
Menelek and Khalifah 'Abdullahi was revealed to the Italian
Ambassador at St. Petersburg. Salisbury was not sure whether
this rumor of concerted action against the Italians by the Sudanese
and the Abyssinians was true or not, but, in his opinion, an attack
by the Khalifah on Kasalah was not impossible. 'Do you think that
a demonstration in the neighborhood of Wadi Halfa would be
useful to create a diversion and do you see any objection to such
a step being taken?' [1] Cromer replied that Kitchener was absent
from Cairo, but it was known that the military authorities were
strongly opposed to anything in the nature of mere demonstration.
These authorities held the opinion that to advance and then to
retire would inevitably increase the prestige of the Dervishes
especially if actual collision took place. They maintained that no
demonstration would appreciably affect the Italian position and
that any ground taken from the Dervishes should be permanently
held. Cromer agreed with this view and added that there would be
much difficulty in persuading the Egyptian ministers to spend
money merely for helping the Italians unless it was proved to them
that Egypt would gain. In Cromer's opinion, there were two courses
open; the first was to collect an Egyptian force at Wadi Halfa
and move to Suarda or perhaps to Dongola, where the opposition
was composed of 8,000 well-armed Dervishes under a capable
leader; the second alternative was to move from Sawakin to Filek
or even to the Atbara, while the Italians might co-operate within
their own territory. 'The latter of these two operations would
probably be less costly and would give more effective help to the
Italians than the former.' [2] Cromer was not able to make any
further definite proposals before again consulting the military

[1] Salisbury to Cromer, No. 1, Jan. 11, 1896, P.R.O., F.O. 78/4986.
[2] Cromer to Salisbury, No. 1, Jan. 13, 1896, P.R.O., F.O. 78/4986.

authorities on the spot and awaited an expression of Salibury's opinion on the general issues involved before entering farther into discussion. He directed the attention of the Government to the financial difficulties, which were considerable but might be over-come. The immediate reaction of Salisbury to this reply was that before going any farther they should wait and see 'if there are any signs of an impending dervish advance.' [1]

On February 24th, 1896 the question of the Sudan was again stirred up in a note written by Sir Thomas Sanderson, the Permanent Under-Secretary of State for Foreign Affairs. He was told by the Italian Ambassador in London that some signs of disaffection were apparent among the native levies in Eritrea. The insubordination, however, was promptly suppressed, but it was a symptom which could not be disregarded. If it recurred it might be necessary for the Italians to withdraw from Kasalah. The Italian Ambassador had no instructions to speak on the subject, but he thought that it was for Britain or Egypt to consider what action should be taken in such an eventuality.[2] Cromer was asked to report whether the military authorities in Cairo, both Egyptian and British, had considered what action was desirable if the Italians were hard pressed at Kasalah or if they should be com-pelled to withdraw.[3] After consulting the military authorities in Cairo, Cromer replied that they considered that the best way to help the Italians would be to send a force from Sawakin to occupy a spot held by friendly tribes at the junction of Khur Langeb and Khur Baraka. After doing this it was considered essential to send another force to occupy Kokreb on the road to Barbar. These two measures might stop the Dervish advance on Italian territories and would pave the way for further operations in the direction of Kasalah. It was maintained by Cromer and the military authorities in Cairo that if an advance had to be made, there should be no subsequent retreat. It was known that the occupation could be effected with ease and with the Egyptian force available at the time. Although there was a manifest danger of being drawn into further operations, yet Cromer was inclined to recommend that the occupation of these two places should be sanctioned. 'It is on

[1] Salisbury to Cromer, No. 2, Jan. 14, 1896, P.R.O., F.O. 78/4986.
[2] A note by Sir Thomas Sanderson, Feb. 24, 1896, P.R.O., 78/4986.
[3] Salisbury to Cromer, No. 10, Secret, Feb. 24, 1896, P.R.O., F.O. 78/4986.

every ground most undesirable that the dervishes should be allowed
to re-establish themselves at Kasalah. If any thing is to be done,
prompt action is necessary.'[1] The military authorities in London,
however, did not agree to this proposal from Cairo. They argued
that the occupation of these two points could not be effected without a fight and the localities were so remote and so far apart that
if they were to be surrounded by the Dervishes, it would be
necessary to send a considerable force for their relief. Salisbury
doubted whether it was worth while to run that risk for nominal
advantages.

We have no great interest in occupation of Kasalah by Italy, who went
there without consulting us and rather against our wish. We have nothing
to gain at present by occupying it ourselves. The Power of the Khalifa tends
steadily to diminish, and a waiting game is the obvious policy. Whenever we
are masters of the valley of the Nile Kasalah will be easily dealt with. Till
then it has little value[2]

On March 2, i.e. the day after the battle of Adua, news reached
Cairo that the Dervishes were before Kasalah and had been fired
at by the Italian fort. It was also reported that the Khalifah had
ordered that trade should cease between Barbar and Sawakin and
also between Barbar and the Nile frontier of Egypt.[3] The first
phase of this question of Italian relief was, therefore, closed by
conflicting views from Cairo and London. The former thought
that operations were feasible in the eastern Sudan for relieving
pressure on the Italians, while the latter saw difficulties in the
realization of this objective. British policy was definitely not
interested in Kasalah and considered it subsidiary to the control
of the Nile valley. But after the defeat of the Italians at Adua the
matter entered a new phase.

On March 10th, 1896 Sir Clare Ford, the British Ambassador at
Rome, telegraphed to Lord Salisbury that it was understood that
Kasalah was completely surrounded by the Dervishes and all
communication was cut with Asmara. The Italian garrison consisted of under 2,000 men with six guns. Fortifications were considered to be sufficient and there were supplies and ammunition

[1] Cromer to Salisbury, No. 17, Secret, Feb. 26, 1896, P.R.O., F.O. 78/4986.
[2] Salisbury to Cromer, No. 11, Secret, Feb. 29, 1896, P.R.O., F.O. 78/4986.
[3] Cromer to Salisbury, No. 22, Mar. 2, 1896, P.R.O., F.O. 78/4986.

sufficient to hold out for three months.[1] Two days later Salisbury received from the Italian Ambassador in London a request to authorize a deversion by the Egyptian troops against the Dervishes who were besieging Kasalah. Salisbury told the Ambassador that Cromer had been given telegraphic instructions authorizing an advance of Egyptian troops to Dongola.[2] The telegram referred to above from Salisbury to Cromer ran as follows:

The Italian Ambassador has pressed me earnestly to take some steps against the dervishes in favor of Kasalah. After consulting the military authorities Her Majesty's Government are of opinion that the occupation of Dongola would be the most effective demonstration, and that the measure will be greatly in the interest of Egypt, and is a charge she may fairly be asked to bear. It will also tend to repel any disposition to attack Egypt which the recent victories of Africans over Europeans may have created among the dervishes. Of course, it is intended to keep Dongola. The War Office is communicating with the military authorities. No secrecy is at all necessary[3]

In a private letter next day Salisbury explained to Cromer that the decision was inspired by a desire to help the Italians at Kasalah and to give no chance to the Dervishes to win a great success which might have important effects. 'In addition we desired to kill two birds with one stone, and to use the same military effort to plant the foot of Egypt rather farther up the Nile.'[4] Sensing that opposition might be raised from the French Government against this move, Salisbury telegraphed to the Marquess of Dufferin, the British Ambassador in Paris, to communicate the decision to the Government there. But it was communicated in such a way as to disarm the expected opposition. 'Please inform French Government that we have been applied to by the Egyptian Government to saction a diversion in favor of Kasalah against the dervishes, and that we have approved an advance of Egyptian troops as far as Dongola.'[5] Salisbury was careful not to mention the assistance to Italy and he said that the request came from the Egyptian Government, which was obviously untrue.

---

[1] Sir Clare Ford to Salisbury, No. 14, Mar. 10, 1896, P.R.O., F.O. 78/4893.
[2] Salisbury to Sir Clare Ford, No. 24, Mar. 12, 1896, P.R.O., F.O. 78/4893.
[3] Salisbury to Cromer, No. 17, Mar. 12, 1896, P.R.O., F. O. 78/4893.
[4] Salisbury to Cromer, Mar. 13, 1896, Zetland, Marquess of, *Lord Cromer* (London, 1932), p. 223.
[5] Salisbury to Dufferin, No. 30, Mar. 12, 1896, P.R.O., F.O. 78/4893.

Cromer replied in two long telegrams on the next day: in the first he discussed the military question and in the second the financial implications of the campaign. He did not deprecate the movement on Dongola and maintained that from the point of view of general policy it was absolutely necessary whatever were the local objections. But from both the military and financial points of view it was obviously much more serious than the movement he had suggested on February 26th, i.e. the one operating from Sawakin. To Cromer the relief of Kasalah, whether in co-operation with the Italians or by the Egyptian army acting alone, could be effected via Tūkar and Khur Langeb. 'If Dongola is occupied, the whole Sudan question will possibly be raised. It is for Her Majesty's Government to judge whether this risk should be run.'[1] No object would be obtained by merely going half-away from Wadi Halfa unless the troops were to go to Dongola. Mere demonstration in favor of the Italians would be impossible to justify to the Khedive and the ministers, with whom Cromer expected to have a good deal of trouble anyway. The only way in which Dongola might be occupied would be if the British Government guaranteed the safety of Sawakin and Cairo and the movement of the whole Egyptian army to the frontier. Perhaps an English battalion would be needed at Wadi Halfa as a backing to the Egyptian troops. 'It is impossible to feel confident that even then the Egyptian army, unaided by British troops, will be able to cope with the business.'[2]

In his second telegram Cromer earnestly required the British Government to consider fully the financial side before anything was definitely decided. 'Pray read first two pages of my recent report. The expedition will be very expensive, and the increased annual charge thrown on the Egyptian Treasury will be heavy.'[3] The expedition would necessitate conferring a greater financial liberty of action on the Egyptian Government, which would meet with many difficulties, and Cromer urged his Government to settle this question. He thought that the movement was being undertaken mainly in Italian interests, because from an English and Egyptian point of view it was certainly premature. For this reason the Italian Government should be moved to instruct their com-

[1] Cromer to Salisbury, No. 27, Mar. 13, 1896, P.R.O., F.O. 78/4893.
[2] Ibid.
[3] Cromer to Salisbury, No. 28, Mar. 13, 1896, P.R.O., F.O. 78/4893.

missioner of the *caisse de la dette* to support a proposal 'that a credit of at least half a million on the general reserve fund should be opened in favor of the Egyptian Government.'[4] If this arrangement was not made, there would be difficulties even about cash. Cromer proposed that the Austrian and the German governments should be approached for the same purpose.

Generally speaking the point of view which I venture to urge on the earnest attention of Her Majesty's Government is this: that advance on Dongola, advisable though in many respects it may be, cannot be considered by itself, or exclusively on its own merits. It will almost certainly bring on a crisis in Egyptian affairs and oblige us to depart from the expectant and doubtful attitude which has been adopted for the last thirteen years. This may or may not be desirable, but of the fact I have little doubt, and I think it my duty to lay before Her Majesty's Government my view of the ultimate consequences before any final decision is taken.[1]

The British Government was so anxious to give publicity to the decision to advance on Dongola that they resorted to announcing the expedition in *The Times* in form of a telegram written in London, but purporting to come from Cairo. Cromer described the publicity in this manner as somewhat unfortunate, as he was not able to see the Khedive or any of his ministers on the subject.[2] On the next day Cromer spoke to the Egyptian Prime Minister about the advance to Dongola. His remarks were described by Cromer as most reasonable. He recognized the advantages that would accrue to Egypt from the movement, but he emphasized the necessity of guarding against any military reverse. At the same time he drew the serious attention of the British Government to the financial aspects. The Prime Minister then saw the Khedive and reported to Cromer. It was fortunate that the Khedive did not hear the decision from others. 'I can see from what he says, as I anticipated, the Khedive does not like the idea, which he considers is conceived mainly in Italian interests. I daresay His Higness may be overcome, but no active support or help is likely to be obtained from him.'[3] But Sir E. Palmer, the British financial adviser to the Egyptian Government, reported to Cromer that the meeting of the

[4] Ibid.
[1] Ibid.
[2] Cromer to Salisbury, No. 29, Mar. 13, 1896, P.R.O., F.O. 78/4893.
[3] Cromer to Salisbury, No. 30, Mar. 13, 1896, P.R.O., F.O. 78/4893.

council of ministers on the subject went off fairly well. 'The sore point with the Khedive is the employment of English troops.' [1]

The Italian Cabinet, to which the disaster of Adua was attributed, fell, and was succeeded by a new one which came to a resolution to evacuate Kasalah. They therefore requested the British Government to suspend all military preparations for forty-eight hours. 'If they adhere to this policy, it relieves us of the necessity of any immediate action. This decision is to be regretted but I do not think Her Majesty's Government will be disposed to urge Egyptian action when the main object of our interest in it has disappeared.' [2] Cromer was asked to keep this secret. But in the afternoon of the same day the Italian Cabinet resolved not to abandon Kasalah. 'Better not publish these oscillations of policy more than you can help.' [3]

When everything was set for the campaign Salisbury immediately entered into the financial question. On March 15, 1896, he circulated a letter through his ambassadors to the Governments of France, Austria, Germany, Russia, and Italy. He pointed out that the British Government had been for some time in consultation with the military authorities in Egypt on the movements by the Dervishes which were threatening the Egyptian posts around Sawakin. In case of a successful Dervish attack on Kasalah, or even if for military considerations the Italians should evacuate the place, it was clear that a renewal of fanaticism might ensue, that the Khalifah would gain in prestige, and that the defense of the Egyptian frontier would be difficult. Acting under the expert advise of their military authorities, the British Government had come to the decision to authorize an advance from Wadi Halfa to take and retain Dongola. The operation, however, would require and expenditure in excess of the amount which the Egyptian Government had at their own absolute disposal. 'Her Majesty's Government trust therefore that the commissioners of the caisse will authorize for the object the expenditure of £500,000 out of the General Reserve Fund of £2,000 000 which has been accumulated and is held applicable to extraordinary expenses.' [4] Salisbury considered the matter very pressing.

[1] Cromer to Salisbury, No. 32, Mar. 14, 1896, P.R.O., F.O. 78/4893.
[2] Salisbury to Cromer, No. 20, Mar. 14, 1896, P.R.O., F.O. 78/4893.
[3] Salisbury to Cromer, No. 21, Mar. 14, 1896, P.R.O., F.O. 78/4893.
[4] Salisbury to Sir Clare Ford, No. 28, Mar. 15, 1896, P.R.O., F.O. 78/4893.

The Italian, the Austrian, after some hesitation and the German Governments agreed to the proposal and instructed their respective agents of the *caisse* accordingly. Opposition was expected from Russia and France. The latter had many reasons to oppose, among which was their project to reach the Nile before the British. It will be recalled that in their final authorization of Marchand's mission the French were looking at the matter as a race towards the upper Nile between them and the British operating from Uganda. The British decision to operate from the north on behalf of Egypt placed France in an inconvenient position because the French had always declared their intention to respect the rights of the Khedive. All this happened only a few days after the French Colonial Minister signed his final instructions to Liotard and Marchand. This change of front took the French completely by surprise. In a casual and unofficial interview with Lord Dufferin, the French Minister for Foreign Affairs stated that the contemplated move to Dongola would prove very displeasing to French public opinion. He further told Dufferin that the financial question would have to be carefully considered by the council of ministers before a reply could be given. The French at the time held the view that the request for sanctioning expenditure of money should be accompanied by an invitation to enter upon a discussion about Egypt, which might be satisfactory to France.[1] The French, together with the Russian commissioner, therefore, opposed the authorization of the Egyptian Government to receive the half-million pounds for expenditure on the campaign. The French Government, at the same time, did not change the plan of their advance towards the Nile. Cromer considered it necessary not only on financial but on political grounds that Britain should succeed in getting the half-million pounds approved. He reported that the 'native anglophobe opposition which was very strong against the whole policy has for the moment centered itself on this issue. This opposition is certainly encouraged by the Khedive.'[2]

The French opposition was not only direct but they also instigated the Sultan of Turkey to use his legal rights in frustrating

[1] Dufferin to Salisbury, No. 7, Confidential, Mar. 16, 1896, P.R.O., F.O. 78/4893.

[2] Cromer to Salisbury, No. 39, Confidential, Mar. 17, 1896, P.R.O., F.O. 78/4893.

the Dongola expedition The French Embassy at Constantinople addressed a communication to the Turkish Ministry of Foreign Affairs on the Egyptian question. The note related the story of the British request to France to sanction the payment of half a million out of the reserve fund and the refusal of both France and Russia. The Frech note maintained that the expedition would modify the character of the existing occupation and would expose Egypt to dangers. 'The Sultan should not permit Egypt to go to war without his previous approval and consent, and, in any case, the Sultan should recognize that this expedition is a further proof of the necessity for him to come to no arrangement with England in regard to Egypt without the consent and approval of France and Russia.'[1]

The Sultan's response to this French note was immediate as he stated to the British Ambassador that he heard of the expedition but that no official notification had reached him. He would like to be informed about the nature and objects of the expedition. The tone of the communication was described by Sir Philip Currie as courteous and moderate.[2] At the same time the Sultan telegraphed to the Khedive asking him for an explanation of the decision to send an expedition to Dongola without previous consultation of him (the Sultan).[3] The British Government replied to the Sultan that the object of the expedition was the interior defense of Egypt, which was recognized in the Imperial firmans as the duty of the Egyptian army. The British reply maintained that a part of the territories entrused by the Sultan to the Khedive was overrun by rebel tribes. The present expedition had as its objective the defense of what remained to the Khedive from further incursions. 'It will also, we trust, have the result of restoring the Khedive's authority over portions of the territory now withdrawn from their obedience to himself and to the Porte. But nothing has been done or is contemplated, which is beyond the Khedive's competence or requires any special authority from the Sultan.'[4] As to the application to the *caisse de la dette*, Salisbury explained that it was merely for the use of money set apart for certain purposes and available

---

[1] French note to Turkey, quoted in Sir P. Currie to Salisbury, No. 112, Secret, Mar. 24, 1896, P.R.O., F.O. 78/4893.
[2] Sir P. Currie to Salisbury, No. 113, Mar. 24, 1896, P.R.O., F.O. 78/4893.
[3] Cromer to Salisbury, No. 61, Mar. 25, 1896, P.R.O., F.O. 78/4893.
[4] Salisbury to Currie, No. 55, Mar. 25, 1896, P.R.O., F.O. 78/4893.

for extraordinary expenses. There was no question of fresh loans or of increasing the Egyptian army beyond the number authorized by the firman. 'There is nothing which need cause the Sultan anxiety, or is likely to alter the political situation of Egypt.'[1]

The Khedive was caused to reply that the expedition was sent by the British and Egyptian governments, who both agreed that the moment was opportune for attempting to restore Dongola to the Egyptian administration. Under the terms of the firmans the Khedive considered previous consultation unnecessary.[2] The Sultan was not content with this reply and sent a long telegram couched in strong terms. 'Any dispatch of Egyptian troops, more especially to act against Mussulmans, depends absolutely and entirely on the will and permission of His Imperial Majesty. . . . It is absolutely impossible that this military expedition should be sanctioned by the Imperial Government.'[3] Cromer had seen Mustafa Fahmi Pasha, the Egyptian Prime Minister, about this Turkish ultimatum and advised him that the reply should be in the general sense of the British reply. Cromer told Mustafa Pasha that the Khedive could rest assured that he could rely on the cordial support of Her Majesty's Government in resisting the attempts of the Sultan to go beyond his rights as set forth in the firmans. In a postscript Cromer stated that it was understood that the Khedive at first intended to reply saying that he disapproved of the expedition but was powerless against the British pressure. The Prime Minister objected to this course. Then Cromer thought it advisable to defer the Khedive's reply until they could hear from London. In Cromer's opinion the Khedive was evidently much frightened. 'His behavior is fairly satisfactory, and I think with a very clear statement to the effect that we will guarantee him against any action from the Sultan, he may be kept straight for the time being.'[4] The reply which was finally agreed upon was couched in conciliatory and, at the same time, respectful language. The Khedive dwelt on the fact that the Dervishes were not true Muhammadans and that the firmans were not infringed. 'The military expedition against Dongola was not originally conceived

---

[1] Ibid.
[2] Cromer to Salisbury, No. 62, Mar. 25, 1896, P.F.O., F.O. 78/4893.
[3] Cromer to Salisbury, No. 69, Mar. 28, 1896, P.R.O., F.O. 78/4893.
[4] Ibid.

by the Egyptian Government. It is the result of agreement with the views and proposals of the British Government, which is now in military occupation of Egypt.'¹ The matter was closed by a telegram from the Sultan to the Khedive in very friendly terms thanking him for his message.² The Sultan's attitude was evidently dictated by pressure from France and Russia. They both instigated him to take a strong line about the Dongola expedition, but he was unwilling to go so far as to alienate Britain.

In the course of two days, the 12th and 13th, orders and counter-orders to the British officer commanding in Egypt, to Cromer, and to Sir Clare Ford were issued. It was not clear whether the British General or Cromer was to control the affairs of the expedition. It was also not clear whether it was finally decided to carry the expedition to Dongola or to make it merely a demonstration. In these circumstances Cromer wrote to Salisbury on March 14 noting that he had seen the instructions to the General. As the British Government's agent he had to carry out what he understood to be the wishes of Her Majesty's Government, but for the time being control of the whole machine had to a great extent passed out of his hands. He stated that orders were being issued and heavy expenditure incurred without 'the Khedive and his advisers, whose army is to be used and who will apparently have to pay the whole charge, having had any adequate opportunity for considering the matter.'³

Cromer urged the importance of coming to an early decision about the advance, whether it was to have Dongola as its objective or whether it was to be limited to a demonstration to 'Akāshah. The former would very likely involve employment of British troops in addition to the great expense it would incur. The latter alternative would be of no use to the Italians and be unjustifiable from an Egyptian point of view. 'As it appears definitely decided that a movement of some sort is to be made, I maintain my opinion that, in spite of very serious difficulties which I see ahead advance should be made to Dongola.'⁴

¹ Cromer to Salisbury, No. 74, Mar. 30, 1896, P.R.O., F.O. 78/4893.
² Cromer to Salisbury, No. 81, Apr. 1, 1896, P.R.O., F.O. 78/4893.
³ Cromer to Salisbury, No. 31, Mar. 14, 1896, P.R.O., F.O. 78/4893.
⁴ Ibid.

On March 16th, the Cabinet discussed all the telegrams from Cromer with the commander-in-chief and with General Sir Francis Grenfell, whose military advice was also sought. They reached the decision that the movement would have two objects; the first was to keep the Dervishes off the Italians; the second was to restore some of the lost territory to Egypt. For the first object a demonstration would be sufficient, but it would make the Egyptians think that they were badly treated. The proposal, therefore, was that an advance should be made beyond the Murrat wells, but that the troops would ultimately retire. At the same time 'Akāshah would at once be occupied with the intention of going to Dongola. There would be no haste to go to Dongola, as the season would be getting hot and it was intended to drag the railway after the troops to 'Akāshah and to Abu Fatmah. After the latter place there would be open water far beyond Dongola, and the town would be at the mercy of the advancing army. This was, in the opinion of Salisbury, a more prudent policy and less likely to involve military or financial trouble than an attempt to rush Dongola: 'It is true that dervishes will reinforce it, but that very act will take the strain off the Italians.' [1]

Cromer replied that he would endeavor to carry out the program of Her Majesty's Government, but again he urged the full realization of both military and financial difficulties. The slow movement, in his opinion, would cost more than the rapid advance. He maintained that the whole future would depend on the behavior of the Egyptian troops when they were first brought into contact with the enemy. 'Whatever position be occupied in the Nile valley, Dongola will not be at our mercy until the main body of dervishes has been defeated.' [2] Kitchener was told to go on collecting supplies and transport on the assumption of a movement on Dongola. Sleepers were being sent up the line to 'Akāshah. From a military point of view the British officer commanding in Egypt was of opinion that some British troops should be sent to Egypt as reinforcement against eventualities. Cromer had no objection to such purely technical matters, but he was rather worried at the expense they might entail. He, however, suggested that such

[1] Salisbury to Cromer, No. 23, Mar. 16, 1896, P.R.O., F.O. 78/4893.
[2] Cromer to Salisbury, No. 40, Mar. 17, 1896, P.R.O., F.O. 78/4893.

reinforcements should stay at Malta if it was not intended to send them immediately to the field.[1]

The question of the ability of the Egyptian army to stand the opposition of the Dervishes unaided was raised at an early stage of the expedition by Mukhtar Pasha, the Turkish Commissioner, who warned Cromer against placing too much reliance on the fellaheen troops. 'IIe has confidence in the Blacks, but thinks that if we are to go to Dongola we must certainly employ English troops. He is an excellent authority on a point of this sort.'[2] Sir Herbert Kitchener, the sirdar, who had to lead the Egyptian army, assured Cromer that the best spirit prevailed among native officers and men of his army, 'but from what he says and from what I hear from others it is clear to me that the English officers have little confidence in their fallaheen men.'[3] Kitchener held the view that sending two more battalions of British troops would have great moral effect. Cromer thought there was no military necessity at the time for them; and in addition there were obvious objections on the score of expense. On the other hand, no one could predict what would happen on the frontier; and in case of a sudden reverse British troops would have to be sent immediately and trouble might be expected in Egypt. 'There can be no doubt that policy of advance is very unpopular among the most noisy part of the population, who declare that it is not dictated by regard for Egyptian interests.'[4]

On March 19th, Cromer reported that the Khedive was expected to create considerable trouble. Cromer failed to persuade him to address his troops before leaving Cairo in a sense which would make it clear that he was in favor of partial reoccupation of the Sudan. He did not think that the Khedive would commit any serious act which would call for complaint, 'but his language to almost every one leaves no doubt of his extreme hostility.'[5] His two complaints were that the advance was for Italian interests and that he was not consulted beforehand. 'He is actively encouraging the circulation of the most anglophobe newspapers.' Although difficulties of all kinds were very great, yet they could be overcome

---

[1] Cromer to Salisbury, No. 37, Mar. 16, 1896, P.R.O., F.O. 78/4893.
[2] Cromer to Salisbury, No. 35, Mar. 15, 1896, P.R.O., F.O. 78/4893.
[3] Cromer to Salisbury, No. 41, Mar. 18, 1896, P.R.O., F.O. 78/4893.
[4] Cromer to Salisbury, No. 41, Mar. 18, 1896, P.R.O., F.O. 78/4893.
[5] Cromer to Salisbury, No. 44, Mar. 19, 1896, P.R.O., F O. 78/4893.

if the British showed a firm front to the French and determination to advance to Dongola. 'After what has happened we are indeed bound to go so far, whatever may be the difficulties.' From this point of view Cromer thought that the dispatch of two additional British battalions would help.

With all the above remarks and observations of Cromer before them, the British Government, in consultation with their military advisers in London, this time stated their policy with more detail and precision. They instructed that the advance should be gradual, accompanied by the extention of the railway communication. No additional British troops were to be sent at that early stage. It was considered of great importance to improve river communication above Wadi Halfa and for this purpose they recommended the immediate placement of orders for certain steamers and river craft. As regards expenses the Egyptian Government should bear any expenditure incurred by bringing in more British troops up to the limit of £200,000 fixed in 1885. Any additional expenses that might be caused by the movements of British troops beyond Wadi Halfa would be subject to further discussion.[1]

In his reply to the above instructions Cromer touched on questions of principles for the conduct of war. He stated that he would show the opinions of the War Office to Kitchener not as instructions to be obeyed, but mere views of military advisers, which he would carefully consider. 'It will then be for him to lay such proposals before the Egyptian Government as he may think desirable.'[2] As to the rapidity or slowness of the move Cromer maintained that he was not yet in a position to form an opinion. He would wait until he heard what Kitchener had to say and what was the position with respect to the Dervishes themselves. He would say nothing to the Egyptian Government about the charge of £200,000; Cromer thought it was impossible to say whether Egypt would be able to pay such a sum. The War Office program appeared to Cromer to be manifestly expensive and 'if once financial difficulties are raised great political trouble will ensue.' The War Office should order nothing suggested by the Foreign Office without distinct authority from Cairo.

Cromer was very much worried about the excited state of public

[1] Salisbury to Cromer, No. 50, Mar. 26, 1896, P.R.O., F.O. 78/4893.
[2] Cromer to Salisbury, No. 66, Mar. 27, 1896, P.R.O., F.O. 78/4893.

opinion in Egypt and knew that great attention would be paid to the debate which he suspected would take place in Parliament about the campaign. He suggested to Salisbury that stress should be laid on the fact that the Egyptians considered it a grievance that under British advice the Sudan was abandoned and that Egyptian public opinion was urgently demanding its reconquest. He, however, urged that any statement implying that this particular expedition had been undertaken at the request of the Egyptian Government should be avoided.[1]

The concentration in the Nile frontier left only two battalions at Tūkar and Sawakin with no reserves in Cairo. Cromer maintained that it would be impossible for the Egyptian army to fight on two fronts simultaneously. The situation would be very much aggravated if Kasalah should fall. He, therefore, would direct the attention of Her Majesty's Government to such an eventuality and the necessity that might thus arise of employing British troops.[2] On the next day reports from Sawakin stated that large numbers of Arabs were flocking towards Sawakin, which was an indication that 'Uthman Diqna was on the move. The black battalion at Tūkar that had been ordered to leave for the Nile frontier had to remain where it was. Kitchener's opinion was that if the situation deteriorated at Sawakin and British troops were not sent there, it would be necessary to reinforce it from the Nile. This would mean that the permanent occupation of 'Akāshah would be rendered difficult and there could be no idea of further movement south. 'Egyptian army is insufficient to carry out active operations at both places at the same time. Please press on Her Majesty's Government that an early reply is necessary.'[3] Cromer asked for a more definite military policy. His own view was that the expedition to Dongola should be carried to a successful issue, whatever might be the difficulties and objections. He suggested that Her Majesty's Government should guarantee the defense of Sawakin and Tūkar, though immediate dispatch of English or Indian troops was not necessary.[4]

Her Majesty's Government's reply emphasized that the advance should ultimately go to Dongola, but should be slow, because the

[1] Cromer to Salisbury, unnumbered, Mar. 18, 1896, P.R.O., F.O. 78/4893.
[2] Cromer to Salisbury, No. 73, Mar. 30, 1896, P.R.O., F.O. 78/4893.
[3] Kitchener to Cromer, quoted in Cromer to Salisbury, No. 76, Mar. 31, 1896, P.R.O., F.O. 78/4893.
[4] Cromer to Salisbury, No. 76, Mar. 31, 1896, P.R.O., F.O. 78/4893.

Nile could not be used till July. The railway should be extended not only to Farkah but, if possible, to Abu Fatmah. They asked whether Cromer by the guarantee of Sawakin and Tūkar meant of necessity the employment of British or Indian troops. In any case even if they had to be sent it would be of a great advantage to defer their being sent till after the hot weather.[1] Cromer refrained from speaking positively on the Sawakin front until events should develop. He was of opinion that the force at Tūkar was quite sufficient to hold its own for the time being, but if the town was invested, no Egyptian troops would be available to send as a relieving force. He advised that the Sirdar should be told not to decrease the Sawakin and Tūkar garrisons below their present strength without instructions. He should also be informed not to send further reinforcements there. At the same time, if assistance were needed at Sawakin, it would be British assistance, 'but I do not think any immediate decision is necessary.'[2] Cromer explained what he meant by more definite military policy. He wished that 'all doubt should be removed as to whether the Government really mean to move on to Dongola, or whether they are only aiming at diversion.' He himself would adhere to the former policy; he thought it would involve very serious difficulties of all kinds if the latter was pursued which he thought wholly indefensible.

When 'Akáshah, a point south of Wadi Halfa, had been successfully occupied, Cromer thought of informing Kitchener fully about the object of the expedition and also about the possibility of employment of British troops. The immediate objective of the expedition was the capture of Dongola, although in the remote future there would be the possibility of a further advance. 'There is at present no question of a general reconquest of the Sudan. Pray bear this carefully in mind.'[3] From this point of view the construction of the Kurusko-Abu Hamad line, demanded by Kitchener, was unnecessary. It was the policy to take Dongola and consolidate the Egyptian position there, and a further forward movement would be reconsidered. Kitchener was told that it would be undesirable to employ British troops either at Sawakin

[1] Salisbury to Cromer, No. 54, Secret, Mar. 31, 1896, P.R.O., F.O. 78/4893.
[2] Cromer to Salisbury, unnumbered, Apr. 1, 1896, P.R.O., F.O. 78/4893.
[3] Cromer to Kitchener, record of telegraphic conversation, enclosed in Cromer to Salisbury, No. 39, Apr. 7, 1896, P.R.O., F.O. 78/3762.

or in the Nile valley. Considerations on this subject should be based on purely military reasons. In this conversation Kitchener asked permission to move to Farkah, about thirteen miles south of 'Akāshah, as he considered it to be safer. Cromer gave him discretion to move to Farkah or not, but no advance beyond it should be made without further communication with Cromer.

Reports received from Sawakin were somewhat alarming and Cromer urged the sending of Indian troops to that town with a view to the adoption of an offensive policy. He reiterated his previous opinion that it would be beyond the unaided military resources of Egypt to deal with the situation both on the Nile and at Sawakin.[1] After receiving answers from Cromer to some questions, explaining and elaborating certain points, the Cabinet came to the decision that they were very strongly opposed to sending additional British regiments to the Sudan from home. 'But they are willing that, if expedient, Indian troops should be sent to Sawakin, and that all the Egyptian and English forces now in Egypt should be sent to the Sudan.'[2]

As soon as it was known that there was an idea of garrisoning Sawakin with English or Indian troops it was interpreted in Turkey that Sawakin was going to be handed over to the British. The Grand Vizier wrote to the Khedive that if his forces were insufficient for the protection of Sawakin, Ottoman troops would be dispatched there. Cromer proposed to advise the Khedive to reply that the Sultan had been misinformed and what took place was nothing but ordinary changes in the Egyptian garrisons. Cromer suggested also that Her Majesty's Government should intimate to the Sultan in some form or another that the dispatch of Ottoman troops to Sawakin was unnecessary and could not be countenanced.[3] The Sultan was not content with his communication to the Khedive, but requested the British Government to put in his hands the administration of Sawakin in order to enable him to consolidate his religious authority in the Hijaz and the Red Sea. 'He would be prepared to facilitate in every way the extension of British commerce by building railways, making roads

---

[1] Cromer to Salisbury, No. 117, Apr. 21, 1896, P.R.O., F.O. 78/4893.
[2] Salisbury to Cromer, No. 64, Apr. 22, 1896, P.R.O., F.O. 78/4893.
[3] Cromer to Salisbury, No. 121, Apr. 24, 1896, P.R.O., F.O. 78/4893.

etc.'[1] The Turkish Ambassador in London told Salisbury that if the rumor of sending British troops to Sawakin were true it would be exceedingly displeasing to the Sultan. 'I stated that no such movement had been ordered by Her Majesty's Government but that I could not admit that the Sultan had any right to object to the dispatch of British or Indian troops to Sawakin. It had been done more than once before, and was well within the discretionary rights of the Khedive, if he thought such a measure necessary.'[2] The Khedive replied in the sense suggested by Cromer. He, however, strongly objected to the resumption of the administration of Sawakin by the Sultan and would much prefer the garrisoning of the place by Indian rather than Turkish troops. He was evidently very nervous that the Sultan might do him harm and that in the end he would not be supported by the British. 'It would help me greatly if you would let me say that in the event of Indian troops being sent to Sawakin Her Majesty's Government will take the responsibility and that he will be guaranteed against any action Sultan may wish to take against him on that account.'[3] Salisbury replied that the Khedive could rest assured of Her Majesty's Government's support.[4] The Sultan sent a further telegram to the Khedive requesting a specific reply as to whether he was certain that Sawakin would not be occupied by foreign troops. Cromer advised the Khedive to reply that as Egypt was occupied by foreign troops 'Her Majesty's Government may consider it necessary to send a force to Sawakin as they have done on previous occasions.'[5] Cromer thought that some further direct communication should be sent by Her Majesty's Government to the Sultan on this subject so as to relieve the Khedive of responsibility. Sir Philip Currie was instructed to inform the Porte that 'if for the purpose of protecting it against the dervishes it is found necessary to garrison Sawakin with foreign troops, the responsibility for that measure will rest with Her Majesty's Government as it has rested more than once before.'[6] This controversy over Sawakin, which

[1] Currier to Salisbury, No. 134, Apr. 24, 1896, P.R.O., F.O. 78/4893.
[2] Salisbury to Currie, No. 68, Apr. 24, 1896, P.R.O., F.O. 78/4893.
[3] Cromer to Salisbury, No. 124, Secret, Apr. 25, 1896, P.R.O., F.O. 78/4893.
[4] Salisbury to Cromer, No. 69, Apr. 25, 1896, P.R.O., F.O. 78/4893.
[5] Cromer to Salisbury, No. 126, Apr. 27, 1896, P.R.O., F.O. 78/4893.
[6] Salisbury to Currie, No. 69, Apr. 27, 1896, P.R.O., F.O. 78/4893.

continued for four days between London, Constantinople, and Cairo, was closed.

Kitchener proposed to start the advance on Dongola about July 10 so as to take full advantage of the rising river. As he would have the entire Sawakin garrison at his disposal, it would not be necessary to do more than move the British battalion at Wadi Halfa to the rail-head and replace it by another from Cairo. He considered that three Indian battalions should be sent to Sawakin, which would enable the whole Egyptian garrison to be sent to the Nile valley. He wished the Indian contingent to arrive at Sawakin not later than June 1. 'I need hardly point out that all this means heavy expenses. It is, however, premature to discuss the financial question at present. Military success must be secured.'[1] Cromer expected some trouble or at least misunderstanding from the Khedive and the Egyptian Government. For this reason he thought it desirable that no announcement should be made about the Indian contingent until he had spoken to the Khedive and the Egyptian ministers. He requested to be authorized to state that the Indian troops would be withdrawn as soon as Egyptians were able to regarrison the town, that there was no idea of making a railway from Sawakin to Barbar, and that an officer of the Egyptian army would be maintained as a civil governor of Sawakin.[2] Salisbury approved the proposed language.[3] The Khedive agreed to the proposed garrisoning of Sawakin by Indian troops, but he desired one Egyptian battalion to stay. Kitchener raised no objection to this desire and allowed a reserve battalion of fellaheen to stay in the town. This would mean that only two Indian battalions would be required instead of three.[4]

The Defense Committee of the British Cabinet considered all Cromer's recent telegrams on the affairs of the campaign and had their observations to make on various points. They understood that Kitchener proposed to commence his advance about July 10. By this date the railway would not reach Abu Fatmah or even Farkah. It would, therefore, imply that the Sirdar would advance before his communications by river and rail were complete and

[1] Cromer to Salisbury, No. 122, Apr. 24, 1896, P.R.O., F.O. 78/4893.
[2] Cromer to Salisbury, No. 123, Apr. 24, 1896, P.R.O., F.O. 78/4893.
[3] Salisbury to Cromer, No. 67, Apr. 24, 1896, P.R.O., F.O. 78/4893.
[4] Cromer to Salisbury, No. 125, Apr. 26, 1896, P.R.O., F.O. 78/4893.

consequently would depend on camels. From another telegram from Cromer the committee inferred that Kitchener was opposed to an advance depending on camels. 'If it is necessary to defer the advance till later in order to avoid dependence on camel communications; it must be deferred so far as is necessary for that purpose.'[1] In reply, Cromer maintained that the various communications he received from London were somewhat perplexing and explained what plans he proposed to carry out with the approval of Her Majesty's Government. He considered it quite essential that no unreasonable risk should be run. But at the same time it would be undesirable to allow the state of affairs obtaining at the time to drag on for an indefinite period. He urged the return to normal conditions as soon as it was consistent with reasonable prudence in the conduct of the operations. He saw no reason why the operations should not be concluded in that year. By July the railway would reach 'Akāshah and the time would be ripe for getting the steamers over the cataracts and there would be no excuse for delaying the advance. In any case the transport would be partly by camels and partly by river. Cromer thought that no advance of any kind beyond 'Akāshah would be possible until the frontier force was reinforced. 'I earnestly beg, therefore, that there should be no further delay in sending Indian troops to Sawakin in order to set free Egyptian garrison there.'[2]

Lord Wolseley, the commander-in-chief, when reviewing the situation, recommended in a memorandum to Lord Lansdowne, Secretary of State for War, that the Sirdar with Cromer would be responsible for the operations and that the War Office would only give advice. Wolseley presumed that the Government had full confidence in Kitchener and his plan of campaign. 'The plan of campaign is unknown to me and my knowledge of Sir H. Kitchener is not sufficient to enable me to judge of his capacity for command.'[3] It was also difficult for him to pass judgment on the value of the Egyptian army by itself, or only slightly stiffened by British troops. He had no doubt about the fighting qualities of the Sudanese battalions in the Egyptian army and on the whole he

---

[1] Salisbury to Cromer, No. 72, May 1, 1896, P.R.O., F.O. 78/4893.
[2] Cromer to Salisbury, No. 132, May 5, 1896, P.R.O., F.O. 78/4893.
[3] Memorandum by Lord Wolseley to Lord Lansdowne, May 8, 1896, P.R.O., F.O. 78/4894.

408 THE INDEPENDENT SUDAN

felt reasonable confidence that the Egyptian army would be equal
to the task before it if stiffened as proposed by English troops.
Wolseley proposed that in future he would not criticize Kitchener's
arrangements or call attention to any measures which might appear
to him to entail avoidable risk unless desired to do so by the
Secretary of State. Lansdowne did not agree with Wolseley on this
latter point. He told Wolseley that although Her Majesty's Government did not desire the War Department to interfere unnecessarily
with Cromer's arrangements, yet all information received with
regard to the campaign would be regularly communicated to the
War Office for comment. 'If anything goes seriously wrong, the
intervention of the War Office will certainly be required, and it
should be given every facility for watching events in order that it
may be able, if necessary, to advise Her Majesty's Government on
any important question that may arise.' [1]

As regards the actual operations in the field we left the Sirdar
concentrating his troops at 'Akāshah. He was allowed discretion
by Cromer to advance to Farkah, which was considered a better
place from a strategic point of view. At dawn on June 7 he surprised the Dervishes at Farkah under the leadership of Hamūda
Idris, and a battle ensued. In spite of the superiority of numbers
and arms on Kitchener's side, the Dervishes 'resisted gallantly, holding hills and village,' [2] but they were completely defeated in every
position by the Egyptian army, which sustained slight casualties.
'All troops behaved magnificently.' The Egyptian army, therefore, stood the first test, and the military success which Cromer
needed for an easy solution of his difficulties, particularly the
financial ones, was secured. Reports received by the Sirdar told
of the loss of morale of the Dervishes at Dongola brought about
by their defeat at Farkah and their huge losses. Unfortunately
for Kitchener he was expected to fight another enemy perhaps
more formidable, cholera. He heard that the epidemic had broken
out at Aswan and Kurusko.[3] The army had by necessity to halt
because of the expected fight against the epidemic, and also to
wait for the rise of the Nile before using the river steamboats.

[1] Lansdowne's comment on ibid.
[2] General Officer Commanding in Egypt to Secretary of State for War, No.
34, June 7, 1896, P.R.O., F.O. 78/4894.
[3] Cromer to Salisbury, No. 174, une 15, 1896, P.R.O., 78/4894.

Cholera spread southwards to the camp. Notwithstanding all the strenuous efforts to stem its tide, it took a toll of about 800 persons from soldiers and camp followers.

The advance to Dongola started in September by the occupation of Karma, which was evacuated by the Mahdists, who crossed to the left bank at Hafir. The gunboats, assisted by the fire of battalions on the east bank, carried out the bombardment of the Dervishes' position at Hafir and continued on their way southwards towards Dongola, while the Sirdar with his forces remained at Karma pending further news of the Dervish movements.[1] On the next day it became clear that the Dervishes had evacuated Hafir and the Egyptian army began crossing the river to occupy the deserted position.[2] The advance towards Dongola was resumed as soon as the army was in a position to move from Hafir, and on September 23, the town was enveloped in a semicircle by the Egyptian army approaching from the desert side with the boats bombarding it from the river. Wad Bishara, the Amir of the place, beat a hurried retreat, evacuating the town. Those who stayed behind surrendered and the Egyptian flag was hoisted on the old building of the province headquarters.[3] Kitchener had to occupy the rest of the province up to Marawi, and Cromer just returning from leave reported that so far as he could gather the 'Sudan campaign is virtually over.'[4]

[1] Rodd to Salisbury, No. 233, Sept. 19, 1896, P.R.O., F.O. 78/4894.
[2] Rodd to Salisbury, No. 234, Sept. 20, 1896, P.R.O., F.O. 78/4894.
[3] Rodd to Salisbury, No. 240, Sept. 23, 1896, P.R.O., F.O. 78/4894.
[4] Cromer to Salisbury, No.242, Sept. 24, 1896, P.R.O., F.O. 78/4895.

XVI

KHARTUM CAMPAIGN

As soon as Dongola was successfully captured, the Egyptian ministers nursed the hope of a further advance. The British Government required a respite before they could think of advancing into the interior. From a military point of view the Sirdar considered it essential to reach Marawi so that the cataracts of the Manasir country would afford a barrier on the river, while the desert south of al-Dabba would form a natural frontier. Cromer believed that there were 'no insuperable military objections to a further advance, now that the dervishes have received a severe blow.'[1] In his opinion the question was wholly one of money, and it was quite certain that Egypt could not pay if the campaign had to continue. If the British Government were not willing to pay there would be no question of advance. Salisbury's reaction was that he should give his colleagues time to think very carefully of the matter before they gave a decision. After full discussion in the Cabinet the British Government replied to Cromer as follows: 'There is no change in our policy with respect to the Sudan advance. Financial considerations do not, in our judgment, make it possible to carry our occupation further than Marawi this year.'[2] In a letter Salisbury explained why they objected to any immediate advance. They thought that it would be impossible to advance without more railway. They suggested to Cromer that he should send a reconnoitering party to ascertain what railway was needed. 'Ought it to strike Barbar or Matammah or any point between the two? and from what point between al-Dabbah and Marawi should the railway start?'[3] Salisbury informed Cromer that their alienation from Germay seemed to be progressing and they therefore could no longer rely on her co-operation for their Egyptian policy.

For expenditure on the Dongola campaign we left the Egyp-

[1] Cromer to Salisbury, No. 245, Confidential, Sept. 27, 1896, P.R.O., F.O. 78/4894.

[2] Salisbury to Cromer, No. 111, Oct. 5, 1896, P.R.O., F.O. 78/4895.

[3] Salisbury to Cromer, No. 112, Oct. 5, 1896, P.R.O., F.O. 78/4895.

tian Government applying to the *caisse la de dette* for half a million pounds from the general reserve fund; and the British Government had succeeded in persuading Italy, Germany, and Austria to instruct their agents in the *caisse* to support this application. The commissioners of the *caisse* accordingly approved the measure, the French and Russian commissioners objecting. It was thought on the British side that a majority was sufficient decision, while the French and the Russian commissioners held the view that the decision was illegal, and brought an action against the Egyptian Government in the Mixed Tribunals. The Court of First Instance passed judgment against Egypt and ordered the Egyptian Government to return the money to the *caisse*. Egypt, however, appealed to the Mixed Court of Appeal, but it was clear to Cromer that most probably Egypt would lose the case and an alternative should be sought.

With this probability of Egypt losing the case in mind, Cromer saw nothing for it but that either Her Majesty's Government should pay or advance the money to Egypt. 'If this is done we should certainly announce that we intend to control administration and therefore Revenue and Expenditure of the reconquered Provinces.' [1] On the 2nd of December 1896 the Mixed Court of Appeal passed their judgment confirming the decision of the Court of First Instance and thus Egypt had to pay back the half-million pounds. On the same day Cromer was authorized by the Chancellor of the Exchequer to state that Her Majesty's Government would be prepared 'to advance so much as they are satisfied that the Egyptian Treasury is unable to provide on conditions as to interest and repayment of capital which will be settled hereafter.' [2] As this advance of money to Egypt would require a parliamentary vote, the Chancellor of the Exchequer asked Cromer some relevant questions as regards the legal situation in Dongola in order to be able to reply to questions that might arise. [3] Before receiving these queries, Cromer had already sent his suggestions on how to proceed with this question of advance of money. He suggested that the English treasury should advance a sum not exceeding one million pounds and the Egyptian Government

[1] Cromer to Salisbury, No. 255, Oct. 21, 1896, P.R.O., F.O. 78/4895.
[2] Salisbury to Cromer, No. 121, Dec. 2, 1896, P.R.O., F.O. 78/4895.
[3] Salisbury to Cromer, No. 123, Dec. 3, 1896, P.R.O., F.O. 78/4895.

would pay interest and sinking fund at the rate of 4 per cent. Until the interest were repaid, Dongola and further territory reconquered would be administered by the Sirdar in the name of Her Majesty's Government acting under orders from Cromer. In practice the Sirdar would be under the financial adviser to the Egyptian Government. To guard against interference from the *caisse*, the revenue and expenditure of the Sudan should be kept separate. Cromer anticipated a deficit for the first three years and recommended that Her Majesty's Government should be responsible for its payment. 'Looking to situation generally it would appear desirable not to lose the present very favorable opportunity of strengthening our position in Egypt and the Sudan.'[1] Cromer in his reply to the Chancellor's queries stated that the arrangement proposed would be opposed by the Khedive but he attached no importance to this point. The ministers would really not mind and perhaps would be pleased. But Cromer maintained that the ministers would not be persuaded to give assent to the political part of the arrangement suggested by him. 'By far the best plan will be not to consult them but to communicate to them decision of Her Majesty's Government. I am sure that this is what they would prefer.'[2] Sir Thomas Sanderson, the Permanent Under-Secretary of State for Foreign Affairs, minuted under the above dispatch of Cromer:

> Logically it will not be very easy to defend a proclamation by the Khedive's Commander in chief that he is administering and occupying the Sudan with the Khedive's officers and troops on behalf of Her Majesty's Government and by their orders. Such a course is also at variance with our original announcement that we had authorized an Egyptian advance into the Sudan.

It was quite natural to find this divergence of view between Cromer and the Foreign Office. Taking the local conditions alone the former considered it feasible, but the latter envisaged the international difficulties it might entail. Acting on Sanderson's minute Salisbury telegraphed to Cromer pointing out that the proceeding suggested by him would be too illogical and would offend most of the sovereigns and ministers on the Continent in

---

[1] Cromer to Salisbury, No. 275, Dec. 4, 1896, P.R.O., F.O. 78/4895.
[2] Cromer to Salisbury, No. 276, Dec. 4, 1896, P.R.O., F.O. 78/4895.

addition to the grave criticism that might arise from Parliament. 'You must not count on Germany's support as a certainty. If she saw us in a difficulty she would attempt to blackmail.'[1]

This advance of money from the British Government to Egypt after an adverse decision by the Mixed Tribunal seemed to have had a great effect on the Khedive's relation with the British. He presided at a council of ministers in which it was decided to send an official letter expressing in warm terms the gratitude of the Egyptian Government to Her Majesty's Government for the financial help offered to them.[2] Two days later Cromer reported that the attitude of the Khedive about the Sudan affairs was for the time being by no means unfavorable.[3]

The advance beyond Dongola seemed to have been agreed upon, but again financial and transport considerations had unavoidably delayed it. It was Kitchener's opinion from the beginning that for any advance towards Barbar and Khartum the spanning of the desert between Kurusko and Abu Hamad by a railway would be preferable to the old project of a railway from Dongola Province in the neighborhood of al-Dabba to Barbar or to Matammah. The great difficulty of the Kurusko-Abu Hamad railway was water, but Kitchener thought it could be provided by the Murrat wells, half-way. After making a preliminary survey, Kitchener decided to make Wadi Halfa the starting-point for the railway and not Kurusko.[4] In the new year of 1897 work on this railway had actually started.

Among the preparations for the proposed advance beyond Dongola, some additional Nile boats had to be ordered through the British Admiralty. This raised the whole question of expenses over and above the half-million pounds advanced by Her Majesty's Government. Cromer maintained that if an advance had to be made beyond Abu Hamad in 1897 the half-million pounds should be augmented by an additional sum.[5] Salisbury replied that the amount of assistance to be given by Her Majesty's Government would depend upon the surplus which the Chancellor of the Exchequer could find towards the end of the financial year. Subject

[1] Salisbury to Cromer, No. 125, Secret, Dec. 5, 1896, P.R.O., F.O. 78/4895.
[2] Cromer to Salisbury, No. 279, Dec. 5, 1896, P.R.O., F.O. 78/4895.
[3] Cromer to Salisbury, No. 283, Dec. 7, 1896, P.R.O., F.O. 78/4895.
[4] Cromer to Salisbury, No. 290, Dec. 12, 1896, P.R.O., F.O. 78/4895.
[5] Cromer to Salisbury, No. 294, Dec. 16, 1896, P.R.O., F.O. 78/4895.

to this consideration the British Government would advance to Egypt in addition to the half-million £E.240,000 for the purchase of railway material for the Wadi Halfa-Abu Hamad line. The interest would be 2⅔ per cent. and no sinking fund. But the Egyptian Government 'will record an understanding with Her Majesty's Government that the principal shall be repaid by such payments from the annual Egyptian surplus as may be from time to time possible.' [1] Any surplus from the Sudan budget would go to this purpose and Her Majesty's Government could not undertake the responsibility for future Sudanese deficit. Salisbury made it clear that the above arrangement would not imply that they sanctioned any advance beyond Barbar during 1897.

When Kitchener left for the Sudan to enter on the new phase of the Sudan campaign he had discussed all aspects of the advance beyond Dongola. In a long dispatch Cromer discussed all the probabilities of the future. The chief military fact was that the Khalifah's power was still intact and it had to be encountered somewhere. Taking the strength of the Egyptian army, whether of the existing battalions or of those in process of formation and allowing for the necessity of not reducing the garrisons of Sawakin and Tūkar, there would be no reserves, and a serious reverse to the main body of the Egyptian army would make it inevitable to fall back on British help. Although the Egyptian army did well in the recent campaign, yet absolute reliance on it was still a matter of doubt. It would depend on the conditions under which they had to fight. Past experience of fighting with the Mahdiya troops illustrated the principle that where a disciplined army opposes an undisciplined one the former has a great advantage provided that the commander can select his own ground. It was not possible, however, to feel certain that the Egyptian commander would always be in a position to choose his own battlefield. Reports coming from the Khalifah's side as regards the extent of his preparations and the direction in which he might move were confusing and unreliable. It would be impossible to prepare a plan to meet with the danger coming from that quarter. The commander had to be constantly on the watch and to be prepared, so far as possible, for all emergencies as circumstances might dictate. If things went off normally the plan would be to collect railway material at Wadi

[1] Salisbury to Cromer, No. 137, Dec. 20, 1896, P.R.O., F.O. 78/4895.

Halfa, to push on the railway a part of the way southwards to Abu Hamad, then to march troops up the river from Marawi to Abu Hamad and finish the line to that place. The next task would be the general consolidation of the position at Abu Hamad before contemplating any further advance. It would be a great advantage if the Khalifah decided to have the encounter to the north of Omdurman in the neighborhood of Barbar, as it was preferable that it should take place nearer to Egypt rather than to Khartum.

The general instructions to Kitchener from Cromer laid emphasis on the fact that if Kitchener at any time found himself in a military position he could not cope with, he should not hesitate to inform Cromer of the fact. Although it would be unreasonable to ask a military commander to guarantee success, yet Cromer maintained the utmost confidence in Kitchener's military knowledge and discretion. 'He is cautious and at the same time has that amount of dash without which no military commander can hope to succeed.' [1] Looking to the difficulties of marching a large force across the Jakdul desert, it was improbable that the Dervishes would come in sufficient numbers down to Dongola Province to attack Egyptian positions there. Yet all the Egyptian troops in Dongola were either already entrenched or would be so very shortly. For the time being Kitchener proposed to maintain a defensive attitude. Cromer could not give an opinion on the time when the advance on Abu Hamad could be made nor on the time required for the completion of the railway.

It is interesting to note the resolution adopted by the Committee of the International Arbitration and Peace Association about this advance into the Sudan:

This Committee learns with profound regret that the British Government contemplates a further advance of troops towards Omdurman. The International Arbitration and Peace Association has for several years past protested against the unduly prolonged occupation of Egypt by British forces as calculated to alienate the sympathies of other powers through being open to the interpretation of a breach of faith. The step now contemplated will undoubtedly arouse new jealousies and cause more protests and in the event of the advance leading to the occupation of further territory and thus to the expansion of British interest, the sentiment of suspicion and hostility on the part of other nations might not impossibly result in an ultimatum

[1] Cromer to Salisbury, No. 25, Secret, Feb. 17, 1897, P.R.O., F.O. 78/4895.

presented to Great Britain involving national humiliation or the prospect and peril of war.

The Committee would again urge on Her Majesty's Government the desirability of entering into peaceful negotiations with the leaders of the native tribes with a view to the extension of legitimate trade and commerce and the permanent pacification of the Sudan.[1]

When the railway from Wadi Halfa to Abu Hamad progressed and was approaching the latter place, it was inevitable that the place would have to be captured from the Mahdiya. Hunter Pasha, the commander of the infantry in the Egyptian army, advanced with a column over the Manasir country and after a severe battle he managed to capture Abu Hamad on the morning of August 7, 1897.[2] Hunter had some very anxious moments at Abu Hamad, for his was a comparatively small force detached from the main body of the army. If the Khalifa determined to send his Barbar garrison with reinforcement from the south, the isolation and ultimate annihilation of that little band at Abu Hamad was more than probable. But, fortunately for Hunter, the Khalifah guessed that the invading army would repeat Lord Wolseley's plan by sending a column across the desert to Matammah. In this case the Barbar garrison would serve no purpose and thus Zaki 'Uthman, the Amir of Barbar, received orders to evacuate the place, which was subsequently occupied by the Egyptian army without a fight.

In November 1897 it became evident to the military authorities in Cairo that in spite of the successes of the Egyptian army and the defeats sustained by the Khalifah's troops, the situation was that Dervish resistance had crystallized rather than that their forces had been disrupted. The General Officer Commanding in Egypt was of opinion that the 'Egyptian Army is unable, without danger, to continue their advance without support.'[2] The occupation of Barbar had brought the two forces almost within striking distance of one another, 'and should the enemy undertake offensive operations in almost any direction, no one could view the situation without disquiet.' The situation as it appeared to the General

---

[1] July 28, 1897, P.R.O., F.O. 78/4895.
[2] De Salis to Salisbury, No. 79, Aug. 9, 1897, P.R.O., F.O. 78/4895.
[3] General Officer Commanding in Egypt to Under-Secretary of State for War, No. 7700/8476, Nov. 19, 1897, P.R.O., F.O. 78/4895.

Officer Commanding in Egypt was that there was no doubt of the ability of the Egyptian army to repel any attack, but owing to the great distance separating the various detachments and the state of the river, combined action by the whole army would be difficult.

The above warning did not move the British Government to action on the question of support, but reports received about the Khalifah's movements began to be alarming. It was known that a large force collected at Omdurman was ready to move to Matammah. Saltin Pasha, who was in the intelligence service of the Egyptian army, thought that it might have been the intention of the Khalifah to drive the Egyptians out of Barbar.[1] In order to meet that probable threat the units of the Egyptian army at Marawi and Abu Hamad were hurried to Barbar to meet the Khalifah's troops on the line of the Atbara river.[2] At the same time Cromer telegraphed to Kitchener expressing his anxiety about the military situation in the Sudan. He required Kitchener to state whether the force under his command was strong enough to meet the attack which seemed to be impending. If it was not sufficient Kitchener was urged to give warning while there was time.[3] Cromer was reluctant to ask for British assistance if it could possibly be avoided. On the other hand, the Sirdar should be told to give timely warning if he urgently needed assistance. The General Officer Commanding in Egypt assured Cromer that two British battalions in Cairo could, in case of need, reach Barbar in about a fortnight.[4] This was made possible because the railway had reached Abu Hamad and continued beyond it southwards.

Leaving the Egyptian army concentrating at Barbar, let us go to Omdurman and see the reaction of the Khalifah, especially with respect to that force of his that moved to Matammah as mentioned above. It was the Khalifah's guess that the invading army would follow the same route as that of Wolseley's desert column. The line of defense, therefore, should be on the river at Matammah. It was the Khalifah's plan to meet the Egyptian army somewhere in the neighborhood of Matammah when it would be emerging from the desert in an exhausted state and block their march to the river.

[1] Cromer to Salisbury, No. 152, Dec. 21, 1897, P.R.O., F.O. 78/7895.
[2] General Officer Commanding to Secretary of State for War, Dec. 22, 1897, P.R.O., F.O. 78/7895.
[3] Cromer to Salisbury, No. 154, Dec. 22, 1897, P.R.O., F.O. 78/4895.
[4] Cromer to Salisbury, No. 155, Dec. 22, 1897, P.R.O., F.O. 78/4895.

It was his idea to entrust this job to the Ja'alin themselves, the inhabitants of the place, but if they failed to perform the task his own troops would proceed to Matammah and occupy it, and its inhabitants should be evacuated to Shandi on the eastern bank of the river. 'Abdallah Wad Sa'ad, the chief of the Ja'alin, seemed to have shown his inability to stop the advance of the army, and the other alternative, the evacuation of Matammah, became inevitable. 'Abdallah left Omdurman with the understanding that the Khalifah's army would very soon proceed to Matammah to occupy it. But in his heart 'Abdallah seemed to be determined not to co-operate with the Khalifah whether by fighting his battle for him or by evacuating the capital of the Ja'alin country. When once back in his town 'Abdallah with a relatively small number of his tribe determined to oppose the Khalifah's army. Mahmud, the general commanding the Khalifah's forces, was resisted when he approached the town and it was unavoidable that a battle should decide the issue. It was a foregone conclusion that superiority of arms and numbers was on Mahmud's side and the town was subjected to the sword, which left it in a pitiable state. 'Abdallah's non-cooperative attitude to the Khalifh could be understood when we recall his attempts to collaborate with Kitchener in a revolt against the Mahdiya in 1894. Mahmud, after breaking the Ja'alin resistance, had to sit at Matammah waiting for Kitchener's army to emerge from the desert and then encounter it. It was this march of Mahmud's army from Omdurman that alarmed Cromer and the General Officer Commanding in Egypt and which was interpreted by them to mean an advance to Barbar.

Towards the end of December 1897, reports, which were confirmed by Kitchener's gunboats that patrolled the Nile, indicated that the Khalifah was intending to move at the head of reinforcements to join Mahmud at Matammah. It was expected that he would be in that town on the 25th of January 1898. Kitchener asked that English troops should be ready to move up the Nile. Consequently the General Officer Commanding asked permission to use the Lincolnshire regiment, which was under orders for India, if necessary.[1] In the new year of 1898 Hunter at Barbar reported the news of the Khalifah's advance: 'It appears,' Kitchener

[1] General Officer Commanding to Secretary of State for War, No. 7700/8513, Dec. 31, 1897, P.R.O., F.O. 78/4895.

wrote, 'as if the fight for the Sudan would be at Barbar.' [1] On this same day two British battalions were placed under orders to proceed to Wadi Halfa and the Sirdar was asked to telegraph his recommendations for any additional force.[2] The military authorities in London were somewhat worried about the precarious position of Kitchener's army if the Dervishes were to make use of their opportunity. The secretary of State for War asked the General Officer Commanding in Egypt whether he was satisfied that a brigade would suffice to enable Kitchener to defeat the enemy or even to hold his position. 'Let me have timely warning should more troops be required.' [3] General Grenfell replied that a brigade would be sufficient to repel any attack from the Mahdiya but Kitchener should have enough forces not only to repel attack but to follow the enemy up and take Matammah under any circumstances that winter. In Grenfell's opinion the War Office should be prepared to send three more battalions and replace any cavalry and artillery sent from Cairo.[4] When Kitchener was given time to survey his force he reported that with the British assistance he already had his army was sufficient to resist attack. But if he had eventually to take the offensive he would require, in addition to the four battalions which would shortly be available, four further battalions, a regiment of cavalry, a battery of field artillery, and a detachment of forty-pounders.[5] The whole military question seemed to be perplexing to Cromer, who realized that the choice was between evils. He was opposed to keeping British troops for a long time in the Sudan. At the same time an attack by the Dervishes was probable at any moment. He was not certain what instructions to give to Kitchener; and in the case of an attack from the Khalifah being repulsed, whether to allow him to follow up his victories or not.[6] On the 19th of January Kitchener telegraphed that he would be able to cope with anything but a very exceptional

[1] Kitchener to Cromer, quoted in Cromer to Salisbury, No. 1, Jan. 1, 1898, P.R.O., F.O. 78/5049.
[2] Cromer to Salisbury, No. 2, Jan. 1, 1989, P.R.O., F.O. 78/5049.
[3] Secretary of State for War to General Officer Commanding, Jan. 5, 1898,
[4] General Officer Commanding to Secretary of State for War, Jan. 5, 1898, P.R.O., F.O. 78/5049.
[5] Cromer to Salisbury, No. 11, Jan. 6, 1898, P.R.O., F.O. 78/5049.
P.R.O., F.O. 78/5049.
[6] Cromer to Salisbury, No. 16, Jan. 7, 1898, P.R.O., F.O. 78/5049.

movement on the part of the Dervishes with only three battalions,
and so the reinforcements he asked for some days previously were
ordered to remain in Cairo and thus the estimate of expenditure
was reduced.[1] On the 31st of January, 1898 it was reported to the
Sirdar that the Khalifah had relinquished his plans for taking the
offensive and was busy building forts at Omdurman for defensive
purposes.[2]

Kitchener, therefore, had a respite in which he could consolidate
his position and extend his railway southwards. But on the 25th of
February it was reported that Mahmud was going to attack Atbara
Fort with his force of 12,000 men. This news necessitated the
sending of the British Brigade, which was under orders to join
Kitchener's army at any moment.[3] Sir Francis Grenfell happened
to be in the Sudan at that time. Cromer wished to remove any
doubt about the responsibility for conducting war operations. He
telegraphed to Kitchener stating that in spite of Grenfell's presence
in the Sudan, he was exclusively responsible for all military operations south of Daraw whether they were undertaken by British or
Egyptian troops.[4] When it was confirmed to Kitchener that Mahmud had actually crossed the river to Shandi and moved northwards, he concentrated his troops at Kennur to the north of
Atbara fort. On the Mahdiya side, however, there was some
difference of opinion between Mahmud the Commander and 'Uthman Diqna his subordinate, about the line of march. The difference
was referred to the Khalifah, who decided in favor of 'Uthman.
'Uthman's plan was to strike into the desert and then outflank the
Egyptian army at Atbara and descend on the Nile at Barbar behind
their lines, thus cutting their line of retreat. In execution of this
plan Mahmud left the river at 'Alyab and proceeded in an easterly
direction. Kitchener had to make his plans in accordance with
this strategy and these tactics and had, therefore, to move along
the Atbara river so as to block the enemy' path. Mahmud, however, came to the Atbara river at al-Nikhailah and knowing that
Kitchener was determined not to be outflanked, he entrenched
inside a zaribah on the river bank waiting to repulse an attack that

[1] Cromer to Salisbury, No. 33, Jan. 19, 1898, P.R.O., F.O. 78/5049.
[2] Cromer to Salisbury, No. 41, Jan. 31, 1898, P.R.O., F.O. 78/5049.
[3] Cromer to Salisbury, No. 57, Feb. 25, 1898, P.R.O., F.O. 78/5049.
[4] Cromer to Salisbury, No. 58, Feb. 25, 1898, P.R.O., F.O. 78/5049.

seemed to him to be imminent. Kitchener on his part encamped on the Atbara waiting for Mahmud's attack. Both sides were reconnoitring each other's positions, with skirmishes between these reconnoitring parties attended by casualties on both sides.

The reason why Kitchener avoided attacking Mahmud was that the latter was entrenched in thick bush in a position not at all favorable to the British and Egyptian forces, while in front of him there was a fairly good fighting ground, and he hoped that Mahmud would come out of the thick bush. Cromer replied to the above that he understood Kitchener's reason for not advancing and had no doubt that that was the correct attitude. Past experience went to show the inadvisability of risking a general action on unfavorable ground. 'Your conduct of the operations inspires me with fullest confidence and I am sure that this confidence is fully shared by all responsible authorities in England.'[1] Cromer further told Kitchener to telegraph any news which he did not want to leak out in Foreign Office cypher. When sending the above to Kitchener, Cromer had in mind the disposition in military circles to criticize Kitchener for not going on and Cromer did not at all want Kitchener's hand to be forced. 'All the information received goes to show that the Khalifah 'Abdullah is determined to make a great effort and to fight it out to the bitter end.'[2]

The military problem for Kitchener was how to ascertain the enemy's position, entrenched behind a zariba in thick bush. A sufficient force under General Hunter went out to reconnoitre until they came within 300 yards of Mahmud's trenches, which were found to be in a strong position with a zariba and in heavy bush. 'It was so thick that they were unable to get more than a partial view of the encampment. Enemy were lying in the trenches, which were in some places in three rows, one behind the other.'[3] This reconnaissance, however, did not give Kitchener a clear picture of Mahmud's position as the Dervishes did not leave their trenches, probably waiting for an attack at close quarters. He telegraphed to Cromer that the situation was rather perplexing, as they could not know the intentions of Mahmud, whether he

[1] Cromer to Kitchener, quoted in Cromer to Sanderson, Private, Mar. 4, 1898, P.R.O., F.O. 78/5049.

[2] Cromer to Sanderson, Private, Mar. 4, 1898, P.R.O., F.O. 78/5049.

[3] Sirdar to Cromer, quoted in Cromer to Foreign Office, No. 110, Mar. 31, 1898, P.R.O., F.O. 78/5049.

would assume an offensive or continue in his defensive position. Discussion of the situation with Hunter, commander of the Egyptian infantry, and Gatacre, commander of the British Brigade, revealed that Hunter preferred waiting rather than attacking Mahmud in that unsuitable position. Kitchener, however, maintained that they would undoubtedly have a great advantage if only Mahmud would advance. On the other hand, if he should retire, they would have lost the opportunity of dealing a blow that would probably considerably affect future resistance in the Sudan. 'I have little doubt our attack on his present entrenched position would be successful though it would probably entail considerable loss.' [1] Kitchener, therefore, decided not to change his present position for three days, before which he hoped to know something definite and asked for Cromer's views.

Cromer sent his views to Kitchener remarking that they should not be regarded as instructions but merely as observations on the position as it struck him at a distance. 'I have no desire to cripple your full liberty of action in case you should think it desirable to act contrary to the view to which I incline. Whatever you may decide to do I wish to assure you that you will receive full support both from myself and I am sure I may add from the authorities at home.' [2] Cromer in agreement with Grenfell put forward five reasons why the policy of waiting and letting Mahmud attack was preferable; it was very important on local and general grounds to obviate so far as possible any risk of a reverse; it would be imprudent to try the Egyptian army too highly; all former experience of warfare in the Sudan had shown the great importance of choosing ground for an engagement which would be favorable to the action of a disciplined and well-armed force; Cromer attached great weight to the opinion of Hunter, who had seen the Dervish position and who had more experience of Sudan warfare and was better acquainted with the Egyptian army than Gatacre; it was highly probable that Mahmud could not stay for long where he was and if he retired without fighting, he would be discredited. On the other hand, the argument that the retirement of Mahmud would

[1] Kitchener to Cromer, quoted in Cromer to Foreign Office, No. 111, Apr. 1, 1898, P.R.O., F.O. 78/5049.
[2] Cromer to Kitchener, quoted in Cromer to Foreign Office, No. 112, Apr. 2, 1898, P.R.O., F.O. 78/5049.

strengthen future resistance appeared to Cromer not to be sufficiently weighty to counterbalance the arguments on the other side.
'My inclination, therefore, is to advise patience. I am disposed to
think you had better not attack for the present, but allow events to
develop and wait for your opportunity for action.'[1] The reaction
of the Foreign Office was that unless Kitchener wished for military
opinion, they would refrain from offering any remarks which
would interfere with his absolute discretion. 'He may count on our
support whichever course he decides on adopting.'[2]

Before receiving Cromer's comments Kitchener, in agreement
with Hunter and Gatacre, had decided to attack Mahmud's position, probably on April 6th. But if Cromer's reaction should prove
unfavorable to the attack, he would postpone the forward
movement. Cromer immediately told Kitchener not to be deterred
by observations made at a distance if it was thought advisable
to attack. Cromer admitted that it was very difficult to give any
valuable opinion from Cairo. The situation appeared to have been
materially altered, from Cromer's point of view, since Hunter,
who was opposed to the advance, had come round to the other
point of view: 'I must leave the decision to you, only again assuring
you that whatever you decide you will be fully supported.'[3]
Kitchener's reaction to Cromer's telegram with the observation
preferring waiting was to postpone the attack on Mahmud's position for the time being.[4] But when he received the two telegrams
from Cromer and the Foreign Office allowing him absolute discretion, he again decided to advance but more slowly and with greater
deliberation than he had originally intended, so that by careful
reconnaissances he would assure the success of the attack.

I shall not commit myself to a general attack, until, as far as I can judge,
the right moment has arrived. My present difficulty is to know with any
certainty how long the dervishes can hold out under the privations they are
undergoing, and I think that by getting nearer them I shall have better
opportunity of ascertaining this.[5]

[1] Ibid.
[2] Foreign Office to Cromer, No. 31, Apr. 2, 1898, P.R.O., F.O. 78/5049.
[3] Cromer to Kitchener, quoted in Cromer to Foreign Office, No. 113. Apr. 3,
1898, P.R.O., F.O. 78/5049.
[4] Cromer to Foregin Office, No. 114, Apr. 3, 1898, P.R.O., F.O. 78/5049.
[5] Kitchener to Cromer, quoted in Cromer to Foreign Office, No. 115, Apr. 4,
1898, P.R.O., F.O. 78/5049.

When the Sirdar came nearer Mahmud's position and before ordering a general attack on his enemy's entrenched position, he thought of carrying out a last reconnaissance. Mahmud's horsemen and footmen, who came out of the zaribah, engaged this reconnoitring party and casualties were sustained on both sides, but Mahmud's losses were by far the greater. 'Troops all behaved well. General Hunter who was in command specially mentioned value of Maxims.'[1] Kitchener, who feared Mahmud might receive supplies at any time, ordered a general attack for the morning of April 8th. At 6:15 on the morning of April 8th the first guns were fired on Mahmud's zaribah, and were replied to by sustained firing from the Dervishes. The whole army lined up in an attacking formation and rushed the zaribah until they reached the river. It was inevitable that Mahmud's losses should be heavy, because his men stuck stubbornly to their posts. On the other hand, the losses of Kitchener's army were more than they would have sustained if they had chosen their own battle ground. Mahmud himself was taken prisoner and the cavalry pursued the retreating Dervishes.[2]

Leaving Kitchener now preparing for the advance on Omdurman, we turn to the attempts of the British Government to establish cordial relations with Abyssinia on the assumption that sooner or later there might arise frontier problems with the King of Kings. This necessity arose when it was evident that the advance should be carried beyond Dongola and ultimately to Khartum and southwards. A mission, at the head of which was Mr. Rennel Rodd, was formed to proceed to Addis Ababa. His instructions contained an assurance to King Menelek from Her Majesty's Government of friendly feeling on their part towards Abyssinia and of their desire to maintain the most cordial relations with him. Rodd had to explain to Menelek that the operations undertaken by the Egyptian Government were solely for the restoration of provinces which were formerly under Egypt and were not moved by any hostility towards Abyssinia. Broadly speaking the British Government would entertain no objection to recognizing an Abyssinian frontier between the tenth and fifteenth parallels of north latitude which

---

[1] Kitchener to Cromer, quoted in Cromer to Foreign Office, No. 119, Apr. 6, 1898, P.R.O., F.O. 78/5049.
[2] Kitchener to Cromer, quoted in Cromer to Foreign Office, No. 122, Apr. 8, 1898, P.R.O., F.O. 78/5049.

would not exceed the sphere of influence assigned to Italy by the protocol of April 15th, 1891.

They would, indeed, be ready to agree to a further extension of the frontier as far as that portion of the Blue Nile which lies between Karkuj and Famaka, if it should be necessary for the purpose of securing King Menelek's alliance and cooperation against the dervishes. But the matter is one which largely concerns Egyptian interests.[1]

Mr. Rodd had to be guided in his negotiations on this point by the information and advice which he would receive from Lord Cromer before leaving Cairo.

When Rodd arrived at Addis Ababa he was cordially welcomed by Menelek and the appearance of the British mission made a good impression on him. It was known there that the Khailfah had sent two missions to Menelek. Rodd could not obtain the details of these Dervish missions but it was understood that their object was to secure more friendly relations with Menelek in view of the threatened Anglo-Egyptian advance south of Dongola. The Emperor's reaction was reported to be one of disinterested neutrality. It appeared that he told the Khalifah's representatives that he was not intending to renew hostilities against the Mahdiya but at the same time he did not give any promise of aid. During their stay in Addis Ababa the Khalifah's ambassadors were lodged in the house of Archbishop Mathios and were not permitted to hold communication with any persons in the town. The head of the second mission was Muhammad 'Uthman Wad Hajj Khalid al-'Umarabi.[2]

When beginning actual negotiations with Menelek Rodd discovered that the utmost concession which he had been authorized to give to Abyssinia even in the case of common action against the Mahdists fell far short of the territory which the Emperor actually claimed as part of his empire, in addition to the large area to which he asserted a theoretical claim which he showed his intention to maintain. The idea which Menelek held and which was carefully fostered by his French advisers was that he might enlarge his borders in the direction of the Sudan without fear of encountering

[1] Foreign Office to Mr. Rood, Feb. 1897, F.O. 1/32.
[2] Memorandum by Lt.-Col. Wingate with the assistance of Capt. Count Gleichon, enclosed in Rodd to Salisbury, No. 18, Confidential, May 9, 1897, P.R.O., F.O. 1/32.

active opposition on the part of the British. This move on the part of Menelek would have the full countenance and moral support of the French. Rodd found no argument to dispel this idea. 'Should the recapture of Omdurman be decided on, and should a fleet of powerful steamers eventually patrol the long reach of Nile, which extends without obstacle from Khartum to Fashoda, we should have that moral force behind us in stating our claims and those of Egypt in explicit terms, which is wholly wanting now.' [1] Acting on the information supplied by Rodd's mission, it was found necessary that Her Majesty's Government should have a resident agent in Addis Ababa to handle on the spot all outstanding problems with Abyssinia and to be prepared for the coming territorial diputes when the Anglo-Egyptian army had captured Khartum and advanced southwards. Cromer suggested explaining to Menelek by telegram the reasons why British troops were sent to the Sudan and that he should await further explanation on the arrival of the British agent. 'It is very desirable to keep him in a good humor and it will perhaps be as well that he should not hear the first news of the movement from other sources.' [2]

After the battle of Atbara, Kitchener sent his troops to their summer quarters between Atbara and 'Abidiya to give them some respite before he could resume his advance towards Omdurman. He reinforced his army still further by three more British battalions and a contingent of Arab friendlies to protect his desert flank in the advance. The Khalifah, on his part, determined to fight in defense of his capital by concentrating all his available soldiers at Omdurman and by fortifying the town and laying mines in the Nile to impede the progress of his enemy's boats. When all was set for resumption of the advance, Kitchener was favored by the friendly and co-operative attitude of the inhabitants on the Nile between Atbara and Omdurman and the occupation of Kasalah by the Egyptian troops through agreement with the Italians, who handed it over to Parsons Pasha, the commander of the Egyptian detachment. There were no difficult problems of transport and supplies and the line of communication with Egypt was efficiently maintained by the railway which by this time was approaching

[1] Rodd to Salisbury, No. 21, Very Confidential, May 14, 1897, P.R.O., F.O. 1/32.

[2] Cromer to Salisbury, No. 15, Confidential, Jan. 7, 1898, P.R.O., F.O. 78/5049.

Atbara. Kitchener's army encamped some few miles to the north of Omdurman and the Khalifah decided to fight his decisive battle for that town outside it. On the morning of September 2nd, 1898, the enthusiastic troops of the Mahdiya advanced in close formation towards Kitchener's zaribah affording a good target for the disciplined army's fire, especially for the Maxim guns. In spite of the large casualties sustained by them, those who were spared by the first shots jumped over the dead bodies of their comrades to fall, in their turn, in front of them. The total casualties of the Mahdiya amounted to about 12,000 men and the remnants retreated only after recognizing that it would be impossible to reach their enemy's zaribah against that incessant hail of bullets. When Kitchener was sure that the battle was decided in his favor, he ordered a general march towards Omdurman. Some of the Khalifah's troops, however, put up a last effort to impede the advance of the army, and although they gave anxious moments to a Sudanese brigade of the Egyptian army, the attempt failed and the road to Omdurman was cleared for the victorious army. The battle was decisive as far as the Mahdiya was concerned, but the Khalifah resolved to retreat to the west to strengthen himself in order to offer stronger resistance. Kitchener's preoccupation after Omdurman was chiefly about Fashoda, about which he received instructions and which we shall deal with in the next chapter. Before leaving for Fashoda he recommended the extension of the railway to the Blue Nile opposite Khartum in order to avoid the Sabaloqa cataracts which impeded the Nile navigation. Apart from its military advantages the extended railway would open up the country for trade.[1]

[1] Kitchener to Rodd, enclosed in Rodd to Salisbury, No. 139, Confidential, Sept. 10, 1898, P.R.O., F.O. 78/5050.

XVII

FASHODA CRISIS

We have seen how the expedition to Dongola was an unhappy surprise to the French, who calculated on the English advance from Uganda. Moreover, France had always proclaimed her respect for the rights of the Khedive in the Sudan. But this new situation did not deter them from proceeding with their project of the march to the Nile. They tried to frustrate the Dongola expedition by applying pressure on the Sultan and by using their financial veto. On April 18, 1896 Leon Bourgeois, the Foreign Minister at the time, received Captain Marchand, who declared that he would act in perfect accord with Liotard, that he woud deal with the Mahdists in an entirely peaceful manner, and that the extreme goal of his march would be the Nile at Fashoda. Marchand thought that he would reach a point in Bahr al-Ghazal near the Nile in eighteen months. 'No one can get there before the French, as they are by far the nearest to this point at Zemio.' [1]

Ten days later the Bourgeois cabinet resigned and was replaced by the Meline cabinet in which Hanotaux again became Foreign Minister and André Lebon was Colonial Minister. Lebon sent new instructions to Liotard saying that with the impending arrival of Marchand French action would enter upon a decisive phase. To him the policy was still the establishment of French influence in the Nile basin. Again the mission was described as a civilian and not a military undertaking. Plans of conquest could not be thought of in terms of small forces. To keep this exclusively peaceful character of the mission it should avoid coming to grips with the Dervishes. The official documents on the French side about this march to the Nile are not easily understood unless they are interpreted against the political atmosphere of the time. In France at that time the colonial group played a large part and carried great weight, as is evidenced by the personal welcome they met with from ministers and even from the President of the Republic. The public in Great Britain supported their Govern-

[1] Renouvin, Pierre, in*Revue Historique*, Oct.—Dec. 1948, p. 194.

428

ment, who looked upon the Nile valley as a vital British interest. Apart from this highly charged atmosphere the object that was maintained through all these French attempts was nothing but to plant the French flag on the Nile in order to reopen the question of Egypt. The French Government persistently continued to foster the project in spite of warning given in a private statement by Dufferin and a public statement by Grey that the French project if executed would ultimately lead to conflict. The French were of opinion that in face of a *fait accompli* the British Government would resign itself to negotiate. This was an error, as the Nile question was vital to the British and they would accept no negotiation on it.[1]

Rumors reached Kitchener as early an January 1898 about the presence of the French in the south and next he heard that the Khalifah had sent a force to intercept them.[2] In March 1898 one 'Abbadi Amir escaping from Omdurman told Kitchener that the presence of the French in Bahr al-Ghazal was known at Omdurman but there was no definite news about their occupation of any point on the Nile. The Khalifah was also aware of an Abyssinian advance towards Bani-Shangul.[3] By June 1898 it became clear that most probably the French would reach a point on the Nile and the Abyssinians would advance along the Blue Nile taking advantage of the Khalifah's occupation with the bigger danger from the north. In order to be prepared for both these eventualities, Cromer suggested sending a flotilla up each of the two Niles as soon as Omdurman was conquered and the Khalifah defeated. The White Nile expedition, which would probably encounter the French, should be larger and commanded by the Sirdar in person. The Bule Nile one should also be led by a senior British officer serving in the Egyptian army, but it would be composed of a smaller force. If a technical difficulty arose about which government these officers served, Cromer suggested that they should wear the distinctive marks of British and not of Egyptian uniform and that they should be considered as on a temporary transfer from one servise to the other. Instructions to the two commanders would

[1] Renouvin, op. cit., pp. 196-7.
[2] Sirdar to Cromer, quoted in Cromer to Salisbury, No. 37, Jan. 23, 1898, P.R.O., F.O. 78/5049.
[3] Sidar to Cromer, quoted in Cromer to Salisbury, No. 87, Mar. 9, 1898, P.R.O., F.O. 78/5049.

include defending themselves if they were attacked, but in respect of any French or Abyssinian force with which they might come in contact, they were on no account to take the offensive. 'Further, that they are to avoid so far as is possible, any action calculated to provoke an attack on themselves.' [1]

If the French flag was found flying on any spot on the Nile, Cromer suggested that the officer in command should be instructed to protest against the presence of a French force and 'formally to lay claim to the territory occupied. But is he to lay claim to the territory in the name of the English Government, or of the Khedive, or of both combined? definite instructions should be issued on this point which is obviously one of much importance.' [2]

On July 1st, Sir E. Monson, the British Ambassador in Paris, sent his impressions about the new cabinet to Salisbury. He was of opinion that M. Delcassé, the now Foreign Minister, would be a very combative minister. An Anglophobe writer in *Figaro* welcomed Delcassé's advent to the Quai d'Orsay 'in the confident hope that he will signalize it by vigor in dealing with the Egyptian Question.' [3] In another dispatch Monson maintained that Russia would most probably support France in case of conflict with Britain. [4]

Lord Cromer's memorandum of June 5th, was circulated to the members of the cabinet for discussion and instructions based on Cromer's suggestion were sent to Cairo. Kitchener, as commander of the White Nile flotilla, was instructed that in his dealing with any French or Abyssinian authorities who might be met, 'nothing should be said or done which would in any way imply a recognition on behalf of Her Majesty's Government of a title to possession on behalf of France or Abyssinia to any portion of the Nile valley.' [5] As regards France, in particular, the views of Her Majesty's Government were made clear in a note addressed to M. Hanotaux by Sir Edmund Monson on December 10th, 1897. The note contained the following relevant extract:

[1] Memorandum by Cromer to Salisbury, June 15, 1898, P.R.O., F.O. 78/4956.
[2] Ibid.
[3] Monson to Salisbury, July 1, 1898, *British Documents on the Origins of the War 1898-1941* (London, 927, edited by Gooch, G.P., and Temperly, Harold, with the assistance of Penson, Lillian M.), vol. i, p. 158.
[4] Monson to Salisbury, July 4, 1898, ibid., p. 159.
[5] Silisbury to Cromer, Aug. 2, 1898, ibid., pp. 159-61.

Her Majesty's Government must not be understood to admit that any other European power than Great Britain has any claim to occupy any part of the valley of the Nile. The views of the British Government upon this matter were plainly stated in Parliament by Sir Edward Grey some years ago, during the administration of the Earl of Rosebery, and were formally communicated to the French Government at the time. Her Majesty's present Government entirely adhere to the language that was on this occasion employed by their predecessors.[1]

Kitchener was urged to avoid any collision with the forces of the Emperor Menelek and his language should be that of referring any dispute to their respective governments. In the possible contingency of a French force actually in occupation of a point on the Nile, the attitude which Kitchener should adopt would depend on the local circumstances and Her Majesty's Government wished to give him discretion on that point. They felt that Kitchener should endeavor to convince the French commander that 'the presence of the latter in the Nile valley is an infringement of the rights both of Great Britain and of the Khedive.' In the case of an encounter with Belgians in the Lado area, they should be told that by the agreement of May 1894 they had no title to permanent possession but according to the agreement the British Government would not interfere with the temporary lease of certain specified territory.

When the results of the battle of Omdurman were known to the world, the French Government was sure that there would be a meeting between Marchand's mission, which was known to be well on its way to the Nile, and the Anglo-Egyptian force. On the 7th of September 1898 M. Delcassé received the diplomatic body as usual. On talking to Sir Edmund Monson Delcassé lost no time in congratulating him upon the Sudan victory. He stated that difference of opinion between the two countries about Egypt 'could not affect the judgment passed by France upon this brilliant feat of arms.'[2] Then the French Minister proceeded to the important subject of Marchand's mission. He told the British Ambassador that in the probable contingency of the two expeditions meeting on the upper Nile he wished to make it clear that Marchand had strict and definite instructions that he was nothing but an 'emissary to civilization' and under no circumstances had he to create local

---

[1] Salisbury to Cromer, Aug. 2, 1898, *British Documents*, p. 160.
[2] Monson to Salisbury, Sept. 8, 1898, ibid., p. 163.

conflicts about rights. All those subjects of principle would be taken up by the respective Governments at home. Delcassé wished that the British Government would convey the same instructions to her commanding officer so that a collision might be prevented. Delcassé referred to a previous conversation in which he maintained that all outstanding differences between Britain and France might be amicably settled in a patient spirit of conciliation. Monson tried by various questions to elicit something positive about the French mission but did not succeed, as the French Minister seemed to have no recent information about it. Monson's opinion at that time indicated that the French people and Government realized that they would gain nothing by blustering about Egypt. This did not mean that they would not create a storm about the British occupation of Egypt in both the press and Parliament. 'But while they very naturally try to argue that "logically" that occupation should now come to an end, they see clearly enough that the recent operations have simply clinched our hold upon Egypt more tightly, and that British "practice" cannot be assimilated to French "logic".'[1] Salisbury requested Monson, should Delcassé revert to the subject, to point out to him 'that by the military events of last week, all territories which were subject to the Khalifa passed to the British and Egyptian Governments by right of conquest. Her Majesty's Government do not consider that this right is open to discussion, but they would be prepared to deal in the manner suggested by His Excellency with any territorial controversies now existing in regard to those regions which are not affected by this assertion.'[2] When Delcassé was shown the tenor of this telegram, he confined himself to commenting upon the expression 'territories which were subject to the Khalifa,' which in his opinion was vague.[3]

In a further conversation reported by Monson, Delcassé inquired whether it was the opinion of Her Majesty's Government that Marchand had no right to be on the Nile. Monson replied that Britain openly warned France that any incursion into the Nile valley would be considered an unfriendly act and wondered why the French sent the Marchand mission knowing quite clearly that

---

[1] Ibid.
[2] Salisbury to Monson, Sept. 9, 1898, *British Documents*, p. 164.
[3] Monson to Salisbury, Sept. 10, 1898, ibid., pp. 164-5.

it might lead to a conflict. Delcassé reminded Monson that the French Government had never recognized the British sphere of influence. He resented the term 'Marchand Mission.' Marchand was nothing but a subordinate appointed by his superior M. Liotard, Commissioner of the upper Ubangi, to secure French interests in the north-east. Delcassé maintained that for a long time past the whole region of Bahr al-Ghazal had been out of the Khalifah's jurisdiction, and if the newspapers were correct there was some doubt whether Fashoda itself had been an occupied post of the Khalifah when Marchand took possession of it. Finally, Delcassé wished to impress upon Monson that 'if Her Majesty's Government would meet that of France in a friendly spirit, there could be no reason why a satisfactory arrangement should not be quickly arrived at.'[1] Monson replied that Fashoda was considered by Her Majesty's Government as part of the Khalifah's dominion and that they held to the decision already announced to him and would not consent to a compromise. Monson concluded the conversation: 'For the rest we had no wish to pick a quarrel; but having long ago given a warning, I could not see how we could now cause surprise if we resent a step which we had cautioned France not to take.'

Kitchener, leading the White Nile flotilla in person, found Captain Marchand with eight officers and 120 soldiers lodged in the old Government buildings at Fashoda and flying the French flag. In a reply to Kitchener's letter announcing his approach, Marchand stated that in accordance with instructions from his Government he occupied Bahr al-Ghaza land all the land west of the Nile up to Fashoda. He had concluded a treaty with the chief of the Shulluks, who placed his country under French protection. He described the fight that took place between him and the Derveishes and while waiting for the probable renewed attack by them, he sent a steamer to the south for reinforcements, but the arrival of Kitchener had averted the war with the Dervishes. In a meeting with Marchand Kitchener stated that 'the presence of a French force at Fashoda and in the valley of the Nile was regarded as a direct infringement of the rights of the Egyptian Government and of that of Great Britain, and I protested in the strongest terms against their occupation of Fashoda and their hoisting the French flag in

[1] Monson to Salisbury, Sept. 18, 1898, *British Documents*, p. 165.

the dominions of His Highness the Khedive.'[1] Marchand maintained that he had executed his Government's instructions and would not retire without receiving orders to this effect. On being pressed by Kitchener whether he would resist the hoisting of the Egyptian flag at Fashoda, Marchand 'hesitated and replied that resistance was impossible.' Then Kitchener caused the Egyptian flag to be hoisted on the ruins of an old Egyptian fortification about 500 yards south of the French flag. Leaving Major Jackson in command at Fashoda with a Sudanese battalion, Kitchener left for the Sūbāt, where he ascertained that there were no Abyssinians. Before leaving for the Sūbāt, however, Kitchener handed to Marchand a formal protest in writing, 'on behalf of the British and Egyptian Governments against any occupation by France of any part of the Nile valley, such occupation being an infringement of the rights of these Governments which I could not recognize.' On the position of Marchand at Fashoda Kitchener remarked that it was as impossible as it was absurd. He was cut off from the interior and his water transport was inadequate in addition to shortage of ammunition and supplies. He had no following in the country as the Shulluk chief and his tribe were delighted to return to their former allegiance and 'nothing could have saved him and his expedition from being annihilated by the dervishes had we been a fortnight later in crushing the Khalifah.' Marchand himself, according to Kitchener's report, realized the futility of his efforts. 'In his present position, he is powerless, but I hope that Her Majesty's Government will take the necessary steps for his removal as soon as possible, as the presence of a French force and flag on the Nile is manifestly extremely undesirable.' Kitchener was prepared to send a steamer up to Fashoda to bring the explorer Marchand and his company down the Nile if the French Government would instruct him by telegraph to leave Fashoda.[2]

It is very interesting to give Marchand's account of the incident, which was given by him to *Figaro* six years later, and a copy of which was forwarded by Monson to Lord Lansdowne on August 26th 1904. In it Marchand attempted to make fun of Lord Kitchener's spoken French. He asserted that he could easily have prevented Kitchener's landing and with the slightest encouragement from

[1] Kitchener to Rodd, received Sept. 25, 1898, ibid., p. 167.
[2] Ibid., p. 168.

him the majority of Kitchener's troops would have gone over to the French side. Monson's comments on this report described it as 'ignorant, malevolent, and wilfully untruthful.'[1] To Monson this report was evidence enough of the correctness of judgment of the French military authorities who had just accepted Marchand's resignation from the army on account of his insurbordinate conduct.

Monson was instructed to read to the French Minister for Foreign affairs Kitchener's reports and leave no copy with him. At the same time he was to say that Her Majesty's Government entirely approved the Sirdar's proceedings and language. Declassé submitted what he remembered of Kitchener's report read to him by Monson to the French cabinet. As it was mentioned in these reports that Marchand had sent a report to his Government through Abyssinia and the French Congo, they could not come to a decision before they had received information from their accredited agent. It was clear that it would take time before this information could reach Paris, but the Government of the Republic would be obliged if a telegram were allowed to be sent by the French agent at Cairo to Khartum with a view to forwarding it up the Nile to Marchand instructing him to send as quickly as possible a copy of his report down the Nile.[2] Then Delcassé proceeded to convey to Monson the great desire of the French Government to avoid any serious difficulty and he was convinced, after knowing the conduct of the Sirdar, that Her Majesty's Government was not less desirous in that respect. On pressing the question whether the French Government was about to order Marchand's immediate recall, Declassé replied that he and his colleagues were prepared to make great concessions, but they should not be asked for the impossible. He informed Monson that 'he would be ready to enter into discussion, negotiation, or whatever it might be called without receiving the Report but this was all he could do.'[3] Monson reminded Delcassé of Her Majesty's Government's decision of not entering into discussion upon such questions as the rights of Egypt to Fashoda. Declassé replied that if there was not going to be discussion a rupture could not be avoided. They would like to have more explicit definition of what Her Majesty's Government.

---

[1] Ibid., p. 168, footnote.
[2] Monson to Salisbury, Sept. 27, 1898, *British Documents,* p. 169.
[3] Ibid.

considered to be the claims of Egypt. The French right to Fashoda was no less valid than the Belgian right to Lado. Declassé seemed to have been driven to his stand by some of the Paris papers which were circulating the rumor that Marchand was abandoned by his Government, and which described Delcassé as the 'author of national disgrace.'

Salisbury replied that he would send instructions to Rodd in Cairo to send the suggested message to Marchand, but it should be understood that Her Majesty's Government would accept no 'responsibility for any consequences to M. Marchand's health or safety which may result from delay in his departure from his present position.' [1] Salisbury requested Monson to tell Delcassé that Her Majesty's Government might be compelled to publish the facts if the present situation was prolonged and caused uneasiness in Britain. To prepare for this eventuality he wished to ascertain from Delcassé how much of his recent communications to Monson he would like to release for publication. But if it could be announced that Marchand was leaving Fashoda, publication would be unnecessary.

In conversation with Monson, Delcassé repeated his belief in the right of France to occupy territory practically abandoned by Egypt and 'contested the right of Great Britain to warn off other powers which had not recognized her sphere of influence or to assert that France was committing an unfriendly act in advancing on Upper Nile.' [2] He reiterated his deep conviction that honest discussion would remove all causes of misunderstanding, and that France would prefer to have Britain as an ally rather than Russia. He begged Monson to take into account the state of public excitement in France which was becoming dangerous and might break into overt action. He admitted the strength of feeling on the other side of the channel but stated that the British were not so excitable as the French. Again he repeated what he had stated on the previous day. 'Do not ask me for the impossible; do not drive me into a corner.' The general impression created in Monson's mind after this conversation was that there was little hope of their recalling Marchand, but Delcassé had several times referred to the possibility of 'transaction.'

[1] Salisbury to Monson, Sept. 28, 1898, ibid., pp. 170-1.
[2] Monson to Salisbury, Sept. 28, 1898, ibid., p. 171.

The Parisian press raised the conflict to a high pitch, which was reflected in the attitude of the Government. Declassé unofficially told Monson that 'it is impossible for the French Government to give up Fashoda, their right to occupy which Her Majesty's Government do not even choose to discuss. Neither this nor any other Ministry could submit to what would be the humiliation of France. Any formal demand of this nature would be considered as an ultimatum and rejected.'[1] Declassé informed Monson that the Sirdar by occupation of Sūbāt had already performed what practically amounted to an act of war or at least to more than an unfriendly act. He emphasized that the whole of that conversation was unofficial but it was 'embodying a decision which would not be retracted.' All France would resent 'such an insult to the national honor' as was implied in the proposal to recall Marchand. Delcassé did not think that England would wish to go to war over such a question, 'but France would, however unwillingly, accept war rather than submit.' Monson confined himself in that conversation to saying that his Government had already made clear their point of view and he could not see how they 'could possibly retract from it.' Against this strong language coming from the French Her Majesty's Government instructed Kitchener to make Marchand's position as untenable as possible. No reinforcements or munitions of war should be allowed to reach him. If he was in need of food supplies, nothing should be furnished him except in case of extreme necessity.[2] On their part Her Majesty's Government wished to make it clear to the French that, by complying with their request to transmit messages to Marchand, it should not be implied that they modified their views previously expressed.

You should add that, whether in times of Egyptian or of dervish dominion, the region in which M. Marchand was found has never been without an owner, and that in the view of Her Majesty's Government his expedition into it with an escort of 100 Senegalese troops has no political effect, nor can any political significance be attached to it.

In view of the high pitch of feeling to which the French public had been worked by the Parisian press and the effect of this on the ministers, it was thought desirable to instruct their Ambassador

[1] Monson to Salisbury, Sept. 30, 1898, ibid., p. 172.
[2] Salisbury to Rodd, Oct. 10, *British Documents*, pp. 172-3.

in London to interview Salisbury. The interview lasted for nearly two hours and the topic of conversation was Fashoda. The French point of view was repeated by their Ambassador, which was that Egypt had lost her claim by her abandonment of the Sudan, that the French had a right to a position on the Nile as much as the Germans or the Belgians, and that the French had retained for themselves freedom of action on the Nile by the reservations which they had made when the subject was mentioned. Salisbury replied that 'the Egyptian title to the banks of the Nile had certainly been rendered dormant by the military successes of the Mahdi; but that the amount of right, whatever it was, which by those events had been alienated from Egypt, had been entirely transferred to the conqueror.'[1] Salisbury maintained that the dispute of title over the Nile valley was between Egypt and the Mahdiya and its fluctuation from one side to the other was decided on the battlefield.

There is no ground in international law for asserting that the dispute of title between them which had been inclined one day by military superiority in one direction, and a few years later had been inclined in the other, could give any authority or title to another power to come in and seize the disputed region as vacant or relinquished territory.

The Mahdiya's power extended as far south as Bor and it was superseded by the conquering army. It was poined out to the French Ambassador that Marchand with his little band might have been annihilated had it not been for the timely arrival of Kitchener and that France had received several warnings that occupation of territory on the Nile valley would not be accepted. 'At all events, if she thought fit to try, in face of these warnings, to establish a title over the vast territory to which they applied, by a secret expedition of a handful of men, she must not be recognized by us.' The French Ambassador stated that Marchand might return by the way he came if it was given out that negotiations were going on about the delimitation between the two powers and he added that it was unjust to exclude France from the Nile while Germany and Belgium were given access. Salisbury gave no countenance to the proposal of delimitation, which, as described by the Ambassador, gave France a considerable stretch of the left bank of the Nile. To Salisbury a German position on the shores of Lake Victoria

[1] Salisbury to Monson, Oct. 6, 1898, ibid., pp. 173-4.

could hardly be called a position on the Nile; and whatever territory was leased to the Congo State was only for the lifetime of the King of the Belgians. 'We separated without coming to any conclusion; for I had no communication to make except the reiteration of our claim of right; and he made no suggestion of any arrangement by which that right could be reconciled with the present pretensions or desires of France.' [1]

After French feelings had reached their highest pitch, determination to retain Fashoda and whatever other territory they had occupied, the French entered, in view of the British stand, a period of trying to convince Britain to negotiate and of preparedness to recall Marchand. The Government-inspired paper *Le Matin* moderated its tone and stated that the abandonment of Fashoda would be compatible with the national honor. It appreciated the great achievement of Marchand and his little band, but it would be imprudent on the part of the French Government to encumber herself with useless territory practically inaccessible from the French possessions on the Atlantic coast. It was evident to the French Government that Britain was determined to allow no French title to the Nile valley and that no negotiation on this subject would be considered; but to yield to the British was considered by the French nation as a disgrace to the national honor. The repeated request of Delcassé and the French Ambassador in London for an announcement of negotiations accompanied by the recall of Marchand was a plea for a bridge over which they could gracefully retreat without giving the appearance that France was humiliated and insulted. Delcassé complained of the tone of the British press, which made his position untenable and made the French retreat difficult. The French Government knew quite well that if the matter was not settled very soon, they would be subjected to severe criticism in the Chamber, which was about to open. Also, it is probable that Russia advised France not to provoke a war over Fashoda, although officially the Russians showed their agreement with the French attitude and their willingness to support them.

Marchand, however, decided to go to Cairo to report in person. Delcassé was irritated by the behavior of Marchand, who had quitted his post without permission. It was decided to send an

[1] Ibid.

envoy from Paris to Cairo to carry instructions to Marchand, who would be ordered back to Fashoda. Delcassé, in an interview with Monson, again made it clear that his continuance in office would be dependent upon a definite answer being given to his 'request that the French Government should, in some way or another, be assured that their order to Marchand to evacuate Fashoda would be followed by an undertaking that England will negotiate on the principle of the grant to France of an outlet for her commerce to the Nile.' [1] Without this Delcassé thought that a humiliation would be inflicted on France, which he could not accept. As he was averse to the possibility of war with England and equally averse to the humiliation of France, he would have no choice but to resign his post. In London a second interview took place between Salisbury and the French Ambassador, in which the former maintained that so long as the French flag was floating at Fashoda, any discussion on the subject would be impossible because it would imply that Her Majesty's Government admitted the legality of Marchand's position. The French Ambassador, however, 'repudiated the doctrine that M. Marchand's position was illegal.' [1] He stated to Salisbury that reports received from Marchand seemed to show that Fashoda could not furnish an outlet on the Nile for France; 'and that, therefore, it was of no use to her. He thought it, therefore, not improbable that M. Marchand would receive orders to retire.' Salisbury was glad to receive this information although it was accompained by claims of right, which he could not admit. If the French Government would give orders to Marchand to evacuate and then raise the question of frontiers, Her Majesty's Government would be prepared to consider it in just the same way as with any other European power. From the tone of the French Ambassador there was no doubt that the French Government was about to evacuate Fashoda. On the 4th of November Salisbury was able to send the following telegram to Monson: 'The French Ambassador informed me today that the decision had been taken by his Government to withdraw M. Marchand's party from Fashoda and to send him back there to carry out that decision, and that orders to that effect had been sent to Cairo.' [2]

[1] Monson to Salisbury, Oct. 29, 1898, *British Documents,* p. 186.
[1] Salisbury to Monson, Oct. 30, 1898., ibid., p. 187.
[2] Salisbury to Monson, Nov. 4, 1898, ibid., p. 188.

XVIII

THE CONDOMINIUM AGREEMENT

It will be recalled that the reconquest of the Sudan was initiated by the British Government and that both the Khedive and his ministers, although wishing their lost dominion to be restored, were actually surprised by the decision to advance into Dongola. The Khedive objected on the two grounds that it was merely to assist Italy and that he was not consulted beforehand. His subsequent attitude was that of neutrality and indifference rather than co-operation. As late as April 1898, after the battle of Atbara, Cromer reported that the Khedive had probably no clear ideas of what he wanted either in Egypt or the Sudan, 'but in this particular case he cannot get over the feeling that any advantage now gained in the Sudan constitutes an English rather than an Egyptian success.'[1] Notwithstanding the Khedive's indifference it was assumed up to June 1898 that the reconquest was nothing but the restoration of the Sudan to Egypt, although Cromer had in mind a kind of administration which would not repeat the injustices of the pre-Mahdiya period.

The first document which ushered in a new attitude to the title to the Sudan was dated June 3, 1898. Lord Salisbury told Lord Cromer that a message from the Sultan, though friendly, indicated that he might annoy the British in Egypt by his technical and moral power over the Khedive. Salisbury guessed that this might be due to French suggestion.

In view of this state, we must be careful of acknowledging Egyptian title by itselt any further south. Would it not be wise, if you take Khartum, to fly the British and Egyptian flags *side by side?* We might treat Khartum as the capital of the Mahdi state and the capture of Khartum would deliver by right of conquest the whole of the Mahdi state from Halfa to Wadelai into the power of the capturing army. That army would consist of two allied contingents. Sirdar commands the whole by virtue of his personal position as Marlborough commanded British and German contingents without trenching on the independent rights of the allied Governments.[2]

[1] Cromer to Salisbury, No. 57, Secret, Apr. 12, 1898, P.R.O., F.O. 78/4956.
[2] Salisbury to Cromer, No. 47, Secret, June 3, 1898, P.R.O., F.O. 78/5050.

In Salisbury's opinion this position would remove a great deal of diplomatic difficulty and he requested Cromer to have this consideration in mind when increasing the size of the British contingent.

Cromer thought the argument was conclusive in favor of having an extra battalion, but he would wait to see Kitchener before replying to the War office in this sense. He thought also that as the railway question was not yet finally settled, the hoisting of the two flags together might be a useful means of applying pressure pending a settlement. 'But I am inclined to think if we can obtain all we practically want without a radical change of the political status of the Sudan, this will perhaps be the best policy to adopt, although the alternative project has some obvious attractions.' [1] Cromer reminded Salisbury that control over the Sudan south of Wadi Halfa would necessitate the taking of Sawakin also. This would introduce another difficult political issue. Unless Egypt continued to pay for the whole of the army in the Sudan the share of the burden on England would be heavy. He saw, in addition to the Sultan's opposition, the difficulty of making a suitable arrangement with a private company for taking over the Sudan railways. His suggestion was to tell Sir E. Palmer, the financial adviser, how the matter stood and to authorize him to continue negotiations. There would be no harm if the negotiations dragged on till the autumn. 'When an arrangement has been made, I would then propose to present it to the Khedive and insist on his accepting it in spite of any opposition on the part of the Sultan. My belief is that he will yield.' In the meantime Cromer suggested that he should tell the Khedive and his ministers that the opposition of the Sultan would not change the views of Her Majesty's Government, which they intended to insist upon when the question was ripe for decision. The Khedive should accept whatever proposals might be then made to him. 'For general local reasons it is very important that neither the opposition of the Sultan nor that of the Khedive should be allowed to prevail.' It is clear, therefore, that Cromer was at first doubtful about the two-flag business and what worried him most was the question of the railways. But a week later he wrote privately to Salisbury. 'I have been thinking over the two-flag idea and the more I think over it the more I like it.' [2]

[1] Cromer to Salisbury, No. 163, Secret, June 4, 1898, P.R.O., F.O. 78/5050.
[2] Cromer to Salisbury, June 11, 1898, Zetland, Marquess of, *Lord Cromer*, p. 238.

When Cromer was thoroughly convinced of the soundness of a condominium government for the Sudan he drew up a memorandum in which he stated the various issues which appeared to him to need to be decided. As an observation of a general nature he begged that the effect of the Sudan policy on the Egyptian policy should not be lost sight of.

It seems quite clear that we are now pledged to the occupation of Egypt for an indefinite period. It is also certain that so long as the occupation lasts the Khedive and the small but influential class, which looks to the Khedive for guidance, will maintain a position of irreconcilable hostility. From this point of view, it becomes almost a political necessity that the mass of the people, should be in such a condition of material prosperity as to render them well nigh proof against appeals made to sentiment of race hatred and religious fanaticism.[1]

For this reason Cromer was anxious to revert to fiscal reforms. Under normal conditions a forward policy in the Sudan would necessarily involve heavy expenditure. But at the same time the future would be very uncertain, especially in the expectation of difficulties from Menelek, where the main danger lay. 'We may possibly find ourselves in the presence of a condition of things, which will not only involve a prolonged adjournment of fiscal reforms in Egypt, but may also conceivably tax Egyptian resources beyond what they are capable of bearing.'

Cromer maintained that he did not make these remarks in order to advocate a policy of inaction, but on the contrary he deprecated 'halting midway in the execution of the Sudan policy.' What he was driving at was that the procedure should be essentially a cautious one with avoidance of risks of rupture with Abyssinia. This clearly indicates that people on the spot in Cairo were thinking in terms of possible conflict with Abyssinia rather than with France. Cromer urged that occupation should be limited for the time being to territories 'absolutely necessary for the execution of our general policy, that is to say, mainly to the banks of the White Nile and a portion of the Blue Nile.'

Proceeding from these general remarks Cromer asked: 'What is to be the political status of the reoccupied territory?' He admitted that he misunderstood the suggestion of the two flags, but he now

[1] Memorandum by Cromer to Salisbury, June 15, 1898, P.R.O., F.O. 78/4956.

came round to the idea that it merited careful consideration. It would be wise to use it at least as a temporary measure. To him the hoisting of the two flags would only 'give outward and visible expression to a *de facto* position which already exists. The Khedive knows perfectly well that neither in Egypt nor in the Sudan can he take any important step without the consent of Her Majesty's Government.' Menelek was plainly told that in treating Egyptian affairs he had to deal with Britain and not with Egypt. It would in general bring the theory into harmony with the practice. 'It would emphasize the fact that the khedive is not free to act in the Sudan without the consent of his senior partner. It would afford a salutory warning to the Sultan, and it would be a clear indication to the French and the Abyssinians that the control of the Nile is more an English than an Egyptian question.'

There appeared some sort of difficulty in flying the British flag at Wadi Halfa unless it was also flown at Aswan, a step which would obviously bring its crop of difficulties. The Sirdar stated that, for administrative convenience, Aswan was administered from Wadi Halfa in what was known as the 'Frontier Province.' Kitchener's opinion was that it would be sufficient for practical purposes to hoist the two flags at Khartum. 'He would consider Khartum as the capital of the Sudan, and administer the whole of the rest of the country down to Sawakin on the Red Sea and to Aswan in the Nile valley, from Khartum.' Cromer considered this to be on the whole the best policy to adopt, as it would involve the minimum amount of political disturbance. To Cromer the hoisting of the British flag at Wadi Halfa, Aswan, and Sawakin, especially in the case of the last two places, would excite strong opposition for many obvious reasons, and it would be difficult to justify. In case of a French complaint about the British flag, it would be pointed out to the French that they, but a short time ago, had invited the Khalifah to make use of the French flag.[1]

In order to justify their legal participation in the administration of the Sudan Her Majesty's Government decided that, in addition to the military assistance given to Egypt in terms of one division, they should bear their share in the financial expenditure. It will

---

[1] There was a rumour at the time that the French made an offer to the Khalifah and Cromer was of opinion that it was correct, but subsequent events did not confirm it.

be recalled that the British Government decided to advance to the Egyptian Government the half-million pounds returned to the *caisse* as a result of the Mixed Tribunal's judgment against Egypt. It was found later that the expenditure on the railways would necessitate a further sum of a little less than £E.300,000. On July 5, 1898 Salisbury sent to Cromer the information that on the proposal of the Chancellor of the Exchequer the Committee of Ways and Means of the House of Commons passed the following resolution: 'That it is expedient that the grant-in-aid of £798,802 to the Government of the Khedive of Egypt should not be repaid.' [1] It was understood that the Egyptian Government, released from the obligation in regard to this sum, would be able to provide for all expenses connected with the Sudan.

Cromer's memorandum referred to above was circulated to the members of the cabinet. It contained, in addition, to the discussion of the future status of the Sudan, instructions which he suggested for the commanders of the two flotillas acting from Khartum on the two Niles. As regards the two-flag suggestion the following were the relevant instructions:

In view of the substantial military and financial co-operation which has recently been afforded by Her Majesty's Government to the Government of the Khedive, Her Majesty's Government have decided that at Khartoum the British and Egyptian flags should be hoisted side by side. This decision will have no reference to the manner in which the occupied countries are to be administered in the future. It is not necessary at present to define their political status with any great precision. These matters can be considered at a later period. You will, however, explain to the Khedive and to his Ministers that the procedure I have indicated is intended to emphasize the fact that Her Majesty's Government consider that they have a predominant voice in all matters connected with the Sudan, and that they expect that any advice which they may think fit to tender to the Egyptian Government, in respect to Sudan affairs, will be followed.[2]

The day before the battle for Omdurman, Rodd, in the absence of Cromer, informed the British Government that when Khartum was occupied he would communicate to the Egyptian Government paragraph two of their instructions contained in the dispatch

[1] Salisbury to Cromer, No. 92, July 5, 1898, P.R.O., F.O. 78/4955.
[2] Salisbury to Cromer, Aug. 2, 1898, *British Documents*, p. 159.

from Salisbury to Cromer of August 2, 1898.[1] Rodd received the authorization from Mr. Balfour on the same day.[2] On the 4th day of September Rodd sent the following communication to his Excellency Butros Ghali Pasha, the Egyptian Foreign Minister.

I have the honor to bring to your Excellency's knowledge that, in view of the substantial military and financial co-operation which has been afforded by Her Majesty's Government to the Government of His Highness the Khedive, Her Majesty's Government have decided that at Khartum the British and Egyptian flags should be hoisted side by side. This decision will have no reference to the manner in which the occupied countries are to be administered in the future, but the procedure is intended to emphasize the fact that Her Majesty's Government consider that they have a predominant voice in all matters connected with the Sudan, and that they expect that any advice which they may think fit to tender to the Egyptian Government in respect to Sudan affairs will be followed.[1]

All that the Khedive had to do as a reaction to this British procedure was to instruct his ministers to telegraph confidentially to the Sultan the fact that British and Egyptian flags had been hoisted at Khartum. The ministers carried out the instructions by communicating this information to the Grand Vizier without comment.[4] The Sultan sent a message to the British Ambassador at Constantinople telling him that he heard of the proposal of flying the British with the Turkish flag at Khartum. 'His Highness appeals to Her Majesty's Government to reconsider this decision, which if carried out would place him in a difficult position.'[5] The Ambassador asked whether Salisbury would wish him to communicate to the Sultan's First Secretary in reply the substance of the note addressed by Rodd to the Egyptian Foreign Minister explaining the intentions of Her Majesty's Government with regard to this matter. Under this Salisbury minuted: 'Certainly do not communicate. I am doubtful whether any answer at all is desirable.' In this way the question was closed as far as the Sultan's opposition was concerned.

The communication made by Rodd to Butros Ghali was not

[1] Rodd to Balfour, No. 208, Secret, Sept. 1, 1898, P.R.O., F.O. 78/5050.
[2] Balfour to Rodd, No. 72, Confidential, Sept. 2, 1898, P.R.O., F.O. 78/5050.
[3] Rodd to Butros Ghali, enclosed in Rodd to Salisbury, No. 134, Sept. 4, 1898, P.R.O., F.O. 78/5050.
[4] Rodd to Salisbury, No. 226, Sept. 8, 1898, P.R.O., F.O. 78/5050.
[5] De Bunsen to Salisbury, No. 174, Sept. 15, 1898, P.R.O., F.O. 78/5050.

kept absolutely secret and what leaked out proceeded incorrect versions and the French representative in Cairo was persistent in his inquiries on the subject. In order to prevent all misunderstanding Rodd asked whether he should publish the exact text.[1] Salisbury replied that the part of the note stating that the decision to hoist the two flags, which had no reference to the manner in which the occupied territories were to be administered in future, was 'somewhat ambiguous and might give rise to embarrassing comment. I think it will be better not to publish it.'[2] Rodd took this to be an unfavorable remark on the note and defended himself by pointing out to Sir Thomas Sanderson that what he had communicated to Butros Ghali was taken word for word from the original instruction of the British Government.[3] Sanderson replied that Lord Salisbury's remark was meant as an explanation of the reasons for thinking that publication of the note would be undesirable at the time.[4]

In November 1898 Cromer completed his discussions with the various authorities in Cairo and drafted an agreement with the Egyptian Government, which he forwarded to London with an explanatory note. He mentioned to the President of the Egyptian council of ministers and to the Foreign Minister that such an agreement was considered necessary. 'So far as I can gather from what they let fall in conversation, they fully agree in the general principles involved. I have, however, not attempted to discuss the details with them. Some opposition from the Khedive is, I presume, to be anticipated.'[5] As Kitchener was in England at this time, Cromer suggested that he should be consulted on the subject. From the point of view of administration it was desirable that this question should be settled with as little delay as possible. Whether the Anglo-French controversy over the upper Nile would postpone its consideration or not was to Cromer a point on which he could express no opinion.

In his memorandum[6] Cromer maintained that it would be quite

[1] Rodd to Salisbury, No. 82, Sept. 22, 1898, P.R.O., F.O. 78/5050.
[2] Salisbury to Rodd, No. 82, Sept. 22, 1898, P.R.O., F.O. 78/5050.
[3] Rodd to Sanderson, Sept. 23, 1898, P.R.O., F.O. 78/5051.
[4] Sanderson to Rodd, Sept. 24, 1898, P.R.O., F.O. 78/5051.
[5] Cromer to Salisbury, Separate and Secret, Nov. 10, 1898, P.R.O., F.O. 78/4957.
[6] Memorandum by Cromer, marked Confidential, enclosed in ibid.

possible to settle each point of difficulty on its own merits, if it was only a question of dealing with the inhabitants of the Sudan.

The purely native requirements are, in fact, very simple. A light system of taxation, some very simple forms for the administration of civil and criminal justice, and the appointment of a few carefully selected officials with a somewhat wide discretionary power to deal with local details, are all that for the time being is necessary.

But they had also to deal with Europeans who had already submitted numerous demands for residence, investment of capital, acquisition of real property, or trade with the conquered country. 'It is obviously both impossible to exclude them and undesirable to do so, for without European capital and assistance no real progress can be made.' One of the great difficulties of the situation, in Cromer's opinion, was the contrast between the primitive institutions which would be quite sufficient for the Sudanese for a time and the more complex administrative and judicial system which the presence of Europeans would necessitate. Europeans should be told that if they chose to trade with or reside in a country just emerging from barbarism, they must be content with the best judicial and administrative system that the Government could afford. The best would, for a time, be defective even if judged by Egyptian standards.

The big problem as it appeared to Cromer was how to prevent 'the acquisition of rights and the recognition of priviliges to Europeans similar to the rights and privileges which exist in Egypt.' If Europeans were allowed to reside in, hold property in, and trade with the Sudan without a distinct declaration of the régime which would in future exist in the country, seeds of future trouble would be sown. 'In default of any authoritative declaration they may not unnaturally consider, and many of them will certainly consider, that the status of Europeans resident in the Sudan is similar to that which obtains in Egypt.' On these grounds, as well as because of the necessity to define the British position from the beginning as precisely as possible, 'some public act laying down the political status of the Sudan is necessary.'

The first alternative for the political status of the Sudan would be annexation by Great Britain. This would solve all the difficulties of the situation. But for obvious political and financial reasons this course could not be followed. The second alternative would be the consideration of the Sudan as part of the Ottoman dominions. This would certainly perpetuate all the international difficulties of which the British had complained during the last fifteen years in Egypt and which had somewhat hampered reform and progress. Under such circumstances the solution would lie in some form of compromise, 'but it is to be remembered that we shall be creating a status hitherto unknown to the law of Europe.' It would, therefore, be difficult to put down on paper any arrangement which would be workable and convincing. Cromer thought that this arrangement should take the form of a convention or agreement with the Egyptian Government.

Cromer admitted that the validity of such a document might be challenged on some grounds. In the first place it might be argued that the Ottoman firmans made it clear that the Khedive had no right to make any treaty with foreign powers except commercial and customs conventions. Moreover, it was laid down in the firman appointing 'Abbas II that he 'shall not, on any pretext or motive abandon to others in whole or in part, the privileges accorded to Egypt, which are intrusted to him, and which pertain to the inherent rights of the Sovereign Power, nor any portion of the territory.' Cromer had two answers to this. The first would be that the convention was not a proper treaty. The Khedive was merely exercising his acknowledged right of making arrangement for the internal administration of his territory. The hoisting of the Egyptian flag in the Sudan was an evidence that the Turkish suzerainty was, at least in part, recognized. This argument appeared weak to Cromer, 'for the more we dwell on whatever fragment of the Sultan's Suzerainty, which will remain, the more difficult will it be to differentiate the Sudan from the rest of the Ottoman dominions in respect to the treatment of Europeans and other subjects.' The second answer would be that

the Egyptian army, which forms part of the Ottoman army, was unable to maintain its position in the Sudan, and would unaided have been quite unable to reconquer that country; that the reconquest has been effected by English money, English troops, and Egyptian troops officered and trained by Englishmen; that this fact confers on Her Majesty's Government, on the recognized principles of international law, predominant rights in the determination of the future régime of the country; that the question of whether the Khedive is acting within his rights is therefore beside the mark, for that, rather than ceding anything to England, he is obtaining concessions from England.

Cromer then proceeded to give some explanatory remarks on the articles of the proposed convention.

Preamble. Allusion was made incidentally to the rights of the Khedive before the Mahdiya, but the rights of the British by virtue of the reconquest were given more prominence. 'It appears necessary to state these rights, as they alone constitute the real justification for the creation of a political and adminstrative status in the Sudan different to that which exists in Egypt.'

Article I. The frontiers of the conquered territories included Wadi Halfa. To be consistent with the principle set forth in the preamble Wadi Halfa should not be included as it had never formed part of the Mahdiya administration and remained in Egyptian hands all through. But its exclusion would create great administrative inconvenience. Yet Cromer finds an argument for including both Wadi Halfa and Sawakin in the Sudan by the fact that were it not for 'the defensive action taken from time to time by British troops and under British auspices, they would certainly have been lost to Egypt during the rebellion.' So Cromer found a way, in framing the article, to divide the territories to which the name Sudan applied into three categories. The first was the territory which had never been evacuated by the Egyptian army since 1882. 'This formula has been adopted in order to include Wadi Halfa and Sawakin.' The second referred to those territories which were administered by His Highness the Khedive before the Mahdist rebellion, and which in this way were temporarily lost to Egypt but had been reconquered by 'Her Majesty's Government and the Egyptian Government acting in concert.' This would include all territories recently conquered. Cromer maintained that there would be an objection to using the term 'all the territory which formerly belonged to Egypt' without limiting it to those conquered by an Anglo-Egyptian force. Without such a limitation it might be interpreted to include part of the Equatorial Province, Zeyla, and Barbara, which, 'of course, are not intended to be included in the present agreement.' The third category would be those territories which might be conquered later by the two governments acting in concert. 'This provision has been so worded as to include extensions southwards or westwards, acquired by Anglo-Egyptian action, and at the same time to exclude extensions from Uganda northwards, made by the English Government acting alone.'

Article II. In the proposed draft agreement it was suggested to hoist the two flags all through the Sudan with the exception of Sawakin in order to make it uniform with Khartum. This would make it clear that the status of the whole country was the same. Hoisting the British flag at Sawakin would raise a great outcry and Cromer saw no necessity to do so, as the jurisdiction of the Mixed Tribunals was applied to Sawakin.

Articles III and IV. These were the most important provisions of the agreement as they regulated the manner by which supreme authority would be exercised in the Sudan. The proposal provided for vesting the supreme military and civil command in the hands of one officer to be termed the 'Governor-General of the Sudan.' Of the desirability of this measure Cromer had no doubt. It was suggested that his appointment should be by a Khedivial decree on the recommendation of Her Majesty's Government. It was the same procedure as for the nomination of the commissioners of the debt and some other officials.

I should add that I should prefer that allusion should be specifically made in the preamble of the Decree to the fact that English sanction has been obtained to the nomination, though the adoption of this course is not altogether necessary for the Khedive is under an obligation to follow English advice in all important matters so long as the occupation lasts.

It was proposed that all proclamations issued by the Governor-General should have the force of law, but it was provided that in important matters the previous consent of the Khedive through his council of ministers and of Her Majesty's Government through their representative in Cairo should be obtained. Cromer thought that it was necessary that the Governor-General should be under some sort of control and the only really effective control would be that of the British Government through their Consul-General; 'but the Khedive must also be mentioned, both because, *ex-hypothesi,* the Sudan though possessing a separate political status, is still to be Egyptian territory and because the financial responsibilities assumed by Egypt render it both necessary and desirable

that the voice of the Egyptian Government should be heard.'
Whether in case of each proclamation the previous consent of the
two Governments should be obtained was left an open question by
Cromer. But he was of opinion that the Governor-General should
be made 'absolutely supreme in the eyes of the population of the
Sudan.' Although Cromer advocated control over the Governor-
General, yet he thought it to be a great mistake to centralize the
administration of the Sudan in any authority in Cairo.

It is proposed, therefore, to take power in the convention to dispense with
the previous assent of the Khedive and of the English Diplomatic agent in
certain matters. The detailed points in respect to which a free hand shall be
left to the Governor-General can form the subject of subsequent discussion.

Article V. This deals with laws applicable in the Sudan. It was
at first proposed that no Egyptian law should be valid in the Sudan
unless it was proclaimed by the Governor-General as such. The
objection raised to this procedure was that the Sudan would be in
a state of lawlessness for some time to come before a body of laws
could be framed. It was thought better to apply Egyptian laws
which were strictly speaking considered to be still in force in the
Sudan. On this basis Cromer was advised that the only laws that
would be applicable to the Sudan were those in force previous to
the year 1884, which year witnessed the collapse of the Egyptian
authority in that country. This would include all Egyptian laws
promulgated in 1883. But it was intended to limit all future Egyptian laws to those of which the Governor-General should choose
to be specifically applied to the Sudan. 'It will be borne in mind
that under Article IV all existing Egyptian laws may be altered or
abrogated by proclamation of the Governor-General.'

Article VI. It was considered to be undesirable to allow the
caisse de la dette to interfere in the Sudan finance. After full discussion with his financial advisers Cromer decided not to make any
allusion in the convention to this subject. The arrangement at the
time was that the net charge on account of the Sudan appeared on
the expenditure side of the Egyptian accounts, to which the *caisse*
had agreed. No question would, therefore, be raised by the *caisse*
until the Sudan yielded a surplus and it would take a long time
before the Sudan could produce such a surplus. Cromer doubted,
however, whether any provision in this agreement would help

towards a settlement if any difficulty arose with the *caisse* in this respect. 'I think we had better leave this branch of the question alone for the present.'

It was proposed that all the revenue of the Sudan should be at the disposal of the Egyptian Government which would be solely responsible for the civil and ordinary military expenditure. Cromer stated that the Egyptian treasury would be able to bear such expenditure without 'making any call for British assistance,' and the Sudan figures worked out much more favorably than he anticipated. Cromer agreed to the proposal made by the British military authorities in Egypt, who saw the necessity for keeping a British force of about two companies (250 men) permanently at Khartum. 'Their presence will give confidence to every one, and will be a very useful enterprise in the event of any difficulties occurring with the native, notably the black troops.' Cromer thought that it would be awkward to ask the Egyptian Government to pay for them and that their expenses would be a fair charge on the British treasury.

Article VII. This article asserted the right to lay down conditions under which foreigners might reside in, trade with, and hold property in the Sudan. Cromer had already, in his general remarks, stated that this right might be challenged. This is unfortunate but it cannot be helped. We are in possession and shall be able to assert our rights even although we may not be able to convince others of the regularity of our position, or the validity of our arguments. In the meantime laying down the principle of the "open door" trade for all might mitigate hostility.'

Article VIII. This dealt with the customs duties. It was 'conceived in a sense, from which the right to separate the commercial régime of the Sudan from that of Egypt may be inferred even if it be not expressly stated.' This right might be contested and Cromer suggested no alternative in that case but to 'fall back on the right of conquest argument.' He, however, did not propose any extra import duty on goods entering the Sudan from Egypt or from the ports of the Red Sea comprised in the term 'Sudan.' 'On the other hand care has been taken to draft Article VIII in such a manner as to preserve complete liberty of action in respect to trade entering the Sudan not from Egypt or the Red Sea but from other directions.' As to the export duties it might become necessary to impose a higher duty than 1 per cent on some articles such as gum and ostrich feathers. 'It is proposed, therefore, to maintain our liberty of action on that point.'

Article IX.   This provided that the jurisdiction of the Mixed Tribunals would not extend to the Sudan. Some legal authorities maintained that there would be doubt whether their jurisdiction might be extended to the Sudan, even if its political status were not changed. Cromer thought that it would be unwise to depend on this argument, as the Mixed Courts had the tendency to extend their jurisdiction and as a safeguard against such eventuality their limits should be specified. Sawakin was rather a difficult case. For better or for worse the jurisdiction of the Mixed Courts had for many years been recognized there and it would raise an outcry if any change was now made. Cromer was averse to such a change as it was undesirable.

Article X.   For the time being martial law would prevail in the Sudan except at Sawakin. This would strengthen the position against allowing the jurisdiction of the Mixed Courts to extend to the Sudan, 'for I conceive that many judges, who would refuse to admit the validity of our rights based on reconquest, would recognize that so long as the ordinary civil law was in abeyance the courts could exercise no jurisdiction.' It was not mainly for this reason that Cromer proposed proclamation of martial law. It was known that the country was still disturbed and that it was necessary that the Governor-General should have ample powers for maintenance of order including the right to expel any individual from the country whether European or native. This should not be interpreted to mean absence of law-courts, as they were already instituted in Dongola and provision in the budget was made for extension of these institutions.

'The spirit, therefore, in which I propose the proclamation of martial law is this; that the extreme powers which will thus be vested in the Governor-General shall only be used in exceptional cases; and, further that, as time goes on, every endeavor shall be made to bring the administration of the law in the Sudan into harmony with the generally recognized principles of civil jurisprudence.'

Article XI.   No consular authorities were to reside in the Sudan except with the permission of Her Majesty's Government. Again

Cromer remarked that it might be challenged by those 'who hold that the political status of the Sudan in no way differs from that of other parts of the Ottoman dominion.'

Article XII. While Cromer was strongly of the opinion that the importation or exportation of slaves should be at once forbidden, he admitted that the case of domestic slavery was much more difficult and better left alone for the time being.

Article XIII. This dealt with arms and alcoholic drinks; 'although such a course is not absolutely necessary it may perhaps be as well to draw special attention to the provisions of the Brussels act as regards the sale and importation of arms and spiritous liquors.'

When the proposed draft agreement was shown to Kitchener in London he had two main observations to make on Article IV which included provision for a future arrangement as regards the powers of the Governor-General. Kitchener thought that such powers should be laid down at once, as the Khedive would dislike the clause and it 'will only cause fresh disputes when the details have to be decided on and until this is done the powers and position of the Governor-General will be undermined.' Then he proceeded to make an actual amendment to a portion of the proposed article. Cromer had proposed the following:

> Proclamations of the Governor-General shall be issued only with the prior consent of His Highness, the Khedive, acting under the advice of his council of ministers, and of Her Britannic Majesty's Government through Her Britannic Majesty's Agent and Consul-General.
>
> Nevertheless the parties whose consent is so required may, from time to time, exempt from the obligations to receive such prior consent proclamations of the Governor-General in respect of all such classes of administrative or executive matters as may be specified in any instrument conferring such exemption.
>
> Proclamations issued without prior consent, by virtue of exemption, shall be forthwith notified to Her Britannic Majesty's Agent and Consul-General in Cairo, and to the President of the council of ministers of His Highness the Khedive, and shall be subject to such power of revision or rescission as may be reserved by the instrument creating the exemption.

Kitchener's amendment ran as follows:

> All such proclamations or ordinances of the Governor-General shall after promulgation be forthwith notified to the President of the council of ministers

of His Highness the Khedive and to Her Majesty's Government's Agent and Consul-General in Cairo and shall be in all cases subject to such revision or rescission as they may jointly decide.

On Article VI Kitchener did not see the object of declaring that the whole of the Sudan revenue should be at the disposal of the Egyptian Government. If it was meant to be interpreted that the finances of the Sudan would be administered by the Finance Ministry in Cairo, it appeared to Kitchener to be very undesirable. If such was the intention it would mean that Sudan revenue, being an integral part of Egyptian revenue, would provide a cause for interference from Cairo in every detail of law and administration of the Sudan.

If this is not intended I do not see the object of the statement as it may eventually turn out to be a very inconvenient declaration to have made and might admit of the intervention of the *caisse* in the regulation of expenditure, which Lord Cromer desires to avoid.

Kitchener, therefore, suggested that the article should be framed to read as follows:

The administration of the Finances of the Sudan will be under the direction of the Governor-General assisted by the Financial Secretary to the Sudan, who will be appointed by Khedivial Decree in a similar manner to the Governor-General—the control and supervision of these finances will be vested in the Ministry of Finance in Cairo, the Egyptian Government being solely responsible for all civil and ordinary military expenditure in the Sudan.

Salisbury seems to have been impressed by Kitchener's observations, because he privately told Cromer that he discussed his 'Sudanese constitution with the Sirdar. I by no means pledge myself to his verbal criticism, but in the two main points on which he insists I think he is probably right.'[1] While agreeing to a certain amount of control over the Governor-General, Salisbury held that he should not be unduly hampered by the necessity of obtaining approval beforehand. Too much centralization would reduce the machinery of Government to 'that mania for paper-piling which is the endemic pest of British Departments.'[2] Cromer was not worried about these two remarks on his draft proposal for the agreement.

[1] Salisbury to Cromer, Dec. 9, 1898 Zetland, op. cit., pp. 238-9.
[2] Ibid

I very much hope that you will not let the Sudan convention question drop. The two points about which you wrote to me admit of being settled without much difficulty. The main points, however, are twofold. First, to take steps, which should not be too long delayed, to keep internationalism out of the Sudan; and secondly to devise a plan which will give some legal sanction to legislative and administrative measures. If these two problems are solved I do not care about the rest.[3]

After receiving the comments of Kitchener and the British Cabinet the proposed draft was handed over to the legal experts in Cairo to put it in its final legal form. The document as it appeared in its final form was simpler and the financial arrangements were made the subject of further discussion and a separate agreement. Before the actual signature Cromer took a journey to the Sudan and to an assembly of the inhabitants at Omdurman he delivered a speech. He first congratulated the assembled people on having been delivered from the tyranny of the Dervish rule by the 'military skill of the Sirdar and his officers, and gallantry of the British and Egyptian troops.'[1] He told them that the two flags were an indication that they would be governed in future by Her Majesty the Queen and His Highness the Khedive represented by the Governor-General. 'No attempt will be made to govern the country from Cairo, still less from London. You must look to the Sirdar alone for justice and good government, and I do not doubt that you will have no cause for disappointment.' Then he proceeded to describe how other Muslims were living under the rule of Her Majesty the Queen and how contented they were under that merciful rule, and how their religion was respected. 'You may feel sure that the same principle will be adopted in the Sudan. There will be no interference whatever in your religion.' At this, one of the shaikhs present asked whether this would mean the application of the Muhammadan sacred law. Cromer replied in the affirmative. He continued to mention that many abuses were committed during the old Egyptian régime. 'You need be under no fear that these abuses will be repeated. You will, without doubt, have heard that the Egyptian Government of the present day is animated by a very different spirit to that which existed in former

[3] Ibid., p. 246.
[1] Cromer's speech at Omdurman, enclosed in Rodd to Salisbury, No. 3, Jan. 5, 1899, P.R.O., F.O. 78/5022.

times.' He assured them that the taxes which they would have to pay would not be heavy, no irregular exactions would be allowed, and a few British officers would be resident in each district 'in order to ensure strict compliance with these principles.'

On the 19th of January 1899 the Condominium Agreement was signed by the representatives of both governments, Cromer for the British and Butros Ghali for the Egyptian. On the same day a Khedivial decree was issued appointing Lord Kitchener as the Governor-General of the Sudan by virtue of Article III of the Agreement. Cromer forwarded copies both of the Agreement and the decree to Kitchener and added that he was directed by Her Majesty's Government to give the following instructions:

The Governor-General of the Sudan is to obey whatever instructions he may from time to time receive from Her Britannic Majesty's Agent and Consul-General in Cairo, and is to keep the latter fully informed of all important current events connected with the affairs of the Sudan. The main object of the agreement which has been signed between the two Governments concerned is to enable an adequate control to be exercised by Her Majesty's Government, acting in concert with the Khedivial Government over all important matters connected with the Sudan, whilst at the same time sufficient powers are conferred on the Governor-General to settle all matters of local detail on the spot without reference to Cairo or London. In pursuance of this principle, you should, before issue, submit to Her Britannic Majesty's Agent and Consul-General the draft of all important measures and especially all laws, and regulations of general application, which you may propose to enact under the powers conferred upon you by Articles IV, V and VI of the Agreement. You should also refer to Her Britannic Majesty's Agent and Consul-General for instructions in respect to all matters concerning the external relations of the Sudan. I have further to request that at the close of each year you will address to me a report on the administration of the Sudan for submission to Her Majesty's Government and to the Government of the Khedive.[1]

The new machinery of government was set up, but the Khalifah was still in the west and determined to resist. An attempt was made by Colonel Kitchener, who was sent at the head of an expedition, to defeat the Khalifah but failed because Colonel Kitchener thought the force under his command was insufficient and it would be

---

[1] Cromer to Kitchener, Jan. 19, 1899, enclosed in Cromer to Salisbury, No. 15, Jan. 22, 1899, P.R.O., F.O. 78/5022.

a risky movement if the Khalifah chose to fight. It was only in November 1899 that Colonel Wingate was able to defeat the Khalifah at a place west of the present Kusti. Losing hope of victory the Khalifah chose to meet his end in the traditional Sudanese manner under such circumstances by spreading his sheepskin on the ground and sitting on it with all his faithful adherents around and waiting for Wingate's bullets to send him from this world to the world to come.

An administrative machinery was thus established under the Sirdar as governor-general with British officers in the Egyptian army as provincial governors and inspectors, and Egyptian officers in junior administrative posts. The Boer War necessitated the recall of many British officers from the Egyptian service and the Sudan Government had to substitute civilians graduated from Oxford and Cambridge, and in this way the nucleus of the Sudan Civil Service was formed. The one fact that stands out quite clearly from the study of British policy in the Sudan is that the Sudan question all through was considered as subsidiary to the Egyptian question.

XIX

THE SUDAN BEFORE THE 1914 WAR

In addition to his post as Sirdar of the Egyptian Army Kitchener was appointed as the first Governor-General of the Sudan. Provincial administration was under British officers seconded to the Egyptian Army and districts were under Egyptian officers. Their salaries were charged to the Egyptian Treasury as officers in the Egyptian Army. Kitchener's circulars to the provincial governors emphasized that respect and loyalty to the Government depended on personal contact with influential people and inspectors should establish familiar relations with leaders in their districts. Through such leaders and men of influence rulers would control the people. Freedom of worship was to be assured, but religious organizations which might result in fanatic uprising would not be allowed. British district inspectors supervised the work of the Egyptian Mamurs. The latter were instructed to prove that they were agents of a just, benevolent government. It would be their duty to show that the new government was eminently better than the previous one. They were warned against corruption and bribes. People were to be encouraged to increase their agricultural plots and carry their crops to markets. The Mamur in his district was the police authority, magistrate, registrar of lands and the economic adviser for the people.

Kitchener had to issue his first laws and ordinances regulating land tenure especially in towns like Khartum, Barbar and Dongola, and also for the levy and collection of taxes. A criminal code and civil justice ordinance were an immediate necessity for administration. Mr. William Brunyate, an official of the Ministry of Justice in Egypt, and Mr. Bonham Carter, the Legal Secretary of the Sudan Government, cooperated in creating a Sudan penal code and criminal procedure. The code was based on Indian criminal law as applied in Zanzibar.

Kitchener was recalled for service in the Boer war in South Africa and Sir Reginald Wingate succeeded him as the Sirdar of the Egyptian Army and Governor-General of the Sudan. He was

460

at a great advantage when he took over. For many years before the conquest of the Sudan he was the head of the intelligence service of the Egyptian Army in Cairo. In this capacity he collected a store of information about the Sudan, its Government, people, and geography and was very familiar with the administrative machinery of the Mahdiya. The first problem to face him on his appointment was a mutiny in a battalion of the Egyptian Army stationed at Omdurman.

The background for this mutiny and other occasions of discontent among the Egyptians and on certain occasions among some Sudanese goes back to the Condominium Agreement of 1899. It is to be remembered that although that document on its face looked like a genuine legal document, in practice it was nothing but a complete British control over the Sudan with Egypt simply as a nominal partner. The Governor General, departmental heads and inspectors were all Britishers. Salaries of all officers whether British or Egyptians were paid by the Egyptian Treasury; Deficits in the Sudan Budget were met by Egypt up to 1913, the defense of the country was undertaken mainly by the Egyptian Army, which was a charge on the Egyptian finances; the Sudan was restored in the name of the Khedive, an argument which was maintained against all other European powers and used with effect against France in the Fashoda incident.

The British suffered some reverses in the Boer War and rumors spread in the Egyptian Army that the purely Sudanese Battalions were to be sent to South Africa in support of the British Army which was reported to be in difficulties. Maxwell Pasha, the Acting Sirdar, started to collect ammunition which was in the hands of soldiers. Some Egyptian officers induced their Sudanese soldiers not to hand over their ammunition. They actually attacked the stores to restore what they had handed over before. The 14th Sudanese battalion totally disobeyed the instructions to give up their ammunition. Hearing of these mutinous activities in Cairo, Wingate took with him messages from the Khedive deprecating such activities and ordering his soldiers to surrender to authority. On arrival in Khartum Wingate managed to restore authority and the officers responsible for the trouble were tried and sent to Cairo.

The first Anniversary of the Condominium Agreement witnessed the birth of a Nationalist Egyptian paper, al-Liwa, with the young nationalist Mustafa Kamil as an editor. On the 20th of January, 1900, he wrote a fiery leader in his paper inciting the Egyptians to look upon the day of the Condominium Agreement as a day of mourning. It was the day in which the Sudan became a British colony not with British money and blood but with the Egyptians'. That was the tone of al-Liwa for many years to come and in this way an increasing number of Egyptians and Sudanese who felt their community of interest with Egypt became aware of the necessity of common efforts against the British in the Nile Valley. I have dwelt at this beginning of a common struggle to throw off the British yoke in order to remove the misconception that this move started only in 1919. On reading those early issues of al-Liwa the news of the Sudan towns and provinces were reported together with those of Egypt as though they were one country.

In reaction to such an anti-British movement, Cromer in his annual reports developed the arguments of how Egypt benefited from the restoration of the Sudan; her southern frontiers were secure forever, the regular supply of the Nile water for Egyptian irrigation was assured and trade between the two countries was revived. Both Egypt and Britain could be proud of returning the Sudan to civilization.

The Sudan was, therefore, conquered in the name of the Khedive as a restoration of his dominion lost to him by the Mahdist revolution, but without his prior consultation. An agreement for the administration of the newly conquered territory was signed, but the British were the actual rulers. The high-ranking officers including the Sirdar who were supposed to be the Khedive's servants were in practice obeying British instructions and policy. By the Agreement the Governor-General was almost a dictator, but in 1910 he practised his authority with a council which although advisory, was shouldering with him the responsibility of administration. They were his subordinates, who were in charge of Departments.

Although the first few years of the new regime were spent in establishing law and order and a workable machinery of government, yet economic and educational developments were thought of at the start. With the military railway and telegraph lines as a nucleus expansion in them was the first concern of the administration. The main difficulty was how to finance these projects especially the railway lines, which were considered essential to any economic development. Cromer was faced with the problem and his first impulse was to entrust the new railway projects to a company because of costs which could not be met by the meager revenue of the Sudan, nor by the already burdened Egyptian Treasury. The British Treasury as a source was out of the question. It was just a thought in Cromer's mind, but he was not enthusiastic about it and the Egyptian Government objected. The only alternative was, therefore, for the Egyptian Government to advance some loan for reasonable development along this line. The Halfa railway was extended from Atbara to Khartum North and an Atbara-Red Sea railway also built, but Port Sudan took the place of the old historic town of Sawakin. Before the outbreak of the First World War al-Ubayyid was linked to Khartum.

As the main reason for the restoration of the Sudan was control of the Nile water for the benefit of Egypt, it was only natural that the British engineers in the irrigation service of Egypt should make a thorough survey of the main Nile and its tributaries. The immediate concern of that survey were the needs of Egypt, but it was envisaged also that the Sudan should make use of the Nile water for big irrigational projects. The Jazirah was the possible area for such schemes. The original project was the building of a dam somewhere between Sennar and Roseris with two main canals taking off both on the east and west sides of the river for irrigating the Jazirah and the eastern parts of the Blue Nile. The plan was to use flood water only and to cultivate wheat, which would find ready markets in Arab countries and perhaps would compete with Indian wheat in European markets.

While these irrigational projects were being considered by experts, others were exploring the possibilities of cotton production and the first experiments proved a success. The whole project was revised along the line of cotton rather than wheat. The area to be irrigated was restricted to the Jazirah and a reservoir for storing water was provided for. Land had to be registered and the railway line which ultimately reached al-Ubayyid had to be laid in the area. The Empire Cotton-producing Society gave its support to the scheme and a deputation waited on the Prime Minister in London requesting the British Government's support also. A loan of three million pounds for the execution was guaranteed by the British Treasury for the dam, reservoir and canalization. Work had already begun in 1914, but the war stopped it.

It has already been pointed out that in those early years of the

Condominium administration, there was always a deficit in the
Sudan Government Budget even without spending a penny on defense
which was the exclusive responsibility of the Egyptian Army. The
table below shows the Budget of the first four years in Egyptian
pounds:—

YEAR	REVENUE	EXPENDITURE
1899	126,569	230,238
1900	156,888	331,918
1901	242,309	475,335
1902	270,226	516,945

It was intentional on the part of the new administration to make
the burden of taxation as light as possible, having in mind how
taxes and methods for their collection were the curse of the Turco-
Egyptian period before the Mahdiya. Cromer was very much
impressed by the system of the Mahdiya taxes which was based on
Muhammadan Law and it was followed with some modification
in the case of animals and land produces.

Kitchener went on leave on Christmas of 1898 and immediately
launched an appeal to the British public for a subscription in order
to commemorate Gordon by an educational institution in Khartum.
In a short time he managed to collect 100,000 pounds. The sort of
education which he wanted at the time was the practical rather than
the academic and the Arabic language was to be given a dominant
place. There were at the time the Egyptian schools in Aswan and
Wadi Halfa as a model. In Cromer's opinion no further stand as
be taken without consultation with educational experts. Elementary
schools were to be established in the big towns which would stand as
a model for others in the various parts of the country. A primary
school was started at Omdurman to be followed by similar institutions in selected towns. In Kitchener's own opinion these funds collected in memory of Gordon should be spent for development of
primary education and the secondary stage should come at later
date.

In 1900 James Currie was appointed as the first Director of
Education to take over what was already established from his
colleague Bonham Carter, the legal secretary, and to plan for future
development. He thought that progress in education should go hand
in hand gradually with economic development. Schools and other

educational institutions should, therefore, aim at what would lead to economic revival and understanding of the new administrative machinery. That would mean training young Sudanese to be artisans and junior Government Officials. It would further aim at educating the people in the understanding of administrative machinery. For the implementation of this policy various kinds of schools were established, technical for the training of artisans, elementary for the 3 R's, primary for junior officials, and training colleges for teachers.

The battle of um Dwikrat in which Khalifah 'Abdullahi' met his end in a noble fashion by spreading his sheep-skin and sitting waiting for the bullets of Wingate was the last serious resistance to the new regime. But from time to time there was an uprising mainly religious, which was ended only by military action. A man from the west called Sharif Muhammad al-Amin and claiming descent from the prophet Muhammad rose in Taqali Hills in the Nuba Mountains with those who believed in his religious mission. An expedition under Mahon Pasha, the Governor of Kurdufan, defeated him. In 1904 a man near Singa claimed to be Nabi Isa (Jesus), rebelled with a few followers, but was very soon suppressed. In 1906 a rebellion in Talodi (Nuba Mountains) killed many soldiers, policemen, merchants and the Mamur.

Perhaps the most serious revolt in the Sudan before 1914 was the rebellion of Abd al-Qadir Wadd Habbuba in al-Jazirah between Hasa-Heisa and Kamlin. He belonged to the Halawin tribe, who took a great share in the fighting of al-Mahdi. Abd al-Qadir himself was a fighter in al-Nujumi's expedition that invaded Egypt. He was one of the determined group who kept themselves in readiness for restoring the power of the Mahdiya. His attitude and way of life made the Government authorities suspect him. His own relatives gave information about his preparations for an uprising. A British inspector and an Egyptian Mamur went to him to find out for themselves whether news about his rebellious attitude were true or not, but they were murdered. Troops were marched against him and although they suffered a comparatively big loss in a night surprise attack by 'Abd al-Qadir and his followers, in the end he was defeated and hanged.*

*My Authority for this Chapter is 'al-Sudan Fi Qarn' (Cairo 1957 second edition.) by the Author.

XX

THE SUDAN DURING THE 1914-18 WAR

When war broke out in Europe, it was the policy of the Sudan Government to explain the case of the Allied powers in general and that of Britain in particular. It was known from the beginning that Turkey would most probably gravitate to the side of Germany. Turkey was supposed to be officially the leader of Islamic people by virtue of its Sultan being at the same time the Khalifah of all Muslims. It was, therefore, a general British policy to be prepared to combat any propaganda that might emanate from Turkey inciting all Muslims to declare a holy war on the side of Turkey against the infidels who were the allies. There was a flaw in that Turkish argument, because the central powers were non-Muslims as well as the Allied powers and such a kind of appeal for a holy war would not carry great weight.

In October 1914 Sir Reginald Wingate, the Governor General, toured the country and contacted chiefs of tribes and men of influence, religious leaders and senior officials explaining to them the general situation in Europe and the noble purposes for which England was standing in that war. In Khartum, Labib Juridini, the editor of *al-Sudan,* the only paper at the time, was writing the same sort of propaganda as that of the Governor-General.

On November 6th news was received in Khartum declaring that hostilities had started between Britain and Turkey. The next day Sir Reginald invited to his palace Senior officers in the Egyptian army informing them that the Sudan would be standing in that war on the side of England. He continued to explain the situation and the power of both sides and the ultimate result of the war in favor of the Allies. He appealed to them to remain faithful and loyal to their duties and he showed his willingness to exempt those officers descending from Turkish origin from carrying arms against Turkey if they felt that their conscience would not permit them to do so. On November 8th he invited to the palace 'Ulama (learned men), chiefs, notables and men of religious influence. After telling them the story of the war and the position of the two camps, he enumer-

466

ated to them the benefits that accrued to the country from the present administration and the support that was given to Muslims and Islam by Britain. They immediately signed a document in which they pledged themselves to support Britain in that war. Others who were not present at the meeting sent messages in the same spirit and similar expressions of loyalty were exhibited in the provinces. *Al-Sudan* published all these expressions of loyalty which were subsequently reprinted in a book called the "Book of Loyalty."

Just by way of illustration I quote here below some of such expressions of loyalty by some prominent personalities:

"We, the undersigned, 'Ulema, Religious Sheikhs and Notables of the Sudan, beg to submit to our just Government the expression of our deepest and most cordial sincerity and loyalty. We affirm hereby that we have never experienced other than the greatest respect for our religion; that material support has been given to our places of worship; that Ulema have been appointed to teach the precepts of our religion, and judges to settle all questions pertaining to the Muhammadan Law; . . . . We are with our present Government heart and soul and have no bond with Turkey, which power has followed the advice of Germany and has declared war in conjunction with Her."

"We regret exceedingly and our hearts are filled with grief at Turkey's action in participating in a war against Great Britain. This act is assuredly against the desires of the Sultan and his wise councillors and has given great offense to the Muslims in all four quarters of the Globe. . . . We beg hereby to declare our most sincere and loyal attachment, on behalf of ourselves and the Sudan population, to Great Britain, that just Government whose great respect for our religion and interest in our welfare is proved by the progress which has been made in our country through justice and civilization. The justice of England embraces ninety millions of our Muhammadan brethren all over the world: England is the true and close friend of all Muhammadans."

"I, the undersigned, on behalf of myself and of my family and tribe, descended from the old Arab tribes of Quraish and Hashim, and others in the Sudan whose opinion I represent, beg to offer an expression of our most sincere loyalty, both to your just Government and to your beloved person. . . . We are witnesses that the 16 years passed under your rule are unparalleled in the history of the Sudan. Under your flag, which protects many millions of other Muhammadans, we are enjoying full liberty in the exercise of our religious duties, as well as our daily work, in the same way as all other millions of Muhammadans under your rule."

It seems, therefore, that the country was loyal to the cause of the allied powers and particularly to Britain when war was declared in spite of the Turkish propaganda for a holy war. But still there were individuals, who were either of Turkish origin or their feeling of religious affinity with Turkey was so strong that they chose to stage a counter-propaganda in the form of circulars sent to religious leaders. The Government promptly reacted and arrested those who were considered to be the makers of such circulars and others who were suspected to be of doubtful loyalty. With the exception of this and rumors that magnified German victories, the country remained as a whole peaceful except in Darfur and some uprisings in the Nuba mountains. The Sudan contributed to the war efforts in the form of transport camels for the Palestinian expedition, cattle and sheep for meat, and such produces as Dura (millet).

There were two local disturbances in the Nuba mountains during the war, one in the Nyma, Dilling District under the leadership of Agabna and the other in Miri, Kadugli under Faki 'Ali. The first was the more serious one as the patrol that was sent against it totalled about 3,000 in officers and men and it took them several months before they could suppress the revolt.

Darfur had its own history after the restoration in 1898. When Kitchener was at Atbara before his final march on Omdurman, he sent Ibrahim 'Ali, who was a soldier in the defeated army of Mahmud and who claimed descent from the royal family of Darfur to that country in order to pave the way for the authority of the conquering army. Kitchener took that step because he was aware of the remoteness of Darfur with the inherent difficulties of transport and water and the several occasions of defying the authority, whether that of the Turco-Egyptian period or that of the Mahdiya. Ibrahim 'Ali, the chosen emissary, did not succeed in his mission, but the same objective was attained by another man, a member of the Darfur Royal Family called 'Ali Dinar, Son of Zakaria.

Ali Dinar was appointed by the Mahdiya authority as a nominal Sultan of part of Darfur, but he very soon fell under suspicion of being disloyal to the regime and so was brought to Omdurman under supervision, though not actually in prison. He was staying there up to the day previous to the Omdurman battle, when he took the opportunity of fleeing to the west with a group of chosen friends who numbered less than ten. While passing through Kurdufan and the northeastern parts of Darfur a number of men gathered around him until he, it is stated, reached the heart of Darfur with at least two thousand men ready to stand by him and give him support in the re-establishment of the illustrious Sultanate of Darfur. The Mahdiya authorities at al-Fashir handed over to him everything, because by this time the Khalifa's power was practically overthrown. When Kitchener heard of the rivalry between Ali Dinar and his emissary Ibrahim 'Ali he requested both to wait until he could decide who would have more influence in the area. But Ibrahim 'Ali solved the problem by resigning in favor of 'Ali Dinar.

It was the policy of the Sudan Government, at the time, to let 'Ali Dinar be completely autonomous internally, but provided with advisers who would reside with him in his capital. Dinar, on the other hand, ascended a throne of his ancestors by his own power and initiative and the Sudan Government did nothing to help him. He was willing to fly the two flags of the Sudan and to pay a yearly tribute but things should stop at that. Various attempts and approaches were made to let him accept advisers or to enter into negotiations, but he was adamant and would not accept any interference of any kind. Though that was an unpleasant situation for the Sudan Government, yet they accepted the *fait accompli,* because they were not desirous at that early stage to assume direct responsibility of Government in that remote territory with the attendant expenses.

To pacify Darfur and impose his authority on the vast province was not an easy task for Dinar. He was dealing with petty chiefs and Baggara tribes of power who were proud of occasional periods of independence. Ever since it was conquered by al-Zubair in the Turco-Egyptian period and all through the Mahdiya period there were always disturbances and rebellions. Dinar, however, managed to have a relative success in that respect. Just before the First World War he had to deal with a European people over border questions. The French penetrated into the heart of Africa and very soon clashed with Dinar over frontiers and he started handling the question himself with the French. The Sudan Government instructed him to stop any negotiations over such questions and leave it to the British Government to take it up with the French on behalf of the Sudan. They maintained that it was foreign policy and not internal problems. This conflict was submerged in the war and ultimately bigger issues led to war with Dinar.

In 1912 the railway line reached al-Ubayyid in Kurdufan and some of the problems of transport to Darfur began to be partly solved. The Sudan by this time was reasonably pacified. Dinar began to handle questions of foreign policy which he ought not to have touched at all. All attempts to approach him with a view of establishing more contacts and better relations were a failure. Dinar, on the other hand, consolidated his position and his rule was accepted in the territory of his grandfathers and was known as an illustrious Muslim Emir in the heart of Africa. He had definite complaints against the Sudan Government. His requests for rifles and ammunition were not attended to, his own emissary for buying such weapons from Arabia was not allowed to do so, chiefs and tribesmen taking refuge in Kurdufan from Darfur were not returned and aggressions of Kurdufan tribes into Darfur were not stopped or punished. Slatin Pasha, the inspector general who was handling relations with Darfur, seemed to have been a bit rude in his correspondence with Dinar. That was the state of affairs when war broke out in 1914.

The news of the outbreak of war and the relative positions of the hostile forces were conveyed to Dinar by the Governor-General in a letter. Wingate advised Dinar to follow the events of the war in the columns of al-Sudan and not to listen to other unfounded rumors. But the news of German successes reached Dinar from the other camp especially after the entrance of Turkey into the war. Unlike the other chiefs and notables of the Sudan Dinar as a Muslim Emir recognized the Sultan of Turkey as the Khalifa of all Muslims. When we add to this the issues of conflict and misunderstanding between him and the Sudan Government just before the war, we should not be surprised to find Dinar seizing the opportunity of sending a letter to the Khalifa asking for help. We have no evidence to know for certain whether that letter found its way to Istanbul or not. At the same time Turkish propaganda was active harping on the tone of the holy war against the infidels. Dinar re ceived a letter from Turkey giving a version of the causes and events of the war different to what Wingate told Dinar, and he immediately replied that he was in a state of preparedness to defy infidels' authority.

The intelligence service of the Sudan Government was sure of the hostile attitude of Dinar and his intention to invade their territory. In spite of the need for their military forces to be used in other fields the Sudan Government decided to send an expedition against Dinar to resolve that problem once and for all. A force of about 3,000 soldiers was collected while a number of messages were sent from the religious leaders, notables and official circles advising Dinar to stop his preparations for war. Although it was relatively a small force, yet the difficulties of transport and water were great especially west of al-Nuhud during the dry season. When the Government troops were about 12 miles north of al-Fashir they felt the presence of other forces near the village of Bringieh. It was the plan of Dinar to hide in ambush to surprise the Govern-ment forces and thus annihilate them. But a scouting party discovered the positions of the Fur army and retreated to take their positions in the square of the invading forces. The Fur army came out in the open and launched and attack on the square. The Government army was in a position and formation which enabled them to repel the attack which was pressed with courage and determination. But after a large number of casualties, including some only ten yards in front of the square, they had to retreat and in this way their resistance was broken. Ali Dinar had to evacuate the capital to take refuge in the Marra mountain area, where he would be in a good defensive position and would ultimately attack.

The first phase of the campaign was concluded and companies of the army were sent to occupy certain selected posts in the province waiting for orders to start the second phase of the campaign. It was understood that when Dinar finally located himself in the Marra mountain area with its good natural defense position, it would need a renewed campaign, which could not be carried out success-fully during the rainy season which was just starting in Darfur. But Miralai Huddleston (later the Governor-General of the Sudan during the Second World War) who was in charge of a small force near the position of the Sultan had another point of view. He thought that it was time that the Sultan should be attacked and thus the Government saved effort, worry, and more expenses. Contrary to his instructions he moved with his forces and attacked Dinar. A stray bullet killed the Sultan and in this way the resistance was finally broken and all Darfur lay at the disposal of the Sudan Government. From that date in November, 1916, Darfur was just a province of the Sudan like the others and the period of its autonomous rule was brought to an end.

XXI

EVENTS OF 1924

When hostilities came to an end in November 1918 a deputation of Sudanese composed of the religious leaders, 'Ulama and tribal chiefs travelled to London to congratulate the King. Men of influence in the country expressed their loyalty to the British and were true to their word during the war and now crowned their good faith by this deputation. It was the close of a phase and opening of a new one by the young educated or enlightened generation. This new anti-British feeling, which was in marked contrast to the old manifestation of loyalty synchronized with the revival of Egyptian nationalism and was closely associated with and influenced by it.

Towards the close of the war all politically minded groups and individuals in Egypt came to a common understanding as to the way in which they would like to present their case to the British. A deputation of three including Sa' ad Zaghlul had a meeting with Sir Reginald Wingate, the British High Commissioner, on the 13th of November, 1918. Wingate was not in a position to submit a plan for future development in Egypt and replied that he considered the meeting unofficial and thanked them for coming to see him. The delegates pointed out that they were asking for the independence of Egypt and giving guaranties for important British interests. Finding no satisfactory answer from the High Commissioner they asked for leave to travel to London and present their case to the British Government. This was refused and followed by the arrest of Sa' ad and other leaders on the pretext of a disturbance of public security. On hearing of the deportation of those leaders to Malta, the anti-British feeling all over Egypt broke out in the forms of demonstrations, attacks on the British and cutting the means of communication. The British military authorities suppressed this popular eruption of feeling by sheer force. Mr. Lloyd George appointed General Allenby with extraordinary powers in Egypt so that the British Government would be free to deal with more important issues in the Peace Conference. The deportees were released and instead of returning they went to the Peace Conference hoping to get a hearing, but without success.

A Commission under Lord Milner was appointed to investigate the Egyptian situation and to report with their recommendations. Although the Commission were boycotted, yet they could collect information which enabled them to get a somewhat clear picture. 'Adly Pasha persuaded Sa' ad and his colleagues, who were in Paris at the time, to go to London to meet members of the Commission who had returned by this time. The Egyptian delegates submitted a draft of agreement in which they reserved the right for a separate agreement on the Sudan. Milner on the other hand expressed the view that he recognized the vital problem of the regular flow of water to Egypt and the British Government would guarantee this. When a compromise draft was reached it was presented to other leaders and members of the Wafd in Egypt, who refused it and this first attempt failed.

The second attempt was by an official delegation under 'Adly Pasha, after prolonged negotiation with Lord Curzon. The British side submitted to 'Adly a draft agreement, which he could not accept. What is of interest to us is the part dealing with the Sudan. The British in their draft assured the Egyptians their fair portion of the Nile water and that no new irrigational projects would be built south of Wari Halfa without the approval of a Committee of three representing Egypt, the Sudan and Uganda. Against this Egypt would be required to continue giving the same military assistance or a subvention adequate for the purpose. All Egyptian forces in the Sudan should be under the authority of the Governor-General. When ultimately a unilateral declaration was made by the British Government on the 28th of February, 1922, abolishing the protectorate and declaring Egypt an independent Sovereign State with four reservations, the Sudan was one of these four, i.e. no change until superseded by new agreements. So far the Egyptian point of view about the Sudan was to avoid discussing it, because they would like to open it in a way favorable to them and that would be after obtaining their independence. The British on the other hand would not like the present British administration to be disturbed and insisted that the status quo should be maintained.

The question of the Sudan came again to the forefront when the Committee set up in Egypt to write a constitution based on the declaration of February 28th, 1922. Any group of Egyptians entrusted with the task of making a constitution for Egypt could not avoid the question of the Sudan. If it was ignored by them it would be taken as an evidence they were abandoning their rights. They recommended that the title of the King should be that of Egypt and the Sudan, but its administration would be decided by a special law. The British opposed the draft and after an ultimatum it was agreed that the title of King of Egypt would be decided after reaching a final agreement about the Sudan. In the meantime the implementation of this constitution in Egypt alone would not prejudice whatever right the Egyptians had over the Sudan.

The elections that were held after passing the constitution brought a majority for the Wafd Party under Sa' ad Zaghlul Pasha who formed the Cabinet early in 1924. Debates and questions in parliament brought up the question of the Sudan in one way or another. On one occasion the command of the Egyptian Army by a foreigner, who resided in the Sudan in his capacity as Governor-General, was bitterly criticised. In another a member demanded that the Sudan Government Budget should be presented to parliament in the same way as it used to be in the legislative assembly before the war. Some members raised the question of the use of coercive methods by the British in preventing Sudanese going to Egypt in order to show their loyalty to the crown and Egypt.

This incessant discussion and questions about the Sudan in the Egyptian parliament made the British state their policy. In the House of Lords the Government spokesman stated that the Sudan question was a matter of concern only for the British Government and the Sudanese, that the British would not abandon the Sudan and that no change in the present Sudan Administration would take place without the consent of the British Parliament. Zughlul responded immediately to these declarations of statement of policy. He declared that Egypt would not abandon the Sudan and that they would spare no effort to remove the injustice by lawful means.

The above account was a brief description of the political atmosphere between 1919 and 1924. The young generation of the Sudanese who received any education beyond the elementary were following the development of Egyptian nationalism with eagerness. They used to read what appeared in the papers and Zaghlul stood out as a leader not for Egypt but for the Sudan as well. The Egyptian Army whose units were stationed in the Sudan comprised

Sudanese units and officers who were treated on an equal footing with their Egyptian comrades and took the oath of loyalty to the King of Egypt. Egyptians were working in the schools and offices with their Sudanese colleagues and the discussion of political developments was the main topic of conversation among them. They had seen how the Egyptians crowned their struggle by independence and a democratic constitutional Government. They (the Sudanese) should follow the same methods and should get the support of Egypt against the common enemy—the British. It is in this kind of atmosphere and that line of thought that the Sudanese reacted.

Early in 1921 the headmaster of Gordon College, who maintained a fatherly relationship with his former pupils and graduates of the college, read to some of them an article which appeared in the *Times* about the Sudan. The general impression formed was that the Sudan was for the Sudanese and that the British policy should be directed towards that aim. The news of that meeting and the question it raised were conveyed to other graduates and senior pupils still pursuing their studies. It cannot be established whether that movement on the part of the British in the Sudan had any connection with the secret society formed by the politically-minded Sudanese later in the year. The aim of that Society which was called 'Society for the Sudanese Union' was the liberation of the Sudan from British Imperialism with the support of Egypt, without specifying the relation between the two countries. Their methods included posters and circulars pasted to the walls during the night in which they incited people against the British and called upon them to shake off the British yoke. As they were largely government officials and senior schoolboys, they chose to carry out their activities secretly. They were instrumental in sending some pupils to Egypt to pursue their education there in a freer atmosphere.

The next development in the national movement was for others to work in the open and the group that followed that method were to be the founders of the 'White League Flag' who aimed at uniting their struggle with that of the Egyptians. Unlike the other secret Society this had its leader in a young courageous Sudanese officer, the late 'Ali Abdel Lateef. They maintained their activities in the form of telegrams to authorities in Egypt and the Sudan supporting Egyptian claims, especially when Zaghlul became Prime Minister and they staged many anti-British demonstrations in the main towns of the Sudan. As they were not careful about their papers and records and as many quite openly led those demonstrations, the government arrested nearly all of them and sent them to prison. Their movement reached its climax in 1924. Their demonstrations, coming after the posters of the secret society and during the time when the Egyptians were pursuing their struggle, achieved a partial success. All these brought politics to the notice of the ordinary people in the Sudan.

The same year 1924 which saw the first constitutional government in Egypt under Zaghlul brought to power in Britain the first Labor Government. In a cordial telegram Mr. Macdonald, the Prime Minister, conveyed his hearty good wishes to the 'newest of Parliaments' 'I believe,' the telegram continued, 'that Egypt and Great Britain will be tied by a strong bond of friendship, our desire being to see this bond made stronger on a permanent basis. For this purpose the Government of His Majesty the King is ready now, and at any time, to negotiate with the Egyptian Government.' This telegram was read to the Egyptian Parliament in March, 1924, on its opening day. In the same meeting the speech from the throne which stated the Zaghlul Government's policy declared; 'You have before you one of the most grave and delicate tasks upon which the future of Egypt depends, the task of realizing her complete independence in the true meaning of the word. My Government is ready to enter into negotiations, free of all restrictions, with the British Government, so as to realize our national aspirations with regard to Egypt and the Sudan.'

It became clear that Zaghlul was determined that he was not asking for negotiations to settle the outstanding problems of Egypt alone, but that of the Sudan. While Macdonald showed his mere willingness for negotiations, Zaghlul made it a policy of his aspirations which were nothing other than independence. Those declarations of policy on the part of Egypt and especially their reference to the Sudan, with some Britishers being murdered in Egypt from time to time, annoyed the British Government and made Macdonald hesitate to fulfil his promise of opening negotiations. But Lord Allenby, the High Commissioner, insisted that nothing should stop them and argued that it was too late to retreat.

The effect in the Sudan of 1924 events was most favorable to

Egypt. The Egyptians were not going to speak for Egypt alone but they would take up the problem of the Sudan in a way which would ultimately remove or at least diminish the British influence. As a manifestation of this support the White League Flag intensified its activities. The cadets of the military school in Khartum staged an armed demonstration in which they displayed their anti-British sentiment and their feeling towards Egypt. When returning to their school they were disarmed after a cordon of the British Army was stationed around them and then were taken to boats in the middle of river and finally sent to prison with the political prisoners.

Negotiations in London came to nothing. Their failure was not a surprise knowing that Macdonald was hesitant even to open them and that Zaghlul would not like to be tainted with the stigma of legalizing the declaration of November 1922. The British were ready to give in on some points but were adamant about the Suez Canal and the status quo in the Sudan. Just before the start of the negotiations Macdonald held a conference with the British High Commissioner in Egypt and the Governor-General of the Sudan and the upshot of the meeting was that the view of His Majesty's Government was that if Egypt refused to play the game in the Sudan they should be told to quit it altogether. The implications of that policy would be to form a purely Sudanese force and the additional expenses should be sought in acceleration of cotton production. In the White paper which Macdonald published after the failure of negotiations it was affirmed that the British Government considered herself a trustee for the Sudan and her responsibility in that respect could only be handed over to the Sudanese.

On November 19th, 1924, Sir Lee Stack, Governor-General of the Sudan and Sirdar of the Egyptian Army, was murdered in the streets of Cairo. The crime, coming soon after the failure of negotiations and anti-British activities in the Sudan, brought an ultimatum which was presented by Britain to Egypt that included the withdrawal of Egyptian officers and purely Egyptian units from the Sudan. The Commandant of the Egyptian artillery refused to leave without explicit instructions from King Fuad. This news spread among the Sudanese officers and Sudanese units of the Egyptian Army. Some officers leading Sudanese companies marched with their arms and ammunition to join the battalion which refused to leave. They clashed with the British Army who were in the buildings of Gordon

College and the battle that followed could only come to a stop after the Sudanese fired all their ammunition. The casualties among the British were relatively heavy.

By December 1924 after the withdrawal of the Egyptian units the acting Governor-General in full agreement with the acting Sirdar telegraphed to the High Commissioner in Cairo for transmission to London: 'Foundations of Condominium are proved utterly untrustworthy and we cannot rebuild army on double allegiance. It is impossible to guarantee that we shall not have another mutiny: we can deal with it if it occurs with our present forces, but every life lost on both sides in suppressing it will be due to our not doing what, according to all opinion here, we should have done on the morning after Stack's death, viz. declaring abolition of Egyptian authority. The chance of a further mutiny will be very greatly reduced by lowering the Egyptian flag.' British authorities in Cairo and London did not agree to make such a drastic change at so late a stage.*

* My main sources for this chapter are:

1. Lord Lloyd: Egypt since Cromer (London 1934).

2. Muhammad Shafig Ghurbal: Tarikh al-Mufawadat al-Masria al-Inglizia 1882-1936. (Cairo 1952).

3. Special issue of *al-Rai al'Am* newspaper commemerating the Independence of the Sudan (Khartum, March 1956).

XXII

EVENTS BETWEEN 1924 AND 1950

1924 was a black year for the Sudan. The first genuine struggle for freedom from the British after the battle of Um-Duwikrat when Khalifah Abdalla fell was ruthlessly suppressed. Leaders and members of the White Flag League and the Military Cadets were in prison, officers who resisted the British Army were shot and a general policy of repression was followed. Boys of the Gordon Memorial College were made to clean their rooms, make their beds and remove the mounds of sands in the afternoon. Children in the elementary schools had to squat on native mats instead of sitting on benches when attending classes. The program of establishing native courts with somewhat discretionary powers on the pretext of following native customs and traditions was accelerated. Movements between Egypt and the Sudan were restricted and the reading of Egyptian newspapers amounted to an offence, especially among school boys.' Between 1924 and 1935 there were two attempts to come to an agreement about the four reserved points between Egypt and Britain, but all failed.

In the second half of 1928 the first batch of Sudanese graduates from the American University of Beirut arrived in Khartum to teach in the Gordon Memorial College. They very soon began to influence their pupils and awaken them to the repressive atmosphere in which they were living. They cultivated in them the spirit of social work and cooperation among themselves. That new spirit had to have its first test in 1931. The Sudan Government on the pretext of the economic depression had to reduce the starting salaries of graduates of the college. The reaction of the pupils was immediate. After discussing the question they decided on a strike from lessons in a peaceful atmosphere without exhibiting any form of violence. In pursuing that course they wanted to avoid the most certain result of closing down the College indefinitely if violence were used. It was only after the intermediary of the graduates of the college and Sayyid Abd al-Rahman al-Mahdi that the Government raised the salaries a bit and the pupils were persuaded to return to their

480

classes. It was the generation which attended schools after the repressive policy that followed 1924 and those who experienced the events of the 1931 strike, who led the struggle for liberation culminating in independence.

When the Anglo-Egyptian Treaty of 1936 was concluded the structure of the 1899 Condominium was maintained and the only addition was that the object of Sudan administration would be the welfare of the Sudanese. By this time the politically-minded educated Sudanese were concentrating their activities in the literary and debating societies, either in their clubs or in private houses, and in contributing to the press, but they did not yet come out in the open as had the people of 1924. Discussion in such societies very naturally touched on the political situation and particularly about the conclusion of a Treaty which partially concerned the Sudan, the people of which were not consulted in any manner whatsoever. The activities of Wad Madani Society culminated in the idea of a Congress of enlightened Sudanese to define their political aims and to work for them. The Sudan Schools club of Omdurman was selected to be the headquarters of the new congress and it was intended that it should have branches all over the Sudan. The membership was open for any one with educational qualifications above the elementary.

The movement found a ready response among the people who were qualified to be members. It was in the last years of the period between the wars; countries of the Middle East like Egypt, Iraq, Syria and Lebanon had already settled their relations with Britain and France on a Treaty basis. India was gaining progress in her struggle towards independence. The enlightened Sudanese were reading such news and were impressed by the progress towards independence and self-government in those countries and saw that there was no indication of similar movements in their country. All hopes were pinned on the graduates' congress for the fulfilment of national aspirations. Although the founders and promoters were very careful to include in their objectives the interests of the graduates as well as public interests, they were, right from the start, intending that the vague reference to public interest would be interpreted as political aspirations. In the first few years they were busy in increasing membership and promotion of education, in which they attained considerable success.

By 1942 the Congress had been accepted as representative of the political aspirations of the country by the enlightened Sudanese. It had proved its worth by its fine educational program. The Sudan defense force was fighting beyond its frontiers with the British and the Sudan produces were used for war efforts by a British corporation fixing peace-time prices for them. It was not, therefore, a surprise that the Congress should ask officially on behalf of the Sudanese for more association with the government of their country and a promise by the Condomini Governments that the Sudanese would be granted the right of self-determination after the cessation of hostilities. These demands were conveyed in a memorandum addressed to the Governor-General through the Civil Secretary.

Although the tone of the memorandum containing these demands was quite moderate and admitted that the congress itself was a fruit of the Condomini yet the reaction of the Sudan Government was a flat refusal of the demands and the return of the memorandum. This was a blow even to those who believed in cooperating with the British for attainment of self-government. In his reply the Civil Secretary denied to the Congress the representation of the Sudanese and reminded them of the previous correspondence between the Congress and his predecessor in which they did not claim a representation other than their members. The Governor-General and his advisers, the Congress was told, were aware of the legitimate aspiration of the enlightened Sudanese for more association with the government of their country, but the pace of progress along that line would be for the Sudan Government alone to decide.

The Government, on their side, thought that the legitimate aspiration at the time could be satisfied by an advisory council for the Northern Sudan (Arabic speaking part). The Congress by this time extended its membership to include the two main religious fraternities of the Ansar and the Khatmia to compete for the control of the Congress. In 1943 the group which received the support of the Khatimia won the Congress elections and the Ansar left the Congress and formed the Umma party as a straightforward political party demanding independence for the Sudan. The Khatmia-supported group formed the Ashiqqa party, which was seeking some sort of federal relations with Egypt. The political struggle after the formation of these two political parties began to take a definite shape. The Ansar forming the main group of the Umma were standing for independence and both the British Government and the British officials in the Sudan showed no objection at all, for such an objective would mean hostility to Egyptian claims. This was interpreted by their opponents as a kind of independence in which the British would be the advisers and would dominate the political scene. The Khatmia-supported-group argued that the only way to avoid this British sponsored independence would be the pooling of political resources with those of Egypt. The traditional rivalry between the Ansar and the Khatmia was at the root of this perplexing situation.

Late in 1945 it was agreed between the British and Egyptian Governments to enter into negotiations for the revision of the 1936 Treaty. All Sudanese were in agreement that this time their voice should be heard and that nothing should be arrived at between the negotiating parties affecting the Sudan without their consultation. As the negotiations were to start in Cairo, political parties prepared themselves to send their delegations to observe and if possible to be a party in all matters relating to their country. Although the two main parties had quite different objectives, it was thought that there should be one united delegation with demands which should be a compromise of the two points of view. There was a public pressure on the parties to proceed to Cairo as one delegation rather than two distinct groups. These efforts succeeded at the last moment and the Sudanese found themselves in Cairo to follow the negotiations. The delegation of the Independence-front withdrew when it was made clear to them that the Egyptian side was advising an undefined permanent unity under the Egyptian Crown. This was not a surprise since solidarity of the Sudanese delegation was known to be shaking between two groups of such divergent objectives. Members of the Unity Parties stayed in Cairo observing the progress of the negotiations.

When the Cairo negotiations failed Sidki Pasha, the Egyptian Premier and Mr. Bevin, the British Foreign Secretary, reached a compromise agreement, which they initialled in October, 1946 in London. What concerns us here is that part of the agreement, which referred to the Sudan. It was embodied in a draft Sudan Protocol which recognized a symbolic and a temporary Egyptian Sovereignty over the Sudan. Sidki Pasha was reported to have said that he brought the Egyptian Sovereignty over the Sudan. Serious disorders and clashes broke out in Khartum between the Independence and

Unity Parties. Press reports and official utterances in Cairo confirmed that their interpretation of the Sudan Protocol was a permanent unity of the two countries under the Egyptian Crown. The British, on the other hand, did not read into it more than a temporary and symbolic unity. Because of these two different interpretations it became clear that no agreement on the Sudan question could be reached. By January 1947 negotiations broke off.

The Egyptian Government took the dispute to the Security Council of the United Nations. The Egyptian delegation headed by the Prime Minister argued that the unity of the Nile Valley was an historical fact, the unity of two peoples geographically, culturally and politically. Even the conquest of Muhammad Ali in 1820 was interpreted to be a consolidation rather than a conquest. This line of argument led to the conclusion that there was no question of self-determination, but any problem between the two peoples inhabiting the Nile Valley could be solved between themselves without interference from outside. The British were accused of making the question of preparing the Sudanese for self-government as a pretext for prolonging their stay in the Sudan to serve their own interests. 'I must reiterate,' Premier Nakrashy continued, 'the intention of the Egyptian Government to work in season and out of season to protect the Sudan from dismemberment, to make it possible for our Sudanese brethren to direct their own affairs within the framework of the unity of the Nile Valley under the Crown of Egypt.' The British, who were alien to the Sudanese in every respect in Nakrashy's opinion, could not guide the Sudanese and prepare them for self-government. The Egyptian delegation asked the Security Council to end the regime established in Sudan since 1899 and let the Sudanese join their fellow-countrymen in Egypt. The Sudanese, as it would be expected, sent to the United Nations their delegations as observers with their different points of view. The British delegation reiterated the same arguments adopted by their government in negotiations i.e. no change without consultation with the Sudanese themselves.

In the course of discussion members of the Security Council supported the right of the Sudanese to determine their future status. The Polish and Russian delegations in particular, were outspoken in upholding the principle of self-determination and ascertaining the wishes of the Sudanese. The mere fact that the Sudanese sent two delegations was a clear evidence that they were not in agreement as to the status of their country in the future. In reply to these arguments Nakrashy Pasha, the Egyptian Premier, expressed the view that Egypt would not object to the principle of self-determination for the Sudanese but they would object to that right being exercised under British rule or with British aid. He was confident that when the Sudanese were free they would reach a satisfactory solution with the Egyptians. The whole question was shelved when the Security Council failed to adopt any resolution.

Even before the departure of the United Sudanese delegation to Cairo in 1946, members of the advisory council for the Northern Sudan were assured by the Governor-General that they would be consulted before any settlement for the Sudan question could be reached. On March 26, 1946, Mr. Bevin declared in the House of Commons that His Majesty's Government would look forward to the day when the Sudanese would be able finally to decide their poltical future for themselves. He added that no change would be made in the Sudan administration as a result of Treaty revision before the Sudanese were consulted through constitutional channels.

In 1948 the Advisory council was superseded by a legislative assembly and executive council, but the whole organization was within the framework of the Condominium Agreement of 1899. The ordinance initiating that new step forward for associating the Sudanese with the Government was agreed to at first between the British Ambassador in Cairo and the Egyptian Foreign Minister but was rejected by the Foreign Relations Committee of the Egyptian Senate. The British Government authorized the Governor-General to proceed with the implementation of the ordinance. But he incorporated in the ordinance the recommendations of the British Ambassador and the Egyptian Foreign Minister. The Unity Parties opposed the ordinance, boycotted the elections and staged demonstrations in Khartum and the main towns. A number of their leaders were tried and sent to prison. The Legislative Assembly and the Executive Council were, therefore, accepted by the Independence Front alone.†

† My authorities are:
    1. The special issue of *al-Rai al-'Am* on Independence referred to before.
    2. Mekki Abbas 'The Sudan Question.' (London 1952)

XXIII

THE LAST STEPS TOWARDS INDEPENDENCE

The Sudan question came to the forefront again in 1950 after the failure of the Security Council to adjudicate in the Anglo-Egyptian dispute in 1947. The Wafdist Government under al-Nahhas Pasha declared in Parliament their determination to achieve national aspirations, i.e. evacuation of British Troops from Egyptian soil and unity of Egypt and the Sudan under the Egyptian Crown. Talks were resumed, but it was clear right from the start that the two parties (British and Egyptians) held diametrically opposite views; Egypt looked upon the two main questions of defense in the Middle East and the Sudan as one inseparable issue, while Britain considered them as distinct and separate. Talks dragged on without any sign of either party yielding to the demands of the other or even to a compromise.

When the Egyptian Government was pressed for results the Minister for Foreign Affairs gave a statement in May of 1951:—

"God knows that I want to get results as soon as possible, whether they are good or bad. If you want me to summarize the position precisely, and dot some i's and cross some t's then I will say, firstly, that the British proposals are as far as could be from meeting our national demands; secondly, that the Egyptian Government has answered these proposals with counter proposals which are nothing but the full Egyptian demands for complete evacuation and unity of the Nile Valley; thirdly, that if we have not reached the point of breaking off negotiations we have reached a critical stage at which either Britain concedes our demands, or the result will be what you are asking."

In August of 1951 the British came out with proposals which made the security of the Middle East an allied (Britain, France, America and Turkey) responsibility. But the Egyptian Government was fed up with such talks which were now heading towards the interference of other powers. The long-waited for bomb was delivered on October 8th by al-Nahhas Pasha in Parliament. He anounced that the Egyptian Government abrogated the 1936 Treaty alliance and the 1899 condominium Agreements of the Sudan. Bills for a constitution of the

486

Sudan were presented to Parliament and passed. They proclaimed Farouk 'King of Egypt and the Sudan' and provided for a constituent assembly and a Sudanese Cabinet. Foreign affairs, defense, army and currency were reserved for the King.

On October 13th the British came out with new definite proposals for the Sudan. They included an International Commission to reside in the Sudan for watching over the constitutional development and tendering advice to Britain and Egypt and an agreed fixed date by which the Sudanese would attain Self-government leading to Self-determination. But it was too late for the Egyptian Government to enter into negotiations after declaring their policy and passing of their bills. It was evident that the new Egyptian constitution for the Sudan could not be enforced and both the British Government and the Governor-General declared emphatically that there would be no change.

In January 1952 suggestions for a new self-government constitution were published. They were debated in the legislative assembly and comments were invited from the general public. They were finally considered by the Executive Council and formally passed by the legislative assembly. The final draft provided for a wholly elected House of Representatives and a Senate partly elected and partly appointed. An all-Sudanese Cabinet was responsible to the parliament for internal administration. The Governor-General was the Head of the Constitution who was exclusively responsible for Foreign Affairs and specially responsible for the public service and the Southern Provinces.

The Egyptian Government under Naguib al-Hilali approached al-Sayyid Abd al-Rahman al-Mahdi for talks which might end in understanding. In response al-Mahdi sent a personal mission that would not commit the Umma Party. Nothing came out of this, but it was clear that the Egyptian Government was hankering after some form of unity nominal though it might appear. After the fall of al-Hilali's Cabinet, his successor, Husain Sirri Pasha, invited Sayyid 'Abd al-Rahman in person. It was agreed that he would do so towards the end of July when on his way to Switzerland. But the military coup d'etat on the 23rd of July, 1952, put an end to the old relations between Egypt and the Sudan and opened a new phase.

The political groupings in the Sudan when the regime was changed in Egypt were as follows: The Umma Party led by Sayyid Abd al-

Rahman al-Mahdi, who were standing for independence both from Britain and Egypt. The Sayyid himself was already in London in the fall of 1952 for political talks; the socialist Republican Party with membership largely of tribal chiefs, who were also standing for independence, but for stronger links with Britain. Although they were an independence party, yet they were not allying themselves with the Umma and claiming support of the Khatmia, followers of Sayyid 'Ali al-Mirghani. The unity parties, i.e. the Ashiqqa, the National Front and the Unity of the Nile Valley. The first two also claimed the support of Sayyid Mirghani. It was a perplexing situation for those three parties each alleging the support of the Khatmia. The British Government gave their consent to the draft (Constitution) of Self-Government and waited for the Egyptian Government to give their consent before it could be implemented.

The head of the revolutionary regime in Egypt, General Naguib, and his two lieutenants in the Sudan question handled the situation admirably well. Previously the main flaws in the Egyptian attitude when handling the Sudan were two; firstly they were extremely reluctant to concede the right of Self-determination for the Sudan and secondly they favored the unity parties and called the Independence Parties the separatists. With his Sudanese background and education Naguib was known to be treating the Sudanese alike whether they were standing for unity or Independence and both liked and trusted him. He was known to be an intimate friend of Sayyid al-Mahdi. By October 1952 the Egyptian Government had before it the draft constitution for the Sudan for consent or mutual amendments. They took the right attitude when they sought to reach an agreement with the Sudanese first and with the Umma Party in particular.

On the 20th of October, 1952 Sayyid Abd al-Rahman arrived from London in Cairo with some of his advisers. Both in the aerodrome and the Palace that was set aside for his residence, he was given almost a royal welcome. Talks started between the Egyptian Government and the Umma Party and an agreement was reached, which brought rejoicings both in Egypt and the Sudan. The next step was for the Unity Parties to come together and accept amalgamation in one party. That was successful and the National unionist party was born in Cairo and it was definitely known that Sayyid Ali al-Mirghani gave it his blessing and the support of the Khatmia.

The stage had now been prepared for settling things between the Egyptians and representatives of the main Sudanese parties before the Condominium Powers would turn them into a legal document. The basis for the detailed discussion was the constitution of the Self-Government for the Sudan. The modifications that were made aimed at restricting the powers of the Governor-General by a commission composed of two Sudanese, one Egyptian, one British and a neutral chairman. The maximum period for Self-Government was to be three years after which a plebiscite had to be held for either complete independence or some form of union with Egypt in a free atmosphere by withdrawing the British and Egyptian armies and all British and Egyptian officials who might influence Sudanese opinion in the plebiscite.

Early in 1953 Major Salah Salim had to fly to Khartum and the southern Sudan to convince what ever shades of opinion existed in the North and South of the advantages in the new arrangements. His mission was a success and on the 10th of January 1953 a document was signed by all Sudanese Parties signifying their agreements to all points of difference in the Self-Government constitution. What is more important was that they all agreed to boycott the elections if their agreed constitution was not accepted.

Armed with this document in his pocket Major Salim flew back to Cairo to start negotiations with the British for the final agreement. It took about a month after this most important event to sign the Treaty on the 12th of February 1953. The new regime in Egypt took the initiative from the hands of the British by abandoning the old Egyptian slogan of Sovereignty over the Sudan and assuring the agreement with all the Sudanese before entering into negotiations with the British. It was a change of front for the British, because they were appearing as the champions of Sudanese Independence and Self-determination while the Egyptians were claiming legal sovereignty and unity of the Nile Valley as indisputable principles.

The 20th of February 1953 witnessed the celebrations of rejoicings in the Khalifa's square in Omdurman where there were no differences and where law and order was not kept by the security forces of the state but by the people themselves. It was one of those occasions where Sudanese solidarity was manifested in a spectacular way.

The Electoral Commission provided for by the agreement met on the 6th of April 1953 with one Egyptian, one British, one American member, three Sudanese members and an Indian Chairman. They reviewed the Electoral Law and made changes, most important of which was the appreciable increase in the number of direct electoral constituencies. This removed the protection that was given to tribal chiefs by the system of indirect election and allowed the ordinary voter to elect his representative directly to the assembly. There was brisk competition for the elections fixed for November between the Umma Party supported by Sayyid Abd al-Rahman al Mahdi and the National Unionist Party supported by Sayyid Ali al-Mirghani. The National Unionist won 51 out of the 97 seats in the lower House and 22 out of the 30 electoral seats in the Upper House. The reaction to this revolt was interpreted in Khartum, Cairo and London to be a victory of the pro-Egyptian elements to those of the pro-British and members of the British civil service in the Sudan did not conceal their disappointments.

In accordance with the provisions of the constitution Sayyid Ismail al-Azhari, leader of the National Unionist Party, was appointed Prime Minister and he formed his cabinet exclusively from his Party. Although Parliament met on the 1st of January 1954, the official opening was fixed for March 1st, to which delegates from many countries were invited to witness the historical occasion. The event was, however, not celebrated owing to a very unfortunate incident. The Umma Party attributed their defeat in the elections to Egyptian money lavishly spent in support of the N.U.P. in the election campaign. They thought that this Egyptian behavior was a breach of the "Gentlemen's Agreement" of non-interference in the campaign. Knowing that General Naguib was coming to Khartum for the occasion of the inaugural ceremonies, they staged a procession in protest to meet him at the airport and to march to the Governor-General's palace. Outside the walls of the palace the situation deteriorated into a riot and a number of casualties from both the demonstrators and members of the police force was the result. What was prepared to be an occasion of rejoicing was turned into national mourning.

The main task before the new government was the preparation of the neutral atmosphere for self-determination within three years. It meant discharging Egyptian and British officials who might influence public opinion, and replacing them by either Sudanese or neutral expatriates. They had to be lavishly compensated which meant a substantial amount of money. When we know that nearly all the key posts in the civil service and the technical departments were occupied by the British and that there was a lack of qualified and experienced Sudanese to take over from them, it is a great credit to the Sudanese that they rose to the occasion and could keep the machinery of administration functioning with a reasonable degree of efficiency.

May 1955 was a turning point in the political history of the Sudan. So far it was known that the N.U.P. were standing for some form of union with Egypt and the Umma Party for complete independence. The plebiscite which would be held at the end of the Self-Government stage should determine the future of the country for one or the other of the two rival theories. But Sayyid Ismail al-Azhari, the Prime Minister and Leader of N.U.P. declared in May, on the occasion of the Muslim Bairam celebration, his pledge to work for independence and full sovereignty. He kept repeating that pledge on every occasion in which he had to state his policy. In August Parliament passed a resolution declaring that Sudanization had been completed and expressed the desire that arrangements for self-determination should start.

In August 1955 the Southern units of the Sudan Army mutinied at Torit in Equatoria Province. It was followed by the massacre of several hundreds of northerners working in the south as merchants or officials. A state of lawlessness continued for some months in many parts of Equatoria before the government could resume control. Many causes were attributed to that unfortunate and sad incident; the traditional enmity, or at least, lack of understanding between the Arabs in the north and the Nilotics in the south, the British policy of practically closing the south from northern contact and influence, the hostile propaganda carried out by foreign missionaries in the south against the Muslim north—these and other causes were mentioned by various people as the roots of the trouble.

Although self-determination through some form of plebiscite was accepted by all, yet it was felt that it would be unnecessary since the N.U.P. declared their policy of Independence. Yet the two co-Domini were asked to amend the Agreements to provide for a plebiscite. Negotiations about formation of a commission to conduct it were entered into. On the other hand the idea that Parliament should declare independence and do away with all the complications of the plebiscite was discussed by Sudanese public opinion. On

December 15th Azhari announced that he would table a Resolution calling for immediate recognition of independence. On the 19th the Resolution was unanimously passed by Parliament. The Self-Government Constitution was amended to meet with the new situation. A supreme commission of five was elected by Parliament to be the Head of State and to replace the Governor-General. January 1st, 1956 was, to the Sudanese, a historic Day which marked their emergence as a full Sovereign State in the Comity of Nations.

APPENDIX

AGREEMENT FOR THE ADMINISTRATION OF THE SUDAN

Agreement between Her Britannic Majesty's Government and the Government of His Highness the Khedive of Egypt relative to the future Administration of the Sudan.

Whereas certain provinces in the Sudan which were in rebellion against the authority of His Highness the Khedive have now been reconquered by the joint military and financial efforts of Her Britannic Majesty's Government and the Government of His Highness the Khedive;

And whereas it has become necessary to decide upon a system for the administration of and for the making of laws for the said reconquered provinces, under which due allowance may be made for the backward and unsettled condition of large portions thereof, and for the varying requirements of different localities;

And whereas it is desired to give effect to the claims which have accrued to Her Britannic Majesty's Government by right of conquest, to share in the present settlement and future working and development of the said system of administration and legislation;

And whereas it is conceived that for many purposes Wadi Halfa and Suakin may be most effectively administered in conjunction with the reconquered provinces to which they are respectively adjacent;

Now it is hereby agreed and declared by and between the undersigned, duly authorized for that purpose, as follows:—

ARTICLE I

The word 'Sudan' in this agreement means all the territories south of the 22nd parallel of latitude, which:

(1) have never been evacuated by Egyptian troops since the year 1882: or

(2) which having before the late rebellion in the Sudan been administered by the Government of His Highness the Khedive were temporarily lost to Egypt and have been reconquered by her Majesty's Government and the Egyptian Government, acting in concert: or

(3) which may hereafter be reconquered by the two Governments acting in concert.

ARTICLE II

The British and Egyptian flags shall be used together both on land and water, throughout the Sudan, except in the town of Suakin, in which locality the Egyptian flag alone shall be used.

ARTICLE III

The supreme military and civil command in the Sudan shall be vested in one officer, termed the 'Governor-General of the Sudan.' He shall be appointed by Khedivial Decree on the recommendation of Her Britannic Majesty's Government, and shall be removed only by Khedivial Decree, with the consent of Her Britannic Majesty's Government.

ARTICLE IV

Laws, as also Orders and Regulations with the full force of law, for the good government of the Sudan, and for regulating the holding dosposal and devolution of property of every kind therein situated may from time to time be made altered or abrogated by Proclamation of the Governor-General. Such Laws, Orders, and Regulations may apply to the whole or any named part of the Sudan, and may, either explicitly or by necessary implication, alter or abrogate any existing Law or Regulation.

All such Proclamations shall be forthwith notified to Her Britannic Majesty's Agent and Consul-General in Cairo, and to the President of the Council of Ministers of His Highness the Khedive.

ARTICLE V

No Egyptian Law, Decree, Ministerial Arrêté, or other enactment hereafter to be made or promulgated shall apply to the Sudan or any part thereof, save in so far as the same shall be applied by Proclamation of the Governor-General in manner hereinafter provided.

ARTICLE VI

In the definition by Proclamation of the conditions under which Europeans, of whatever nationality, shall be a liberty to trade with or reside in the Sudan, or to hold property within its limits, no special privileges shall be accorded to the subjects of any one or more Power.

ARTICLE VII

Import duties on entering the Sudan shall not be payable on goods coming from Egyptian territory. Such duties may however be levied on goods coming from elsewhere than Egyptian territory, but in the case of goods entering the Sudan at Suakin or any other port on the Red Sea littoral, they shall not exceed the corresponding duties for the time being leviable on goods entering Egypt from abroad. Duties may be levied on goods leaving the Sudan, at such rates as may from time to time be prescribed by Proclamation.

ARTICLE VIII

The jurisdiction of the Mixed Tribunals shall not extend, nor be recognized for any purpose whatsoever, in any part of the Sudan, except in the town of Suakin.

ARTICLE IX

Until, and save so far as it shall be otherwise determined by Proclamation, the Sudan, with the exception of the town of Suakin, shall be and remain under martial law.

ARTICLE X

No Consuls, Vice-Consuls, or Consular Agents shall be accredited in respect of nor allowed to reside in the Sudan, without the previous consent of Her Britannic Majesty's Government.

ARTICLE XI

The importation of slaves into the Sudan, as also their exportation, is absolutely prohibited. Provision shall be made by Proclamation for the enforcement of this Regulation.

ARTICLE XII

It is agreed between the two Governments that special attention shall be paid to the enforcement of the Brussels Act of the 2nd of July 1890, in respect of the import, sale, and manufacture of firearms and their munitions, and distilled or spirituous liquors.

Done in Cairo, the 19th January 1890.

Signed: { BOUTROS GHALI
{ CROMER

SUPPLEMENTAL AGREEMENT FOR THE ADMINISTRATION OF THE SUDAN

Agreement made between the British and Egyptian Governments Supplemental to the Agreement made between the two Governments on 19th January 1899 for the future administration of the Sudan.

Whereas under our Agreement made the 19th day of January 1899, relative to the future administration of the Sudan, it it provided by Article VIII, that the jurisdiction of the Mixed Tribunals shall not extend nor be recognized for any purpose whatsoever in any part of the Sudan except in the town of Suakin:

And whereas no Mixed Tribunal has ever been established at Suakin and it has been found to be inexpedient to establish any such tribunal in that locality by reason notably of the expense which the adoption of this measure would occasion:

And whereas grievous injustice is caused to the inhabitants of Suakin by the absence of any local jurisdiction for the settlement of their disputes and it is expedient that the town of Suakin should be placed upon the same footing as the rest of the Sudan:

And whereas we have decided to modify our said Agreement accordingly in manner hereinafter appearing:

Now, it is hereby agreed and declared by and between the undersigned duly authorized for that purpose, as follows:—

ARTICLE I

Those provisions of our Agreement of the 19th day of January 1899 by which the town of Suakin was excepted from the general régime established by the said Agreement for the future administration of the Sudan, are hereby abrogated.

Done at Cairo, the 10th of July 1899.

Signed: { BOUTROS GHALI
{ CROMER

BIBLIOGRAPHY

A. *In London*

1. *In the Public Record Office*
   (a) F.O. 78 Egypt. Official correspondence between the British Consul-General in Cairo and the Foreign Office in London.
   (b) W.O. 33/44. War Office correspondence dealing mainly with the military aspect of the question of the Sudan, and giving details of the actions in which the British troops took part.
   (c) G.D. 29. The Granville Private Papers. These contain Granville's private telegrams and letters to Malet and Baring in Cairo and to his colleagues in the Government.
2. *In the British Museum*
   Add. MSS. The Gladstone Private Papers. These contain Gladstone's private correspondence with his colleagues, particularly with Granville and Hartington on the question of the Sudan.

B. *In Cairo*

1. 'Abdin Palace, Arabic Department. The 'In' and 'Out' Telegram Books contain the telegrams between the Khedive and the Governor-General in Khartum. They are not to be confused with the Historical Archives of 'Abdin Palace which contain the records of the reigns of Muhammad 'Ali, 'Abbas I, Sa'id, and Isma'il, but not those of the reign of Tawfiq.
2. The Egyptian Government Archives at the Citadel. The personnel files of the generals, officers, and Government officials are kept there.

C. *In Khartum*

1. Newbold Library, University College of Khartum.
   (a) 'Abbas Afandi's diary.
   'Abbas Afandi Hilmi accompanied 'Ala al-Din Pasha as his mu'awin (assistant) on Hicks's expedition. He kept a diary of the detailed daily happenings in a small notebook in pencil. This was evidently found on the body of the author when the army was annihilated and kept by an ansari until it was handed over to the intelligence branch of the Egyptian army in 1899 after the battle of Omdurman. It was then translated into English and the version preserved in Khartum is not the original but the English translation.
   The authorship of the diary can now be established with reasonable certainty. The file of 'Abbas Afandi confirms that he accompanied the expedition as an assistant to 'Ala al-Din. The accuracy of the document is proved by checking it with Hicks's last letter to Cairo and with statements given by Muhammad Nur al-Barudi, one of Hicks's cooks who

498   THE INDEPENDENT SUDAN

survived the annihilation. The original is kept in the Royal Library
of Windsor.
(b) Statements given to the intelligence branch of the Egyptian army
in Egypt by some of those who escaped from the Sudan.
2. Sir al-Sayyid 'Abd al-Rahman al-Mahdi's collections. These are papers
consisting of al-Mahdi's letters and circulars, statements given by ansar
who took part in the events they narrated, and also sayings of al-Mahdi
indicating his religious teachings and reforms.
3. *Sudan Notes and Records* (Khartum). A periodical containing historical
commandants in the field and provincial governors.

II. OFFICIAL PUBLICATIONS

1. *British Documents on the Origins of the War*, 1898-1914, vol. i, edited
by G. P. Gooch and Harold Temperley (London, 1927).
2. *Hansard's Parliamentary Debates*, 1881-5.
3. *Parliamentary Papers*. These provide little material for the study of
the subject as the original correspondence provides all that is required.

III. NEWSPAPERS AND PERIODICALS

1. *The Times*. This newspaper had two very able correspondents—Mr.
Moberly Bell in Cairo and Mr. Power in Khartum—who kept the
English public informed of the events in the Sudan. Questions in
Parliament were mainly the result of news appearing in *The Times*.
In addition, letters to the Editor appeared from time to time on some
aspect of the Sudan problem.
2. *Pall Mall Gazette*. This is the paper which sponsored Gordon's mission
to the Sudan and published Gordon's views on the whole question of
the Sudan a few days before he proceeded to Khartum.
3. *Sudan Notes and Records* (Khartum). A periodical containing historical
articles and notes and statements of eyewitnesses.
4. *Revue Historique* (Paris).

IV. BIOGRAPHIES, LETTERS, MEMOIRS, AND JOURNALS

Allen, Bernard M. *Gordon and the Sudan* (London, 1931).
This is the best and latest account of Gordon's life in the Sudan.
Bell, E. H. C. Moberly (daughter). *The Life and Letters of C. F. Moberly
Bell* (London, 1927).
Black, Charles E. Drummond. *The Marquess of Dufferin and Ava* (London,
1903).
Cecil, Lady Gwendolen. *Life of Robert, Marquis of Salisbury*, 4 vols.
(London, 1932).
Childers, S. *The Life and Correspondence of the Right Hon. C. E.
Childers 1827-1896* 2 vols. (London, 1901).
Fitzmaurice, Lord Edmond. *The Life of Granville, George Leveson Gower,
Second Earl of Granville, 1815-1891*, 2 vols. (London,1905).

Gardiner, A. G. *The Life of Sir William Harcourt*, 2 vols. (London, 1923).

Gordon, Major-General C. G. *The Journals of Gordon at Khartum*, introduction and notes by A. Egmont Hake (London, 1885). This is Gordon's diary of the daily events in Khartum from September 24th 1884 to December 14th 1884. It was supposed to have been a continuation of Stewart's diary. Steward left Khartum on September 24th 1884 and was killed in the Manasir country on the Nile west of Abu Hamad and his diary was lost. Stewart kept a diary from the time he and Gordon left Charing Cross station on January 18th 1884 and sent it regularly to Baring in Cairo until March 8th 1884. His diary from March 9th to September 23rd was, however, lost.

Gordon, M. A. (editor). *Letters of C. G. Gordon to his sister, M. A. Gordon* (London, 1888).

Gwynn, S. L., and Tuckwell, Gertrude M. *The Life of the Rt. Hon. Sir Charles W. Dilke, Bart., M. P.*, 2 vols. (London, 1917).

Holland, Bernard. *Life of Spencer Compton, 8th Duke of Devonshire*, 2 vols. (London, 1911).

Jackson, H. C. *Osman Diqna* (London, 1926).
A biography of 'Uthman Diqna, al-Mahdi's general in the eastern Sudan. It is particularly important, because it includes the record of statements of eyewitnesses.

Jerrold, Walter. *Sir Redvers H. Buller, V.C. The Story of his Life and Campaigns* (London, 1908).

Mallet, Sir Bernard. *Thomas George, Earl of Northbrook, A Memoir* (London, 1908).

Maurice, Sir F., and Arthur, Sir George. *The Life of Lord Wolseley* (London, 1924).

Morley, John. *The Life of William Ewart Gladstone*, 3 vols. (London, 1903).

Ohrwalder, Joseph (translated from German into English by Wingate, F.R.). *Ten Years' Captivity in the Mahdi's Camp* (London, 1892). Father Ohrwalder was an Austrian missionary in the Nuba mountains when the Mahdist revolution broke out. He was taken prisoner while al-Mahdi was still in Kurdufan and remained a prisoner for ten years, after which he escaped from Omdurman to Egypt where he recorded his narrative of the Mahdiya from memory and not from notes recorded at the time. Ohrwalder's original manuscript was translated into English by Wingate.

Palmer, Roundell, Earl of Selborne. *Memorials, Personal and Political*, 2 vols. (London, 1898).

Power, Frank. *Letters from Khartum* (London, 1885).

Sartorius, Ernestine, *Three Months in the Sudan* (London, 1885). The record of events in the eastern Sudan when Mrs. Sartorius was with her husband, General Sartorius, at Sawakin taking part in Baker's expedition.

500   THE INDEPENDENT SUDAN

Schweitzer, Georg. *Emin Pasha, his Life and Work,* 2 vols. (London, 1898.
  Deals with the events of the revolution in Equatoria Province where Amin Pasha was the last mudir.
Slatin, Rudolf, C. (translated from German into English by Wingate, F.R.). *Fire and Sword in the Sudan* (London and New York, 1896).
  Slatin was the last governor-general of Darfur and surrendered to al-Mahdi's emissary, Muhammad Khalid Zuqal. His narrative of events in Darfur is that of an eyewitness and a responsible official who took part in the struggle, but it was recorded from memory about thirteen years after the events which he described had taken place.
The Letters of Queen Victoria, 2nd series (third volume), edited by George Earle Buckle (London, 1928).
Vetch, R. H. *Life of Lieut.-General the Hon. Sir Andrew Clarke* (London, 1905).
—— *Life, Letters, and Diaries of Lieut.-General Sir Gerald Graham* (Edinburgh and London, 1901).
Ware, J. R., and Mann, R. K. *The Life and Times of Colonel Fred Burnaby* (London, 1885).
Watson, Sir Charles M. *The Life of Major-General Sir Charles William Wilson* (London, 1909).
Whyte, Frederick. *The Life of W. T. Stead,* 2 vols (London, 1925).
Wilson, Sir C. W. *From Korti to Khartum* (London, 1886).
  A journal of the desert march from Korti to Gubat and the ascent of the Nile in General Gordon's steamers.
Wolseley, Garnet J. *The Letters of Lord and Lady Wolseley,* edited by Sir George Arthur (London, 1922).
Zetland, Marquess of. *Lord Cromer* (London, 1932).

V. OTHER WORKS ETC.

Burleigh, B. *Desert Warfare* (London, 1884).
  The chronicle of the eastern Sudan campaign.
Colborne, J. *With Hicks Pasha in the Sudan* (London, 1884).
  An account of the battles in al-Jazirah and the White Nile under Hicks by an officer who took part in them.
Colvile, H. E. *History of the Sudan Campaign,* 2 parts (London, 1899).
  Compiled in the Intelligence Division of the War Office.
  The official record of Wolseley's campaign on the Nile and Graham's from Sawakin. It describes all the battles fought and contains all the military reports and correspondence.
Cromer, the Earl of. *Modern Egypt,* 2 vols. (London 1908).
Golvin, Sir Auckland. *The Making of Modern Egypt* (London, 1908).
Graham, Lieut.-General Sir Gerald. *Last Words with Gordon* (London, 1887).
Langer, Professor William L. *The Diplomacy of Imperialism,* 1890-1902 2 vols. (New York and London, 1935).

Milner, Sir Alfred. *England in Egypt* (London, 1902).

Temperly, Harold, and Penson, Lillian M. *Foundations of British Foreign Policy* (Cambridge, 1938).

Wingate, F. R. *Mahdiism and the Egyptian Sudan* (London, 1891).
Sir Reginald Wingate compiled all accounts about the revolution from people who escaped to Egypt or from prisoners taken after the battle of Tuski when the Mahdist army led by 'Abd al-Rahman al-Nujumi was defeated. This work also contains translations of some of al-Mahdi's letters and circulars. Wingate's official position in the military intelligence section of the Egyptian army afforded him the opportunity of collecting information about the Mahdiya. Wingate was assisted by his chief clerk Na'um Bey Shuqair, who published almost the same material in an Arabic book (*Tarikh al-Sudan,* Cairo, 1903). Na'um, however, supplemented these accounts taken in Cairo with others taken in Khartum and Omdurman after the reconquest of the Sudan in 1898).

Wylde, A. B. '83 *to* '87 *in the Sudan* (London, 1888).
Wylde, an English merchant at Sawakin, recorded accounts of events in the Sawakin area with his own comments. He was in close contact with the senior English officers who operated on that front.

INDEX

503

Date Due